Developing Management Skills

The Scott, Foresman Series in Management and Organizations

Lyman W. Porter, and Joseph W. McGuire, *Editors*

Developing Management Skills

David A. Whetten
University of Illinois at Urbana-Champaign

Kim S. Cameron
*National Center for Higher Education Management Systems and
University of Colorado*

Scott, Foresman and Company

Glenview, Illinois

Dallas, Texas   Oakland, New Jersey   Palo Alto, California
Tucker, Georgia   London, England

Acknowledgments

Acknowledgments for literary selections and illustrations appear at the back of the book on pp. 500–3, which are extensions of the copyright page.

Library of Congress Cataloging in Publication Data

Whetten, David A. (David Allred), 1946–
  Developing management skills.

  Includes bibliographies and index.
    1. Management—Study and teaching. 2. Management —
Problems, exercises, etc. 3. Role playing. I. Cameron, Kim S.
II. Title.
HD30.4.W46 1984   658.4′007′1173   83–20325
ISBN 0-673-15590-0

To Renée, Zina, and Melinda.

■ Preface

The impetus for writing *Developing Management Skills* grew out of our frustration with teaching management courses following conventional methods. When we used texts based on the traditional "principles of management" framework, we felt uncomfortable with their lack of theoretical and research grounding. Because principles of management have been generally derived from the recollections and interpretations of practicing managers, empirical research and theory regarding their validity in modern organizations is limited. When we used a "watered-down organizational behavior" approach, colleagues teaching the OB courses reported that students complained about redundancy. The same topics were covered in organizational behavior and management books, and neither considered ways to make students better managers. When we emphasized the "experiential learning" approach centered around simulations, case discussions, and games, students complained they weren't gaining enough substantive knowledge about how to be effective managers. Few students brought enough practical experience, theoretical knowledge, or self-analytic skills to those exercises to get much meaning from them. The exercises were entertaining, but not very useful. We determined that each approach had its place in management education, and each could contribute to a student's education, but none could, taken alone, help students develop into competent managers.

In our search for alternatives, we asked recent graduates to evaluate the organizational behavior and management curricula in terms of their experiences as managers. In general, these graduates criticized behavioral science courses for not teaching them job-relevant skills. They were acutely aware of the challenges posed by "people problems" in their work, and they felt that their education had not prepared them for that component of their job.

Based on this feedback, we began an experiment to develop an approach to teaching management based on skill competency. In formulating the teaching methodology, we examined the way skills are taught in other professional schools, such as education, social work, engineering, medicine, and law. We also drew heavily on recent innovations in training programs for practicing managers that emphasize behavior modification through role modeling. To identify the relevant management skills, we surveyed over 400 managers in public and private organizations and combed the professional literature for statements by management experts regarding the characteristics of effective managers. As our teaching model began to evolve, it became apparent that a supporting textbook would need to be developed, since none existed. Further, it would necessarily have to be a hybrid, containing diverse teaching methods and materials that gave equal emphasis to theory and practice.

We also recognized that a book devoted to developing management skills would have to adopt a radical view regarding what behavioral science courses should offer management students. These courses typically present an array of general principles and concepts derived from research in industrial/organizational psychology, sociology, OB, industrial administration, and so on. They describe management practice and provide students with frameworks for analyzing common people problems encountered by managers. While this exposure to conceptual and analytic frameworks is useful and necessary, it is an incomplete method for developing skilled managers.

We have found that focusing on behavioral skills rather than theories of behavior not only increases students' interest in and acceptance of the theoretical material, but also significantly increases their ability to apply the concepts they have learned. Overall, the preparation of students for managerial positions is markedly improved by participation in a management skills course. In fact, we have discovered that competence in certain personal and interpersonal skills is just as essential to the success of managers as competence in the analytic and quantitative skills taught in accounting, finance, and operations and marketing research courses.

Writing a textbook, especially one that is nontraditional, requires a great deal of support and sustenance. In the development of this text, the contributions of several individuals stand out as particularly critical. Our institutional leaders have provided considerable support for our experimental teaching activities, both in the classroom and in outside executive training settings. The teaching assistants for BA 210 at the University of Illinois contributed many useful comments on the multiple iterations of our course structure and content. Without their willingness to help test our ideas, we could never have come this far. In addition, the secretarial support of Judy Butler, Dee Lowrance, Debbie Loos, and Barbara Lucas was crucial in enabling us to meet our deadlines.

We are especially grateful to Jim Sitlington and John Nolan at Scott, Foresman, who had the courage and foresight to guarantee a publishing outlet when our plans were little more than a fuzzy and quite radical dream. Their moral and financial support during the developmental phase was critical. Other members of the staff at Scott, Foresman provided valuable technical assistance in transforming our drafts into a final product, but the help of Diane Culhane and Carol Karton was particularly important.

We would also like to thank our numerous colleagues who reviewed early versions of various chapters. While they obviously bear no responsibility for the final product, their feedback was very helpful in shaping our thinking. These include John Bigelow, Oregon State University; Lyman Porter, University of California, Irvine; Sue Mohrman, University of Southern California; Noel Tichy, University of Michigan; Robert Miles, Harvard University; Lloyd Baird, Boston University; Jon L. Pierce, University of Minnesota;

David J. Cherrington, Brigham Young University; Mary Lippitt Nichols, University of Minnesota; Richard E. Hunt, Rockhurst College; and Michael Lombardo, Center for Creative Leadership.

Finally, but most important, we are grateful to our families, who willingly provided the necessary emotional support. We especially appreciate their patience and understanding during our numerous evening and weekend absences. It is our fervent hope that, in return, we can learn to better implement the skills described herein where they matter most, in our own homes.

Contents

Introduction to Management Skill Development

Introduction   2
Supplementary Material   11
     Personal Assessment   11
     Interviewing Managers   13
     What Makes a Top Executive?   14
     The Tampa Pump & Valve Company   21

1   Developing Self-Awareness   34

Skill Preassessment   35
     Self-Awareness Preassessment   35
Skill Learning   36
     Three Critical Areas of Self-Awareness   36
Skill Analysis   64
     Brainwashing   64
     The Boy, the Girl, the Ferryboat Captain, and the Hermits   66
Skill Practice   68
     The Defining Issues Test   68
     The Cognitive Style Instrument   76
     Fundamental Interpersonal Relations Orientation–Behavior   80
     Group Discussion Exercise   83
Skill Application   84
     Application Exercises   84

2   Managing Personal Stress   85

Skill Preassessment   86
     Social Readjustment Rating Scale   86
     Type A Behavior Pattern Inventory   87
Skill Learning   89
     The Management of Stress and Time   89
Skill Analysis   123
     The Day at the Beach   123
     The Case of the Missing Time   127
Skill Practice   133
     The Controller's Report   133
     The Stress of Success   137
Skill Application   138
     Application Exercises   138

3   Solving Problems Creatively   139

Skill Preassessment   140
     How Creative Are You?   140
Skill Learning   144
     Becoming a More Creative Problem-Solver   144
Skill Analysis   180
     Admiral Kimmel's Failure at Pearl Harbor   180
     The Double Helix   183
Skill Practice   188
     Tidewater College   188
     Acks and Blogs   190
Skill Application   191
     Application Exercises   191

4   Establishing Supportive Communication   192

Skill Preassessment   193
     Response Inventory   193
     Managing the Management Course   196
Skill Learning   199
     Resolving Interpersonal Problems Through Communication   199
Skill Analysis   232
     Get Off My Back   232
     Rejected Plans   234
Skill Practice   236
     United Chemical Company   236
     Empathy Exercise   239
     Reflective Listening Exercise   241
Skill Application   242
     Application Exercises   242

5   Gaining Power and Influence   243

Skill Preassessment   244
     Empowerment Profile   244
     Preferred Influence Strategies   246
Skill Learning   247
     Building a Strong Power Base and Using Influence Effectively   247
Skill Analysis   284
     Why I Quit General Motors   284
     Wild Ride for John DeLorean   288
Skill Practice   294
     Repairing Power Failures in Management Circuits   294
     Ann Lindner   296
Skill Application   300
     Application Exercises   300

6   **Improving Employee Performance Through Motivation**   301

Skill Preassessment   302
    Coming to Grips with Motivational Issues and Problems   302
Skill Learning   304
    Increasing Employee Motivation and Shaping Constructive Behavior   304
Skill Analysis   334
    Elizabeth Sternberg and Judith Greene   334
Skill Practice   345
    Behavior Modification at Tampa Pump & Valve   345
Skill Application   347
    Application Exercises   347

7   **Delegating and Decision Making**   348

Skill Preassessment   349
    Delegating at the South Seas Gift Shop   349
    Inclinations Toward Delegation   351
Skill Learning   353
    How, When, Why, What, and to Whom to Delegate   353
Skill Analysis   385
    Case Analysis   385
    Minding the Store   387
Skill Practice   389
    Meeting at Hartford Manufacturing Company   389
Skill Application   398
    Application Exercises   398

8   **Managing Conflict**   399

Skill Preassessment   400
    General Strategies for Handling Interpersonal Conflicts   400
    Where's My Talk?   401
Skill Learning   403
    Interpersonal Conflict Management   403
Skill Analysis   435
    The Harried Supervisor   435
    Webster Arsenal   437
Skill Practice   442
    Win as Much as You Can   442
    Responding to Conflictual Encounters   443
Skill Application   448
    Application Exercises   448

9 Conducting Effective Group Meetings 449

Skill Preassessment   450
    Johnny Rocco   450
Skill Learning   454
    Improving Group Decision Making   454
Skill Analysis   484
    It Wasn't "Just Another Dull Meeting"   484
Skill Practice   489
    First Management Staff Meeting at Tampa Pump & Valve   489
    Quality Circles at Battle Creek Foods   491
Skill Application   498
    Application Exercises   498

Developing Management Skills

Introduction to Management Skill Development

■ *Introduction*

■ *Supplementary Material*

Personal Assessment
Interviewing Managers
What Makes a Top Executive?
The Tampa Pump & Valve Company

■ Introduction

Many management school graduates have a hard time adjusting to organizational reality. They are long on analytic skills but short on implementation skills. The best solution in the world is worthless unless you can get others to support it. We call this malady "paralysis by analysis."

Vice president of a major computer manufacturer

The higher up the organization you go, the less relevant technical knowledge becomes. It is important for your first couple of promotions, but after that, people skills are what count.

Partner in a "big eight" accounting firm

I can't believe it. I went for my second interview with a company last week and I spent the first half-day participating in simulation exercises with ten other job candidates. They videotaped me playing the role of a salesman handling an irate customer, a new director of personnel putting down a revolt by the "old guard," and a plant manager trying to convince his people of the need to install a radically new production process. Boy, was I unprepared for that!"

Recent management school graduate

The message behind these statements is clear—competence in interpersonal skills is a critical prerequisite for a successful career in management. Strong analytical and quantitative skills are important, but not sufficient. Successful managers must also be able to work effectively with people. Organizational leaders are becoming increasingly cognizant of this fact and are placing greater emphasis on it in hiring and promotion decisions. Our purpose in writing this text is to foster your development in this vital aspect of management.

To accomplish this, we emphasize *practicing* management skills, rather than merely reading about what managers do, or what researchers surmise managers ought to do. The need for this type of approach has been noted by several scholars. For example, Henry Mintzberg (1975, p. 60) argues:

Management schools will begin the serious training of managers when skill training takes [its] place next to cognitive learning. Cognitive learning is detached and informational, like reading a book or listening to a lecture. No doubt much important cognitive material must be assimilated by the manager-to-be. But cognitive learning no more makes a manager than it does a swimmer. The latter will drown the first time he jumps into the water if his coach never takes him out of the lecture hall, gets him wet, and gives him feedback on his performance. Our management schools need to identify the skills managers use, select students who show potential in these skills, put the students into situations where these skills can be practiced, and then give them systematic feedback on their performance.

The skill development approach raises two specific questions, which we shall discuss in turn—how can one best learn management skills, and which skills should we focus on?

THE LEARNING MODEL

This text can best be described as a management skills practicum. We use the term "practicum" to denote a combination of conceptual learning and behavioral practice, since both are necessary for effective skill development. Education that involves teaching behavioral guidelines but provides no opportunity for practice ignores the precarious link between knowledge and application (Whetten & Cameron, 1983). Similarly, training programs that do not provide a broad conceptual understanding of skill topics and instead emphasize rote behavior modeling overlook the need for flexible application. The metamanagement skill is adaptability. Our approach to learning draws heavily on social learning theory (Bandura, 1977; Davis & Luthans, 1980). Variations on this general approach have been used widely in on-the-job supervisory skill training programs (Goldstein & Sorcher, 1974), as well as in allied professional education classroom settings, such as teacher development and social work (Rose, Cayner, & Edleson, 1977; Singleton, Spurgeon, & Stammers, 1980).

The learning model used most widely for skill training in industry usually consists of four steps: first, the presentation of principles (sometimes called behavioral guidelines or key action steps) based on data collected from successful practicing managers or derived from general theories of human behavior; second, demonstration of the principles to participants by the instructor, a videotaped incident, or written scripts; third, opportunities to practice the principles in role plays or exercises; and fourth, feedback on personal performance received from the instructor, experts, or peers.

Research on the effectiveness of training programs using this general format has shown that it produces results superior to those based on the traditional lecture/discussion approach (Moses & Ritchie, 1976; Burnaska, 1976; Smith, 1976; Latham & Saari, 1979; Porras & Anderson, 1981). Consequently, we have organized each chapter in the book around these four learning activities, with three important modifications.

First, we have emphasized conceptual learning, since it is important to understand the *whys* behind the *hows*. This enhances one's ability to adapt to changing circumstances and also prepares one for a vital function of management—teaching these skills to others.

Second, because many of you do not have extensive managerial experience in organizations, you are probably unaware of your current level of competence in management skills. Moreover, because of this lack of experience, you may not recognize the importance of developing some of these skills. Therefore, we have inserted a preassessment activity at the beginning of each chapter to help you determine how well you can perform the skill now and to motivate you to improve your performance.

Third, an application activity is placed at the end of each chapter to help you apply that skill in a setting similar to one you will face on the job. Most of the suggested application activities require that you record your experiences and analyze your degree of success or failure.

The chapters in this book follow the format shown in Table 1. First, at the beginning of each chapter, before engaging in any learning activities, you assess your current level of understanding and competence in each skill. This *Skill Preassessment* involves filling out a questionnaire, answering questions about a brief case, or participating in a role play or other experiential activity. Its purpose is to increase the efficiency of the learning process by focusing attention on deficiencies in knowledge or performance.

Conceptual text material is contained in the *Skill Learning* section. The purpose of this section is to present the most essential and relevant material available on each subject. Lengthy theoretical discussions are avoided. Our objective is to provide a sound rationale for the behavioral principles summarized at the end of the section. These guidelines serve as the foundation for subsequent practice and application activities.

In the *Skill Analysis* section, you are asked to analyze one or two brief cases that have been selected to reflect good or bad applications of the behavioral principles. The purpose of this section is to bridge the gap between in-

TABLE 1 *Organization of Each Chapter*

Component	Contents	Objectives
Skill preassessment	Survey instruments Role plays	Assess current level of skill competence and knowledge.
Skill learning	Written text Behavioral guidelines	Teach correct principles and present rationale for behavioral guidelines.
Skill analysis	Cases	Provide examples of appropriate and inappropriate skill performance. Analyze behavioral guidelines and reasons they work.
Skill practice	Exercises Simulations Role plays	Practice behavioral guidelines. Adapt general prescriptions to personal style. Receive feedback and assistance.
Skill application	Assignments (behavioral and written)	Transfer classroom learning to real-life situations. Foster ongoing personal development.

tellectual assimilation and behavioral application. Critiquing the performance of the managers in these cases gives you an opportunity to check comprehension of the skill learning material prior to practicing it yourself, and to analyze a model of the skill being performed.

The *Skill Practice* section allows you to begin experimenting with the behavioral guidelines in the supportive atmosphere of the classroom. It is important that you avoid simply mimicking the style or mannerisms of a role model (either written or visual). Instead, you should experiment, adapting each set of behavioral principles to your own personality.

The *Skill Application* section contains assignments to facilitate the transfer of classroom learning to everyday practice. You may be directed to teach the skill to someone else (an excellent test of understanding), to report on the impact friends and associates have on others when they succeed or fail in using the behavioral principles, or to report on a personal effort to apply the principles in an appropriate setting.

THE NINE CRITICAL MANAGEMENT SKILLS

The chapters in this book focus on nine critical management skills. We selected these skills based on the results of an extensive survey of the literature (Livingston, 1971; Miner, 1973; Ghiselli, 1963; Mintzberg, 1975; Boyatzis, 1982; Katz, 1974; Flanders, 1981), as well as our own study of over 400 practicing managers in a variety of public and private organizations (Cameron & Whetten, 1980). Our final list includes several characteristics:

1. It contains a combination of personal (e.g., stress management) and interpersonal (e.g., conflict resolution) skills, since both are critical prerequisites for effective management.

2. It focuses on proven characteristics of high-performing managers. We have avoided faddish management topics in favor of sticking with fundamental subjects that are grounded in mainstream organizational behavior theory and research.

3. It contains only characteristics that have trainable behavioral components. We have not included topics like leadership that involve a broad range of behaviors, and we have avoided traits like responsibility, fairness, and initiative that lack a well-defined behavioral component.

4. It avoids highly situation-specific supervisory techniques that are best suited for on-the-job training. Some kinds of skills are difficult to learn outside the organizational setting in which they are to be performed (e.g., hiring and firing procedures). The skills we have selected are applicable in most organizations and hierarchical positions.

Our final list of chapters, shown in Table 2, proceeds from personal to interpersonal skills. This sequence is based on the premise that individuals must be in control of their personal affairs before they can effectively manage the affairs of others. As the playwright Messinger remarked, "He that would govern others first should master himself."

TABLE 2 *Critical Management Skills and Subskills*

1. Developing Self-Awareness

   Determining cognitive style, level of values development, and interpersonal orientation
   Becoming aware of personal strengths and weaknesses
   Understanding the impact of your interpersonal style on others

2. Managing Personal Stress

   Developing effective time management techniques
   Identifying major stressors in daily life
   Developing effective coping mechanisms for stress

3. Solving Problems Creatively

   Developing competence in rational problem solving
   Overcoming conceptual blocks
   Creating flexibility in thinking

4. Establishing Supportive Communication

   Becoming adept at active listening
   Developing the ability to be empathetic
   Using the appropriate response formats

5. Gaining Power and Influence

   Establishing a strong power base
   Converting power into influence
   Avoiding abuses of power

6. Improving Employee Performance Through Motivation

   Distinguishing between problems of ability and motivation
   Providing highly valued incentives
   Making rewards contingent on performance
   Timing rewards for maximum impact

7. Delegating and Decision Making

   Developing competence in assigning tasks to others
   Fostering successful task completion in others
   Determining when to involve others in making decisions

8. Managing Conflict

   Balancing assertiveness and sensitivity
   Handling personal criticisms
   Registering complaints effectively
   Mediating conflicts between subordinates

9. Conducting Effective Group Meetings

   Making adequate preparations
   Effectively managing both task and process aspects of meetings
   Making effective presentations

Inasmuch as the key to effective personal life management is self-awareness, in Chapter 1 you have an opportunity to learn more about your personal values, cognitive style, and interpersonal orientation. The insights gained in this chapter will facilitate assimilation of the remaining skills. Our purpose is not to fundamentally alter your personality, value system, or ways of thinking. While some marginal changes may occur in these areas during this course, our objective in Chapter 1 is much more modest. Once you understand yourself better in terms of these three core dimensions, you can adapt the specific behavioral guidelines presented in subsequent chapters to make them consistent with your own "style." While the behavioral guidelines have demonstrated validity, not all effective managers implement them in exactly the same way. Consequently, one broad objective of this text is to help you develop an integrated, congruent approach to management that is consistent with both your core personal characteristics and the guidelines for each skill.

In Chapter 2 we argue that self-awareness is necessary, but not sufficient, for effective personal life management. Managers must also learn how to effectively control stress on the job. "Job burnout" and "midlife crisis" are popular terms for stress-related personal problems experienced by a large number of managers. As we discuss in Chapter 2, an estimated 10 percent of our annual gross national product is lost each year to absenteeism, alcohol and drug abuse, and sabotage caused by job-induced stress. In this chapter we examine the common causes of stress and alternative approaches to maintaining an optimal level of stress in one's life. Since a common source of stress is poor time management, we present a variety of techniques for managing time better. We also discuss several related topics, such as balancing personal and work life activities, establishing realistic long-term goals, and successfully implementing a program of personal development.

Chapter 3 addresses one of the most vital management skills, the ability to break through conceptual logjams. Our emphasis on creativity does not mean that managers should always place a premium on unusual solutions. In this chapter we focus more on the problem-solving process than on the outcome. Managers often get into conceptual ruts, relying habitually on certain traditional patterns of thinking. When they confront a new problem, they have great difficulty coping with it. To help you avoid such ruts, we discuss techniques for approaching apparently unsolvable problems and provide guidelines for divergent and lateral approaches to problem solving.

Beginning with Chapter 4, we focus on interpersonal skills. While stress management and problem solving might involve some interaction with others, interpersonal contact is not central to these activities. In contrast, the remaining skills focus explicitly on the responsibilities of managers that directly involve others. In Chapter 4 we establish a basic framework for these interactions by discussing supportive communication. We pay particular attention to the impact of the message on the sender-listener relationship. It is important not only to communicate a message accurately, but to ensure that the communication process strengthens the relationship between the participants. This skill includes the ability to send messages in a supportive way, to listen supportively, to empathize, and to respond appropriately to others' messages.

Chapter 5 contains a discussion of a second skill that pervades all interpersonal relationships—gaining power and influence. Power is a prerequisite for effective management. Weak managers are unable to implement decisions, defend the interests of their work group, or obtain special rewards for deserving subordinates. To assist in the development of a strong power base, we discuss sources of power originating from the attributes of individuals and the characteristics of organizational positions. A second theme is the proper use of power, once it has been obtained. Many individuals have a reputation for being powerful but not very influential. This is because they are ineffective in using their power to motivate others to accomplish a common objective. Such individuals have often abused their prerogatives, creating resentment and alienation in peers and subordinates.

Chapter 6 focuses on a pressing problem in American management, the need to improve employee performance. Managers are expected to help their organizations achieve the maximum return on their investment in human capital. For this to occur, workers' skill levels must be matched with assigned task difficulty and organizational rewards must satisfy workers' needs and expectations. A thorough understanding of the motivational processes involved in the work place will improve a manager's ability to diagnose the causes of poor worker performance. This is a critical managerial skill. Too often managers unskilled in this area feel that it takes less effort to get rid of poor performers than to investigate the causes of their problems.

After discussing how to communicate supportively, use power sensibly, and motivate effectively, we focus on three management skills that build on these three interpersonal skills. In Chapter 7 we examine one of the most common sources of ineffectiveness among managers—their inability, or unwillingness, to delegate. Managers often have difficulty determining what tasks to delegate, to whom, when, and with what amount of supervision. Delegating is difficult because it means allowing others to make mistakes while retaining responsibility for those mistakes. This chapter combines a prescription for delegating successfully with a model for decision making to help determine what and to whom to delegate responsibilities.

One of the least pleasant aspects of a manager's job is dealing with conflict, the subject of Chapter 8. Most people feel very uncomfortable when they are confronted with an emotionally charged, adversarial situation. This might involve two subordinates arguing over the merits of their respective proposals, or a subordinate criticizing the way the manager allocates work. These situations require slightly different conflict management skills. In the first case the manager would be intervening to mediate the conflict and would have little personal investment in its resolution. His or her principal concern would be ensuring that the better proposal is accepted and the decision-making process does not damage ongoing working relationships. In the second case the manager would be directly involved in the conflict. Indeed, he or she would allegedly be the source of it. Handling this type of criticism in a nondefensive manner is viewed by some experts as the most severe test of a manager's interpersonal skills.

The final skill topic, presented in Chapter 9, is improving group decision making. Members of business organizations often spend a large part of each day in group meetings to coordinate their activities in task forces, management committees, or ongoing work teams. A common perception is that many such meetings are a waste of time. Research on this subject has shown that the villain is generally not the decision to hold the meeting, but the way it is managed. In this chapter we focus on the role of the meeting chairperson and examine ways to make meetings more efficient and relevant. However, since the typical manager will have many more opportunities to make presentations in meetings than to chair them, we also present guidelines for making formal presentations. We have chosen to emphasize this skill since a well-organized, forceful presentation before a management committee can greatly advance a young career.

SUMMARY AND BEHAVIORAL GUIDELINES

There is considerable evidence that individuals planning long-term careers in management must be able to work effectively with people. This requires a wide range of personal, interpersonal, and group management skills. We have chosen to focus on nine core skills identified frequently in the literature and our study of over 400 managers.

It is also apparent that the traditional lecture-discussion approach to teaching is inadequate for developing these critical management skills. This book is designed specifically to facilitate skill development using a format that balances conceptual understanding with behavioral training. Each chapter begins with an assessment of your current skill level and understanding. Next, a set of behavioral guidelines is derived from the scholarly literature and experiences of managers. These guidelines provide the basis for analyzing the actions of managers portrayed in case examples. They also serve as the foundation for skill enhancement during the practice exercises. Finally, transferral of learned behaviors to your day-to-day interactions is facilitated by a series of application assignments.

To better acquaint you with the management skill development approach, the following section contains several learning activities.

REFERENCES

Bandura, A. *Social learning theory.* Englewood Cliffs, N.J.: Prentice-Hall, 1977.

Boyatzis, R. E. *The competent manager.* New York: John Wiley and Sons, 1982.

Burnaska, R. F. The effects of behavior modeling training upon managers' behavior and employees' perceptions. *Personnel Psychology,* 1976, *29,* 329–335.

Cameron, K. S., & Whetten, D. A. An assessment of salient management skills. University of Wisconsin School of Business, working paper, 1980.

Davis, T. R., & Luthans, F. A social learning approach to organizational behavior. *Academy of Management Review,* 1980, *5,* 281–290.

Flanders, L. R. *Report I from the federal manager's job and role survey: Analysis of responses by SES and mid-management levels executive and management development division.* Washington, D.C.: U.S. Office of Personnel Management.

Ghiselli, E. E. Managerial talent. *American Psychologist,* 1963, *18,* 631–642.

Goldstein, A. P., & Sorcher, M. *Changing supervisor behavior,* New York: Pergamon Press, 1974.

Katz, R. L. Skills of an effective administrator. *Harvard Business Review,* 1974, *51,* 90–102.

Latham, G. P., & Saari, L. M. Application of social-learning theory to training supervisors through behavioral modeling. *Journal of Applied Psychology,* 1979, *64,* 239–246.

Livingston, J. S. Myth of the well-educated manager. *Harvard Business Review,* 1971, *49,* 79–89.

Miner, J. B. The real crunch in managerial manpower. *Harvard Business Review,* 1973, *51,* 146–158.

Mintzberg, H. The manager's job: Folklore and fact. *Harvard Business Review*, 1975, *53*, 49–61.

Moses, J. L., & Ritchie, R. J. Supervisory relationships training: A behavioral evaluation of a behavior modeling program. *Personnel Psychology*, 1976, *29*, 337–343.

Porras, J. I., & Anderson, B. Improving managerial effectiveness through modeling-based training. *Organizational Dynamics*, 1981, *9*, 60–77.

Rose, S. D., Cayner, J. J., & Edleson, J. L. Measuring interpersonal competence. *Social Work*, 1977, *22*, 125–129.

Singleton, W. T., Spurgeon, P., & Stammers, R. B. *The analysis of social skill.* New York: Plenum Press, 1980.

Smith, P. E. Management modeling training to improve morale and customer satisfaction. *Personnel Psychology*, 1976, *29*, 351–359.

Whetten, D. A., & Cameron, K. S. Skill development—A needed addition to the management curriculum. *Exchange*, in press.   ∎

■ Supplementary Material

Personal Assessment

Rate yourself according to the following characteristics. The closer you mark to a characteristic, the more it is typical of you. Rate yourself as you *are*, not as you would like to be. Candor is extremely important in this exercise.

1. Prefer to work with others   ___:___:___:___:___   Prefer to do work by myself

2. Often seek leadership opportunities   ___:___:___:___:___   Often avoid leadership opportunities

3. Assertive   ___:___:___:___:___   Not assertive

4. Priorities well-established   ___:___:___:___:___   Priorities not yet well-established

5. Inclined to take pleasure from others' successes   ___:___:___:___:___   Inclined to be jealous of others' successes

6. Inclined to let others do their own thing   ___:___:___:___:___   Have strong desire to influence others

7. Generally unwilling to take responsibility for what others do   ___:___:___:___:___   Generally willing to take responsibility for others' behavior

8. Inclined to exercise power or authority   ___:___:___:___:___   Not inclined to exercise power or authority

9. Easy to identify with others' feelings   ___:___:___:___:___   Difficult to identify with others' feelings

10. Have trouble making decisions   ___:___:___:___:___   Have no trouble making decisions

11. Inclined to be upset and anxious at having lots of time demands   ___:___:___:___:___   Have no difficulty tolerating numerous time demands

12. Inclined to leave things as they are, even when dissatisfied   ___:___:___:___:___   Inclined to suggest and initiate change when needed

13. Am not in control of the use of my time   ___:___:___:___:___   Largely control the use of my time

14. Feel that I know myself intimately   ___:___:___:___:___   Feel frequently out of touch with myself

15. Can generally find all needed information prior to making decisions   ___:___:___:___:___   Frequently have difficulty obtaining information needed to make a decision

16. Not very competitive   ___:___:___:___:___   Very competitive

17. Uncomfortable when distinctive or singled out   ___:___:___:___:___   Enjoy being distinctive or singled out

18. Have little trouble being criticized   ___:___:___:___:___   Bothers me a lot to be criticized

19. Generally rebel against authority   ___:___:___:___:___   Generally obey authority

20. Self-confident   ___:___:___:___:___   Not self-confident

21. Have trouble expressing myself verbally   ___:___:___:___:___   Generally do well expressing myself verbally

22. Trusted by others   ___:___:___:___:___   Often distrusted by others

23. Uncomfortable giving straightforward negative feedback to others   ___:___:___:___:___   No trouble giving straightforward negative feedback to others

24. Have few or no close interpersonal relationships   ___:___:___:___:___   Have many close interpersonal relationships

25. High need to achieve   ___:___:___:___:___   Low need to achieve

26. Have a strong desire to exercise power   ___:___:___:___:___   Not interested in pursuing positions of power

27. Able to effectively resolve disagreements to the satisfaction of both parties   ___:___:___:___:___   Have difficulty resolving disagreements to the satisfaction of both parties

28. Can absorb criticism without becoming defensive   ___:___:___:___:___   Become very defensive when criticized

29. Likely to assume a leadership role in a group when a formal leader has not been appointed   ___:___:___:___:___   Inclined to let others assume a leadership role in a group

30. Feel comfortable giving formal presentations or talks   ___:___:___:___:___   Have great difficulty giving a formal presentation or talk

These items identify certain management skills found to be important for success as a manager. Your instructor has the scoring key.

Interviewing Managers

Your assignment is to interview at least three managers who are employed full time. You should use the questions below in your interviews, but you are not restricted to them. The purpose of these interviews is to give you a chance to learn about critical managerial skills from those who have to use them.

Treat the interviews as confidential. The names of the individuals do not matter, only their opinions, perceptions, and behaviors. Assure the managers that no one will be able to identify them from these responses.

Keep notes on your interviews. These notes should be as detailed as possible so you can reconstruct the interviews for class. Be sure to keep a record of each person's job title and a brief description of his or her organization.

1. Please describe a typical day at work.

2. What are the most time-consuming activities that occupy your workday?

3. What are the most critical problems you face as a manager?

4. What are the most critical skills needed to be a successful manager in your line of work?

5. What are the major reasons managers fail in positions like yours?

6. If you could design a college course to help students become successful managers, what would the course include?

7. On a scale of 1 (very rarely) to 5 (constantly), can you rate the extent to which you use the following skills or behaviors during your workday?

_____ Managing personal stress	_____ Orchestrating change
_____ Managing time	_____ Appraising others' performance
_____ Setting goals	_____ Facilitating group decision making
_____ Making individual decisions	_____ Listening
_____ Defining or recognizing problems	_____ Disciplining others
_____ Using verbal communication skills	_____ Achieving self-awareness
_____ Delegating	_____ Empathizing
_____ Motivating others	_____ Team building
_____ Managing conflict	_____ Solving problems
_____ Interviewing	_____ Conducting meetings
_____ Gaining and using power	_____ Negotiating

What Makes a Top Executive?

Morgan W. McCall, Jr., and Michael M. Lombardo

> *Senior Executive:* At one time, Jim was the leading, perhaps the only, candidate for chief executive officer. And then he ran into something he'd never faced before—an unprofitable operation. He seemed to go on a downward spiral after that, becoming more remote each day, unable to work with key subordinates.
>
> *Interviewer:* Why do you think he derailed?
>
> *Senior Executive:* Some of it was bad luck, because the business was going down when he inherited it. Some of it was surrounding himself with specialists, who inevitably wear the blinders of their particular field. And some of it was that he had never learned to delegate. He had no idea of how to lead by listening.

The case of Jim is by no means unusual. Many executives of formidable talent rise to very high levels, yet are denied the ultimate positions. The quick explanations for what might be called their derailment are the ever-popular Peter Principle—they rose past their level of competence—or, more darkly, they possessed some fatal flaw.

The grain of truth in these explanations masks the actual complexity of the process. So we learned from a study that we recently did here at the Center for Creative Leadership, a nonprofit research and educational institution in Greensboro, North Carolina, formed to improve the practice of management.

When we compared 21 derailed executives—successful people who were expected to go even higher in the organization but who reached a plateau late in their careers, were fired, or were forced to retire early—with 20 "arrivers"—those who made it all the way to the top—we found the two groups astonishingly alike. Every one of the 41 executives possessed remarkable strengths, and every one was flawed by one or more significant weaknesses.

Insensitivity to others was cited as a reason for derailment more often than any other flaw. But it was never the only reason. Most often, it was a combination of personal qualities and external circumstances that put an end to an executive's rise. Some of the executives found themselves in a changed situation, in which strengths that had served them well earlier in their careers became liabilities that threw them off track. Others found that weaknesses they'd had all along, once outweighed by assets, became crucial defects in a new situation requiring particular skills to resolve some particular problem.

Our goal was to find out what makes an effective executive, and our original plan was to concentrate on arrivers. But we soon realized that, paradoxically, we could learn a lot about effectiveness by taking a close look at executives who had failed to live up to their apparent potential.

SOURCE: Morgan M. McCall, Jr., and Michael M. Lombardo, What makes a top executive? *Psychology Today,* 1983, 26, 28–31.

We and our associate, Ann Morrison, worked with several Fortune-500 corporations to identify "savvy insiders"—people who had seen many top executives come and go and who were intimately familiar with their careers. In each corporation one of us interviewed several insiders, usually a few of the top 10 executives and a few senior "human resources professionals," people who help to decide who moves up. We asked them to tell both a success story and a story of derailment.

FATAL FLAWS

Asked to say what had sealed the fate of the men (they were all men) who fell short of ultimate success, our sources named 65 factors, which we boiled down to ten categories:

1. Insensitive to others: abrasive, intimidating, bullying style.
2. Cold, aloof, arrogant.
3. Betrayal of trust.
4. Overly ambitious: thinking of next job, playing politics.
5. Specific performance problems with the business.
6. Overmanaging: unable to delegate or build a team.
7. Unable to staff effectively.
8. Unable to think strategically.
9. Unable to adapt to boss with different style.
10. Overdependent on advocate or mentor.

No executive had all the flaws cited; indeed, only two were found in the average derailed executive.

As we have noted, the most frequent cause for derailment was insensitivity to other people. "He wouldn't negotiate; there was no room for countervailing views. He could follow a bull through a china shop and still break the china," one senior executive said of a derailed colleague.

Under stress, some of the derailed managers became abrasive and intimidating. One walked into a subordinate's office, interrupting a meeting, and said, "I need to see you." When the subordinate tried to explain that he was occupied, his boss snarled, "I don't give a goddam. I said I wanted to see you now."

Others were so brilliant that they became arrogant, intimidating others with their knowledge. Common remarks were: "He made others feel stupid" or "He wouldn't give you the time of day unless you were brilliant too."

In an incredibly complex and confusing job, being able to trust others absolutely is a necessity. Some executives committed what is perhaps management's only unforgivable sin: They betrayed a trust. This rarely had anything to do with honesty, which was a given in almost all cases. Rather, it was a one-upping of others, or a failure to follow through on promises that wreaked havoc in terms of organizational efficiency. One executive didn't implement a decision as he had promised to do, causing conflicts between the marketing and the production divisions that reverberated downward through four levels of frustrated subordinates.

Others, like Cassius, were overly ambitious. They seemed to be always thinking of their next job, they bruised people in their haste, and they spent too much time trying to please upper management. This sometimes led to staying with a single advocate or mentor too long. When the mentor fell from favor, so did they. Even if the mentor remained in power, people questioned the executive's ability to make independent judgments. Could he stand alone? One executive had worked for the same boss for the better part of 15 years, following him from one assignment to another. Then top management changed, and the boss no longer fit in with the plans of the new regime. The executive, having no reputation of his own, was viewed as a clone of his boss and was passed over as well.

A series of performance problems sometimes emerged. Managers failed to meet profit goals, got lazy, or demonstrated that they couldn't handle certain kinds of jobs (usually new ventures or jobs requiring great powers of persuasion). More important in such cases, managers showed that they couldn't change; they failed to admit their problems, covered them up, or tried to blame them on others. One executive flouted senior management by failing to work with a man specifically sent in to fix a profit problem.

After a certain point in their careers, managers must cease to do the work themselves, and must become executives who see that it is done. But some of the men we studied never made this transition, never learning to delegate or to build a team beneath them. Although overmanaging is irritating at any level, it can be fatal at the executive level. When executives meddle, they are meddling not with low-level subordinates but with other executives, most of whom know much more about their particular area of expertise than their boss ever will. One external-affairs executive who knew little about government regulation tried to direct an expert with 30 years' experience. The expert balked, and the executive lost a battle that should never have begun.

Others got along with their staff, but simply picked the wrong people. Sometimes they staffed in their own image, choosing, for instance, an engineer like themselves when a person with marketing experience would have been better suited for the task at hand. Or sometimes they simply picked people who later bombed.

Inability to think strategically—to take a broad, long-term view—was masked by attention to detail and a miring in technical problems, as some executives simply couldn't go from being doers to being planners. Another common failure appeared as a conflict of style with a new boss. One manager who couldn't change from a go-getter to a thinker/planner eventually ran afoul of a slower-paced, more reflective boss. Although the successful managers sometimes had similar problems, they didn't get into wars over them, and rarely let the issues get personal. Derailed managers exhibited a host of unproductive responses—got peevish, tried to shout the boss down, or just sulked.

In summary, we concluded that executives derail for four basic reasons, all connected to the fact that situations change as one ascends the organizational hierarchy:

1. *Strengths become weaknesses.* Loyalty becomes overdependence, narrowness, or cronyism. Ambition is eventually viewed as politicking and destroys an executive's support base.
2. *Deficiencies eventually matter.* If talented enough, a person can get by with insensitivity at lower levels, but not at higher ones, where subordinates and peers are powerful and probably brilliant also. Those who are charming but not brilliant find that the job gets too big and problems too complex to get by on interpersonal skills.
3. *Success goes to their heads.* After being told how good they are for so long, some executives simply lose their humility and become cold and arrogant. Once this happens, their information sources begin to dry up and people no longer wish to work with them.
4. *Events conspire.* A few of the derailed apparently did little wrong. They were done in politically, or by economic upheavals. Essentially, they just weren't lucky.

While conducting the interviews, we heard few stories about waterwalkers. In fact, the executive who came closest to fitting that category, the one "natural leader," derailed precisely because everyone assumed that he could do absolutely anything. At higher levels of management, he became lost in detail, concentrated too much on his subordinates, and seemed to lack the intellectual ability to deal with complex issues. Still, no one helped him; it was assumed that he would succeed regardless.

In short, both the arrivers and those who derailed had plenty of warts, although these generally became apparent only late in the men's careers. The events that exposed the flaws were seldom cataclysmic. More often, the flaws themselves had a cumulative impact. As one executive put it, "Careers last such a long time. Leave a trail of mistakes and you eventually find yourself encircled by your past."

In general, the flaws of both the arrivers and the derailed executives showed up when one of five things happened to them: (1) They lost a boss who had covered, or compensated for, their weaknesses. (2) They entered a job for which they were not prepared, either because it entailed much greater responsibility or because it required the executives to perform functions that were new to them. Usually, the difficulties were compounded by the fact that the executives went to work for a new boss whose style was very different from that of his newly promoted subordinate. (3) They left behind a trail of little problems or bruised people, either because they handled them poorly or moved through so quickly that they failed to handle them at all. (4) They moved up during an organizational shake-up and weren't scrutinized until the shake-down period. (5) They entered the executive suite, where getting along with others is critical.

One or more of these events happened to most of the executives, so the event itself was telling only in that its impact began to separate the two groups. How one person dealt with his flaws under stress went a long way toward explaining why some men arrived and some jumped the tracks just short of town. A bit of dialogue from one interview underscores this point:

> *Senior Executive:* Successful people don't like to admit that they make big mistakes, but they make whoppers nevertheless. I've never known a CEO [chief executive officer] who didn't make at least one big one and lots of little ones, but it never hurt them.
> *Interviewer:* Why?
> *Senior Executive:* Because they know how to handle adversity.

Part of handling adversity lies in knowing what *not* to do. As we learned, lots of different management behavioral patterns were acceptable to others. The key was in knowing which ones colleagues and superiors would find intolerable.

As we said at the beginning, both groups were amazingly similar: incredibly bright, identified as promising early in their careers, outstanding in their track records, ambitious, willing to sacrifice—and imperfect. A closer look does reveal some differences, however, and at the levels of excellence characteristic of executives, even a small difference is more than sufficient to create winners and losers.

THE ARRIVERS AND THE DERAILED COMPARED

In the first place, derailed executives had a series of successes, but usually in similar kinds of situations. They had turned two businesses around, or managed progressively larger jobs in the same function. By contrast, the arrivers had more diversity in their successes—they had turned a business around *and* successfully moved from line to staff and back, or started a new business from scratch *and* completed a special assignment with distinction. They built plants in the wilderness and the Amazonian jungle, salvaged disastrous operations, resolved all-out wars between corporate divisions without bloodshed. One even built a town.

Derailed managers were often described as moody or volatile under pressure. One could control his temper with top management he sought to impress, but was openly jealous of peers he saw as competitors. His too-frequent angry outbursts eroded the cooperation necessary for success, as peers began to wonder whether he was trying to do them in. In contrast, the arrivers were calm, confident, and predictable. People knew how they would react and could plan their own actions accordingly.

Although neither group made many mistakes, all of the arrivers handled theirs with poise and grace. Almost uniformly, they admitted the mistake, forewarned others so they wouldn't be blind-sided by it, then set about analyzing and fixing it. Also telling were two things the arrivers didn't do: They didn't blame others, and once they had handled the situation, they didn't dwell on it.

Moreover, derailed executives tended to react to failure by going on the defensive, trying to keep it under wraps while they fixed it, or, once the problem was visible, blaming it on someone else.

Although both groups were good at going after problems, arrivers were particularly single-minded. This "What's the problem?" mentality spared them three of the common flaws of the derailed: They were too busy worrying about their present job to appear overly eager for their next position; they demanded excellence from their people in problem solving; and they developed many contacts, saving themselves from the sole-mentor syndrome. In fact, almost no successful manager reported having a single mentor.

Lastly, the arrivers, perhaps due to the diversity of their backgrounds, had the ability to get along with all types of people. They either possessed or developed the skills required to be outspoken without offending people. They were not seen as charming-but-political or direct-but-tactless, but as direct-and-diplomatic. One arriver disagreed strongly with a business strategy favored by his boss. He presented his objections candidly and gave the reasons for his concerns as well as the alternative he preferred. But when the decision went against him, he put his energy behind making the decision work. When his boss turned out to be wrong, the arriver didn't gloat about it; he let the situation speak for itself without further embarrassing his boss.

One of the senior executives we interviewed made a simple but not simplistic distinction between the two groups. Only two things, he said, differentiated the successful from the derailed: total integrity, and understanding other people.

Integrity seems to have a special meaning to executives. The word does not refer to simple honesty, but embodies a consistency and predictability built over time that says, "I will do exactly what I say I will do when I say I will do it. If I change my mind, I will tell you well in advance so you will not be harmed by my actions." Such a statement is partly a matter of ethics, but, even more, a question of vital practicality. This kind of integrity seems to be the core element in keeping a large, amorphous organization from collapsing in its own confusion.

Ability—or inability—to understand other people's perspectives was the most glaring difference between the arrivers and the derailed. Only 25 percent of the derailed were described as having a special ability with people; among arrivers, the figure was 75 percent.

Interestingly, two of the arrivers were cold and asinine when younger, but somehow completely changed their style. "I have no idea how he did it," one executive said. "It was as if he went to bed one night and woke up a different person." In general, a certain awareness of self and willingness to change characterized the arrivers. That same flexibility, of course, is also what is needed to get along with all types of people.

A final word—a lesson, perhaps, to be drawn from our findings. Over the years, "experts" have generated long lists of critical skills in an attempt to define the complete manager. In retrospect it seems obvious that no one, the talented executive included, can possess all of those skills. As we came to realize, executives, like the rest of us, are a patchwork of strengths *and* weaknesses. The reasons that some executives ultimately derailed and others made it all the way up the ladder confirm what we all know but have hesitated to admit: There is no one best way to succeed (or even to fail). The foolproof, step-by-step formula is not just elusive; it is, as Kierkegaard said of truth, like searching a pitchdark room for a black cat that isn't there.

ASSIGNMENT

Identify your ideal career path for the next 15–20 years. Begin with the entry-level management position you are aiming for after graduation, proceed through at least two promotions, and describe your ultimate goal as a manager. (Don't be overly modest, but also don't be unrealistic—this is for your benefit.) Now look through the remainder of the chapters in this book, as well as your results on the Personal Assessment test, and write down several personal learning objectives for this course. Consider the skills that will be critical at each stage in your career. Next, write down several guidelines from this article that will help you reduce the chances of becoming "derailed" as you proceed along your career path.

The Tampa Pump & Valve Company

R. E. Dutton and R. C. Sherman

The Tampa Pump & Valve Company, whose plant manager had been John Manners, is a subsidiary of Florida Chemical & Equipment Corporation. Its operations have been quite successful. Beginning with a capital investment of slightly less than $750,000 shortly after the end of World War II, its capital investment today is in excess of $65,000,000. The Tampa Pump & Valve Company possesses a newly constructed office building and a manufacturing and assembly plant. There are two sales outlets—one in Tampa and one in Jacksonville.

The company, excluding top management, is currently staffed with sixty engineers and thirty-two technicians. Approximately 1000 persons are employed in the production department, working two forty-hour shifts a week.

Joe O'Malley is the general superintendent in charge of production. All valves and pump assemblies and components that are not purchased are manufactured and assembled in the production department according to job and design specifications. These are shipped to various sites and locations according to orders, or they are stored in the company's two warehouses in Jacksonville and Tampa. Centralized product and planning enables the company to maintain rigid production and quality controls over all units that become a part of completed products. In addition, carefully planned production and shipping schedules reduce the amount of time that completed units must be stored at receiving stations. Thus, shipping costs are reduced, and the company is better able to insure that contracted completion dates are met.

The research and development division, currently under the direction of Tom Everts, has grown from two engineers to its present size of thirty engineers and twelve technicians and draftsmen. Partly because of the plant manager's intense interest, 10 percent of the company's profits are allocated to research and development. The research division recently developed a less expensive and longer lasting rust inhibitor than that previously manufactured. New rotary arc-welding units for the plant have also been developed, as well as a new method for testing the strength and quality of welded unions. Also, the division was responsible for the design of expansion joints which are formed and assembled in the company's plant, ready for immediate installation at construction sites.

In addition to being the controller, Bill Marshall is general counsel for the plant. A staff of two attorneys and three legal assistants report directly to him, as does the chief accountant and his staff. The accounting department employs approximately fifteen people.

SOURCE: D. D. White and H. W. Vroman (Eds.), *Action in organizations* (Boston: Allyn & Bacon, 1978) pp. 441–449.

The industrial and employee relations department, under A. C. Cushwell, has a staff of approximately fifteen people. A total of eighty-two employees are employed in the marketing department, which is headed by James Barber. . . .

John Manners suffered a severe heart attack on April 12 and died. It had been noticed that he appeared tired and overworked recently. At this time, Richard West was transferred from the Orlando Pump and Valve Plant, which is a slightly smaller subsidiary of Florida Chemical & Equipment Corporation, to fill the position.

INSTRUCTIONS

Today is Sunday, April 14, 1975. Richard West has just come into the office, for the first time, at 6:45 P.M. He must leave in time to catch the 10:00 P.M. plane for Caracas, Venezuela, for an important meeting. He will not be back until next Monday, April 23. His secretary is Pearl Powell, who was secretary to John Manners before he died.

The materials in this packet [Items 1–12] were left in the in-basket on his desk by his secretary (Pearl Powell). You are to assume the role of Richard West and go through the entire packet of materials, taking whatever action you deem appropriate for each item. Every action [you wish] to take should be written down, including memos to the secretary, memos to "yourself" (Richard West), etc. Draft letters where appropriate, write out any plans or agenda for meetings or conferences that you plan. These letters, memos, notes, etc., may be in "rough draft" form.

Remember! The day is Sunday, April 14, time: 6:45 P.M. Write down every action you take on any item. You cannot call on anyone for assistance. The telephone switchboard is not operating. You must work with the materials at hand. You will be out of the office from 9:45 tonight until Monday, April 23. Be sure to record every action, whether memo, letter, meeting plan, etc.   ▪

Item 1A

April 13, 1975

OFFICE MEMORANDUM

TO: Richard West

FROM: Pearl Powell

SUBJECT: SAM Presentation (see attached)

Mr. West:

   Just a note to let you know that Mr. Manners did nothing toward
developing the program scheduled April 25, except to send the title
to Mr. Johnson via phone. The title was announced to the members
some time ago. I don't think Mr. Manners discussed the matter with
any of the department heads.

Pearl

Item 1B

THE SOCIETY FOR THE ADVANCEMENT OF MANAGEMENT
Dallas Chapter
P.O. Box 9106
Dallas, Texas

April 4, 1975

Mr. John Manners
Plant Manager
Tampa Pump & Valve Company
Tampa, Florida 33601

Dear John:

This is a reminder that we are counting on you and on the
Tampa Pump & Valve Company to provide us with the three-hour
evening program for our meeting April 25.

I know you and your boys will provide a stimulating and
worthwhile program. The title of the program you are to present,
"The Image of Today's Executive," sounds very interesting and
already the dinner and program is a "sell-out." Therefore, you
can look forward to a full house on the night of your presentation.

Could you prepare a brief outline of the program and text of
any speeches that will be presented indicating who will present
them so we can go ahead with the programs and press releases?

We are all looking forward to seeing you then.

Best regards,

Paul Johnson,
Secretary Dallas
Chapter, Society
for the Advancement
of Management

PJ:am

Item 2

P E R S O N A L

April 10, 1975

OFFICE MEMORANDUM

TO: John Manners

FROM: A. C. Cushwell, Industrial and Employee Relations

SUBJECT: Frank Batt

I have heard through the grapevine and "unimpeachable" sources that Frank Batt has been looking around and has had an outside job offer on which he is going to give a firm answer next week. I don't think anyone else knows this yet. I just happened to run on to it. I understand that he has been offered more money than we can offer him now based on present wage and salary policy. As you know, Batt has only been with the company a short time and is already making somewhat more than others at his rank. This presents a problem which needs to be ironed out. I am afraid I mentioned the possibility of just such a situation as this when you instituted the plan last November. Perhaps we need to reconsider some of the aspects of your plan before we make offers to June graduates.

I know that you and Everts feel that Frank is one of the most valuable men in research and development, and I thought I would let you know about this for whatever action you want to take.

A. C. Cushwell

Item 3

April 7, 1975

OFFICE MEMORANDUM

TO: John Manners

FROM: A. C. Cushwell, Industrial and Employee Relations

SUBJECT: Testing Program

You recently suggested that we institute a testing program for hiring secretarial and clerical personnel. The following are some suggested tests and other criteria that we might want to consider. Do you have any further suggestions for types of tests or other hiring procedures which we might want to look into before we finalize a program?

(1) Clerical Personnel:

    (a) Whitney General Clerical Survey (includes measures on spelling, arithmetic, alphabetizing, and general aptitude).

    (b) Mann-Watson Typing Test

    (c) Age to 40

(2) Secretarial Personnel:

    (a) Whitney General Clerical Survey

    (b) Mann-Watson Typing Test

    (c) Collins Shorthand Skill Inventory (via recording)

    (d) High School Diploma

    (e) Age to 40

A. C. Cushwell

Item 4

April 10, 1975

OFFICE MEMORANDUM

TO: John Manners

FROM: Bill Marshall

SUBJECT: Termination of Robert Roberts, Employee #6897

This is a summary of my reasons for terminating Robert Roberts.
As you know, Mr. Roberts was employed as a legal assistant on
March 4, 19xx. For almost two years he has been working for us on
a full-time basis while attending law school at night. He has
continually been a source of irritation to those who have been
working closely with him. The problem in general has been one of
overstepping his authority. He has frequently been involved in
controversies with the legal staff over problems with which we felt
he was not adequately prepared to deal nor were any of his concern
since they did not involve his own work assignments. In general,
he did an adequate job on the work he was assigned, but many of the
staff felt that he was not putting forth a full effort because he
seemed to have a lot of free time which he spent in the coffee bar
or in conversations with others in the department. The incident
that caused his termination took place about three days before his
termination. He was told to contact a party concerning a pending
contract. All he was to do was to secure the necessary signatures
from the other party. The attorney handling the contract for our
company in the particular case was George Slavin. Mr. Roberts,
instead of simply securing signatures, evidently discussed the
contract with the outside party, recommending changes, and in
general so disrupted proceedings that now the whole contract is
in question. After the customer contacted George, George
immediately discussed the occurrence with me, and we felt that the
incident was serious enough to warrant dismissal.

Bill

Item 5

April 6, 1975

OFFICE MEMORANDUM

TO: John Manners

FROM: James Barber

SUBJECT: Sales Promotion of Rust Inhibitor

As you know, we are moving into our campaign to push the new rust inhibitor. I would like to have your permission to set up a contest among our sales representatives with a trip to Hawaii for the sales representative who sells the highest dollar volume in the next six-month period. I want to make the prize good enough to tempt the sales force.

Jim

Item 6

April 11, 1975

OFFICE MEMORANDUM

TO: John Manners

FROM: A. C. Cushwell

SUBJECT: Employment of John Jones, Engineer

I would like to bring you up to date on my feelings concerning the engineer, John Jones, whom Everts wishes to employ. Everts is from Chicago, and I don't think that he fully understands the morale problems we would have if we hired a black engineer who would have supervision over several white assistants. I realize that we are going to have to protect our interests in government contracts, but I think we can find a better way to do so than starting at this level. I would suggest that you talk with Everts about this problem and the possible complications that could arise.

A. C. Cushwell

Item 7

April 9, 1975

OFFICE MEMORANDUM

TO: John Manners

FROM: Bill Marshall

SUBJECT: Annual Budget Requests

    We are late in turning in our budget proposal to Florida Chemical and Equipment Company for the next fiscal year since the report from R & D is still not in. All other department heads have turned in sound budgets which, if approved, should greatly facilitate the cutting of costs next year. Can you do something to speed up action?

                                       Bill Marshall

Item 8

April 6, 1975

OFFICE MEMORANDUM

TO: John Manners

FROM: Bill Marshall

SUBJECT: Coffee Breaks

    This morning I timed a number of people who took 40 minutes standing in line and drinking their coffee. These people were mainly from the production and research departments. I am able to control this in my department, and I feel you should see that this matter is taken care of by the heads of the other departments. I estimate that the waste amounts to 125,000 man hours (approximately $500.00) a year.

                                       Bill

Item 9

April 9, 1975

OFFICE MEMORANDUM

TO: John Manners

FROM: Tom Everts

SUBJECT: Allocations for Research

This department has been successful in developing an efficient method for extracting certain basic compounds from slag and other similar by-products that are currently classified as waste by a large number of chemical plants within this area.

It is my recommendation that this company take every step necessary to commercially develop this extraction method. I have brought this matter to Bill Marshall's attention on two separate occasions, requesting that the necessary funds be allocated to fully develop this program. I have been advised by him both times that the funds could not possibly be made available within the next fiscal year. He has also indicated that we should de-emphasize research in the chemical area, since this is unnecessary duplication of functions with the Orlando and Lake City plants.

It is my opinion that this company should capitalize on its advantageous position now, before our competitors are able to perfect a similar method.

The above is for your consideration and recommendations.

Tom Everts

cc: Mr. O. J. Thompson, Vice-President
Research & Development

Item 10

AMERCIAN FEDERATION OF FOUNDRY WORKERS
Local 801
Tampa, Florida

April 6, 1975

Mr. John Manners, Manager
Tampa Pump & Valve Company
Tampa, Florida 33601

Dear Sir:

On several recent occasions, I have noticed that you and
your staff have employed your company newspaper as a vehicle for
undermining the present union administration.

In addition, a series of supervisory bulletins have been
circulated that were designed to cause supervisory personnel to
influence the thinking of union members in the forthcoming union
election. I am also well aware of your "support" for Jessie Sims
and others, who have been more than sympathetic towards company
management.

As you know, such behavior as I have described is in direct
violation of Section 101, Subsection 9 (a) of the Labor-Management
Relations Act, as well as being a violation of Article 21 of our
contract with your company. I am sure that you are also aware
of the negative impact the filing of a charge of unfair management
practices could have on future elections and negotiations.

I trust such action will not become necessary and that you
will take steps to prevent any further discrimination against this
administration.

Sincerely yours,

R. L. Loper, President
A. F. F. W., Local 801

RLL:jg

cc: Mr. A. C. Cushwell

Item 11

April 10, 1975

OFFICE MEMORANDUM

TO: John Manners

FROM: Joe O'Malley

SUBJECT: Quality Control

   The marketing department has put pressure on us to increase production for the next two months so that promised deliveries can be made. At the present time we cannot increase production without some risk in terms of quality. The problem is that marketing does not check with us before committing us to specific delivery dates. This problem has come up before, but nothing has been done. Could I meet with you in the near future to discuss the situation?

                                        Joe

Item 12

OFFICE MEMORANDUM

TO: John Manners

FROM: Joe O'Malley

SUBJECT: Pay rate for maintenance men who worked on the U. S.
          National Day of Mourning

    It was necessary for me to bring in seven maintenance men last
Monday in spite of your order that we would observe the National
Day of Mourning due to the sudden death of President Harris.

    The question has arisen as to whether these men should be paid
straight time for the work or double time, which is customary for
work during holidays. I also had 40 people on vacation during
this period. Ordinarily, when a legal holiday falls during their
vacation they are given an extra day. Since this was an unusual
situation I am not sure how to handle it and would like your
recommendation.

                                                 Joe

1 Developing Self-Awareness

- **Skill Preassessment**

  Self-Awareness Preassessment

- **Skill Learning**

  Three Critical Areas of Self-Awareness

- **Skill Analysis**

  Brainwashing

  The Boy, the Girl, the Ferryboat Captain, and the Hermits

- **Skill Practice**

  Defining Issues Test

  The Cognitive Style Instrument

  FIRO-B

  Group Discussion Exercise

- **Skill Application**

  Application Exercises

■ *Skill Preassessment*

Self-Awareness Preassessment

Please respond to these items on the basis of how typical each statement is of you. The purpose of the instrument is to help you determine how self-aware you are. Therefore, answer as accurately as you can. Use the following scale: 5—strongly agree, 4—agree, 3—neither, 2—disagree, 1—strongly disagree.

_____ 1. I have articulated a clear set of principles that guide my behavior.

_____ 2. I often hear things about myself from others that I think are untrue or unrepresentative of the way I really am.

_____ 3. In interpersonal relationships, I seldom am able to be completely at ease.

_____ 4. I don't know how to improve my ability to learn new things.

_____ 5. I frequently have close, personal talks about myself with someone I know well.

_____ 6. I frequently have been offended by others' behavior toward me.

_____ 7. I seldom have really gotten below the surface in a conversation with a friend.

_____ 8. I can resolve interpersonal difficulties with someone I know relatively easily.

_____ 9. The decisions I make about how to behave are always consistent with my values.

_____ 10. I think about things differently than many people do.   ■

■ *Skill Learning*

Three Critical Areas of Self-Awareness

For more than three hundred years, knowledge of the self has been considered to be at the very core of human behavior. The ancient dictum "Know thyself" has been variously attributed to Plato, Pythagoras, Thales, and Socrates. Plutarch noted that this inscription was carved on the Delphic Oracle, that mystical sanctuary where kings and generals sought advice on matters of greatest importance to them. As early as 42 B.C., Publilius Syrus proposed, "It matters not what you are thought to be, but what you are." Alfred Lord Tennyson said, "Self-reverence, self-knowledge, self-control, these three alone lead to sovereign power." And probably the most oft-quoted passage on the self is Polonius' advice in *Hamlet:* "To thine own self be true, and it must follow as the night the day, thou canst not then be false to any man."

Students of human behavior have long known that knowledge of the self—self-awareness, self-insight, self-understanding—is a prerequisite for productive personal and interpersonal functioning, and a host of techniques and methods for achieving that goal have been devised. Various therapies, group methods, meditation techniques, and exercise programs have been touted as enhancing insight into the self and inner peace. This chapter does not aim to summarize those procedures, nor does it espouse one particular method of reaching that goal. Rather, we discuss here the importance of self-awareness in relation to managerial behavior, and we present a series of self-assessment instruments that research has shown to have a relationship to managerial success. Our emphasis is on scientifically validated information linking self-awareness to the behavior of managers, and we try to avoid common-sense generalizations that have not been tested in research.

THE ENIGMA OF SELF-AWARENESS

Erich Fromm (1939) was one of the first behavioral scientists to observe the close connection between the self-concept and feelings about others: "Hatred against oneself is inseparable from hatred against others." Carl Rogers (1961) later proposed that self-awareness and self-acceptance are prerequisites for psychological health, personal growth, and the ability to know and accept others. In fact, Rogers suggested that the basic human need is for self-regard, which he found to be more powerful in his clinical cases than physiological needs. Hayakawa (1962) has asserted that the first law of life is not *self*-preservation, but *self-image* preservation. "The self-concept," he states, "is the fundamental determinant of all our behavior. Indeed, since it is an organization of our past experiences and perceptions as well as our values and goals, it determines the character of the reality we see" (p. 229). There is considerable empirical evidence that self-awareness and self-acceptance are strongly related to personal adjustment, interpersonal relationships, and life success. Brouwer (1964, p. 156) has asserted:

> The function of self-examination is to lay the groundwork for insight, without which no growth can occur. Insight is the "oh, I see now" feeling which must consciously or unconsciously precede change in behavior. Insights—real, genuine glimpses of ourselves as we really are—are reached only with difficulty and sometimes with real psychic pain. But they are the building blocks of growth. Thus, self-examination is a preparation for insight, a groundbreaking for the seeds of self-understanding which gradually bloom into changed behavior.

There is little question that the knowledge we possess about ourselves, which serves to make up our self-concept, is critical to improving our management skills. We cannot improve ourselves or develop new capabilities unless and until we know what level of capability we currently possess. On the other hand, several authors point out that self-knowledge may inhibit personal improvement, rather than facilitate it. They point out that individuals frequently evade personal growth and new self-knowledge because of fear. That is, individuals resist acquiring additional information to protect their self-esteem or self-respect. If they acquire new knowledge about themselves, there is always the possibility that it will be negative or make them uncomfortable in some way. The new knowledge might lead to feelings of inferiority, weakness, evilness, or shame, so it is avoided. As Maslow (1962, p. 57) notes,

> We tend to be afraid of any knowledge that would cause us to despise ourselves or to make us feel inferior, weak, worthless, evil, shameful. We protect ourselves and our ideal image of ourselves by repression and similar defenses, which are essentially techniques by which we avoid becoming conscious of unpleasantness or dangerous truths.

The implication is that personal growth is avoided for fear of finding out that we are not all that we would like to be. If there is a better way to be, the current state must therefore be inadequate or inferior. That realization—that one is not totally adequate or knowledgeable—is difficult for many people to accept. They end up resisting personal improvement through a "denying of our best side, of our talents, of our finest impulses, of our highest potentialities, of our creativeness. In brief, this is the struggle against our own greatness" (Maslow, 1962, p. 58). That is why Freud (1956) asserted that to be completely honest with oneself is the best effort an individual can make, because complete honesty requires a continual search for more information about the self and a desire for self-improvement.

Seeking knowledge of the self, therefore, seems to be an enigma. It is a prerequisite for and motivator of growth and improvement, but it may also inhibit growth and improvement. It may lead to stagnation because of fear of knowing more. How, then, can improvement be accomplished? How can management skills be developed if they are being resisted?

THE SENSITIVE LINE

One answer relies on the concept of the "sensitive line." This concept refers to the point at which individuals become defensive or protective when encountering information about themselves that is inconsistent with their self-concept or when encountering pressure to alter their behavior. Most people regularly experience information about themselves that doesn't quite fit or that is marginally inconsistent. For example, a friend might say, "You look tired today. Are you feeling okay?" If you were feeling fine, the information would be inconsistent with your self-awareness. But because the discrepancy would be relatively minor, it would not be likely to offend you or to evoke a strong defensive reaction. That is, it would probably not require that you reexamine and change your self-concept. On the other hand, the more discrepant the information or the more serious its implications for your self-concept, the closer it would approach your sensitive line, and you would feel a need to defend yourself against it. For example, having a co-worker judge your work incompetent may cross your sensitive line if you think you have done a good job. This would be especially true if the co-worker were an influential person. Your response would likely be to defend yourself against the information to protect the image you held of yourself.

Hayakawa (1962, p. 230) states the point differently. He asserts that the self-concept "tends to rigidify under threat," so that if an individual encounters discrepant information that is threatening, the current self-concept is reasserted with redoubled force. Haney (1979) refers to a "comfort zone" similar to a thermostat. When the situation becomes too uncomfortable, protective measures are brought into play that bring the situation back to normal. When marked discrepancies in the self-image are experienced, in other words, the validity of the information or its source is denied or other defensive mechanisms are used to ensure that the self-concept remains stable.

In light of this defensiveness, then, how can personal change and increased self-knowledge ever occur? There are at least two answers. One is that information that is verifiable, predictable, and controllable is less likely to cross the sensitive line than information without those characteristics. That is, if an individual can test the validity of the discrepant information (e.g., if some objective standard exists), if the information is not unexpected or "out-of-the-blue" (e.g., if it is received at regular intervals), and if there is some control over when and how much information is received, it is more likely to be heard and accepted. The information you receive about yourself in this chapter possesses those three characteristics. You will be asked to complete three self-assessment instruments that have been used extensively in research. Their reliability and validity have been established. Moreover, they have been found to be associated with managerial success. Therefore, by completing them honestly, you can gain important insight that can prove helpful to you.

A second answer to the problem of overcoming defensiveness in self-awareness lies in the role other people can play in helping this insight to occur. It is almost impossible to increase skill in self-awareness without interacting with and disclosing ourselves to others. Unless one is willing to open up to others, to discuss aspects of the self that seem ambiguous or unknown, little growth can ever occur. Self-disclosure, therefore, is a key to improvement in self-awareness. Harris (1981) points out:

> In order to know oneself, no amount of introspection or self-examination will suffice. You can analyze yourself for weeks, or meditate for months, and you will not get an inch further—any more than you can smell your own breath or laugh when you tickle yourself.
>
> You must first be open to the other person before you catch a glimmering of yourself. Our self-reflection in a mirror does not tell us what we are like; only our reflection in other people. We are essentially social creatures, and our personality resides in association, not in isolation.

As you complete instruments and engage in exercises in this chapter, therefore, it is important that you discuss your insights with someone else. This is because a lack of self-disclosure not only inhibits self-awareness, but also may affect adversely other aspects of managerial skill development. For example, several studies have shown that low self-disclosers are less healthy and more self-alienated than high self-disclosers. College students give the highest ratings for interpersonal competence to high self-disclosers. Individuals are liked best who are high self-disclosers, and excessive or insufficient self-disclosure results in less liking and acceptance by others (see, for example, Jourard, 1964). Some of the exercises in this chapter will require you to discuss your experiences with others. This is done because involving others in your acquisition of self-understanding will be a critical aspect of your personal growth.

One can overcome the enigma of self-awareness, then, by exercising some control over what kind of information one receives about oneself, and when, and by involving others through self-disclosure. The social support individuals receive from others during the process of self-disclosure, besides maintaining an incremental approach to self-insight (i.e., controlling the information flow), helps them accept information that increases self-awareness without crossing the sensitive line.

IMPORTANT AREAS OF SELF-AWARENESS

We shall focus on three major areas of self-awareness that have been found to be key in developing successful management: personal values, cognitive style, and interpersonal orientation. Personal values will be discussed first because they are "the core of the dynamics of behavior, and play so large a part in unifying personality" (Allport, Gordon, & Vernon, 1931, p. 2). That is, all other attitudes, orientations, and behaviors arise out of individuals' values. Two major types of values will be considered—instrumental and terminal (Rokeach, 1973). We shall present research findings that relate personal development on these two types of values to successful managerial performance. An instrument designed to assess your values development will be discussed later, along with information concerning the scores of other groups of people so that you can compare your scores with those of more and less successful managers.

The second area of self-awareness is "cognitive style," which refers to the manner in which individuals process information. A discussion of three critical dimensions of cognitive style will be presented, along with an instrument for assessing your own style. Empirical research linking cognitive style to various managerial behaviors and the relevance of your cognitive style for learning in school will be discussed. This discussion will help you relate your score to academic success and future managerial performance.

Finally, interpersonal orientation, or the tendency to interact in certain ways with other people, will be explained. An instrument for measuring certain aspects of interpersonal orientation is included later, along with an explanation of its relevance to managerial behavior. By completing the instrument and analyzing your scores, you can obtain useful insights not only into yourself, but into your interrelationships with others in social interactions.

These three areas of self-awareness—values, cognitive style, and interpersonal orientation—constitute the very core of the self-concept. Values define an individual's basic *standards* about what is good and bad, worthwhile and worthless, desirable and undesirable, true and false, moral and immoral. Cognitive style determines individual *thought processes* and perceptions. It determines not only what kind of information is received by an individual, but how that information is interpreted, judged, and responded to. Interpersonal orientation determines the *behavior patterns* that are most likely to emerge in interactions with others. The extent to which an individual is open or closed, assertive or retiring, controlling or dependent, affectionate or aloof depends to a large degree on interpersonal orientation. Figure 1.1 summarizes these three aspects of self-awareness, along with their functions in defining the self-concept.

Figure 1.1   *Three Core Aspects of the Self-Concept*

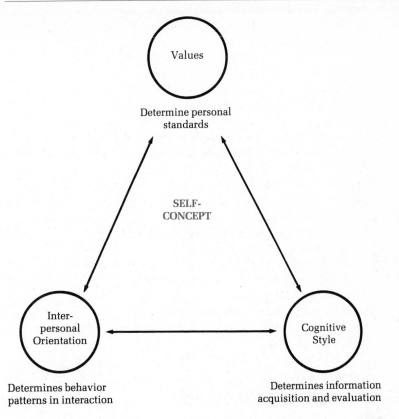

VALUES

Values are among the most stable and enduring characteristics of individuals. They are the basis upon which attitudes and personal preferences are formed. On the other hand, as Simon (1974) and others have suggested, people sometimes are not conscious of their own values, and they often behave in ways that are inconsistent with those values. That is, they pursue lower priorities at the expense of higher priorities, and they substitute goals with immediate pay-offs for more long-term, central values. The pursuit of immediate wealth or status when one values family happiness and inner peace more highly is an example. Not being cognizant of one's own value priorities can lead to long-term frustration and personal ineffectiveness.

Rokeach (1973) argues that the total number of values people possess is relatively small, and that all individuals possess the same values, only in different degrees. That is, everyone values peace, but some make it a higher priority than others. Two general types of values have been identified by

Rokeach, and independent priority ratings have been found to exist for each type (i.e., the two sets of values are largely unrelated). One general type of values is labeled *instrumental,* or means-oriented; the other type is *terminal,* or ends-oriented.

Instrumental values prescribe desirable modes of conduct or methods for attaining an end. Two types of instrumental values relate to morality and competence. Violating moral values (e.g., behaving dishonestly) causes feelings of guilt, while violating competence values (e.g., behaving stupidly) brings about feelings of shame.

Terminal values prescribe desirable ends or goals for the individual. There are fewer of them, according to Rokeach, than there are instrumental values, so the sum total for all individuals in all societies can be identified. Terminal values are either personal (e.g., peace of mind) or social (e.g., world peace). Rokeach has found that an increase in the priority of one personal value tends to increase the priority of other personal values and decrease the priority of social values. Conversely, an increase in the priority of one social value tends to increase the priority of other social values and decrease the value of personal values. Individuals who increase their priority for "a world at peace," for example, would also increase their priority for "equality" while decreasing their priority for "pleasure," "salvation," or "self-respect." Table 1.1 lists the eighteen terminal values, as well as eighteen instrumental values "judged to represent the most important values in American society" (Rokeach, 1973, p. 29).

TABLE 1.1 *Terminal and Instrumental Values*

Terminal Values	*Instrumental Values*
A comfortable life (a prosperous life)	Ambitious (hard-working, aspiring)
An exciting life (a stimulating, active life)	Broadminded (open-minded)
A sense of accomplishment (lasting contribution)	Capable (competent, effective)
A world at peace (free of war and conflict)	Cheerful (lighthearted, joyful)
A world of beauty (beauty of nature and the arts)	Clean (neat, tidy)
Equality (brotherhood, equal opportunity for all)	Courageous (standing up for your beliefs)
Family security (taking care of loved ones)	Forgiving (willing to pardon others)
Freedom (independence, free choice)	Helpful (working for the welfare of others)
Happiness (contentedness)	Honest (sincere, truthful)
Inner harmony (freedom from inner conflict)	Imaginative (daring, creative)
Mature love (sexual and spiritual intimacy)	Independent (self-reliant, self-sufficient)
National security (protection from attack)	Intellectual (intelligent, reflective)
Pleasure (an enjoyable, leisurely life)	Logical (consistent, rational)
Salvation (saved, eternal life)	Loving (affectionate, tender)
Self-respect (self-esteem)	Obedient (dutiful, respectful)
Social recognition (respect, admiration)	Polite (courteous, well-mannered)
True friendship (close companionship)	Responsible (dependable, reliable)
Wisdom (a mature understanding of life)	Self-controlled (restrained, self-disciplined)

SOURCE: Milton Rokeach, *The nature of human values* (New York: Free Press, 1973), p. 28.

Value differences exist among people in terms of both stability and priority. For example, honors students and students planning to go on for advanced degrees have been found to have more stable values than students in general, and women's value priorities generally are more stable than men's. Individuals majoring in business and those selecting business as a career or teaching specialty (i.e., business professors) have been found to value "ambition," "capability," "freedom," and "responsibility" more highly than others (Rokeach, 1973). In a study of managers' values, Singer (1975) used a broader classification scheme than that in Table 1.1 to assess the six categories of values developed by Allport, Vernon, and Lindzey (1960). These included theoretical values (e.g., logic, pursuit of truth), economic values (e.g., industriousness, accumulation of wealth), aesthetic values (e.g., beauty, harmony), social values (e.g., friendship, equality), political values (e.g., power, recognition), and religious values (e.g., salvation, ultimate purpose). Managers were classified as highly successful, moderately successful, and unsuccessful based on their salaries, positions, and rates of salary increase over the past ten years. A comparison of the values of these three groups revealed significant differences. Successful male managers scored higher on economic, political, and religious values than their less successful counterparts. Successful female managers held economic and political values in substantially higher priority than did their less successful counterparts, college women in general, and male managers.

In comparison with the population in general, managers have been found to place substantially more value on "sense of accomplishment," "self-respect," "a comfortable life," and "independence" (Clare & Sanford, 1979). The instrumental value held highest by managers, in fact, was "ambition," and the highest held terminal value was "sense of accomplishment." Personal values and those oriented toward achievement, in other words, seem to predominate among managers.

Simply esteeming certain personal and achievement-oriented values does not mean, of course, that one will be a successful manager. On the other hand, it is clear that values do affect individual behavior. For example, Kohlberg (1969) proposes that the behavior displayed by individuals (i.e., the means used to achieve their valued ends) is a product of their level of values maturity (or what he calls moral maturity). Individuals differ in their level of moral maturity, according to Kohlberg, so different sets of instrumental values are held by individuals at different stages of development. People progress from one level of maturity to another, and as they do, their value priorities change. A qualitatively different set of instrumental values is possessed by individuals who have progressed to more mature levels of values development than individuals who are at less mature levels.

This theory of values or moral development has received a great deal of attention from researchers, and research findings have some important implications for self-awareness and managerial effectiveness. Therefore, we shall discuss in some detail this notion of values maturity.

Kohlberg's model of values maturity consists of three major levels, with each level containing two stages. Table 1.2 summarizes the characteristics of each stage. In brief, the stages are sequential (for example, a person can't progress to stage 3 before passing through stage 2), and each stage represents a higher level of maturity.

The first level of maturity, called the *preconventional* level, contains the first two stages of values development. Moral reasoning and instrumental values are based on personal needs or wants and on the consequences of an act. For example, something could be judged as right or good if it helped an individual obtain a reward or avoid punishment and if the consequences were not negative for someone else. Stealing $50,000 is worse than stealing $500 in a preconventional level because the consequences (i.e., loss) are more negative for someone else.

The second, or *conventional,* level contains stages 3 and 4. Moral reasoning is based on conforming to and upholding the conventions and expectations of society. This level is sometimes referred to as the "law and order" level because the emphasis is on conformity to laws and norms. Right and wrong are judged on the basis of whether or not behaviors conform to the rules of those in authority. Stealing $50,000 and stealing $500 are equally wrong in this level because both violate the law. Most adults function at this level of values maturity.

Third is the *postconventional* level. It contains the final two stages of maturity, and represents the most mature level of moral reasoning and the most mature set of instrumental values. Right and wrong are judged on the basis of the internalized principles of the individual. That is, judgments are made on the basis of a set of principles that have been developed from individual experience. In the highest stage of maturity, this set of principles is comprehensive (it covers all contingencies), consistent (it is never violated), and universal (it does not change with the situation or circumstance). Thus, stealing $50,000 and stealing $500 are still judged to be wrong, but the basis for the judgment is not the violation of laws or rules, but the violation of a comprehensive, consistent, universal principle developed by the individual. Few individuals, according to Kohlberg, reach this final level of maturity.

In short, preconventional individuals view rules and laws as outside themselves, but they obey because, by doing so, they may get rewarded or avoid punishment. Conventional individuals view rules and laws as outside themselves, but they obey because they have learned and accepted those rules and laws. Postconventional individuals examine the rules and laws and develop a set of internal principles. If there is a choice to be made between obeying a rule or obeying a principle, they choose the principle. Internalized principles supersede rules and laws in postconventional individuals.

To understand the different levels of values maturity, consider the following story used by Kohlberg (1969):

In Europe a woman was near death from a special kind of cancer. There was one drug that the doctors thought might save her. It was a form of

TABLE 1.2 *Classification of Moral Judgment into Levels and Stages of Development*

Level	Basis of Moral Judgment	Stage of Development
I	Moral value resides in external, quasiphysical happenings, in bad acts, or in quasiphysical needs, rather than in persons and standards.	1. Obedience and punishment orientation. Egocentric deference to superior power or prestige, or a trouble-avoiding set. Objective responsibility. 2. Naively egoistic orientation. Right action is that instrumentally satisfying the self's needs and occasionally others'. Awareness of relativism of value to each actor's needs and perspectives. Naive egalitarianism and orientation to exchange and reciprocity.
II	Moral value resides in performing good or right roles, in maintaining the conventional order and the expectancies of others.	3. Good-boy orientation. Orientation to approval and to pleasing and helping others. Conformity to stereotypical images of majority or natural role behavior, and judgment by intentions. 4. Orientation to "doing duty," showing respect for authority, and maintaining the social order for its own sake. Regard for earned expectations of others.
III	Moral value resides in conformity by the self to shared or shareable standards, rights, or duties.	5. Contractual legalistic orientation. Recognition of an arbitrary element or starting point in rules or expectations for the sake of agreement. Duty defined in terms of contract, general avoidance of violation of the will or rights of others, and majority will and welfare. 6. Conscience of principle orientation. Orientation not only to actually ordained social rules, but to principles of choice involving appeal to logical universality and consistency. Orientation to conscience as a directing agent and to mutual respect and trust.

SOURCE: Lawrence Kohlberg, The cognitive-developmental approach to socialization, in D. A. Goslin (ed.), *Handbook of socialization theory and research* (Chicago: Rand McNally, 1969), p. 376.

radium that a druggist in the same town had recently discovered. The drug was expensive to make, but the druggist was charging ten times what the drug cost to make. He paid $200 for radium and charged $2000 for a small dose of the drug. The sick woman's husband, Heinz, went to everyone he knew to borrow the money, but he could get together only about $1000, which was half of what it cost. He told the druggist that his wife was dying and asked him to sell it cheaper or let him pay later. But the druggist said, "No, I discovered the drug and I'm going to make money from it." So Heinz grew desperate and began to think about breaking into the store to steal the drug for his wife.

Now answer the following questions.

1. Would it be wrong for Heinz to break into the store?
2. Did the druggist have the right to charge that much for the product?
3. Did Heinz have an obligation to steal the drug for his wife?
4. What if Heinz and his wife did not get along. Should Heinz steal the drug for her?
5. Suppose it wasn't Heinz's wife that was dying of cancer, but his best friend. Should Heinz steal the drug for his friend?
6. Suppose the person dying was not close to Heinz personally. Should Heinz steal the drug?
7. Suppose Heinz read in the paper about a woman dying of cancer. Should he steal the drug for her?
8. Would you steal the drug to save your own life?
9. Suppose Heinz was caught breaking in and brought before a judge. Should he be sentenced to jail?

For individuals on the preconventional level of maturity, stealing the drug might be justified because Heinz's wife had instrumental value—she could cook and clean, look after Heinz, and so on. A stranger, however, would not have the same instrumental value for Heinz, so it would be wrong to steal the drug for a stranger. Individuals on the conventional level would base their judgments on the closeness of the relationship and on law and authority. Heinz has an obligation to steal for family members, according to this reasoning, but not for nonfamily members. The governing principle is always whether it is against the law (or society's expectations) or not. Postconventional individuals base their judgments on a set of universal, comprehensive, and consistent principles. They may answer any question yes or no, but their reasoning will be based on their own principles, not on externally imposed standards or expectations. (For example, they might feel an obligation to steal the drug for anyone because human life is valued more than property.)

Research on Kohlberg's model of values development has revealed some interesting findings that have relevance to managerial behavior. For example, moral judgment stories were administered to college students who had earlier participated in Milgram's (1963) obedience study. Milgram's subjects had been directed to give increasingly intense shocks to a person who was observed to be in great pain under the guise of a reinforcement-learning experiment. Of the respondents at the postconventional level (stages 5 and 6), 75 percent refused to administer the shocks, while only 12.5 percent of the respondents at the conventional level refused. Higher levels of values development, in other words, are associated with an unwillingness to hurt other people. Haan, Smith, and Block (1968) found that both postconventional and preconventional individuals are inclined to join in massive social protests, such as the Berkeley free speech movement, but the motives of preconventional individuals are directed toward bettering themselves individually, while the postconventional individuals are motivated by justice and the rights of the larger community.

Becoming more mature in values development requires that individuals develop a set of internalized principles by which they can govern their behavior. The development of those principles is enhanced and values maturity is increased as value-based issues are confronted, discussed, and thought about. Lickona (1976, p. 25) notes, "Simply increasing the amount of reciprocal communication that occurs among people is likely to enhance moral development."

To help you determine your own level of values maturity, an instrument developed by James Rest (1979) is included on pp. 68–72. It has been used extensively in research because it is easier to administer than Kohlberg's method for assessing maturity. According to Kohlberg (1976, p. 47), "Rest's approach does give a rough estimate of an individual's moral maturity level." Rather than placing a person in one single level of values maturity, it identifies the stages that the person relies on most. That is, it assumes that individuals use more than one level of maturity (or set of instrumental values), but that one level generally predominates. By completing this instrument, therefore, you can identify your predominant level of values maturity. We encourage you to take time now to complete the instrument.

This instrument should stimulate you to examine your level of values maturity and the priorities you hold most important. Be sure to complete the instrument as you really are, not as you think you should be. By discussing your scores and answers with others, not only will values clarification occur, but higher levels of maturity will be reached as well.

COGNITIVE STYLE

Cognitive style is the second core area of the self-concept. Cognitive style consists of a large number of cognitive factors that relate to the way individuals perceive, interpret, and respond to information. Table 1.3 lists thirty-two cognitive factors that have been used in research on cognitive style (see, for an elaboration, Eckstrom, French, & Harman, 1979). However, this list is only a partial one (Nunney, 1978; Vernon, 1970); many other factors could be listed as well, so it is impossible to assess, or to be aware of, all the aspects of cognitive style that may affect managerial behavior.

In this chapter, we cannot discuss each of the many factors used to define cognitive style, nor can we provide ways to measure each of them. Instead, we shall discuss three major dimensions of cognitive style that have appeared in research on management and that have been shown to have particular relevance for managerial behavior.

Among the most important aspects of cognitive style is the manner in which individuals gather, evaluate, and act on the information they receive. Three cognitive activities in particular—information gathering, information evaluation, and information response—have received considerable attention from management researchers and trainers (McKenney & Keen, 1974; Kolb, 1974; Myers, 1980). The basic premise is that every individual is faced with an overwhelming amount of information, and only part of it can be given attention and acted upon. Individuals therefore develop strategies for dealing with the information they receive. These are neither inherently good nor inherently bad, and not everyone adopts an identifiable set of strategies that become part of their cognitive style. However, most individuals do develop, mostly unconsciously, a preferred set over time, and these make up their unique cognitive style.

The Cognitive Style Instrument (p. 75) assesses three dimensions of your cognitive style. You should complete this instrument now before going on. Your score will be more valid if you do so before reading the explanation of the dimensions and research findings linking cognitive style to managerial behavior.

In order for your scores on the cognitive style instrument to be meaningful to you, you must understand the theories on which it is based. One theory was developed by James McKenney and his colleagues, who developed a model of cognitive style based on two dimensions—information gathering and information evaluation (McKenney & Keen, 1974). Figure 1.2 illustrates that model. The information-gathering dimension of the model divides a *receptive* strategy from a *preceptive* strategy, and the information evaluation dimension separates a *systematic* strategy from an *intuitive* strategy.

Different strategies for taking in, coding, and storing information (information gathering) develop as a result of certain cognitive filters used by individuals to select the information they pay attention to. A *preceptive* strategy emphasizes concepts and generalizations, or the relationships among the various elements of data, in gathering information. Preceptive thinkers frequently have preconceived notions about what sort of information may be relevant, and they look at various items of information to find commonalities or consistencies with their preconceptions. They tend to be convergent thinkers.

The *receptive* strategy focuses on detail, or on the specific attributes of each element of data, rather than on relationships among the elements. Recep-

TABLE 1.3 *Aspects of Cognitive Style*

Cognitive Factor	Definition
Flexibility of closure	The ability to keep one or more configurations in mind despite distraction
Speed of closure	The ability to unify a complex set of data
Associational fluency	The ability to produce words with a certain meaning
Expressional fluency	The ability to think rapidly of appropriate wording for ideas
Ideational fluency	The ability to generate a large number of ideas
Word fluency	The ability to produce words of a certain kind, regardless of their meaning
Induction	The ability to put together different ideas to find a general principle
Associative memory	The ability to remember bits of unrelated material
Span memory	The ability to remember a series of items in the correct order
Number facility	The ability to do arithmetic problems rapidly
Originality	The ability to produce clever or uncommon responses
Perceptual speed	Speed in accurately perceiving phenomena
General reasoning	The ability to solve a broad range of reasoning problems
Semantic redefinition	The ability to use an object or idea in a new way
Syllogistic reasoning	The ability to reason from a premise to a conclusion
Spatial orientation	The ability to perceive spatial arrangements and patterns
Sensitivity to problems	The ability to recognize practical problems
Spatial scanning	Speed in visually exploring complex phenomena
Verbal comprehension	The ability to understand language
Visualization	The ability to transform one pattern into another
Figural adaptive flexibility	The ability to try out various alternatives mentally and to converge on the one best alternative
Spontaneous semantic flexibility	The ability to express a variety of ideas
Automatic processes	The ability to apply rules automatically to a problem
Behavioral relations and systems	The ability to judge an interaction between two people so the feelings of the people are known
Chunking memory	The ability to use a small number of symbols to represent a large amount of data
Concept formation	The ability to find the common elements among a diverse set of symbols
Estimation	The ability to estimate a solution to a problem prior to having sufficient evidence to solve it
Figural illusions and perceptual alterations	The ability to form mental illusions and to switch from one alternative to another quickly
Integration	The ability to keep in mind several alternatives simultaneously
Meaningful memory	The ability to retain elements that are related to existing knowledge
Visual memory	The ability to memorize based on visual stimuli
Verbal closure	The ability to solve problems when some of the data are missing or confused

SOURCE: R. B. Eckstrom, V. W. French, and H. H. Harmon, Cognitive factors: Their identification and replication, *Multivariate Behavioral Research Monographs*, 1979, *72*, 3–84.

Figure 1.2   *Model of Cognitive Style Based on Two Dimensions*

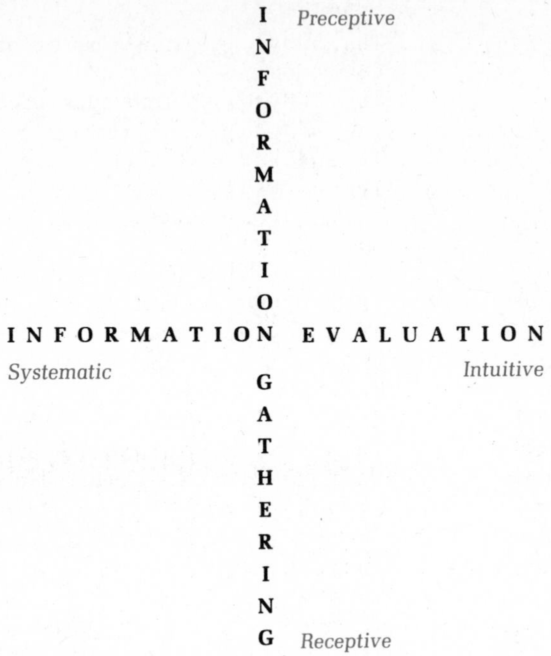

```
                              I   Preceptive
                              N
                              F
                              O
                              R
                              M
                              A
                              T
                              I
                              O
        INFORMATION  EVALUATION
        Systematic            G            Intuitive
                              A
                              T
                              H
                              E
                              R
                              I
                              N
                              G   Receptive
```

tive thinkers have few preconceptions about what may be relevant, so they insist on a close and thorough examination of all data. They tend to be divergent thinkers.

In simplified terms, a preceptive strategy focuses on the whole, a receptive strategy on the parts of the whole. A preceptive strategy looks for commonalities and overall categories, a receptive strategy for uniqueness, detail, and exceptions to the general rule.

The second dimension of the model refers to strategies for interpreting and judging information (information evaluation). These strategies develop as a result of reliance on a particular problem-solving pattern. A *systematic* strategy approaches a problem from the standpoint of a method or plan with specific sequential steps. There is a focus on appropriate methods and logical progressions. People who solve problems systematically conduct an orderly search for information. They generally rely on objective data. Attempts are made to fit problems into a known, logical model or framework. When such people defend their solutions, they emphasize the methods and procedures used to solve the problems. Vertinsky (1976) refers to these individuals as members of a "continuous culture."

An *intuitive* strategy, on the other hand, approaches a problem on the basis of "gut feel," or an internal sense of how to respond. The problem is often defined and redefined, and approaches are tried on a trial-and-error basis, rather than through a logical procedure. Intuitive individuals have a penchant for subjective or impressionistic rather than objective data, and they frequently cannot describe their own problem-solving processes. Problem solutions are often found through seeing analogies or unusual relationships between the problem and a past experience. Vertinsky (1976) refers to these individuals as members of a "discontinuous culture."

These different strategies have important implications for managerial behavior. Receptive managers, for example, because they focus on detail, experience information overload and personal stress more readily than preceptive managers when faced with a large amount of data. When they encounter too much detail, receptive managers become overloaded because each detail receives attention. Preceptive managers, on the other hand, who focus on the relationships among elements and the whole, handle additions of detail relatively easily. However, when wide diversity or ambiguity is encountered in the information or when aberrations from the expected sequence occur and overall categories don't fit, preceptive managers are likely to have more difficulty coping than receptive managers. Encountering exceptions or the absence of a clear set of relationships among elements is particularly problematic for preceptive managers. Receptive managers are likely to handle these situations more easily because of their tendency to do "fine-grained analyses" of problems. They analyze one element at a time and can therefore identify sources of conflict or ambiguity.

Systematic managers are less likely to be effective when encountering problems requiring creativity and discontinuous thinking, or when encountering highly ambiguous problems with partial information. When no apparent system exists for solving a problem, these individuals are likely to have more difficulty than intuitive managers. On the other hand, when one program or system will solve a variety of problems, intuitive managers are less effective because of their tendency to try new approaches, to redefine problems, and to reinvent the solution over and over without following past programs. This generally leads to overload. Systematic managers have less difficulty in such situations.

The third commonly used dimension of information processing concerns *information response,* the extent to which individuals are inclined to act or reflect on the information they receive. This dimension separates *active* strategies from *reflective.* Figure 1.3 adds the information response dimension to the two dimensions illustrated in Figure 1.2.

Individuals employing an active strategy are inclined to experiment with or to execute a behavior as a result of receiving information. They are doers rather than thinkers, and they are more interested in practical application than in theoretical elegance. Actives feel impatient if a solution or action is not forthcoming when they are confronted with a problem.

Individuals employing a reflective strategy, on the other hand, are inclined to ponder information for a longer time before deciding to take action.

Figure 1.3   *Model of Cognitive Style Based on Three Dimensions*

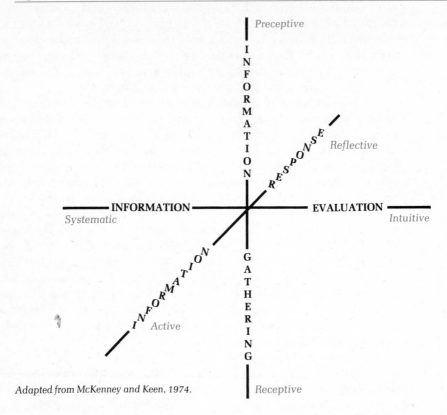

Adapted from McKenney and Keen, 1974.

They tend to observe rather than to actively participate, and the practical application of information is not nearly so important to them as its meaning and conceptual logic. They are thinkers, not doers.

Active managers are likely to be most effective when quick decisions are needed and execution and application of information are required. However, when a wider search for information is required or long-term implications must be considered, the active managers' tendency to respond quickly may lead them to be less effective than reflecters.

Reflective managers are likely to be most effective when complex or contradictory information requires in-depth analysis rather than action. Thinking through a problem thoroughly, for example, may reduce the chances of making a move too quickly. On the other hand, when time is short and the situation requires immediate action based on limited information, reflectives may be too tentative and deliberate, and thus less effective than actives.

Research on these cognitive dimensions has some relevance for helping you interpret your scores. For example, McKenney and Keen (1974) and

Mitroff and Kilmann (1975) have found that no matter what type of problem they face, individuals use their preferred cognitive style to approach it. Moreover, when given a choice, individuals prefer decision situations and problem types that are consistent with their own cognitive style (e.g., individuals scoring high on systematic prefer problems with a step-by-step method of solution). Henderson and Nutt (1980) have found that differences in cognitive style also produce different decision-making processes in managers. Managers who are more systematic than intuitive, for example, implement more computer-based systems and rational processes than do intuitives (Mulkowsky & Freeman, 1979).

Research by Kolb (1974) clearly links cognitive style to academic major and career choices. Kolb separated *actives* from *reflectives* and individuals with a general, conceptual orientation *(preceptives)* from those with a specific, concrete orientation *(receptives)* (Figure 1.4). He found, just as Plovnick (1971)

Figure 1.4 *Undergraduate Majors of 630 Managers with Different Cognitive Styles*

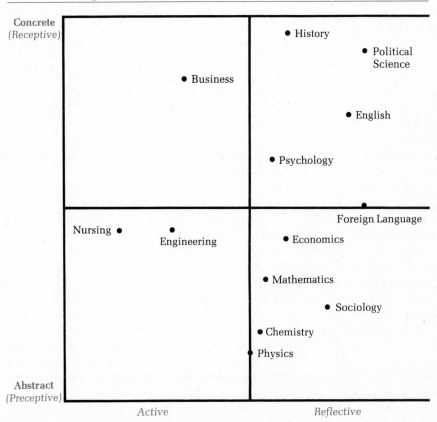

did, that individuals with certain cognitive styles gravitate toward academic majors that reinforce those styles (e.g., business reinforces active, receptive styles; mathematics reinforces reflective, preceptive styles). Moreover, he discovered that cognitive styles also affect managerial behavior. For example, managers who held high-risk, high-pressure jobs in the trust department of a bank tended to be active and receptive. Managers in low-risk, low-discretion jobs tended to be reflective and preceptive (Stabell, 1973). Similarly, receptive managers tended to rely on information from other people in their investment decisions, whereas preceptives relied on analytically oriented printed material.

What these research results suggest is that individuals with different cognitive styles use different decision-making strategies, are effective in different business environments, and select different academic majors in college. In addition, individuals with different cognitive styles approach learning differently, and different kinds of educational experiences hold meaning for different types of people. For example, individuals who emphasize preceptive strategies tend to do better in conceptual courses and learn more easily through reading and through discussing general relationships. Exams with one right answer may be easier for them than for those who are receptive. Individuals who emphasize receptive strategies tend to do better in factual courses or courses in which attention to detail and dissimilarity is important. Critical and analytical learning activities (e.g., debates) facilitate learning, and exams emphasizing implications and creativity may be easiest for these individuals.

Individuals who emphasize a systematic strategy do best in courses that take an orderly, step-by-step approach to the subject, courses in which what is learned builds on, and follows directly from, what was learned earlier (e.g., mathematics). On the other hand, intuitive individuals do best in courses requiring creativity and idea generation. Learning activities in which the student must rely on a personal sense of what is appropriate (e.g., sculpturing) are likely to be preferred by these individuals.

Individuals who are strongest in active strategies do best in courses that emphasize experimentation and action. Trying out the information in a practical setting is an attractive alternative for learning, and exams in which demonstration or application is required may be easiest for these individuals. Individuals who emphasize reflective strategies, on the other hand, do best in courses dealing with abstract ideas and theoretical models. Pondering meanings and implications of information is a valued learning activity for these individuals, and exams are easiest that allow for a thoughtful presentation of ideas.

In short, knowing your own cognitive style should prove advantageous not only in planning your career, but also in capitalizing on your academic strengths and in enhancing your potential for managerial success. While many aspects of your cognitive style are important, these three dimensions related to information processing are especially critical in management.

INTERPERSONAL ORIENTATION

The third critical area of self-awareness is interpersonal orientation. Because the manager's job has been characterized as overwhelmingly interpersonal, interpersonal orientation, or the tendency to behave in certain ways around other people, is an especially important aspect of self-awareness. Sayles (1964, p. 38) suggests that management involves virtually constant contact with people, and managers whose personalities do not dispose them toward a high amount of interpersonal activity are likely to be frustrated and dissatisfied. The quality and type of this interpersonal activity can vary widely, however. Therefore, it is important for you to know your own interpersonal tendencies and inclinations to maximize the probabilities of successful interactions.

"Interpersonal orientation" does not refer to the actual behavior patterns displayed in interpersonal situations. Rather, it refers to the underlying tendencies to behave in certain ways regardless of the other person involved or the circumstance. Interpersonal orientation generally arises from certain basic needs in the individual that relate to relationships with others.

A very well-known and thoroughly researched theory of interpersonal orientation was proposed by Schutz (1958). The basic assumption of his model is that people need people, that all individuals seek to establish compatible relationships with other individuals in their social interactions. Striving for compatibility in interactions leads to the development of three primary interpersonal needs that must be satisfied if the individual is to avoid personal stress and unsatisfactory relationships. The first is the need for *inclusion*. This is a need to maintain a relationship with other people, to be included in their activities, or to include them in the individual's own activities. To some extent all individuals seek to belong to a group, but at the same time they want to be left alone. There is always a trade-off between tendencies toward introversion and tendencies toward extroversion. Therefore, individuals differ in their relative need strength on two aspects of the need for inclusion: the need to include others, or *expressed inclusion,* and the need to be included by others, or *wanted inclusion.*

A second interpersonal need is the need for *control.* This is the need to maintain a satisfactory balance of power and influence in relationships. All individuals need to exert control, direction, or structure over other people, while also remaining independent from them. All individuals also need to be controlled, directed, or structured by others, but at the same time to maintain freedom and discretion. Essentially, there is a trade-off between authoritarianism and antiauthoritarianism. Individual differences arise, therefore, in the need to control others, or *expressed control,* and the need to be controlled by others, or *wanted control.*

A third need relates to *affection,* or the need to form close personal relationships with others. This need is not restricted to physical affection or romantic relationships, but includes needs for warmth, intimacy, and love apart from overt behaviors. All individuals need to form close, personal relationships with other people, but at the same time want to avoid becoming over-committed or smothered. All individuals need to have others show a great deal of warmth and affection to them, but also to maintain some distance. This is a trade-off between high affiliative needs and high independence needs. Individuals therefore vary in their needs for *expressing affection* toward other people and for *wanting affection* to be expressed toward them.

In short, each of the three interpersonal needs has two aspects, a desire to *express* the need and a desire to *receive* the needed behavior from others. These three needs determine an individual's interpersonal orientation. That is, individuals differ uniquely in their needs to give or receive certain behaviors when interacting with others. Figure 1.5 summarizes these three needs and illustrates characteristics of each.

In the Skill Practice section is the instrument Schutz developed to assess inclusion, control, and affection needs (p. 80). Take time to complete that instrument now. Using the scoring sheet and instructions, compute your score for each interpersonal need. The discussion of interpersonal orientation in this section will be more meaningful to you if you have already generated your own scores on the instrument. It should take you only about ten minutes.

There are several ways your scores on this questionnaire can be analyzed and interpreted. For example, you can compare your expressed total with your wanted total to determine the extent to which you are willing to give as much behavior as you want to get. Individuals who have high expressed scores and low wanted scores are called "controllers" by Ryan (1970) because they want to express but are unwilling to accept in return. The reverse pattern, high wanted scores and low expressed scores, is called a "passive" pattern by Ryan because these individuals want to receive but are unwilling to initiate any interaction.

By comparing each need score, you can determine which is your most important interpersonal need. Your highest score may indicate the need that is being least satisfied.

Figure 1.5   *Descriptors of Fundamental Interpersonal Relations Orientation-Behavior (FIRO-B) Needs*

	Inclusion	Control	Affection
Expressed Toward Others	I join other people, and I include others.	I take charge, and I influence people.	I get close and personal with people.
Wanted from Others	I want other people to include me.	I want others to lead me or give me directions.	I want people to get close and personal with me.

Another way to interpret your scores is to compare them with the national norm data in Figure 1.6. The numbers at the top of each box (e.g., 4 to 7) refer to the average range of scores. At least 50 percent of adults fall within that range. The numbers at the bottom (e.g., 5.4) refer to the average scores in the cells. At least 50 percent of adults score within 1.5 of those scores. If you scored 6 in the expressed control cell, you score higher than 75 percent of the people on that need; if you scored 2 in the expressed affection cell, you score lower than 75 percent.

The score in the lower right-hand corner (the total of the expressed and wanted scores) is called the social interaction index. This score represents the overall interpersonal need level. The highest possible score is 54. Individuals with high scores have strong needs to interact with other people. They are likely to be gregarious, friendly, and involved with others. Low scores are more typical of shy, reserved people.

Hill (1974) has found that business school students differ significantly on the social interaction index, depending on their majors. Accounting and systems analysis students in his study had means of 22.3 and 22.6, respectively (lower than average), while marketing and personnel majors had means of 31.0 and 31.9, respectively (higher than average). Finance, small business, and engi-

Figure 1.6   *Average FIRO-B Scores and Ranges*

	Inclusion	Control	Affection	
Expressed Toward Others	4 to 7 5.4	2 to 5 3.9	3 to 6 4.1	9 to 18 13.4
Wanted from Others	5 to 8 6.5	3 to 6 4.6	3 to 6 4.8	11 to 20 15.9
	9 to 15 11.9	5 to 11 8.5	6 to 12 8.9	20 to 38 29.3

neering students were in the middle. This difference turned out to be statistically significant, which suggests that career selection may have something to do with interpersonal orientation.

Probably the greatest usefulness of the scores lies in analyzing interpersonal compatibility—that is, in matching one person's scores with another person's. Individuals can be interpersonally incompatible in three ways. To explain these three incompatibilities, two hypothetical scores are used in Figure 1.7.

The first type of incompatibility is called *reciprocal incompatibility*. It refers to the match between one person's expressed behavior and another person's wanted behavior. For example, if one person has a high need to express control but the other person does not want to be controlled, there is a reciprocal incompatibility. The formula for computing reciprocal incompatibility is

$$| \text{Manager's } e - \text{Subordinate's } w | + | \text{Subordinate's } e - \text{Manager's } w |$$

The straight lines indicate absolute values (no minus numbers). The data in Figure 1.7 show that in the inclusion area, for example, a reciprocal incompatibility exists between the manager and the subordinate. Using the formula above, we have

$$| 9 - 2 | + | 3 - 8 | = 12$$

Any score higher than 6 means that there is a strong possibility of incompatibility. In this case, the manager has strong needs to include others and

Figure 1.7   *Examples of Two FIRO-B Scores*

Manager

	Inclusion	Control	Affection	
Expressed (*e*)	9	9	1	19
Wanted (*w*)	8	4	3	15
	17	13	4	34

Subordinate

	Inclusion	Control	Affection	
Expressed (*e*)	3	8	6	17
Wanted (*w*)	2	2	8	12
	5	10	14	29

to be included by them, but the subordinate has low needs in both aspects of inclusion. There is a potential for interpersonal conflict to arise in this area, particularly if inclusion behavior is required in the relationship.

The second type of incompatibility is called *originator incompatibility*. It refers to the match between the expressed scores of both individuals. Originator incompatibility occurs when both people want to initiate in an area or neither wants to initiate. The formula for computing originator incompatibility is

(Manager's *e* − Manager's *w*) + (Subordinate's *e* − Subordinate's *w*)

The parentheses indicate that minus numbers should be computed. The data from Figure 1.7 in the control area make clear that an originator incompatibility exists. Both the manager and the subordinate want to control, and neither has a high need to be controlled. Their incompatibility score is computed as follows

$$(9 - 4) + (8 - 2) = +11$$

Any score higher than +6 indicates high *competitive* originator incompatibility. A score of less than -6 indicates high *apathetic* originator incompatibility. Apathetic incompatibility occurs when neither individual wants to initiate in the area. In such a case, neither person wants to control or take charge; both want the other to do it.

The third type of incompatibility is *interchange incompatibility*. It refers to the extent to which two individuals emphasize the same or different interpersonal needs. For example, interchange incompatibility exists if one person emphasizes control needs highly while the other emphasizes affection needs highly. When interpersonal problems arise, one person would likely define the problem as one of control, direction, or influence, while the other person would likely define the problem as one of closeness, warmth, and affection. The difficulty would be in getting the two people to see the situation as the same problem. The formula for computing interchange incompatibility is

| Manager's *e* + Manager's *w* | − | Subordinate's *e* + Subordinate's *w* |

Again, the straight lines in the formula refer to absolute values. In the affection area in Figure 1.7, an interchange incompatibility exists. Affection is a high need area for the subordinate but a low need area for the manager. (The reverse case exists in the inclusion area.) Computing the interchange incompatibility score gives us

$$|1 + 3| - |6 + 8| = 10$$

Scores above 6 indicate a strong possibility of incompatibility. The need of the subordinate in the affection area is likely to be ignored or rejected in the relationship.

TABLE 1.4 *Incompatibility Scores for a Hypothetical Manager and Subordinate*

	Inclusion	Control	Affection
Reciprocal incompatibility	12	11	10
Originator incompatibility	2	11	-4
Interchange incompatibility	12	3	10
Total incompatibility (Sum of absolute values)			75

Using these three incompatibility formulas allows us to compute a *total incompatibility* score, which combines the three types of incompatibilities in the three need areas. These are computed in Table 1.4 for the hypothetical manager and subordinate.

The incompatibility scores indicate that this manager and subordinate have a high probability of interpersonal difficulty in their relationship. Potential problems of not meeting one another's needs in any of the three need categories (reciprocal incompatibility), of both wanting to control but not wanting to be controlled (originator incompatibility in the control area), and of having different need emphases (interchange incompatibility in the inclusion and affection areas) would probably lead these two people to have a relatively conflict-ridden relationship.

Research confirms this prediction. For example, DiMarco (1974) has found that low incompatibility scores result in more favorable attitudes of subordinates toward managers. Obradovic (1962) has found teacher attitudes are more favorable toward students when compatibility scores are high. Hutcherson (1963) has found that students achieve higher levels in classes when compatibility with the teacher is high. Friends have also been found to be chosen more often from among those with compatible scores. Sapolsky (1965) and Mendelsohn and Rankin (1969) have even found that the success of therapist–patient treatment is affected by interpersonal compatibility. This last finding is somewhat controversial, however, since other studies have shown that while patients *like* therapists more whose scores are compatible with theirs, the actual therapeutic outcome is not significantly different between compatible and incompatible matches (Gassner, 1970).

There is strong evidence that groups composed of compatible individuals are more satisfying to members and more effective than groups composed of incompatible individuals. The following are some characteristics that studies (Hewett, O'Brien, & Hornik, 1974; Liddell & Slocum, 1976; Reddy & Byrnes, 1972; Shalinsky, 1969; Schutz, 1958; Smith & Haythorn, 1973) have found typical of interpersonally compatible groups:

1. More interpersonal attraction among members,
2. More positive group climate,
3. More cooperative behavior on tasks,

4. More productivity in accomplishing tasks,
5. Faster problem solving,
6. Fewer errors in solving problems,
7. Less hostility among members.

Knowing your interpersonal orientation, then, can be an important factor in your managerial success. Not only does it enhance good interpersonal relations by helping you diagnose potential areas of incompatibility, but it helps you generate alternatives for behavior when you attempt to solve interpersonal difficulties. For example, some problems can be solved simply by increasing inclusion activities, by allowing someone else to express a little more control, or by redefining the issue as an affection problem instead of a control problem.

SUMMARY AND BEHAVIORAL GUIDELINES

As we have pointed out in this chapter, developing self-awareness is a critical first step in becoming an effective manager. Awareness of three areas in the self-concept are particularly important: values, cognitive style, and interpersonal orientation. These three factors lie at the root not only of human behavior, but also of individual perceptions and interpretations of the outside world.

Most of the following chapters relate to skills in interpersonal or group interaction, but successful skill development in those areas will occur only if you have a firm foundation in self-awareness. There is an interesting paradox in human behavior: We can know others only by knowing ourselves, but we can know ourselves only by knowing others. Our knowledge of others, and therefore our ability to manage or interact successfully with them, comes from relating what we see in them to our own experience. If we are not self-aware, we have no basis for knowing certain things about others. Self-recognition leads to recognition and understanding of others. As Harris (1981) puts it:

> Nothing is really personal that is not first interpersonal, beginning with the infant's shock of separation from the umbilical cord. What we know about ourselves comes only from the outside, and is interpreted by the kind of experiences we have had; and what we know about others comes only from analogy with our own network of feelings.

Below are the behavioral guidelines relating to the improvement of self-awareness. These guidelines are provided as a summary to aid your efforts at self-improvement.

1. Become aware of your sensitive line. Determine what information about yourself you are most likely to defend against.

2. Become aware of your terminal and instrumental value priorities and identify a comprehensive, consistent, and universal set of principles on which to base your bahavior.
3. Become aware of your cognitive style as it relates to gathering, evaluating, and responding to information. Determine the implications of your cognitive style for learning new material in school.
4. Become aware of your interpersonal orientation. Compute incompatibility scores with those you regularly interact with and determine strategies for dealing with areas of potential conflict.
5. Engage in productive self-disclosure with someone who is close to you and accepting of you. Check out aspects of your self that you are not sure of.

REFERENCES

Allport, G., Gordon, R., & Vernon, P. *The study of values manual.* Boston: Houghton Mifflin Co., 1931.

Allport, G., Vernon, P., & Lindzey, G. *Study of values.* Boston: Houghton Mifflin Co., 1960.

Brouwer, P. J. The power to see ourselves. *Harvard Business Review,* 1964, *42,* 156–165.

Clare, D. A., & Sanford, D. G. Mapping personal value space: A study of managers in four organizations. *Human Relations,* 1979, *32,* 659–666.

DiMarco, N. J. Supervisor–subordinate life style and interpersonal need compatibilities as determinants of subordinate's attitudes toward the supervisor. *Academy of Management Journal,* 1974, *17,* 575–578.

Eckstrom, R. B., French, J. W., & Harmon, H. H. Cognitive factors: Their identification and replication. *Multivariate Behavioral Research Monographs,* 1979, *72,* 3–84.

Freud, S. *Collected papers* (Vols. 3 and 4). London: Hogarth, 1956.

Fromm, E. Selfishness and self love. *Psychiatry,* 1939, *2,* 507–523.

Gassner, S. M. Relationship between patient–therapist compatibility and treatment effectiveness. *Journal of Counseling and Clinical Psychology,* 1970, *34,* 408–414.

Haan, N., Smith, M. B., & Block, J. Moral reasoning of young adults: Political-social behavior, family background, and personality correlates. *Journal of Personality and Social Psychology,* 1968, *10,* 183–201.

Haney, W. V. *Communication and interpersonal relations.* Homewood, Ill.: Irwin, 1979.

Harris, S. Know yourself? It's a paradox. Associated Press, Oct. 6, 1981.

Hayakawa, S. I. *The use and misuse of language.* New York: Fawcett World Library, Crest, Gold Medal, & Premier Books, 1962.

Henderson, J. C., & Nutt, P. C. The influence of decision style on decision making behavior. *Management Science,* 1980, *26,* 371–386.

Hewett, T. T., O'Brien, G. E., & Hornik, J. The effects of work organization, leadership style, and member compatibility upon the productivity of small groups working on a manipulative task. *Organizational Behavior and Human Performance,* 1974, *11,* 283–301.

Hill, R. E. Interpersonal needs and functional area of management. *Journal of Vocational Behavior,* 1974, *4,* 15–24.

Hutcherson, D. E. *Relationships among teacher–pupil compatibility, social studies grades, and selected factors.* Unpublished doctoral dissertation, University of California, Berkeley, 1963.

Jourard, S. M. *The transparent self.* Princeton, N.J.: D. Von Nostrand Company, 1964.

Kohlberg, L. The cognitive-developmental approach to socialization. In D. A. Goslin (Ed.), *Handbook of socialization theory and research.* Chicago: Rand McNally, 1969.

Kohlberg, L. Moral stages and moralization, the cognitive-developmental approach. In T. Lickona (Ed.), *Moral development and behavior*. New York: Holt, Rinehart & Winston, 1976.

Kolb, D. A. On management and the learning process. In D. Kolb, I. Rubin, & J. McIntyre (Eds.), *Organizational psychology: A book of readings* (2nd ed.). Englewood Cliffs, N.J.: Prentice-Hall, 1974.

Lickona, T. Critical issues in the study of moral development and behavior. In T. Lickona (Ed.), *Moral development and behavior: Theory, research, and social issues*. New York: Holt, Rinehart & Winston, 1976.

Liddell, W. W., & Slocum, J. W., Jr. The effects of individual-role compatibility upon group performance: An extension of Schutz's FIRO theory. *Academy of Management Journal*, 1976, *19*, 413–426.

Maslow, A. H. *Toward a psychology of being*. Princeton, N.J.: D. Von Nostrand Company, 1962.

McKenney, J. L., & Keen, P. G. W. How managers' minds work. *Harvard Business Review*, 1974, *51*, 79–90.

Mendelsohn, G. A., & Rankin, N. O. Client–counselor compatibility and the outcome of counseling. *Journal of Abnormal Psychology*, 1969, *74*, 157–163.

Milgram, S. Behavioral study of obedience. *Journal of Abnormal and Social Psychology*, 1963, *67*, 371–378.

Mitroff, I. I., & Kilmann, R. On evaluating scientific research: The contributions of the philosophy of science. *Technological Forecasting and Social Change*, 1975, *8*, 163–174.

Mulkowsky, G. P., & Freeman, M. J. The impact of managerial orientation on implementing decisions. *Human Resource Management*, 1979, *18*, 6–14.

Myers, I. B. *Introduction to type*. Palo Alto, Calif.: Consulting Psychologists Press, 1980.

Nunney, D. N. Cognitive style mapping. *Training and Development Journal*, 1978, *32*, 50–57.

Obradovic, S. M. *Interpersonal factors in the supervisor–teacher relationship*. Unpublished doctoral dissertation, University of California, Berkeley, 1962.

Plovnick, M. S. *A cognitive ability theory of occupational roles*. Working paper #524-71, Massachusetts Institute of Technology, Sloan School of Management, Spring 1971.

Reddy, W. B., & Byrnes, A. Effects of interpersonal group composition on the problem-solving behavior of middle managers. *Journal of Applied Psychology*. 1972, *56*, 516–517.

Rest, J. R. *Revised manual for the Defining Issues Test: An objective test of moral judgment development*. Minneapolis: Minnesota Moral Research Projects, 1979.

Rogers, C. R. *On becoming a person*. Boston: Houghton Mifflin Co., 1961.

Rokeach, M. *The nature of human values*. New York: Free Press, 1973.

Ryan, L. R. *Clinical interpretation of the FIRO-B*, Palo Alto, Calif.: Consulting Psychologists Press. 1970.

Sapolsky, A. Relationship between patient–doctor compatibility, mutual perception, and outcome of treatment. *Journal of Abnormal Psychology*, 1965, *70*, 70–76.

Sayles, L. *Managerial behavior*. New York: McGraw-Hill, 1964.

Schutz, W. C. *FIRO: A three-dimensional theory of interpersonal behavior*. New York: Holt, Rinehart & Winston, 1958.

Shalinsky, W. Group composition as a factor in assembly effects. *Human Relations*, 1969, *22*, 457–464.

Simon, S. B. *Meeting yourself halfway: 31 value clarification strategies for daily living*. Niles, Ill.: Argus Communications, 1974.

Smith, S., & Haythorn, W. W. Effects of compatibility, crowding, group size, and leadership seniority on stress, anxiety, hostility, and annoyance in isolated groups. *Journal of Personality and Social Psychology*, 1973, *22*, 67–79.

Stabell, C. *The impact of a conversational computer system on human problem solving behavior*. Unpublished working paper, Massachusetts Institute of Technology, Sloan School of Management, 1973.

Vernon, P. E. (Ed.). *Creativity*. New York: Penguin Books, 1970.

Vertinsky, I. *Implementation II: A multi-paradigm approach*. Working paper presented at International Conference on the Implementation of Management Science in Social Organizations. University of Pittsburgh, February 1976.

■ *Skill Analysis*

Brainwashing

Edgar H. Schein

To find examples of a more intensive destruction of identification with family and reference groups, and the destruction of social role and self-image, we must turn to the experiences of civilian political prisoners interned within Chinese Communist prisons.

. . . In such prisons the total regimen, consisting of physical privation, prolonged interrogation, total isolation from former relationships and sources of information, detailed regimentation of all daily activities, and deliberate humiliation and degradation, was geared to producing a complete confession of alleged crimes, and the assumption of a penitent role depicting the adoption of a Communist frame of reference. The prisoner was not informed what his crimes were, nor was it permissible to evade the issue by making up a false confession. Instead, what the prisoner learned he must do was re-evaluate his past from the point of view of the Communists and recognize that most of his former attitudes and behavior were actually criminal from this point of view. For example, a priest who had dispensed food to needy peasants in his mission church had to recognize that he was actually a tool of imperialism and was using his missionary activities as cover for exploitation of the peasants. Even worse, he may have had to recognize that he was using food as blackmail to accomplish his aims.

The key technique used by the Communists to produce social alienation to a degree sufficient to allow such redefinition and reevaluation to occur was to put the prisoner into a cell with four or more other prisoners who were somewhat more advanced in their "thought reform" than he. Such a cell usually had one leader who was responsible to the prison authorities, and the progress of the whole cell was made contingent upon the progress of the least "reformed" member. This condition meant in practice that four or more cell members devoted all their energies to getting their least "reformed" member to recognize the truth about himself and to confess. To accomplish this they typically swore at, harangued, beat, denounced, humiliated, reviled, and brutalized their victim twenty-four hours a day, sometimes for weeks or months on end. If the authorities felt that the prisoner was basically uncooperative, they manacled his hands behind his back and chained his ankles, which made him

SOURCE: E. H. Schein, Interpersonal communication, group solidarity, and social influence, *Sociometry*, 1960, 23, 148–161.

completely dependent on his cell mates for the fulfillment of his basic needs. It was this reduction to an animal-like existence in front of other humans which, I believe, constituted the ultimate humiliation and led most reliably to the destruction of the prisoner's image of himself. Even in his own eyes he became something which was not worthy of the regard of his fellow man.

If, to avoid complete physical and personal destruction, the prisoner began to confess in the manner desired of him, he was usually forced to prove his sincerity by making irrevocable behavioral commitments, such as denouncing and implicating his friends and relatives in his own newly recognized crimes. Once he had done this he became further alienated from his former self, even in his own eyes, and could seek security only in a new identity and new social relationships. Aiding this process of confessing was the fact that the crimes gave the prisoner something concrete to which to attach the free-floating guilt which the accusing environment and his own humiliation usually stimulated.

. . . A good example was the plight of the sick and wounded prisoners of war who, because of their physical confinement, were unable to escape from continual contact with their interrogator or instructor, and who therefore often ended up forming a close relationship with him. Chinese Communist instructors often encouraged prisoners to take long walks or have informal talks with them and offered as incentives cigarettes, tea, and other rewards. If the prisoner was willing to cooperate and become a "progressive," he could join with other "progressives" in an active group life.

Within the political prison, the group cell not only provided the forces toward alienation but also offered the road to a "new self." Not only were there available among the fellow prisoners individuals with whom the prisoner could identify because of their shared plight, but once he showed any tendency to seek a new identity by truly trying to re-evaluate his past, he received again a whole range of rewards, of which perhaps the most important was the interpersonal information that he was again a person worthy of respect and regard. . . .

DISCUSSION QUESTIONS

1. To what extent is the self-concept a product of situational factors?

2. What is the relationship between self-knowledge and social pressure?

3. Is self-awareness constant, or do people become more and less self-aware over time?

4. What mechanisms could have been used by prisoners of war to resist the destruction of their self-concepts?

5. What could have been done to facilitate the reform of the self-concepts of prisoners? What can be done to enhance a positive self-concept?

The Boy, the Girl, the Ferryboat Captain, and the Hermits

There was an island, and on this island there lived a girl. A short distance away there was another island, and on this island there lived a boy. Now the boy and the girl were very much in love with each other and had been deeply in love for several years.

Eventually the boy had to leave his island and go far away, and he would be gone for a very long time. The girl felt that she must see the boy one more time before he went away. There was only one way to get from the island where the girl lived to the boy's island, and that was on a ferryboat that was run by a ferryboat captain. And so the girl went down to the dock and asked the ferryboat captain to take her to the island where the boy lived. The ferryboat captain agreed and asked her for the fare. The girl told the ferryboat captain that she did not have any money. The ferryboat captain told her that money was not necessary: "I will take you to the other island if you will stay with me tonight."

The girl did not know what to do, so she went up into the hills on her island until she came to a hut where a hermit lived. We will call him hermit 1. She related the whole story to hermit 1 and asked for his advice. Hermit 1 told her, "I cannot advise you. You must weigh the alternatives and the sacrifices that are involved and come to a decision within your own heart. I cannot advise you."

And so the girl went back down to the dock and accepted the ferryboat captain's offer.

The next day, when the girl arrived on the other island, the boy was waiting at the dock to greet her. They embraced, and then the boy asked her how she got over to his island, for he knew she did not have any money. The girl explained the ferryboat captain's offer and what she did. The boy pushed her away from him and said, "We're through. That's the end. Go away from me, I never want to see you again," and he left.

The girl was very upset and did not know what to do, so she went up into the hills of the boy's island to a hut where a hermit lived. We will call him hermit 2. She told the whole story to hermit 2 and asked him what she should do. Hermit 2 told her that there was nothing she could do, that she was welcome to stay in his hut, to partake of his food, and to rest on his bed while he went down into the town and begged for enough money to pay the girl's fare back to her own island.

When hermit 2 returned with the money for her, the girl asked him how she could repay him. Hermit 2 answered, "You owe me nothing. We owe this to each other. I was only too happy to be of help." And so the girl went back down to the dock and returned to her own island.

DISCUSSION QUESTIONS

1. List in order the characters in this story that you like, from most to least.

2. Why do you like some more than others?

3. What values help govern your choices?

4. In a small group, discuss your choices with others and identify reasons for the different rank orderings.   ■

■ *Skill Practice*

The Defining Issues Test

This instrument is aimed at assessing your opinions about controversial social issues. Different people make decisions about these issues in different ways. Therefore, you should answer the questions for yourself without discussing them with others.

The underlying question upon which this instrument is based is: In making a decision about these social problems, what should be the most important questions a person asks him/herself? On what general basis would you want people to determine what is crucial to solving these problems?

You are presented with three problem stories. Following each problem story there are twelve statements. Your first task after reading the story is to rate *each* of the twelve statements in terms of its importance in making a decision. After rating each item individually, select the four most important statements and rank them from one to four in the spaces provided. The statements should be rated and ranked in terms of how important that statement is in making a decision. That is, which is the crucial question that a person should focus on in making a decision?

Some statements will raise important issues, but you should ask yourself, should the decision rest on that issue? Some statements sound high and lofty but are largely gibberish. If you cannot make sense of a statement, or if you don't understand its meaning, mark it of *no* importance.

You will be given thirty minutes to complete the questionnaire. This should be ample time to consider each item carefully and respond to the three stories.

Use the following rating scale for your responses:

Of great importance	This statement makes a big, crucial difference one way or the other in making a decision about the problem.
Of much importance	This statement is something that a person should clearly be aware of in making a decision. It would make a difference in your decision, but not a big, crucial difference.
Of some importance	This statement says something you care about, but something that is not of crucial importance in deciding about this problem.
Of little importance	This statement concerns something that is not sufficiently important to consider in this case.
Of no importance	This statement is not important in making a decision. You would waste your time thinking about this in making your decision.

ESCAPED PRISONER

A man had been sentenced to prison for 10 years. After one year, however, he escaped from prison, moved to a new area of the country, and took on the name of Thompson. For 8 years he worked hard, and gradually he saved enough money to buy his own business. He was fair to his customers, gave his employees top wages, and gave most of his own profits to charity. Then one day, Mrs. Jones, an old neighbor, recognized him as the man who had escaped from prison 8 years before, and whom the police had been looking for.

Should Mrs. Jones report Mr. Thompson to the police and have him sent back to prison? (Check one.)

Should report him _____   Can't decide _____   Should not report him _____

IMPORTANCE

Great Much Some Little No

___ ___ ___ ___ ___ **1.** Hasn't Mr. Thompson been good enough for such a long time to prove he isn't a bad person?

___ ___ ___ ___ ___ **2.** Every time someone escapes punishment for a crime, doesn't that just encourage more crime?

___ ___ ___ ___ ___ **3.** Wouldn't we be better off without prisons and the oppression of our legal systems?

___ ___ ___ ___ ___ **4.** Has Mr. Thompson really paid his debt to society?

___ ___ ___ ___ ___ **5.** Would society be failing what Mr. Thompson should fairly expect?

___ ___ ___ ___ ___ **6.** What benefit would prison be apart from society, especially for a charitable man?

___ ___ ___ ___ ___ **7.** How could anyone be so cruel and heartless as to send Mr. Thompson to prison?

___ ___ ___ ___ ___ **8.** Would it be fair to all the prisoners who had to serve out their full sentences if Mr. Thompson was let off?

___ ___ ___ ___ ___ **9.** Was Mrs. Jones a good friend of Mr. Thompson?

___ ___ ___ ___ ___ **10.** Wouldn't it be a citizen's duty to report an escaped criminal, regardless of the circumstances?

___ ___ ___ ___ ___ **11.** How would the will of the people and the public good best be served?

_____ _____ _____ _____ _____   **12.** Would going to prison do any good for Mr. Thompson or protect anybody?

From the list of questions above, select the four most important:

Most important _____   Second most important _____

Third most important _____   Fourth most important _____

THE DOCTOR'S DILEMMA

A lady was dying of cancer which could not be cured and she had only about six months to live. She was in terrible pain, but she was so weak that a good dose of pain-killer like morphine would make her die sooner. She was delirious and almost crazy with pain, and in her calm periods, she would ask the doctor to give her enough morphine to kill her. She said she couldn't stand the pain and that she was going to die in a few months anyway.

What should the doctor do? (Check one.)

He should give the lady an overdose that will make her die _____   Can't decide _____   Should not give the overdose _____

IMPORTANCE

Great Much Some Little No

_____ _____ _____ _____ _____   **1.** Whether the woman's family is in favor of giving her the overdose or not.

_____ _____ _____ _____ _____   **2.** Is the doctor obligated by the same laws as everybody else if giving her an overdose would be the same as killing her?

_____ _____ _____ _____ _____   **3.** Whether people would be much better off without society regimenting their lives and even their deaths.

_____ _____ _____ _____ _____   **4.** Whether the doctor could make it appear like an accident.

_____ _____ _____ _____ _____   **5.** Does the state have the right to force continued existence on those who don't want to live?

_____ _____ _____ _____ _____   **6.** What is the value of death prior to society's perspective on personal values?

7. Whether the doctor has sympathy for the woman's suffering or cares more about what society might think.

___ ___ ___ ___ ___

8. Is helping to end another's life ever a responsible act of cooperation?

___ ___ ___ ___ ___

9. Whether only God should decide when a person's life should end.

___ ___ ___ ___ ___

10. What values the doctor has set for himself in his own personal code of behavior.

___ ___ ___ ___ ___

11. Can society afford to let everybody end their lives when they want to?

___ ___ ___ ___ ___

12. Can society allow suicides or mercy killings and still protect the lives of individuals who want to live?

From the list of questions above, select the four most important:

Most important ___   Second most important ___

Third most important ___   Fourth most important ___

NEWSPAPER

Fred, a senior in high school, wanted to publish a mimeographed newspaper for students so that he could express many of his opinions. He wanted to speak out against the war in Viet Nam and to speak out against some of the school's rules, like the rule forbidding boys to wear long hair.

When Fred started his newspaper, he asked his principal for permission. The principal said it would be all right if before every publication Fred would turn in all his articles for the principal's approval. Fred agreed and turned in several articles for approval. The principal approved all of them and Fred published two issues of the paper in the next two weeks.

But the principal had not expected that Fred's newspaper would receive so much attention. Students were so excited by the paper that they began to organize protests against the hair regulation and other school rules. Angry parents objected to Fred's opinions. They phoned the principal telling him that the newspaper was unpatriotic and should not be published. As a result of the rising excitement, the principal ordered Fred to stop publishing. He gave as a reason that Fred's activities were disruptive to the operation of the school.

Should stop it ___   Can't decide ___   Should not stop it ___

IMPORTANCE

Great Much Some Little No

1. Is the principal more responsible to the students or to the parents?

2. Did the principal give his word that the newspaper could be published for a long time, or did he just promise to approve the newspaper one issue at a time?

3. Would the students start protesting even more if the principal stopped the newspaper?

4. When the welfare of the school is threatened, does the principal have the right to give orders to students?

5. Does the principal have the freedom of speech to say "no" in this case?

6. If the principal stopped the newspaper, would he be preventing full discussion of important problems?

7. Whether the principal's order would make Fred lose faith in the principal.

8. Whether Fred was really loyal to his school and patriotic to his country.

9. What effect would stopping the paper have on the students' education in critical thinking and judgments?

10. Whether Fred was in any way violating the rights of others in publishing his own opinions.

11. Whether the principal should be influenced by some angry parents when it is the principal that knows best what is going on in the school.

12. Whether Fred was using the newspaper to stir up hatred and discontent.

From the list of questions above, select the four most important:

Most important _____   Second most important _____

Third most important _____   Fourth most important _____

INTERPRETING THE DEFINING ISSUES TEST

The possibility of misusing and misinterpreting this instrument is high enough that its author, James Rest, maintains control over the scoring procedure associated with its use. Some people may interpret the results of this instrument to be an indication of inherent morality, honesty, or personal worth, none of which the instrument is intended to assess. A scoring manual may be obtained from James Rest, Minnesota Moral Research Center, Burton Hall, University of Minnesota, Minneapolis, MN 55455.

Our purpose is to help you become aware of the stage of moral development you rely on most when facing moral dilemmas. To help determine that, the following lists present the stage of moral development each statement associated with each story reflects. By looking at the four statements you selected as most important in deciding what action to take in each situation, you can determine which stage of development you use most often.

After you have done this, you should discuss which action you would take in each situation and why, and why you selected the statements you did as the most important ones to consider.

Escaped Prisoner

1. Hasn't Mr. Thompson been good enough for such a long time to prove he isn't a bad person? (Stage 3)

2. Every time someone escapes punishment for a crime, doesn't that just encourage more crime? (Stage 4)

3. Wouldn't we be better off without prisons and the oppression of our legal system? (Indicates antiauthoritarian attitudes.)

4. Has Mr. Thompson really paid his debt to society? (Stage 4)

5. Would society be failing what Mr. Thompson should fairly expect? (Stage 6)

6. What benefits would prison be apart from society, especially for a charitable man? (Nonsense alternative, designed to identify people picking high-sounding alternatives.)

7. How could anyone be so cruel and heartless as to send Mr. Thompson to prison? (Stage 3)

8. Would it be fair to all the prisoners who had to serve out their full sentences if Mr. Thompson was let off? (Stage 4)

9. Was Mrs. Jones a good friend of Mr. Thompson? (Stage 3)

10. Wouldn't it be a citizen's duty to report an escaped criminal, regardless of circumstances? (Stage 4)

11. How would the will of the people and the public good best be served? (Stage 5)

12. Would going to prison do any good for Mr. Thompson or protect anybody? (Stage 5)

The Doctor's Dilemma

1. Whether the woman's family is in favor of giving her an overdose or not. (Stage 3)

2. Is the doctor obligated by the same laws as everybody else if giving her an overdose would be the same as killing her? (Stage 4)

3. Whether people would be much better off without society regimenting their lives and even their deaths. (Indicates antiauthoritarian attitudes.)

4. Whether the doctor could make it appear like an accident. (Stage 2)

5. Does the state have the right to force continued existence on those who don't want to live? (Stage 5)

6. What is the value of death prior to society's perspective on personal values? (Nonsense alternative, designed to identify people picking high-sounding alternatives.)

7. Whether the doctor has sympathy for the woman's suffering or cares more about what society might think. (Stage 3)

8. Is helping to end another's life ever a responsible act of cooperation? (Stage 6)

9. Whether only God should decide when a person's life should end. (Stage 4)

10. What values the doctor has set for himself in his own personal code of behavior. (Stage 5)

11. Can society afford to let everybody end their lives when they want to? (Stage 4)

12. Can society allow suicides or mercy killing and still protect the lives of individuals who want to live? (Stage 5)

Newspaper

1. Is the principal more responsible to students or to the parents? (Stage 4)

2. Did the principal give his word that the newspaper could be published for a long time, or did he just promise to approve the newspaper one issue at a time? (Stage 4)

3. Would the students start protesting even more if the principal stopped the newspaper? (Stage 2)

4. When the welfare of the school is threatened, does the principal have the right to give orders to students? (Stage 4)

5. Does the principal have the freedom of speech to say "no" in this case? (Nonsense alternative, designed to identify people picking high-sounding alternatives.)

6. If the principal stopped the newspaper, would he be preventing full discussion of important matters? (Stage 5)

7. Whether the principal's order would make Fred lose faith in the principal. (Stage 3)

8. Whether Fred was really loyal to his school and patriotic to his country. (Stage 3)

9. What effect would stopping the paper have on the students' education in critical thinking and judgments? (Stage 5)

10. Whether Fred was in any way violating the rights of others in publishing his own opinions. (Stage 5)

11. Whether the principal should be influenced by some angry parents when it is the principal that knows best what is going on in the school. (Stage 4)

12. Whether Fred was using the newspaper to stir up hatred and discontent. (Stage 3)

The Cognitive Style Instrument

In this instrument you must put yourself in the position of someone who must gather, evaluate, or respond to information. The purpose is to investigate the ways you think about information you encounter. There are no right or wrong answers, and one alternative is just as good as another. Therefore, try to indicate the ways you *do* or *would* respond, not the ways you think you *should* respond.

For each scenario there are three pairs of alternatives. For each pair, select the alternative that is more like the way you would respond. Answer each item. If you are not sure, guess.

Suppose you are a scientist at NASA whose job it is to gather information about the moons of Saturn. Which of the following would you be more interested in investigating?

1. (a) How the moons are similar to one another

   (b) How the moons differ from one another

2. (a) How the whole system of moons operates

   (b) The characteristics of each moon

3. (a) How Saturn and its moons are unique compared to Earth and its moon

   (b) How Saturn and its moons are similar to Earth and its moon

Suppose you are the chief executive of a company and have asked division heads to make presentations at the end of the year. Which of the following would be more appealing to you?

4. (a) A presentation analyzing the details of the data

   (b) A presentation oriented toward presenting the conceptual whole

5. (a) A presentation showing how the division contributed to the company as a whole

   (b) A presentation showing the unique contributions of the division

6. (a) Details of how the division performed

   (b) General summaries of performance data

Suppose you are visiting the Orient, and you are writing home to tell about your trip. Which of the following would be most typical of the letter you would write?

7. (a) A detailed description of people and events

   (b) General impressions and feelings

8. (a) A focus on similarities of our culture and theirs

   (b) A focus on the uniquenesses of their culture

9. (a) Overall, general impressions of the experience

   (b) Separate, unique impressions of parts of the experience

Suppose you are attending a concert featuring a famous symphony orchestra. Which of the following would you be most likely to do?

10. (a) Listen for the parts of individual instruments

(b) Listen for the blend of all the instruments together

11. (a) Pay attention to the overall mood associated with the music

(b) Pay attention to the separate feelings associated with different parts of the music

12. (a) Focus on the overall style of the conductor

(b) Focus on how the conductor conducts different parts of the score

Suppose you are considering taking a job with a certain organization. Which of the following would you be more likely to do in deciding whether or not to take the job?

13. (a) Systematically collect information on the organization

(b) Rely on personal intuition or inspiration

14. (a) Consider primarily the fit between you and the job

(b) Consider primarily the methods needed to succeed in the organization

15. (a) Be methodical in collecting data and making a choice

(b) Give attention mostly to your personal instincts and gut feelings

Suppose you inherit some money and decide to invest it. You learn of a new high-technology firm that has just issued stock. Which of the following is most likely to be true of your decision to purchase the firm's stock?

16. (a) You would invest on a hunch

(b) You would invest only after an organized investigation of the firm

17. (a) You would be somewhat impulsive in deciding to invest

(b) You would follow a sequential pattern in making your decision

18. (a) You could rationally justify your decision to invest in this firm and not in another

(b) It would probably be difficult to rationally justify your decision to invest in this firm and not in another

Suppose you are being interviewed on TV, and you are asked the following questions. Which alternative would you be most likely to select?

19. How are you more likely to cook?
(a) With a recipe

(b) Without a recipe

20. How would you predict the Super Bowl winner next year?
(a) After systematically researching the personnel and records of the teams

(b) On a hunch or by intuition

21. Which games do you prefer?
(a) Games of chance (like Bingo)

(b) Chess, checkers, or Scrabble

Suppose you are a manager and need to hire an executive assistant. Which of the following would you be most likely to do in the process?

22. (a) Interview each applicant using a set outline of questions

(b) Concentrate on your personal feelings and instincts about applicants in the interview

23. (a) Consider primarily the fit between yourself and the candidates

(b) Systematically consider the match of personal skills and position requirements

24. (a) Rely on factual and historical data on each candidate in making a choice

(b) Rely on personal intuition or inspiration in making a choice

Suppose you are a newly appointed member of a university board of trustees. They are discussing how to solve an important problem. Which of the following is most likely to be typical of your behavior?

25. (a) You would actively participate in the discussion

(b) You would mostly observe

26. (a) You would favor taking action one way or the other

(b) You would favor thinking about it for a while

27. (a) You would recommend deliberation and sifting through the issue before making a decision

(b) You would become impatient unless a solution were reached relatively soon

Suppose you develop a new type of photographic film that significantly improves the quality of photographs. After two weeks or so, however, the photographs begin to fade. Which of the following would you be most likely to do?

28. (a) Ponder and thoughtfully consider possible solutions

(b) Immediately begin to experiment with new alternatives and conditions

29. (a) Take immediate action to try to correct the problem

(b) Be patient and reflect on what might be done to solve the problem

30. (a) Concern yourself with the longer-term implications of the problem

(b) Concern yourself with the practical, immediate concerns of getting it to work

Suppose you are at a party where you know only a few people. Which of the following would be typical of your behavior?

31. (a) Introduce people you know

(b) Wait to be introduced by people you know

32. (a) Actively go from group to group to try to meet people

(b) Sit back and observe the behavior of others

33. (a) Try to create the impression that you are a doer rather than a thinker

(b) Try to create the impression that you are a thinker rather than a doer

Which of the following types of people are most appealing to you?

34. (a) A decisive, dynamic manager

(b) A thoughtful, careful manager

35. (a) The inventor of useful items

(b) The developer of an elegant scientific theory

36. (a) A deliberate problem solver

(b) An aggressive problem solver

SCORING KEY

To determine your score on the three dimensions of cognitive style, circle the items below that you checked on this instrument. Then count up the number of circled items and put your scores in the spaces below.

Gathering Information		Evaluating Information		Responding to Information	
Preceptive	Receptive	Systematic	Intuitive	Active	Reflective
1a	1b	13a	13b	25a	25b
2a	2b	14b	14a	26a	26b
3b	3a	15a	15b	27b	27a
4b	4a	16b	16a	28b	28a
5a	5b	17b	17a	29a	29b
6b	6a	18a	18b	30b	30a
7b	7a	19a	19b	31a	31b
8a	8b	20a	20b	32a	32b
9a	9b	21b	21a	33a	33b
10b	10a	22a	22b	34a	34b
11a	11b	23b	23a	35a	35b
12a	12b	24a	24b	36b	36a

Preceptive Score	Receptive Score	Systematic Score	Intuitive Score	Active Score	Reflective Score
_____	_____	_____	_____	_____	_____

Your instructor has been provided with some comparison data from other respondent groups. These will help you compare your own scores with those of others outside your own small group.

Fundamental Interpersonal Relations Orientation–Behavior

For each statement below, decide which of the following answers best applies to you. Place the number of the answer at the left of the statement.

1. Usually   2. Often   3. Sometimes   4. Occasionally   5. Rarely   6. Never

_____ 1. I try to be with people.

_____ 2. I let other people decide what to do.

_____ 3. I join social groups.

_____ 4. I try to have close relationships with people.

_____ 5. I tend to join social organizations when I have an opportunity.

_____ 6. I let other people strongly influence my actions.

_____ 7. I try to be included in informal social activities.

_____ 8. I try to have close, personal relationships with people.

_____ 9. I try to include other people in my plans.

_____ 10. I let other people control my actions.

_____ 11. I try to have people around me.

_____ 12. I try to get close and personal with people.

_____ 13. When people are doing things together I tend to join them.

_____ 14. I am easily led by people.

_____ 15. I try to avoid being alone.

_____ 16. I try to participate in group activities.

For each of the next group statements, choose one of the following answers:

1. Most people   2. Many people   3. Some people   4. A few people   5. One or two people   6. Nobody

_____ 17. I try to be friendly to people.

_____ 18. I let other people decide what to do.

_____ 19. My personal relations with people are cool and distant.

_____ 20. I let other people take charge of things.

_____ 21. I try to have close relationships with people.

_____ 22. I let other people strongly influence my actions.

_____ 23. I try to get close and personal with people.

_____ 24. I let other people control my actions.

_____ 25. I act cool and distant with people.

_____ 26. I am easily led by people.

_____ 27. I try to have close, personal relationships with people.

SOURCE: *FIRO: A three-dimensional theory of interpersonal behavior* (New York: Rinehart & Co., 1958).

For each of the next group of statements, choose one of the following answers:

1. Most people	2. Many people	3. Some people	4. A few people	5. One or two people	6. Nobody

_____ **28.** I like people to invite me to things.

_____ **29.** I like people to act close and personal with me.

_____ **30.** I try to influence strongly other people's actions.

_____ **31.** I like people to invite me to join in their activities.

_____ **32.** I like people to act close toward me.

_____ **33.** I try to take charge of things when I am with people.

_____ **34.** I like people to include me in their activities.

_____ **35.** I like people to act cool and distant toward me.

_____ **36.** I try to have other people do things the way I want them done.

_____ **37.** I like people to ask me to participate in their discussions.

_____ **38.** I like people to act friendly toward me.

_____ **39.** I like people to invite me to participate in their activities.

_____ **40.** I like people to act distant toward me.

For each of the next group of statements, choose one of the following answers:

1. Usually	2. Often	3. Sometimes	4. Occasionally	5. Rarely	6. Never

_____ **41.** I try to be the dominant person when I am with people.

_____ **42.** I like people to invite me to things.

_____ **43.** I like people to act close toward me.

_____ **44.** I try to have other people do things I want done.

_____ **45.** I like people to invite me to join their activities.

_____ **46.** I like people to act cool and distant toward me.

_____ **47.** I try to influence strongly other people's actions.

_____ **48.** I like people to include me in their activities.

_____ **49.** I like people to act close and personal with me.

_____ **50.** I try to take charge of things when I'm with people.

_____ **51.** I like people to invite me to participate in their activities.

_____ **52.** I like people to act distant toward me.

_____ **53.** I try to have other people do things the way I want them done.

_____ **54.** I take charge of things when I'm with people.

INSTRUCTIONS FOR SCORING

To derive your interpersonal orientation scores, refer to the table below. Note that there are six columns, each with *items* and *keys*. Each column refers to an interpersonal need listed in the chart at the bottom of the page. *Items* in the column refer to question numbers on the questionnaire; *keys* refer to answers on each of those items. If you answered an item using any of the alternatives in the corresponding key column, circle the item number on this sheet. When you have checked all of the items for a single column, count up the number of circled items and place that number in the corresponding box in the chart. These numbers will give you your strength of interpersonal need in each of the six areas. The highest possible score is 9. The lowest score is 0. Refer to the explanations in the chapter in order to interpret your scores.

Expressed Inclusion		Wanted Inclusion		Expressed Control		Wanted Control		Expressed Affection		Wanted Affection	
Item	Key	Item	Key	Item	Key	Item	Key	Item	Key	Item	Key
1	1–2–3	28	1–2	30	1–2–3	2	1–2–3–4	4	1–2	29	1–2
3	1–2–3–4	31	1–2	33	1–2–3	6	1–2–3–4	8	1–2	32	1–2
5	1–2–3–4	34	1–2	36	1–2	10	1–2–3	12	1	35	5–6
7	1–2–3	37	1	41	1–2–3–4	14	1–2–3	17	1–2	38	1–2
9	1–2	39	1	44	1–2–3	18	1–2–3	19	4–5–6	40	5–6
11	1–2	42	1–2	47	1–2–3	20	1–2–3	21	1–2	43	1
13	1–2	45	1–2	50	1–2	22	1–2–3–4	23	1–2	46	5–6
15	1	48	1–2	53	1–2	24	1–2–3	25	4–5–6	49	1–2
16	1	51	1–2	54	1–2	26	1–2–3	27	1–2	52	5–6

	Inclusion	Control	Affection	
Expressed Behavior Toward Others				___
Wanted Behavior from Others				___
	___	___	___	[ ]

Group Discussion Exercise

Form groups of three or four individuals and share your scores on the values, cognitive style, and interpersonal orientation instruments. Discuss the following among yourselves:

1. What is the meaning of your scores on the values and moral development instrument? What are the implications for your own behavior and for your future? What incidents in your recent past have illustrated your orientation?

2. How are your scores on this instrument similar to or different from others' scores in the group? What do the differences imply?

3. What is the meaning of your cognitive style scores? What consistencies and inconsistencies are there in terms of the way you think about yourself?

4. How should you study in school to maximize your cognitive strengths? What kind of career would you do best in?

5. What are the implications of your interpersonal orientation scores for your relationships with friends or family members?

6. What incompatibilities exist in your group? What are the implications of those incompatibilities for future relationships?   ■

■ *Skill Application*

Application Exercises

1. Now that you have completed several personal assessment instruments and have had an opportunity to discuss the meaning of the results, write an essay responding to the question "Who am I?"

2. Keep a journal for at least the remainder of this course. Record significant discoveries, insights, learnings, and personal recollections, not just daily activities. Give yourself some feedback.

3. Write down the comprehensive, consistent, and universal principles that guide your behavior under all circumstances and that you rarely violate.

4. Spend an evening with a close friend or relative discussing your values, cognitive style, and interpersonal orientation. You may want to have that person complete the instruments as well so you can compare and contrast your scores. Discuss implications for your future and for your relationship.

5. Teach someone else the value of self-awareness in managerial success, and explain the relevance of values maturity, cognitive style, and interpersonal orientation. Describe the experience in your journal (see 2, above). ■

2 Managing Personal Stress

■ *Skill Preassessment*
Social Readjustment Rating Scale
Type A Behavior Pattern Inventory

■ *Skill Learning*
The Management of Stress and Time

■ *Skill Analysis*
The Day at the Beach
The Case of the Missing Time

■ *Skill Practice*
The Controller's Report
The Stress of Success

■ *Skill Application*
Application Exercises

■ Skill Preassessment

Social Readjustment Rating Scale

Which of the following have you experienced in the past year? Using the weightings at the right, total up your score.

Life Event	Mean Value
1. Death of spouse	100
2. Divorce	73
3. Marital separation from mate	65
4. Detention in jail or other institution	63
5. Death of a close family member	63
6. Major personal injury or illness	53
7. Marriage	50
8. Being fired at work	47
9. Marital reconciliation with mate	45
10. Retirement from work	45
11. Major change in the health or behavior of a family member	44
12. Pregnancy	40
13. Sexual difficulties	39
14. Gaining a new family member (e.g., through birth, adoption, oldster moving in, etc.)	39
15. Major business readjustment (e.g., merger, reorganization, bankruptcy, etc.)	39
16. Major change in financial state (e.g., a lot worse off or a lot better off than usual)	38
17. Death of a close friend	37
18. Changing to a different line of work	36
19. Major change in the number of arguments with spouse (e.g., either a lot more or a lot less than usual regarding childrearing, personal habits, etc.)	35
20. Taking out a mortgage or loan for a major purchase (e.g., for a home, business, etc.)	31
21. Foreclosure on a mortgage or loan	30
22. Major change in responsibilities at work (e.g., promotion, demotion, lateral transfer)	29
23. Son or daughter leaving home (e.g., marriage, attending college, etc.)	29
24. Trouble with in-laws	29
25. Outstanding personal achievement	28
26. Wife beginning or ceasing work outside the home	26
27. Beginning or ceasing formal schooling	26
28. Major change in living conditions (e.g., building a new home, remodeling, deterioration of home or neighborhood)	25
29. Revision of personal habits (dress, manners, association, etc.)	24
30. Troubles with the boss	23
31. Major change in working hours or conditions	20
32. Change in residence	20

SOURCE: T. H. Holmes and R. H. Rahe, Social readjustment rating scale, *Journal of Psychosomatic Research*, 1967, 11, 213–218.

33. Changing to a new school   20
34. Major change in usual type and/or amount of recreation   19
35. Major change in church activities (e.g., a lot more or a lot less than usual)   19
36. Major change in social activities (e.g., clubs, dancing, movies, visiting, etc.)   18
37. Taking out a mortgage or loan for a lesser purchase (e.g., for a car, TV, freezer, etc.)   17
38. Major change in sleeping habits (a lot more or a lot less sleep, or change in part of day when asleep)   16
39. Major change in number of family get-togethers (e.g., a lot more or a lot less than usual)   15
40. Major change in eating habits (a lot more or a lot less food intake, or very different meal hours or surroundings)   15
41. Vacation   13
42. Christmas   12
43. Minor violations of the law (e.g., traffic tickets, jaywalking, disturbing the peace, etc.)   11

Type A Behavior Pattern Inventory

Rate the extent to which each of the following statements is typical of you *most of the time.* Try to describe your general way of behaving or feeling, not isolated incidents. There are no correct answers. Scoring instructions for the instrument will be provided by the instructor. In responding to each statement, use the following scale:

> 5—The statement is *true.* It is *typical* of me.
> 4—The statement is *somewhat true.* It is *somewhat typical* of me.
> 3—The statement is *neither true nor untrue,* or I *can't decide.*
> 2—The statement is *somewhat untrue.* It is *somewhat atypical* of me.
> 1—The statement is *untrue.* It is *not typical* of me at all.

_____ **1.** I am involved in a job that "stirs me into action."

_____ **2.** When I was younger, I was hard driving and competitive.

_____ **3.** Nowadays, I am still hard driving and competitive.

_____ **4.** I am rated as being hard driving and competitive by my spouse and friends.

_____ **5.** I am rated as being too active (engaged in too many activities) by my spouse and friends.

_____ **6.** I give much more effort to my work than the average worker.

_____ **7.** I consider myself to be more responsible than the average worker.

Adapted from Stephen J. Zyzanski and C. David Jenkins, Basic dimensions within the coronary-prone behavior pattern. *Journal of Chronic Diseases,* 1970, 22, 781–795.

——————— **8.** I hurry in my work more than the average worker.

——————— **9.** I consider myself to be more precise than the average worker.

——————— **10.** I approach life more seriously than the average worker.

——————— **11.** I often have trouble finding time for a haircut.

——————— **12.** I eat more rapidly than most people.

——————— **13.** I am often told that I eat too fast.

——————— **14.** I frequently hurry a speaker to make the point.

——————— **15.** I frequently put words into the speaker's mouth.

——————— **16.** I find myself often inattentive to lengthy comments.

——————— **17.** I often think of other things when listening to someone talk.

——————— **18.** I find everyday life filled with challenges to be met.

——————— **19.** I frequently set deadlines for myself at home.

——————— **20.** I generally keep two jobs moving forward simultaneously.

——————— **21.** I prefer a promotion to an increase in pay.

——————— **22.** My income has considerably increased in the last three years.

——————— **23.** I have more responsibility in my work than I did 10 years ago.

——————— **24.** My present work has more prestige than it did 10 years ago.

——————— **25.** I frequently do not leave work until well after closing time.

——————— **26.** I frequently bring work home to do during the evenings.

——————— **27.** I have held an office in an activity group while in school.

Total score for the total instrument:
Total score for items 1 through 10:
Total score for items 11 through 17:
Total score for items 18 through 27:

■ Skill Learning

The Management of Stress and Time

The United States Clearing House for Mental Health Information estimates that U.S. industry experiences a loss in productive capacity of $17 billion annually because of stress-induced mental dysfunction. Ivancevich and Matteson (1980) place the cost of stress conservatively at $75–90 billion annually (10 percent of the gross national product), based on various government, industry, and health organization estimates. Albrecht (1979) reports costs associated with stress-related alcoholism, drug abuse, disease, and emotional trauma to be in the $142 billion range. Over 130,000 publications on stress have now been produced, and a large number of organizations (e.g., Xerox, Weyerhauser, IBM) have invested large sums in stress reduction training programs. In a recent survey, Sailer, Schlacter, and Edwards (1982) found that 80 percent of responding job holders wanted information on the management of stress. In short, the ability to manage stress has become recognized as a critical area of concern by the medical profession as well as practicing managers. Stress directly affects higher-order mental processes, personal productivity, motivation, life satisfaction, interpersonal relations, and physical health (Selye, 1976).

Consider the following story reported by the Associated Press in December 1979.

> BALTIMORE (AP)   The job was getting to the ambulance attendant. He felt disturbed by the recurring tragedy, isolated by the long shifts. His marriage was in trouble. He was drinking too much.
>
> One night it all blew up.
>
> He rode in back that night. His partner drove. Their first call was for a man whose leg had been cut off by a train. His screaming and agony were horrifying, but the second call was worse.
>
> It was a child beating. As the attendant treated the youngster's bruised body and snapped bones, he thought of his own child. His fury grew.
>
> Immediately after leaving the child at the hospital, the attendants were sent out to help a heart attack victim seen lying in a street.
>
> When they arrived, however, they found not a cardiac patient but a drunk—a wino passed out.
>
> As they lifted the man into the ambulance, their frustration and anger came to a head. They decided to give the wino a ride he would remember.
>
> The ambulance vaulted over railroad tracks at high speed. The driver took the corners as fast as he could, flinging the wino from side to side in the back. To the attendants, it was a joke.

Suddenly, the wino began having a real heart attack. The attendant in back leaned over the wino and started shouting.

"Die, you mother!" he yelled, "Die!"

He watched as the wino shuddered. He watched as the wino died.

By the time they reached the hospital, they had their stories straight. Dead on arrival, they said. Nothing we could do.

The attendant, who must remain anonymous, talked about that night at a recent counseling session on "professional burnout"—a growing problem in high-stress jobs.

As this story illustrates, stress frequently has devastating effects on individuals who encounter it. Personal consequences can range from inability to concentrate, anxiety, and depression to mental breakdown and coronary heart disease. For organizations, consequences range from absenteeism and job dissatisfaction to high accident rates and turnover (Sailer, Schlacter, & Edwards, 1982).

In this chapter we shall explain why burnout and even more serious consequences occur as a result of stress. Our purpose is to help you understand and learn to recognize the factors that are stressful for managers, and to present principles and action guidelines that will be useful for coping with stress. This discussion is important because, despite the high personal, organizational, and even societal costs of stress, relatively little is known about ways of adapting to it. Most of the scholarly literature on stress focuses on relationships between stress and its consequences; hardly any relates to effective coping strategies (Jenkins, 1979; Payne, Jick, & Burke, 1982). As Toffler (1970, p. 2) has pointed out, we still know relatively little about how to adapt to the pressures we face:

I gradually came to be appalled by how little is actually known about adaptivity, either by those who call for and create vast changes in our society, or by those who supposedly prepare us to cope with those changes. Earnest intellectuals talk bravely about "educating for change," or "preparing people for the future." But we know virtually nothing about how to do it. In the most rapidly changing environment to which man has ever been exposed, we remain pitifully ignorant of how the human animal copes.

We shall begin this chapter by presenting a framework that will be useful for understanding stress and learning how to cope with it. This model explains the major types of stressors faced by managers, the primary reactions to stress, and reasons some people experience more negative reactions (e.g., burnout) than others. The last section presents principles for adapting to stress, along with some specific examples and action guidelines.

UNDERSTANDING STRESS

One way to understand the dynamics of stress is to think of it as the product of a "force field" (Lewin, 1951). Kurt Lewin suggests that all individuals (and organizations) exist in an environment filled with reinforcing as well as opposing forces or pressures. These forces act to stimulate or inhibit the performance desired by the individual. As illustrated in Figure 2.1, a manager's level of personal functioning in an organization results from factors that may either complement or contradict one another. Certain forces drive or motivate changes in behavior, but other forces restrain or block those changes.

According to Lewin's theory, the forces affecting individuals are normally balanced in the force field. The strength of the driving forces is matched exactly by the strength of the restraining forces. (In the figure, longer arrows indicate stronger forces.) Behavior changes when the forces become imbalanced. That is, if the driving forces become stronger than the restraining forces, or more numerous or long-lasting, change occurs. Conversely, if the restraining forces become stronger or more numerous than the driving forces, change occurs in the opposite direction.

Stress results from the occurrence of certain "stressors" inside or outside the individual. These stressors can be thought of as the driving forces in the model. That is, they put pressure on the individual to change present levels of functioning physiologically, psychologically, and interpersonally. Unrestrained, those forces lead to pathological results (e.g., coronary heart disease, mental breakdown). However, most people have developed certain restraining forces that counter stressors and inhibit pathological results. These restraining forces are behavior patterns, psychological characteristics, and social support

Figure 2.1   *Model of Force Field Analysis*

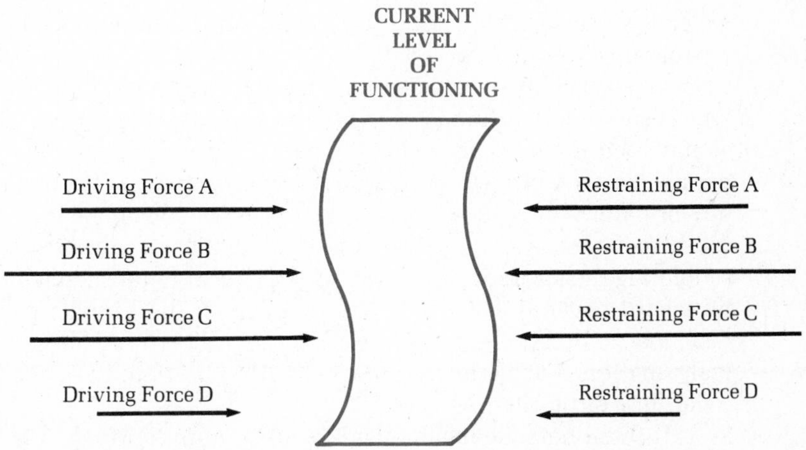

CURRENT
LEVEL
OF
FUNCTIONING

Driving Force A   Restraining Force A

Driving Force B   Restraining Force B

Driving Force C   Restraining Force C

Driving Force D   Restraining Force D

mechanisms that people use to cope with stress. Strong restraining forces lead to low heart rates, good interpersonal relations, emotional stability, and effective management. An absence of restraining forces leads to the reverse.

When stressors overpower the adaptive capacities of individuals, chronic stress is experienced and negative personal consequences generally follow. However, when the adaptive capacities of individuals are strongly developed, chronic stress is less apt to be experienced and negative consequences are unlikely. Figure 2.2 shows the major categories of stressors faced by managers, the major restraining forces that moderate the effects of stressors, and the major behavioral and psychological reactions to stress. In the next section, we shall discuss each of those categories and review relevant research that shows links between these factors and stress.

Reactions to Stress

An individual's current level of functioning is a product of the stressors and resistance factors operating in opposition to one another. Stress may be experienced temporarily when a stressor occurs, but equilibrium can be restored quickly if sufficient restraining forces are present. In the case of the ambulance driver, multiple stressors overpowered the available restraining forces and burnout occurred. Before that extreme state is reached, however, individuals progress through three stages of reactions. Hans Selye (1976), the father of stress research, identifies these as the *alarm* stage, the *resistance* stage, and the *exhaustion* stage.

The alarm stage is characterized by acute increases in anxiety or fear if the stressor is a threat, or marked increases in sorrow or depression if the stressor is a loss. A feeling of shock or confusion may result if the stressor is particularly acute. Physically, the immediate release of adrenalin mobilizes the individual's energy resources, increasing the heart rate and raising the blood pressure. These reactions are largely self-correcting if the stressor is only of brief duration. However, if it continues, the individual enters the resistance stage, in which defense mechanisms predominate and the body begins to store up extra energy.

Five types of defense mechanisms are most characteristic of individuals who respond to continued stressors (Cofer & Appley, 1964). The first is *aggression,* which involves attacking the stressor directly, or attacking oneself, other people, or even objects. A second is *regression,* which is the adoption of a behavior pattern or response that was successful at some earlier time. A third defense mechanism, *repression,* involves denial of the stressor, forgetting, or redefining the stressor. *Withdrawal* is a fourth defense mechanism, and it may take both psychological and physical forms. Individuals may engage in fantasy, inattention, or purposive forgetting, or they may actually leave the physical situation. A fifth defense mechanism is *fixation,* or persisting in a response regardless of its effectiveness.

If these defense mechanisms reduce an individual's feelings of stress, he or she will seldom display such negative reactions as high blood pressure, anxiety, or mental disorder (Jenkins, 1979). The primary evidence for stress may simply be an increase in psychological defensiveness. However, when stressors are so pronounced as to overwhelm defenses or so enduring that they outlast available energy for defensiveness, pathological end-states, or what Selye calls "exhaustion," may result.

Pathological end-states can occur psychologically (e.g., severe depression), interpersonally (e.g., dissolution of a marriage), or physically (e.g., coronary heart disease). They are thought to result from damage done to the individual for which there was no defense (e.g., psychotic reactions among prisoners of war), from an inability to defend continuously against a stressor (e.g., becoming exhausted), from an overreaction to a stressor (e.g., stomach ulcers resulting from an oversecretion of body chemicals), or from lack of self-awareness so that stress goes unacknowledged. While each reaction stage may have negative consequences for the individual, this third stage is most severe.

Driving Forces

The story of the ambulance driver illustrates the four major stressors in Figure 2.2. The first, *anticipatory stressors,* are potentially disagreeable events that

Figure 2.2   *Model of Stress in Terms of Force Field Analysis*

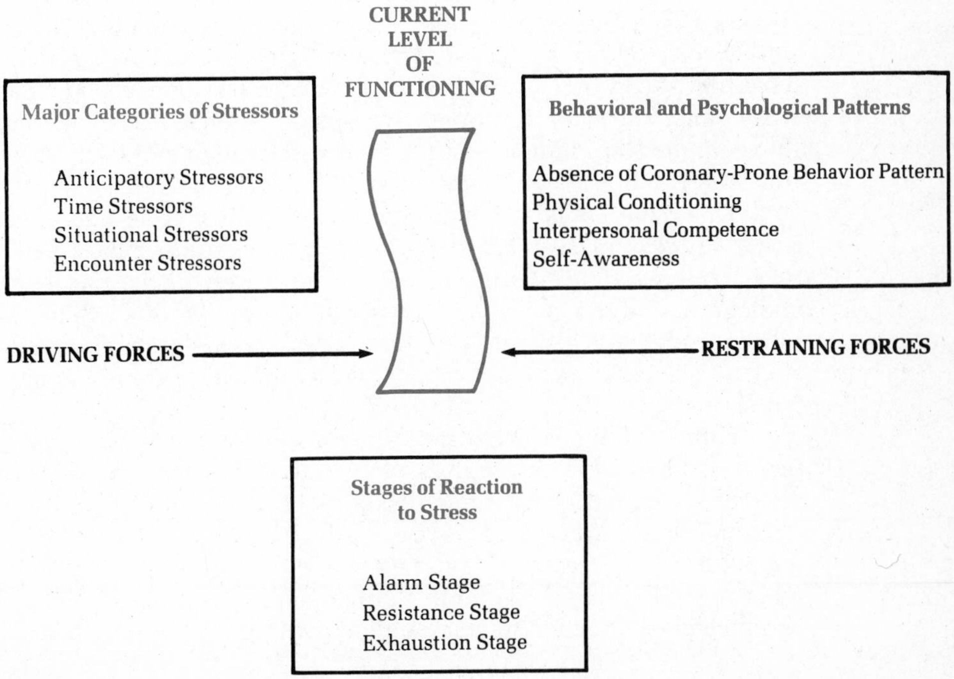

CURRENT
LEVEL
OF
FUNCTIONING

Major Categories of Stressors

Anticipatory Stressors
Time Stressors
Situational Stressors
Encounter Stressors

Behavioral and Psychological Patterns

Absence of Coronary-Prone Behavior Pattern
Physical Conditioning
Interpersonal Competence
Self-Awareness

DRIVING FORCES —————→   ←————— **RESTRAINING FORCES**

Stages of Reaction
to Stress

Alarm Stage
Resistance Stage
Exhaustion Stage

threaten to occur. Something unpleasant that has not yet happened but might happen serves as an anticipatory stressor. In the case of the ambulance driver, the constant threat of having to witness human suffering or having a patient die is an anticipatory stressor. Threats of death by Iranian guards of the American hostages in 1980 were reported to be great stressors by the hostages, and Schein (1960) reports dramatic behavioral and psychological changes occurred in American prisoners in the Korean War. He identifies anticipatory stressors (e.g., threat of severe punishment) as major contributors to psychological and physiological pathology among the prisoners.

Anticipatory stressors need not be highly unpleasant or severe, however, to produce stress. Schachter (1959), Milgram (1963), and others have induced high levels of stress by telling individuals that they would experience a loud noise or a mild shock, or that someone else might become uncomfortable because of their actions. Fear of failure or fear of embarrassment in front of peers is a common anticipatory stressor. Anxieties about retirement and losing vitality during middle age have been identified by Levinson (1978), Hall (1976), and others as common maladies.

A second category of stressors is *time stressors*, which result from having too much to do in too little time. This has been identified as the most common and most pervasive source of stress faced by managers in American organizations (Mintzberg, 1973; Carlson, 1951; Sayles, 1964). One reason is that American culture is extremely time conscious, and it is becoming more so with the development of digital watches. Fifteen years ago when asked for the time, for example, a person might have responded, "It's about 2:30." Now the response is more likely, "It's 2:28," or even, "It's 2:28 and 43 seconds." The emphasis on time is also evidence by the many ways we have of talking about time. We have time, keep time, buy time, save time, mark time, spend time, sell time, waste time, kill time, pass time, give time, take time, and make time. Contrast this with the Hopi Indians in the Southwest, who do not even have a word for time! They only have past, present, and future tense words.

This remarkable fascination with time makes it an important source of stress. French and Caplan (1972), for example, studied the relationships between role overload and chronic time pressures on the one hand and psychological and physiological dysfunction on the other. They found significant relationships between time stressors and job dissatisfaction, tension, perceived threat, heart rate, cholesterol levels, skin resistance, and other factors.

In the ambulance story, time stressors are evidenced by *role overload,* or feeling compelled to accomplish a large number of tasks in a short time. They also are illustrated by *not being in control* of one's time. When experienced on a chronic basis, these stressors can be highly dysfunctional. The presence of temporary time stressors may serve as motivators in getting the work done, and some individuals accomplish much more when faced with an immediate deadline than when left to work at their own pace. However, constant states of time pressure, having too much to do, and not feeling able to control the use of time generally are negatively stressful.

The third category of stressors is *situational stressors,* which arise from the environment in which a person exists or from an individual's circumstances. For the ambulance driver, the continual presence of crises, long hours, and isolation from colleagues were situational stressors.

One of the most well-researched links between situational stressors and negative consequences involves the effects of changes in life events (Wolff, Wolf, & Hare, 1950; Holmes & Rahe, 1970). The Social Readjustment Rating Scale (SRRS) was introduced in 1967 to track the number of changes individuals had experienced over the past twelve months. Since changes in some events were thought to be more stressful than others, a scaling method was used to assign weights to each life event. Numerous studies among a variety of cultures, age groups, and occupations have confirmed the relative weightings in the 1967 instrument (see Rahe, Ryman, & Ward, 1980). That is, the weightings generally hold true regardless of culture, age, or occupation. You completed this instrument in the preassessment section.

Statistical relationships between the amount of life events change and physical illness and injury have been found consistently among managers (Kobasa, 1979), sports figures (Holmes & Masuda, 1974), naval personnel (Rahe, 1974), and the general population (Jenkins, 1976). For example, scores of 150 points or below result in a probability of less than 33 percent that a serious illness will occur in the next two years, but the probability increases to about 50 percent with scores of 150–300. Those who score over 300 on the SRRS have an 80 percent chance of serious illness (Holmes & Rahe, 1967).

Several studies have been conducted using college and high school football players to determine if life event change is related to injury as well as to illness (Bramwell, Masuda, Wagner, & Holmes, 1975; Coddington & Troxell, 1980). Bramwell et al. found that college players with the lowest scores on the SRRS had a rate of injury (they missed three or more practices) of 35 percent. Those with medium scores had an injury rate of 44 percent, and those with high scores were injured at the amazing rate of 72 percent. Coddington and Troxell's results showed an injury rate five times as great for high scorers on the SRRS as for low scorers among high school athletes. Holmes and Holmes (1970) studied the extent to which daily health changes occurred as a result of life event changes. Rather than focusing on major illnesses or injuries, they recorded minor symptoms such as headache, nausea, fever, backache, eyestrain, etc., over 1300 workdays. The results revealed high correlations between life event change scores and the presence of these symptoms on an everyday basis.

We must caution, of course, that simply scoring high on the SRRS does not mean a person is going to become ill or get injured. A variety of coping skills and personal characteristics may moderate those probabilities, and they will be discussed later. The point to be made here is that situational stressors are important factors to consider in learning to manage stress skillfully.

The last category of stressors includes *encounter stressors,* or those stressors that result from interpersonal interactions. Most people have experienced the debilitating effects of a quarrel with a friend, roommate, or spouse, of trying to work with an employee or supervisor with whom there has been an interpersonal conflict, or trying to accomplish a task in a group that is divided by lack of trust and cohesion. Each of these is a stressor resulting from interpersonal encounters. Encounter stressors are especially common for managers. They generally arise from three types of conflicts—*role conflicts,* in which roles performed by group members are incompatible; *issue conflicts,* in which disagreement exists over how to define or solve a problem; and *interaction conflicts,* in which individuals do not get along well because of antagonism toward one another (Hamner & Organ, 1978).

A number of authors have demonstrated that encounter stressors in organizations have significant negative effects on productivity and satisfaction (e.g., Argyris, 1964; Likert, 1967), and encounter stressors are identified by Schutz (1958) as being at the heart of most organizational dysfunction. Encounter stressors arise more frequently, of course, when managers have responsibility for people, as opposed to having responsibility for equipment. That is, the highest levels of encounter stress exist among managers who interact frequently with others and who have responsibility for others in the work place (French & Caplan, 1972). Particularly high levels of stress have been found when relations with others are poor. Zand (1972) reviewed literature on interpersonal trust, for example, and reported that lack of trust among individuals not only blocks quality communication, information-sharing, decision competence, and problem-solving capabilities, but results in high levels of personal stress.

These four major categories of stressors—anticipatory, time, situational, and encounter—can produce the same kinds of negative personal and organizational consequences. However, their occurrence does not affect all people the same way. Some people seem to be unaffected by the same levels of stress that prove devastating to others. For example, over 25 percent of World War II concentration camp victims survived their ordeals with no evidence of psychological or physiological disorders (Antonovsky, 1971). Some individuals even seem to thrive on increased stress. For example, some athletes and teams do better in "the big game," while others do worse. Some managers appear to be brilliant strategists when the stakes are high; others fold under the pressure.

What differentiates individuals who have positive responses to stressors from those who have negative responses? One answer is the presence or absence of well-developed restraining forces in those individuals. Just as vaccinations help inoculate people against certain infectious diseases, so the negative effects of stressors can be mitigated by certain individual characteristics. At the same time, the negative effects of stress can be enhanced by the presence of certain individual characteristics.

Restraining Forces

Four main categories of restraining forces have been found to have important moderating effects on stress in individuals. The first is the *absence of the coronary-prone behavior pattern*. To explain this restraining force, it is useful to discuss the main elements that make up the coronary-prone behavior pattern and their relationship to stress. Then it will be possible to identify alternatives to that pattern.

The Coronary-Prone Behavior Pattern

The coronary-prone pattern of behavior consists of three main elements: type A personality (Friedman & Rosenman, 1974), the lethal aspects of the male role (Jourard, 1964), and workaholism (Macklowicz, 1978). The presence of these three elements is strongly associated with negative stress reactions, while their absence inhibits the negative effects of stress. For example, with coronary heart disease (CHD) being the leading cause of death in the United States and with its increasing frequency among younger people, a large amount of medical research has been conducted to identify its causes. Most research until 1965 focused on blood pressure, serum lipids, cholesterol levels, cigarette smoking, obesity, and sedentary life conditions. However, more recently, increased emphasis has been given to social and psychological factors, particularly stress, and remarkable associations have been discovered. Meyer Friedman and Ray Rosenman (1974), for example, identified a particular personality type that seems conducive to CHD. It is characterized by extreme competitiveness, striving for achievement, haste, impatience, restlessness, hyperalertness, explosiveness of speech, tenseness of facial muscles, and feelings of being under time pressures and challenges of responsibility. Friedman and Rosenman identified this personality type by observing the behaviors individuals displayed during interviews. Subsequent research found that individuals who displayed this personality type (called *type A personality*) were significantly more likely to develop heart disease than those who did not. For example, in the best and most extensive research done to date, 3400 men in eleven corporations in California were categorized as type A or type B in 1960 (type B being characterized by the absence of type A characteristics). Yearly assessments of both physiological and behavioral patterns followed over the next twenty years. Results revealed that type A individuals in the 39–49-year age group had approximately 6.5 times the likelihood of CHD that type B's did, and the likelihood was 1.9 times greater in the 50–59-year age group. Even when factors such as cigarette usage, parental history of CHD, blood pressure, and cholesterol levels were controlled for, the type A personality alone still resulted in a 2 to 3 times greater likelihood of heart disease than the type B. Type A behavior, in fact, is a better predictor of CHD than physiological factors.

A self-report instrument developed by Jenkins, Rosenman, and Friedman (1967) allows type A personality to be assessed without using the difficult interview strategy developed by Friedman and Rosenman. Results with this self-report instrument have been found to be reliable and valid and to correlate highly with categorizations made through the interview method (Jenkins, Zyzanski, & Rosenman, 1971; Jenkins, Rosenman, & Zyzanski, 1974). You completed a similar instrument in the preassessment section. High scores on the "hard driving" and "speed and impatience" dimensions have been found to be associated with development of heart disease (Jenkins, Zyzanski, & Rosenman, 1971; Rowland & Sokol, 1972).

A second element in the coronary-prone behavior pattern is *lethal aspects of the male role.* That is, the strong, macho, emotionally immune image of "maleness" has been claimed by Jourard (1964), Goldberg (1976), and others to be a major cause of stress-related illness, even death. Coronary heart disease is largely a male disease, and the gap between male and female life expectancies is widening. In 1900 women lived an average of 2 years longer than men, in 1970 the difference was 7.7 years, and estimates are that by the year 2000 the gap will be more than 12 years. Jourard attributes these trends to traditional male characteristics that are incompatible with effective stress management. He claims that men are less self-disclosing, less emotionally involved with others, less aware of their own feelings, less competent in loving and being loved, less inspired by the beauty and meaning of existence, less empathetic, and more defensive than women. Goldberg (1976, p. 15) refers to the tendency of men to want to dominate in social settings and in their relationships with women as the "masculine privilege" that is costing them their health:

> Men evaluate each other and are evaluated by many women largely by the degree to which they approximate the masculine ideal. . . . They have lost touch with, or are running away from, their feelings and awareness of themselves as people. They have confused their social masks for their essence, and they are destroying themselves while fulfilling the traditional definitions of masculine-appropriate behavior.

On the other hand, as more females enter the work force, the incidence of heart disease, peptic ulcers, high blood pressure, and other stress-related pathologies is increasing among women. Suicide rates, which are twice as high among men as women in the general population, are higher among professional women than professional men. The lethal aspects of the male role, therefore, are not sex-linked traits. Rather, they are behavioral patterns that equate self-disclosure, emotional display, and sensitivity with weakness. Individuals subscribing to this traditional pattern are likely to experience more negative reactions to stress than those with opposite characteristics.

The third element in the coronary-prone behavior pattern is *workaholism,* or a tendency to allow one's life to be dominated by work-related activities. Many managers feel that to succeed they must be at the office 18 to 20 hours a day, constantly bring work home, or be working on some organizationally related matter all the time. Many prominent individuals have developed this pattern as a way of getting ahead, and many success stories can be cited that resulted from this workaholic tendency. On the other hand, there are risks involved with workaholism, as evidenced by the associations of this pattern with negative reactions to stress. For example, research has shown that individuals who work excessively long hours (i.e., more than 48 hours a week) have twice the rate of CHD as those who work fewer hours (Buell & Breslow, 1960). Zohman (1973) has found that excessive work hours and time spent on the job result in ineffective coping with the stressors commonly experienced by managers. High social, psychological, and physiological costs have been attributed to an overemphasis on work-related activities (also see Selye, 1976; Macklowicz, 1978).

On the other hand, Albrecht's (1979) work on stress reduction has demonstrated that individuals who live "balanced lives"—that is, lives in which emphasis is given to physical, spiritual, cultural, intellectual, social, and personal activities, as well as to work—can cope more effectively with stressors. In a way, this finding appears counterintuitive. If individuals are overburdened at work by time and situational stressors, a natural reaction is to give more time and emphasis to work activities in an attempt to ameliorate the stressors. If a manager is facing role overload, for example, one way to cope is to spend longer hours at the office to get the work done. While this may be an effective strategy, it may also lead to an increased likelihood of negative stress reactions and to a reduction in the efficiency of time spent in work. Individuals who have developed outside-of-work activities are better able to cope with stressors when they occur than those who overemphasize work. Rather than adding to an overload condition, development of outside activities helps restore energy levels and enhance effective coping.

In summary, the absence of these three major elements of coronary-prone behavior—type A personality, lethal aspects of the male role, and workaholism—serves as a major restraining force for stress. Individuals who develop opposite characteristics—type B personality, sensitivity, empathy, a willingness to get close to others, and well-developed interests outside of work—are more likely to resist the potential negative consequences of stressors.

Physical Conditioning

Henry Ford is reputed to have stated, "Exercise is bunk. If you are healthy, you don't need it. If you are sick, you shouldn't take it." American business has not taken Ford's advice, however, since over one thousand major corporations now have in-house fitness facilities. This emphasis on physical conditioning in business has resulted partly from the overwhelming evidence that individuals in good physical condition are better able to cope with stressors than those in poor physical condition. The attempted assassination of Ronald Reagan in 1981 illustrated this point well. Medical doctors labelled the President's physiological and emotional recovery "remarkable" and attributed it largely to his excellent physical conditioning. Kostrubala (1976, p. 169), in propagating the advantages of running for physical fitness, noted, "There has never been a proved death reported from coronary heart disease . . . in anyone who has finished a marathon within seven years after finishing." Research on stress among air traffic controllers (among the highest stress occupations) has concluded that the state of the physique, nutrition, and vigor (i.e., physical conditioning) are important moderators of the effects of stress on the individual (Jenkins, 1979). Natural immunities against pathologies such as CHD are higher in individuals who maintain good physical conditioning.

The results of research into the effects of this restraining force on the ability to cope with stressors are summarized in Table 2.1. They illustrate how individuals in good physical condition are better able than others to avoid the negative effects of stressors.

Interpersonal Competence

A third major restraining force is skill in getting along with other people. This means skill in relating to individuals not only at work, but also at home and in social gatherings. When managers identified major sources of stress in a recent study, for example, work-related stress was the most common (57 percent of the cases), but not getting along with family members was the second most common (45 percent of the cases) (Cooper & Melhuish, 1980).

The importance of interpersonal competence in families is illustrated by research conducted by Hansen (1965), who found that families composed of interpersonally competent individuals adapt much more effectively to stress-

TABLE 2.1 *Confirmed Benefits of Regular Vigorous Exercise*

Blood pressure is lowered.

Resting heart rate is lowered, meaning that the heart does not have to work as hard to get blood to the rest of the body.

Cardiac output is increased, meaning that the heart is better able to distribute blood where needed under stress.

Number of red blood cells is increased, meaning that more oxygen can be carried per quart of blood.

Elasticity of arteries is increased.

Triglyceride level is lowered.

Blood cholesterol level is decreased. High-density cholesterol, which is more protective of blood vessels than low-density cholesterol, is proportionately increased.

Adrenal secretions in response to emotional stress are lowered.

Lactic acid is more efficiently eliminated from the muscles (this has been associated with decreased fatigue and tension).

Fibrin, a protein that aids in the formation of blood clots, is decreased.

Additional routes of blood supply are built up in the heart.

SOURCE: H. Goldberg, *Executive health* (New York: McGraw-Hill, 1978), p. 133.

ors such as loss of a family member, disability, deprivation, or loss of job than families with less competent members. Interpersonal competence in this case was defined as having family members display behavior such as clarifying role and positional expectations, meeting other family members' needs, performing voluntary actions on behalf of others, and providing mutual support.

The presence of social support—having well-developed relationships with others that can be relied on to provide emotional support and empathy—has been found to be a significant moderator of stress. Close interpersonal relationships with family members, social support groups, or colleagues at work is an important restraining force in coping with stressors.

It is not only close relationships that are needed, however, but the ability to form new relationships and to maintain cordial and mutually supportive relationships with people one is not close to. For example, several researchers have determined that lack of interpersonal competence in individuals contributes to hypertension (Harris, Sokolow, Carpenter, Freedman, & Hunt, 1953; Kalis, Harris, Sokolow, & Carpenter, 1957). Individuals with low interpersonal skill levels react with significantly higher blood pressures and heart rates when exposed to stressful role-play situations than interpersonally skilled individuals. Moreover, less skilled individuals later develop hypertension to a significantly greater degree than their more skilled counterparts. (Interpersonal skill in these studies was rated by trained observers on the basis of certain behaviors displayed.) Other studies have found that individuals who display less self-control, who create negative social impressions, who display lower levels of interpersonal trust, and who have more extreme anger, pain, and fear reactions also have significantly higher levels of hypertension and risk of CHD than individuals without those characteristics (Weiner, Singer, & Reiser, 1962; Schacter, 1959; Sapira, Scheib, Moriarty, & Shapiro, 1971; Williams, Kemball, & Williard, 1972). In fact, after reviewing the literature on social coping behavior and hypertension, Linden and Feuerstein (1981, p. 31) concluded that "the behavioral response style that appears to characterize hypertensives corresponds closely with patterns observed in individuals with low social competence. . . . The hypothesis emerges that social competence may act as a mediating factor in essential hypertension." In short, there is evidence that level of interpersonal skill affects how well individuals cope with stress.

Self-Awareness

The fourth major restraining force in the model of stress in Figure 2.2 is self-awareness. It has been found that individuals not in touch with themselves are more likely to have difficulty coping with stressors because they are not aware of their own reactions to stress, nor are they aware of what strategies are available to them for coping with stress. Physical illness can occur, for example, without the self-alienated person's being aware that something is wrong. Jourard (1964) argues that self-alienation, or an absence of self-awareness, is the primary root of both psychological and physiological illness.

Research has shown that self-awareness relative to three areas—values development, cognitive style, and need for power—is a particularly important moderator of negative reactions to stress. (These were discussed in detail in Chapter 1.) With regard to values development, individuals who are more religious and who operate on a higher level of moral maturity (i.e., the principled level) have been found to have significantly lower rates of CHD than others (Comstock & Partridge, 1972). Jenkins (1979) also reported significantly lower rates of impulse control problems among a group of air traffic controllers with characteristics indicative of higher values maturity. Managers who scored in the high-stress group on the Holmes and Rahe (1970) SRRS instrument but had a clear, stable sense of values and goals and an unshakable sense of meaningfulness in their life plan had significantly less stress-related illness than managers who scored low on values development and meaningfulness (Kobasa, 1979). Clarity of values and principles, therefore, appears to act as an important restraining force.

It has also been found that awareness of one's own cognitive style serves as an important moderator of stress. For example, McKenney and Keen (1974) showed that managers with different cognitive styles experienced stress from different kinds of stressors. "Receptive managers" (who focus on detail) are most affected by time stressors such as role or information overload. "Preceptive managers" (who focus on the whole) are most affected by situational stressors such as role conflict or role ambiguity, in which aberrations from expected sequences occur. "Systematic managers" (who rely on logical methods) are most stressed by problems requiring creativity and trial-and-error testing, and "intuitive managers" (who rely on intuition) are most stressed by problems requiring programmed, parsimonious solutions. Awareness of cognitive style, therefore, helps managers anticipate the sources of greatest stress and enhances their ability to cope with it effectively (see Chapter 1).

A second aspect of cognitive style is locus of control. Individuals with an internal locus of control feel they have power over critical events and activities in their lives. In contrast, individuals with an external locus of control feel they are at the mercy of environmental factors. Managers with an internal locus of control have been found to be much less likely to show negative reactions to stressors (i.e., less physical illness and emotional strain) than externally controlled managers (Kobasa, 1979). This is because they feel a stressor can be handled by some personal action. Internally controlled individuals are also less likely to perceive stressors as threatening than are externally controlled individuals and therefore manifest fewer adverse reactions (Chan, 1977). In short, individuals with an external locus of control appear more susceptible to pathological reactions to stress than internally controlled individuals, and awareness of one's own tendencies toward locus of control can serve as an important precondition for coping.

The third area of self-awareness, need for power, has also been found to be a moderator of reactions to stress. Individuals who score high in need for power have been found to be more argumentative, more competitive, and more prone toward conspicuous consumption and prestige symbols, and to engage in more self-enhancing behaviors than those low in need for power (McClelland, 1975). However, managers differ in the ways they display need for power in that some are more socially inhibited than others. Inhibition essentially moderates the display of the need for power so that it is channeled into socially accepted behaviors. For example, one may work hard for a promotion, instead of sabotaging the work of a rival to appear more promotable. A number of studies have reported that individuals with a high need for power that is inhibited are more likely to become ill, more often and more severely, than individuals with a low need for power and low inhibition (McClelland, Locke, & Williams, 1979; McClelland, Floor, Davidson, & Saron, 1980). These individuals also report more temporary headaches, backaches, nausea, depression, and anxiety than those with lower need levels, and are more likely to develop long-term stress-related pathologies such as high blood pressure and CHD over time. Men characterized by the inhibited power motive in their early thirties developed significantly more hypertension twenty years later than others. In fact, as need-for-power scores increase over time, signs of stress-related pathologies show a correlated increase (McClelland, 1979).

On the other hand, neither a need for power nor activity inhibition is inherently unhealthy. In fact, men who have a high need for power but *low* inhibition scores drink more alcohol, lie more, seek more sexual conquests, and are more impulsive and aggressive than those with high power and *high* inhibition (McClelland, 1975; McClelland, Davis, Kalin, & Wanner, 1972). Furthermore, McClelland and Burnham (1976) point out that persons with high needs for power and high inhibition make the most successful managers, since they seek to influence others in a controlled way. Despite the association between high inhibited power needs and susceptibility to stress-related pathologies, therefore, many writers argue that such an orientation is critical to managerial success.

Thus far, we have pointed out that managers face four major kinds of stressors—anticipatory, time, situational, and encounter. These stressors can produce a variety of negative reactions in individuals, ranging from headache and tension to coronary heart disease and death. However, the negative consequences of these stressors are not inevitable because of restraining forces present in most people. The stronger those restraining forces are, the less likely are negative reactions to stress. Developing behavior patterns that are opposite from the coronary-prone behavior pattern, such as achieving good physical conditioning, developing close interpersonal relationships and increased interpersonal competence, and increasing self-awareness relative to a consistent set of values, cognitive style, and need for power, is an important restraining force in coping with stress. In the next section, we shall point out practical ways to develop some of these restraining forces and present a simple formula for dealing with stress.

WAYS TO MANAGE STRESS

Combining what we know about stress with force field analysis makes clear that there are at least three types of strategies for managing stress. Force field analysis suggests that, to change current levels of functioning, one can eliminate the negative forces keeping behaviors from getting better, add positive forces that induce better behavior, or implement a new behavioral alternative, regardless of the forces in the field. Research has shown that the most effective strategy is eliminating negatives, followed by introducing positives, with trying new alternatives being the least effective (Benne & Birnbaum, 1969).

In coping with stressors, therefore, one should follow a particular ordering of strategies. First, one should use strategies that directly attack the stressors (the negative forces)—that is, change them or remove them. The most longlasting way to cope with a stressor is to eliminate it altogether. However, many stressors cannot be eliminated directly, and individuals don't have total control of their environments. Therefore, if these strategies are unavailable or don't work, the next best strategies are those that strengthen restraining forces. These forces induce positive change. The advantages of these strategies is that they "inoculate" the individual, or make the person better able to cope with stress over the long term by enhancing positive behavioral and psychological patterns. They also help the person cope with a variety of types of stressors. The disadvantage is that they take time to develop and implement. If this second category of strategies is not available (for example, because of lack of know-how or resources) or if there is particular urgency, the third type of strategies should be used. These relate only to the immediate behavioral or psychological reaction to stressors, or to the short-term change that has occurred because of the stressor. They make an individual feel better, but they must be repeated each time stressors are encountered. The force field remains intact. They remove discomfort temporarily, but their recurrent use may contribute to more stress in the long run (e.g., addictions). Their main advantage is that they can be used to "buy time" so other strategies can be developed or implemented that relate to driving or restraining forces.

Figure 2.3 summarizes these three types of strategies. As the figure illustrates, these strategies differ in terms of their permanence and implementation time. Eliminating stressors has the most permanent effect, while dealing only with the reactions to stressors is the least permanent. However, eliminating stressors and developing restraining forces generally take a long time to accomplish, whereas implementing strategies to cope with reactions to stressors can be done almost immediately. We shall discuss examples of each type of strategy and present some rules of thumb for implementing them.

Figure 2.3 *Three Types of Strategies for Coping with Stress*

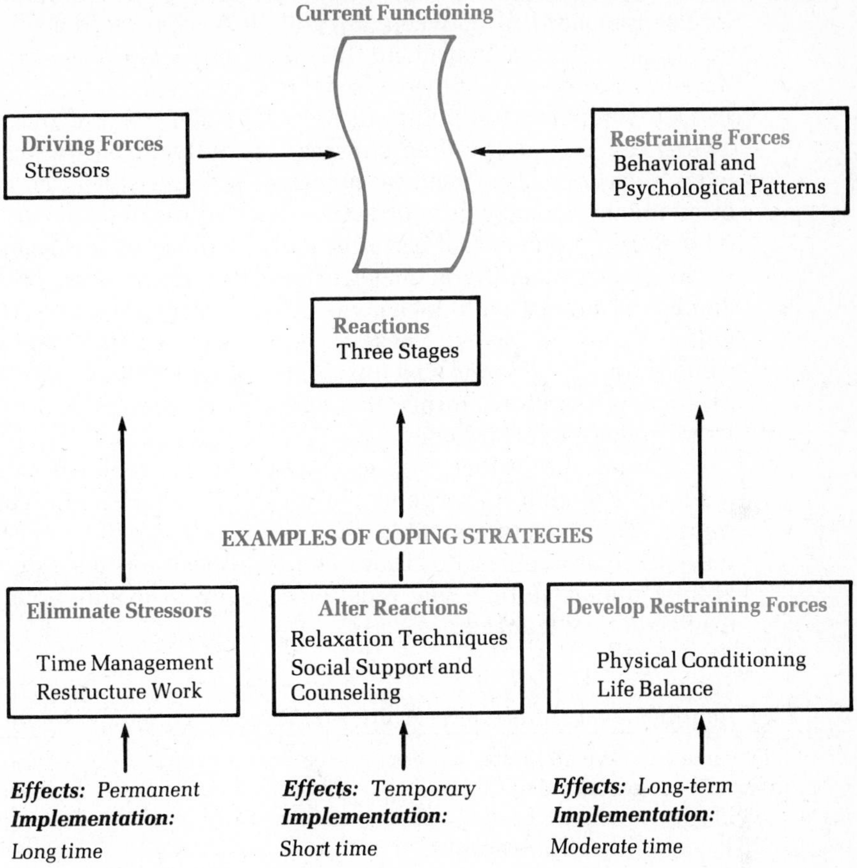

Current Functioning

Driving Forces		Restraining Forces
Stressors		Behavioral and Psychological Patterns

Reactions
Three Stages

EXAMPLES OF COPING STRATEGIES

Eliminate Stressors	Alter Reactions	Develop Restraining Forces
Time Management Restructure Work	Relaxation Techniques Social Support and Counseling	Physical Conditioning Life Balance

Effects: Permanent
Implementation:
Long time

Effects: Temporary
Implementation:
Short time

Effects: Long-term
Implementation:
Moderate time

Eliminating Stressors

The external environment frequently is immutable. That is, no matter what one does, some stressors cannot be eliminated or neutralized. On the other hand, individuals often are more able to eliminate stressors than they realize merely by implementing some simple procedures for time and work management. In this section principles of time management are discussed first, followed by principles of work management.

As pointed out earlier, time stressors often are the greatest source of stress for managers. Mintzberg's (1973) research shows, for example, that managers are frequently interrupted (over 50 percent of their activities last nine minutes or less), they engage in hardly any long-range activities, and fragmentation, brevity, and variety characterize their time use. Another study, by Carlson (1951), found that no manager worked more than twenty minutes at a time without interruption, and most of the manager's time was controlled by the most bothersome and energetic people. Guest (1956) found that industrial foremen engaged in between 237 and 1073 separate incidents a day with no real breaks. Time management, therefore, appears to be an important strategy for eliminating many of the stressors managers encounter.

It is important to point out how dependent time management is on self-awareness. Frequently time stressors are brought on by personal characteristics, such as a strong need for power, a cognitive style that focuses on details, or a tendency to take on too much work. Unless one is aware of these needs, tendencies, or behavioral patterns, it does little good to suggest rules of thumb for managing time. If a manager displays a type A behavioral pattern, for example, the suggestion to take a vacation or to step back and reassess priorities will probably be useless. These suggestions are antithetical to the type A personality, and vacations just turn into work sessions. The chapter on self-awareness, therefore, forms an important base on which to build time and stress management strategies.

Implementing time management strategies requires being aware of the tendencies of almost everyone to use time in certain ways. The list of propositions in Table 2.2, for example, shows the general patterns of behavior of most individuals in their use of time. These propositions act as constraints on the ability to manage time that must be recognized if individuals are to become proficient time managers.

TABLE 2.2 *Potential Constraints on the Ability to Manage Time Effectively*

We do what we like to do before we do what we don't like to do.	We do things that are scheduled (for example, meetings) before nonscheduled things.	We do interesting things before uninteresting things.	We respond on the basis of the consequences to us of doing or not doing something.
We do the things we know how to do faster than the things we do not know how to do.	We sometimes do things that are planned before things that are unplanned.	We do things that advance our personal objectives or that are politically expedient.	We tackle small jobs before large jobs.
We do the things that are easiest before things that are difficult.	We respond to demands from others before demands from ourselves.	We wait until a deadline approaches before we really get moving.	We work on things in the order of their arrival.
We do things that require a little time before things that require a lot of time.	We do things that are urgent before things that are important.	We do things that provide the most immediate closure.	We work on the basis of the squeaky-wheel principle (the squeaky wheel gets the grease).
We do things for which the resources are available	We readily respond to crises and emergencies.	We respond on the basis of who wants it.	We work on the basis of consequences to the group.

Time is such a universal stressor, and time management is such an effective means for coping with stress, that we include in the next section a detailed discussion of ways to improve use of time to reduce stress. In Table 2.3, for example, are thirty-four rules of thumb that have been derived from research on the management of time. These are divided into two categories—seventeen with applicability to almost anyone in his or her daily activities,

TABLE 2.3 *Some Rules of Thumb for Managing Time*

General Strategies

1. Make a list of tasks to perform today.
2. Prioritize your tasks on the basis of importance and urgency.
3. Make a list of five- or ten-minute discretionary tasks.
4. Determine which 20 percent of your tasks will produce 80 percent of the results.
5. Evaluate the result, not the means or the effort.
6. Periodically keep a time log.
7. As much as possible, respond to demands on your time when you select.
8. Do redundant or busy work at one set time during the day.
9. Delegate routine tasks.
10. Schedule some time each day for personal, alone time.
11. Set deadlines for yourself.
12. Don't habitually procrastinate. Do it today.
13. Save your best time during the day for important matters.
14. Divide large projects into separate stages.
15. Concentrate on one important thing at a time, but do multiple trivial things at once.
16. Have a place for everything.
17. Read selectively, and underline or mark what is important.

Strategies Especially for Managers

1. Hold routine meetings at the end of the day.
2. Hold all short meetings standing up.
3. Set a time limit at the outset of each meeting.
4. Cancel meetings once in a while.
5. Have a written agenda for every meeting.
6. Stick to the agenda.
7. Assign someone to take minutes and watch the time in every meeting.
8. Start all meetings on time.
9. Prepare minutes of meetings promptly, and follow up promptly.
10. Insist that subordinates suggest solutions for every problem they raise.
11. Meet visitors to your office outside or in the doorway.
12. Go to the subordinate's office when possible.
13. Come early rather than staying late.
14. If you have a secretary, have him or her answer all calls.
15. Have one place where, if necessary, you can work uninterrupted.
16. Do something permanent with every piece of paper you handle.
17. Make a worry list.

and seventeen with particular relevance to managers in the work place. While stress can result from having too much unused time available (i.e., boredom), this is unusual for managers and these rules assume that the stressor is the opposite—having too much to do in too little time.

Rules of Thumb for Managing Time

Rule 1, *make a list of things to perform today,* is a common-sense rule that implies that some advance planning must occur for each day and that you should not rely solely on memory. (Also implied is that you should have only one list, not multiple scraps of paper.) Rule 2, *prioritize your tasks,* means that you should work *first* on the task that is *both* the most important and the most urgent. One must take care, of course, not to wait until a crisis arises before paying attention to a matter. An individual can produce more stress by always being in an urgent frame of mind. On the other hand, many individuals drive out important tasks by doing less important and easier tasks first. During World War II, with an overwhelming number of tasks to perform, General Dwight D. Eisenhower successfully managed his time by following rule 2 strictly. He reasoned that if it was not urgent, it could wait; if it was not important, it could be done by someone else (Mackenzie, 1970).

Rule 3, *list some five- or ten-minute discretionary tasks,* helps use the small bits of time almost everyone has during his or her day (such as when waiting for something to begin, between meetings or events, or even while talking on the telephone). A danger that must be guarded against, of course, is spending all the time doing these small discretionary tasks and not getting to the number 1 priority.

Rule 4, *determine the critical 20 percent of your tasks,* refers to Pareto's law, which states, essentially, that only 20 percent of tasks produce 80 percent of results. Therefore, it is important to analyze which are the most important 20 percent and spend the bulk of your time on those. Rule 5, *evaluate the result,* is related to rule 4. It suggests that the results of the day's work should be evaluated (not the effort expended, the processes used, etc.) and time spent on results-oriented activities.

Rule 6, *periodically keep a time log,* is essential to most time management strategies. It is impossible to improve the management of time, or to decrease time stressors, unless it is known how time is spent. Time logs should be kept in short enough intervals that they capture the activities, but not so short as to create a recording burden. One way to analyze a time log after it has been recorded is to use the rating scales in Table 2.4. (For an elaboration of these ideas, see Trickett, 1962.) Eliminate those activities that consistently receive C's and D's.

Rule 7 states, as much as possible, *respond to demands when you select.* As Carlson (1951) points out, managers are often like puppets, but their strings are pulled by a crowd of unknown and unorganized people. The more self-control that can be maintained over how time is spent, the better time management will be.

TABLE 2.4 *A Model for Analyzing Time Logs*

Each activity is analyzed and rated on these dimensions:

1. *Importance*
   a. Very important—must be done.
   b. Important—should be done.
   c. Not so important—may be useful, but is not necessary.
   d. Unimportant—doesn't accomplish anything.

2. *Urgency*
   a. Very urgent—must be done now.
   b. Urgent—should be done soon.
   c. Not urgent—can be done sometime later.
   d. Time is not a factor.

3. *Delegation*
   a. I am the only one who can do it.
   b. It can be delegated to someone close to me (e.g., child, immediate subordinate).
   c. It can be delegated to someone far from me (e.g., outside of family, staff).

4. *Interactions*
   a. I must see these people every day.
   b. I need to see these people frequently (not daily).
   c. I should see these people sometime.
   d. I don't need to see these people.

Rule 8, *do busywork at one time,* prevents trivia from driving out more important tasks. By refusing to answer mail or read the newspaper until a specified time, for example, you can ensure that priority items are not superseded. Rule 9, *delegate routine tasks,* is discussed in detail in Chapter 7. Effective delegation skill is probably the most needed tool in the time manager's repertoire.

Rule 10, *schedule in personal time,* refers to time when no interruptions occur, when individuals get off the "fast track" for a while so they can be alone with themselves. This time can be used to plan, prioritize, take stock, pray, meditate, or just relax. Personal time helps people maintain self-awareness. Rule 11, *set deadlines,* helps improve efficiency of time use. Work always expands to fill the time available, so if a termination time is not specified, tasks tend to continue longer than they need to. An important rule of thumb is to reach closure on at least one thing every day. Having nothing completely finished (even a ten-minute task) at the end of a day serves to increase the sense of overload and time stress.

Rule 12, *don't keep procrastinating,* suggests that many tasks can be done right now, and they take less time and effort than if they are put off. Of course, you must guard against spending all your time on trivial, immediate concerns that drive out more important tasks. The line between procrastination and time wasting is a fine one, but keeping in mind rules 2, 7 and 8 in Table 2.3 helps prevent procrastination and being overburdened by trivia. Rule 13, *save your best time for important matters,* suggests that time spent on trivial tasks should not be your "best" time. Do routine work when your energy level is low, your mind is not sharp, or you aren't on top of things. Reserve your best times for accomplishing the most important and urgent tasks. In addition, don't let other people interrupt your best time. You should control your best time, not others.

Rule 14, *divide up large projects,* helps you avoid feeling overwhelmed by large, important, urgent tasks. Feeling that a task is too big to accomplish contributes to a feeling of overload and to procrastination. Rule 15, *do one important thing but multiple trivial things at a time,* means that much can be accomplished if more than one thing at a time is done when tasks are routine or trivial or require little thought. This rule allows managers to get rid of multiple trivial tasks in less time (e.g., signing letters while talking on the phone).

Rule 16 is to *have a place for everything.* Having things out of place robs time in two ways: more time is required to find something when you need it, and you are tempted to interrupt the task you are doing to do something else. For example, if material for several projects is scattered on top of your desk, you will be continually tempted to switch from one project to another as your gaze changes or papers are moved. Rule 17, *read selectively,* is applicable mostly to individuals who find themselves with too much to read—mail, magazines, newspapers, books, brochures, instructions, and so on. Except when you read for relaxation or pleasure, most reading should be done the way you read a newspaper. Skim most of it, but stop to read what seems most important. Even the most important items frequently need not be read thoroughly, since important points are generally at the beginnings of paragraphs or sections. Furthermore, if you underline or note what you find important, it can be reviewed very quickly when you need to refer to it again.

Rules of Thumb for Managers

The second list of rules is of more relevance to practicing managers than to students. These relate primarily to the activities managers engage in at work. For example, the first nine rules deal with conducting meetings. Since managers report that approximately 70 percent of their time is spent in meetings (Mintzberg, 1973; Cooper & Davidson, 1982), these rules of thumb can be particularly useful in eliminating wasted meeting time.

The purpose of rule 1, *hold routine meetings at the end of the day,* is to hold meetings for which high energy and creativity are not required at a time when these attributes are not likely to be present. Furthermore, an automatic deadline (i.e., quitting time) will help the meeting finish on time. Rule 2, *hold short meetings standing up,* simply guarantees that meetings *will* be short. Getting comfortable helps prolong meetings. Rule 3, *set a time limit,* establishes an expectation of when the meeting should end and creates pressure to conform to a time boundary. Rule 4, *cancel meetings once in a while,* is designed to send the message that meetings will be held only if they are needed. This helps make the meetings that are held more productive and more time efficient.

Rules 5, 6 and 7, *have agendas, stick to them,* and *keep minutes and time,* can help individuals stay on the subject, prepare in advance of the meeting, and remain work oriented. Many items will be handled outside of meetings if they have to appear on a formal agenda. Even impromptu meetings can have a verbal agenda set at the beginning. Keeping a record of the meeting ensures that assignments made are not forgotten. Rule 8, *start meetings on time,* helps guarantee that people will arrive on time. (Some managers set meetings for odd times, such as 10:13 A.M., to make attendees time conscious.) Rule 9, *prepare minutes promptly and follow up,* keeps items from appearing again in a meeting without having been resolved. It also creates the expectation that most work should be done outside the meeting.

Rule 10, *insist that subordinates suggest solutions to problems,* is discussed more in the chapter on delegation. Its purpose is to eliminate a tendency for upward delegation (that is, for subordinates to delegate difficult problems back to managers by asking for their ideas and solutions). It is more efficient for managers to choose among alternatives than to generate their own alternatives.

Rule 11, *meet visitors in the doorway,* helps managers maintain control of their time by controlling the use of their office space. It is more difficult to keep a meeting short if you are sitting in your office, rather than standing in the doorway. Rule 12, *go to subordinates' offices,* is useful if it is practical. The advantage is that it helps managers control when they leave and how long the meeting lasts. Of course, if managers spend a great deal of time traveling between subordinates' offices, the rule is not useful.

Rule 13, *come early rather than staying late,* suggests that if managers are going to put in extra time at work, they are less likely to be interrupted before rather than after hours. Rule 14, *have your secretary answer calls,* simply helps provide managers with a buffer from interruptions. Rule 15, *have a place to work uninterrupted,* helps guarantee that when a deadline is near, the manager can work without interruption. (This will probably not be the office.) Rule 16, *do something permanent with the paperwork handled,* helps keep managers from shuffling paper or recycling the same items over and over. Finally, rule 17, *make a "worry list,"* recommends listing things that are of concern to you. Worry about those things only at a specified time, not all the time. Don't let worry keep you from attending to other problems.

Remember that these rules of thumb for managing time are a *means* to an end, not the end itself. If trying to implement all the rules creates more rather than less stress, they should not be applied. However, research has indicated that managers who use these kinds of strategies are in more control of their time, accomplish more in less time, have better relations with subordinates, and eliminate many of the time stressors most managers ordinarily encounter. Therefore, many of these ideas are useful for individuals aspiring to be better managers.

Restructure Work

A second set of strategies that helps eliminate stressors relates to restructuring the work itself. A great deal of research has indicated that the nature of the tasks performed by managers serves as a major source of stress (Turner & Lawrence, 1965; Hackman & Lawler, 1971; Hackman & Oldham, 1975; French & Caplan, 1972). However, it also has been found that changing the *structure* of those tasks, rather than the tasks themselves, can help eliminate many negative stress reactions. For example, in a study of administrators, engineers, and scientists at the Goddard Space Flight Center, French and Caplan (1972) found that individuals provided with more discretion regarding how and when to perform tasks and more participation in making decisions about assigning tasks experienced fewer time stressors (e.g., role overload), stituational stressors (e.g., role ambiguity), encounter stressors (e.g., interpersonal conflict), and anticipatory stressors (e.g., job-related threat). Individuals without discretion and participation experienced significantly more of these stressors.

Hackman (1977) and his colleagues have found that negative reactions to work stress can be overcome by designing the structure of tasks. They have found that certain psychological states are closely connected to the nature of the work being performed. These states determine whether an individual likes a job, is comfortable with it, and is motivated, as well as to what extent negative reactions to job-related stress occur. The three psychological states are (1) the experienced *meaningfulness* of the work—that is, the extent to which the work seems important and worthwhile; (2) the experienced *responsibility* for the outcomes of the work—that is, the extent to which individuals feel personally accountable for the results of their work; and (3) *knowledge of the results* of the work activity—that is, knowing to what extent the results of the work are satisfactory. When the work being performed provides a sense of meaningfulness, responsibility, and knowledge of results, fewer negative reactions to stress are experienced than would otherwise be true.

Figure 2.4 shows the relationship between certain characteristics of work and the three critical psychological states. The more *variety* in the skills a person can use in performing the work, the more experienced meaningfulness results. Similarly, the more an individual can perform a complete job from beginning to end (i.e., *task identity*) and the more the work has a direct effect on the lives of other people (i.e., *task significance*), the more experienced meaningfulness results. On the other hand, when the work requires few skills, only part of a task is performed, and there seems to be little or no effect on other people from doing a good job, experienced meaningfulness is low.

The more *autonomy* in the work, or the more individuals are free to choose what job to do, when, and how, the more responsible they feel for their successes and failures. Finally, the more *feedback* individuals get from the work itself (not from a co-worker or manager), the more knowledge of results there is. That is, if it is possible to tell how well one is doing as the work is being performed, knowledge of results increases and negative reactions to stress decrease.

Figure 2.4 *Core Job Dimensions and Critical Psychological States*

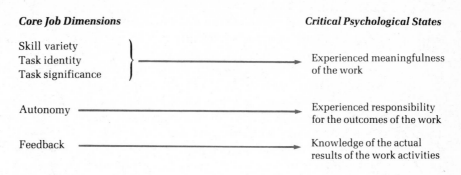

Adapted from Hackman et al., 1975.

One example of positive results from restructuring of work occurred at the Travelers Insurance Companies. When management increased these five characteristics of the work being performed (i.e., variety, identity, significance, autonomy, and feedback), productivity increased dramatically, absenteeism and errors fell sharply, and the amount of distractions and stresses experienced by managers decreased significantly (Hackman, Oldham, Janson, & Purdy, 1975).

One way to eliminate stressors, therefore, is to increase these attributes of the work being performed. This restructuring can be oriented toward both subordinates' and managers' work. Less stressed employees create less stressed managers in the organization. This restructuring is not easy, of course, but it can be accomplished by (1) grouping tasks or individuals together or rotating assignments to increase variety, significance, and identity of tasks; (2) increasing direct contacts with clients or opening up feedback channels to improve knowledge of results; and (3) instituting flexible work schedules, decentralizing decision making, or removing selected formalized controls to increase autonomy. The goal of redesigning work is to decrease stressors, so as with time management, it should be used as a means to the end, not the end itself.

Developing Restraining Forces

Eliminating stressors is not always possible, and some stressors may occur regardless of efforts to avoid them. Consequently, it is important for individuals to develop behavioral and psychological patterns that help restrain the negative effects of those stressors. Among the many possible restraining forces available, two are discussed here because of their almost universal applicability for people faced with stress.

Physical Conditioning

We already have explained the need for physical conditioning in moderating the effects of stressors. In this section we simply suggest a few practical ways to improve physical conditioning through an exercise program, good diet, adequate rest, and avoidance of some substances. This discussion is particularly important if you have frequently experienced such physiological symptoms as tension headaches, depression, excessive daydreaming, or high blood pressure. Each of these is a danger sign that more severe negative reactions to stress may be imminent (Goldberg, 1976).

Regular exercise inoculates the body against stress by subjecting it to small amounts of stress so it can cope better with the stresses faced during the workday. Cardiovascular fitness is particularly important as part of physical conditioning. Unfortunately, it does not result from short-term or sporatic exercise programs. In fact, more harm than good may be done unless there is regular, sustained exercise. The important thing is that you should raise your heart beat up to 140 beats a minute for twenty minutes or longer at least three times each week. Another yardstick is to burn up at least 2000 calories a week. This could be achieved by one hour of tennis (420–430 calories), one hour of squash (660), one hour of cycling at twelve miles an hour (430–600), and one hour of running at 6 miles an hour (660) each week. There are a variety of ways to exercise, including jogging, bicycling, rope skipping, swimming, dancing, weight training, rock climbing, and participating in competitive athletics. The important thing is that the exercising should be done regularly, and it should have both cardiovascular and muscle tone advantages. One helpful hint for beginning and maintaining an exercise program is to get someone else to do it with you. Social support and public commitment are good motivators for engaging in such a program, particularly when other stressors threaten to take up the time required.

The benefits of regular exercise are greatly diminished if it is not coupled with good nutrition, proper rest, and avoidance of harmful substances. Eating several small meals instead of two or three big ones, making certain that all food groups are represented in the daily diet, avoiding or drastically reducing addicting substances such as alcohol, nicotine, and caffeine, carefully controlling intake of sugar and salt, and getting seven hours of sleep a night are some components of a good physical conditioning program. Each helps serve as an inoculation against stress-related illnesses and psychological exhaustion (Selye, 1976; Albrecht, 1979).

Life Balance

A second strategy for developing restraining forces is to develop a balanced pattern of living. Earlier we mentioned that individuals who emphasize one activity to the exclusion of others (i.e., workaholics) have much higher rates of heart disease and other health problems than those who lead more balanced lives. An important inoculation strategy for stress, therefore, is to develop a variety of interests and activities. Figure 2.5 shows seven areas that are especially important in stress reduction (Albrecht, 1979). Assume the edge of the circle is the ideal level of development in each area. Starting in the center, shade in the portion of each section that represents the degree to which you emphasize that area of your life. Small shaded areas and lopsided figures do not indicate as healthy a pattern as large, round shaded figures. Write down two or three specific activities you could perform that would improve your development in those areas that need work. For example, you may go to a classical music concert or visit a museum for the cultural area. Sending a card to a friend or inviting someone over might be appropriate for the social area. Engaging in regular prayer or reading inspiring literature could be helpful in the spiritual area. Whatever activities you list for yourself, make them practical and doable. Remember that the purpose is not to add to your stressors by multiplying activities, but to develop and grow in areas that may have been neglected. As you become more balanced, the efficiency of time you spend at work will increase and pathological reactions to stress will become less likely.

Figure 2.5   *Balancing Life Activities*

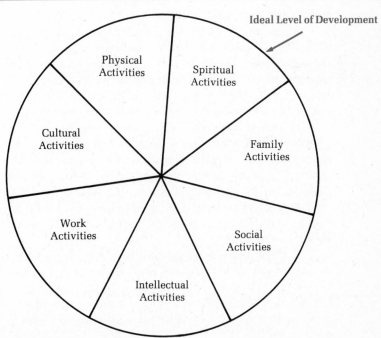

Altering Reactions

Eliminating stressors and developing restraining forces have long-term effects on reducing stress, but they also require substantial amounts of time to implement. It takes a while, for example, to get in good physical condition. Most people need to reduce the stress they are feeling immediately, however, because experiencing stress decreases mental proficiency, reasoning power, and creativity (Ivancevich & Matteson, 1980). To effectively cope with stress on a long-term basis, therefore, you must reduce stress in the short term.

A general reaction of many people to stress is to engage in behaviors that reduce immediately the uncomfortable feelings (i.e., altering reactions), but then to never pursue strategies that are more long-term or permanent. For example, many people react to stress by smoking, drinking alcohol, taking a pill, eating, daydreaming, getting irritated, and so on, and never implement long-term strategies. The problem with most of these behaviors is that they provide only temporary means for dealing with stress and must be introduced over and over again, each time stressors are encountered. Furthermore, they may produce detrimental effects, especially if engaged in to excess.

We shall discuss two general strategies for obtaining temporary and immediate relief from stress. Unlike some other reactions to stress, repetition of these strategies does not produce negative consequences. Furthermore, they may be implemented immediately with little preparation.

Relaxation Techniques

There are at least five kinds of temporary relaxation techniques. One, called *progressive relaxation,* consists of relaxing different muscle groups throughout the body in turn. The technique involves tightening up a single muscle group for ten seconds and then completely relaxing it. By starting with the feet and progressing through the calves, thighs, stomach, and on to the neck and face, you can relieve much of the tension you are experiencing.

A second technique is the use of *diversions.* To use this technique, pick a pleasant past experience, a favorite song, a picture of your family, a poem, a conversation, or any other diversion and concentrate on it for a short time, instead of on your anxious thoughts. That is, sing the song to yourself, recite the poem, recreate the conversation, describe the pleasant experience, or whatever, to give your mind a break. If you concentrate on the diversionary experience, even for a few seconds, you can release some of the nervousness that accompanies stress.

A third technique is *rehearsal.* This involves talking through a situation with yourself, sometimes out loud. Carry on a dialogue with yourself. Play out various alternatives. Practice using a positive response to those alternatives. Make yourself comfortable with the situation you are facing by responding to it privately over and over. Rehearse just as you would when reciting a speech in front of a mirror. You may even want to jot down a few notes by way of a reminder. The point is to rehearse the situation and your response often enough that it becomes nonstressful.

A fourth technique, *deep breathing,* consists of taking several successive slow, deep breaths and exhaling completely. This technique can be used when you are asked a question you can't answer, when you become embarrassed and don't know what to say, or almost anytime you must respond immediately but find it stressful. Some managers take a long, slow puff on a pipe. Others simply look off into space for a few moments before attempting a response. Whatever the process, taking a few seconds to be silent, to regain control, and to relax helps clear the mind and reduce stress.

A fifth technique is *meditation.* There is a growing amount of evidence that engaging in various forms of meditation can decrease heart and respiratory rates, oxygen consumption, blood sugar levels, blood pressure, and cholesterol levels (Cooper & Aygen, 1979; Stone & Deleo, 1976; Orme-Johnson, 1973; Beary & Benson, 1977; Benson, 1975). All meditation techniques emphasize the following:

1. *A quiet environment.*
2. *A mental focus.* Transcendental meditation (TM) advocates recommend concentrating on one word or phrase. Benson (1975) suggests the word "one" or any other neutral, one-syllable word or object (e.g., a vase). The idea is to rid the mind of all thoughts by focusing on the word or object.
3. *Controlled breathing.* Breathe deliberately, with pauses between breaths.
4. *A passive attitude.* If other thoughts enter the mind, ignore them.
5. *A comfortable position.* Minimize muscular effort.
6. *Repetition.* Try to meditate at least twenty to thirty minutes a day.

Each of these techniques is simple, but all can be used immediately to reduce the level of experienced stress. Their purpose is to give the individual time to cope with the stressor on a more long-term basis by reducing the immediate negative reaction. Some strategies having more permanent effects cannot be implemented as long as high levels of stress are being experienced.

Social Support and Counseling

A second general strategy for coping with stress on an immediate basis is to involve other people. In general, simply having someone to talk to, someone with whom you can let off steam or who will act as a sounding board, is a productive way to temporarily cope with stress. Talking about the stress not only tends to decrease it, but also may help you discover more long-term coping strategies.

In general, this kind of interaction should occur with someone who will listen and empathize, rather than give advice. Advice is usually not as useful in this situation as is a chance to get something off your chest. Furthermore, the interaction should be with someone who can affirm you as a person, rather than evaluate you negatively because of what you say. This suggests that you should not use just anyone to unload your stress on. With some people you may find that your level of stress increases rather than decreases. Therefore, you should interact with someone with whom you have established a relationship. A family member is more likely to understand your stress and accept you as a person than is an individual who hasn't shared experiences with you. Therapists or counselors are another good source of stress-reducing interaction, but the expense of such relationships may be prohibitive. On the other hand, the purpose of the social support strategy is to relieve feelings of stress so more effective, long-term strategies can be implemented. And sometimes counselors or therapists are the best sources of insights into ways to inhibit stressors altogether or to develop strong restraining forces.

SUMMARY AND BEHAVIORAL GUIDELINES

We have discussed a comprehensive model of stress in this chapter. Stress has been described as a product of a force field. Stressors serve as driving forces, while individual behavioral and psychological patterns serve as restraining forces. Positive or negative reactions to stress occur only as an imbalance is created in those driving and restraining forces.

There are four general categories of stressors—anticipatory, time, situational, and encounter. The effects of these stressors on individuals are moderated by certain individual characteristics. Four behavioral and psychological patterns are especially important moderators—the absence of the coronary-prone behavior pattern, physical conditioning, interpersonal competence, and self-awareness. Reactions to stress occur in three stages—the alarm stage, the resistance stage, and the exhaustion stage. Pathological reactions to stress occur only when stressors are too strong, too long-lasting, or too numerous to be managed adequately by the individual in the alarm or resistance stage and exhaustion occurs.

Three types of strategies can help individuals manage stress more effectively. These strategies can be categorized as those that attack the stressors directly, those that serve as inoculators against stress by strengthening restraining forces, and those that relate only to the immediate reaction to the experienced stress. These strategies should be implemented in the order listed. That is, try first to eliminate the stressor, then work on inoculation strategies, and finally implement strategies that pertain only to the immediate stressful feelings.

Behavioral guidelines are presented below that summarize the steps presented in the chapter. Use them as rules of thumb to guide your skill practice activities.

1. Institute good time management practices, such as those listed in Table 2.3.
2. Engage in some activities at least monthly that help you develop culturally, physically, spiritually, socially, intellectually, and in your family relationships. That is, develop yourself in a variety of areas, and don't let work activities inhibit that development.
3. Develop an open, trusting, sharing relationship with at least one other person. Rely on that relationship to affirm your worth as a person and to provide social support during periods of stress.
4. Find some time during the day for complete privacy. Be alone with yourself at least twenty minutes a day. Use that time to meditate, relax, pray, set priorities, or engage in other stress-relieving activities. Don't waste private time.
5. Get into good physical shape. Engage in a regular program of exercise and form sensible eating habits. As much as possible, cut out habit-forming drugs and foods with "empty" calories.
6. Learn at least one relaxation technique and apply it regularly.

REFERENCES

Albrecht, K. *Stress and the manager, making it work for you.* Englewood Cliffs, N.J.: Prentice Hall, 1979.

Antonovsky, A. Twenty-five years later: A limited study of the sequelae of the concentration camp experience. *Psychiatry,* 1971, *6,* 186–193.

Argyris, C. *Integrating the individual and the organization.* New York: John Wiley, 1964.

Beary, J. F., & Benson, H. A simple psychophysiologic technique which elicits the hypometabolic changes of the relaxation response. *Psychosomatic Medicine,* 1977, *36,* 115–120.

Benne, K. D., & Birnbaum, M. Change does not have to be haphazard. *The School Review.* Chicago: University of Chicago Press, 1969.

Benson, H. *The relaxation response.* New York: William Morrow, 1975.

Bramwell, S. T., Masuda, M., Wagner, N. N., & Holmes, T. H. Psychosocial factors in athletic injuries. *Journal of Human Stress,* 1975, *1,* 6.

Buell, P., & Breslow, L. Mortality from coronary heart disease in California men who work long hours. *Journal of Chronic Diseases,* 1960, *11,* 615–626.

Carlson, S. *Executive behaviour: A Study of the work load and the working methods of managing directors.* Stockholm: Strombergs, 1951.

Chan, K. B. Individual differences in reactions to stress and their personality and situational determinants. *Social Science and Medicine,* 1977, *11,* 89–103.

Coddington, R. D., & Troxell, J. R. The effect of emotional factors on football injury rates—A pilot study. *Journal of Human Stress,* 1980, *6,* 3–5.

Cofer, C. N., & Appley, M. H. *Motivation: Theory and research.* New York: John Wiley, 1964.

Comstock, G. W., & Partridge, K. B. Church attendance and health. *Journal of Chronic Diseases,* 1972, *25,* 665–672.

Cooper, C. L., & Davidson, M. J. The high cost of stress on women managers. *Organizational Dynamics*, 1982, *11*, 44–53.

Cooper, C. L., & Melhuish, A. Occupational stress and managers. *Journal of Occupational Medicine*, 1980, *22*, 588–592.

Cooper, M. J., & Aygen, M. M. A relaxation technique in the management of hypercholesterolemia. *Journal of Human Stress*, 1979, *5*, 24–27.

French, J. R. P., & Caplan, R. D. Organizational stress and individual strain. In A. J. Marrow (Ed.), *The failure of success*. New York: AMACOM, 1972.

Friedman, M., & Rosenman, R. H. *Type A behavior and your heart*. New York: Knopf, 1974.

Goldberg, H. *The hazards of being male*. New York: Nash Publishing, 1976.

Guest, R. H. Of time and the foreman. *Personnel*, 1956, *32*, 478–486.

Hackman, J. R. Work design. In J. R. Hackman & J. L. Suttle (Eds.), *Improving life at work: Behavioral science approaches to organizational change*. Santa Monica, Calif.: Goodyear, 1977.

Hackman, J. R., & Lawler, E. E. Employee reactions to job characteristics. *Journal of Applied Psychology*, 1971, *55*, 259–286.

Hackman, J. R., & Oldham, G. R. Development of the job diagnostic survey. *Journal of Applied Psychology*, 1975, *60*, 159–170.

Hackman, J. R., Oldham, G. R., Janson, R., & Purdy, K. A new strategy for job enrichment. *California Management Review*, 1975, *17*, 57–71.

Hall, D. T. *Careers in organizations*. Santa Monica, Calif.: Goodyear, 1976.

Hamner, W. C., & Organ, D. W. *Organizational behavior: An applied psychological approach*. Dallas: Business Publications, 1978.

Hansen, D. Personal and positional influence in formal groups: Propositions and theory for research on family vulnerability to stress. *Social Forces*, 1965, *44*, 202–210.

Harris, R. E., Sokolow, M., Carpenter, L. G., Freedman, M., & Hunt, S. P. Response to psychologic stress in persons who are potentially hypertensive. *Circulation*, 1953, *7*, 874–879.

Holmes, T. H., & Masuda, M. Life change and illness susceptibility. In B. S. Dohrenwend & B. P. Dohrenwend (Eds.), *Stressful life events: Their nature and effects*. New York: John Wiley, 1974.

Holmes, T. H., & Rahe, R. H. The social readjustment rating scale. *Journal of Psychosomatic Research*, 1967, *11*, 213–218.

Holmes, T. H., & Rahe, R. H. The social readjustment rating scale. *Journal of Psychosomatic Research*, 1970, *14*, 121–132.

Holmes, T. S., & Holmes, T. H. Short-term intrusion into life style routine. *Journal of Psychosomatic Research*, 1970, *14*, 121–132.

Ivancevich, J. M., & Matteson, M. T. *Stress and work, a managerial perspective*. Glenview, Ill.: Scott, Foresman and Company, 1980.

Jenkins, C. D. Recent evidence supporting psychological and social risk factors for coronary disease. *New England Journal of Medicine*, 1976, *294*, 1033–1034.

Jenkins, C. D. Psychosocial modifiers of response to stress. *Journal of Human Stress*, 1979, *5*, 3–15.

Jenkins, C. D., Rosenman, R. H., & Friedman, M. Development of an objective psychological test for the determination of coronary-prone behavior pattern in employed men. *Journal of Chronic Disease*, 1967, *20,*, 371–379.

Jenkins, C. D., Rosenman, R. H., & Zyzanski, S. J. Prediction of clinical coronary heart disease by a test for coronary-prone behavior pattern. *New England Journal of Medicine*, 1974, *290*, 1271–1275.

Jenkins, C. D., Zyzanski, S. J., & Rosenman, R. H. Progress toward validation of a computer-scored test for the type A coronary-prone behavior pattern. *Psychosomatic Medicine*, 1971, *33*, 193–202.

Jourard, S. M. *The transparent self*. Princeton, N.J.: D. Von Nostrand Company, 1964.

Kalis, B. L., Harris, R. E., Sokolow, M., & Carpenter, L. G. Response to psychological stress in patients with essential hypertension. *American Heart Journal*, 1957, *53*, 572–578.

Kobasa, S. C. Stressful life events, personality and health: An inquiry into hardiness. *Journal of Personality and Social Psychology,* 1979, *37,* 1–12.

Kostrubala, T. *The joy of running.* Philadelphia: J. B. Lippincott, 1976.

Levinson, D. J. *Seasons of a man's life.* New York: Knopf, 1978.

Lewin, K. *Field theory in social science.* New York: Harper & Row, 1951.

Likert, R. *The human organization.* New York: McGraw-Hill, 1967.

Linden, W., & Feuerstein, M. Essential hypertension and social coping behavior. *Journal of Human Stress,* 1981, *7,* 28–34.

Mackenzie, R. A. *Managing time at the top.* New York: The Presidents Association, 1970.

Macklowicz, M. *Determining the effects of workaholism.* Unpublished doctoral dissertation, Yale University, 1978.

McClelland, D. C. *Power: The inner experience.* New York: Irvington-Halsted-Wiley, 1975.

McClelland, D. C. Inhibited power motivation and high blood pressure in men. *Journal of Abnormal Psychology,* 1979, *88,* 182–190.

McClelland, D. C., & Burnham, D. H. Power is the great motivation. *Harvard Business Review,* 1976, *54,* 100–111.

McClelland, D. C., Davis, W. B., Kalin, R., & Wanner, E. *The drinking man.* New York: Free Press, 1972.

McClelland, D. C., Floor, E., Davidson, R. J., & Saron, C. Stressed power motivation, sympathetic activation, immune function and illness. *Journal of Human Stress,* 1980, *6,* 11–19.

McClelland, D. C., Locke, S. E., & Williams, R. E. *Power motivation, distress and immune functions.* Unpublished report from the Department of Psychology and Social Relations, Harvard University, 1979.

McKenney, J. L., & Keen, P. G. W. How managers' minds work. *Harvard Business Review,* 1974, *11,* 79–90.

Milgram, S. Behavioral study of obedience. *Journal of Abnormal and Social Psychology,* 1963, *63,* 371–378.

Mintzberg, H. *The nature of managerial work.* New York: Harper & Row, 1973.

Orme-Johnson, D. W. Autonomic stability and transcendental meditation. *Psychosomatic Medicine,* 1973, *35,* 341–349.

Payne, R., Jick, T. D., & Burke, R. J. Whither stress research: An agenda for the 1980s. *Journal of Occupational Behavior,* 1982, *3,* 131–145.

Rahe, R. H. The pathway between subjects' recent life change and their near future illness reports: Representative results and methodological issues. In B. S. Dohrenwend & B. P. Dohrenwend (Eds.), *Stressful life events: Their nature and effects.* New York: John Wiley, 1974.

Rahe, R. H., Ryman, D. H., & Ward, H. W. Simplified scaling for life change events. *Journal of Human Stress,* 1980, *6,* 22–27.

Rowland, K. F., & Sokol, B. A review of research examining the coronary-prone behavior pattern. *Journal of Human Stress,* 1972, *3,* 26–33.

Sailer, H. R., Schlacter, J., & Edwards, M. R. Stress: Causes, consequences, and coping strategies. *Personnel,* 1982, *59,* 35–48.

Sapira, J. D., Scheib, E. T., Moriarty, R., & Shapiro, A. O. Differences in perception between hypertensive and normotensive populations. *Psychosomatic Medicine,* 1971, *33,* 239–250.

Sayles, L. R. *Managerial behavior: Administration in complex organizations.* New York: McGraw-Hill, 1964.

Schachter, S. *The psychology of affiliation.* Stanford: Stanford University Press, 1959.

Schein, E. H. Interpersonal communication, group solidarity, and social influence. *Sociometry,* 1960, *23,* 148–161.

Schutz, W. C. *FIRO: A three-dimensional theory of interpersonal behavior.* New York: Holt, Rinehart & Winston, 1958.

Selye, H. *The stress of life* (2nd ed.). New York: McGraw-Hill, 1976.

Stone, R. A., & Deleo, J. Psychotherapeutic control of hypertension. *New England Journal of Medicine,* 1976, *294,* 80–84.

Toffler, A. *Future shock.* New York: Random House, 1970.

Turner, A. N., & Lawrence, P. R. *Industrial jobs and the worker.* Cambridge: Harvard University Press, 1965.

Weiner, H., Singer, M. T., & Reiser, M. F. Cardiovascular responses and their psychological correlates: A study in healthy young adults and patients with peptic ulcer and hypertension. *Psychosomatic Medicine,* 1962, *24,* 477–498.

Williams, R. B., Kemball, C. P., & Williard, H. M. The influence of interpersonal interactions on diastolic blood pressure. *Psychosomatic Medicine,* 1972, *34,* 194–198.

Wolff, H. G., Wolf, S. G., & Hare, C. C. (Eds.). *Life stress and bodily disease.* Baltimore: Williams & Wilkins, 1950.

Zand, D. E. Trust and managerial problem solving. *Administrative Science Quarterly,* 1972, *17,* 229–239.

Zohman, B. L. Emotional factors in coronary disease. *Geriatrics,* 1973, *28,* 110–119.   ■

■ Skill Analysis

The Day at the Beach

Arthur Gordon

Not long ago I came to one of those bleak periods that many of us encounter from time to time, a sudden drastic dip in the graph of living when everything goes stale and flat, energy wanes, enthusiasm dies. The effect on my work was frightening. Every morning I would clench my teeth and mutter: "Today life will take on some of its old meaning. You've got to break through this thing. You've got to!"

But the barren days went by, and the paralysis grew worse. The time came when I knew I had to have help.

The man I turned to was a doctor. Not a psychiatrist, just a doctor. He was older than I, and under his surface gruffness lay great wisdom and compassion. "I don't know what's wrong," I told him miserably, "but I just seem to have come to a dead end. Can you help me?"

"I don't know," he said slowly. He made a tent of his fingers and gazed at me thoughtfully for a long while. Then, abruptly, he asked, "Where were you happiest as a child?"

"As a child?" I echoed. "Why, at the beach, I suppose. We had a summer cottage there. We all loved it."

He looked out the window and watched the October leaves sifting down. "Are you capable of following instructions for a single day?"

"I think so," I said, ready to try anything.

"All right. Here's what I want you to do."

He told me to drive to the beach alone the following morning, arriving not later than nine o'clock. I could take some lunch; but I was not to read, write, listen to the radio or talk to anyone. "In addition," he said, "I'll give you a prescription to be taken every three hours."

He tore off four prescription blanks, wrote a few words on each, folded them, numbered them and handed them to me. "Take these at nine, twelve, three and six."

"Are you serious?" I asked.

He gave me a short bark of laughter.

"You won't think I'm joking when you get my bill!"

The next morning, with little faith, I drove to the beach. It was lonely, all right. A northeaster was blowing; the sea looked gray and angry. I sat in the car, the whole day stretching emptily before me. Then I took out the first of the folded slips of paper. On it was written: LISTEN CAREFULLY.

SOURCE: Arthur Gordon, The day at the beach, *Reader's Digest*, 1960, 76, 79–83.

I stared at the two words. Why, I thought, the man must be mad. He had ruled out music and newscasts and human conversation. What else was there?

I raised my head and I did listen. There were no sounds but the steady roar of the sea, the croaking cry of a gull, the drone of some aircraft high overhead. All these sounds were familiar.

I got out of the car. A gust of wind slammed the door with a sudden clap of sound. Was I supposed, I asked myself, to listen carefully to things like that?

I climbed a dune and looked out over the deserted beach. Here the sea bellowed so loudly that all other sounds were lost. And yet, I thought suddenly, there must be sounds beneath sounds—the soft rasp of drifting sand, the tiny wind-whisperings in the dune grasses—if the listener got close enough to hear them.

On an impulse I ducked down and, feeling fairly ridiculous, thrust my head into a clump of seaweed. Here I made a discovery: if you listen intently, there is a fractional moment in which everything seems to pause, wait. In that instant of stillness, the racing thoughts halt. For a moment, when you truly listen for something outside yourself, you have to silence the clamorous voices within. The mind rests.

I went back to the car and slid behind the wheel. LISTEN CAREFULLY. As I listened again to the deep growl of the sea, I found myself thinking about the white-fanged fury of its storms.

I thought of the lessons it had taught as children. A certain amount of patience: you can't hurry the tides. A great deal of respect: the sea does not suffer fools gladly. An awareness of the vast and mysterious interdependence of things: wind and tide and current, calm and squall and hurricane, all combining to determine the paths of the birds above and the fish below. And the cleanness of it all, with every beach swept twice a day by the great broom of the sea.

Sitting there, I realized I was thinking of things bigger than myself—and there was relief in that.

Even so, the morning passed slowly. The habit of hurling myself at a problem was so strong that I felt lost without it. Once when I was wistfully eyeing the car radio a phrase from Carlyle jumped into my head. "Silence is the element in which great things fashion themselves. . . ."

By noon the wind had polished the clouds out of the sky; and the sea had a hard, polished, and merry sparkle. I unfolded the second "prescription." And again I sat there, half amused and half exasperated. Three words this time: TRY REACHING BACK.

Back to what? To the past, obviously. But why, when all my worries concerned the present or the future?

I left the car and started tramping reflectively along the dunes. The doctor had sent me to the beach because it was a place of happy memories. Maybe that was what I was supposed to reach for: the wealth of happiness that lay half-forgotten behind me.

I decided to experiment: to work on these vague impressions as a painter would retouching the colors, strengthening the outlines. I would choose specific incidents and recapture as many details as possible. I would visualize people complete with dress and gestures. I would listen (carefully) for the exact sound of their voices, the echo of their laughter.

The tide was going out now, but there was still thunder in the surf. So I chose to go back 20 years to the last fishing trip I made with my younger brother. (He died in the Pacific during World War II and was buried in the Philippines.) I found that if I closed my eyes and really tried, I could see him with amazing vividness, even the humor and eagerness in his eyes that far-off morning.

In fact, I could see it all: the ivory scimiter of beach where we were fishing; the eastern sky smeared with sunrise; the great rollers creaming in, stately and slow. I could feel the backwash swirl warm around my knees, see the sudden arc of my brother's rod as he struck a fish, hear his exultant yell. Piece by piece I rebuilt it, clear and unchanged under the transparent varnish of time. Then it was gone.

I sat up slowly, TRY REACHING BACK. Happy people were usually assured, confident people. If, then, you deliberately reached back and touched happiness, might there not be released little flashes of power, tiny sources of strength?

This second period of the day went more quickly. As the sun began its long slant down the sky, my mind ranged eagerly through the past, reliving some episodes, uncovering others that had been completely forgotten. For example, when I was around 13 and my brother 10, Father had promised to take us to the circus. But at lunch there was a phone call: some urgent business required his attention downtown. We braced ourselves for disappointment. Then we heard him say, "No, I won't be down. It'll have to wait."

When he came back to the table, Mother smiled. "The circus keeps coming back, you know."

"I know," said Father. "But childhood doesn't."

Across all the years I remembered this and knew from the sudden glow of warmth that no kindness is ever wasted or ever completely lost.

By three o'clock the tide was out and the sound of the waves was only a rhythmic whisper, like a giant breathing. I stayed in my sandy nest, feeling relaxed and content—and a little complacent. The doctor's prescriptions, I thought, were easy to take.

But I was not prepared for the next one. This time the three words were not a gentle suggestion. They sounded more like a command. REEXAMINE YOUR MOTIVES.

My first reaction was purely defensive. There's nothing wrong with my motives, I said to myself. I want to be successful—who doesn't? I want to have a certain amount of recognition—but so does everybody. I want more security than I've got—and why not?

Maybe, said a small voice somewhere inside my head, those motives aren't good enough. Maybe that's the reason the wheels have stopped going around.

I picked up a handful of sand and let it stream between my fingers. In the past, whenever my work went well, there had always been something spontaneous about it, something uncontrived, something free. Lately it had been calculated, compentent—and dead. Why? Because I had been looking past the job itself to the rewards I hoped it would bring. The work had ceased to be an end in itself, it had been merely a means to make money, pay bills. The sense of giving something, of helping people, of making a contribution, had been lost in a frantic clutch at security.

In a flash of certainty, I saw that if one's motives are wrong, nothing can be right. It makes no difference whether you are a mailman, a hairdresser, an insurance salesman, a housewife—whatever. As long as you feel you are serving others, you do the job well. When you are concerned only with helping yourself, you do it less well. This is a law as inexorable as gravity.

For a long time I sat there. Far out on the bar I heard the murmur of the surf change to a hollow roar as the tide turned. Behind me the spears of light were almost horizontal. My time at the beach had almost run out, and I felt a grudging admiration for the doctor and the "prescriptions" he had so casually and cunningly devised. I saw, now, that in them was a therapeutic progression that might well be of value to anyone facing any difficulty.

LISTEN CAREFULLY: To calm a frantic mind, slow it down, shift the focus from inner problems to outer things.

TRY REACHING BACK: Since the human mind can hold but one idea at a time, you blot out present worry when you touch the happinesses of the past.

REEXAMINE YOUR MOTIVES: This was the hard core of the "treatment," this challenge to reappraise, to bring one's motives into alignment with one's capabilities and conscience. But the mind must be clear and receptive to do this—hence the six hours of quiet that went before.

The western sky was a blaze of crimson as I took out the last slip of paper. Six words this time. I walked slowly out on the beach. A few yards below the high water mark I stopped and read the words again: WRITE YOUR TROUBLES ON THE SAND.

I let the paper blow away, reached down and picked up a fragment of shell. Kneeling there under the vault of sky, I wrote several words on the sand, one above the other. Then I walked away, and I did not look back. I had written my troubles on the sand. And the tide was coming in.

DISCUSSION QUESTIONS

1. What is effective about this strategy for coping with stress?

2. Which of these techniques can be used on a temporary basis without going to the beach?

3. Which techniques can become a habitual part of one's life style in reducing stress?

4. Are these prescriptions effective coping strategies or merely escapes?

5. What other prescriptions could the author take besides the four mentioned here?

The Case of the Missing Time

Thomas J. McNichols

At approximately 7:30 A.M. on Tuesday, June 23, 1959, Chet Craig, manager of the Norris Company's Central Plant, swung his car out of the driveway of his suburban home and headed toward the plant located some six miles away, just inside the Midvale city limits. It was a beautiful day. The sun was shining brightly and a cool, fresh breeze was blowing. The trip to the plant took about twenty minutes and sometimes gave Chet an opportunity to think about plant problems without interruption.

The Norris Company owned and operated three printing plants. Norris enjoyed a nationwide commercial business, specializing in quality color work. It was a closely held company with some 350 employees, nearly half of whom were employed at the Central Plant, the largest of the three Norris production operations. The company's main offices were also located in the Central Plant building.

Chet had started with the Norris Company as an expediter in its Eastern Plant in 1948, just after he graduated from Ohio State. After three years Chet was promoted to production supervisor and two years later he was made assistant to the manager of the Eastern Plant. Early in 1957 he was transferred to the Central Plant as assistant to the plant manager and one month later was promoted to plant manager, when the former manager retired.

Chet was in fine spirits as he relaxed behind the wheel. As his car picked up speed, the hum of the tires on the newly paved highway faded into the background. Various thoughts occurred to him and he said to himself, "This is going to be the day to really get things done."

He began to run through the day's work, first one project, then another, trying to establish priorities. After a few minutes he decided that the open-end unit scheduling was probably the most important, certainly the most urgent. He frowned for a moment as he recalled that on Friday the vice president and general manager had casually asked him if he had given the project any further thought. Chet realized that he had not been giving it much thought lately. He had been meaning to get to work on this idea for over three months, but something else always seemed to crop up. "I haven't had much time to sit down and really work it out," he said to himself. "I'd better get going and hit this one today for sure." With that he began to break down the objectives, pro-

Norris Company Organization Chart

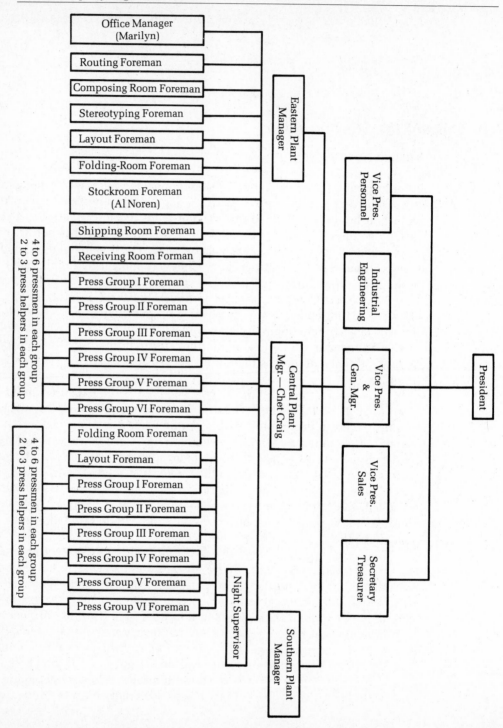

cedures, and installation steps of the project. He grinned as he reviewed the principles involved and calculated roughly the anticipated savings. "It's about time," he told himself. "This idea should have been followed up long ago." Chet remembered that he had first conceived of the open-end unit scheduling idea nearly a year and a half ago, just prior to his leaving Norris's Eastern Plant. He had spoken to his boss, Jim Quince, manager of the Eastern Plant, about it then and both agreed that it was worth looking into. The idea was temporarily shelved when he was transferred to the Central Plant a month later.

A blast from a passing horn startled him, but his thoughts quickly returned to other plant projects he was determined to get under way. He started to think through a procedure for simpler transport of dies to and from the Eastern Plant. Visualizing the notes on his desk, he thought about the inventory analysis he needed to identify and eliminate some of the slow-moving stock items, the packing controls that needed revision, and the need to design a new special-order form. He also decided that this was the day to settle on a job printer to do the simple outside printing of office forms. There were a few other projects he couldn't recall offhand, but he could tend to them after lunch, if not before. "Yes, sir," he said to himself, "this is the day to really get rolling."

Chet's thoughts were interrupted as he pulled into the company parking lot. When he entered the plant Chet knew something was wrong as he met Al Noren, the stockroom foreman, who appeared troubled. "A great morning, Al," Chet greeted him cheerfully.

"Not so good, Chet; my new man isn't in this morning," Noren growled.

"Have you heard from him?" asked Chet.

"No, I haven't," replied Al.

Chet frowned as he commented, "These stock handlers assume you take it for granted that if they're not here, they're not here, and they don't have to call in and verify it. Better ask Personnel to call him."

Al hesitated for a moment before replying. "Okay, Chet, but can you find me a man? I have two cars to unload today."

As Chet turned to leave he said, "I'll call you in half an hour, Al, and let you know."

Making a mental note of the situation, Chet headed for his office. He greeted the group of workers huddled around Marilyn, the office manager, who was discussing the day's work schedule with them. As the meeting broke up, Marilyn picked up a few samples from the clasper, showed them to Chet, and asked if they should be shipped that way or if it would be necessary to inspect them. Before he could answer, Marilyn went on to ask if he could suggest another clerical operator for the sealing machine to replace the regular operator, who was home ill. She also told him that Gene, the industrial engineer, had called and was waiting to hear from Chet.

After telling Marilyn to go ahead and ship the samples, he made a note of the need for a sealer operator for the office and then called Gene. He agreed to stop by Gene's office before lunch and started on his routine morning tour of the plant. He asked each foreman the types and volumes of orders they were running, the number of people present, how the schedules were coming along, and the orders to be run next; helped the folding-room foreman find temporary storage space for consolidating a carload shipment; discussed quality control with a pressman who had been running poor work; arranged to transfer four people temporarily to different departments, including two for Al in the stockroom; and talked to the shipping foreman about pickups and special orders to be delivered that day. As he continued through the plant, he saw to it that reserve stock was moved out of the forward stock area, talked to another pressman about his requested change of vacation schedule, had a "heart-to-heart" talk with a press helper who seemed to need frequent reassurance, and approved two type and one color order okays for different pressmen.

Returning to his office, Chet reviewed the production reports on the larger orders against his initial productions and found that the plant was running behind schedule. He called in the folding-room foreman and together they went over the lineup of machines and made several necessary changes.

During this discussion, the composing-room foreman stopped in to cover several type changes and the routing foreman telephoned for approval of a revised printing schedule. The stockroom foreman called twice, first to inform him that two standard, fast-moving stock items were dangerously low, later to advise him that the paper stock for the urgent Dillion job had finally arrived. Chet made the necessary subsequent calls to inform those concerned.

He then began to put delivery dates on important and difficult inquiries received from customers and salesmen. (The routine inquiries were handled by Marilyn.) While he was doing this he was interrupted twice, once by a sales correspondent calling from the West Coast to ask for a better delivery date than originally scheduled, once by the personnel vice president asking him to set a time when he could hold an initial training and induction interview with a new employee.

After dating the customer and salesmen inquiries, Chet headed for his morning conference in the Executive Offices. At this meeting he answered the sales vice president's questions in connection with "hot" orders, complaints, and the status of large-volume orders and potential new orders. He then met with the general manager to discuss a few ticklish policy matters and to answer "the old man's" questions on several specific production and personnel problems. Before leaving the Executive Offices, he stopped at the office of the secretary-treasurer to inquire about delivery of cartons, paper, and boxes and to place a new order for paper.

On the way back to his own office, Chet conferred with Gene about two current engineering projects concerning which he had called earlier. When he reached his desk, he lit a cigarette and looked at his watch. It was ten minutes before lunch, just time enough to make a few notes of the details he needed to check in order to answer knotty questions raised by the sales manager that morning.

After lunch Chet started again. He began by checking the previous day's production reports, did some rescheduling to get out urgent orders, placed appropriate delivery dates on new orders and inquiries received that morning, and consulted with a foreman on a personal problem. He spent some twenty minutes at the TWX going over mutual problems with the Eastern Plant.

By midafternoon Chet had made another tour of the plant, after which he met with the personnel director to review with him a touchy personal problem raised by one of the clerical employees, the vacation schedules submitted by his foremen, and the pending job evaluation program. Following this conference, Chet hurried back to his office to complete the special statistical report for Universal Waxing Corporation, one of Norris's best customers. As he finished the report, he discovered that it was ten minutes after six and he was the only one left in the office. Chet was tired. He put on his coat and headed through the plant toward the parking lot; on the way he was stopped by both the night supervisor and night layout foremen for approval of type and layout changes.

With both eyes on the traffic, Chet reviewed the day he had just completed. "Busy?" he asked himself. "Too much so—but did I accomplish anything?" His mind raced over the day's activities. "Yes and no" seemed to be the answer. "There was the usual routine, the same as any other day. The plant kept going and I think it must have been a good production day. Any creative or special project-work done?" Chet grimaced as he reluctantly answered, "No."

With a feeling of guilt, he probed further. "Am I an executive? I'm paid like one, respected like one, and have a responsible assignment with the necessary authority to carry it out. Yet one of the greatest values a company derives from an executive is his creative thinking and accomplishments. What have I done about it? An executive needs some time for thinking. Today was a typical day, just like most other days, and I did little, if any, creative work. The projects that I so enthusiastically planned to work on this morning are exactly as they were yesterday. What's more, I have no guarantee that tomorrow night or the next night will bring me any closer to their completion. This is a real problem and there must be an answer."

Chet continued, "Night work? Yes, occasionally. This is understood. But I've been doing too much of this lately. I owe my wife and family some of my time. When you come down to it, they are the people for whom I'm really working. If I am forced to spend much more time away from them, I'm not meeting my own personal objectives. What about church work? Should I eliminate that? I spend a lot of time on this, but I feel I owe God some time, too. Besides, I believe I'm making a worthwhile contribution in this work. Perhaps I can squeeze a little time from my fraternal activities. But where does recreation fit in?"

Chet groped for the solution. "Maybe I'm just rationalizing because I schedule my own work poorly. But I don't think so. I've studied my work habits carefully and I think I plan intelligently and delegate authority. Do I need an assistant? Possibly, but that's a long-time project and I don't believe I could justify the additional overhead expenditure. Anyway, I doubt whether it would solve the problem."

By this time Chet had turned off the highway onto the side street leading to his home—the problem still uppermost in his mind. "I guess I really don't know the answer," he told himself as he pulled into his driveway. "This morning everything seemed so simple but now . . ." His thoughts were interrupted as he saw his son running toward the car calling out, "Mommy, Daddy's home."

DISCUSSION QUESTIONS

1. What personal characteristics possessed by Chet inhibit his effective management of time?

2. What organizational problems exist?

3. What principles of time and stress management are violated in this case?

4. If you were hired as a consultant to Chet, what would you advise him? ■

■ *Skill Practice*

The Controller's Report

> Characters: Flynn Robinson, Vice President of Corporate Development
> Billie-Joe Washington, Controller
> Barbara Nichols, Secretary to Mr. Robinson

Directions: Form groups of four. Three of the group members should each play one of the roles described in this exercise, while the fourth member acts as an observer. Each of the group members should read the description of the setting and his or her own role. *Do not* read the other roles. Part of the purpose of the exercise is to share that information with one another, as well as to practice the time and stress management principles in this chapter. At the end of the exercise, the observer should give personal feedback to each of the other three role players.

SETTING

Today is Monday. The company's Board of Directors is meeting Thursday to make a decision about whether to acquire a small manufacturing firm. This firm is currently a major supplier of some important components needed by the company in producing its product. The decision is an important one because it will involve a substantial investment of company resources, both money and personnel, and it is sure to prove somewhat controversial among stock holders, board members, and management.

Flynn Robinson is the Vice President of Corporate Development. He has been charged with the responsibility of presenting to the Board of Directors the financial and planning documents pertaining to the acquisition. This report is to contain critical information about the financial risks, the market impact, and the future corporate development.

Flynn is extremely capable in his position. He has been with the company for almost fifteen years, and has moved up from a junior accountant position. He is trusted implicitly by the Board of Directors to give them good advice.

Billie-Joe Washington is the company's controller. She is bright, young, and holds two graduate degrees. She has been with the company for only ten months, but she has a reputation for being very competent and extremely hard working. Several company changes have occurred at her suggestion, and they have markedly improved the company's operations.

Billie-Joe is meeting in Flynn's office at his request. He expects her to explain the financial reports pertaining to the acquisition. Barbara Nichols, secretary to Flynn Robinson, has been invited into the meeting to take minutes.

FLYNN ROBINSON, VICE PRESIDENT OF CORPORATE DEVELOPMENT

The report from the company controller is late. It was due on your desk last Friday. The reason it was so important to get the report on time is that it is an integral part of your presentation to the Board of Directors on Thursday. You haven't been able to prepare the rest of your presentation because much of it revolves around the financial data contained in the controller's report. You essentially have wasted a weekend that you could have used to prepare, had you received the report on time.

After you prepare your presentation, it must be typed and bound in presentable form for the board meeting. Also, overhead slides must be made of crucial charts. But by receiving the report this late and not having the weekend to prepare, you may not have enough time to do an adequate job. You have an important speech to give to an investors' group in Chicago tomorrow, so you will not be in the office all day.

One thing that is especially upsetting is that no warning was given that the report would be late. When you checked with Ms. Washington a week ago, things seemed to be coming along fine. And when you tried over the weekend to contact her by phone to get the report, she was unavailable.

Doing a good job in this report to the Board of Directors is extremely important to you. The current president of the company is retiring next year, and this is your chance to impress the board with your qualifications. You probably have a reasonable chance for the position if the presentation comes off well. The board always asks detailed questions and tries to acquire as much information as possible before making a decision. This is especially likely to occur with a decision of this magnitude and long-term impact. This late report, therefore, has really created a lot of stress for you. It may jeopardize both your advancement in the company and the quality of the decision of the Board of Directors concerning the acquisition.

You have left a note for Ms. Washington to meet with you at 8:00 A.M. sharp to explain the report to you. You want her to go over it in detail because you must know the material well. You don't have time to read the report and then contact her later with questions. Your secretary, Barbara Nichols, is a trusted employee and always present at your meetings to take minutes.

BILLIE-JOE WASHINGTON, CONTROLLER

When you were offered the job of controller for the company, it was a real feather in your cap. Previously the job had been held by men, and older men at that. You still suspect that there may be a bias against women in upper management, but you are nevertheless proud of attaining this position. You feel competent in it, and you have helped improve the company since coming.

The past two weeks have been rough for you, however. You have had two major projects to work on, both of which were due last Friday. One project involved providing some financial data to the IRS for the audit it is conducting of the company. The report had to be filed to avoid a fine, as well as some bad publicity. The other project was the financial report to Mr. Robinson about the proposed acquisition of a small manufacturing firm. Both of these projects have been extremely time consuming.

What made things especially bad was that your secretary was called for jury duty last Tuesday. She was not able to work all week because of it. Furthermore, your assistant, who postponed his vacation twice before at your request, left for his vacation two weeks ago. He will be back in the office Monday morning. You have been working until 9:00 or 10:00 P.M. each night this past week at the office. On the weekend you hid away in the company conference room so you wouldn't be disturbed, and you worked all day and most of the night on Saturday to finish Robinson's report. On Sunday, your family had just about run out of patience with your being gone so much. And because you realized that you couldn't finish the report on time anyway, you went home on Sunday to attend church and spend the day with your children.

When you arrived at work this morning at your usual 7:45 A.M. (which is earlier than almost anyone else arrives), there was a note on your desk indicating that Mr. Robinson wanted to see you at 8:00 A.M. to explain the report to him. You have your regular staff meeting at 8:30 A.M., and you have quite a lot of material to prepare for that meeting. You also have an 11:00 A.M. appointment with a representative of the IRS to explain some parts of your report to him. That meeting will also require some preparation. You don't know if your secretary will be in or not.

BARBARA NICHOLS, SECRETARY TO FLYNN ROBINSON

You have been the secretary to Mr. Robinson for over ten years, and you know him well. He relies on you for many personal as well as company appointments, correspondence, special events, etc. You feel that you have a good relationship with him. You also have come to know Ms. Washington somewhat since she arrived at the company ten months ago as the company's first woman controller, but you are not especially close to her.

You have just returned from a weekend seminar entitled "How to Manage Stress." It gave you some new insights and ideas about how to manage your own stress and how to help others manage stress as well. You are hoping to find chances to put into practice some of the knowledge you gained over the weekend, and this meeting might present an opportunity.

While your role in most meetings held by Mr. Robinson is to take minutes, you also feel free to add comments and thoughts when they are important. Once in a while Mr. Robinson has even asked your opinion about an issue, and he seems to value your advice.

OBSERVER

Your task is to observe the other three individuals in the role play and judge the extent to which they engage in various types of behaviors. These behaviors all relate to good time and stress management. At the conclusion of the role play, be prepared to offer feedback, suggestions, and interpretations of what happened.

Position the initials of the different role players on the scales to indicate how much they engaged in the behaviors.

		A Lot				Not at All
1.	Good time management principles were applied in the conduct of the meeting. (See Table 2.3.)	5	4	3	2	1
2.	Mechanisms were used to temporarily release personal stress when it occurred in the meeting, rather than let it build up.	5	4	3	2	1
3.	Actions were taken to eliminate the source of the stress (i.e., permanent resolution).	5	4	3	2	1
4.	Actions were taken and statements made that created stress for others in the meeting.	5	4	3	2	1
5.	When they left the meeting, people felt relaxed and motivated, rather than uptight and angry.	5	4	3	2	1

The Stress of Success

Using force field analysis coupled with the model of stress presented in the text, diagnose this case study. Identify the driving forces (or stressors) and the restraining forces (or inoculators). Suggest realistic and specific strategies that eliminate driving forces and strengthen restraining forces. What should be done first? What should be done second, and so on? Then find a partner and role play this situation. One of you should assume the role of Mark; the other should assume the role of his friend. Then provide both suggestions and a plan of action as part of your advice. Use the model in the text to explain why your suggestions are good. After ten minutes, switch roles.

Mark Hasler is beginning his senior year at an elite Western college. He came to college on a full scholarship after having been student body president at his high school and an all-state football player. Mark has received good grades as a management major in the business school. He currently has a 3.7 GPA.

Mark played football his freshman year, but then quit to devote more time to his studies, student government, and social activities. He joined a prestigious fraternity his sophomore year and almost immediately was given a lot of responsibility. He was elected president of the fraternity in his junior year, and recently was chosen student body vice president for his senior year. In addition, the president of the college has asked Mark to be the student representative on the president's advisory committee, a very prestigious position.

Mark has carried a full course load in school and has had to work at a part-time job this past year to meet expenses. His goal has always been to enter a prestigious law school in the East, and eventually to clerk for a Supreme Court justice. His father, who died recently, had accomplished that goal thirty years earlier.

What no one knows about Mark, however, is that all of this responsibility has created a tremendous amount of stress over the last year or so. He has trouble sleeping at night, and he frequently suffers from headaches and nausea. The death of his father, to whom he had been close, was really the straw that broke the camel's back. Since that time he has had a great deal of trouble coping with his emotions, with school, and with his social activities. He has become more and more depressed. He has even begun to contemplate suicide.

The trouble is, Mark cannot share his feelings with anyone because of the high expectations held for him. He has become a hero of sorts to his family, peers, and many of the faculty. He feels that he cannot let down his image. Besides, the going has been rough in times past, and he has always managed to come through alright. He has considered himself a survivor—that is, until now.

Finally he comes to you as his friend and asks for advice. What will you say? ■

■ *Skill Application*

Application Exercises

1. Pick at least one relaxation technique. Learn it and apply it on a regular basis. Record your progress in your journal.

2. Get a physical examination and then begin a physical fitness program. Even if it is just regular walking, do something physical at least three times a week. Preferably, institute a regular, rigorous cardiovascular fitness program. Record your progress in your journal.

3. Find someone you know well who is experiencing high amounts of stress. Teach him or her how to better manage that stress by applying the concepts, exercises, and instruments in this chapter. Describe your experience in your journal.

4. Do a systematic force field analysis of your job setting, family setting, or academic setting for stressors. Identify the driving and restraining forces. Determine specific strategies for increasing the restraining forces and decreasing the driving forces so you experience less stress. Record your analysis and strategies in your journal.

5. Write a short paper describing when these principles of stress and time management would not work or would be harmful.   ■

3 Solving Problems Creatively

■ *Skill Preassessment*

How Creative Are You?

■ *Skill Learning*

Becoming a More Creative Problem-Solver

■ *Skill Analysis*

Admiral Kimmel's Failure at Pearl Harbor
The Double Helix

■ *Skill Practice*

Tidewater College
Acks and Blogs

■ *Skill Application*

Application Exercises

■ *Skill Preassessment*

How Creative Are You?

After each statement, indicate the degree to which you agree or disagree with it: A—strongly agree, B—agree, C—in between or don't know, D—disagree, E—strongly disagree. Mark your answers as accurately and frankly as possible. Try not to guess how a creative person might respond to each statement.

1. I always work with a great deal of certainty that I'm following the correct procedures for solving a particular problem. _____

2. It would be a waste of time for me to ask questions if I had no hope of obtaining answers. _____

3. I feel that a logical, step-by-step method is best for solving problems. _____

4. I occasionally voice opinions in groups that seem to turn some people off. _____

5. I spend a great deal of time thinking about what others think of me. _____

6. I feel that I may have a special contribution to make to the world. _____

7. It is more important for me to do what I believe to be right than to try to win the approval of others. _____

8. People who seem uncertain about things lose my respect. _____

9. I am able to stick with difficult problems over extended periods of time. _____

10. On occasion I get overly enthusiastic about things. _____

11. I often get my best ideas when doing nothing in particular. _____

12. I rely on intuitive hunches and the feeling of "rightness" or "wrongness" when moving toward the solution of a problem. _____

13. When problem solving, I work faster when analyzing the problem and slower when synthesizing the information I've gathered. _____

14. I like hobbies that involve collecting things. _____

SOURCE: E. Randsepp, *How creative are you?* (New York: G. Putnam's Sons, 1981)

15. Daydreaming has provided the impetus for many of my more important projects. _____

16. If I had to choose, I would rather be a physician than an explorer. _____

17. I can get along more easily with people if they belong to about the same social and business class as I. _____

18. I have a high degree of aesthetic sensitivity. _____

19. Intuitive hunches are unreliable guides in problem solving. _____

20. I am much more interested in coming up with new ideas than I am in trying to sell them to others. _____

21. I tend to avoid situations in which I might feel inferior. _____

22. When I evaluate information, its source is more important to me than its content. _____

23. I like people who follow the rule "Business before pleasure." _____

24. Self-respect is much more important than the respect of others. _____

25. I feel that people who strive for perfection are unwise. _____

26. I like work in which I must influence others. _____

27. It is important for me to have a place for everything and everything in its place. _____

28. People who are willing to entertain "crackpot" ideas are impractical. _____

29. I enjoy fooling around with new ideas, even if there is no practical payoff. _____

30. When a certain approach to a problem doesn't work, I can quickly reorient my thinking. _____

31. I don't like to ask questions that show ignorance. _____

32. I am able to change my interests to pursue a job or career more easily than I can change a job to pursue my interests. _____

33. Inability to solve a problem is frequently due to asking the wrong questions. _____

34. I can frequently anticipate the solution to my problems.   _____

35. It is a waste of time to analyze one's failures.   _____

36. Only fuzzy thinkers resort to metaphors and analogies.   _____

37. At times I have so enjoyed the ingenuity of a crook that I hoped he or she would go scot-free.   _____

38. I frequently begin work on a problem that I can only dimly sense and not yet express.   _____

39. I frequently forget things, such as names of people, streets, highways, small towns, etc.   _____

40. I feel that hard work is the basic factor in success.   _____

41. To be regarded as a good team member is important to me.   _____

42. I know how to keep my inner impulses in check.   _____

43. I am a thoroughly dependable and responsible person.   _____

44. I resent things being uncertain and unpredictable.   _____

45. I prefer to work with others in a team effort, rather than alone.   _____

46. The trouble with many people is that they take things too seriously.   _____

47. I am frequently haunted by my problems and cannot let go of them.   _____

48. I can easily give up immediate gain or comfort to reach the goals I have set.   _____

49. If I were a college professor, I would rather teach factual courses than those involving theory.   _____

50. I'm attracted to the mystery of life.   _____

SCORING INSTRUCTIONS

To compute your percentage score, circle and add up the values assigned to each item.

	A Strongly Agree	B Agree	C In Between or Don't Know	D Disagree	E Strongly Disagree		A Strongly Agree	B Agree	C In Between or Don't Know	D Disagree	E Strongly Disagree
1.	− 2	− 1	0	+1	+2	26.	− 2	− 1	0	+1	+2
2.	− 2	− 1	0	+1	+2	27.	− 2	− 1	0	+1	+2
3.	− 2	− 1	0	+1	+2	28.	− 2	− 1	0	+1	+2
4.	+2	+1	0	− 1	− 2	29.	+2	+1	0	− 1	− 2
5.	− 2	− 1	0	+1	+2	30.	+2	+1	0	− 1	− 2
6.	+2	+1	0	− 1	− 2	31.	− 2	− 1	0	+1	+2
7.	+2	+1	0	− 1	− 2	32.	− 2	− 1	0	+1	+2
8.	− 2	− 1	0	+1	+2	33.	+2	+1	0	− 1	− 2
9.	+2	+1	0	− 1	− 2	34.	+2	+1	0	− 1	− 2
10.	+2	+1	0	− 1	− 2	35.	− 2	− 1	0	+1	+2
11.	+2	+1	0	− 1	− 2	36.	− 2	− 1	0	+1	+2
12.	+2	+1	0	− 1	− 2	37.	+2	+1	0	− 1	− 2
13.	− 2	− 1	0	+1	+2	38.	+2	+1	0	− 1	− 2
14.	− 2	− 1	0	+1	+2	39.	+2	+1	0	− 1	− 2
15.	+2	+1	0	− 1	− 2	40.	+2	+1	0	− 1	− 2
16.	− 2	− 1	0	+1	+2	41.	− 2	− 1	0	+1	+2
17.	− 2	− 1	0	+1	+2	42.	− 2	− 1	0	+1	+2
18.	+2	+1	0	− 1	− 2	43.	− 2	− 1	0	+1	+2
19.	− 2	− 1	0	+1	+2	44.	− 2	− 1	0	+1	+2
20.	+2	+1	0	− 1	− 2	45.	− 2	− 1	0	+1	+2
21.	− 2	− 1	0	+1	+2	46.	+2	+1	0	− 1	− 2
22.	− 2	− 1	0	+1	+2	47.	+2	+1	0	− 1	− 2
23.	− 2	− 1	0	+1	+2	48.	+2	+1	0	− 1	− 2
24.	+2	+1	0	− 1	− 2	49.	− 2	− 1	0	+1	+2
25.	− 2	− 1	0	+1	+2	50.	+2	+1	0	− 1	− 2

Score: _____ (80–100, very creative; 60–79, above average; 40–59, average; 20–39, below average; and 0–19, noncreative) ∎

■ *Skill Learning*

Becoming a More Creative Problem-Solver

Problem solving is a skill that is required of every person in almost every aspect of life. Seldom does an hour go by without most individuals being faced with the need to solve some kind of problem. The job of the manager is inherently a problem-solving job. If there were no problems in organizations, there would be no need for managers. Therefore, it is hard to conceive of an incompetent problem-solver succeeding as a manager.

In this chapter, we shall explain the importance of developing your problem-solving skills, and also present specific guidelines and techniques for you to practice to become a more effective problem-solver.

STEPS IN PROBLEM SOLVING

Most people don't like problems, and try to get rid of them as quickly as they can. Their natural tendency, when faced with a problem, is to select the first reasonable solution that comes to mind (March & Simon, 1958). Unfortunately, that first solution may not be the most appropriate one, and it may lead to more severe problems than the one faced in the first place. Most approaches to managerial problem solving, therefore, try to increase the number of alternatives considered and the probability that the solution finally selected will be the right one.

The most widely accepted model of problem solving involves four general steps, which are summarized in Table 3.1. This information is discussed in more detail in Elbing (1978).

The first step is to *define the problem*. This involves diagnosing the situation so you focus on the *real* problem, not just on the symptoms. For example, suppose an employee consistently failed to get his or her work done on time. Slow work might be the problem, or it might be only a symptom of another problem—say, bad health, low morale, lack of training, or inadequate rewards. Defining the problem, therefore, must be accompanied by a wide search for information. The more information that is acquired, the more likely it is that the problem will be defined accurately. As Charles Kettering put it, "It ain't the things you don't know that'll get you in trouble, but the things you know for sure that ain't so."

The following are among the attributes of a good problem definition:

1. Information of fact is differentiated from opinion or speculation. (Objective data are separated from perceptions and interpretations.)

TABLE 3.1 *A Model of Problem Solving*

Step	Characteristics
1. Define the problem.	Differentate fact from opinion.
	Specify underlying causes.
	Tap all involved individuals for information.
	State the problem explicitly.
	Identify what standard is violated.
	Determine whose problem it is.
	Avoid stating the problem as a disguised solution.
2. Generate alternative solutions.	Postpone evaluating alternatives.
	Be sure all involved individuals generate alternatives.
	Specify alternatives that are consistent with goals.
	Specify both short-term and long-term alternatives.
	Build on previous ideas.
	Specify alternatives that solve the problem.
3. Evaluate and select an alternative.	Evaluate relative to an optimal standard.
	Evaluate systematically.
	Evaluate relative to goals.
	Evaluate main effects and side effects.
	State the selected alternative explicitly.
4. Implement and follow up on the solution.	Implement at the proper time and in the right sequence.
	Provide opportunities for feedback.
	Engender acceptance of others who are being affected.
	Establish an ongoing monitoring system.
	Evaluate based on problem solution.

2. All the individuals involved are tapped as information sources. (As much information is gathered as is necessary before the problem is defined.

3. The problem is stated explicitly. (Stating the problem specifically often helps clarify ambiguities in the definition.)

4. The problem definition identifies what standard or expectation has been violated. (Problems always violate some standard or expectation; otherwise, they are not problems. Be clear about what the standard or expectation is.)

5. The problem definition indicates whose problem it is. (No problems are completely independent of people. It is a problem for *someone*.)

6. The definition is not simply a disguised solution. ("The problem is that we need to fire the slow employee" is inappropriate because the problem is stated as a solution.)

Managers often propose problem solutions before an adequate definition of the problem has been given, and this may lead to solving the wrong problem. The definition step in problem solving, therefore, is extremely important.

The second step is to *generate alternative solutions*. This involves postponing the selection of one solution until several alternatives have been proposed. Maier (1970) has found that the quality of the final problem solution can be significantly enhanced by considering multiple alternatives. Judgment and evaluation, therefore, must be postponed so the first acceptable solution suggested isn't the one that is immediately selected. As Broadwell (1972, p. 121) has noted,

> The problem with evaluating [an alternative] too early is that we may rule out some good ideas by just not getting around to thinking about them. We hit on an idea that sounds good and we go with it, thereby never even thinking of alternatives that may have been better in the long run.

All alternative solutions should be generated without evaluating any of them. A common problem in managerial decision making is that alternatives are evaluated as they are proposed, so the first acceptable (although frequently not optimal) one is selected.

Some attributes of good alternative generation are the following:

1. The evaluation of each proposed alternative is postponed. (All should be proposed before evaluation is allowed.)
2. Alternatives are proposed by all individuals involved in the problem. (A wide search for alternatives improves solution quality and acceptance.)
3. Alternative solutions are consistent with organizational goals or policies. (Subversion and criticism are detrimental to both the organization and the alternative generation process.)
4. Alternatives relate to both the short-term and the long-term.
5. Alternatives build on one another. (Bad ideas may become good ideas if added to by someone else.)
6. Alternatives solve the problem that has been defined. (Another problem may also be important, but it should be ignored if it does not directly affect the problem being considered.)

The third problem-solving step is to *evaluate and select an alternative*. This step involves careful weighing of the advantages and disadvantages of the proposed alternatives before making a final selection. The alternatives must be judged in terms of the extent to which they will solve the problem without causing other unanticipated problems, the extent to which all the in-dividuals involved will accept the alternative, the extent to which implemen-tation of the alternative is likely, and the extent to which the alternative fits within the organizational constraints (e.g., it is consistent with policies, norms, and budget limitations). Care must be taken not to short-circuit these consid-erations by choosing the most conspicuous alternative without considering others. As March and Simon (1958, p. 141) point out,

> Most human decision-making, whether individual or organizational, is con-cerned with the discovery and selection of satisfactory alternatives; only in exceptional cases is it concerned with the discovery and selection of opti-mal alternatives. To optimize requires processes several orders of magni-tude more complex than those required to satisfice. An example is the dif-ference between searching a haystack to find the sharpest needle in it and searching the haystack to find a needle sharp enough to sew with.

Given the natural tendency to select the first satisfactory solution that is proposed, this step deserves particular attention in problem solving.

Some attributes of good evaluation are the following:

1. Alternatives are evaluated relative to an optimal standard (rather than a satisfactory standard).
2. Evaluation of alternatives occurs systematically so each is given consideration. (Short-circuiting evaluation inhibits selection of optimal alternatives.)
3. Alternatives are evaluated in terms of the goals of the organiza-tion and the individuals involved. (Organizational goals should be met while individual preferences are also enhanced.)
4. Alternatives are evaluated in terms of their probable effects. (Both side-effects and direct effects on the problem are considered.)
5. The alternative selected is stated explicitly. (Specifying the alter-native can help uncover latent ambiguities and let others know about the solution selected.)

The final step is to *implement and follow up on the solution.* Implemen-tation of any solution requires sensitivity to possible resistance from those who will be affected by it. Almost any change engenders some resistance. Therefore, the manager must be careful to select a strategy that maximizes the probability that the solution will be accepted and fully implemented. This may involve behaviors ranging from ordering that the solution be imple-mented by others, to "selling" the solution to others, to involving others in the implementation. Tannenbaum and Schmidt (1958) and Vroom and Yetton (1973) provide guidelines for managers to determine which leader behavior is most appropriate under various circumstances. Generally speaking, participation by others in the implementation of a solution will increase its acceptance and decrease resistance.

Effective implementation also requires some follow-up to make certain that implementation is occurring, that negative side-effects are being prevented, and that the problem has really been solved. Follow-up not only helps ensure effective implementation, but serves a feedback function as well by providing information that can be used to improve future problem solutions. Drucker (1974, p. 480) explains,

> A feedback has to be built into the decision to provide continuous testing, against actual events, of the expectations that underlie the decision. Few decisions work out the way they are intended to. Even the best decision usually runs into snags, unexpected obstacles, and all kinds of surprises. Even the most effective decision eventually becomes obsolete. Unless there is feedback from the results of the decision, it is unlikely to produce the desired results.

Some attributes of effective implementation and follow-up can be listed:

1. Implementation occurs at the right time and in a proper sequence. (It does not ignore constraining factors, and it does not come before steps 1, 2, and 3 in the problem-solving process.)
2. Opportunities for feedback are provided in the implementation process. (How well the selected solution works needs to be communicated.)
3. Implementation engenders support and acceptance by those affected by it. (Participation is often the best way to ensure acceptance by others.)
4. An ongoing monitoring system is set up for the implemented solution. (Long-term as well as short-term effects should be assessed.)
5. Evaluation of success is based on problem solution, not on side benefits. (Although the solution may provide positive outcomes, unless it solves the problem being considered, it is unsuccessful.)

LIMITATIONS OF THE PROBLEM-SOLVING MODEL

These steps in problem solving are known by most experienced problem-solvers, and are based on empirical research results and sound rationale (Maier, 1970; Huber, 1980; Elbing, 1978; Filley, House, & Kerr, 1976). Unfortunately, they frequently are not practiced by managers. The demands of the job often pressure managers into circumventing some of these steps, and problem solving suffers as a result. When these four steps are followed, however, problem solving is markedly enhanced.

On the other hand, simply learning about and practicing these four steps of problem solving does not guarantee that an individual will effectively solve all types of problems. There are two reasons why.

First, these problem-solving steps are mainly useful when the problems faced are straightforward, when alternatives are readily available, when relevant information is present, and when a clear standard exists against which to judge the correctness of a solution. Thompson and Tuden (1959) call problems with these characteristics "computational problems," for which the main task is to gather information, generate alternatives, and make an informed choice. The trouble is, many managerial problems are not of this type. Definitions, information, alternatives, and standards are seldom unambiguous or readily available, so knowing the steps in problem solving and being able to implement them are not the same thing.

The second reason is that all individuals encounter certain conceptual blocks in their problem-solving activities—most of which they are not even aware of—that prohibit them from solving problems more effectively. These blocks are largely personal, as opposed to interpersonal or organizational, so personal skill development is required to overcome them. These conceptual blocks relate largely to individual thinking processes and to the ways problem-solvers use their minds when facing problems. Unfortunately, improving mental abilities often is thought of simply as gaining more knowledge or getting exposed to more facts. However, being exposed to more information about problem-solving steps will not improve problem-solving skill. The *process* of thinking must be considered, instead. That is, it is the thinking process that must be improved if individuals are to become more proficient problem-solvers. Consider the following example from Siu (1968, p. 189):

> If you place in a bottle half a dozen bees and the same number of flies, and lay the bottle down horizontally, with its base to the window, you will find that the bees will persist, till they die of exhaustion or hunger, in their endeavor to discover an issue through the glass; while the flies, in less than two minutes, will all have sallied forth through the neck on the opposite side. . . . It is their [the bees'] love of light, it is their very intelligence, that is their undoing in this experiment. They evidently imagine that the issue from every prison must be there where the light shines clearest; and they act in accordance, and persist in too logical action. To them glass is a supernatural mystery they never have met in nature; they have had no experience of this suddenly impenetrable atmosphere; and the greater their intelligence, the more inadmissible, more incomprehensible, will the strange obstacle appear. Whereas the feather-brained flies, careless of logic as of the enigma of crystal, disregarding the call of the light, flutter wildly hither and thither, and meeting here the good fortune that often waits on the simple, who find salvation there where the wiser will perish, necessarily end by discovering the friendly opening that restores their liberty to them.

Frequently, the more educated individuals become, the more formal training they receive, or the more experienced in a job they are, the less able they are to solve problems in creative ways. They become, as bees, stagnant in their thinking processes. They close off the ability to think with experimentation, improvisation, or detours.

A number of researchers have found that training directed toward improving thinking significantly enhances problem-solving abilities and managerial effectiveness (Barron, 1963; Taylor & Barron, 1963; Torrance, 1965). Parnes (1962), for example, found that training in thinking increased the number of good ideas produced in problem-solving by 125 percent. Bower (1965) recorded numerous examples of organizations that increased profitability and efficiency through training in the improvement of thinking skills. Skill development oriented toward improving thinking processes, therefore, is a critical managerial need. John Gardner (1965, pg. 21), in speaking of the development of the mind through traditional formal education, states,

> All too often we are giving our young people cut flowers when we should be teaching them to grow plants. We are stuffing their heads with the products of earlier innovation rather than teaching them to innovate. We think of the mind as a storehouse to be filled when we should be thinking of it as an instrument to be used.

In the remainder of this chapter we shall explain the conceptual blocks that inhibit the thinking processes required for effective problem solving and provide methods for overcoming these blocks. The focus of the discussion is on thinking and the thinking processes used when individuals are faced with a problem. Our goal is to help you understand better how to become an effective problem-solver and to provide you with some techniques for actually doing it. Our point of view is consistent with the conclusions of Olton and Crutchfield (1972, p. 3) in this regard:

> There exists for most individuals a pronounced gap between productive thinking potential and productive thinking performance. . . . [Our research confirms] that direct training in thinking can produce significant increments in thinking skills. Systematic programs for teaching the student how to think should be one of the central concerns of education at all levels and for all types of pupils. For an education without such instruction will produce adults who are destined eventually to become crippled by their own obsolete patterns of thought and by knowledge that is no longer relevant, to become confused and then overwhelmed by a vastly changed future society in which they will no longer know how to participate.

The assertion of Olton and Crutchfield that thought patterns may fall behind the times receives some support from the fact that patents awarded to American inventors declined 16 percent between 1970 and 1975. In the 1950s the U.S. marketed 82 percent of the world's innovations, but it has now been surpassed by several other countries. And Drath (1981) suggests that the 1970s may well be remembered as the "decade of innovation recession." These trends may not be due to waning competence in solving modern problems, but they do indicate that *creative* problem solving in this country is declining.

The basic assumption of this chapter, then, is that if individuals improve their personal thinking skills as they relate to creative problem solving, these skills will enhance their effectiveness in coping with the wide variety of problems they will face in the future.

CONCEPTUAL BLOCKS

The four problem-solving steps discussed above often do not result in effective decisions because conceptual blocks diminish the effectiveness of problem definition, limit the number of alternatives generated, and inhibit selection of the best solution. Conceptual blocks are mental obstacles that constrain the way the problem is defined and the number of alternative solutions thought to be relevant (Allen, 1974). Every individual has conceptual blocks, but they are more numerous and more intense in some people than in others. These blocks are largely unrecognized or unconscious, so the only way individuals can be made aware of them is to be confronted with problems that are unsolvable because of them. Some of these problems are presented in our discussion below to help you diagnose your own conceptual blocks. Self-awareness of conceptual blocks, like other aspects of self-awareness discussed in Chapter 1, can help improve problem-solving competence.

Table 3.2 summarizes eight major conceptual blocks that inhibit creative problem solving. Each is discussed and illustrated below by problems and mini-exercises. We encourage you to complete the mini-exercises and to solve the problems as you read the chapter, because this will help you become aware of the extent of your own conceptual blocks. Later we shall discuss in more detail how to overcome these blocks.

TABLE 3.2 *Conceptual Blocks That Inhibit Problem Solving*

1. *Vertical thinking*—Beginning with a single definition and pursuing problem resolution without considering other possible definitions.
2. *Only one thinking language*—Thinking about a problem only in words, for example, instead of visually, symbolically, emotionally, etc.
3. *Past experiences that cause stereotyping*—Considering present problems only as variations on problems faced in the past.
4. *Separating figure and ground*—Not deleting irrelevant information and filling in needed information that is absent.
5. *Artificially constraining problems*—Defining the boundaries of problems too narrowly.
6. *Not perceiving commonalities*—Failing to see relationships between disparate elements.
7. *Lack of inquisitiveness*—Fearing to appear ignorant if questions are asked.
8. *Bias against thinking*—Tending to be active at the expense of solitary thought time.

Vertical Thinking

One block to creative problem solving is the habit of thinking vertically. Vertical thinking, as defined by deBono (1968), is thinking that begins with a single problem definition and then pursues that train of thought until a conclusion is reached. No alternative definitions are considered. All information gathered and all alternatives generated are consistent with the original definition. It is similar to digging a hole in search of oil. In vertical thinking, a spot for the hole is determined and the hole is dug deeper and deeper until oil is discovered. Lateral thinking, on the other hand, is thinking that generates alternative ways of viewing a problem and produces multiple definitions. Instead of digging one hole deeper and deeper, lateral thinkers pick different places to dig multiple holes in search of oil. The conceptual block arises from not being able to view the problem from multiple perspectives, to dig several holes, or to think laterally *as well as* vertically in problem solving. Problem definition is restricted.

To illustrate, consider the following example from deBono (1968, p. 11):

Many years ago when a person who owed money could be thrown into jail, a merchant in London had the misfortune to owe a huge sum to a moneylender. The moneylender, who was old and ugly, fancied the merchant's beautiful teenage daughter. He proposed a bargain. He said he would cancel the merchant's debt if he could have the girl instead.

Both the merchant and his daughter were horrified at the proposal. So the cunning moneylender proposed that they let Providence decide the matter. He told them that he would put a black pebble and a white pebble into an empty moneybag and then the girl would have to pick out one of the pebbles. If she chose the black pebble she would become his wife and her father's debt would be cancelled. If she chose the white pebble she would stay with her father and the debt would still be cancelled. But if she refused to pick out a pebble her father would be thrown into jail and she would starve.

Reluctantly the merchant agreed. They were standing on a pebble-strewn path in the merchant's garden as they talked and the moneylender stooped down to pick up the two pebbles. As he picked up the pebbles the girl, sharp-eyed with fright, noticed that he picked up two black pebbles and put them into the moneybag. He then asked the girl to pick out the pebble that was to decide her fate and that of her father.

What should she do? Vertical thinkers usually are not much help solving this problem. They usually think the girl has only three alternatives:

1. She could refuse to take a pebble. (She starves and her father goes to jail.)
2. She could accuse the moneylender of cheating. (But she would risk that the moneylender would become angered and cancel the test.)

3. She could take a black pebble. (She could sacrifice herself so her father would not have to go to jail.)

The problem with these alternatives is that all are based on the assumption that taking a pebble will decide the girl's fate. No matter how carefully the solution is worked out vertically, in the end it will be bad for the girl. Lateral thinkers are more apt to consider different ways of solving this problem, and not to assume that the pebble taken will decide the fate of the girl. In the story, the girl put her hand into the bag and quickly withdrew a pebble. But as she did, she let it drop on the path where it was lost among the other pebbles. "Oh, how clumsy of me," she said, "but never mind. If you will look into the bag at the remaining pebble, you will know the color of the pebble I chose." Lateral thinking helped the girl turn a problem with a 0 percent probability of a successful outcome into a problem with a 100 percent probability of a successful outcome. In fact, she was even better off than had the moneylender been honest (a 50 percent chance of a successful outcome).

Use of Only One Thinking Language

A second conceptual block in problem solving is thinking about a problem using only one "language." Most people think in terms of words—that is, they think about a problem and its solution in terms of verbal language. Some writers, in fact, have argued that thinking cannot even occur without words (Vygotsky, 1962). Other thought languages are available, however, such as nonverbal languages (e.g., mathematics), sensory imagery (e.g., smelling or tactile sensation), feelings and emotions (e.g., happiness, fear, or anger), and visual imagery (e.g., mental pictures). The more languages available to problemsolvers, the better and more creative will be their solutions. As Koestler (1967) puts it, "[Verbal] language can become a screen which stands between the thinker and reality. This is the reason that true creativity often starts where [verbal] language ends."

For example, think through and solve the following problem from Leavitt (1972) before going on.

I ask you to throw six dice. They come up like this:

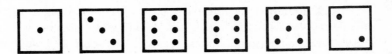

I now tell you that in the set you have just thrown are three windblown roses and six petals. You ask, "What the hell is a 'windblown rose'?" I reply, "That's the game. Your job is to tell me what a windblown rose is and what petals are. So now throw your dice again and tell me how many roses and how many petals you come up with this time."

So you throw again and this time the dice fall like this:

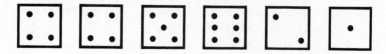

Now how many roses are there? How many petals? The right answer this time is that there are two windblown roses and four petals.

Have you caught on yet? Have you developed a rule? Do you know what a windblown rose and a petal are? If you think you do, or if you think you don't, here are three more samples:

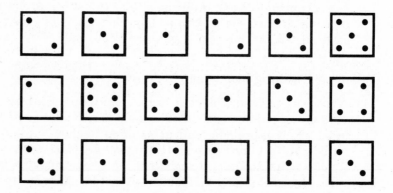

After you have worked on this problem for a few minutes, try to solve it by picturing a rose viewed from its top. A rose is represented on each die by a dot in the middle, surrounded by petals, but some petals are gone. Therefore, in the first roll, only the dice showing one, three, and five dots are roses with petals. Thus, there are three roses and eight petals in that row. Check your answers on the last three rolls with your instructor's answers.

In general, Leavitt (1972) found that women solve this problem more quickly than men, and children more quickly than adults, because they are more inclined to think visually. Logical or mathematical thinking languages in this problem are a common approach used by people, but they simply sidetrack you.

It is difficult to expand the use of thinking languages because they generally are chosen unconsciously. Later, however, as we discuss ways to overcome these conceptual blocks, we will give you a chance to practice using more than one thinking language in solving a problem. But for now, it is important that you recognize that a variety of languages are available to you. When individuals restrict themselves to a single language, not only do they fail to solve many problems creatively and efficiently, but they cannot even recognize that a problem exists.

Past Experiences That Stereotype Present Perceptions

March and Simon (1958) point out that a major obstacle to innovative problem solving is that individuals tend to define present problems in terms of problems they have faced in the past. Current problems are usually seen as variations on some past condition, so the alternatives proposed to solve the current problem are alternatives that have proven successful in coping with past problems. Both problem definition and proposed solution are therefore restricted by the experiences of the past. This restriction is referred to as *perceptual stereotyping* (Allen, 1974). That is, certain preconceptions formed on the basis of past experience determine how an individual defines a situation.

In other words, when individuals receive an initial cue regarding the definition of a problem, all subsequent problems frequently are framed in terms of the initial cue. Of course, this is not all bad, because perceptual stereotyping helps organize problems on the basis of a limited amount of data, and the need to consciously analyze every problem encountered is eliminated. On the other hand, potentially divergent ways of viewing a problem are excised when perceptual stereotyping occurs.

Consider the following problem, which helps test your dependence on past perceptions. Only 5 percent of people who try this problem answer it correctly. Look at Figure 3.1 and determine your answer. Don't read ahead until you have decided on a solution.

There are four volumes of Shakespeare on the shelf. The pages of each volume are exactly two inches thick. The covers are each one-sixteenth of an inch thick. A bookworm started eating at page 1 of Volume 1 and ate through the last page of Volume IV. What is the distance the worm covered?

Most people get this problem wrong because they think of books as starting at page 1 and going to the end, left to right. When the back binding of the book is facing you, however, page 1 is on the right and the last page is on the left. Therefore, the answer to the problem is five inches. Most people answer nine inches because of perceptual stereotyping.

Separation of Figure from Ground

Another conceptual block to problem solving is the inability to differentiate the major problem from irrelevant problems or background information. Problems almost never come clearly specified, so problem-solvers must determine what the real problem is. Inaccurate, misleading, or irrelevant information must be filtered out to correctly define the problem and to generate appropriate alternative solutions. The inability to separate the important from the unimportant serves as a conceptual block because it exaggerates the complexity of the problem and inhibits a simple definition.

Figure 3.1   *Shakespeare Riddle*

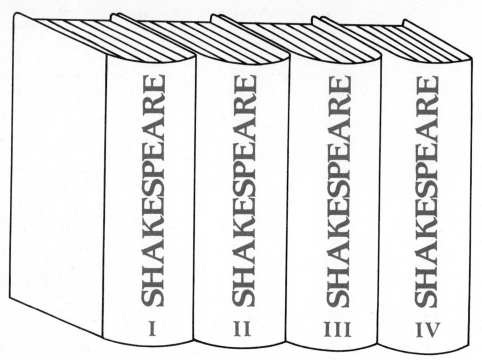

From Raudsepp and Hough, 1977.

For example, consider Figure 3.2. For each pair, find the pattern on the left embedded within the more complex pattern on the right. Draw a line outlining the embedded pattern. How easy is it for you to filter out irrelevant information? Now try to find at least one more figure in each pattern.

This brings us to the other aspect of the figure-ground conceptual block, the inability to fill in necessary details to clarify the problem. This block occurs when you are presented with a certain amount of information about a problem but cannot determine what additional information is needed to clarify that problem. Simple visual examples are presented in Figure 3.3. What do they represent? How easy is it for you to fill in the details?

Sometimes when individuals are given a hint as to what information might be relevant, they find it easier to fill in the missing information. For example, does knowing that the figure on the left is a violin help you identify the figure on the right?

Failing to separate figure from ground, then, can take two forms. Clear problem definition can be blocked because of an inability to filter out superfluous information, or it can be blocked by an inability to fill in additional needed information.

Figure 3.2 Embedded Patterns

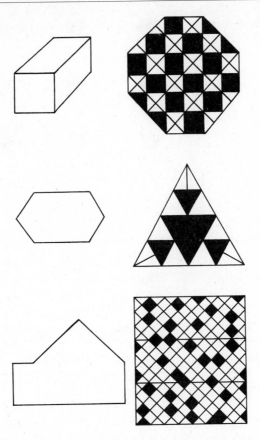

Figure 3.3 Incomplete Figures

From R. H. McKim, *Experiences in visual thinking* (Chicago: University of Chicago, 1972), p. 7. Courtesy of London House Management Consultants, Inc.

Figure 3.4   Dot Problem

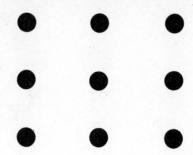

Artificially Constraining Problems

Just as it is difficult to filter out noise and to add missing detail, so it is difficult for many people to avoid ignoring information that is present. That is, they often constrain, or place boundaries around, problems so they are unable to use information that is before them. Constraints arise from hidden assumptions people make about problems they encounter. People assume that some problem definitions or alternative solutions are off limits, and so those are ignored. To illustrate this conceptual block, look at Figure 3.4. Without lifting your pencil from the paper, draw four straight lines that pass through all nine dots. Complete the task before going on.

This problem is difficult to solve if you assume that the boundary of the figure is the outside edge of the nine dots. If you do not constrain the figure artificially, it becomes much easier to find a solution. One solution is shown in Figure 3.5.

By thinking of the figure as constrained more than it actually is, the problem becomes impossible to solve. Now that you have been cued, can you do the same task with only *three* lines? Work on this problem for a minute. If you are successful, try to do the task with only *one* line. Can you determine how to put a single straight line through all nine dots without lifting your pencil from the paper? Your instructor has both the three-line solution and the one-line solution, which were pointed out by Allen (1974).

Constraining problems visually is not, of course, the only way problem-solvers limit themselves. Another way can be illustrated as you answer the following questions.

1. Two men played chess. They played five games, and each man won three. How do you explain this?

2. Answer this question within five seconds. How many animals of each species did Adam take aboard the Ark with him? (Note— The question is *not* how many pairs, but how many animals.)

3. An archaeologist reported that he had discovered two gold coins in the desert near Jerusalem dated 439 B.C. Many of his fellow scientists refused to take his claim seriously. Why?

4. If you had only one match and you entered a room to start a kerosene lamp, an oil heater, and a wood-burning stove, which would you light first and why?

5. Explain the following true boast: "In my bedroom, the nearest lamp that I usually keep turned on is twelve feet from my bed. Alone in the room, without using wires, strings, or any other aids or contraptions, I can turn out the light on that lamp and get into bed before the room is dark."

How long did it take you to answer these five questions? To what extent did you find yourself artificially constraining the problems or making assumptions about possible solutions that you weren't aware of? The answers to the five questions are as follows:

1. The men didn't play each other.
2. None. Adam didn't go on the Ark, Noah did.
3. No one dated anything B.C. until after Christ.
4. You would light the match.
5. The lamp was turned off during the daytime.

Artificially constraining problems, then, means limiting the problem definition and the possible alternatives more than the problem requires. Creative problem solving requires that individuals become adept at recognizing their hidden assumptions and expanding the alternatives they consider. We shall consider ways to do that later.

Figure 3.5   Four-line Solution

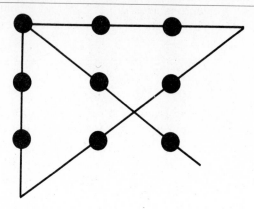

Failure to Identify Commonalities

The inability to identify similarities among seemingly disparate pieces of data is the conceptual block most often identified as standing in the way of creative problem solving. It inhibits the problem-solver's ability to consider all the information available or to acquire an overview of the problem.

Most problems faced by managers require finding underlying commonalities or themes in a wide array of data. This is called "reaching closure" on a problem (McKim, 1972). The ability to find one definition or solution for two seemingly dissimilar problems is a characteristic of creative individuals (Dellas & Gaier, 1970; Steiner, 1978). The inability to do this can overload the problem-solver by requiring that every problem encountered be solved individually. The discovery of penicillin by Sir Alexander Fleming resulted from a problem-solver's seeing a common theme among seemingly isolated events. Fleming was working with some cultures of staphylococci that had accidentally become contaminated. The contamination, the growth of fungi, and isolated clusters of dead staphylococci led Fleming to see a relationship no one else had ever seen previously, and thus to discover a wonder drug (Beveridge, 1960). The famous chemist Friedrich Kekule saw a relationship between his dream of a snake swallowing its own tail and the chemical structure of organic compounds. This creative insight led him to the discovery that organic compounds such as benzene have closed rings rather than open structures (Keostler, 1967).

Identifying commonalities among varied data is more difficult for some than for others. For example, how difficult is it for you to solve the following problem that requires identifying the common element among disparate cues?

For the block of wood in Figure 3.6, describe or draw a single piece of wood that can pass all the way through each hole but also completely fill each hole (i.e., block out the light).

This problem is designed to help you identify the extent to which you may fail to identify commonalities among different elements. If you were unable to solve it, it does not mean that you are uncreative or an ineffective

Figure 3.6 Block Problem

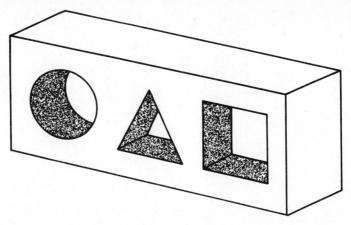

From McKim, 1972.

problem-solver, but it may illustrate an area in your thinking process that deserves more attention. More will be said about this below as we discuss ways to overcome conceptual blocks.

For your information, the solution to the problem is shown in Figure 3.7.

Questioning

Some conceptual blocks in problem solving occur not because of poor thinking habits, but because individuals fear they will appear ignorant or naive if they question or attempt to redefine a problem. Asking questions runs the risk of exposing one's ignorance. It also is threatening to others because it implies that what they accept may not be accurate.

Creative problem solving, by definition, is not tried and tested. That is, a solution wouldn't be creative if it had been tried before and found successful. Therefore, creative approaches may sometimes lead one down the wrong path. Moreover, creative problem definitions or alternative solutions generally must be "sold" to others, and resistance to a changed perspective is likely. For these reasons, individuals frequently refrain from questioning, avoid trying out different perspectives, and act as though they were in the know.

This conceptual block can be illustrated by the following questions:

1. When is the best time to learn a new language, at age five years or thirty-five? Why?
2. How many times in the last month have you attempted something for which the probability of success was below 50 percent?
3. Since mirrors make letters appear backwards, why don't they also make them appear upside down?
4. How does a telephone work? Why can't you hear people's voices when you stand near a telephone line?

Figure 3.7 *Answer for Block Problem*

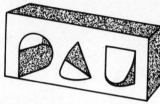

From McKim, 1972.

Individuals often stop being inquisitive as they get older because they learn that it is good to be smart, and being smart is interpreted as already knowing the answers. Consequently, they learn less well at thirty-five than at five, take few risks, and function in the world without trying to understand it. As Allen (1974, p. 77) points out, however, questioning is an important aspect of creative problem solving:

> The questioning attitude is necessary in the broadest sense to motivate conceptualization. If one accepts the status quo unquestioningly, he will have no reason to innovate. He will not be able to see needs and problems, and problem-sensitivity is one of the more important qualities of the creative person.

Biases Against Thinking

The final conceptual block relates to cultural and sometimes personal biases against thinking. When was the last time you heard someone say, "I'm sorry. I can't go to the ballgame (or concert, dance, party, or movie) because I have to think"? Or, "I'll do the dishes tonight. I know you need to catch up on your thinking"? That these statements sound humorous illustrates the bias most people have toward action rather than thought, or against putting their feet up, rocking back in their chair, looking off into space, and engaging in solitary mental activity. This does not mean daydreaming or fantasizing, but *thinking*.

There is a particular conceptual block in our culture against the kind of thinking that uses the right hemisphere of the brain. Left-hemisphere thinking, for most people, is concerned with logical, analytic, linear, or sequential tasks. Thinking using the left hemisphere is apt to be organized, planned, and precise. Language and mathematics are left-hemisphere activities. Right-hemisphere thinking, on the other hand, is concerned with intuition, synthesis, playfulness, and qualitative judgment. It tends to be more simultaneous, imaginative, and emotional than left-hemisphere thinking. The emphasis in most formal education is toward left-hemisphere thought development. Problem solving on the basis of reason, logic, and utility is generally rewarded, while problem solving based on sentiment, intuition, or pleasure is frequently considered tenuous and inferior.

A number of researchers have found that the most creative problem-solvers are ambidextrous in their thinking. That is, they can use both left- and right-hemisphere thinking and easily switch from one to the other (Bruner, 1966; Herrmann, 1981; Martindale, 1975). Creative ideas arise most frequently in the right hemisphere, but must be processed by the left, so creative problem-solvers use both hemispheres equally well.

Maslow (1962) differentiates between *primary* creativity, which arises from the unconscious, and *secondary* creativity, which builds on the work of others. Major breakthroughs in science, Maslow claims, have always been associated with primary creativity, even though almost all support for research and the intellectual emphasis in science is on secondary creativity. Primary creativity is most likely to emerge from right-hemisphere thinking, while secondary creativity is a product of left-hemisphere thinking. Therefore, when individuals become adept at left-hemisphere problem solving at the expense of right-hemisphere problem solving, creative problem solving suffers.

To illustrate the process of ambidextrous thinking, do the following tasks.

1. Using a pen or a pencil, draw the following on a piece of paper.
   a. The smell of bread baking
   b. The laughter of your mother
   c. The taste of licorice
   d. Your ideal job
2. In your mind, decide on the appropriate color for the following:
   a. Trigonometry
   b. The Gettysburg address
   c. Your best friend
   d. Insurance salesmen

How difficult was it for you to accomplish these tasks? What kinds of changes were required in your normal thinking processes? For many people, this task is very difficult because right- and left-hemisphere thinking are not usually combined. These tasks illustrate, however, a potential conceptual block to effective problem solving because translating from one hemisphere to the other is an important part of the creative problem-solving process.

Review of Conceptual Blocks

Up to here we have suggested that certain conceptual blocks prevent individuals from solving problems creatively. These blocks, summarized in Table 3.2, narrow the scope of problem definition, limit the alternative solutions considered, and constrain the selection of an optimal problem solution. Unfortunately, many of these conceptual blocks are unconscious, and it is only by being confronted with problems that are unsolvable because of conceptual blocks that individuals become aware that they exist. In this section we have attempted to make you aware of your own conceptual blocks by asking you to solve problems that require these mental barriers to be overcome. These conceptual blocks, of course, are not all bad because not all solutions can be improved by creative problem solving. Many managerial problems are not amenable to creative problem solving, such as problems that are short-term, fragmented, and computational. But research has shown that individuals who have developed creative problem-solving skills are far more effective with problems that are complex and that require a search for alternative solutions than others who are conceptually blocked (Dauw, 1976; Basadur, 1979; Guilford, 1962; Steiner, 1978).

In the next section we shall discuss ways these blocks can be overcome and creative problem-solving skills improved.

CONCEPTUAL BLOCKBUSTING

Conceptual blocks cannot be overcome all at once because most blocks are a product of years of habit-forming thought processes. Overcoming them requires practice at thinking in different ways over a long period of time. You will not become a skilled creative problem-solver, therefore, just by reading this chapter. On the other hand, by becoming aware of your conceptual blocks and practicing the techniques below, you can enhance your creative problem-solving skills.

Stages in Creative Thought

A first step in overcoming conceptual blocks is simply to recognize that creative problem solving is a skill that can be developed. Being a creative problem-solver is not a quality that some people have and some don't. As Dauw (1976, p. 19) has noted,

> Research results [show] . . . that nurturing creativity is not a question of increasing one's ability to score high on an IQ test, but a matter of improving one's mental attitudes and habits and cultivating creative skills that have lain dormant since childhood.

Researchers generally agree that creative problem solving involves four stages: preparation, incubation, illumination, and verification. (See Haefele, 1962, for a literature review of the stages of creative problem solving.) The preparation stage includes gathering data, defining the problem, generating alternatives, and consciously examining all available information. It is in this stage that training in creative problem solving can significantly improve effectiveness (Allen, 1974; Basadur, 1979; McKim, 1972) because the other three steps are not amenable to conscious mental work. The following discussion, therefore, is limited primarily to improving functioning in this first stage. That is, the incubation stage involves mostly unconscious mental activity in which the mind combines unrelated thoughts in the pursuit of a solution. Conscious effort is not involved. Illumination, the third stage, occurs when an insight is recognized and a creative solution is articulated. Verification is the final stage, which involves evaluating the creative solution relative to some standard of acceptability.

In the preparation stage, two types of techniques are available for improving creative problem-solving abilities. One type helps individuals think about and define the problem more effectively, the other helps individuals gather information and generate alternative solutions to the problem.

The major difference between effective, creative problem-solvers and other people is that creative problem-solvers are less constrained. They allow themselves to have access to a wider array of appropriate information. Their repertoire of problem definitions and alternative solutions is broad. This section, therefore, focuses mostly on techniques and strategies that can help you expand your repertoire of definitions and alternative solutions. As Interaction Associates (1971, p. 15) have explained:

> Flexibility in thinking is critical to good problem solving. A problem-solver should be able to conceptually dance around the problem like a good boxer, jabbing and poking, without getting caught in one place or "fixated." At any given moment, a good problem-solver should be able to apply a large number of strategies [for generating alternative definitions and solutions]. Moreover, a good problem-solver is a person who has developed, through his understanding of strategies and experiences in problem solving, a sense of appropriateness of what is likely to be the most useful strategy at any particular time.

Methods for Improving Problem Definition

Problem definition is probably the most critical step in creative problem solving. Once a definition is clear, solving the problem often is relatively simple. However, Campbell (1952), Medawar (1967), and Schumacher (1977) point out that individuals tend to define those problems they are familiar with. Medawar (1967, Introduction) notes, "Good scientists study the most important problems they think they can solve." When a problem is faced that is strange or does not appear to have a solution (what Schumacher calls "divergent problems"), a clear definition is often avoided. The problem either remains undefined or is redefined in terms of something familiar. Unfortunately, new problems may not be the same as old problems, so relying on past definitions may lead to unsuccessful problem solution (i.e., solving the wrong problem). Training in creative problem definition helps individuals see problems in alternative ways so their definitions are not so narrowly constrained.

Three general principles for improving and expanding problem definition are discussed below. As you read through the principles, take time to do the short exercises associated with each.

Make the Strange Familiar and the Familiar Strange

A well-known technique for improving creative problem solving is called *synectics* (Gordon, 1961). The goal of synectics is to help individuals critically examine their problem definitions so improved solutions can be discovered.

Problem definitions are first formed by an individual (making the strange familiar), and then the definition is made out of focus, distorted, inverted, or transposed (making the familiar strange). As when a child looks between his legs at the world or a person spends a day blindfolded, expanded understanding occurs and problem definitions are often revised when individuals are forced to view a problem differently. The distortion of definition is accomplished in synectics by having individuals use analogies and metaphors. Four types of analogies are prescribed: *personal analogy*, which requires individuals to identify themselves as the problem itself (e.g., "If I were the economy, how would I behave?"); *direct analogy*, which requires the application of parallel facts, technology, or knowledge (e.g., Brunel solved the problem of underwater construction by watching a shipworm tunneling into a tree); *symbolic analogy*, which requires a comparison of the problem with certain symbols or images (e.g., the use of mathematical symbols to conceptualize a definition); and *fantasy analogy*, which requires individuals to ask, "In my wildest fantasy, how would I wish that the problem could be solved?" (e.g., "I wish all employees would work with no supervision.")

The basic purpose of requiring people to engage in these analogies is to force a reconceptualization of a problem. When the problem is framed in terms of an analogy, the problem is temporarily forgotten and the analogy is elaborated and developed. Then when the analogy is applied to the problem, new insights about the problem can emerge from the elaborated analogy. This principle of first making the strange familiar and then making the familiar strange is an important one for creative problem definition. Figure 3.8 illustrates this process through the use of a computer graphics algorithm.

To try out this principle, generate at least four alternative definitions for the following problem:

At State University, morale was falling badly. Faculty did not want to spend time with students, and students constantly complained about the lack of interest shown by the faculty. Neither group liked the administrators.

1. Personal analogy: If I were the faculty (or students or administrators), what would be my problem?
2. Direct analogy: What else is that situation similar to that I have experienced before?

Figure 3.8　　*Making the Familiar Strange*

From Franke, 1971.

3. Symbolic analogy: Is there an image or a model that characterizes the situation?
4. Fantasy analogy: What would the ideal university be like?

Manipulate the Definition

There are a variety of ways to enlarge, alter, or replace a problem definition once it has been specified. One way is to force yourself to generate at least two alternative hypotheses for every problem definition. That is, specify at least two plausible definitions of the problem in addition to the one originally accepted. This is similar to what Rothenburg (1979) refers to as "Janusian thinking." Janus was the Roman god with two faces that looked in opposite directions. Janusian thinking means thinking contradictory thoughts at the same time—that is, conceiving two opposing ideas to be true concurrently. Rothenburg claimed, after studying fifty-four highly creative artists and scientists (e.g., Nobel Prize winners), that most major scientific breakthroughs and artistic masterpieces are a product of Janusian thinking. Creative people who actively formulate antithetical ideas and then resolve them produce the most valuable contributions to the scientific and artistic worlds. Quantum leaps in knowledge often occur.

An example is Einstein's account (1919, p. 1) of having "the happiest thought of my life." He developed the conception that, "for an observer in free fall from the roof of a house, there exists, during his fall, no gravitational field . . . in his immediate vicinity. If the observer releases any objects, they will remain, relative to him, in a state of rest. The [falling] observer is therefore justified in considering his state as one of rest." Einstein concluded, in other words, that two seemingly contradictory states were present simultaneously: motion and rest. This realization lead to the development of his revolutionary general theory of relativity.

In another study of creative potential, Rothenburg (1979) found that, when individuals were presented with a stimulus word and asked to respond with the word that first came to mind, highly creative students, Nobel scientists, and prize-winning artists responded with antonyms significantly more often than did individuals with average creativity. Rothenburg argued, based on these results, that creative people think in terms of opposites more often than do other people.

To develop the skill of Janusian thinking in problem solving, one merely needs to formulate alternative definitions, especially definitions that are contrary to the one that appears to be obvious. If both definitions are considered plausible, the resolution of their seeming contradiction can lead to highly creative solutions. Take the State University example. Specify at least one alternative definition for each one that you listed above. (For example, you might have defined the problem as the faculty being paid too little. An alternative is that they are paid too much, or that *both* conditions exist.)

A second way to manipulate problem definitions is to formulate a question checklist. This is simply a series of questions designed to help individuals think of alternatives to their accepted definitions. Some of the following are helpful questions:

1. Is there anything else?
2. Is the reverse true?
3. Is there a more general problem?
4. Can it be stated differently?
5. Who sees it differently?
6. What past experience is this like?

As an exercise, take a minute now to think of a problem you are currently experiencing. Write it down so it is formally specified. Now manipulate that definition by answering each of the six questions in the checklist.
If you can't think of a problem, try the exercise with this one: "I am not as good-looking as I would like to be."

Reverse the Definition

Reversal is similar to Janusian thinking, but instead of specifying contradictory definitions, one specifies backward definitions. That is, information is turned inside out, upside down, or back to front. Instead of thinking of the problem in the obvious way, one approaches it in reverse. For example, in Aesop's fable, the water was too low in the jug for the bird to drink. But instead of thinking of getting something out of the jug, the bird thought of putting something in. He dropped pebbles into the jug until the water was high enough to drink.

Another illustration is the story of a girl whose father wanted her to marry the richest of her suitors, while she was in love with a poor student. She told her father that she would marry the richest of the lot, but it was not clear who that was. If she asked them, they would probably lie to get her hand. If she asked them for a gift to prove their wealth, they could always borrow the money. She suggested instead that her father give each suitor a present of money, and the one whose lifestyle changed least would surely be the richest. The father praised her for her wisdom and did as she requested, whereupon the daughter eloped with the now-rich student.

Try out the following two problems to practice reversal in problem definition. Both problems were introduced by deBono (1970).

1. Draw the outline of a piece of cardboard that is shaped so that with one straight cut you can divide the piece into four smaller pieces of equal size, shape, and area. (No folding is allowed.)
2. In a single elimination basketball tournament fifty-two teams are entered. You must arrange the pairings. What is the minimum number of games that must be played to determine a winner?

Solve these problems before going on.

The quickest way to solve both problems is to reverse the focus of attention. Instead of focusing on the cut in the first problem, focus on four identical, separate pieces of cardboard and how they could go together with only one straight line between them. (Your instructor has the shapes most commonly used in deBono's studies.) For the second problem, think of the losers instead of the winner. If every team except one has to lose, there are fifty-one games to be played ($N–1$). (Most people approach this problem mathematically ($2n$) or by actually doing the pairings.)

These three principles for improving creative problem definition are summarized in Table 3.3. Their purpose is not to help you generate alternative definitions just for the sake of alternatives, but to broaden your perspectives, to help you overcome conceptual blocks, and to produce more elegant (high quality and parsimonious) solutions.

Information Gathering and Alternative Generation

A common tendency among problem-solvers is to define problems in terms of available solutions (i.e., the problem is defined as a solution) or to select the first acceptable alternative (March & Simon, 1958). This tendency leads to con-

TABLE 3.3 *Principles for Improving Problem Definition*

1. Make the strange familiar and the familiar strange.
2. Manipulate the definition.
3. Reverse the definition.

sideration of a minimal number and narrow range of alternatives in problem solving. In this regard, Guilford (1962), a pioneer in the study of creative problem solving, has asserted that the primary characteristics of highly effective creative problem-solvers are their fluency and their flexibility of thought. *Fluency* refers to the number of ideas or concepts produced in a given length of time. *Flexibility* refers to the diversity of ideas or concepts generated. While most problem-solvers consider a few homogeneous alternatives, creative problem-solvers consider many heterogeneous alternatives. The following principles are designed to help you improve your ability to generate many varied alternatives when faced with problems. They are summarized in Table 3.4.

Defer Judgment

The first principle asserts that judging alternatives should be postponed until a sufficient number have been proposed. Unfortunately, this is not always easy to do because most people tend to make quick judgments about the validity of the information they encounter. A variety of techniques have been proposed to help individuals generate alternatives for problem solution without prematurely evaluating, and hence discarding, them. Most of those techniques are based on the notion of brainstorming developed by Osborn (1953). Four main rules govern brainstorming:

1. No evaluation of any kind is permitted as alternatives are being generated. Individual energy is spent on generating ideas, not on defending them.
2. The wildest possible ideas are encouraged. It is easier to tighten alternatives up than to loosen them.
3. The quantity of ideas takes precedence over the quality. Emphasizing quality engenders judgment and evaluation.
4. Participants should build on or modify the ideas of others. Poor ideas that are added to or altered often become good ideas.

Brainstorming techniques are best used in a group setting so individuals can stimulate ideas in one another. In fact, generating alternatives in a group setting produces more and better ideas than can be produced alone (Maier, 1967). One caution about brainstorming should be made, however. Often, after a rush of common alternatives are produced at the outset of a brainstorming session, the quantity of ideas rapidly subsides. To stop there is an ineffective use of brainstorming. Only when no common solutions are available are truly creative alternatives produced in brainstorming groups.

TABLE 3.4 *Principles for Improving the Generation of Alternative Solutions.*

1. Defer judgment.
2. Expand current alternatives.
3. Combine unrelated attributes.

It is almost impossible to understand how brainstorming works without experiencing it, so you may want to try the following exercise. With two or three classmates, select a problem of common interest and spend at least a half an hour brainstorming alternative solutions. Be sure to state the problem precisely at the outset. If you can't think of a common problem, you may want to try one of these:

1. What are some alternatives to a military draft?
2. How can students have more say regarding the policies of the university (e.g., admissions, grading, or graduation requirements)?
3. What kind of compensation system best motivates employees?
4. How could all automobile deaths be eliminated on the highways?
5. What kind of sport could be introduced that could involve everyone from age two years to 102?

The purpose of this exercise is to give you experience in generating ideas that you probably hadn't thought of before. Remember to follow the four rules discussed earlier, and above all, avoid making evaluative statements about your own or others' alternatives (e.g., don't begin by saying, "This isn't a very good idea, but . . . " or, "I just had a great idea, and here it is.").

Expand Current Alternatives

Sometimes brainstorming in a group is not possible or is too costly in terms of the number of people involved and hours required. Managers pursuing a hectic organizational life often find brainstorming an unrealistic alternative. Moreover, an external stimulus or blockbuster is sometimes needed to help generate new and creative alternatives. In these circumstances, two techniques are useful for expanding the alternatives that are readily available. The first technique relies on implementing a list of manipulator verbs that alter potential solutions. Such lists have been produced by Interaction Associates (1971) and Koberg and Bagnall (1974). For example, consider the following verbs:

Multiply	Distort	Fluff up	Extrude
Divide	Rotate	Bypass	Repel
Eliminate	Flatten	Add	Protect
Subdue	Squeeze	Subtract	Segregate
Invert	Complement	Lighten	Integrate
Separate	Submerge	Repeat	Symbolize
Transpose	Freeze	Thicken	Abstract
Unify	Soften	Stretch	Dissect
Repeat	Cycle	Question	Understate
Exaggerate	Substitute	Organize	Reduce

These verbs represent procedures to be used when alternative problem solutions seem difficult to identify or the problem-solving process is bogged down in some way. For example, what new alternative solutions to the problem of low morale in a university occur when you segregate it (e.g., keep faculty and students apart), subtract it (e.g., remove one of the groups), integrate it (e.g., find ways to bring the groups together), or dissect it (e.g., focus in depth on one of the groups)?

As an illustration of how this works, take the strategy *eliminate.* It is based on the notion that sometimes it is easier to identify what one *doesn't* want than what one *does* want. Think of a college you know well. Write down all the characteristics you can think of that it possesses as an organization. (This strategy works even better if a group generates the characteristics.) Now eliminate all the characteristics you consider less than ideal. The list that remains represents effective traits of your institution. This is one way to generate criteria of organizational effectiveness when it is difficult to do so directly (see Cameron, 1978). Try the same technique using yourself, this class, your family, or one of your problems.

A second way to expand alternative problem solutions is to use the technique of *subdivision.* Subdivision is simply dividing a problem into smaller parts. March and Simon (1958, p. 193) suggest that subdivision improves problem solving by increasing the speed with which alternatives can be generated and selected. They explain,

> The mode of subdivision has an influence on the extent to which planning can proceed simultaneously on the several aspects of the problem. The more detailed the factorization of the problem, the more simultaneous activity is possible, hence, the greater the *speed of problem solving.*

To see how subdivision helps develop more alternatives and speed the process of problem solving, consider the common problem in the creativity literature of listing alternative uses for a common object. For example, in five minutes, how many uses can you list for a Ping-Pong ball? The more uses you list, the greater is your *fluency* in thinking. The more variety in the list, the greater is your *flexibility* in thinking. Uses such as the following might be included: bob for a fishing line, Christmas ornament, toy for a cat, gearshift knob, model for a molecular structure, wind gauge when hung from a string, head for a finger puppet, miniature basketball. Your list, if you did the exercise, would be much longer.

If, after you generated your list, you used the technique of subdivision, you could probably make your list longer still, and more varied. Subdivision would involve identifying specific characteristics of a Ping-Pong ball—that is, dividing it into its component attributes. For example, weight, color, texture, shape, porosity, strength, hardness, chemical properties, and conduction potential are all attributes of Ping-Pong balls that help expand the uses one can think of. By dividing an object mentally into more specific attributes, you can arrive at many more alternative uses (e.g., reflector, holder when cut in half, bug bed, ball for lottery drawing).

To get a feel for how this technique works, try the following exercise. In three minutes, write down all the things you are good at. Now apply the technique of subdivision by dividing your life into small components. What couldn't you do when you were ten years old that you can do now (division by chronology)? What social, physical, emotional, cultural, intellectual, spiritual, and biological skills do you possess (division by domain of activity)? What are your height, weight, hair color, foot size, hand size, waist size, neck size, eye color, and number of teeth (division by physical attributes)? Other questions can be added, but the point is, you can probably now increase the list of things you can do well (e.g., fill out your clothes, blink, cry, look up at people, wear a ring). List more things you are good at now that you have subdivided yourself several ways. Your list will probably at least double in length.

These two techniques—using a list of alternative strategies and sub-dividing—are useful for expanding the alternatives you can think of when try-ing to solve a problem. Not only do they help increase the sheer quantity of ideas, but new insights and higher-quality, more creative solutions often result as well.

Combine Unrelated Attributes

The third principle for improving information gathering and alternative generation helps problem-solvers expand their thinking by forcing seemingly remote elements to be integrated. That is, factors that appear to have nothing in common are compared during problem solving, and interesting new insights are obtained. Research into creative problem solving has shown that this abil-ity to see common relationships among disparate factors is a major factor dif-ferentiating creative individuals from noncreative (see Dellas & Gaier, 1970, for a review of the literature). There are at least two techniques for improving this skill: *morphological forced connections* (Koberg & Bagnall, 1974) and the *relational algorithm* (Crovitz, 1970).

With morphological forced connections, the problem-solver follows a four-step procedure. First, the problem is written down. Second, attributes of the problem situation are listed. Third, alternatives to each attribute are listed. Fourth, alternatives from the attributes list are selected and combined.

To better understand this procedure, suppose you are faced with the problem of a secretary who takes an extended lunch break almost every day despite your reminders to be on time. Think of alternative ways to solve this problem. The first solution that probably comes to mind is to sit down and have a talk with (or threaten) him or her. However, look what other alterna-tives are generated by using morphological connections:

1.   Problem: Secretary takes extended lunches.

2.   Attributes of the situation:
- More than one hour
- Beginning at 12:00
- In cafeteria
- With friends
- Daily

3.   Alternative attributes:

• 30 minutes	• Beginning at 11:00	• At home	• Alone	• Weekly
• 45 minutes	• Beginning at 11:30	• At desk	• With boss	• Every other day
• 90 minutes	• Beginning at 12:00	• In the conference room	• With staff	• Twice a week

4.   Combined attributes:
- A 30-minute lunch beginning at 12:30 in the conference room with the boss once a week.
- A 90-minute lunch beginning at 11:30 in the conference room with staff twice a week.
- A 45-minute lunch beginning at 11:00 in the cafeteria with other staff every other day.
- A 30-minute lunch beginning at 12:00 alone at the desk each day.
- Etc.

Only a few attributes of this problem have been included, so the list of alternative solutions is not as long or diverse as it could be. Even so, some alternatives for solving this problem may come to mind that wouldn't have been considered if the problem were simply stated: How do I keep that secretary from taking too much time at lunch? This technique also allows for a matrix to be devised in which all possible combinations of attributes are considered, as in Figure 3.9.

To gain experience with morphological connections, try to generate solution alternatives for the following problem. Ellen, a CPA with a private office, is continually being interrupted in her work by Rudy, a CPA in the next office, who just wants to talk. List as many attributes of the situation as you think are reasonable, then follow through with the morphological connection steps.

The second technique for combining unrelated attributes in problem solving is the relational algorithm introduced by Crovitz. This involves applying connecting words that force a relationship between two elements. For example, the following is a list of relational words:

About	Among	Because	By	If	Now
Across	And	Before	Down	In	Of
After	As	Between	For	Near	Off
Against	At	But	From	Not	On

Opposite	Over	So	Through	Under	Where
Or	Round	Then	Till	Up	While
Out	Still	Though	to	When	With

To see how this technique works, consider this statement: The manager doesn't get along with the subordinates. The two major elements of this problem are the *manager* and the *subordinates*. They are connected by the phrase "doesn't get along with," which specifies their relationship. With the relational algorithm technique, the relational words in the problem statement are taken out and replaced with other relational words to see if new alternatives for solving the problem occur. For example, instead of the manager *doesn't get along* with subordinates, the following are possibilities for solution:

1. The manager *among* subordinates
2. The manager *as* subordinate
3. The manager *and* subordinates
4. The manager *between* subordinates
5. The manager *for* subordinates
6. The manager *near* subordinates
7. The manager *under* subordinates
8. The manager *with* subordinates

By connecting the two elements of the problem in different ways, you can uncover new possibilities for problem solution. You can also connect single elements in the problem to themselves with the relational words to generate solutions:

Figure 3.9   *Problem-solving Matrix*

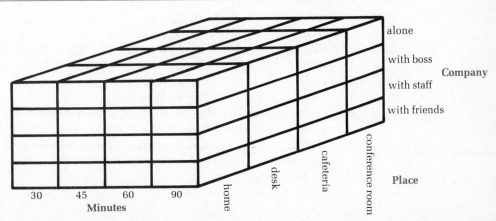

1. Subordinates *opposite* subordinates
2. The manager *through* the manager (management by proxy)
3. Subordinates *over* subordinates
4. The manager *not* the manager (hidden management)

Another option is to reverse the order of the elements in the problem:

1. Subordinates *from* the manager
2. Subordinates *as* the manager
3. Subordinates *round* the manager
4. Subordinates *while* the manager

Problems frequently involve more than two elements, and the relational algorithm is useful with more complex problems as well. For example, in the problem of low morale at the university, the major elements may be students, faculty, administrators, office hours, and classes. Varying the relational words among each of those elements creates a large number of alternatives for solution that may not have been considered otherwise.

These two techniques—morphological forced connections and the relational algorithm—simply help problem-solvers generate alternative solutions by combining problem elements in new ways. As with the other techniques discussed in this chapter, they may not be useful in all types of problems, particularly computational problems for which all information is available and all alternatives are known. However, in most cases when the definition of the problem could be improved by additional information or new ways of thinking or when all the alternative solutions are not known, these techniques can be very helpful in improving the effectiveness of creative problem solving.

SUMMARY AND BEHAVIORAL GUIDELINES

As we have pointed out, a well-developed model exists for solving problems. It consists of four separate and sequential stages: defining the problem, generating alternatives, evaluating and selecting an alternative, and implementing it and following it up. This model, however, is mainly useful for solving straightforward problems. Many problems faced by managers are not of this type, and frequently managers are called on to exercise creative problem-solving skills. That is, they must broaden their perspective of the problem and develop alternative solutions that are not immediately obvious.

We have discussed and illustrated eight major conceptual blocks that inhibit most people's creative problem-solving abilities. Conceptual blocks are mental obstacles that artificially constrain problem definition and solution, and keep most people from being effective creative problem-solvers. The eight conceptual blocks are summarized in Table 3.2.

Overcoming these conceptual blocks is a matter of skill development and practice in thinking, not a matter of innate ability. Everyone can become a skilled creative problem-solver with practice. Just becoming aware of these thinking inhibitors helps individuals overcome them. We also discussed three major principles for improving creative problem definition, and three major principles for improving the creative generation of alternative solutions. Certain techniques were described that can help implement these six principles.

Becoming proficient in creative problem solving takes practice, but we have pointed out specific ways you can do so. Below are specific behavioral action guidelines to help your skill practice:

1. Follow the four-step procedure when solving problems. Keep the steps separate, and do not take shortcuts. (See Table 3.1.)
2. When approaching a difficult problem, try to overcome your conceptual blocks by doing the following:
   a. Using lateral thinking in addition to vertical thinking;
   b. Using several thought languages instead of just one;
   c. Being sensitive to stereotypes based on past problem experience;
   d. Deleting superflous information and filling in important missing information;
   e. Avoiding artificially constraining problem boundaries;
   f. Identifying underlying themes and commonalities in seemingly unrelated factors;
   g. Overcoming a fear of being inquisitive;
   h. Using both right- and left-hemisphere thinking. (See Table 4.2.)
3. When defining a problem, make the strange familiar and the familiar strange by using metaphor and analogy to first focus and then distort and refocus the definition.
4. Manipulate the problem definition by developing at least two alternative (opposite) definitions and applying a question checklist.
5. Reverse the problem definition by beginning with the end result and working backwards.
6. In generating potential problem solutions, defer judging any until all have been proposed. Use the four rules of brainstorming: do not evaluate, encourage wild ideas, encourage quantity, build on others' ideas.
7. Expand the list of current alternative solutions by using a variety of strategies (e.g., eliminate, purge, predict, understate, systematize) or by subdividing the problem into its attributes.
8. Increase the number of possible solutions by combining unrelated problem attributes. Morphological connections and relational algorithms are helpful.

REFERENCES

Allen, J. L. *Conceptual blockbusting.* San Francisco: W. H. Freeman, 1974.

Barron, F. X. *Creativity and psychological health.* New York: Van Nostrand, 1963.

Basadur, M. S. *Training in creative problem solving: Effects of deferred judgment and problem finding and solving in an industrial research organization.* Unpublished doctoral dissertation, University of Cincinnati, 1979.

Beveridge, W. *The art of scientific investigation.* New York: Random House, 1960.

Bower, M. Nurturing innovation in an organization. In G. A. Steiner (Ed.), *The creative organization.* Chicago: University of Chicago Press, 1965.

Broadwell, M. M. *The new supervisor.* Reading, Mass.: Addison-Wesley, 1972.

Bruner, J. S. *On knowing: Essays for the left hand.* Cambridge: Harvard University Press, 1966.

Cameron, K. S. Measuring organizational effectiveness in institutions of higher education. *Administrative Science Quarterly,* 1978, *23,* 604–632.

Campbell, N. *What is science?* New York: Dover, 1952.

Crovitz, H. F. *Galton's walk.* New York: Harper & Row, 1970.

Dauw, D. C. *Creativity and innovation in organizations.* Dubuque, Iowa: Kendall Hunt, 1976.

deBono, E. *New think.* New York: Basic Books, 1968.

Dellas, M., & Gaier, E. L. Identification of creativity: The individual. *Psychological Bulletin,* 1970, *73,* 55–73.

Drath, W. H. Out of the blue. In *Issues and observations.* Greensboro, N.C.: Center for Creative Leadership, 1981.

Drucker, P. F. *Management.* New York: Harper & Row, 1974.

Einstein, A. *Fundamental ideas and methods of relativity theory, presented in their development.* (c. 1919, G. Holton,). Unpublished manuscript.

Elbing, A. *Behavioral decisions in organizations.* Glenview, Ill.: Scott, Foresman, 1978.

Eysenck, H. *Know your own I.Q.* New York: Penguin, 1962.

Filley, A. C., House, R. J., & Kerr, S. *Managerial process and organizational behavior.* Glenview, Ill.: Scott, Foresman, 1976.

Gardner, J. W. *Self-renewal.* New York: Harper & Row, 1965.

Gordon, W. J. J. *Synectics: The development of creative capacity.* New York: Collier, 1961.

Guilford, J. P. Creativity: Its measurement and development. In S. J. Parnes & H. F. Harding (Eds.), *A sourcebook for creative thinking.* New York: Scribner, 1962.

————. *The nature of human intelligence.* New York: McGraw-Hill, 1967.

Haefele, J. W. *Creativity and innovation.* New York: Reinhold, 1962.

Hermann, N. The creative brain. *Training and Development Journal,* 1981, *35,* 11–16.

Hermone, R. Creativity: The supervisor's secret. *Supervisory Management,* 1979, *29,* 24–28.

Huber, G. P. *Managerial decision making.* Glenview, Ill.: Scott, Foresman, 1980.

Interaction Associates. *Tools for change.* San Francisco: Interaction Associates, 1971.

Koberg, D., & Bagnall, J. *The universal traveler: A soft-systems guidebook to creativity, problem solving, and the process of design.* Los Altos, Calif.: William Kaufmann, 1974.

Koestler, A. *The act of creation.* New York: Dell, 1967.

Leavitt, H. J. *Managerial psychology.* Chicago: University of Chicago Press, 1972.

Maier, N. R. F. Assets and liabilities of group problem solving: The need for an integrative function. *Psychological Review,* 1967, *74,* 239–249.

Maier, N. R. F. *Problem solving and creativity in individuals and groups.* Belmont, Calif.: Brooks/Cole, 1970.

March, J. G., & Simon, H. A. *Organizations.* New York: Wiley, 1958.

Martindale, C. What makes creative people different. *Psychology Today,* 1975, *9,* 44–50.

Maslow, A. Emotional blocks to creativity. In S. J. Parnes & H. F. Harding (Eds.), *A sourcebook for creative thinking.* New York: Scribner, 1962.

McKim, R. H. *Experiences in visual thinking.* Monterey, Calif.: Brooks/Cole, 1972.

Medawar, P. B. *The art of the soluable.* London, Methuen, 1967.

Mintzberg, H. *The nature of managerial work.* New York: Harper & Row, 1973.

Olton, R., & Crutchfield, R. Developing the skills of productive thinking. Cited in R. H. McKim (Ed.), *Experiences in visual thinking.* Monterey, Calif.: Brooks/Cole, 1972.

Osborn, A. *Applied imagination.* New York: Sribner, 1953.

Parnes, S. J. Can creativity be increased? In S. J. Parnes & H. F. Harding (Eds.), *A sourcebook for creative thinking.* New York: Sribner, 1962.

Rothenburg, A. *The emerging goddess.* Chicago: University of Chicago Press, 1979.

Rothenburg, A. Creative contradictions. *Psychology Today,* 1979, *13,* 55–62.

Schumacher, E. F. *A guide for the perplexed.* New York: Harper & Row, 1977.

Steiner, G. *The creative organization.* Chicago: University of Chicago Press, 1978.

Tannenbaum, R., & Schmidt, W. H. How to choose a leadership pattern. *Harvard Business Review,* 1958, *3,* 95–101.

Taylor, C. W., & Barron, F. X. *Scientific creativity: Its recognition and development.* New York: Wiley, 1963.

Thompson, J. D., & Tuden, A. Strategies, structures, and processes of organizational decision. In J. D. Thompson & A. Tuden (Eds.), *Comparative studies in administration.* Pittsburgh: University of Pittsburgh Press, 1959.

Torrance, E. P. Scientific views of creativity and factors affecting its growth. *Daedalus,* 1965, *94,* 663–682.

Vroom, V. H., & Yetton, P. W. *Leadership and decision making.* Pittsburgh: University of Pittsburgh Press, 1973.

Vygotsky, L. *Thought and language.* Cambridge, Mass.: MIT Press, 1962.

Watzlawick, P., Weakland, J., & Fisch, R. *Change.* New York: Norton, 1974.

Weick, K. E. *The social psychology of organizing.* Reading, Mass.: Addison-Wesley, 1979.   ∎

■ *Skill Analysis*

Admiral Kimmel's Failure at Pearl Harbor

Irving L. Lanis and Leon Mann

In the summer of 1941, as relations between the United States and Japan were rapidly deteriorating, Admiral Kimmel, Commander in Chief of the Pacific Fleet, received many warnings concerning the imminence of war. During this period he worked out a plan in collaboration with his staff at Pearl Harbor, which gave priority to training key personnel and supplying basic equipment to U.S. outposts in the Far East. The plan took account of the possibility of a long, hard war with Japan and the difficulties of mobilizing scarce resources in manpower and material. At that time, Admiral Kimmel and his staff were keenly aware of the risks of being unprepared for war with Japan, as well as of the high costs and risks involved in preparing for war. They appear to have been relatively optimistic about being able to develop a satisfactory military plan and about having sufficient time in which to implement it. In short, all the conditions were present for vigilance, and it seems likely that this coping pattern characterized their planning activity.

But during the late fall of 1941, as the warnings became increasingly more ominous, a different pattern of coping behavior emerged. Admiral Kimmel and his staff continued to cling to the policy to which they had committed themselves, discounting each fresh warning and failing to note that more and more signs were pointing to the possibility that Pearl Harbor might be a target for a surprise air attack. They repeatedly renewed their decision to continue using the available resources primarily for training green sailors and soldiers and for supplying bases close to Japan, rather than instituting an adequate alert that would give priority to defending Pearl Harbor against enemy attack.

Knowing that their sector and the rest of the U.S. military organization were not ready for a shooting war, they clung to an unwarranted set of rationalizations. The Japanese, they thought, would not launch an attack against any American possession; and if by some remote chance they decided to do so, it certainly wouldn't be at Pearl Harbor. Admiral Kimmel and his staff acknowledged that Japan *could* launch a surprise attack in any direction, but remained convinced that it would not be launched in their direction. They saw no reason to change their course. Therefore, they continued to give peacetime weekend leave to the majority of the naval forces in Hawaii and allowed the many warships in the Pacific Fleet to remain anchored at Pearl Harbor, as sitting ducks . . . Kimmel regularly discussed each warning with members of his staff. At times he became emotionally aroused and obtained reassurance from

SOURCE: I. L. Janis and L. Mann, *Decision making* (New York: Free Press, 1977), pp. 120–123.

the members of his in-group. He shared with them a number of rationalizations that bolstered his decision to ignore the warnings. On November 27, 1941, for example, he received an explicit "war warning" from the chief of naval operations in Washington, which stirred up his concern but did not impel him to take any new protective action. This message was intended as a strong follow-up to an earlier warning, which Kimmel had received only three days earlier, stating that war with Japan was imminent and that "a surprise aggressive movement in any direction including attack on Philippines or Guam is a possibility." The new warning asserted that "an aggressive move by Japan is expected within the next few days" and instructed Kimmel to "execute appropriate defensive deployment" preparatory to carrying out the naval war plan. The threat conveyed by this warning was evidently strong enough to induce Kimmel to engage in prolonged discussion with his staff about what should be done. But their vigilance seems to have been confined to paying careful attention to the way the warning was worded. During the meeting, members of the staff pointed out to Kimmel that Hawaii was not specifically mentioned as a possible target in either of the two war warnings, whereas other places—the Philippines, Malaya, and other remote areas—were explicitly named. Kimmel went along with the interpretation that the ambiguities they had detected in the wording must have meant that Pearl Harbor was not supposed to be regarded as a likely target, even though the message seemed to be saying that it was. The defensive quality that entered into this judgment is revealed by the fact that Kimmel made no effort to use his available channels of communication to Washington to find out what really had been meant. He ended up agreeing with the members of his advisory group that "there was no chance of a surprise air attack on Hawaii at that particular time."

Since he judged Pearl Harbor not to be vulnerable, Kimmel decided that the limited-alert condition that had been instituted months earlier would be sufficient. He assumed, however, that all U.S. Army units in Hawaii had gone on a full alert in response to this war warning, so that antiaircraft and radar units under army control would be fully activated. But, again, reflecting his defensive lack of interest in carrying out tasks that required acknowledging the threat, Kimmel failed to inquire of Army headquarters exactly what was being done. As a result, he did not discover until after the disaster on December 7 that the Army, too, was on only a limited alert, designed exclusively to protect military installations against local sabotage.

On December 3, 1941, Kimmel engaged in intensive discussion with two members of his staff upon receiving a fresh warning from naval headquarters in Washington stating that U.S. cryptographers had decoded a secret message from Tokyo to all diplomatic missions in the United States and other countries, ordering them to destroy their secret codes. Kimmel realized that this type of order could mean that Japan was making last-minute preparations before launching an attack against the United States. Again, he and his advisers devoted considerable attention to the exact wording of this new, worrisome warning. They made much of the fact that the dispatch said "most" of the codes but not "all." They concluded that the destruction of the codes should be interpreted as a routine precautionary measure and not as a sign that Japan was planning to attack an American possession. Again, no effort was made to find out from Washington how the intelligence units there interpreted the message. But the lengthy discussions and the close attention paid to the wording of these messages imply that they did succeed in at least temporarily inducing decisional conflict.

By December 6, 1941, the day before the attack, Kimmel was aware of a large accumulation of extremely ominous signs. In addition to receiving the official war warnings during the preceding week, he had received a private letter three days earlier from Admiral Stark in Washington stating that both President Roosevelt and Secretary of State Hull now thought that the Japanese were getting ready to launch a surprise attack. Then on December 6, Kimmel received another message from Admiral Stark containing emergency war orders pertaining to the destruction of secret and confidential documents in American bases on outlying Pacific islands. On that same day, the FBI in Hawaii informed Kimmel that the local Japanese consulate had been burning its papers for the last two days. Furthermore, Kimmel's chief naval intelligence officer had reported to him that day, as he had on the preceding days, that despite fresh efforts to pick up Japanese naval signal calls, the whereabouts of all six of Japan's aircraft carriers still remained a mystery. (U.S. Naval Combat Intelligence had lost track of the Japanese aircraft carriers in mid-November, when they started to move toward Hawaii for the planned attack on Pearl Harbor.)

Although the various warning signs, taken together, clearly indicated that Japan was getting ready to launch an attack against the United States, they remained ambiguous as to exactly where the attack was likely to be. There was also considerable "noise" mixed in with the warning signals, including intelligence reports that huge Japanese naval forces were moving toward Malaya. But, inexplicably, there was a poverty of imagination on the part of Kimmel and his staff with regard to considering the possibility that Pearl Harbor itself might be one of the targets of a Japanese attack.

The accumulated warnings, however, were sufficiently impressive to Kimmel to generate considerable concern. On the afternoon of December 6, as he was pondering alternative courses of action, he openly expressed his anxiety to two of his staff officers. He told them he was worried about the safety of the fleet at Pearl Harbor in view of all the disturbing indications that Japan was getting ready for a massive attack somewhere. One member of the staff immediately reassured him that "the Japanese could not possibly be able to proceed in force against Pearl Harbor when they had so much strength concentrated in their Asiatic operations." Another told him that the limited-alert condition he had ordered many weeks earlier would certainly be sufficient and nothing more was needed. "We finally decided," Kimmel subsequently recalled, "that what we had [already] done was still good and we would stick to it." At the end of the discussion Kimmel "put his worries aside" and went off to a dinner party.

DISCUSSION QUESTIONS

1.   What conceptual blocks are illustrated in this case?

2.   Was the problem-solving model discussed at the beginning of the chapter followed by Kimmel and his advisors? What mistakes were made on their use of the model?

3.   What kinds of conceptual block-busters could have been useful to Kimmel? If you were his advisor, what would you have suggested to help his problem-solving processes?

4.   What kinds of formalized structures or procedures could have been established to help protect Kimmel against poor problem solving? When faced with a potential problem of war, what mechanisms could have been used to aid the problem-solving process?

The Double Helix

James D. Watson

The following are excerpts from James D. Watson's description of his discovery of the double helix structure of DNA. This discovery not only won him a Nobel Prize, but revolutionized biology. Watson was working at Cambridge University with Francis Crick (a co-winner of the Nobel Prize) when they became obsessed with finding the structure for DNA. Watson describes the breakthroughs, following months of studying the results of chemical and X-ray tests, that led to his discovery.

The next few days saw Francis becoming increasingly agitated by my failure to stick close to the molecular models. It did not matter that before his tenish entrance I was usually in the lab. Almost every afternoon, knowing that I was on the tennis court, he would fretfully twist his head away from his work to see the polynucleotide backbone unattended. Moreover, after tea I would show up for only a few minutes of minor fiddling before dashing away to have sherry with the girls at Pop's. Francis' grumbles did not disturb me, however, because further refining of our latest backbone without a solution to the bases would not represent a real step forward.

  I went ahead spending most evenings at the films, vaguely dreaming that any moment the answer would suddenly hit me . . .

  Even during good films I found it almost impossible to forget the bases.

SOURCE: James D. Watson, *The double helix* (New York: Mentor Books, 1969), pp. 114–17, 120, 123, 125, 127, and 128.

The fact that we had at last produced a stereochemically reasonable configuration for the backbone was always in the back of my head . . .

Generally, it was late in the evening after I got back to my rooms that I tried to puzzle out the mystery of the bases. Their formulas were written out in J. N. Davidson's little book *The Biochemistry of Nucleic Acids,* a copy of which I kept in Clare. So I could be sure that I had the correct structures when I drew tiny pictures of the bases on sheets of Cavendish notepaper. My aim was somehow to arrange the centrally located bases in such a way that the backbones on the outside were completely regular—that is, giving the sugar-phosphate groups of each nucleotide identical three-dimensional configurations. But each time I tried to come up with a solution I ran into the obstacle that the four bases each had a quite different shape. Moreover, there were many reasons to believe that the sequences of the bases of a given polynucleotide chain were very irregular. Thus, unless some very special trick existed, randomly twisting two polynucleotide chains around one another should result in a mess. In some places the bigger bases must touch each other, while in other regions, where the smaller bases would lie opposite each other, there must exist a gap or else their backbone regions must buckle in . . .

My doodling of the bases on paper at first got nowhere, regardless of whether or not I had been to a film. Even the necessity to expunge *Ecstasy* from my mind did not lead to passable hydrogen bonds, and I fell asleep hoping that an undergraduate party the next afternoon at Downing would be full of pretty girls. But my expectations were dashed as soon as I arrived to spot a group of healthy hockey players and several pallid debutantes. Bertrand also instantly perceived he was out of place, and as we passed a polite interval before scooting out, I explained how I was racing Peter's father [Linus Pauling] for the Nobel Prize.

Not until the middle of the next week, however, did a nontrivial idea emerge. It came while I was drawing the fused rings of adenine on paper. Suddenly, I realized the potentially profound implications of a DNA structure in which the adenine residue formed hydrogen bonds similar to those found in crystals of pure adenine. If DNA was like this, each adenine residue would form two hydrogen bonds to an adenine residue related to it by a 180-degree rotation. Most important, two symmetrical hydrogen bonds could also hold together pairs of guanine, cytosine, or thymine. I thus started wondering whether each DNA molecule consisted of two chains with identical base sequences held together by hydrogen bonds between pairs of identical bases. There was the complication, however, that such a structure could not have a regular backbone, since the purines (adenine and guanine) and the pyrimidines (thymine and cytosine) have different shapes. The resulting backbone would have to show minor in-and-out buckles depending upon whether pairs of purines or pyrimidines were in the center.

Despite the messy backbone, my pulse began to race. If this was DNA, I should create a bombshell by announcing its discovery. The existence of two intertwined chains with identical base sequences could not be a chance matter. Instead it would strongly suggest that one chain in each molecule had at some earlier stage served as the template for the synthesis of the other chain ...

As the clock went past midnight I was becoming more and more pleased. There had been far too many days when Francis and I worried that the DNA structure might turn out to be superficially very dull, suggesting nothing about either its replication or its function in controlling cell biochemistry. But now, to my delight and amazement, the answer was turning out to be profoundly interesting. For over two hours I happily lay awake with pairs of adenine residues whirling in front of my closed eyes. Only for brief moments did the fear shoot through me that an idea this good could be wrong ...

... My scheme was torn to shreds by the following noon. Against me was the awkward chemical fact that I had chosen the wrong tautomeric forms of guanine and thymine ...

When I got to our still empty office the following morning, I quickly cleared away the papers from my desk top so that I would have a large, flat surface on which to form pairs of bases held together by hydrogen bonds. Though I initially went back to my like-with-like prejudices, I saw all too well that they led nowhere. When Jerry came in I looked up, saw that it was not Francis, and began shifting the bases in and out of various other pairing possibilities. Suddenly I became aware that an adenine-thymine pair held together by two hydrogen bonds was identical in shape to a guanine-cytosine pair held together by at least two hydrogen bonds. All the hydrogen bonds seemed to form naturally; no fudging was required to make the two types of base pairs identical in shape. Quickly I called Jerry over to ask him whether this time he had any objection to my new base pairs.

When he said no, my morale skyrocketed, for I suspected that we now had the answer to the riddle of why the number of purine residues exactly equaled the number of pyrimidine residues. Two irregular sequences of bases could be regularly packed in the center of a helix if a purine always hydrogen-bonded to a pyrimidine. Furthermore, the hydrogen-bonding requirement meant that adenine would always pair with thymine, while guanine could pair only with cytosine. Chargaff's rules then suddenly stood out as a consequence of a double-helical structure for DNA. Even more exciting, this type of double helix suggested a replication scheme much more satisfactory than my briefly considered like-with-like pairing ...

Upon his arrival Francis did not get more than halfway through the door before I let loose that the answer to everything was in our hands. Though as a matter of principle he maintained skepticism for a few moments, the similarly shaped A-T and G-C pairs had their expected impact. His quickly pushing the bases together in a number of different ways did not reveal any other way to satisfy Chargaff's rules.

... Francis' preoccupation with DNA quickly became full-time. The first afternoon following the discovery that A-T and G-C base pairs had similar shapes, he went back to his thesis measurements, but his effort was ineffectual. Constantly he would pop up from his chair, worriedly look at the cardboard models, fiddle with other combinations, and then, the period of momentary uncertainty over, look satisfied and tell me how important our work was. I enjoyed Francis' words, even though they lacked the casual sense of understatement known to be the correct way to behave in Cambridge. It seemed almost unbelievable that the DNA structure was solved, that the answer was incredibly exciting, and that our names would be associated with the double helix as Pauling's was with the alpha helix . . .

The following morning I felt marvelously alive when I awoke. On the way to the Whim I slowly walked toward the Clare Bridge, staring up at the gothic pinnacles of the King's College Chapel that stood out sharply against the spring sky. I briefly stopped and looked over at the perfect Georgian features of the recently cleaned Gibbs Building, thinking that much of our success was due to the long uneventful periods when we walked among the colleges or unobtrusively read the new books that came into Heffer's Bookstore. After contentedly poring over *The Times,* I wandered into the lab to see Francis, unquestionably early, flipping the cardboard base pairs about an imaginary line. As far as a compass and ruler could tell him, both sets of base pairs neatly fitted into the backbone configuration. As the morning wore on, Max and John successively came by to see if we still thought we had it. Each got a quick, concise lecture from Francis, during the second of which I wandered down to see if the shop could be speeded up to produce the purines and pyrimidines later than afternoon.

Only a little encouragement was needed to get the final soldering accomplished in the next couple of hours. The brightly shining metal plates were then immediately used to make a model in which for the first time all the DNA components were present. In about an hour I had arranged the atoms in positions which satisfied both the X-ray data and the laws of stereochemistry. The resulting helix was right-handed with the two chains running in opposite directions. Only one person can easily play with a model, and so Francis did not try to check my work until I backed away and said that I thought everything fitted. While one interatomic contact was slightly shorter than optimal, it was not out of line with several published values, and I was not disturbed. Another fifteen minutes' fiddling by Francis failed to find anything wrong, though for brief intervals my stomach felt uneasy when I saw him frowning. In each case he became satisfied and moved on to verify that another interatomic contact was reasonable. Everything thus looked very good when we went back to have supper with Odile.

DISCUSSION QUESTIONS

1. What kinds of conceptual block-busting activities did Watson engage in while he was trying to figure out the DNA structure?

2. What principles of creating problem solving can you derive from this brief account? (For a more complete account, read Watson's *The Double Helix*, Mentor, 1968.)

3. How many thinking languages are evidenced in this account?

4. In what ways is the problem of the structure of DNA similar to the ambiguous problems that arise in organizations? ■

■ *Skill Practice*

Tidewater College

In a small group, define and solve the problem(s) discussed in this case. Use the principles described in the behavioral guidelines. An observer should provide feedback on the extent to which group members applied these principles effectively, using the form that follows.

Tidewater College was founded by a local church in 1925 to give local residents of this rural, mountain area an opportunity to get a college education. For thirty-five years the college had taught about 450 students a year, focusing on liberal arts and teacher preparation. Then, during the 1960s, because of the baby boom, the student body increased to 1,750 students a year. Faculty teaching loads were greatly overextended, and the Old Main building, which comprised the entire campus, began to be woefully inadequate.

The president, who clearly based his planning decisions on faith, decided that a whole new campus was in order. At the end of the spring semester, 1969, ground was broken for this new campus, which eventually included four five-story buildings in the meadow behind Old Main. The new campus was completed in August 1971, the year enrollments peaked. Unfortunately, the buildings were not financed by a local bond issue or fund-raising campaign. Therefore, to pay for the indebtedness on the new buildings, government grants were obtained which promised to provide many programs, but which Tidewater was not equipped to handle.

The current situation can be described as follows:

1. Enrollment is down to 600.
2. Government grants have dried up.
3. The college is still responsible to the government for the completion of certain programs.
4. Because of the government contracts, the college has experienced "program proliferation," and there is no coordination of the courses being offered. Additionally, teachers are forced to teach courses they know little about.
5. Student morale is very low, and student vandalism has averaged about $500 a week for several years.
6. Teacher morale is also low, since teachers much teach courses outside their areas of expertise and have not received a pay raise in four years.
7. The college is located in a mountain community of 2,000 people. The closest town is twenty miles away and has a population of 30,000 and no major industry, and there are three other small,

private colleges in the area. A popular state college is within fifty miles.

8. The college has a reputation in town for being poorly managed and having unruly students whom the trustees will not allow to be disciplined.
9. The last president resigned in despair.
10. The college still has a large capital debt, due to the building boom in the late 1960s.

If you were the new president of Tidewater, how would you creatively solve these problems?

OBSERVATION SHEET

Research on group problem solving has shown that four separate stages should be identifiable in effective problem solving. These questions will help you look for and identify the extent to which the group engages in each stage.

1.   Was the problem defined explicitly?
  a. To what extent was information sought from all group members?

  b. Did the group avoid defining the problem as a disguised solution?

  c. What techniques were used to expand or alter the definition of the problem?

2.   Were alternatives proposed before any alternative solution was evaluated?
  a. Did all group members help generate alternative solutions?

  b. Did people build on the alternatives proposed by others?

  c. What techniques were used to generate more creative alternatives for solving the problem?

3.   Was the optimal solution selected?
  a. Were alternatives evaluated systematically?

  b. Was consideration given to the probable long-term effects of each alternative?

4.   Was consideration given to how and when the solution should be implemented?

a. Was an opportunity for feedback and evaluation provided in the implementation of the solution?

b. Was the solution accepted because it solved the problem under consideration, or because of other benefits it provided?

5. Were these four steps identifiable in the group's problem-solving process:
    a. Problem definition

    b. Generation of alternatives (without evaluation)

    c. Evaluation and selection of alternatives

    d. Consideration of implementation and follow-up

6. How creative was the group in defining and solving the problem?

7. What techniques of conceptual block busting did the group use?

Acks and Blogs

This exercise presents a problem that will require you to work in a group. Groups of five or six people are best. One person should serve as an observer to record the methods used by the group and individuals within the group to solve the problem. The goal is to have the group solve the problem as quickly as possible.

Pretend that ACKS and BLOGS represent a new way of measuring distance, and that CEPES, DATS, and FUMMS represent a new way of measuring time. A woman catches a train in Giz City and travels to Hakk City. She must travel through Jel City and Kyt City on her way. The task of your group is to determine how many DATS the entire trip took. Do not select a formal leader for your group. Work on the problem using whatever strategy you think will bring you the right answer the most quickly.

Each of the group members will have several items of information presented to them by the instructor. These items may be shared orally with other group members, but they cannot be written down and passed to others. When you have reached a solution that *all* members of the group can agree on, raise your hand.

After you have solved this problem, analyze the strategies used by the group and the individuals in it to solve the problem. Which strategies seemed to work best? Which problem-solving strategies did you feel most comfortable with? Which thinking language did you use? What conceptual blocks needed to be overcome? How did you overcome them?   ■

■ *Skill Application*

Application Exercises

1. Teach someone else how to solve problems creatively. Record your experience in your journal.

2. Think of a problem that is important to you right now for which there is no obvious solution. Use the principles and techniques discussed in the chapter to work out a creative solution to that problem. Spend the time it takes to do a good job. (It may take several days or longer.) Describe the experience in your journal.

3. Help direct a group (your family, roommates, social club, church, or whatever) in a creative problem-solving exercise using any techniques discussed in the chapter that seem to apply. Record your experience in your journal.

4. Write a short paper answering the following questions:
   a. Under what conditions is creative problem solving most needed in management?
   b. Under what conditions is creative problem solving inappropriate in management? ■

4 Establishing Supportive Communication

■ *Skill Preassessment*

Response Inventory
Managing the Management Course

■ *Skill Learning*

Resolving Interpersonal Problems Through Communication

■ *Skill Analysis*

Get Off My Back
Rejected Plans

■ *Skill Practice*

United Chemical Company
Empathy Exercise
Reflective Listening Exercise

■ *Skill Application*

Application Exercises

■ *Skill Preassessment*

Response Inventory

In this exercise are a series of statements by a person about an aspect of a situation he or she faces. Following each statement are six possible responses. Circle the letter before the one that best represents what you would say to the speaker if you were attempting to be helpful.

1. I've planned all of my life to go to an Ivy League law school, and nothing is going to stand in my way. I've got to have a good grade point average to make it, and I'm not afraid to do what I have to do to get what I want. I'll never be satisfied with second best.

    a. You see yourself as a really ambitious person, don't you?
    b. It sounds as if you may be reacting to some insecurities about your intellectual abilities by making high grades so important.
    c. Why do you feel that going to an Ivy League law school is so important?
    d. Not being satisfied with second best doesn't mean you have to emphasize grades at the expense of everything else, does it?
    e. Oh, I'm sure you'll do well enough to get into law school. I wouldn't worry so much about it if I were you.
    f. I think you're putting too much emphasis on grades and Ivy League schools.

2. I've been in this job now for six months, and I hardly know anyone at all in the company. I just can't seem to make friends or to be accepted by other people. Most people are out for themselves anyway, and they really don't care to go out of their way to be friendly. The people in this place are mostly very cold.

    a. Don't be upset about not making friends so soon. Things will get better, you'll see.
    b. When you first meet people, what do you say? Are you friendly to them first?
    c. You say that you don't know anyone, and yet you say they are cold. How do you know they're cold if you don't know them?
    d. You're feeling that people haven't accepted you in this company?
    e. I'll bet that you must be feeling pretty lonely and insecure after six months of this.
    f. It's not as bad as you make it out to be. When I first joined the company it took me more than six months to get adjusted, and I still don't feel accepted by the secretarial staff.

3. Since coming to school last fall I've really felt sick. It makes me so depressed because I can't concentrate in classes and I can't study very well. The trouble is, I'm afraid to go to the doctor because I'm afraid it might be cancer. My mother had it, and my grandmother and my aunt. I've lived with this fear all my life. I just don't know what to do.

   a. Aside from your fear, have you any symptoms of cancer?
   b. It sounds as if you really have a terrific fear of cancer.
   c. I think you're wrong not to go to the doctor. That's just being immature.
   d. I'm sure you're OK. The chances of your having cancer are almost nil. Besides, it's not hereditary.
   e. Your anxiety about not doing well in classes and not being able to study may be the thing that's causing your illness. It could be self-perpetuating.
   f. I've had the same feeling sometimes. Especially last year when I thought I had a bleeding ulcer. Boy, I was scared.

4. I hate my boss. He is the most autocratic demagogue you can image. I've never worked around anyone I despise more than him. If I could, without getting fired, I'd punch him out. I don't like feeling like this about another person, but he's such a turkey.

   a. You sound as if you're having difficulty dealing with rigid control and authority.
   b. I know how you feel because last year we had a woman in the department who would drive anybody crazy. She was the ultimate in the dominating mother-figure.
   c. I'm sure you'll work it out. Things will get better, I'm sure.
   d. You're going to have real problems unless you work this out. I think you're overreacting.
   e. You sound as if you would really prefer having a different boss.
   f. Why is it that you're feeling so strongly about him?

5. What I want to know is, what happened on the last promotion decision? I thought I was in line for it. In fact, no one else in the department has had my performance record, and to hear people talk, they thought it was a foregone conclusion. I'm really disappointed that someone from outside was appointed over me. I really don't think it's fair. Just what does it take to get a promotion around here, anyway?

   a. Has something happened, George, that makes you bring this up at this time?
   b. Don't be discouraged, George, we like your work. Just be patient and I'm sure a promotion will come along. We'll do all we can to help you get ready.
   c. I hate to say it, George, but I think you're wrong about this. You really weren't in line for this job.

d. In other words, George, you feel kind of puzzled about just where you stand with the company. Is that it?

e. It seems to me that you're just insecure in your job, and you seem to be interpreting being passed over as a challenge to your personal competence.

f. I felt the same way on my first job, George. When Mary Hansen was promoted before I was, I was sure it was because she was a woman and not because of performance. It really frosted me.

6. Boy, I'm in a terrible fix. I'm in love with a really great girl, and she loves me. I'm sure of that. But I'm not good enough for her. I can't ask her to marry me. I've had affairs with other girls, but she has saved herself just for me—for our marriage. She doesn't know about all the other girls, but I know it will come up someday. No, I couldn't marry her and have children and have her—and them—find out there have been other women.

a. Well, why don't you just go ahead and tell her? It sounds like you're being a coward.

b. You seem to be saying that you're afraid to face her because she might break up with you, and you couldn't stand the rejection.

c. Why are you so sure that she wouldn't accept you if she knew your past? Have you talked honestly with her about other things?

d. A person who loves someone should be totally honest with her.

e. Don't worry so much about it. Nothing bad is going to happen either way.

f. It sounds as if deep down you are feeling guilty about violating your moral code, and you don't know how to deal with it. Is that right?

7. I got out of school last month and thought, "Now what?" I looked for a job, but in this area, nothing is ever available. I couldn't make up my mind what to do. I thought maybe I'd try to get into graduate school, but maybe I'd be happier in the Navy. Then I looked for some part-time jobs, but nothing stood out as a clear choice. Everything looked bad; I couldn't do any of them. Well, what's the use? Am I going crazy? I don't seem to be able to get any direction in my life.

a. I know how you feel because I had a lot of trouble getting a job last summer. I needed the money to be able to go to school, but I just couldn't get work anywhere. It was really a lousy summer.

b. Most people feel like you do sometime. It's not so bad. It will disappear in time if you stay busy.

c. Where have you looked for a job? Have you checked with the placement office or an employment agency?

d. You don't need to remain messed up. You may be confused right now, but that's just a product of your new social environment. This is a real change for you in life.

    e. Don't feel so bad. There are lots of college graduates who can't find jobs. You're not unusual.

    f. It sounds like you are feeling that you really need direction in your life right now, right?

8. Hey, Bob, what's the idea of not approving my requisition for a new filing cabinet? You know we need it in the office. We've got files stacked all over the place. And don't give me the old line about tight company resources again. I've been in line for some new equipment for a long time now.

    a. You sound really upset over not getting your request approved, Ben.

    b. Just because you've waited a long time doesn't mean the resources are there to get a new cabinet for you.

    c. Why do you say you've been in line for new equipment for a long time?

    d. You know, Ben, several other offices are a lot worse off than yours is. Some of them don't have any filing cabinets at all.

    e. I know you're upset, Ben. But I'm sure we can work out a solution.

    f. You're wrong, Ben, in inferring that tight resources aren't a good reason for turning the request down. That's exactly it.

Managing the Management Course

In this role play exercise, two students will interact to try to solve some problems. At least one observer should be assigned to give you feedback on his or her impressions of your communication competency.

Read only the description for the role you are assigned. The role play will be both less realistic and less useful for you if you read both role descriptions. In this situation, neither person would know about the role of the other.

Your assignment is to read the description of the setting and your assigned role, and then engage in the role play. The student should begin the interaction. After ten or fifteen minutes, the observer should provide feedback on what communication processes were used and how effective the two role-players were.

SETTING

The undergraduate course in management has been taught at this college for years. It has always been a relatively popular course, although when the instructor changes, it always takes a semester or two to get the course on track. Student ratings inevitably decline during that period.

Recently Professor Jones has taken over the course and has revised substantially the way it is taught. This is the second semester Professor Jones has taught the course this way.

Professor Jones has an appointment with a student in this course to discuss how things are going.

ROLE OF THE STUDENT

You have taken two other courses in this department, so you feel you have some idea what is and should be expected of students. You are bothered by how this course is being taught and what is being covered. You've also heard a number of other students express some dissatisfaction as well.

Several things bother you:

1. The examples used by Professor Jones seem always to relate to an Ivy League school or a Wall Street firm, which seems a little elitist.
2. The room in which the class meets is too big. This seems to stifle class participation.
3. The class is held at 8:00 A.M., and hardly anyone feels like sitting in class at that time of day.
4. Other courses are very demanding of your time (e.g., accounting), and you resent the amount of reading assigned by Professor Jones that doesn't get discussed much in class.
5. You've heard that Professor Jones is a very hard grader, and you feel uncomfortable with that. Grades are very important to you.
6. A lot of exercises and small group discussions are held in the class, and you feel that they are largely a waste of time. It would be nice if Professor Jones would just give you the material, tell you what's important, and move on.

You'd like to tell Professor Jones about your feelings partly to get them off your chest, but also to improve the class. But how do you tell a professor these things?

ROLE OF PROFESSOR JONES

As far as you are concerned, this course is going pretty well. In your first semester of teaching the course, student feedback was very positive. You were quite surprised that the students adapted so well to your innovative way of teaching this course.

This semester students seem a little less enthusiastic, but you haven't heard any negative feedback as yet. Anyway, you are not worried about it because the semester is only about half over and a lot of interesting things are yet to be covered.

The student coming to see you generally sits toward the back of the room, and may not really be paying attention. The student participates very little on a volunteer basis. You would like to help him or her take a more active role in the class.

OBSERVATION SHEET

As the observer, you are to watch the interaction of the other two individuals and be prepared to provide feedback on their behaviors. The following questions identify some important characteristics of effective interpersonal communication. These are among the principles discussed in the text.

1. To what extent were the two people *honest and open* in expressing their views? Did they try to manipulate one another?

2. Were comments focused on the other *person*—or were they focused on the *problems*?

3. To what extent did one or the other person get *defensive*? What caused this reaction (or lack of reaction)?

4. How much *empathy* was shown by both individuals?

5. How *flexible* were the two people in trying to reach a mutually agreeable solution?

6. Did one person monopolize the *talk time*, or was it a joint interaction?

7. Would you have felt *comfortable* in the interaction had you been a part of it? Why or why not?

■ *Skill Learning*

Resolving Interpersonal Problems Through Communication

Surveys have shown consistently that the ability to communicate is the characteristic judged by managers to be most critical in determining promotability (see surveys reported by Randle, 1956; Bowman, 1964; and Fielden, 1964). In a study of eighty-eight profit and nonprofit organizations, for example, Crocker (1978) found that, of thirty-one skills assessed, interpersonal communication and listening skills were rated as the most important. Thorton (1966, p. 237) summarized a variety of survey results by stating, "A manager's number one problem can be summed up in one word: communication."

At least 80 percent of an individual's waking hours are spent in verbal communication activity, so it is not surprising that serious attention has been given to a plethora of procedures to improve interpersonal communication. Parent effectiveness training, transactional analysis, est, sensitivity sessions, rolfing, encounter therapy, and even hot tubs have all been used to clear away barriers to effective communication and strengthen interpersonal relationships. Scholars and researchers have written extensively on communicology, semantics, rhetoric, linguistics, cybernetics, syntactics, pragmatics, proxemics, and canalization, and library shelves are filled with books on the physics of the communication process—encoding, decoding, transmission, media, perception, reception, and noise.

Even with all these approaches to improved communication, misunderstandings, damaged relationships, and ambiguity still proliferate because most people generally lack skill in verbal communication. Ironically, unlike many other managerial skills discussed in this book, effective verbal communication is a skill in which most people feel they are highly proficient. Haney (1979, p. 219) reported on a survey of over eight thousand people in universities, businesses, military units, government agencies, and hospitals in which "virtually everyone felt that he or she was communicating at least as well as and, in many cases, better than almost everyone else in the organization. Most people readily admit that their organization is fraught with faulty communication, but it is almost always 'those other people' who are responsible." Thus, while proficiency in verbal communication is critical to managerial success, most individuals don't feel a strong need to improve their own skill level.

FOCUS ON COMMUNICATION ACCURACY

Much of the writing on interpersonal communication focuses on the *accuracy* of the information being communicated. The concern generally is with making certain that the message is transmitted and received with little alteration or variation from intent. The communication skill of most concern is the ability to transmit clear, precise messages. The following incidents illustrate problems that result from inaccurate communication.

A motorist was driving on the Merritt Parkway outside New York City when his engine stalled. He quickly determined that his battery was dead and managed to stop another driver who consented to push his car to get it started.

"My car has an automatic transmission," he explained, "so you'll have to get up to 30 to 35 miles per hour to get me started."

The second motorist nodded and walked back to the car. The first motorist climbed into his own car and waited for the good Samaritan to pull up behind him. He waited—and waited. Finally, he turned around to see what was wrong.

There was the good Samaritan—coming at his car at 30 to 35 miles per hour!

The damage to his car amounted to $800 (Haney, 1979, p. 285).

A woman of 35 came in one day to tell me that she wanted a baby but that she had been told that she had a certain type of heart disease which might not interfere with a normal life but would be dangerous if she ever had a baby. From her description, I thought at once of mitral stenosis. This condition is characterized by a rather distinctive rumbling murmur near the apex of the heart, and especially by a peculiar vibration felt by the examining finger on the patient's chest. The vibration is known as the "thrill" of mitral stenosis.

When this woman had been undressed and was lying on my table in her white kimono, my stethoscope quickly found the heart sounds I had expected. Dictating to my nurse, I described them carefully. I put my stethoscope aside and felt intently for the typical vibration which may be found in a small but variable area of the left chest.

I closed my eyes for better concentration, and felt long and carefully for the tremor. I did not find it, and with my hand still on the woman's bare breast, lifting it upward and out of the way, I finally turned to the nurse and said: "No thrill."

The patient's black eyes snapped open, and with venom in her voice she said: "Well, isn't that just too bad? Perhaps it's just as well you don't get one. That isn't what I came for."

My nurse almost choked, and my explanation still seems a nightmare of futile words (Loomis, 1939, p. 47).

When accuracy of communication is the primary consideration, attempts to improve communication generally center on explanations of the *components* of effective communication processes. Generally those components include transmitters and receivers, encoding and decoding, sources and destinations, and noise.

Fortunately, much progress has been made recently in improving the transmission of accurate messages—that is, in improving their clarity and precision. Primarily through the development of a sophisticated information-based technology, major strides have been taken to enhance communication speed and accuracy in organizations. As Haney (1979, p. 223) puts it,

> In the last two decades, particularly, we have witnessed incredible advances in communication "hardware"—computers, magnetic tapes, television, lasers, and many others.
>
> Information technology has developed machines capable of performing highly complex manufacturing tasks, such as assembling automobiles. Doctors can dial an electrocardiogram to a computer in Washington, D.C., which can analyze it faster and sometimes more accurately than a human mind.
>
> It is now possible with "laser writing" to transmit coast to coast a full newspaper page complete with photographs in a second or so. If you had a receiver at home, the publisher could "deliver" your paper by radio or telephone.
>
> The Josephson logic gate can make a binary decision in 10 trillionths of a second. This will render our already rapid computers 100 times faster.
>
> Ordinary books will soon be available to the blind with the aid of a computer that converts English into natural-sounding speech.
>
> Similarly, the deaf will be aided by having speech converted directly into writing.
>
> The day is near when you will be able to phone a computer, ask a question, and receive an immediate, clearly enunciated answer. The computer could recite a page from a medical text for a doctor, inventory status for a stock manager, or flight information for an airline agent.

However, comparable progress has not occurred in the *interpersonal* aspects of communication. People still become offended at one another, make insulting statements, and communicate unskillfully. By the interpersonal aspects of communication we mean the nature of the relationship between the communicators. The effect of who says what to whom, what is said, and how it is said on the relationship between two people has important implications for the effectiveness of the communication, aside from the accuracy of the statement. A statement Josiah Stamp made over eighty years ago illustrates this point.

> The government are very keen on amassing statistics. They collect them, add them, raise them to the nth power, take the cube root and prepare wonderful diagrams. But you must never forget that every one of these figures comes in the first instance from the village watchman, who just puts down what he damn pleases.

Similarly, irrespective of the availability of sophisticated information technologies and elaborately developed models of communication processes, individuals still communicate pretty much as they please—which is often in abrasive, insensitive, and unproductive ways. And more often than not, it is the *interpersonal* aspect of communication that stands in the way of effective message delivery, rather than the inability to deliver accurate information.

Ineffective communication may lead individuals to dislike each other, be offended by one another, lose confidence in one another, refuse to listen to one another, and disagree with one another, as well as a host of other interpersonal problems. These interpersonal problems, in turn, generally lead to restricted communication flow, inaccurate messages, and misinterpretations of meanings. Figure 4.1 summarizes this process.

Consider the following situation. Cal is trying to introduce his new goal-setting program to the organization as a way to overcome some of their productivity problems. After Cal's carefully prepared presentation in the management council meeting, Jedd raises his hand and bursts out, "In my opinion, this has been a very naive approach to solving our organizational problems. The considerations are much more complex than you seem to realize, and I don't think we should waste our time by pursuing this alternative any further." Jedd may, in fact, be trying to be objective in this comment, but the manner in which the message is delivered will probably eliminate any hope of the message's being dealt with objectively. Instead, Cal will probably hear a message such as "I don't like you, and I don't like your proposal. You come across as being really naive." We wouldn't be surprised if Cal's response was hostile. Any good feelings between the two will probably be destroyed, and the communication will become focused on defensiveness. The merits of the proposal will be smothered by this defensiveness.

In this chapter we shall present principles of effective interpersonal communication that have been found to enhance interpersonal relationships among communicators, thereby leading to effective message delivery and reception. These principles are especially useful when the relationship between two individuals may be negatively affected by the communication. People generally have much less trouble giving others positive feedback than negative in-

Figure 4.1   *Relationship Between Unskillful Communication and Interpersonal Relationships*

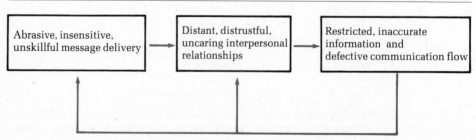

formation. For example, when an awkward interpersonal issue must be resolved, an unwilling listener must be confronted, or an employee must be terminated, most people have difficulty effectively resolving these issues and building the relationship at the same time. Interpersonal relationships suffer as a result of unskillful communication.

SUPPORTIVE COMMUNICATION

Effective interpersonal communication is *supportive communication.* This means that not only is the message delivered accurately, but the relationship between the two communicating parties is supported and enhanced by the interaction, even in problematic or negative circumstances. The focus is on face-to-face interactions in which the interpersonal relationship has important implications for the effectiveness of the communication.

When individuals are required to resolve differences or confront problems, there are two major barriers to effective communication (Gibb, 1961; Sieburg, 1978). One is the presence of *defensiveness* in one of the communicating parties. If an individual feels threatened or punished by the communication, both the message and the interpersonal relationship will be blocked. Self-protection will become paramount. Aggression, anger, competitiveness and avoidance behaviors are common results. The second barrier is *disconfirmation.* This occurs when one of the communicating parties feels put down, ineffectual, or insignificant because of the interaction. Reactions are frequently withdrawal, loss of motivation, and dissatisfaction with both the interpersonal relationship and the communication itself. Recipients of the communication feel they are regarded as worthless by the communicator.

The purpose of supportive communication is not only to effectively pass along a message, but to overcome these two barriers to effective interpersonal communication. The ten principles below are aimed at reducing defensiveness and confirming the worth of the interacting parties.

1. *Supportive communication is based on congruence, not incongruence.* Rogers (1961), Dyer (1972), and others argue that the best interpersonal communications, and the best relationships, are based on *congruence,* or the accurate matching of thoughts and feelings with communication and behavior. If an individual behaves congruently, what is communicated, verbally and nonverbally, matches exactly what the individual is thinking and feeling.

Two kinds of incongruence are possible. One is a mismatch between what one is experiencing and what one is aware of. For example, an individual may not even be aware that he or she is experiencing anger toward another person, even though the anger is really there. Therapists must frequently help individuals reach greater congruence between experience and awareness. A second kind of incongruence, and the one more closely related to supportive communication, is a mismatch between what one experiences and what one communicates. For example, an individual may be aware of a feeling of anger but deny having that feeling.

Rogers (1961, pp. 344–345) suggests that congruence in communication leads to a "general law of interpersonal relationships":

> The greater the congruence of experience, awareness, and communication on the part of one individual, the more the ensuing relationship will involve: a tendency toward reciprocal communication with increasing congruence; a tendency toward more mutually accurate understanding of the communications; improved psychological adjustment and functioning in both parties; mutual satisfaction in the relationship.
>
> Conversely the greater the communicated incongruence of experience and awareness, the more the ensuing relationship will involve: further communication with the same quality; disintegration of accurate understanding; less adequate psychological adjustment and functioning in both parties; mutual dissatisfaction in the relationship.

Striving for congruence, of course, does not mean that one should blow off steam immediately on getting upset, nor does it mean that one cannot repress certain inappropriate feelings (e.g., anger, disappointment, attraction). Other principles of supportive communication must also be practiced, and achieving congruence at the expense of all other considerations is not productive. On the other hand, in problematic interactions, individuals are more likely to express too little congruence than too much. This is because many people are afraid to respond in a completely honest way, or are not sure how to communicate congruently without being offensive. By saying exactly what you feel, you can sometimes offend the other person.

Consider the problem of a subordinate who is not performing up to expectations and displays a nonchalant attitude when his or her superior points out the division's rating is being negatively affected. What could be said that would strengthen the interpersonal feelings between the subordinate and his or her superior and still resolve the problem? Other principles of supportive communication provide some guidelines.

2. *Supportive communication is descriptive, not evaluative.*   When individuals use evaluative communication, a judgment is made or a label placed on other individuals or on their behavior—"You are bad," "You are doing it wrong," "You are incompetent." This evaluation generally makes the other person feel under attack or punished and begin to defend against it. A likely response is, "No, I'm not bad." "I'm not doing it wrong." "I am as competent as you are." Arguments, bad feelings, and a weakening of the interpersonal relationship result.

The tendency to evaluate others is strongest when the issue involves emotions or when a person is made personally uncomfortable. When people have strong feelings about an issue or experience anxiety as a result of a situation, they often make negative evaluations of others' behavior. They try to restore their own good feelings or reduce their own anxiety by placing a label on others—"You are bad, and that implies I am good. Therefore, I feel better."

The problem with this approach is that evaluative communication is likely to be self-perpetuating. Your placing a label on another generally leads that person to respond by placing a label on you, which makes you defensive in return. Feelings therefore deteriorate, rather than improve.

An alternative to evaluation is the use of descriptive communication. Because it is difficult to avoid evaluating other people without some alternative strategy, the use of descriptive communication helps eliminate the tendency to evaluate or to perpetuate a defensive interaction. Descriptive communication involves three steps.

First, one should describe as objectively as possible the event that occurred. This description should be objective in the sense that it relies on elements of the event that can be confirmed or that could be observed by another person. Subjective impressions or attributions about the motives of another person, for example, would not be helpful in the description of the event. The description "You have finished fewer projects this month than anyone else in the division" can be confirmed (an objective record can be made available) and relates strictly to the event, not to the motives or personal characteristics of the subordinate. There is less likelihood of the subordinate's feeling threatened, since no evaluative label is being placed on the event and no attack is being made on the person. Describing an event, as opposed to evaluating an event, is relatively neutral.

Second, one's reactions to the event or its consequences should be described. Rather than projecting onto another person the cause of the problem, the focus should be on the reactions the event has produced. This requires that communicators be aware of their own reactions and able to describe them. Using one-word descriptors for feelings is often the best method—"I feel annoyed," "I was disappointed when I saw the report," "I'm concerned about our productivity." Again, there is no need for defensiveness in the interaction since the problem is framed in terms of the feelings of the communicator. If those feelings are not described in an accusing way, the major energies of the communicators can be focused on problem solving, rather than on defending against evaluations.

Third, a more acceptable alternative should be suggested. This helps the other person save face (Goffman, 1955) and feel valued (Sieburg, 1978) by separating the individual from the behavior. The worth of the person is confirmed; it is just the behavior that should be modified. Care should be taken not to give the message "I don't like the way things are, so what are *you* going to do about it?" The change need not be the responsibility of only one of the communicating parties. Rather, the emphasis should be on finding a solution that is acceptable to both, not on deciding who is right and who is wrong, or who should change and who shouldn't—"I'd like to suggest that you set a goal this month of completing six more projects than last month," or "I would like you to identify the things that are standing in the way of higher performance."

In following these three steps of descriptive communication, it is important that the communicators be aware of their own feelings and that there is some empathy in the relationship. For example, the other person may respond after step 2, "I don't care how you feel," or, "It's too bad if this annoys you. I'm not going to change." This lack of concern now becomes the priority problem. That is, without willingness to strengthen the relationship and work on the problem together, effective communication and problem solving are difficult at best. The focus should switch, therefore, from the immediate problem (low performance) to the nature of the relationship (lack of caring).

The supervisor might respond, "I am surprised to hear you say you don't care how I feel about this [step 1]. That is of great concern to me [step 2], and I'd like to talk with you about your reactions to me and our relationship [step 3]."

The steps of descriptive communication do not imply that one person should do all the changing. Frequently a middle ground must be reached on which both individuals are satisfied (e.g., one person becomes more tolerant of deliberate work and the other person becomes more conscious of working faster).

When it is necessary to make evaluative statements, the evaluations should be made in terms of some established criteria (e.g., the behavior does not meet the prescribed standard), probable outcomes (e.g., continuation of the behavior will lead to worse consequences), or more appropriate behavior performed by the same individual (e.g., this behavior is not as good as your past behavior). The important point is to avoid disconfirming the other person or arousing defensiveness.

3. *Supportive communication is problem oriented, not person oriented.* This principle follows directly from the previous one. Person-oriented communication focuses on the characteristics of the individual, not the event, and it communicates the impression that the individual is inadequate. One problem with person-oriented communication is that, while most people can change their behavior, few can change their basic characteristics. Because nothing can generally be done to accommodate person-oriented communication, it leads to a deterioration in the relationship, rather than to problem solving. Person-oriented messages often are oriented toward persuading the other individual that "this is how you should feel" or "this is what kind of person you are" (e.g., "You are an incompetent manager, a lazy worker, or an insensitive officemate"). But since most individuals accept themselves pretty much as they are, the common reaction to person-oriented communication is to defend against it or reject it outright. Even when communication is positive (e.g., "You are a wonderful person"), it may not be viewed as trustworthy since it is not tied to a behavior or an accomplishment. The absence of a meaningful referent is the key weakness in person-oriented communication.

Problem-oriented communication focuses on the problem and its solutions, rather than on personal traits. It is useful even when personal appraisals are called for, since it focuses on behaviors and events. "You are an autocrat" and "You are insensitive" are person oriented, for example, while "I seldom meet with you to help make decisions" and "Our relationship is deteriorating" are more descriptive of problems. Imputing motives to an individual is person oriented (e.g., "It's because you are unconcerned about others"), whereas expressing concern with overt manifestations of behavior is problem oriented (e.g., "You made several sarcastic comments in the meeting today").

4. *Supportive communication is equality oriented, not superiority oriented.*   Communication that is superiority oriented gives the impression that the communicator is informed and others ignorant, adequate and others inadequate, competent and others incompetent, or powerful and others impotent. It creates a carrier between the communicator and those to whom the message is sent.

Superiority-oriented communication can take the form of put-downs, in which others are made to look bad so the communicator looks good. Or it can take the form of "one-upmanship," in which the communicator tries to elevate himself or herself in the esteem of others. One of the most common forms of superiority-oriented communication is the use of jargon, or words used in such a way as to exclude others or to create barriers in a relationship. John Kenneth Galbraith (1975) has stated:

> Complexity and obscurity have professional value: they are the academic equivalent of apprenticeship rules in the building trades. They exclude the outsiders, keep down the competition, preserve the image of a privileged or priestly class. The man who makes things clear, depending on the metaphor, is a recusant or a scab. He is criticized not only for his clarity but for his treachery.

Doctors, lawyers, and many other professionals are well known for their use of jargon to exclude others, rather than to clarify a message. Michael Crichton (1977), a physician and novelist, notes, for example, that some doctors are beginning to fear that they will be underrated "because they wrote their papers too clearly, because they made their ideas too simple. . . . [As a result] only recently have physicians begun to use language to conceal knowledge from one another."

Individuals who are not associated with academia or the professions may also use language to appear superior. One way to do that is to use polysyllabic words or complex phrases. For example, the words in the columns below, from the "Systematic Buzz Phase Projector" (Haney, 1979, pp. 306–307), can be combined to produce impressive-sounding, verbose, but largely nonsensical phrases. For example, pick any three-digit number from the columns on the next page and combine the corresponding words. The number 269 produces "systematized transitional contingency." Sounds impressive, doesn't it? But it's nonsense. Superiority communication, in like manner, is designed to sound impressive, but it obscures effective communication.

Column 1	Column 2	Column 3
0. integrates	0. management	0. options
1. total	1. organizational	1. flexibility
2. systematized	2. monitored	2. capability
3. parallel	3. reciprocal	3. mobility
4. functional	4. digital	4. programming
5. responsive	5. logic	5. concept
6. optical	6. transitional	6. time-phase
7. synchronized	7. incremental	7. projection
8. compatible	8. third-generation	8. hardware
9. balanced	9. policy	9. contingency

Egalitarian communication, on the other hand, is oriented toward the maintenance of a reciprocal relationship. Both parties in the communication are treated as worthwhile, competent, and capable of making a meaningful contribution to the interaction. The emphasis is on using language that is understood by both parties and on communicating in such a way that both parties win, instead of one party being elevated at the expense of the other. In hierarchical organizations, in which superiors clearly have more information or power than subordinates, this principle is especially important. Rather than communicating in an exclusionary or condescending way, superiors must take care to communicate in ways that display egalitarian characteristics.

5. Supportive communication validates rather than invalidates individuals. Therapists and others in the helping professions have long been aware that the ways people communicate can facilitate personal and interpersonal growth and security or inhibit growth and security. Barnlund (1968, p. 618) suggests that all too often interpersonal communication is destructive:

> People do not take time, do not listen, do not try to understand, but interrupt, anticipate, criticize, or disregard what is said: in their own remarks they are frequently vague, inconsistent, verbose, insincere, or dogmatic. As a result, people often conclude conversations feeling more inadequate, more misunderstood and more alienated than when they started them.

Communication that is invalidating arouses negative feelings about self-worth, identity, and relatedness to others. It denies the presence, uniqueness, or importance of other individuals. Especially important are communications that invalidate people by conveying three qualities: indifference, imperviousness, and disqualification (Sieburg, 1976).

Indifference is communicated when the other person's existence or importance is not acknowledged. A person may do this by using silence, by making no verbal response to the other's staements, by avoiding eye contact or any facial expression, by interrupting the other person frequently, by using impersonal words ("one should not" instead of "you should not"), or by engaging in unrelated activity during a conversation. The communicator appears not to *care* about the other person.

Through imperviousness a communicator fails to acknowledge the validity of the other person's feelings or perceptions. He or she denies that the feelings or perceptions reported by the other person are real, legitimate, or reasonable—"I'm sure you don't mean that," "You shouldn't feel that way," "It is ridiculous to get upset over this."

Communication is disqualifying when it denies the other the chance to form an interpersonal relationship with the communicator. The recipient of the communication is thus disqualified from entering into a reciprocal relationship. This occurs when one person does not allow the other to finish a thought, when a competitive (win-lose) stance is taken, or when confusing messages are given—"You wouldn't understand," "You're wrong. It's really this way."

Invalidating communication, then, "reflects unawareness of others, misperception of them, rejection of their attempt to communicate, denial of their self-experience, or disaffiliation with them [Sieburg, 1978, p. 146]." Invalidation is even more destructive to relationships than criticism or disagreement, because criticism and disagreement validate the other person by recognizing that what was said or done is worth responding to (Jacobs, 1973). As William James (1965) stated, "No more fiendish punishment could be devised, even were such a thing physically possible, than that one could be turned loose in a society and remain absolutely unnoticed by all the members thereof."

Validating communication, on the other hand, helps people feel recognized, understood, accepted, and valued. It has five attributes:

1. It recognizes the other person's existence.
2. It recognizes the person's uniqueness as an individual, rather than treating him or her as a role or a job.
3. It acknowledges the worth of the other person.
4. It acknowledges the validity of the other person's perception of the world.
5. It expresses willingness to be involved with the other person, at least during the communication.

In practical terms, a good way to express validation in communication is to identify an important point made by the other person before pointing out trivial ones, to identify an area of agreement before pointing out disagreements, to identify an advantage before pointing out disadvantages, to identify a compliment before pointing out criticisms, and so on. The point is not to be incongruent or artificial, but to validate the other person before delivering messages that may be threatening.

6. *Supportive communication is flexible, not rigid.*   "Know-it-alls," rigid people who require no additional information or seem to have the answers at their fingertips, are frequently perceived as insecure, dogmatic, or both. Gibb (1961) suggests that they are often individuals who would rather win an argument than solve a problem, who need to appear to be right, and who are intolerant of opposing views. The likely response to such rigid communication is competitiveness, reciprocal rigidity, and defensiveness.

Rigidity in communication can be displayed in a variety of ways:

1. Never expressing agreement with anyone else, or when agreement is expressed, expressing it in terms of "they agree with me," not "I agree with them."
2. Reinterpreting all other viewpoints to conform to one's own.
3. Never saying, "I don't know," but having an answer for everything.
4. Not expressing openness to others' opinions or information.
5. Using evaluative and invalidating statements, instead of communicating understanding and validation for others.
6. Appearing unwilling to tolerate criticisms or alternative points of view.
7. Reducing complex issues to simplistic definitions.
8. Using all-encompassing and overgeneralized statements (that is, communicating the message that everything worthwhile that can be said about the subject has just been said).
9. Merging definitions of problems with solutions so alternatives are not considered.
10. Placing exclamation points after statements so the impression is created that the statement is final, complete, or unqualified.

Flexibility in communication, on the other hand, means that the communicator is willing to accept additional data, that other alternatives may exist, and that other individuals may be able to make significant contributions to the conversation and the relationship. It means communicating genuine humility—not self-abasement or demonstrated weakness, but *openness to truth*. As Bertrand Russell stated, "One's certainty varies inversely with one's knowledge." Disraeli noted, "To be conscious that you are ignorant is a first great step toward knowledge."

Perceptions and opinions are not presented as facts in flexible communication, but are stated provisionally. That is, a distinction is made between facts and opinions, between evidence and assumptions, and no claim is made for the truthfulness of opinions and assumptions. Rather, they are identified as being changeable if more data become available. Flexible communication conveys a willingness to enter into a coequal interaction, rather than to control the other person or to assume a master-teacher role. Being flexible is not synonymous with being wishy-washy, however; rather, it indicates a willingness to learn and grow. "Gee, I can't make up my mind" is wishy-washy, whereas "I have my preferences, but what do you think?" suggests flexibility.

A witness being sworn in at a trial, as reported by Haney (1979, p. 357), exemplified the ultimate in flexibility:

> *Bailiff:* Do you swear to tell the truth, the whole truth, and nothing but the
> truth, so help you God?
> *Witness:* Look, if I knew the truth, the whole truth, and nothing but the
> truth, I would be God!

7. *Supportive communication is specific (and useful), not global (and not useful).*   In general, the more specific a communication is, the more useful it is. For example, the statement "You are domineering" is too general to be useful, whereas "You interrupted me three times just now" provides specific information that can serve as a basis for behavioral change. "You are a poor communicator" is not nearly as useful as a more specific "In this role play, you used evaluative statements 60 percent of the time and descriptive statements 10 percent of the time."

Specific communication avoids extremes and absolutes. The following are extreme statements that lead to defensiveness or disconfirmation:

> "You *never* ask for my advice."
>   "Yes, I do, I *always* consult you before making a decision."

> "You have *no* consideration for others' feelings."
>   "I do so. I am *very* considerate."

> "This class is *boring.*"
>   "It is not. The instructor is *terrific.*"

Another common type of global communication is the either-or statement, such as, "You either do what I say or I'll fire you," "Life is either a daring adventure or nothing [Helen Keller]," "There are but two objects in marriage, either love or money. If you marry for love, you will have some very happy days, and probably many very uneasy ones; if for money, you will have no happy days and probably no uneasy ones [Lord Chesterfield]."

The uselessness of extreme and either-or statements lies in their prohibition of any alternatives other than the stated extremes. The possible responses of the recipient of the communication are severely constrained. About the only response to such a statement is to contradict or deny it. A statement of Adolf Hitler in 1933 illustrates the point: "Everyone in Germany is a National Socialist—the few outside the party are either lunatics or idiots."

Specific statements are more useful because they focus on behavioral events and indicate gradations in positions. More useful forms of the examples above are the following:

"You made that decision yesterday without asking for my advice."
"Yes, I did. While I generally like to get your opinions, I didn't think it was necessary in this case."

"By using sarcasm in your response to my request, you give me the impression you don't care about my feelings."
"I'm sorry. I know I am often sarcastic without thinking how it affects others."

The readings in this class are hard to understand."
"That may be so, but I find the instructor's illustrations very helpful."

As these examples point out, the use of qualifier words such as "generally," "frequently," "appears to be," "may be," "about," "seldom," "quite," "very," and so on, help avoid global connotations, as does linking the statement to a specific event. To see how this works, list antonyms for each of the following words.

good   _____   light   _____
happy   _____   hot   _____

You probably found this relatively simple. Now take the same words and provide some gradations between the two extremes. The middle words will be more specific than the two words on the ends of the continuum.

good   _____ _____ _____ _____ bad
happy _____ _____ _____ _____ sad
light _____ _____ _____ _____ dark
hot   _____ _____ _____ _____ cold

Not all specific statements are useful just because they are grounded in a behavioral referent or qualified in some way. Specific statements may not be useful if they focus on things over which another person has no control. "I hate it when it rains," for example, may relieve some personal frustration, but the referent of the statement is something about which nothing can be done, so interpersonally the communication is not very useful. Similarly, communicating the message (even implicitly) "I don't like people of your background" or "Your personality bothers me" only proves frustrating for the interacting individuals. Specific communication is useful to the extent that it focuses on an identifiable problem or behavior about which something can be done (e.g., "I'm bothered that you checked up on me four times today.").

8. *Supportive communication is conjunctive, not disjunctive.*   Conjunctive communication is joined to previous messages in some way. It flows smoothly. Disjunctive communication is disconnected from what was stated before.

Communication can appear disjunctive in at least three ways. First, there can be an absence of synchronization of speaking turns. When one person interrupts another, when one person dominates by controlling "air time", or when two or more communicators try to speak at the same time, the communication is disjunctive. The transitions between speaking partners simply do not flow smoothly. Second, extended pauses are disjunctive. When speakers pause for long periods in their statements or when there are long pauses before responses, the communication is disjunctive. Pauses need not be total silence, for the space may be filled with "umm," "aaa," or a repeating of what was stated earlier, but the communication does not progress. Third, topic control can be disjointed. When one person decides unilaterally what the topic of conversation will be (as opposed to having it decided bilaterally), the communication is disjunctive. Individuals may switch topics, for example, with no reference to what was just said, or they may control the other person's communication topic by directing what should be responded to. Sieburg (1969) found this problem a severe one in her analysis of interacting groups. Over 25 percent of the statements made in small group discussions failed to refer to or even acknowledge prior speakers or their statements.

These three factors—synchronization of speaking turns, management of timing, and topic control—contribute to what Wiemann (1977) calls "interaction management." They have been found to be absolutely critical to effective supportive communication. In an empirical study of perceived communication competence, Wiemann (1977, p. 104) found that "the smoother the management of the interaction [of the three factors above], the more competent the communicator was perceived to be." In fact, interaction management was concluded to be the most powerful determinant of perceived communication competence in his experimental study. Individuals who used conjunctive communication were rated as being significantly more competent in interpersonal communication than were those whose communication was disjunctive. This is because conjunctive communication confirms the worth of the other person's statements. It makes both parties feel valued.

This suggests that skilled communicators manage communication situations so they are conjunctive rather than disjunctive by eliminating long pauses, facilitating synchronized turn-taking, and relating statements to what went before. A continuum may exist for conjunctive communication. For example, statements that relate to the immediately preceding statement are most conjunctive, while statements that relate to something that occurred earlier in the conversation are somewhat less so, statements that relate to something in the immediate environment are less conjunctive still, and statements that relate to none of these factors are the least conjunctive.

9. *Supportive communication is owned, not disowned.* "Owning" communication means taking responsibility for one's statements, acknowledging that the sources of the ideas are one's self, not another person or group. Using first-person words such as "I", "me", and "mine", indicates owning of communication. Disowning communication is suggested by use of third-person or first-person plural words—"We think," "They said," or "One might say." The disowned communication is attributed to an unknown person, group, or to some external source (e.g., "Lots of people think"). The communicator avoids taking responsibility for the message, and therefore avoids investing in the interaction. This conveys the message that the communicator is aloof or uncaring about the receiver, or is not confident enough in the ideas expressed to take responsibility for them.

Glasser (1965) bases his approach to mental health—reality therapy—on the concept of responsibility or owning of communication and behavior. According to Glasser, individuals are mentally healthy if they accept responsibility for their statements and behaviors. They are ill if they avoid taking responsibility. According to this theory, taking responsibility for one's communication builds self-confidence and a sense of self-worth in the communicator, as well as confidence in the receiver of the communication by confirming that his or her worth is valued.

One result of disowning communication is that the listener is never sure whose point of view the message represents, and misinterpretation is more likely—"How can I respond if I don't know whom I am responding to?" "If I don't understand the message, whom can I ask?" Moreover, an implicit message associated with disowned communication is, "I want to keep distance between you and me." This is done by communicating as a representative rather than as a person, or as a message-conveyer rather than as an interested individual. Owning communication, on the other hand, indicates a willingness to invest oneself in the relationship and to act as a colleague or a helper.

10. *Supportive communication is appropriately intimate, not overbearing or aloof.* Another way an interpersonal relationship can be damaged is by communication at an inappropriate level of intimacy. "Level of intimacy" refers to how personal a message is. Messages that imply a greater investment of the person are more intimate than messages that imply little personal investment. For example, sharing personal information or expressing inner feelings at the beginning of a relationship may be interpreted as coming on too strong because too much personal investment is expressed too soon. Consider the following:

> *Bob, near the water cooler:* "Hi, I'm Bob."
> *Mary:* "Glad to meet you, Bob. My name is Mary."
> *Bob:* "It's really nice to find someone to talk to. I hardly know anyone around here. Actually, I'm pretty lonely. The other people I work with don't seem to like me very much. It must be because of my weight. People are just not very understanding of people who are fat, and . . ."

> *Mary:* "Oh, golly, Bob. I've got to get to a meeting. Sorry I can't stay and
> talk. See you later."
> *Bob:* "OK."

In this situation, Bob began making statements that were too personal for his superficial relationship with Mary. This led to discomfort and withdrawal on Mary's part. A less intimate level of conversation would have been more appropriate in such a situation.

On the other hand, communication that remains impersonal when the individuals have known each other a long time can also produce defensiveness. Consider the following dialogue between two people who once worked in the same department for five years:

> *John:* "Hi, Joan. Gee, I'm glad I ran into you. How are things?"
> *Joan:* "Fine."
> *John:* "It seems like I haven't seen you for a long time. What have you been
> up to?"
> *Joan:* "Not much."
> *John:* "Boy. This past month has really been hectic for me. I've had to work
> late almost every night."
> *Joan:* "Hmmm . . . "
> *John:* "Ah . . . well . . . I guess I'd better be going."
> *Joan:* "OK."

John is likely to interpret Joan's lack of reciprocal intimacy as a sign of disinterest or uncaring. His reponse will likely be to decrease his own expressions of intimacy, thereby making the relationship more and more superficial. Eventually, with only superficial messages being exchanged, the relationship may cease.

Figure 4.2 summarizes two primary dimensions on which the various levels of intimacy in communication are based. One dimension refers to the *focus* of the communication—i.e., what subject is being talked about. The other refers to the *type* of the communication—i.e., the kind of messages being sent. As the focus of communication moves from left to right, it becomes more intimate. Similarly, as the process of communication moves from top to bottom, intimacy also increases. A brief description of the categories in the model will help explain its usefulness in supportive communication.

Interpersonal communication can focus on any of four subject areas. The first, and least intimate, is *external issues*. The weather, the economy, the Middle East situation, and the Superbowl are examples for most people. This level of intimacy is most appropriate for the early stages of interactions and for new, formal, or superficial relationships. The next subject, *the common group*, refers to people or experiences communicators have in common. A class that they are taking, a common acquaintance, and a club both belong to

Figure 4.2   *Matrix on Intimacy of Communication*

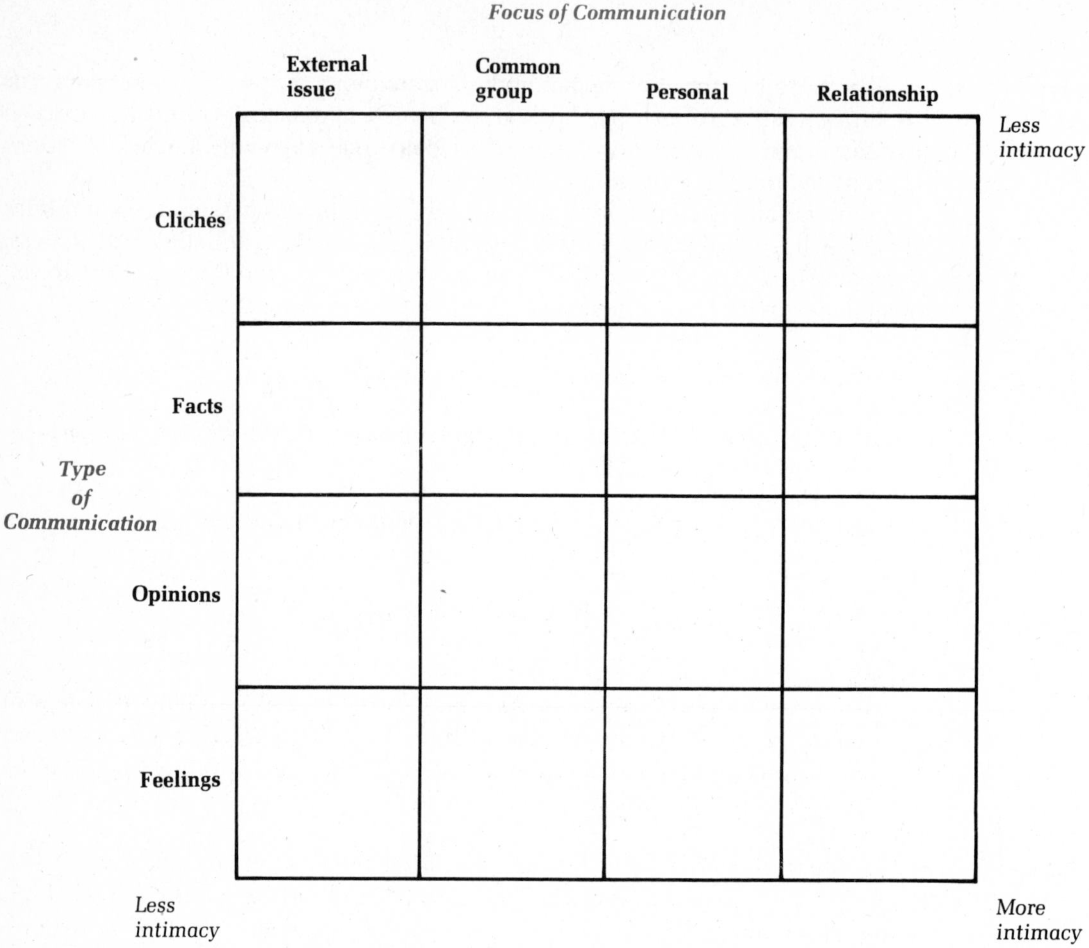

Focus of Communication

	External issue	**Common group**	**Personal**	**Relationship**	
Clichés					*Less intimacy*
Facts					
Opinions					
Feelings					

Type of Communication

Less intimacy   *More intimacy*

are somewhat more intimate subjects than external issues, but still fairly safe (i.e., they imply only marginal personal investment). To feel closer to someone they have just met, people often search for some common group phenomenon to talk about. The third subject, *personal information*, is more intimate than the previous two. It refers to disclosure of personal information that the listener could not obtain otherwise, such as likes and dislikes, family history, career plans, and so forth. Discussing personal information too soon in a relationship, as in the example of Bob and Mary, gives the impression of being too pushy and too familiar. Never discussing personal information, however, may keep the relationship superficial, as in John and Joan's case. The fourth and most intimate subject is the *relationship* itself. This refers to discussions of "us", how you feel about or react to someone else, and vice versa. The statement "I want to tell you how I feel about us" would be entirely inappropriate in the early stages of a relationship.

In some relationships, intimate levels of communication might never be appropriate. An example might be a relationship that is formally circumscribed by protocol or in which only limited involvement is prescribed (e.g., a college dean–student relationship). More often, even when one person is a superior and the other a subordinate, the nature of the interpersonal relationship is an important part of effective communication, and increasing intimacy is an important goal.

The other dimension of intimacy in Figure 4.2 is the type of communication. Four types of communication can be used to deliver messages—clichés, facts, opinions, and feelings. Clichés require the least investment of the person in the communication, and feelings require the most. The value of differentiating among these four types is that miscommunication and defensiveness can result not only from using an inappropriate kind of message, but also from having the interacting parties use mismatching types so that one is consistently more intimate than the other (recall the examples of Bob and Mary, and John and Joan).

Clichés are statements that usually are not meant to be taken literally. They merely acknowledge the presence of the other person and convey that the conversation should remain superficial: "Howdy, how are things?" (external issue) "How's school going?" (common group) "How are you feeling?" (personal) "Let's get together sometime." (relationship) Clichés generally serve to introduce people to one another, renew a relationship, or convey the level of personal investment desired by the communicators.

A more intimate level of communication is conveyed by using *facts*. Facts provide information to the receiver and require more personal investment than clichés: "It's cold outside, isn't it?" (external issue) "We're going to have an exam Friday." (common group) "I'm starting to come down with a cold." (personal) "We laugh a lot when we're together." (relationship)

Opinions express the attitudes and impressions of the communicator. By expressing opinions, communicators invest much more of themselves in the communication than by using clichés or facts: "I'm still for the President's economic program, aren't you?" (external issue) "This class has really been helpful to me so far." (common group) "I had a great time at the party last night." (personal) "I think the morale in our work group here is really suffering." (relationship).

Expressing *feelings* is the most intimate type of communication that can be used. The expression of feelings conveys a strong personal investment in the relationship because such messages imply trust that the feelings will not be misused or ignored, and that the intimacy will be reciprocated by the receiver. Feelings differ from opinions in that they are less cognitive and more emotional: "I feel really anxious about interviewing for a new job this week." (external issue) "I'm feeling really good about the progress we're making on our group report." (common group) "I'm pretty lonesome living off campus." (personal) "I would like to get to know you better." (relationship)

When confronting interpersonal problems, individuals should be careful not to communicate at a level of intimacy that is overbearing or aloof. Sometimes, to communicate in the most supportive way, warm-up time using clichés and facts and focused on topics or the common group is needed before more intimate—and more direct—statements can be made. The goal is to communicate in a supportive way, and the appropriate level of intimacy is one important consideration.

Table 4.1 summarizes these ten characteristics of supportive communication and provides appropriate and inappropriate examples of each. The underlying purpose of using these ten attributes of supportive communication is to address interpersonal issues, or provide negative information, and at the same time strengthen the relationship. Of course, it is possible to become overly concerned with technique in trying to incorporate these ten principles and defeat the goal of being supportive. That is, it is possible to become incongruent by focusing on technique rather than on honest, caring communication. But if the principles are practiced and consciously implemented in everyday conversation, they will become a part of your skill repertoire and an important addition to your managerial competence.

SUPPORTIVE LISTENING

Up to now we have focused exclusively on the delivery of messages—that is, on communication in which the message originates with you. But another aspect of supportive communication is at least as important as delivering supportive messages, and that is listening and responding effectively to someone else's statements. As Maier, Solem, and Maier (1973, p. 311) stated: "In any conversation the person who talks the most is the one who learns the least about the other person. The good supervisor therefore must become a good listener."

In a survey of personnel directors in three hundred businesses and industries conducted to determine what skills are most important in becoming a manager, Crocker (1978) reported that effective listening was ranked highest. Despite its importance in managerial success, however, and despite the fact that most people spend at least 45 percent of their communication time listening, most people have underdeveloped listening skills. Tests have shown, for example, that individuals are usually about 25 percent effective in listening (Huseman, Lahiff, & Hatfield, 1976). Even when asked to rate the extent to which they are skilled listeners, 85 percent of all individuals rate themselves as average or worse. Only 5 percent rate themselves as highly skilled (Steil, 1980). And it is particularly unfortunate that listening skills are poorest when

TABLE 4.1 *Key Characteristics of Supportive Communication*

1. *Congruent,* Not Incongruent "I must tell you that your reaction in the meeting really upset me."	NOT	"Oh, do I seem upset? No, every- thing is fine."
2. *Descriptive,* Not Evaluative "This is what happened, and this is how I felt about it. I'd like to suggest an alternative that would be more acceptable to me."	NOT	"You are wrong for doing what you did."
3. *Problem Oriented,* Not Person Oriented "How can we solve this problem?"	NOT	"Why are you so slow?"
4. *Equality Oriented,* Not Superiority Oriented "I have some ideas, but do you have any suggestions?"	NOT	"Your suggestion is dumb. This is the way to handle this problem."
5. *Validating,* Not Invalidating "That is an interesting sug- gestion."	NOT	"I can't believe you could think such a thing."
6. *Flexible,* Not Closed-Minded "I have some questions, but let's explore it further."	NOT	"Whatever made you think that that would work?"
7. *Specific,* Not Global "You did not give me equal time to cover my material in that pre- sentation."	NOT	"You are always seeking all the recognition for our work."
8. *Conjunctive,* Not Disjunctive "Relating to your earlier point about X, I'd like to discuss Y."	NOT	"As long as you are here, I've been wanting to talk to you about Y."
9. *Owned,* Not Disowned "I've decided to turn down your request, because . . ."	NOT	"You have a pretty good idea, but you know how it is in an organiza- tion—everyone can't get every- thing they want."
10. *Appropriately Intimate,* Not Overbearing or Aloof "Since we have known each other a long time, I'd like to tell you how I feel about our relationship."	NOT	"I know we just met, but I really need to tell you something per- sonal."

people interact with those closest to them, such as family members and co-workers.

The major roadblocks to effective listening are the personal character-istics of the listener, such as attitudes, biases, and personal needs. When individuals are preoccupied with meeting their own needs (e.g., saving face, persuading someone else, winning a point, avoiding getting involved), when they have already made a prior judgment, or when they hold negative attitudes toward the communicator or the message, effective listening is curtailed. Because effective listening can occur at the rate of 500 words a minute but normal speech occurs at 125 to 250 words a minute, the listener's mind can dwell on other things over half the time. Therefore, the attitudes, biases, and personal needs of the listener can inhibit effective listening because the listener has so much time to dwell on them.

Extensive research on listening behavior has identified one technique that is especially effective in helping listeners concentrate on the message instead of on these barriers. It is called *supportive listening*. The goal of supportive listening is to both hear and understand the message being sent and to enhance the interpersonal relationship of the communicating parties. Rogers and Farson (1976, p. 99) suggest that this kind of listening conveys the idea that "I'm interested in you as a person, and I think what you feel is important. I respect your thoughts, and even if I don't agree with them, I know they are valid for you. I feel sure you have a contribution to make. I think you're worth listening to, and I want you to know that I'm the kind of person you can talk to."

Competence in supportive listening depends on the ability to empathize with another individual and the ability to select appropriate responses to the message. Each of these is discussed below to help clarify their relationship with the concept of supportive listening.

Empathy

The ability of a manager to empathize has been found to significantly affect subordinates' behavior and attitudes. For example, Rogers (1961) cites several research studies suggesting that positive behavioral and attitude change and interpersonal growth are significantly associated with a display of empathy by the superior in an interaction. Egan (1975), Gladstein (1977), and Truax and Carcuff (1967) have found evidence that self-awareness, self-exploration, therapeutic success, and satisfaction are enhanced in individuals exposed to empathetic superiors. Carcuff (1967, p. 173) concludes that "empathy is the key ingredient of helping. Its explicit communication, particularly during the early phases of [interaction], is critical."

Most people think of themselves as relatively empathetic. In fact, most of us easily feel empathy for others who are experiencing what we have experienced before. But true empathy is a skill, not a memory. Individuals who have developed the ability to empathize can display it even when encountering individuals with whom they have little in common.

Heilman (1972) has identified three main characteristics of the ability to empathize. First, empathy involves accurately perceiving the *content* of the message of another person. Second, attention is given to the *emotional* components and unexpressed *core meanings* of the message. Third, an *"as if"* quality is maintained. Empathetic individuals attend to the feelings of the other but maintain an "as if" perspective, while sympathetic individuals adopt those feelings as their own (Wispe, 1968). Empathy involves understanding and relating to another's feelings; sympathy involves adopting those feelings.

These three attributes of empathy are the key mechanisms that underlie the ability to listen supportively. The listener attends to the content of the message, to the feelings and unexpressed meanings underlying the message, and to the intention of the message (insofar as possible) from the standpoint of the communicator. Because listening in this way requires much more effort than just hearing words, it tends to drive out considerations of one's own agenda. That is, it requires attention to multiple parts of the message, not just the explicitly stated agenda. It also helps the communicator feel that he or she is valued and important, and that the message is genuinely understood by the listener.

Supportive listening involving empathy requires more than simply saying, "I understand." In fact, two levels of empathy are necessary for competent supportive listening. The first is the *interchange* or primary level. Communicating on this level entails conveying understanding and acceptance of the content and emotion of the message. The empathizer understands both cognitively and emotionally the speaker's explicit message. The second level of empathy is called the *additive* or advanced level. This involves attending not only to what the communicator expresses, but also to what is implied but left unstated in the message. In additive empathy, attention is directed to the core meaning, or implicit message, of the statement, in addition to overt expressions. An example of these two levels of empathy has been provided by Egan (1975, p. 135):

> *Communicator:* "I don't know what's going on. I study hard, but I just don't get good grades. I think I study as hard as anyone else, but all of my efforts seem to go down the drain. I don't know what else I can do."
>
> *Interchange Response:* "You seem to feel frustrated because even when you try hard you fail."
>
> *Additive Response:* "It's depressing to put in as much effort as those who pass and still fail. It gets you down and maybe even makes you feel a little sorry for yourself."

The interchange respondent in the example is trying to understand the message from the communicator's point of view. This involves reflecting back the explicit message to the communicator. The additive respondent attends to messages that were not verbally expressed but that may be manifest in tone of voice or nonverbal cues—namely, that the communicator may be feeling sorry for himself or herself. Additive empathy does not mean trying to outguess another's communication. Rather, this level of empathy involves a consideration of the messages that are present but not made explicit (and maybe not even recognized) by the communicator.

Competent supportive listeners have four main abilities with regard to these two types of empathy. First, they can display both levels separately. For example, a communicator may feel threatened or defensive if additive empathy is displayed early in an interaction. On the other hand, interchange empathy may appear superficial and insincere in a relationship that is more intimate. It is best, therefore, to use interchange empathy (to focus on the explicit message) in the beginning stages of communication, moving on to additive empathy (implicit messages) in later stages.

Second, competent supportive listeners can separate a focus on content from a focus on feelings. While attending to both the content and the feelings behind the message is usually best, communicators may be uncomfortable dealing with personal feelings in the early stages of communication. Sometimes listeners must begin with a focus on content and move gradually to feelings to avoid producing defensiveness. One way to give feelings some legitimacy in the conversation is for listeners to state how they might feel in similar circumstances. In addition, Rogers (1961) suggests that expressing a *desire* to understand helps communicators feel valued and free to express more sensitive thoughts and feelings.

Third, competent supportive listeners can postpone evaluation and bias when hearing a message. That is, they listen objectively to communication without labelling it good or bad, right or wrong. They can accept individuals without feeling compelled to agree with them. Agreement and disagreement are postponed as much as possible.

Fourth, competent supportive listeners remain sensitive to signs of resistance and defensiveness that may arise from misperceiving communications or being inaccurate in responses. Sometimes listeners may inappropriately respond on the additive level instead of the interchange level, or may focus on underlying feelings too soon. Another mistake can be to not match the communicator's level of intensity in the response (e.g., if communicators are animated and excited in the message but receive calm, low-key responses, they probably will not feel understood). In each of these circumstances, supportive listeners should be sensitive to cues that communication is closing off, becoming guarded, or focusing on superficials because of their responses.

In summary, empathetic supportive listeners do the following:

1. Attend both to content and to feelings and underlying meanings being expressed in the message.
2. Look at the world from the communicator's frame of reference, postpone personal evaluation, and respond with an intensity similar to that being communicated.
3. Begin with the interchange level of empathy (focusing on content) in early stages of the interaction, then move gradually toward the additive level (attending to emotions, deeper meanings, and implied messages).
4. Are sensitive to indications of defensiveness or resistance that may arise because of inaccurate perceptions or inappropriate responses.

Alternative Responses

As we pointed out earlier, communicators cannot know they are being supportively listened to unless some response is made by the listener. The type of response most closely associated with empathetic abilities is the *reflective* or *understanding* response, which is advocated widely as the most appropriate response type for managers to develop (Rogers, 1961; Rogers & Farson, 1976; Athos & Garbarro, 1978; Maier, 1973). While this is a very useful and effective response to communicate supportive listening, it is not the only appropriate type of response, and its usefulness may even be limited in certain circumstances. Moreover, those of you who have been on the receiving end of repeated reflective responses know that they can sometimes be unnerving because they may be redundant, gimmicky, superficial, and one-sided. Competent supportive listeners have a repertoire of response alternatives, and they select carefully to clarify the communication, as well as to strengthen the interpersonal relationship. The second key ability of supportive listeners, then, is competence in selecting appropriate responses to others' statements.

The appropriateness of alternative response types depends largely on two factors: the goal of the communication and the intimacy of the relationship. For example, if the goal of the communication is to express a complaint, to identify or solve a problem, or to express personal feelings, an open, nondirective response is probably more appropriate. On the other hand, when direction is requested or an evaluation is called for, a closed, directive response is probably more appropriate. In a relationship that is still on a superficial level, responses are more appropriate that build trust and openness and express acceptance (open responses). When the relationship is more intimate, responses can be more confrontational or express personal feelings (closed responses).

Figure 4.3 lists seven response types and arranges them on a continuum from most closed or directive to most open or nondirective. Closed responses eliminate topics from consideration by providing direction to the conversation. They also allow for more personal opinions and feelings to be expressed. Open responses, on the other hand, free communicators to pursue the topic of their choice by providing no direction or personal opinions.

What is ironic about this ordering is that many individuals reverse this pattern when they respond to others' statements. Evaluative responses are generally used first, and it is not until much later in a relationship that understanding/reflective responses are employed. For example, agreement or disagreement is a common first response to someone's statement, as is confronting others with a fallacy or omission in their statement. Expressing acceptance of the message and being concerned with the communicator's feelings often occur only after a relationship has been developed.

Each of these alternative responses is described below to clarify when certain responses should and should not be used.

Figure 4.3 *Seven Response Types, from Most Closed to Most Open*

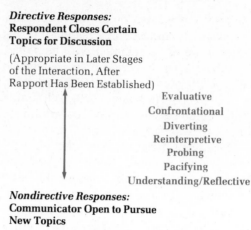

Directive Responses:
Respondent Closes Certain
Topics for Discussion

(Appropriate in Later Stages
of the Interaction, After
Rapport Has Been Established)

Evaluative
Confrontational
Diverting
Reinterpretive
Probing
Pacifying
Understanding/Reflective

Nondirective Responses:
Communicator Open to Pursue
New Topics

(Appropriate in Early Stages
of the Interaction)

Evaluative Responses

Rogers (1961) reports that evaluative responses are the most frequently used. Most individuals feel obliged to make judgments about communications they encounter. An evaluative response, then, passes judgment, expresses approval or disapproval, or offers advice. Such a response imposes on the communicator the framework of the listener, and generally retards or closes off further exploration of the topic area. Evaluative responses are most useful in later stages of an interaction when the topic of conversation has been explored in depth, when specific advice or direction is asked for *and* the listener has some idea of the frame of reference of the communicator, when the position of the listener makes clear that advice or direction should be given (e.g., the listener is an expert), or when the personal feelings or opinions of the listener are requested.

Ineffective use of evaluative responses may inhibit effective communication by putting communicators on the defensive, by implying they must justify the message communicated, or by unilaterally controlling the topics discussed (i.e., disjunctive communication). Managers might best use evaluative responses when they are viewed as experts, their advice is sought, and they can compare their evaluation to an accepted standard. The following exchange illustrates an evaluative response:

> *Subordinate:* "As a manager, you are supervising my work so closely that it is becoming disruptive."

> *Evaluative Response:* "That's because you aren't experienced enough to perform by yourself."

Confrontational Responses

A confrontational response challenges the communicator to clarify the message, usually by pointing out inconsistencies in what was just stated. Contradicting what was just said is a confrontational response. Confrontation can generally help communicators clarify their thoughts and feelings or attend to something they are avoiding. It is most useful in later stages of the interaction, when trust, empathy, and acceptance have been fostered. In other cases confrontation may produce defensiveness and competitiveness by being interpreted as argumentative. Inappropriate confrontation can be interpreted as an attack. Managers might best use confrontational responses when the communicator does not recognize a mistake or omission in his or her communication, or when clarity is needed.

> *Subordinate:* "As a manager, you are supervising my work so closely that it is becoming disruptive."
> *Confrontational Response:* "I see it another way. You seem hesitant to accept suggestions in spite of your past mistakes."

Diverting Responses

A diverting response switches the focus from the communicator's problem to one selected by the listener. It essentially involves changing the subject. Listeners may substitute their own experience for that of the communicator (e.g., "Let me tell you something similar that happened to me."), or an entirely new topic may be introduced (e.g., "That reminds me of [something else]."). A diverting response is useful when a comparison is needed or the communicator needs to know someone else has experienced the same thing for reassurance. In these circumstances diversion can be confirmatory and encourage the communicator to pursue the topic in more depth. On the other hand, a diverting response may imply that the communicator's topic is not worthwhile or that the experience of the listener is more important than that of the communicator. In these circumstances it produces competitiveness and feelings of being one-upped. In general, diverting responses should be used in later stages of interactions, when the point of view of each person is understood and inclinations toward competitiveness are not present. One good way for managers to use diverting responses is to share personal experiences or feelings that are similar to the communicator's to show support or reassurance. One example of diverting is the following:

> *Subordinate:* "As a manager, you are supervising my work so closely that it is becoming disruptive."
> *Diverting Response:* "Your statement reminds me of my feelings about the manager I had in my first job who used to . . . [etc.]."

Probing Responses

A probing response asks a question about what the communicator just said (in which case it is more open and conjunctive) or about a topic selected by the listener from his or her own perspective (in which case it is more closed and disjunctive). Probing responses are useful when the listener needs *specific* information to understand the message or when the responder must introduce another topic to make the communication clearer. On the other hand, probing is not useful when it switches the focus of attention from the message communicated to underlying reasons behind it. For example, a communicator may feel forced to justify a feeling or perception, rather than just reporting it (e.g., "Why do you feel that way?"). Similarly, probing responses can serve as a mechanism for escaping discussion of a topic (e.g., "Instead of pursuing your feelings about supervision, tell me why you're not happy on the job."), or they can force the listener to direct the conversation (e.g., "I'll only talk about what you ask me to talk about."). "Why" questions are more likely to produce escape and speculative communication than "what" questions. That is, it is usually better to ask, "*What* do you mean by that?" rather than, "*Why* do you feel that way?" An example of a probing response is the following:

> *Subordinate:* "As a manager, you are supervising my work so closely that it is becoming disruptive."
>
> *Probing Response:* "Can you tell me specifically what it is I do to cause you to feel that way?" (Not: "*Why* are you so upset with me?")

Reinterpretive Responses

A reinterpretive response attempts to get at an underlying cause, meaning, or interpretation of the message. Reinterpretive responses attempt to present the communication in a new light by emphasizing an implicit or underlying theme. They are similar to responses used to demonstrate the additive level of empathy.

The usefulness of this response type is that it can clarify a message for both the communicator and the listener, or it can encourage the communicator to pursue the topic in more depth. On the other hand, reinterpretive responses can be perceived as "psychoanalyzing." The listener may be viewed as somewhat presumptuous, especially if reinterpretation is used early in the interaction, before there is a full understanding of what is being experienced. The message "*I* know what you are saying but *you* don't" may be conveyed by this response, which can produce defensiveness and a superior–inferior relationship. Reinterpretive responses, therefore, should be used in later stages of communication, and only when they will enhance understanding and the free flow of communication between individuals. Managers might best use reinterpretive responses when the communicator is not aware of the implications of his or her message, and it will be helpful to make that underlying message explicit. For example,

Subordinate: "As a manager, you are supervising my work so closely that it
    is becoming disruptive."
Reinterpretive Response: "You seem to feel a need to work more by
    yourself."

Pacifying Responses

A pacifying response is designed to reassure the other person or to reduce the
intensity of emotions associated with a message. It says essentially, "Don't
worry, things will be fine." Pacifying responses are most useful when individuals need to be reassured before they go on communicating, or when intense
feelings are inhibiting communication. An outraged subordinate may need
pacifying, for example, before he or she can communicate clearly.

Pacifying responses may be useful in the early stages of the communication because they can remove obstacles to more in-depth communication.
On the other hand, one must take care not to pacify emotions that may enhance the communication. Pacifying can suggest that it is inappropriate to experience or discuss the emotions (e.g., "Now, now, don't feel so bad."). This
may make the communicator feel guilty or defensive and less willing to communicate feelings congruently. Pacifying responses might best be used when
the communicator's emotions inhibit effective, rational communication. Pacifying should be avoided when the problem is the emotions, or when the emotions energize the communicator to talk honestly. Consider the following:

Subordinate: "As a manager, you are supervising my work so closely that it
    is becoming disruptive."
Pacifying Response: "There's no need to worry about your performance.
    You're doing fine."

Understanding/Reflective Responses

The primary purpose of the understanding/reflective response is to reflect to
the communicator what was heard and to communicate understanding and acceptance of that person. Reflecting the message *in different words* allows the
speaker to feel listened to, understood, and free to explore the topic in more
depth. Rogers (1961), Benjamin (1969), Athos and Gabarro (1978) and others argue that this response should be used most of the time in the beginning stages
of interaction, since it leads to the most clear communication and intimate
relationships. It is also appropriate in later stages of an interaction.

Understanding/reflective responding involves paraphrasing and clarifying the message. Instead of simply mimicking the communication, listeners
contribute meaning, understanding, and acceptance to the conversation while
still allowing communicators to pursue topics of their choosing. A potential
disadvantage of understanding/reflective responses is that communicators can
get the impression that they are not being understood or heard. If the communicator continually receives a reflection back of what he or she just said, the

response might begin to be: "I just said that. Didn't you hear me?" The best understanding/reflective responses do the following:

1. Avoid repeating the same response over and over, such as "You feel that . . ." "Are you saying that . . . ?" or "What I heard you say was . . ."
2. Avoid an exchange in which listeners do not contribute equally to the conversation, but serve only as mimics. (One can use understanding/reflective responses while still taking equal responsibility for the depth and meaning of the communication).
3. Respond to the personal rather than the impersonal. For example, to the statement by the subordinate about close supervision and feelings of incompetence and annoyance, an understanding/reflective response would focus on personal feelings, rather than on supervision style.
4. Respond to expressed feelings before responding to content. When expressed, feelings are the most important part of the message to the person, and may stand in the way of the ability to communicate clearly.
5. Respond with empathy and acceptance, rather than complete objectivity, detachment, or distance on the one hand, or over-identification (accepting the feelings as one's own) on the other.
6. Avoid expressing agreement or disagreement with the statements.

An understanding/reflective response is indicated below:

Subordinate: "As a manager, you are supervising my work so closely that it is becoming disruptive."
Understanding/reflective response: "You are annoyed because I check up on you so often."

SUMMARY AND BEHAVIORAL GUIDELINES

The most important barriers to effective communication in organizations are interpersonal. Much progress has been made in the last two decades on improving the accuracy of message delivery in organizations, but communication problems still persist between managers and their subordinates and peers. A major reason for these problems is that the kind of communication used does not support a strong interpersonal relationship. Instead, it frequently engenders distrust, hostility, defensiveness, and feelings of disconfirmation and low self-esteem.

These results are seldom associated with situations in which compliments are given, congratulations are made, a bonus is awarded, or other positive interactions occur. Most people have little trouble communicating effectively in such situations. Instead, potentially harmful communication patterns are most likely to emerge when one is giving feedback on poor performance, saying no to a proposal that has been in preparation for six months, resolving a difference of opinion between two subordinates, correcting problem behaviors, receiving criticism from others, or facing other negative interactions. Management of negative situations in a way that fosters interpersonal growth and a strengthening of relationships is one mark of an effective manager.

In this chapter we have pointed out that effective communicators employ characteristics of supportive communication and supportive listening. The goal in this kind of communication and listening is to clarify and understand the message while making the other person feel accepted, valued, and understood. Behavioral guidelines that can help you practice this kind of communication include the following:

1. Communicate congruently by acknowledging your inner feelings but not acting them out in damaging ways.
2. Use descriptive, not evaluative, statements by describing objectively what occurred, describing your reactions to it, and suggesting an alternative that is acceptable to you.
3. Use problem-oriented statements, rather than person-oriented statements, by identifying behavioral referents or characteristics of events, not attributes of the person.
4. Use equality-oriented statements by giving the message that the recipient is valued and worthwhile, and that you want the interaction to be mutually satisfying.
5. Use validating statements that acknowledge the other person's importance and uniqueness and that communicate willingness to enter into a relationship by identifying areas of agreement or positive characteristics before pointing out areas of disagreement or negative characteristics.
6. Use flexible statements by separating facts from opinions, by expressing openness to additional information, and by avoiding dogmatic assertions.
7. Make specific statements that do not present the world in either-or, black or white, terms by using qualifier words that allow for finer gradations and by focusing on things over which some control is possible.
8. Use conjunctive statements that flow smoothly from what was said before by synchronizing speaking turns, not causing long pauses, not completely controlling the topic, and acknowledging what was stated before.
9. Own your statements by using personal words ("I"), rather than impersonal ("they").

10. Use appropriate levels of intimacy by matching the strength of the relationship with the intimacy of the subject discussed (external issues, common group, personal data, relationship) and the types of statements used to discuss it (clichés, facts, opinions, feelings).

11. Use empathy in listening to the statements of others by paying attention to the content of the message, the feelings behind the message, and any implicit meanings that may underlie the message.

12. Be sensitive to signs of resistance or defensiveness that result from misperceiving meanings or feelings or from responding inappropriately.

13. Use a variety of responses to others' statements, depending on the goal of the communication and the strength of the relationship, not just one response.

REFERENCES

Athos, A. & Gabarro, J. *Interpersonal behavior.* Englewood Cliffs, N.J.: Prentice-Hall, 1978.

Barnlund, D. C. *Interpersonal communication: Survey and studies.* Boston: Houghton Mifflin, 1968.

Bejamin, A. *The helping interview.* Boston: Houghton Mifflin, 1969.

Bowman, G. W. What helps or harms promotability? *Harvard Business Review,* 1964, 42, 14.

Carcuff, R. R. *Helping and human relations.* New York: Holt, Rinehart and Winston, 1969.

Crichton, M. *Chicago Tribune,* May 22, 1977.

Crocker, J. *Speech communication instruction based on employers' perceptions of the importance of selected communication skills for employees on the job.* Paper presented at the Speech Communication Association meeting, Minneapolis, Minn., 1978.

Dyer, W. G. Congruence. In *The sensitive manipulator.* Provo, Utah: Brigham Young University Press, 1972.

Egan, E. *The skilled helper: A model for systematic helping and interpersonal relating.* Belmont, Calif.: Brooks/Cole, 1975.

Fielden, J. What do you mean I can't write? *Harvard Business Review,* 1964, 42, 144–156.

Galbraith, J. K. Are you Mark Epernay? The literary Galbraith on the art of writing. *Christian Science Monitor,* December 9, 1975, p. 19.

Gibb, J. R. Defensive communication. *Journal of Communication,* 1961, 11, 141–148.

Gladstein, G. A. Empathy and counseling outcomes: An empirical and conceptual review. *Counseling Psychologist,* 1977, 6, 70–79.

Glasser, W. *Reality therapy: A new approach to psychiatry.* New York: Harper & Row, 1965.

Goffman, E. On face-work: An analysis of ritual elements in social interaction. *Psychiatry,* 1955, 18, 213–231.

Haney, W. V. *Communication and interpersonal relations.* Homewood, Ill.: Irwin, 1979.

Heilman, K. *Empathy: The construct and its measurement.* Ann Arbor, Mich.: University Microfilms International, 1972.

Huseman, R. C., Lahiff, J. M., & Hatfield, J. D. *Interpersonal communication in organizations.* Boston: Holbrook Press, 1976.

Jacobs, M. *Levels of confirmation and disconfirmation in interpersonal communication.* Unpublished doctoral dissertation, University of Denver, 1973.

James, W. Cited in R. D. Laing, Mystification, confusion, and conflict. In I. Boszormenya-Nagy, J. L. Framo, (Eds.), *Intensive family therapy*. New York: Harper & Row, 1965.

Lerner, L. Cited in W. V. Haney, *Communication and interpersonal relations*. Homewood, Ill.: Irwin, 1979.

Loomis, F. *The consultation room*. New York: Knopf, 1939.

Maier, N. R. F., Solem, A. R., & Maier, A. A. Counseling, interviewing, and job contacts. In N. R. F. Maier (Ed.), *Psychology of industrial organizations*. Boston: Houghton Mifflin, 1973.

Randle, C. W. How to identify promotable executives. *Harvard Business Review*, 1956, *34*, 122.

Rogers, C. *On becoming a person*. Boston: Houghton Mifflin, 1961.

Rogers, C. and Farson, R. *Active listening*. Chicago: Industrial Relations Center, 1976.

Shannon, C. E., & Weaver, W. *The mathematical theory of communication*. Champaign, Ill.: University of Illinois Press, 1949.

Sieburg, E. *Dysfunctional communication and interpersonal responsiveness in small groups*. Unpublished doctoral dissertation, University of Denver, 1969.

Sieburg, E. *Confirming and disconfirming organizational communication*. Working paper, University of Denver, 1978.

Steil, L. K. *Your listening profile*. Minneapolis: Sperry Corporation, 1980.

Thorton, B. B. As you were saying—The number one problem. *Personnel Journal*, 1966, *45*, 237–238.

Truax, C. B., & Carcuff, R. *Toward effective counseling and psychotherapy*. Chicago: Aldine, 1967.

Wienmann, J. M. Explication and test of a model of communicative competence. *Human Communication Research*, 1977, *3*, 195–213.

Wispe, L. G. Sympathy and empathy. In D. L. Sills (Ed.), *International encyclopedia of the social sciences* (Vol. 15). New York: Macmillan, 1968. ■

■ *Skill Analysis*

Get Off My Back

Joe Toby, director of management services, schedules a counseling session with Herman Sutherland, a management consultant on his staff:

Joe: As you know, Herman, I've scheduled this meeting with you because I want to talk about certain aspects of your work. And my comments are not all that favorable.

Herman: Since you have formal authority over me, I guess I'll have to go along with the session. Go ahead.

Joe: I'm not a judge reading a verdict to you. This is supposed to be a two-way interchange.

Herman: But you called the meeting, go ahead with your complaints. Particularly any with foundation. I remember once when we were having lunch you told me that you didn't like the fact that I wore a brown knitted suit with a blue shirt. I would put that in the category of unfounded.

Joe: I'm glad you brought appearance up. I think you create a substandard impression to clients because of your appearance. A consultant is supposed to look sharp, particularly at the rates we charge clients. You often create the impression that you cannot afford good clothing. Your pants are baggy. Your ties are unstylish and often food-stained.

Herman: The firm may charge those high rates, but as a junior the money I receive does not allow me to purchase fancy clothing. Besides, I have very little interest in trying to dazzle clients with my clothing. I have heard no complaints from them.

Joe: Nevertheless, I think that your appearance should be more business-like. Let's talk about something else I have on my list of things in which I would like to see some improvements. A routine audit of your expense account shows a practice that I think is improper. You charged one client for a Thursday night dinner for three consecutive weeks, yet your airline ticket receipt shows that you returned home at three in the afternoon. That kind of behavior is unprofessional. How do you explain your charges for these phantom dinners?

Herman: The flight ticket may say 3 P.M. but with our unpredictable weather, the flight could very well be delayed. If I eat at the airport, then my wife won't have to run the risk of preparing a dinner for me that goes to waste. Food is very expensive.

Joe: But how can you eat dinner at 3 P.M. at the airport?

Herman: I consider any meal after 1 in the afternoon to be dinner.

SOURCE: Andrew J. DuBrin, *Human relations: A job oriented approach*, second edition, (Reston, Va.: Reston Publishing Company, 1981), pp. 236–37.

Joe: Okay for now. I want to comment on your reports to clients. They are much more careless than they should be. I know that you are capable of more meticulous work. I saw an article you prepared for publication that was first rate and professional. Yet on one report you misspelled the name of the client company. That's atrocious.

Herman: A good secretary should have caught that mistake. Besides, I never claimed that I was able to write perfect reports. There are only so many hours in the working day to spend on writing up reports.

Joe: Another thing that requires immediate improvement is the appearance of your office. It's a mess. You have the worst-looking office in our branch. In fact, you have the worst-looking office I have ever seen in a CPA or management-consulting office. Why can't you have a well-organized, cool-looking office?

Herman: What's the difference? Clients never visit me in this office. It's just a work place. Incidentally, Joe, could you do me one favor?

Joe: What's that?

Herman: Get off my back.

DISCUSSION QUESTIONS

1.   What principles of supportive communication and supportive listening are violated in this case?

2.   How could the interaction have been changed to produce a better outcome?

3.   Categorize each of the statements in terms of the rule of supportive communication that is illustrated or violated.

Rejected Plans

Richard Hurst

The following dialogue occurred between two employees in a large firm. The conversation illustrates several aspects of empathy and different types of responses.

Ellen: How did your meeting go with Mr. Peterson yesterday?

Bob: Well, uh, it went . . . aaa . . . it was no big deal.

Ellen: It looks as if you're pretty upset about it.

Bob: Yeah, I am. It was a totally frustrating experience. I, uh, well, let's just say I would like to forget the whole thing.

Ellen: Things must not have gone as well as you had hoped they would.

Bob: I'll say! That guy was impossible. I thought the plans I submitted were very clear and well-thought-out. Then he rejected the entire package.

Ellen: You mean he didn't accept any of them?

Bob: You got it.

Ellen: I have seen your work before, Bob. You have always done a first-rate job. It's hard for me to figure out why your plans were rejected by Peterson. What did he say about them?

Bob: He said they were unrealistic and too difficult to implement, and . . .

Ellen: Really?

Bob: Yeah, and when he said that I felt he was attacking me personally. But, on the other hand, I was also angry because I thought my plans were very good, and, you know, I paid close attention to every detail in those plans.

Ellen: I'm certain that you did.

Bob: It just really ticks me off.

Ellen: I'll bet it does. I would be upset, too.

Bob: Peterson must have something against me.

Ellen: After all the effort you put into those plans, you still couldn't figure out whether Peterson was rejecting *you* or *your plans,* right?

Bob: Yeah. Right. How could you tell?

Ellen: I can really understand the confusion and uncertainty that were caused when you felt Peterson's actions were unreasonable.

Bob: I just don't understand why he did what he did.

Ellen: Sure. If he said your plans were unrealistic, what does that mean? I mean, how can you deal with a rationale like that? It's just too general . . . meaningless, even. Did he mention anything specific? Did you ask him to point out some problems or explain the reasons for his rejection more clearly?

Bob: Good point, but, uh, you know . . . I was so disappointed at the rejection that I was kinda like in outer space. You know what I mean?

Ellen: Yeah. It's an incapacitating experience. You have so much invested personally that you try to divest as fast as you can to save what little self-respect is left.

Bob: That's it alright. I just wanted to get out of there before I said something I would be sorry for.

Ellen: Yet, in the back of your mind, you probably figured that Peterson wouldn't risk the company's future just because he didn't like you personally. But then, well . . . the plans were good! It's hard to deal with that contradiction on the spot, isn't it?

Bob: Exactly. I knew I should have pushed him for more information, but, uh, I just stood there like a dummy. But, what can you do about it now? It's spilled milk.

Ellen: I don't think it's a total loss, Bob. I mean, from what you have told me—what he said and what you said—I don't think a conclusion can be reached. Maybe he doesn't understand the plans, or maybe it was just his off day. Who knows, it could be a lot of things. What would you think about pinning Peterson down by asking for his objections, point by point? Do you think it would help to talk to him again?

Bob: Well, I would sure know a lot more than I know now. As it is, I wouldn't know where to begin revising or modifying the plans. And you're right, I really don't know what Peterson thinks about me or my work. Sometimes I just react and interpret with little or no evidence.

Ellen: Maybe, uh . . . maybe another meeting would be a good thing then.

Bob: Well, I guess I should get off my duff and schedule an appointment with him for next week. I am curious to find out what the problem is with the plans, or me. (Pause) Thanks, Ellen, for helping me work through this thing.

DISCUSSION QUESTIONS

1. Categorize each statement in the case according to the type of response style it represents, the amount of empathy displayed, and the extent to which each typifies characteristics of supportive communication. For example, the first statement by Bob obviously is not very congruent, but the second one is much more so.

2. Which statements in the conversation were most helpful? Which do you think would produce defensiveness or close off the conversation?

3. What are the potential disadvantages of giving outright advise for solving Bob's problem? Why doesn't Ellen just tell Bob what he ought to do? Is it incongruent to ask Bob what he thinks is the best solution?

4. Identify the statements in the conversation that illustrate empathy, different types of responses, and different principles of supportive communication. ∎

■ Skill Practice

United Chemical Company

In this exercise you should apply the principles of supportive communication and supportive listening you have read about in this chapter. First, you will need to form groups of four people each. Next, read the case and assign the following roles in your group: Max, Sue, Jack, and an observer. Assume that a meeting is being held with Max, Sue, and Jack immediately after the incidents below end. Play the roles you have been assigned and try to resolve the problems. The observer should provide feedback to the other three individuals at the end of the role play.

The United Chemical Company is a large producer and distributor of commodity chemicals with five chemical production plants in the United States. The operations at the main plant in Baytown, Texas, include not only production equipment, but also the company's research and engineering center.

The process design group consists of eight male engineers and the supervisor, Max Kane. The group has worked together steadily for a number of years, and good relationships have developed among all members. When the workload began to increase, Max hired a new design engineer, Sue Davis, a recent masters degree graduate from one of the foremost engineering schools in the country. Sue was assigned to a project involving expansion of one of the existing plant facilities' capacity. Three other design engineers were assigned to the project along with Sue: Jack Keller (age thirty-eight, fifteen years with the company), Sam Sims (age forty, ten years with the company), and Lance Madison (age thirty-two, eight years with the company).

As a new employee, Sue was very enthusiastic about the opportunity to work at United. She liked her work very much because it was challenging and it offered her a chance to apply much of the knowledge she had gained in her university studies. On the job, Sue kept fairly much to herself and her design work. Her relations with her fellow project members were friendly, but she did not go out of her way to have informal conversations during or after working hours.

Sue was a diligent employee who took her work quite seriously. On occasions when a difficult problem arose, she would stay after hours in order to come up with a solution. Because of her persistence, coupled with her more current education, Sue completed her portion of the various project stages usually a number of days before her colleagues. This was somewhat irritating

SOURCE: A. D. Szilagyi and M. J. Wallace, *Organizational behavior and performance*, 3rd ed. (Glenview, Ill.: Scott, Foresman and Co., 1983), pp. 204–205.

to her because on these occasions she went to Max to ask for additional work to keep her busy until her fellow workers caught up to her. Initially, she had offered to help Jack, Sam, and Lance with their part of the project, but each time she was turned down very tersely.

About five months after Sue had joined the design group, Jack asked to see Max about a problem the group was having. The conversation between Max and Jack was as follows:

Max: Jack, I understand you wanted to discuss a problem with me.

Jack: Yes, Max. I didn't want to waste your time, but some of the other design engineers wanted me to discuss Sue with you. She is irritating everyone with her know-it-all, pompous attitude. She just is not the kind of person that we want to work with.

Max: I can't understand that, Jack. She's an excellent worker whose design work is always well done and usually flawless. She's doing everything the company wants her to do.

Jack: The company never asked her to disturb the morale of the group or to tell us how to do our work. The animosity of the group can eventually result in lower-quality work for the whole unit.

Max: I'll tell you what I'll do. Sue has a meeting with me next week to discuss her *six-month* performance. I'll keep your thoughts in mind, but I can't promise an improvement in what you and the others believe is a pompous attitude.

Jack: Immediate improvement in her behavior is not the problem, it's her coaching others when she has no right to engage in publicly showing others what to do. You'd think she was lecturing an advance class in design with all her high-power, useless equations and formulas. She'd better back off soon, or some of us will quit or transfer.

During the next week, Max thought carefully about his meeting with Jack. He knew that Jack was the informal leader of the design engineers and generally spoke for the other group members. On Thursday of the following week, Max called Sue into his office for her midyear review. One portion of the conversation was as follows:

Max: There is one other aspect I'd like to discuss with you about your performance. As I just related to you, your technical performance has been excellent; however, there are some questions about your relationships with the other workers.

Sue: I don't understand—what questions are you talking about?

Max: Well, to be specific, certain members of the design group have complained about your apparent "know-it-all attitude" and the manner in which you try to tell them how to do their job. You're going to have to be patient with them and not publicly call them out about their performance. This is a good group of engineers, and their work over the years has been more than acceptable. I don't want any problems that will cause the group to produce less effectively.

Sue: Let me make a few comments. First of all, I have never publicly criticized their performance to them or to you. Initially, when I was finished ahead of them, I offered to help them with their work, but was bluntly told to mind my own business. I took the hint and concentrated only on my part of the work.

What you don't understand is that after five months of working in this group I have come to the conclusion that what is going on is a "rip-off" of the company. The other engineers are "goldbricking" and setting a work pace much slower than they're capable of. They're more interested in the music from Sam's radio, the local football team, and the bar they're going to go to for TGIF. I'm sorry, but this is just not the way I was raised or trained. And finally, they've never looked on me as a qualified engineer, but as a woman who has broken their professional barrier.

OBSERVATION SHEET

As the observer, rate the extent to which the role-players performed the following behaviors effectively. Place initials of individuals on the scale in the place that represents their performance.

		A Lot				Not at All
1.	Communicated congruently.	5	4	3	2	1
2.	Used descriptive communication.	5	4	3	2	1
3.	Used problem-oriented communication.	5	4	3	2	1
4.	Used validating communication.	5	4	3	2	1
5.	Used specific and qualified communication.	5	4	3	2	1
6.	Used conjunctive communication.	5	4	3	2	1
7.	Owned statements and used personal words.	5	4	3	2	1
8.	Listened intentively.	5	4	3	2	1
9.	Displayed empathy.	5	4	3	2	1
10.	Used a variety of response alternatives.	5	4	3	2	1

Empathy Exercise

This exercise is designed to help you experience empathy on an interchange as well as an additive level. You should pair up with another member of the class and use interchange empathy skills to understand both cognitively and emotionally the frame of reference of the other person. After a brief interaction, you should attempt to display additive empathy by "becoming" the other person and introducing him or her to the rest of the class. This will give you a chance to express in your own words the point of view of the other person, with particular emphasis on thoughts and feelings that were not overtly expressed.

This exercise is conducted by forming two circles with the same number of people, one inside the other. Each person in the outer circle becomes the partner of the nearest person in the inner circle. Partners should spend five to ten minutes interacting, with the outer circle member serving as the empathizer and the inner circle member serving as the communicator. The empathizer should find out about, and empathize with, the frame of reference of the communicator. After this interaction time, the empathizers should introduce their partners to the rest of the class. Start with whoever wants to be first.

Introductions should last three to four minutes each, depending on the size of the group. The introductions must follow these rules:

1. The empathizer must place his or her hands on the shoulders of the person being introduced and maintain physical contact throughout the introduction.
2. The empathizer must use first-person speech in the introduction ("Hi, *I'm* John.") and take the role of the person he or she is introducing.
3. The introduction should not be a repetition of factual information. Rather, the introducer should display additive empathy by revealing the frame of reference of the other person. ("If I were you, here is how I would view life, how I would feel, what I would think, etc.")

After all members of the inner circle have been introduced, the two circles should change places and the partners reverse roles. A few minutes should be spent repeating the interaction with the new empathizer listening to the new communicator. Introductions should again be made after the interactions.

Because this exercise may be a little awkward at first for those who haven't had much experience with additive empathy, some may be tempted to avoid doing the work necessary to really experience empathy. Watch out for behaviors that serve as escapes, such as the following:

This is based on an idea suggested by J. M. Pfeiffer and J. E. Jones, *Annual handbook for group facilitators, 1973* (LaJolla, Calif.: University Associates, 1973), p. 7.

- Not maintaining physical contact.
- Not using first-person language.
- Laughing or joking about "becoming" another person, especially a member of the opposite sex.
- Saying only what one heard the partner say.
- Sticking strictly to facts, rather than describing feelings, meanings, and points of view.
- Treating this as a memory exercise, rather than an empathy exercise.

You may want to discuss the following on completion of this exercise:

1. How difficult was it to empathize? What are the major barriers to experiencing additive empathy?
2. What did you learn about yourself as you tried to empathize? Did you feel threatened?
3. What is the difference between additive empathy and interchange empathy, based on your experience?
4. What advice would you give someone on how to develop empathy?

Reflective Listening Exercise

Indicate the extent to which you agree or disagree with each statement below. Express your honest feelings, even though they may not be particularly popular.

Use the following scale for your ratings. Notice there are no 3's; you must take sides on each item. 5—definitely agree, 4—agree somewhat, 2—disagree somewhat, 1—definitely disagree.

_____ **1.** To climb the executive hierarchy, women must become more selfish, more demanding, and less caring of others.

_____ **2.** Women who stay in the home are usually better mothers than those who work outside the home on a full-time basis.

_____ **3.** For a woman to be a successful executive, she must sacrifice some of her femininity.

_____ **4.** Women have an obligation to move with their husbands when they get better jobs in another city, even if it means giving up a job.

_____ **5.** Most men think of women in the work place in sexual terms.

_____ **6.** Men have a fear (albeit generally hidden) of intelligent and powerful women.

_____ **7.** Most women cannot be totally fulfilled unless they have an opportunity for employment outside the home.

_____ **8.** A woman's first obligation is to her home and family.

Calculate your score for these items by reversing the scoring for items 5 through 8 and adding up your total score. Now find someone who has an opposite opinion from yours on most of these items (that is, a person who has a score at least 15 points different from yours). Try to influence that person to change his or her opinions so they are more compatible with yours. In your conversation, before you can reply to what your partner said, you must first reflect back to his or her satisfaction what you think the message was. Both of you must do this before you reply. The goal is to practice listening empathetically even when you feel differently from the person you are communicating with.   ■

■ *Skill Application*

Application Exercises

1. Tape-record an interview with someone other than your best friend or spouse. Then categorize your responses to the person on the basis of the seven response types discussed in this module. The Rejected Plans case provides an example of such an interview. Your goal is to listen supportively and to use appropriate response types.

2. Teach someone you know the concepts of supportive communication and supportive listening. Provide your own explanations and illustrations so the person understands what you are talking about. Describe your experience in your journal.

3. Think of an interpersonal problem you share with someone, such as a roommate, parent, friend, or instructor. Discuss the problem with that person using supportive communication. Write up the experience in as much detail as possible. Concentrate on the extent to which you and the other person used the ten principles of supportive communication. Record and describe areas in which you need to improve.

4. Think of situations (such as your job) in which supportive communication could help you solve problems. Describe those problems in your journal and explain what you would say to resolve them.   ■

5 Gaining Power and Influence

■ *Skill Preassessment*

Empowerment Profile
Preferred Influence Strategies

■ *Skill Learning*

Building a Strong Power Base and Using Influence Effectively

■ *Skill Analysis*

Why I Quit General Motors
Wild Ride for John DeLorean

■ *Skill Practice*

Repairing Power Failures in Management Circuits
Ann Lindner

■ *Skill Application*

Application Exercises

■ *Skill Preassessment*

Empowerment Profile

Pamela Cuming

For each of the following items, select the alternative with which you feel more comfortable. While for some items you may feel that both a and b describe you or neither is ever applicable you should select the alternative that better describes you most of the time.

1. When I have to give a talk or write a paper, I . . .
   _____ a. Base the content of my talk or paper on my own ideas.
   _____ b. Do a lot of research, and present the findings of others in my paper or talk.

2. When I read something I disagree with, I . . .
   _____ a. Assume my position is correct.
   _____ b. Assume what's presented in the written word is correct.

3. When someone makes me extremely angry, I . . .
   _____ a. Ask the other person to stop the behavior that is offensive to me.
   _____ b. Say little, not quite knowing how to state my position.

4. When I do a good job, it is important to me that . . .
   _____ a. The job represents the best I can do.
   _____ b. Others take notice of the job I've done.

5. When I buy new clothes, I . . .
   _____ a. Buy what looks best on me.
   _____ b. Try to dress in accordance with the latest fashion.

6. When something goes wrong, I . . .
   _____ a. Try to solve the problem.
   _____ b. Try to find out who's at fault.

7. As I anticipate my future, I . . .
   _____ a. Am confident I will be able to lead the kind of life I want to lead.
   _____ b. Worry about being able to live up to my obligations.

8. When examining my own resources and capacities, I . . .
   _____ a. Like what I find.
   _____ b. Find all kinds of things I wish were different.

9. When someone treats me unfairly, I . . .
   _____ a. Put my energies into getting what I want.
   _____ b. Tell others about the injustice.

SOURCE: Pamela Cuming, *The power handbook* (Boston: CBI Publishing Co., 1980) pp. 3–4.

10. When someone criticizes my efforts, I . . .
    _____ a. Ask questions in order to understand the basis for the criticism.
    _____ b. Defend my actions or decisions, trying to make my critic understand why I did what I did.

11. When I engage in an activity, it is very important to me that . . .
    _____ a. I live up to my own expectations.
    _____ b. I live up to the expectations of others.

12. When I let someone else down or disappoint them, I . . .
    _____ a. Resolve to do things differently next time.
    _____ b. Feel guilty, and wish I had done things differently.

13. I try to surround myself with people . . .
    _____ a. Whom I respect.
    _____ b. Who respect me.

14. I try to develop friendships with people who . . .
    _____ a. Are challenging and exciting.
    _____ b. Can make me feel a little safer and a little more secure.

15. I make my best efforts when . . .
    _____ a. I do something I want to do when I want to do it.
    _____ b. Someone else gives me an assignment, a deadline, and a reward for performing.

16. When I love a person, I . . .
    _____ a. Encourage him or her to be free and choose for himself or herself.
    _____ b. Encourage him or her to do the same thing I do and to make choices similar to mine.

17. When I play a competitive game, it is important to me that I . . .
    _____ a. Do the best I can.
    _____ b. Win.

18. I really like being around people who . . .
    _____ a. Can broaden my horizons and teach me something.
    _____ b. Can and want to learn from me.

19. My best days are those that . . .
    _____ a. Present unexpected opportunities.
    _____ b. Go according to plan.

20. When I get behind in my work, I . . .
    _____ a. Do the best I can and don't worry.
    _____ b. Worry or push myself harder than I should.

_____ Total of all a scores.

_____ Total of all b scores.

Preferred Influence Strategies

An important use of influence in managerial situations is getting others to do what you request. To better understand your preferences for obtaining compliance, rank order the following strategies from 1 (most preferred) to 6 (least preferred).

——————— **1.** People need to know you're the boss by your manner. If I ask others to do something and they drag their feet or ignore me, I don't threaten them directly, but they know by my tone of voice and general behavior that I will not tolerate that.

——————— **2.** If you expect to get things done, people need to know you have clout and aren't afraid to use it. Therefore, when I'm in charge, I make sure others know that if they don't do what they are told, they're in real trouble. I tell them exactly what to do and how to do it. All they have to do is follow my instructions and we'll get along just fine.

——————— **3.** The best way to get things done is to make people feel obligated to do your bidding. If you're friendly to people, do them small favors, and turn your back when they bend a rule or two, they'll come through for you in the clutch.

——————— **4.** It is important that people feel they are being treated fairly. If I ask someone to do something for me, I make it clear to them what they will receive in return— "what's in it for them."

——————— **5.** People's actions reflect their general values and beliefs. When I make a request, I tie it into those things that are salient to that individual. For example, if they feel that being a loyal team member is very important, I imply that loyal people would do what I'm asking.

——————— **6.** People like to understand why they are doing something. Therefore, when I make a request, I present the facts justifying the need for the action up front. This way there is no misunderstanding about the purpose or urgency of the task.

The influence strategies characterized by these six behavioral styles are shown in Table 5.2 on p. 267.   ■

■ *Skill Learning*

Building a Strong Power Base and Using Influence Effectively

Newspaper columnist James Kilpatrick once noted, "The name of the game is power. Nothing else. Who has power, how he gets it, how power is delegated, how power is restrained, how power is exercised—these are the questions that absorb us" (Kipnis, 1976, p. 2). These are clearly the questions that absorb managers. Abraham Zaleznick (1970, pp. 47–48), a professor at Harvard University Business School, has argued,

> Whatever else organizations may be (problem-solving instruments, sociotechnical systems, reward systems, and so on), they are political structures. This means that organizations operate by distributing authority and setting a stage for the exercise of power. It is no wonder, therefore, that individuals who are highly motivated to secure and use power find a familiar and hospitable environment in business.

Individuals planning careers in business organizations must understand the political nature of organizations and prepare themselves to succeed in that environment. Observers of organizations point out that the core internal processes consist of competition between coalitions for control over limited resources. If the R&D department is to continue testing a new prototype, it needs more money. If the production department is to remain competitive, in terms of cost per unit of production, it must continually upgrade its equipment. To increase market penetration, the sales department needs additional sales personnel. To satisfy their members, union leaders must demand that larger and larger shares of company profits be converted into salaries and benefits. Seeking to increase short-term returns on their investments, stockholders pressure top management to hold down costs and convert profits into dividends, rather than plowing them back into the firm.

Which of these interest groups is right? Isn't it possible to simply assess each request on its merits and make an informed, logical decision based on the objective evidence supporting each? While this is an attractive portrayal of the decision-making process in organizations, it is not realistic (Pfeffer, 1981). Management is such an inexact science that we cannot produce a simple algorithm that can be used to weigh the merits of every proposal for how a company's resources should be allocated. Certainly over time an experienced manager develops a feel for what is more or less important in a particular organization, based on emerging trends in the industry and the strategic plans of competitors. But these decisions are also influenced by a number of intangible, subjective assessments. For example, will your very qualified, bright head of sales quit your organization if his request is turned down? Will the union strike if the improvements in working conditions you promised are deferred until the next fiscal year? Will the morale in the production department management team be irreparably damaged if you turn down its request to update its equipment so you can channel more resources into sales to beat back threatening encroachments from competition? Given that your president is production oriented, what impact will your allocation decision have on the promotion he or she has promised you?

These considerations are basically assessments of political ramifications. They reflect the type of political assessment an astute manager will consider in making an important decision—in addition to considering the objective merits of the proposal. It is, therefore, important for students planning careers in management to increase their awareness of the political undercurrents in organizations and to cultivate the skills required to navigate those successfully. This requires first developing a healthy orientation towards the exercise of power in organizations.

For many people, power is a four-letter word connoting vulgar and distasteful activities they feel uncomfortable discussing. It conjures up images of vindictive, domineering bosses and manipulative, cunning subordinates. It is associated with dirty office politics engaged in by ruthless individuals who use as their handbooks for guerrilla warfare books like *Winning Through Intimidation* and *Man the Manipulator* and who subscribe to the philosophy of Heinrich von Treitscheke: "Your neighbor, even though he may look upon you as a natural ally against another power which is feared by you both, is always ready, at the first opportunity, as soon as it can be done with safety, to better himself at your expense. . . . Whoever fails to increase his power, must decrease it, if others increase theirs" (Korda, 1975, p. 4). Those who share this distaste for power argue that to train students in contemporary American business schools how to increase their power is tantamount to sanctioning the use of primitive forms of leadership.

This, however, is a very narrow view of power. Power need not be associated with aggression, brute force, craftiness, or deceit. Power can also be viewed as a sign of personal efficacy. It is the ability to mobilize resources to accomplish productive work. People with power shape their environment, while the powerless are molded by theirs. Rollo May, in *Power and Innocence* (1972), suggests that those who are unwilling to exercise power and influence are condemned to experience unhappiness throughout their lives.

Rosabeth Kanter (1979) has pointed out that powerful managers not only can accomplish more personally, but can also pass on more information and make more resources available to subordinates. For this reason, people tend to prefer bosses with "clout." Subordinates tend to feel that they have higher status in the organization and their morale is higher when they perceive that their boss has considerable upward influence. In contrast, Kanter argues, powerlessness tends to foster bossiness, rather than true leadership. "In large organizations, at least," she notes, "it is powerlessness that often creates ineffective, desultory management and petty, dictatorial, rules-minded managerial styles (p. 65).

Kanter has identified eight indicators of a manager's upward and outward power in an organization. A powerful manager can intercede favorably on behalf of someone in trouble with the organization, get a desirable placement for a talented subordinate, get approval for expenditures beyond the budget, get above-average salary increases for subordinates, get items on the agenda at policy meetings, get fast access to top decision-makers, maintain regular frequent contact with top decision-makers, and get early information about decisions and policy shifts (Kanter, 1979).

The plight of powerless members of organizations has been described as demeaning and dehumanizing. For example, the authors of *Organizational America* argue that, in our society, organizations have replaced individuals as the basic unit of productive activity (Scott & Hart, 1979). Because of the increased complexity of our environment, the lone individual as a productive enterprise is ineffectual, and only large groups of individuals, properly organized and managed, can hope to compete. These authors propose that the result of this shift from the individual to the organizational imperative has been an erosion of human rights in organizations.

Of course, this concern has been expressed before. It is at the core of Marx's economic and social philosophies, and it was graphically portrayed in Charlie Chaplin's classic movie *Modern Times*. However, the argument is especially salient to young people beginning their careers at a time when American firms are rushing to solve their productivity problems by replacing workers with mechanical robots and government is reducing the barriers to corporate mergers. The result of these actions is the creation of an increasingly impersonal and inhospitable working environment, especially for newcomers.

We believe that these conditions increase the need for powerful managers. Only strong managers can protect their subordinates from the dehumanizing forces set in motion by business's relentless preoccupation with improving the "bottom line." Unless you can get an exception to the rule authorized, unbudgeted but vital expenditures approved, innovative improvisations supported, and meritorious work in your unit recognized, you and your subordinates will feel victimized by the organizational imperative. There is nothing more demoralizing than to feel you have a creative new idea or a unique insight into a significant organizational problem and then come face to face with your organizational impotence. Only the naive believe that the best recommendations always get selected, the most capable individuals always get the promotion, and the deserving units always get their fair share of the budget. These are political decisions heavily influenced by the interests of the powerful. An adequate preparation for a career in the modern business organization should therefore include development of an in-depth understanding of how to build a strong power base.

Two basic factors determine a person's power in any organization: position characteristics and personal attributes. Naturally, the importance of each factor varies with the overall organization. For example, position title is extremely important in a strong hierarchical system, like the military or civil service. The saying "Rank has its privilege" illustrates the fact that in these organizations rewards are allocated more on the basis of position title than personal merit. In contrast, in a small business in which the organization's survival depends on good customer relations, imaginative ideas for new products, and favorable financial agreements with banks, personal characteristics are the predominant source of power. The work of each employee is highly visible and the unique contribution of the aggressive salesperson or the problem-solving engineer will more likely be recognized and rewarded.

During the course of your career you will find yourself in organizational situations that are more or less responsive to each source of power. However, both sources must generally be developed if one is to build a strong power base. A person occupying a dominant position in an organization who doesn't have the personal skills necessary to capitalize on this strategic advantage will not realize the full potential for power inherent in the position. Also, a person who has the requisite attributes to be a powerful, persuasive powerholder but is in an isolated position doing meaningless work is also not likely to realize his or her full potential. Therefore, in our discussions of power we shall argue that managers seeking influence should try to enhance both the characteristics of their position and their personal attributes.

POSITION CHARACTERISTICS THAT FOSTER POWER

Five important characteristics of a position account for its power potential: centrality, criticality, flexibility, visibility, and relevance.

Centrality and Criticality

Beginning with early research on communication networks in which subjects were arranged in different configurations (e.g., chains, wheels, circles), researchers have observed that persons occupying central positions in a network accrue more power than those in peripheral positions. Because central actors are gatekeepers in these networks, they have the most information about what is happening throughout the network and they can influence which positions receive what information (Boje & Whetten, 1981; Tichy, Tushman, & Fombrun, 1979).

This observation, based on years of laboratory experimentation, has been recently validated in contemporary business organizations by a group of English researchers under the direction of David Hickson (Hinings, Hickson, Pennings, & Schneck, 1974). This group developed the "strategic contingencies" model of power. According to this model, the reason for the uneven distribution of power across units and positions in an organization is that they differ in their ability to control strategic contingencies that would otherwise disrupt the activities of others. A fundamental characteristic of organizational life is task and activity interdependence. Few important activities occur in isolation—what happens in one unit affects what can occur in another. Recognizing this, Hickson and his co-workers are basically arguing that the more pervasive the effect of a unit's activities is throughout the rest of the organization, the more powerful the unit will become. For example, when a division of a large corporation is preparing to submit its annual budget to corporate headquarters, the accounting office's activities represent strategic contingencies for the remaining units in the division. That office's decisions about the way shared costs should be reported, the amount and type of supporting documentation required, and even the format to be used significantly affect the budget development process throughout the division.

According to the strategic contingencies model, the accounting department is powerful because it occupies the most strategic position in this decision-making process. This is best understood when we think of organizations as networks (Moch, 1980; Brass, 1981). Organizations contain two major types of interdependencies: task (sometimes called resource) and information. By identifying the task and communication linkages in an organization, one can identify the most powerful positions in each network. Simply stated, in communication networks, power increases as one approaches the center. In work flow networks, power is based on the extent to which a position's function is unique or critical. The accounting department's power stems from its location in the work flow and communication networks associated with the budget preparation process. Its function in the work flow is unique because no one else is making important decisions and has access to critical information. Also, it is the most central actor in the discussions being held throughout the division on the budget.

The concepts of centrality in a communication network and criticality in a work flow process are illustrated in Figures 5.1 and 5.2. Figure 5.1 illustrates a communication network in a work unit. In this network C is the most central actor since more communication channels involve this position than any other in the network. The person occupying this position is in an ideal location to establish a strong power base because he or she has direct contact with seven of the nine members in the unit. This extensive communication network enables C to gather information and influence the opinions of the other workers. As a result, C will likely become an opinion leader. He or she will be influential in shaping the attitudes of the work group toward company policies, union rules, etc., and thus is most likely to be viewed by others as the spokesperson for this work group.

Figure 5.1   Communication Network for a Work Unit

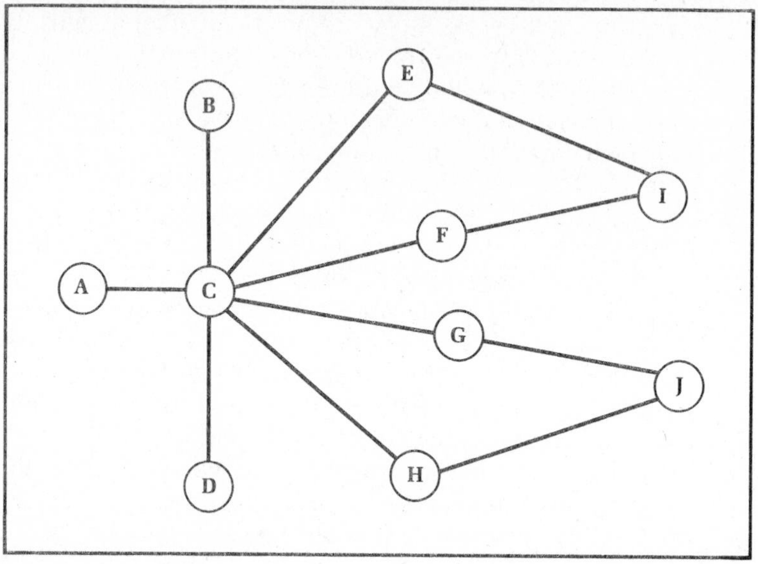

In the work flow diagram (Figure 5.2), C is again the most central actor. As a result, he or she is in an ideal location to build a power base built on resource dependencies. If other members of the network are dependent on C for performing their task assignments adequately, then C controls their strategic contingencies. However, C's power base is very vulnerable in this network because considerable redundancy is built into the work flow. As a result, other members of the unit can perform their work satisfactorily (although possibly not as efficiently) by bypassing C. Thus, to build a strong power base in a work flow network, criticality (that is, non-substitutability) is more important than centrality since it is more likely to create dependence.

A French sociologist, Michel Cozier (1964), has reported an interesting illustration of the relationship between the redundancy of an activity and the power of individuals performing the activity. He conducted many interviews in a tobacco manufacturing facility and found that the maintenance personnel appeared to have enormous power. They dictated their own hours and dress code, and were accorded special treatment by management. Looking into this anomaly further, he discovered that the maintenance personnel had changed the electrical wiring in many critical pieces of equipment so they no longer conformed to the diagrams in the manufacturer's manuals. As a result, management could not replace these maintenance workers with other electricians because only they knew how to fix the equipment when it malfunctioned. Because they were no longer substitutable, others were extremely dependent on them, and as a result they were much more powerful than those several levels above them in the plant's hierarchy.

Figure 5.2 *Work Flow Diagram for a Work Unit*

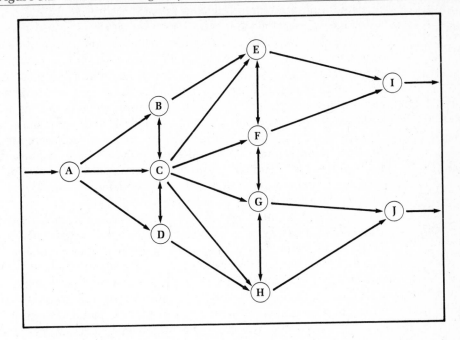

This approach to increasing the amount of power vested in any position in the organization is quite different from conventional strategies. Typically young, aspiring managers strive to increase their power by moving up the hierarchy, their assumption being that power is associated primarily with hierarchical position. But it is also possible to increase your power by expanding the domain of your activities horizontally. This is basically the strategy of the monopolist—increasing market share by buying out competitors. In the terminology of the strategic contingencies model, the effect of reducing competition is to increase non-substitutability. You make your product more critical to consumers by reducing their options for purchasing alternative brands. Within an organization, the same approach can be used to increase personal power. To do this it is necessary to analyze your position in the context of a horizontal network of positions, activities, and transactions, instead of focusing only on its relative location in the vertical hierarchy. If the average middle-level manager spent as much time figuring out ways to increase his or her power through horizontal expansion as scheming how to increase his or her power through promotion, he or she probably would be much more successful. This is especially true in organizations that are not rapidly expanding. In an era of retrenchment, there are simply not as many openings for vice presidents. This means that people motivated to enhance their power and influence will be terribly frustrated unless they orient their aspirations horizontally.

The twin concepts of network centrality and criticality suggest some specific guidelines for expanding your power base horizontally.

First, take actions to increase the uniqueness of your task responsibilities. This suggests that if you have a friend who is a secretary in the steno pool, you should encourage her to either develop expertise in one function and do that exclusively or apply for the first opening available for a private secretary. At this level of technical expertise, generalists have less power than specialists. If you are the director of sales in a corporation, you should insist that all communications between the other departments and your sales personnel are channeled through you. In this manner you can reduce redundant communication channels that could erode your power base. If you are the director of publications for one division and your counterpart in another division is retiring soon, propose a plan that would save the company money by consolidating the two offices under your supervision.

Second, become a central actor in the broadest possible communication network. One of the biggest mistakes made by individuals beginning their management careers is to become isolated. Such people assume that the best way to get ahead in an organization is to get ahead in their department. The result is that they concentrate all their attention on building strong relations with their immediate co-workers. Again, if you think about organizations in terms of horizontal structures, you will see how isolated a communication network in a single department is. It is important to become a central actor in the organization's communication network, not just the department's. This can be done by going to lunch with people in other departments, reading the annual reports of all the divisions, volunteering for interdepartmental task forces, and seeking out boundary-spanning positions that require you to work with other departments.

In addition to the location of a position in the organization's communication network and work flow structure, there are other characteristics of a position that influence the amount of power its occupant is likely to garner. In her research on the determinants of power in business organizations, Kanter (1979) identified three additional critical characteristics: flexibility, visibility, and relevance.

Flexibility

A critical requirement for building a power base is discretion. A person who has no latitude to improvise, to innovate, to demonstrate initiative, will find it extremely difficult to become powerful (except in unusual situations in which meticulous obedience to rules disrupts the system, as in the case of air traffic controllers' slowdowns). Another term for discretion is "flexibility." A flexible position has few rules or established routines governing how work should be done. In addition, when a nonroutine decision needs to be made, it is not necessary to seek the approval of a senior manager. Flexibility tends to be associated with certain types of work assignments, particularly tasks that are high in variety and novelty (Perrow, 1967; Hickson, Hinings, Lee, Schneck, & Pennings, 1971). People in such positions are assigned several types of activities, each of which requires the use of considerable judgment. The more routine the work and the fewer the tasks assigned a person, the easier it is to preprogram the job to eliminate the need for discretion.

Flexibility is also correlated with the life cycle of a position. New tasks are much more difficult to routinize than old ones. Similarly, the number of rules governing a position tends to be positively correlated with the number of individuals who have previously occupied it. Since the intention of rules is to routinize exceptions, the longer a position has been in existence, the more exceptions have likely been discovered. The same logic applies to the life cycle of a decision-making process. The longer a group has been meeting to discuss an issue, the more difficult it is to have any significant influence over its deliberations (unless it becomes hopelessly stalemated). The critical decisions about how discussions will be conducted, what evidence should be examined, and which alternatives are germaine are all made early in a group's history. Therefore, to make a difference, it is important to be a participant from the beginning.

One indication of the amount of flexibility inherent in a position is the reward system governing it. If people occupying a position are rewarded for being reliable and predictable, that suggests the organization will penalize people who use discretion. On the other hand, if people are rewarded for unusual performance and innovation, discretion is encouraged. A "reliable performance" reward system uses as its performance criterion conformity to a set of prescribed means for performing a task, such as a detailed procedure for assembling an electronic circuit. In contrast, an "unusual performance" reward system eschews consistency in favor of initiative. For example, a company may teach salespeople how to close a deal but encourage them to figure out better ways. Individuals with a high need for power should avoid a job that is governed by the reliable performance criteria no matter how attractive it might appear in other respects, since it will strip them of a necessary prerequisite of power.

If you have little choice and find yourself in a position with little discretion, one way to increase the amount of flexibility in the job is to make it more difficult to evaluate. This is the fundamental reason professionals are not closely supervised. Because hospital administrators are not qualified to evaluate the day-to-day performance of physicians, physicians have considerable discretion. There are ways of increasing the professionalization of most organizational positions. These include creating ambiguous job descriptions, developing unique jargon, attending technical training workshops, and joining professional associations. All of these activities convey the importance of developing a unique expertise as a qualification for performing a given task. The implication is that nonexperts (including supervisors) do not have the qualifications to evaluate, let alone meddle in, the activities of those duly trained and certified.

Visibility

A sage corporate executive once counseled a young, aspiring MBA, "The key formula for promotion is excellent performance multiplied by visibility." Obviously, a highly visible, poor performance will not lead to promotion, but the real message of this "formula" is that an excellent but obscure performance won't, either. One measure of visibility is the number of people you normally interact with in your organization. This helps explain why people-oriented positions tend to be more powerful than task-oriented positions. Of course, contacts with some members of the organization are more important than others. It is critical that a position provide you with frequent contact with senior officials. This can be accomplished through participation in company or outside programs, meetings, and conferences. Many a young manager's career has been secured by a strong presentation at a trade association convention or board meeting.

Recognizing this point, an enterprising young junior executive in a large Chicago conglomerate seized on a chance occurrence to impress the chairman of the board. By a strange set of circumstances, he was asked to fill in for the secretary of the board of directors and take notes at a stockholders' meeting. Making sure that he arrived early, he greeted every person who entered the boardroom and then introduced that person to every other member in the room. The fact that this young man was able to put everyone at ease (not to mention remembering the names of a large number of strangers) so impressed the chairman that he subsequently provided several opportunities for him to advance rapidly in the organization.

This example points out an important distinction between centrality and visibility. The purpose of establishing a broad communication network from the perspective of centrality is to help you gain control over the flow of information so others become dependent on you. In contrast, from the point of view of visibility, being in a position that allows you to interact with a large number of influential people increases your power by making your accomplishments more evident to the people who allocate resources, such as choice assignments and promotions.

By far the best way to gain visibility is by means of personal contact. This suggests a prescription: Insist on "going with your report." Often young managers assume that credit for writing an excellent report will be given to the author, but this is not always the case. If one member of a group writes a very good report and another member gives a very good presentation of the report to an executive committee, the presenter will likely receive a disproportionately large share of the credit for the work. Busy executives tend to be more impressed by what they see in a meeting than by what they read in their offices. They have fewer distractions in meetings (no stacks of other reading material or interrupting phone calls), and a slightly positive personal evaluation of a presentation can be transformed into a very strong positive evaluation by the approving nods and smiles of other executives in the meeting.

Another important opportunity for gaining visibility is participation in problem-solving task forces. Simply being asked to serve in this capacity conveys to others that you have valuable expertise. More importantly, if the task force's report is received well by senior officials, your name will be associated with the group responsible for the "breakthrough." Using the language of the strategy contingencies model, problem-solvers gain power by helping others cope with uncertainty. For example, those heads of government whose accomplishments stand out dramatically in a historical perspective proposed remedies to major crises. For example, FDR is credited with bringing this country out of the Great Depression, and Churchill with helping Britain survive World War II. On the smaller scale of a business firm, this truism is equally reliable. The visibility of a person's performance is directly proportional to the significance of the tasks performed and the popularity of the causes championed.

Two additional sources of visibility are name recognition and office location. Elected officials recognize the value of keeping their names before the electorate, so they place signs at state and city boundaries and entrances to public transportation terminals welcoming travelers. In business there are analogous opportunities for keeping your name visible. It is important that you receive proper credit for your written work, especially when it is being circulated widely. If your office regularly sends information to the public or other departments, enclose a signed cover note. If you are new to an organization, introduce yourself to other members. While social etiquette may suggest that it is the older members' responsibility to welcome you to your new job, the fact is that most old-timers have become numbed by the blur of faces coming and going. To distinguish yourself from the transient masses, take the initiative.

One of the most reliable predictors of organizational power is office location. While it is common knowledge that personal power is related to the size and decor of an office, the astute manager does not overlook the advantage of strategic location (Mechanic, 1962; Korda, 1975). Occupants of offices that are central to the interoffice traffic flow are in the best position to tap into the informal communication network. A location adjacent to intersections is ideal. While there are advantages to a quiet, isolated office, the time saved by reducing interruptions is gained at the expense of visibility. To be tied into the power network, individuals in isolated offices must make a conscious effort to seek other opportunities for interaction. One prominent consultant has proposed the following guidelines to desirability in office space: "In is better than out, bigger is better than smaller, private is better than public, and near is better than far" (Athos, 1975).

Relevance

This leads us to the third critical characteristic of powerful positions identified by Kanter. Powerful figures in an organization are generally associated with activities that are directly related to central objectives and issues (Salancik & Pfeffer, 1977). This accounts for the power attributed to problem-solvers, mentioned earlier. But this maxim also holds during periods of normalcy, when there are no major crises to resolve. Charles Perrow (1970) sent a survey to a large number of American firms asking the heads of departments to identify which department had the most power in their organizations. The results showed that sales or marketing was generally viewed as most powerful. Perrow explained that, in an advanced consumer products–oriented economy, sales and marketing represent the central concerns of most businesses. Because other activities in the organization are basically dependent on revenues from sales, the work performed by sales personnel is most relevant to the central concern of organizational survival.

In a similar study, Jay Lorsch and Paul Lawrence (1967) identified the "dominant competitive issue" for companies using different types of technology. The dominant competitive issue is the organizational activity that accounts most for the firm's ability to compete effectively with other members of its industry. Companies using a flow process form of technology, such as oil refineries and chemical plants, were found to be most dependent on effective marketing because of their sizable capital investment and small range of product alternatives. In contrast, companies using a standard mass production (assembly line) form of technology, with a stable line of products and established customers, were most dependent on the efficiency of their production process. Finally, "high-tech" firms or companies producing custom-designed products were most successful when they had strong R&D departments.

These results have significant implications for our discussion of task relevance. An individual who seeks influential positions must be sensitive to the relevance of his or her department's activities for the company. For example, an engineer who works for an oil company is less likely to become influential than one who works for an electronics firm. By the same token, marketing personnel will generally be more powerful in companies that use a flow process form of production, and operations researchers will have more influence in companies with established product lines and an assembly-line production process.

There are other indications of the relevance of assigned activities besides their relationship to the firm's dominant competitive issue. For example, positions that involve working with people outside a work unit or, even better, outside the organization tend to have more power than positions that are internally oriented. The role of representative or advocate is very powerful because it enables a person to become identified with important causes. Another powerful role is that of evaluator. Positions that are designated by the organization as checkpoints become powerful by virtue of the fact that they create dependence. The approval controlled by people in these positions is highly relevant to those individuals who must receive it to obtain organizational rewards.

TABLE 5.1 *Position Determinants of Personal Power*

Characteristic	Description
Centrality	Relationship between positions in a communication network
Criticality	Relationship between tasks performed in a work flow process
Flexibility	Amount of discretion vested in a position
Visibility	Degree to which task performance is seen by influentials in the organization
Relevance	Relationship between a task and organizational priorities

The role of trainer or mentor to new members of a work unit is another powerful position. It places you in a critical position to reduce uncertainty for newcomers and substantially enhance their performance. Newcomers are very dependent and will feel indebted to you for showing them the ropes. Also, successful performance in this developmental role earns you the respect and admiration of those colleagues who stand to benefit from your effective training.

To summarize, we have discussed five aspects of organizational positions that are critical determinants of the amount of power individuals occupying them are likely to achieve (Table 5.1). Centrality and criticality reflect the location of a position in work communication and work flow networks. A position that is both central and critical is powerful because its occupants have access to information and resources and because it fosters dependence. Criticality is related to relevance in that a relevant task tends to be viewed as more critical, but they differ in terms of the mechanism used to produce power. In the case of criticality, power stems from the relationship between the tasks performed by a person and the tasks performed by other individuals. When a task is uniquely attached to one position in a work flow process, that uniqueness (non-substitutability) makes the individual performing the task critical to others in the work group. In contrast, relevance refers to the relationship between a task and the priorities attached to goals and objectives in the organization— e.g., the dominant competitive issue. Powerful positions are those that perform tasks closely aligned with the vital interests of the organization.

Centrality, criticality, and relevance encourage the gaining of power by horizontal expansion, or maneuvering. In other words, a position's potential for power is based on its relationship to other lateral positions and activities in the organization. On the other hand, visibility and flexibility refer more to hierarchical power. Flexibility reflects the amount of discretion vested in a position by superiors. Positions that are closely supervised provide a poor vantage point for establishing a power base. A highly visible position has close ties with higher levels of authority, so a noteworthy performance in a visible position receives more recognition. Recognition is an important prerequisite for upward mobility in an organization.

PERSONAL ATTRIBUTES THAT FOSTER POWER

Not all power stems from location in an organization and activities performed. The personal characteristics you bring to your work also count. There are differences of opinion among organizational scholars regarding the relative importance of these two sources of power (where you are versus who you are) (Kanter, 1979; Potter, 1977; Tedeschi, Schlenker, & Bonoma, 1973). Our interest is not in adding fuel to that debate, but in pointing out that both are critical components in a complete model of power. In particular, three personal characteristics are important sources of power. These are expertise, personal attraction, and effort. Expertise reflects cognitive abilities, personal attraction involves affective appeal, and effort suggests personal commitment.

Expertise

Expertise is an important source of power in an era of technological sophistication. Expertise can result from formal training and education or on-the-job experience. It is especially salient in business organizations because of their preference for a highly rationalized decision-making process (Pfeffer, 1977). In an environment in which choices are supposed to be made by objectively considering information supporting each alternative, a person possessing knowledge accrues power easily. This can become problematic when a subordinate has more expertise than his or her boss. The skillful subordinate makes his or her knowledge available to the superior in a manner that does not threaten the boss's right to make the final decision, but does not erode the subordinate's position of expertise.

Expertise is a strong base of power in large, technologically sophisticated, rapidly changing organizations. In this environment the technical specialist is especially powerful because top management is so far removed from the core work activities of the organization. Management is not aware of new breakthroughs in basic research, the latest product innovations introduced by competitors, or the changing interests of the work force. Consequently, responsibility for monitoring these areas is typically delegated to staff specialists, who develop a monopoly on knowledge and information in their field.

That staff specialists gain power by virtue of their expertise points out the importance of examining both position and personal sources of power. If you were simply to examine the position power of staff specialists, you might conclude that they have very little power. Their position is generally not central in information networks, their function is often substitutable (i.e., others are performing the same duties), their role in the organization is not very visible compared to line management, their tasks are often routine, and their tasks, by themselves, are generally not linked to the most central objectives and concerns of the firm. However, a staff specialist can compensate for weak position power by developing expertise in a particular aspect of organizational life. This might involve a new accounting system, tax loopholes, safety and pollution regulations, or recent legal precedents in acquisitions.

There is, however, a Catch-22 associated with expert power. Becoming an expert on a subject typically requires enormous amounts of time and effort. As a result, it is easy to become typecast as a specialist in one field. If you are interested in moving up in the general management hierarchy, the label of specialist is a hindrance. For example, if you become the company's expert on business-government relations in South America, your knowledge may be viewed as indispensable for a subsidiary with several manufacturing plants in Mexico. Often the more useful you are as a specialist, the less likely it is that you will be considered for a general management position. Aspiring young managers must be careful not to limit advancement opportunities by focusing their attention on very narrow aspects of a business's activities. This is very tempting for individuals who are overly anxious to establish a power base. There are always small niches in an organization that power-hungry novices can quickly lay claim to. Only when they have fallen into the specialist trap do they recognize the value of building a broad base of knowledge about a wide variety of organizational activities to enhance their long-term attractiveness for promotion.

Another critical aspect of expertise is impression management. People judge your expertise not simply on the basis of how many degrees you have accumulated, technical training courses you have completed, or years you have worked in your field; they also pick up clues from the way you conduct yourself (Goffman, 1959). If you continually refer to the way things were done in the past, they may conclude that your knowledge is dated. If you tend to "shoot from the hip" when asked a question in a management meeting, they may wonder whether you really understand the subjects as well as they thought. If you write a report that is long and rambling and filled with technical jargon, your superior may question your ability to communicate effectively. The term "impression management" is sometimes taken to mean deceitful or manipulative practices. However, we use it to refer to the need to respond according to expectation. People have a certain image of how an expert ought to speak and act to make a valid contribution and it is important that those who qualify technically as experts not undermine their credibility by violating those expectations.

Personal Attraction

Personal attraction is manifest in a variety of ways: "He has the look of a strong leader," "When she makes a presentation in a management meeting, her presence is so powerful any message sounds good," "His magnetic personality enables him to attract the most qualified and dedicated people to his department—everyone wants to work for him." There are basically two sources of personal attraction: agreeable behavior and attractive physical appearance.

Social psychologists who have done research on interpersonal attraction have isolated several critical behaviors that determine what they call "likability." These behaviors are the kind one would normally associate with friendship. Indeed, much of this research has been motivated by a desire to understand the essential ingredients of friendships. Studies of this type have identified eight major factors (Canfield & LaGaipa, 1970):

1. Genuineness, or the expectation that a friend will be open, honest, and straightforward.
2. Intimacy potential, or the emotional accessibility of a friend.
3. Acceptance, or unconditional positive regard.
4. Utility potential, or the willingness to endure high costs as the intensity of the relationship increases.
5. Ego reinforcement, or the expectation that a friend will provide social reinforcement in the form of sympathy or empathy.
6. Admiration, or esteem for the friend as an individual.
7. Similarity, in terms of values and interests.
8. Ritualistic social exchange, such as is involved in exchanging birthday and Christmas gifts.

How can we relate this research on friendship to the supposedly hard-nosed world of management? Does this imply that you must become good friends with your co-workers, subordinates, or boss? Not necessarily. Very often people choose to work with others because of their demonstrated expertise—even when they know they will have difficulty getting along (Simons, Berkowitz, & Moyer, 1970). Further, it is often inappropriate to establish a close friendship with someone in your office. Thus, one need not become friends with everyone at work, but people who possess personality characteristics that are attractive to their co-workers (the kind that, if circumstances permitted, would likely lead to a strong friendship) possess a strong base of power (Mechanic, 1962).

This has been demonstrated in a wide range of research. For example, individuals making a persuasive argument are more likely to be effective if they are liked by their audience. This stems from the fact that liked individuals are viewed as more trustworthy and impartial than disliked individuals (Bramel, 1969). Subordinates who are liked by their supervisor also tend to be given the benefit of the doubt in performance appraisals (Jones, 1973). This benevolent orientation is also manifest in the fact that bosses use rewards, rather than coercion, to influence subordinates they like (Schlenker & Tedeschi, 1972; Tedeschi, 1974).

We don't want to overemphasize this point, nor do we mean to suggest that good guys always win, but there is an impressive amount of evidence that individuals with agreeable personalities are more influential than those with disagreeable personalities. Their arguments are given more credence, their influence attempts are less likely to evoke resistance, and co-workers seem less threatened if they are promoted. In general, given a strong cultural distrust of individuals with power, leaders with likable personalities tend to put others at ease, and in so doing gain greater influence.

This conclusion is supported by research on managers' perceptions of the personal characteristics of power-holders. When asked to identify the important characteristics of individuals who were very effective in gaining and exercising power in their organizations, eighty-five managers in the electronics industry indicated that the two most important factors were sensitivity to others and articulateness. These were followed, in order of importance, by social adeptness, competence, popularity, extroversion, self-confidence, aggressiveness, ambition, deviousness, ability to fit in, high intelligence, and logicalness (Allen, Madison, Porter, Renwick, & Mayes, 1979).

There is a second basis for interpersonal attraction that operates independent of personality, or even behavior. This is physical appearance. Research in this area is generally conducted by showing subjects pictures of a variety of individuals and asking them to make attributions about those individuals. Studies have shown that people judged to have an attractive appearance are also judged to have socially desirable personality characteristics and lead highly successful lives. It is further assumed that they hold highly prestigious jobs and are highly successful marriage partners and parents. In addition, attractive individuals are judged to be masters of their own fate—pursuing their own goals, embued with a sense of mission—rather than being buffeted by environmental forces (Dion, Bersheid, & Walster, 1972; Miller, 1970). In general, it appears that people assume attractive individuals are also virtuous and efficacious.

There is considerable evidence that these are not merely fanciful attributions. In some respects attractive people *are* more successful. For example, demographic studies have shown that women who marry above their social class are more likely to be above average in physical attractiveness (Bersheid & Walster, 1974). Attractive students are assumed by teachers to be intelligent and disinclined to get into mischief. This becomes a self-fulfilling prophecy, because teachers are likely to spend more time with such students, which tends to increase their IQ scores and channel their energies into socially approved activities (Jacobson, 1968). In a work setting, the written work of attractive people is more likely to be judged of high quality and attractive people are more likely to receive high performance appraisals from their supervisors than are other people (Jacobson, 1968; Bersheid & Walster, 1974; Landy & Sigall, 1974; Ross & Ferris, 1981).

Thus far, researchers have been unable to validate the attributed connection between physical attractiveness and socially desirable personality characteristics. However, there is some indirect evidence for this. It has been demonstrated that an important source of unpleasant social behavior is low self-esteem. When people who have been judged attractive or unattractive are asked to describe themselves, attractiveness tends to be highly correlated with self-esteem. Attractive people are more likely to feel good about themselves and to have high self-confidence than unattractive people (Keats & Davis, 1970).

This was dramatically borne out in an interesting study in the field of criminal justice (Kurtzberg, Safar & Cavior, 1968). A team of scientists and doctors physically and psychologically screened disfigured inmates in the New York City jail system and randomly placed them into four experimental groups: surgery alone, surgery and social vocational services, social and vocational services without surgery, and no treatment. Disfigurements consisted of things like scars, facial disconformities, and tattoos. Data collected one year after the inmates were released (the surgery was performed immediately on release) showed that the recidivism rate for the inmates receiving surgery was 36 percent lower than for the control group. It is interesting to note the group receiving social and vocational services but no surgery relapsed at a rate 33 percent higher than that for the control group. The experimenters reported that this group appeared to show poorer social relations and tended to become further alienated from society during the one year following their release from jail.

Height is another physical characteristic that influences interpersonal attraction. It has been argued that "American society is a society with a heightist premise: To be tall is to be good and to be short is to be stigmatized (Feldman, 1971, p. 1). Two surveys have indicated that short men are discriminated against in employment situations. One survey of University of Pittsburgh graduates showed that taller students (six feet, two inches and over) received an average starting salary 12.4 percent higher than that for those under six feet. In another survey conducted at a Michigan university, 140 recruiters were asked to make a hypothetical hiring choice for a sales position between two candidates who were equally qualified but differed substantially in height. Seventy-two percent of the recruiters selected the candidate who was six feet, one inch tall, 27 percent expressed no preference, and only 1 percent selected the candidate who was five feet tall (Feldman, 1971).

Further evidence for a relationship between physical height and personal success comes from an intriguing study conducted at yet another university (Wilson, 1968). The experimenter introduced a guest speaker, "Mr. England from Cambridge," to a series of classes. In each class the experimenter altered the speaker's status in the introduction from "student," to "demonstrator," to "lecturer," to "senior lecturer," to "full professor." After the speaker left the classroom, students were asked to estimate his height to the nearest half-inch. The results showed that as Mr. England climbed the contrived academic ladder of success at Cambridge University he grew five inches in the eyes of the students.

Findings on personal attraction are obviously the most difficult to transform into concrete suggestions for personal development. There is not much one can do as an adult to radically transform one's appearance, basic personality, or height. However, this information is still highly relevant for managers for two reasons. First, one can make modest changes to enhance one's attractiveness by being sensitive to principles of good grooming, dress, and posture. One can also emphasize those aspects of one's personality that are consistent with the social norms prevalent in a given organizational context. Second, one can become more sensitive to the way others form impressions and make evaluations. If you suspect you do not measure up very well in this category, despite your best efforts at "accentuating the positive," you should compensate by emphasizing other sources of power. Whether you feel they are fair or not, it is important that you fully understand the biases of others so your choices will be informed.

Effort

In a seminal article entitled "The Power of Lower Participants," David Mechanic (1962) described several ways members of organizations can obtain more power than is warranted by their position in the hierarchy. One strategy he discussed is based on the premise that, because senior members of an organization are unable to attend to all their important business, they are forced to rely on junior members to perform many tasks critical to the goals of the organization. The senior officers thus become highly dependent on their subordinates. If subordinates do not perform well, it reflects poorly on their boss's judgment and ability to supervise. As a result, subordinates are in a position to increase their power by working hard on these vital assignments and thereby gaining favor with their supervisors.

In addition to creating a sense of personal obligation, a high level of effort can also result in an increase in power by setting in motion some of the dynamics previously discussed. For example, individuals who work hard at a task tend to increase their knowledge of the subject. Therefore, they are more likely to be sought out for their advice on that topic. They are also more likely to gather information that is relevant to other members of the organization. This information can often be the key to reducing another person's uncertainty. The proverbial executive secretary who has outlasted four presidents and is the only one in the company who knows where important documents have been filed, how much has actually been spent in the president's expense budget, and so forth, is in a key role to gain influence over his or her boss.

A high level of personal effort can also be parlayed into increased rewards through a process known as cognitive dissonance reduction (Festinger, 1957). A fundamental principle of psychology is that individuals strive to reduce inconsistencies between their personal beliefs and personal behaviors, and between their expectations of others and the behaviors of others. Applied to our discussion of effort, this principle has the following implication. When individuals exert more effort to perform their jobs than is expected according to organizational policy or office norms, an inconsistency occurs. Since the person's rewards are based on the amount of work normally expected, the inconsistency can be eliminated only by reducing the person's effort or increasing his or her rewards. While it is quite common for "rate-busters" in blue-collar jobs to be informed by their co-workers that their unusual effort is unacceptable since it makes the rest of the group look bad, this approach to dissonance reduction is less common in managerial ranks. At that level, extraordinary effort is viewed as a sign of commitment and dedication to be commended and encouraged. Consequently, it is generally rewarded formally or informally by those who benefit. Indeed, as discussed in Chapter 2, many members of organizations are so convinced that greater effort will produce more rewards that they reach the extreme state of job burn-out. They become so obsessed with working harder that they lose their perspective. While this extreme is obviously undesirable, it demonstrates how strong the effort-to-rewards linkage is in the minds of many.

TRANSFORMING POWER INTO INFLUENCE

At this point it is important to differentiate power from influence. As we indicated at the beginning of the chapter, many popular books on this subject suggest power is an end in itself. They bring to mind the old commercials about "98-pound weaklings" who take up body building to punish "bullies" for stealing their girlfriends. We are not interested in helping people gain power for power's sake. When the weak seek power simply because they are tired of being pushed around, tyranny generally follows their ascension. Our interest, instead, is in helping people get more work done in organizations, recognizing that, in general, this requires political clout. The well-meaning but politically naive seldom make major contributions in organizations. Consequently, our focus is on how you can become influential, not simply powerful.

However, we can't talk about influence without discussing power, since power is a necessary precondition for influence. Influential people have power, but not all powerful people have influence. Influence entails actually securing the consent of others to work with you in accomplishing an objective. Many powerful people cannot do that, as can be seen in the chronic inability of American presidents to convince Congress to pass what the president considers essential legislation. The skill of transforming power into influence hinges on implementing the influence attempt in such a way that it minimizes resistance and resentment.

Influence Strategies: The Three R's

Power is converted into influence when the target individual consents to behave according to the desires of the power-holder. Several studies have investigated the influence strategies used by managers to obtain compliance (Kipnis, Schmidt, & Wilkinson, 1980; Allen, Madison, Porter, Renwick, & Mayer, 1979). An examination of these results indicates that most strategies fall into three broad categories: retribution, reciprocity, and reason. Table 5.2 lists these strategies and the corresponding direct and indirect approaches.

TABLE 5.2 *Influence Strategies*

Category	Indirect Approach	Direct Approach
Rely on fear of retribution	Intimidation (demand)	Coercion (threaten)
Invoke norms of reciprocity	Ingratiation (obligate)	Bargaining (exchange)
Use persuasive arguments based on reason	Appeal to personal values (apply general principles)	Present facts (stress immediate needs)

Specific examples of these strategies shown in Table 5.3 are drawn from a review of the compliance strategies literature (Marwell & Schmitt, 1967).

These three influence strategies rely on different mechanisms for obtaining compliance (Etzioni, 1961). Fear of retribution is based on personal threat. The direct form of this approach involves an explicit threat to impose sanctions if the will of the manager is not obeyed. Recognizing their vulnerability to the sanctions controlled by the boss, subordinates generally comply reluctantly. The threat usually involves either the denial of expected rewards or the imposition of punishment.

Intimidation is an indirect form because the threat of retribution is only implied. Behind the manager's forceful demand is the possibility of organizationally based sanctions for noncompliance, but the dominant feature of the demand is an intimidating interpersonal style. Intimidation can take many

TABLE 5.3 *Examples of Compliance-Gaining Strategies*

Fear of Retribution (coercion and intimidation)
   Aversive stimulation—"I will stop punishing you if you comply."
   Threat—"If you do not comply, I will punish you."

Reciprocity (exchange and ingratiation)
   Promise—"If you comply, I will reward you."
   Friendship—"Because we are friends, will you do me a favor?"
   Pregiving—"I will do something you like for you; then will you do this for me?"
   Debt—"You owe me compliance because of past favors."

Reason (persuasion based on facts or appeal to personal values)
   Expertise—"If you comply, you will be rewarded because of the nature of things."
   Esteem—"People you value will think better (worse) of you if you do (do not) comply."
   Altruism—"I need your compliance very badly, so do it for me."
   Moral appeal—"You will feel better (worse) about yourself if you do (do not) comply."
   Altercasting—"A person with good (bad) qualities would (would not) comply."

forms—a manager publicly criticizes a subordinate's report, a member of a management committee is systematically ignored during meetings, or junior executives are given impossible tasks by insecure senior executives.

A novel form of intimidation was used by the Ohio Bell Telephone Company in the late 1970s (Mescon, Albert, & Khedouri, 1977). Employees were shown a film of a fictional newscast set in 1984, in which reporters explained Congress was about to nationalize the telephone system because it was unable to provide adequate service and going broke. As a result, countless Bell employees were about to lose their jobs. The newscaster concluded with a theme he said would have saved the company had it been heeded years ago: "A full day's work for a full day's pay." Bell calculated that increased productivity resulting from showing this film saved the company $29 million over three years.

The second strategy extracts compliance from others by invoking the norm of reciprocity. The direct form of this approach is straightforward bargaining, in which favors and benefits are exchanged. Both parties are aware of the costs and benefits associated with striking a deal, and their negotiations focus on reaching an agreement that is satisfactory to both. Ingratiation is more subtle. It involves using flattery and favors to incur obligations in others. Then, when compliance is required or support is needed, those others are reminded of their obligations.

Reciprocity is used in many ways in organizations. These include striking deals with influential opinion leaders to support a new program, asking subordinates to work overtime in exchange for an extended vacation, doing small favors for the boss so one can take longer lunch hours occasionally, and formally negotiating with staff members to get them to accept undesirable assignments.

While the retribution and reciprocity strategies are both grounded in the manager's control of outcomes valued by others, the dynamics of the influence strategy are quite different. With retribution, aversive stimuli trigger classic pain avoidance behavior, and with reciprocity, approach behavior is induced by making the stimuli appear as attractive as possible. The first strategy ignores the rights of others and the norm of fairness, while the second honors them. Also, the first is insensitive to the quality of the ongoing relationship between the parties, while the second recognizes the value of strengthening their interdependence.

The third approach is based on the persuasive ability of the manager. Instead of seeking compliance by making the instrumental nature of their relationship salient to the target person, this approach appeals to reason. The manager argues that compliance is warranted because of the inherent merits of the request. This is most likely to occur if the manager is perceived as knowledgeable on the subject and possesses personal characteristics that are attractive to the target person. The direct approach to persuasion relies on the compelling nature of the facts supporting the case ("If your shift doesn't work overtime tonight, we will lose $5,000 worth of product"). In the indirect form, the manager appeals to the personal values or goals of the other person. These might include being altruistic, a "loyal team member", or respected as an expert, or helping keep the plant nonunion, or keeping customers satisfied.

Because persuasion is sometimes confused with manipulation, it is important to distinguish between the two. A persuasive appeal is explicit and direct, while a manipulative act is implicit and deceptive. The persuader respects the autonomy of decision-makers and trusts their ability to effectively judge evidence. In contrast, the manipulator has low regard for the abilities of decision-makers and doesn't trust them to make good decisions. Manipulators have the same objectives as authoritarian leaders—they simply use more subtle tactics. Manipulative managers, therefore, often appear to the casual observer to be using a democratic leadership style. In fact, they are actually "illusory democrats"; while their actions may appear democratic, they have no inclination to share power. They use a democratic style only because it makes others less defensive, and therefore more vulnerable to their power initiatives (Whetten & Dyer, 1975).

Each approach has advantages and limitations (Cuming, 1981). The retribution strategy produces immediate action and work is performed exactly according to the manager's specifications. It is best suited to situations in which the goals of the parties are counterdependent (negatively correlated) or independent.This approach is effective only when the target person perceives that the manager has both the power and the will to follow through on his or her threat. Otherwise, the person being influenced may be tempted to call the manager's bluff. Also, the threatened sanctions must be sufficiently severe that disobedience is unthinkable. When it is used repeatedly, this approach produces resentment and alienation that frequently generate overt or covert opposition. Consequently, it should be used extensively only when the ongoing commitment of the target person is not critical, opposition is acceptable (the other can be replaced if necessary), and extensive surveillance is possible. Because these conditions tend to stiffle initiative and innovative behavior, even when individual compliance is obtained, organizational performance will likely suffer because affected individuals have little incentive to bring emerging problems resulting from changing conditions to the attention of their supervisors.

The reciprocity strategy allows the manager to obtain compliance without causing resentment, since both parties benefit from the agreement. Also, because of the instrumental nature of the exchange, it is not necessary to take time to justify the manager's actions. It is most appropriate when each party controls some outcomes valued by the other party and the established rules govern the transaction, including provisions for adjudication of grievances. Even under these conditions, exchanges require some degree of trust—especially those that are not formally documented. If a person has reneged on past agreements, his or her credibility as a negotiating partner becomes suspect. This approach is also best suited to situations in which the power-holder needs the target person to perform specific unambiguous assignments. Consequently, a long-term commitment to general goals and values or the extensive use of personal judgment is not required. An agreement to perform certain tasks according to specified terms is sufficient. When used frequently, the chief disadvantage of this approach is that it engenders a highly instrumental view of work. The target person begins to expect that every request is open for negotiation and every completed assignment will generate a reward of equal value. In its extreme form this approach undercuts organizational commitment, as members take on a highly calculative orientation and downplay the value of working together to achieve organizational goals, regardless of personal gain.

The assets and liabilities of the third approach are more complicated. The objective of the rational strategy is a higher form of compliance—internalized commitment. While the focus of compliance is acceptable behavior, commitment means shared understanding. Commitment relies on teaching correct principles and explaining legitimate needs, and then trusting the good intent and sound judgment of subordinates to act appropriately. In its ideal form, the need for surveillance based on accountability is decreased and subordinates' initiative, commitment, and creativity are enhanced. This approach works best when the worst thing the other person can do is turn down the request, since they have little incentive to hurt the manager. Also, the target person should feel there is little potential for the manager to cause him or her harm. This is typically the case when the target person is a co-worker or superior; when the target person is a subordinate, the manager must demonstrate his or her reluctance to rely on coercion and intimidation in seeking compliance. The principle disadvantage of this approach is the amount of time required to build the trust and mutual understanding required to make it operate effectively. This time increases as the number of individuals involved expands. Also, because the success of this strategy rests largely on the personal characteristics of the manager (rather than the rewards or sanctions he or she controls), long-time associates tend to develop strong personal loyalty to that individual, and interpersonal conflicts with the manager over other issues or a change in managers can seriously jeopardize their commitment.

Effective managers generally use all these strategies for different purposes and under different circumstances (Kipnis, Schmidt, & Wilkinson, 1980). However, managers frequently get into a rut and habitually use only their favorite or most convenient influence strategy and implement it insensitively. When this occurs, a predictable pattern of employee complaints emerges. If these complaints focus on the violation of rights or the apparent insecurity of the manager, coercion and intimidation are probably being overused. If they focus on unfairness, dashed expectations, or the boss's shifting moods, the problem generally stems from the excessive or ineffective use of bargaining and ingratiation. If the subordinates' complaints center on differences of opinion and conflicting perceptions or priorities, the manager is probably using the rational approach excessively or inappropriately.

Avoiding Abuses of Influence:
Two Paradoxes of Power

Up to this point we have discussed ways to gain power and strategies for converting power into influence. Before concluding our discussion, we need to examine the judicious use of influence. Unfortunately, managers often abuse their power by taking advantage of subordinates. The consequences of this practice are best illustrated by two paradoxes of power.

First, when a power relationship is analyzed from the perspective of subordinates, the greater the perceived discrepancy in power, the greater is the subordinates' resistance to influence attempts because they are disturbed by the possibility of the supervisor's causing them great harm or inconvenience (Yukl, 1981). Consequently, the excessive use of power often diminishes a manager's actual influence. When this paradox is related to our earlier discussion of influence strategies, it is apparent that influence attempts based on fear of retribution are most likely to sensitize subordinates to their relative powerlessness. Since the basis for influence is the boss's superior position in the organization, subordinates resent the lack of opportunity to equalize the power in their relationship.

This conclusion is supported by research conducted by Toni Falbo (1977). She asked 141 students to write a paragraph on "How I Get My Way," and then classified these responses into the sixteen general strategies shown in Table 5.4. Using a statistical technique called multidimensional scaling, she clustered these strategies based on their relationships in two dimensions: indirect–direct and rational–nonrational. She then correlated the results with six peer ratings obtained from classmates after they had worked together in small groups during the semester. These results are shown in Figure 5.3. The arrows in this figure depict the relationship between the sixteen influence strategies and the six peer ratings. For example, peer rating 1, "How considerate is this person?", is positively correlated with the rational/indirect strategies, such as persuasion, and negatively related to the nonrational/direct strategies, like threat. It is interesting to note that the peer ratings were all positively related to the use of rational strategies. In other words, individuals did not like working with group members who used either manipulative strategies (indirect/nonrational) or coercive strategies (direct/nonrational).

These six peer ratings focused on social attraction, not task performance. We don't know how individuals using the indirect/nonrational or direct/nonrational strategies would have been rated in terms of their contribution to the group's task. The point of this research is that, if used repeatedly, these strategies are likely to have a negative effect on the superior/subordinate relationship that produces resistance and resentment.

The second paradox of power focuses on the metamorphosis of the power-holder. The frequent use of power (no matter how well intentioned) often leads to easily justified abuses of power. It has long been recognized that the frequent exercise of power tends to distort the power-holder's perception

TABLE 5.4 *Sixteen Strategies*

Strategy	Definition	Example
Assertion	Forcefully asserting one's position	I voice my wishes loudly.
Bargaining	Explicit statement about reciprocating favors and making other two-way exchanges	I tell her that I'll do something for her if she'll do something for me.
Compromise	Both agent and target give up part of their desired goals in order to obtain some of them	More often than not we come to some sort of compromise, if there is a disagreement.
Deceit	Attempts to fool the target into agreeing by the use of flattery or lies	I get my way by doing an amount of fast talking and sometimes by some white lies.
Emotion-agent	Agent alters own facial expression	I put on a sweet face. I try to look sincere.
Emotion-target	Agent attempts to alter emotions of target	I try to put him in a good mood.
Evasion	Doing what one wants by avoiding the person who would disapprove	I got to read novels at work as long as the boss never saw me doing it.
Expertise	Claiming to have superior knowledge or skill	I tell them I have a lot of experience with such matters.
Fait accompli	Openly doing what one wants without avoiding the target	I do what I want anyway.
Hinting	Not openly stating what one wants; indirect attempts at influencing others	I drop hints. I subtly bring up a point.
Persistence	Continuing in one's influence attempts or repeating one's point	I reiterate my point. I keep going despite all obstacles.
Persuasion	Simple statements about using persuasion, convincing, or coaxing	I get my way by convincing others that my way is best.
Reason	Any statement about using reason or rational argument to influence others	I argue logically. I tell all the reasons why my plan is best.
Simple statement	Without supporting evidence or threats, a matter-of-fact statement of one's desires	I simply tell him what I want.
Thought manipulation	Making the target think that the agent's way is the target's own idea	I usually try to get my way by making the other person feel that it is his idea.
Threat	Stating that negative consequences will occur if the agent's plan is not accepted	I'll tell him I will never speak to him again if he doesn't do what I want.

SOURCE: Toni Falbo, Multidimensional scaling of power strategies, *Journal of Personality and Social Psychology*, 1977, 8, 537–547.

Figure 5.3   *Relationship Between Power Strategies and Peer Ratings*

The six peer ratings (PRs) are coded as follows:

PR1 = How considerate is this person?
PR2 = How friendly is this person?
PR3 = How well does this person express himself (herself)?
PR4 = How honest do you think this person is?
PR5 = How much would you like to participate in another discussion group with this
person?
PR6 = How much do you like this person?

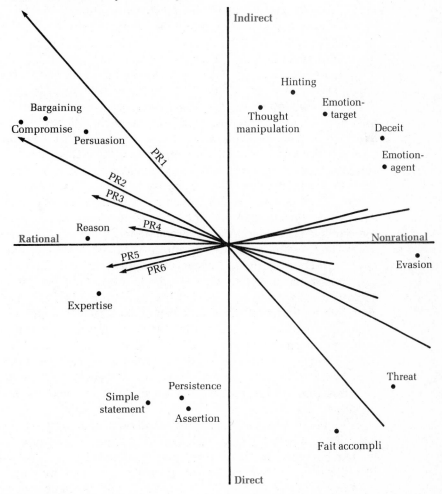

From Falbo, 1977.

of himself or herself and the target person. The result is that the power-holder increasingly exaggerates his or her own worth and denigrates the worth of others. The resulting self-aggrandizement encourages the power-holder to take liberties with subordinates that would otherwise be unthinkable (Kipnis, 1976).

The abuse of power often occurs in a very insidious manner. First, a person is given formal authority to supervise the activities performed by a work group. Second, the very act of designating a leader leads the group to expect direction from that person. Not wanting to step on the toes of the new leader, they wait to be led. Third, the leader interprets this as a lack of personal initiative and concludes that, without direction, the group will become immobilized. Fourth, this leads him or her to conclude that, for the good of the group, he or she must exercise firm control and direction. Fifth, the leader punishes group members who criticize his or her strong leadership, arguing that by attacking the leader they are threatening the well-being of the group as a whole.

This developmental sequence was observed by Robert Michels (1962) in his study of the formation of the German Social Democratic Party before World War I. In response to economic chaos in Germany, the Social Democrats emerged as a populist movement to protect the interests of the workers. Initially the organization was democratically operated. The early elected leaders were ordinary members of the work force. They worked hard to implement the radical goals of the socialist movement and achieved considerable success. As a result, they obtained high status. They were consulted by government officials, courted by businessmen, and quoted by the press. Michels observes that, as the status of the union officials increased, they became more and more conservative. They began advocating goals that were less radical, less ambitious, and less threatening to the established institutions in the society. Further, they suppressed the development of younger leaders in the party who advocated more radical policies. Michels concludes that the leaders' abandonment of their initial idealism and democratic leadership style reflected an emerging personal goal of perpetuating their newfound status. They became so preoccupied with maintaining their positions of power that they avoided the risk of challenging the entrenched interests of government and business, and suppressed criticism of these actions within their own organization.

Michels coined the term "the iron law of oligarchy" to describe this process of a group electing representative leaders, only to find later that those leaders have become so obsessed with protecting their power that their focus has shifted from representing to controlling. "Oligarchy" refers to the rule of the few over the many, and "the iron law" reflects Michels' conviction that this outcome is inevitable in all cases of governance.

There is, unfortunately, considerable evidence to support Michels' pessimism. In our society, "Watergate" has become synonymous with the abuse of power. President Nixon and his staff, bolstered by a record-setting victory over George McGovern, began to feel that their personal political interests were synonymous with the welfare of the nation. They believed their power was absolute and their morality beyond reproach. It is disturbing to observe the similarity between their behavior and that described by a group of anthropologists in the primitive Indian village of Karimpur. The anthropologists described a transformation that occurred among agents of absentee landlords—agents who, once appointed to their positions, exploited their fellow villagers. The researchers (Wiser & Wiser, 1967, p. 113) reported:

> If you were to take one of the most harmless men in the village and put him in the watchman's place, he would be a rascal within six months. . . . The sense of power and sudden popularity which a man experiences on finding himself an agent of some outside authority is in itself a danger. If he tests the new power and finds that he does not inspire fear, he may be content to perform his duties without further ventures. But if he finds his neighbors easily intimidated, and if his personal ambitions urge him on, he repeats his assertions of power until he becomes a hardened tyrant.

Lord Acton's well-known dictum "Power corrupts and absolute power corrupts absolutely" posits a strong relationship between the amount of power a person has and the tendency to abuse the accompanying prerogatives. This is consistent with our discussion of power. Managers must be able to obtain power sufficient to secure the commitments necessary to accomplish important work objectives, but the unbridled use of power tends to be self-defeating.

The observation that the abuse of power tends to be self-checking has been a common theme in literature through the centuries. David Kipnis, in his book *The Powerholders* (1976, p. 169), points out that the Greek dramatists were particularly sensitive to the fate of persons who were at the peak of their power and status:

> In the Greek plays of Sophocles, for instance, the viewer is confronted with the image of great and powerful rulers transformed by their prior successes so that they are filled with a sense of their own worth and importance— with "hubris"—impatient of the advice of others and unwilling to listen to opinions that disagree with their own. Yet, in the end they are destroyed by events, which they discover, to their anguish, that they cannot control. Oedipus is destroyed soon after the crowds say (and he believes) that "he is almost like a God"; King Creon, at the zenith of his political and military power, is brought down as a result of his unjust and unfeeling belief in the infallibility of his judgments. Sophocles warns us never to be envious of the powerful until we see the nature of their endings. Too often arrogance, bred of power, finally causes its own defeat and unhappy ending.

In this context the counsel of A. Bartlett Giamatti, President of Yale University, is particularly appropriate: "Far better to conceive of power as consisting in part of the knowledge of when not to use all the power you have. . . . Whoever knows how to restrain and effectively release power finds, if he is skillful and good, that power flows back to him (1981, p. 169).

Several principles that appear to govern the wise use of power will, if followed, help a leader avoid a situation in which the misuse of power leads to the loss of power.

First, one should place one's desire for power in proper perspective. To be an effective leader, you must be able to establish a strong power base. This enables you to influence critical decisions affecting yourself and your subordinates. However, it is very easy to begin viewing personal power as an end, rather than a means. Once this goal orientation shifts, trouble follows. As we noted earlier, our objection to most of the popular books about how to gain power and intimidate others is that they fail to make this differentiation, and so encourage considerable mischief.

Second, one way to guard against this shift in orientation is to avoid positions that are "all powerful." These are positions that are constrained by too few checks and balances. While these positions are seductive in appearance, they are definitely hazardous to one's long-term career interests, for they encourage injudicious actions and devastating reactions that leave permanent scars on a person's management record. Following Newton's third law that for every action there is an opposite and equal reaction, small abuses of power prompt minor objections that are visible to only a few intimate colleagues. However, egregious abuses sooner or later prompt a backlash of such intensity that it is likely to damage one's career.

Third, one should rely primarily on the persuasion and negotiation influence strategies. Establishing norms that encourage others to disagree with you without fear of recrimination is an effective safeguard against the abuse of power. Tyranny is incompatible with freedom of expression. If you observe yourself relying increasingly on the formal authority of your office to get your way and subordinates are increasingly reluctant to disagree with you, you should take action to counter this shift toward a dominance form of influence.

This discussion leads to a counter-intuitive conclusion. If the loss of power comes from not trusting subordinates enough and jealously hoarding one's power, it follows that managers' influence will be increased if managers share their power with subordinates (Kanter, 1979). David McClelland (1975, p. 263), a Harvard psychologist who has studied organizational power for several decades, has observed:

> The negative . . . face of power is characterized by the dominance submission mode: if I win, you lose. . . . It leads to simple and direct means of feeling powerful (such as being aggressive). It does not often lead to effective social leadership for the reason that such a person tends to treat other people as pawns. People who feel they are pawns tend to be passive and useless to the leader who gets his satisfaction from dominating them. Slaves are the most inefficient form of labor ever devised by man. If a leader wants to have far-reaching influence, he must make his followers feel powerful and able to accomplish things on their own.

Managerial power increases as it is shared with subordinates for two reasons. First, this approach to management encourages subordinates to magnify their talents and abilities. Responding to their boss's encouragement to take the initiative and make recommendations, subordinates get more involved in their work and seek to upgrade their knowledge and skills. The result is that, as commitment increases and skills are upgraded, the performance of the group improves. People with the skills and support necessary to make informed decisions and act quickly generally accomplish more. As the performance of the work group increases, the manager is given credit for getting the most out of the personnel and his or her responsibilities are expanded. This, in turn, expands the manager's power base.

The second reason sharing power expands influence is that delegation enables a manager to take on more responsibility. Training subordinates to do your job enables you to take on more of your boss's responsibilities. Recently a very successful executive visiting a management course was asked several questions about career development. Using his own mercurial advancement as an example, he proposed that the first thing to do on entering an organization is to make sure you are working for a "rising star." Then quickly master your job and train key subordinates to perform all but the most essential and sensitive tasks. Use the time you have freed up to study your boss's job—looking for opportunities to help him or her be more effective. As your boss begins to delegate more work to you, he or she will soon recognize how valuable you have become. As a result, when your boss is promoted, he or she will be anxious to take you along to help meet the challenges of the new assignment.

Michael Maccoby (1976), author of the bestseller *The Gamesman*, underscores this advice. He cites the example of a manager who announced to his staff that he was going to offer a formal class after hours on how to do his job. All were invited to attend. Most of his staff took the course and as a result, after a few months, many of them actually began picking up portions of his work. This enabled him to take on more difficult projects and the staff were gratified that he was encouraging them to expand their knowledge and skills. In the long run, motivation and performance improved in the department and the manager was able to take a more active role in the management of the organization as a whole.

SUMMARY AND BEHAVIORAL GUIDELINES

Our arguments thus far are summarized in the model of power in Figure 5.4. We began by discussing different sources of power, and proposed that these could be grouped into position characteristics and personal attributes. Both are important if one is to maximize one's potential as a power-holder. That is, both the strong person in a weak position and the weak person in a strong po-

Figure 5.4   *Model of Power and Influence*

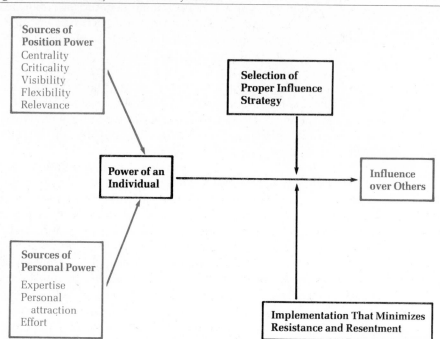

sition are at a disadvantage relative to the strong person in a strong position.

A well-established power base enables a person to be influential in the sense of being able to get work accomplished and obtain commitments to important objectives. However, people often have more power than influence. Consequently, we have also focused on how to translate power into influence. This is done by selecting the appropriate influence strategy and implementing it in such a way that resistance to the exercise of power and resentment of the power-holder are minimized. In general, this is most likely to occur when managers use the higher numbered strategies in Figure 5.3. Persuasion tends to build trust and encourage internalized commitment, while coercion and intimidation erode trust, produce only superficial compliance, and encourage a servile attitude.

The unbridled use of power tends to increase resistance among subordinates, which in turn erodes the power base of the manager. It also tends to transform the orientation of the manager regarding his or her stewardship over subordinates. The more a manager tends to dominate subordinates, the more dependent they become on his or her initiatives. As a result, the manager may overvalue his or her contribution to their work activities ("Without me they would be lost."). This inflated judgment of self-worth encourages abuses of power that may lead superiors, subordinates, union leaders, or the general public to demand the manager's resignation. In this manner, the abuse of power tends to be self-checking.

Key guidelines for gaining power in organizations are the following:

1. Increase your centrality and criticality in the organization by acquiring a more central role in the work flow, having information filtered through you, making at least part of your job responsibilities unique, expanding your network of communication contacts, and occupying an office convenient to main traffic flows.
2. Increase the personal discretion and flexibility of your job by getting rid of routine activities, expanding task variety and novelty, initiating new ideas, getting involved in new projects, participating in the early stages of the decision-making process, and avoiding "reliable performance criteria" for judging your success on the job.
3. Build into your job tasks that are difficult to evaluate by creating an ambiguous job description, developing a unique language or set of labels in your work, obtaining advanced training, becoming more involved in professional associations, and exercising your own judgment.
4. Increase the visibility of your job performance by expanding the number of contacts you have with senior people, making oral presentations of written work, participating in problem-solving task forces, sending out notices of accomplishment that are of interest to the organization, and seeking additional opportunities to increase personal name recognition.
5. Increase the relevance of your tasks to the organization by becoming an internal coordinator or external representative, providing services and information to other units, monitoring and evaluating activities within your own unit, expanding the domain of your work activities, becoming involved in decisions central to the organization's top priority goals, and becoming a trainer or mentor for new members.
6. Enhance your personal power in the organization by developing an area in which you are the acknowledged expert, fostering the eight attributes of friendship (genuineness, intimacy, acceptance, utility, ego reinforcement, admirability, similarity, and social exchange), cultivating critical skills, accentuating pleasant aspects of your personal appearance, and building up personal credits by putting forth more effort than expected.

The key to effectively influencing others lies in selecting the appropriate approach for specific circumstances and avoiding the misuse of power.

Retribution Approaches

1. Use retribution approaches when there is a substantial imbalance of power between the parties, when the ongoing commitment of the other person is not critical, when opposition is acceptable (for example, when personnel replacement is possible, if necessary), and when extensive surveillance is possible.
2. Do not use retribution approaches when quality workmanship and innovation are critical or when acceptance and high commitment are important.
3. Implement retribution strategies by using *aversive stimulation* ("I will stop punishing you if you comply"), *coercion* ("If you do not comply, I will punish you"), or *intimidation* ("You had better comply because of my power over you").

Reciprocity Approaches

4. Use reciprocity approaches when the parties are mutually dependent, when there are clearly specified rules governing interpersonal transactions, and when there is sufficient time to reach satisfactory agreements.
5. Do not use reciprocity approaches when common goals or values are required or when equality in providing mutual rewards is not possible.
6. Implement reciprocity approaches by using *promises* ("If you comply, I will reward you"), *ingratiation* ("I have done something for you, now you do something for me"), *pregiving* ("I will do something for you if you will then do something for me"), *social trading* ("Because we are friends, will you do me a favor?"), or *bargaining* ("Let's find an acceptable alternative in which I get what I want and you get what you want").

Rational Approaches

7. Use rational approaches when there are few time constraints, when initiation and innovation are vital, when interpersonal trust is high, when personal goals are congruent and/or respected by both parties, and when it is important for the other person to understand why the request is being made.
8. Do not use rational strategies when there is high personnel turnover, when relationships are only temporary, when interpersonal conflict is especially high, or when there is a high emotional component to the request.
9. Implement rational approaches by using *presentation of facts* ("The facts indicate that you should comply"), *appeals to exper-*

tise ("I have information that if you comply, you will be rewarded by natural consequences"), *appeals to esteem ("People will think better of you if you comply"), appeals to altruism* ("I need your compliance, and you are a good person; therefore, do it for me"), *appeals to moral values* ("You will feel better about yourself if you comply"), or *altercasting* ("A good person would do it").

Misuse of Power

10. In general, rely on rational and reciprocity strategies and avoid the frequent use of retribution.
11. Use influence strategies to accomplish ends that are not entirely self-serving.
12. Foster a system of checks or constraints on your own use of power to help avoid misuse or overuse of power. Cultivate your subordinates by sharing, rather than hoarding, power.

REFERENCES

Allen, R. W., Madison, D. L., Porter, L. W., Renwick, P. A., & Mayes, B. T. Organizational politics: Tactics and characteristics of its actors. *California Management Review*, 1979, *22*, 77–83.

Athos, A. G. Time, space and things. In R. E. Coffey, A. G. Athos, & P. A. Reynolds (Eds.), *Behavior in organizations* (2nd ed.). Englewood Cliffs: Prentice Hall, 1975.

Berscheid, E., & Walster, E. Physical attractiveness. In N. N. Berkowitz (Ed.), *Advances in experimental psychology*. New York: Academic Press, 1974.

Boje, D. M., & Whetten, D. A. Effects of organizational strategies and contextual constraints on centrality and attributions of influence in interorganizational networks. *Administrative Science Quarterly*, 1981, *26*, 378–395.

Bramel, D. Interpersonal attraction, hostility, and perception. In J. Mills (Ed.), *Experimental social psychology*. New York: Macmillan, 1969.

Brass, D. J. Structural relationships. *Administrative Science Quarterly*, 1981, *26*, 331–348.

Canfield, F. E., & LaGaipa, J. J. *Friendship expectations at different stages in the development of friendship*. Paper read at the annual meeting of the Southeastern Psychological Association, Louisville, April 1970.

Crozier, M. *The bureaucratic phenomenon*. Chicago: University of Chicago Press, 1964.

Cuming, P. *The power handbook*. Boston: CBI Publishing Co., 1981.

Dion, K. K., Berscheid, E., & Walster, E. What is beautiful is good. *Journal of Personality and Social Psychology*, 1972, *24*, 285–290.

Etzioni, A. *A comprehensive analysis of complex organizations*. Glencoe, Ill.: Free Press, 1961.

Falbo, T. Multidimensional scaling of power strategies. *Journal of Personality and Social Psychology*, 1977, *35*, 537–547.

Feldman, S. D. *The presentation of shortness in everyday life and height and heightism in American society: Toward a sociology of stature*. Paper presented before meetings of the American Sociological Association, Denver, Colorado, September 1971.

Festinger, L. *A theory of cognitive dissonance*. Stanford: Stanford University Press, 1957.

Giamatti, A. B. *The university and the public interest*. New York: Antheneum, 1981.

Goffman, E. *The presentation of self in everyday life*. New York: Doubleday, 1959.

Hickson, D. J., Hinings, C. R., Lee, C. A., Schneck, R. E., & Pennings, J. M. Strategic contingencies theory of intraorganizational power. *Administrative Science Quarterly, 1971, 16,* 216–229.

Hinings, C. R., Hickson, D. J., Pennings, J. M., & Schneck, R. E. Structural conditions of intraorganizational power. *Administrative Science Quarterly, 1974, 21,* 22–44.

Jacobson, L. *Pygmalion in the classroom* (Vol. 9). New York: Holt, 1968, 1974.

Jones, S. Self and interpersonal evaluations. *Psychological Bulletin, 1973, 79,* 185–199.

Kanter, R. Power failure in management circuits. *Harvard Business Review,* July-August, 1979, *57,* 65–75.

Keats, G. R., & Davis, K. E. The dynamics of sexual behavior of college students. *Journal of Marriage and the Family, 1970, 32,* 390–399.

Kipnis, D. *The powerholders.* Chicago: University of Chicago Press, 1976.

Kipnis, D., Schmidt, S. M., & Wilkinson, I. Intraorganizational influence tactics: Explorations in getting one's way. *Journal of Applied Psychology, 1980, 65,* 440–452.

Korda, M. *Power: How to get it, how to use it.* New York: Ballantine Books, 1975.

Kotter, J. P. Power, dependence and effective management. *Harvard Business Review,* July-August 1977, *55,* 125–136.

Kurtzberg, R. L., Safar, H., & Cavior, N. Surgical and social rehabilitation of adult offenders. *Proceedings of the 76th Annual Convention of the American Psychological Association, 1968, 3,* 649–650.

Landy, D., & Sigall, H. Beauty is talent: Task evaluation as a function of the performer's physical attractiveness. *Journal of Personality and Social Psychology, 1974, 29,* 299–304.

Lawrence, P. R., & Lorsch, J. W. *Organization and environment.* Homewood, Ill.: Richard D. Irwin, 1969.

McClelland, D. E. *Power: The inner experience.* New York: Irvington Publishers, 1975.

Maccoby, M. Eminent psychologist talks business management. *Boardroom Reports, 1976, 8.*

Marwell, G., & Schmitt, D. R. Dimensions of compliance-gaining behavior: An empirical analysis. *Sociometry, 1967, 30,* 350–364.

May, R. *Power and innocence.* New York: Norton, 1972.

Mechanic, D. Sources of power of lower participants in complex organizations. *Administrative Science Quarterly, 1962, 7,* 349–364.

Mescon, M. H., Albert, M., & Khedouri, F. *Management.* New York: Harper & Row, 1977.

Michels, R. *Political parties.* Glencoe, Ill.: Free Press, 1962.

Miller, A. G. Role of physical attractiveness in impression formation. *Psychonomic Science, 1970, 19,* 241–243.

Moch, M. K. Job involvement, internal motivation, and employees' interaction with networks of work relationships. *Organizational Behavior and Human Performance, 1980, 25,* 15–31.

Perrow, C. Departmental power and perspectives in industrial firms. In M. N. Zold (Ed.), *Power in organizations.* Nashville: Vanderbilt University Press, 1970.

Perrow, C. Framework for comparative analysis of organizations. *American Sociological Review, 1967, 32,* 194–208.

Pfeiffer, J. Power and resource allocation in organizations. In B. Staw and G. Salancik (Eds.), *New directions in organizational behavior.* Chicago: St. Clair Press, 1977.

Pfeiffer, J. *Power in organizations.* Marshfield, Mass.: Pitman, 1981.

Ross, J., & Ferris, K. R. Interpersonal attraction of organizational outcomes: A field examination. *Administrative Science Quarterly, 1981, 26,* 617–632.

Salancik, G. R., & Pfeffer, J. Who gets power—and how they hold on to it: A strategic-contingency model of power. *Organizational Dynamics, 1977, 5,* 3–21.

Schlenker, B. R. *Impression management.* Belmont, Calif.: Wadsworth, Inc., 1980.

Schlenker, B. R., & Tedeschi, J. T. Interpersonal attraction and the use of reward and coercive power. *Human Relations, 1972, 25,* 427–439.

Scott, W. G., & Hart, D. K. *Organizational America.* Boston: Houghton Mifflin, 1979.

Simons, H. W., Berkowitz, N. N., & Moyer, R. J. Similarity, credibility and attitude change: A review and a theory. *Psychological Bulletin, 1970, 73,* 1–16.

Tedeschi, J. T. Attributions, liking and power. In T. L. Huston (Ed.), *Foundations of interpersonal attraction.* New York: Academic Press, 1974.

Tedeschi, J. T., Schlenker, B. R., & Bonoma, T. V. *Conflict power and games: The experimental study of interpersonal relations.* Chicago: Aldine, 1973.

Tichy, N. M., Tuchman, M. L., & Fombrun, C. Social network analysis in organizations. *Academy of Management Review,* 1979, *4,* 507–519.

Whetten, D. A., & Dyer, W. *Leadership and Machiavellianism.* Paper presented at the Midwest Academy of Management, Ann Arbor, Michigan, August 1975.

Wilson, P. R. Perceptual distortion of height as a function of ascribed academic status. *Journal of Social Psychology,* 1968, *74,* 97–102.

Wiser, W., & Wiser, C. *Behind mind walls.* Berkeley, Calif.: University of California Press, 1967.

Yukl, G. *Using power.* Paper presented at the Academy of Management Meetings, San Diego, California, August 1981.

Zaleznik, A. Power and politics in organizational life. *Harvard Business Review,* May-June 1970, *48,* 47–48. ■

■ *Skill Analysis*

Why I Quit General Motors

John Z. DeLorean

It was a shocking experience for me "upstairs." After eight years of running car divisions, I suddenly found myself in the fall of 1972 with no direct operating responsibilities and a non-job as a group executive. I had no business to manage directly. Where I had been a quarterback for eight years, I now was watching the game from the sidelines. I still wanted to play in the games. On the field. These feelings of occupational emptiness were complicated by personalities.

At the time in my career when I was just one of the corporate boys spending my working and non-working hours with General Motors people or the company suppliers, I had a tightly knit group of corporate friends, and I obeyed the corporate dictates in behavior and dress. But as I grew it dawned on me that all of us were becoming too inbred. We were losing contact with America. With our customers. In addition, while I enjoyed work, I've always placed enjoying life high on my list of priorities. So I made a habit of widening my circle of friends and broadening my tastes. This awareness precipitated a seemingly endless chain of personality conflicts, the most difficult of which was with Roger M. Kyes, who was my boss while I was running the Pontiac and Chevrolet divisions. He made life unbearable for me, and he was dedicated to getting me fired; he told me so, many times. Fortunately, I had the protection of my ability as I ran those two divisions to fend off Kyes. But I remember vividly my conflicts with him, especially when he was irritated by my style of dress. The corporate rule was dark suits, light shirts and muted ties. I followed the rule to the letter, only I wore stylish Italian-cut suits, wide-collared off-white shirts and wide ties.

"Goddamnit, John," he'd yell. "Can't you dress like a businessman? And get your hair cut, too."

My hair was ear length with sideburns. I felt both my clothes and hair style were contemporary but not radical. . . .

The fact that I had been divorced, was a health nut and dated generally younger actresses and models didn't set well with the corporate executives or their wives either. And neither did my general disappearance from the corporate social scene. . . .

I thought all of this was an improper intrusion into my personal life, but I didn't pay much attention to it, which I guess perpetuated the problem. I figured I was loyal and dedicated to GM. I did my job and did it well. The com-

SOURCE: J. Patrick Wright, *On a Clear Day You Can See General Motors* (New York: Avon Books, 1980), pp. 9–17.

pany had a right to know how I was spending my business life, but it had no right to know how I was spending my private and non-business life.

Nevertheless, my clothing and lifestyle were increasingly rattling the cages of my superiors, as was the amount of publicity my personal and business lives were generating. I was being resented because my style of living violated an unwritten but widely revered precept that said no personality could outshine General Motors. The executives were supposed to be just as gray and almost as lifeless as the corporate image.

The resentments toward me festered and grew to great proportions without my knowledge. I knew some people disliked me. But since I didn't play the corporate political game, I was not wired into the underground flow of information which would have given me better knowledge about those who viewed themselves as my corporate enemies. . . .

It bothered me when Tom Murphy, my boss during my term at Chevrolet, many times said to me, "You know, John, everybody said I was going to have a helluva lot of trouble with you. But I would really have to say that this is untrue. As far as I am concerned you do the best job of running your division of anyone. You keep me informed of the important things. I know what you are doing. Far and away I have less trouble with you than anybody in the divisions."

Those were kind words from Murphy, the only top manager with whom I felt I had a good rapport. However, the warnings he was getting from other members of management that I was "trouble" indicated to me now that my papers were being graded "upstairs" by something other than my test scores. But my support from Murphy suddenly ended. It was a sinister occurrence which terminated it.

In November 1972, the corporation was staging a massive management meeting of the top 700 GM executives in Greenbrier, West Virginia. These were infrequent gatherings, at least three years apart, which were designed to discuss in total all of the corporation's problems and exchange ideas on how to solve them. Many of The Fourteenth Floor executives were given broad subjects on which to address the conference. As a group executive, I was given the topic of "Product Quality." I prepared a tough talk which in essence said the only way we can remain a success and grow is to deliver real value to the customer. I said that I felt the emphasis at General Motors had switched from this goal to one of taking the last nickel out of every part to improve profits in the short run. I singled out specific products and programs for criticism. The talk was both critical and constructive. It was the kind of talk that was for corporate ears and none other.

As is the required practice, we submitted early drafts of our talks to top management through the public relations department. Management then made corrections and generally edited the draft along the lines it felt was proper. In the process, an executive could wind up writing a speech four or five times or more. After each new draft was prepared, all the copies of the previous version were destroyed. My final draft was toned by management and edited to complement the speeches of the other executives.

Just prior to the conference, my Greenbrier talk turned up in the hands of Bob Irvin, automotive writer for the *Detroit News*. And he printed it. It was not the final version which he wrote about. It was one of the earlier drafts. The only people who had copies of that version were me, the public relations staff and top management. I hadn't leaked it. Nothing in the world could do me more harm personally and internally than to leak this type of a speech. My job was to sell our cars, not criticize them publicly. I was trying, with the talk, to impress people in the corporation with the need for drastic improvement in product quality to counter the growing wave of consumer unrest, fulfill our responsibility to our customers and restore our tarnished image.

The leak destroyed the Greenbrier conference for me and was probably the single thing that hurt me most in the corporation. I could tell that my solid image in Murphy's eyes began to diminish from the day the newspaper story appeared. I was shocked and sick. So was my staff. It was obvious that someone who wanted to give me a good shot to the gut, did.

A short time later, a friend of mine lunching in a downtown Detroit restaurant ran across a private investigator who knew GM's operations and who told him that the speech was leaked by a man on the GM public relations staff.

If I was having my doubts about staying with the corporation, and I was, it was now quite obvious that some people in the corporation were taking steps to see that I couldn't stay. . . .

I balked at becoming a group executive when the job was first offered to me in September. . . . Nevertheless, after two weeks of ceaseless pressure from my bosses, I relented and went upstairs. A non-Chevrolet man was named to the post I was departing. It was not very long before I realized I had made a horrible mistake. On my second day on the new job my boss, Richard Terrell, who succeeded Kyes as executive vice-president for Car and Truck, Body and Assembly, called me into his office. I had heard very little from him when I was running Chevrolet. Not once did we get into a serious discussion about the division's business. I suspect this was his choice since, until he succeeded Kyes, Terrell's entire 36-year GM career was spent in nonautomotive businesses, first with the Electromotive Division and then the Frigidaire Division. He, therefore, knew little directly about GM's automotive operations. This was my first meeting with Terrell in my new capacity. He is moderately tall, with thin gray hair, steel-rimmed glasses, a perpetual smile that looks more like a smirk and a manner that often gives a false sense of authority to what he says.

I walked into his office and sat down in front of his desk. Terrell pushed a button under the cabinet behind his desk which closed the office door, leaned forward in his chair, looked sternly across his desk and said to me in steely tones, "I want you to disappear into the wallpaper up here. I don't want to see you in the newspaper."

Those were not his exact words. He couched his message in terms of "team play," "good of the corporation," and how "no man is above the corporation." But the point of Terrell's message was as obvious to me as the dark suit and white shirt he wore.

"DeLorean, disappear into the boondocks."

I was shocked. And I knew that, while I hadn't heard from Terrell when I was running Chevrolet, I was going to be hearing a lot from him in the secretive quarters of The Fourteenth Floor because I was not protected by my ability and performance as I had been when I ran the car divisions. Up here I had nothing to operate to show that ability. I thought to myself: "Dealing with Terrell is going to be the Kyes situation all over again."

About a week or so later, I was in the office of Elliott M. (Pete) Estes, who was executive vice-president of operations. I was talking to him about some of my doubts about the business in general and life upstairs, and he said, "I've always told them that it's good for GM to have someone like you in the ranks. It shows how democratic we are."

I am sure Pete didn't realize the impact on me of his comment. He didn't say anything about how well I'd managed my business, the people I had developed, or what I'd contributed to the corporation in terms of quality products and substantial profit. All he said was I was sort of a weirdo. Until then, I guess I had deluded myself into thinking I was held in high esteem by my superiors, even if they didn't like me personally, because I was a business success. I had risen faster in the corporation than any of them, and I thought for that reason that I at least had their professional respect.

So I was tragically shocked to realize that this was not the case. Just as the corporation at the time had token blacks, token women and token Chicanos, I was viewed as their token hippie. I just didn't fit in. When I thought over the meetings with Terrell and Estes, I began to realize once again that I could no longer stay with General Motors. I agonized over the prospect of leaving.

The Greenbrier incident made it obvious that someone in the corporation was making an effort to hurt my business reputation. . . . I then began a campaign to leave the corporation which was going to culminate tomorrow morning when I officially resigned. Late Sunday night, I went to sleep.

. . . At about 9:30 A.M., I arrived at the General Motors Building at 59th Street and Fifth Avenue. A minute or so later I walked into the office of Chairman Richard D. Gerstenberg on the twenty-fourth floor. In the room were Gerstenberg, Murphy, by now the vice-chairman, and Kenneth C. MacDonald, who was secretary of the board's bonus and salary committee. . . .

The atmosphere in Gerstenberg's office was neither friendly nor bitter. It was strictly businesslike. The meeting lasted less than 20 minutes. I signed the document of resignation, effective May 31, 1973, which was prepared by the corporation. We all shook hands, and I left the room and headed for the bank of elevators.

Once on the main floor, I walked out into Fifth Avenue. For the first time in a quarter of a century I was out of work in the auto industry. There was a slight feeling of relief because the struggle was over. Bill Finelli took me back to LaGuardia and a flight to Detroit.

The board met that afternoon and approved my resignation. The public relations department prepared a news release—which was made public later in the month—announcing my resignation in which Gerstenberg praised my contributions to General Motors and wished me well in my new ventures. Once back in Detroit I drove home.

As I ate dinner quietly at home that night with my wife, Cristina, and my son, Zachary, I fully realized I had done what few top executives have ever done in the automobile industry. I had quit General Motors.

DISCUSSION QUESTIONS

1. Identify the sources of positional and personal power held by DeLorean in this case. How did DeLorean's views of power differ from others' at GM?

2. What impact did DeLorean's promotion from being the manager of an operating division to a senior executive at corporate headquarters have on his power at GM? Why? His interpersonal style seemed to become more of a liability to his career after this promotion. Given our discussion of the interaction between personal and positional bases of power, why would that happen?

3. John DeLorean argues that managers at GM must totally subjugate their individuality to the corporate image. He complains that there was no place for the unique expression of personal identity. The more he expressed his individuality the less power he appeared to have in the organization. Does conformity increase personal power? What about the rule of thumb that you can tell who is powerful in an organization by how many norms and rules he or she can violate with impunity? Are these observations contradictory? Just what is the relationship between "fitting in" and power?

Wild Ride for John DeLorean

He might have become president of General Motors Corp. By the age of 49, he had raced up the ladder of the giant corporation and, as a group executive, was just one step from the top. But frustrated with a management system that he considered backward, he quit and launched a project that many considered impossible, to build a new car company from the ground up.

For a while, John DeLorean's dream seemed to come true. But suddenly, the man who had done everything right found everything going wrong. Sales of his sleek new sports car dried up, debts began to mount, and the British gov-

SOURCE: How DeLorean went from bold venturer to harried scrambler, *Wall Street Journal*, Oct. 22, 1982, p. 1.

ernment forced his lone manufacturing plant in Northern Ireland into receivership. Mr. DeLorean began a desperate struggle to avoid failure, a struggle that ended Tuesday with his arrest in Los Angeles on drug-trafficking charges.

Friends and associates of the flamboyant auto executive paint a picture of a man who changed drastically as he became increasingly desperate in his attempts to rescue the company he had founded. From the coolly brilliant GM engineer, he became increasingly erratic and dictatorial, taking on many of the characteristics for which he had so sharply criticized his former colleagues at GM. He lost trust in close advisers and began to concentrate in his own hands more and more of the campaign to save the company. In the end, the swashbuckling entrepreneur may have become a victim of his own myth.

At his arraignment in federal court in Los Angeles Wednesday, Mr. DeLorean's attorneys said he would plead innocent to the charges. Federal law enforcement officials have accused him of conspiring to peddle large amounts of cocaine and heroin. The officials say the alleged scheme was a last-ditch effort to "generate large amounts of capital" to keep the fledgling car company afloat. Neither Mr. DeLorean nor his lawyer, Bernard Minsky, responded to requests for interviews.

Regardless of the outcome of the drug charges, the events of the past few days probably have dealt the final blows to Mr. DeLorean's ambitious venture. Almost simultaneously with his arrest on Tuesday, the British government announced that it would permanently close the Belfast manufacturing plant that has produced the DeLorean sports car. Though it still has several hundred cars in stock, DeLorean Motor Co., the parent company and U.S. distributor, is expected to close as well.

REPUTATION ON THE LINE

Almost from the beginning, Mr. DeLorean's actions magnified the consequences of success or failure. He put his personal reputation on the line by thumbing his nose at his former colleagues in Detroit. He declared that he would show the rest of the auto industry "how to build cars" and that his company would produce an "ethical" car that U.S. buyers could afford. He also said it would be far superior to American makes. He identified himself closely with the product, putting his name on the company and the car and his picture in the advertising. "Live the Dream" was the first ad slogan for the luxury auto, a stainless-steel two-seater with distinctive gull-wing doors.

"I think the idea of failure would have been devastating to John DeLorean," says William Collins, one of the founders of the sports-car company and formerly its chief engineer. "John set it up so that he and the company were almost one and the same. If it went down, he went with it."

As the sports-car venture progressed from its inception eight years ago, present and former DeLorean employees say they noticed a change in the boss. They say that initially Mr. DeLorean encouraged team spirit and cooperation within a small but growing corporation, but that then he increasingly began to take charge and give orders, ignoring the advice and recommendations of his subordinates.

The transformation, which accelerated as the company's troubles mounted, caused morale problems and a high level of executive turnover. Robert Dowey resigned in August 1978 as the company's first chief financial officer because, he says, of an argument over money matters that ended with Mr. DeLorean saying: "You do things my way or you can leave." Since then, the company has had two other chief financial officers, and more than 10 high executives have quit or been fired.

"Senior management morale was always very low," Mr. Dewey says. "The problem was we were all just getting orders from John rather than having any say in what the company was doing."

Some executives who joined the company with an enthusiasm stirred by Mr. DeLorean's reputation as an innovative manager say they quickly grew disillusioned. Says one: "He always wanted to be picked up at the airport and stuff like that"—a practice for which Mr. DeLorean had chided GM executives.

Other officials were angry when Mr. DeLorean refused to register the DeLorean Motor stock held by the company's senior management, a stand that made it impossible for them to trade their shares. And according to a former DeLorean public relations official, it also wasn't uncommon for Mr. DeLorean to ask company executives to work on projects involving his personal businesses. "I think one guy must have spent his whole time here working out problems involving a snow-grooming ski-resort equipment company owned by John," he says.

DeLorean employees also resented Mr. DeLorean's jet-set life-style, which continued even after his Northern Ireland plant slid into receivership. He continued to stay at Claridge's, one of London's most prestigious hotels, in rooms costing $160 to $250 a night, and to fly the Concorde between London and New York.

But some employees say Mr. DeLorean's maverick behavior didn't merely cause discord within the company; they contend that it also led directly to its downfall. Against the advice of the company's marketing, manufacturing, and engineering chiefs, Mr. DeLorean late last year—despite a weak auto market world-wide—ordered that car production be doubled at the Belfast plant. He did so because of his confidence that his new product—then profitable—would be scooped up by buyers. But the increased output quickly exceeded sales, and the company was plunged into a cash squeeze.

In February the Belfast manufacturing operation went into voluntary receivership to try to find a way to keep the plant running after the British government had refused to increase its $150 million investment in the facility.

Having lost the company's only assembly plant, Mr. DeLorean began a frantic effort to salvage the factory. But none of his attempts to come up with new financing seemed to work out. A bail-out attempt involving Peter Kalikow, a New York real-estate executive, failed when Mr. Kalikow couldn't agree on final terms with the British receivers.

On other occasions, Mr. DeLorean offhandedly remarked that he had received expressions of interest from a major oil company, a European auto maker, and a big investment-banking firm. Those deals didn't pan out, either.

Moreover, he never would identify these potential rescuers. In fact, the receivers say he was continually changing his prospective partners and his lawyers.

"Problems arose because we never knew who these people were," says Sir Kenneth Cork, one of the two British receivers. "There would be a Telex saying a group of businessmen would put up so much, but always on condition they weren't named."

Doubts arose about Mr. DeLorean's credibility as he kept changing his story. In addition to his references to unnamed rescuers, Mr. DeLorean also kept giving different figures for the amount of money that he needed to regain control of the plant. Early in the summer, he told reporters that he had to come up with at least $60 million; this fall, the figure was $10 million. The British receivers have confirmed that $10 million was the minimum initial investment needed to put the plant back in operation, though automotive experts believe that eventually a much greater sum would have been required.

A WORRIED BANK

At the same time that Mr. DeLorean was searching for a source of funds to recover his plant, problems were developing in the U.S. Worried that it wouldn't be repaid for $18 million in export financing, BankAmerica Corp. moved to repossess the company's inventory of cars on piers on the East and West Coasts.

In a panic, Mr. DeLorean sent a squad of armed men to each facility to get the cars first, according to BankAmerica. At the pier in New Jersey, they succeeded in removing 15 cars to Mr. DeLorean's Bedminster, N.J., mansion, the bank says. But on the West Coast a similar attempt was thwarted, according to C. R. Brown, a DeLorean Motor vice president, who says he called the police. Mr. Brown, who says he was fired the next day because of the incident, felt personally responsible to BankAmerica because he had negotiated the loan.

Mr. DeLorean also was struggling to keep his U.S. dealership network intact. Many dealers were complaining heatedly that they weren't being reimbursed for warranty work and that spare parts were arriving late from the company's warehouse.

The strain apparently began to take its toll on Mr. DeLorean. In Britain, the receivers charged with finding a buyer for the former DeLorean assembly plant began to notice signs of stress in the auto executive. "Sometimes he was in a fairly aggressive state of mind, and sometimes he was far less confident. There was no settled pattern," says Paul Shewell, the other receiver.

USING PERSONAL CHECKS

In an interview this summer, Mr. DeLorean said the only way he could keep the U.S. company running was by writing $2 million in checks on his and his wife's joint account. He said he expected to get that money back when the company recovered.

According to Federal Bureau of Investigation agents, Mr. DeLorean's personal finances are substantial. They estimate his net worth, not including his now-worthless DeLorean Motor stock, at $28 million. In addition to a brick Georgian colonial mansion in New Jersey that he purchased for $3.5 million last year, Mr. DeLorean owns an estate near San Diego, equipped with such opulent touches as a motorized cover on the 41-foot swimming pool, an eight-person hot tub screened by shrubs and flowers, and Mexican-brick fireplaces. He has been trying to sell the San Diego place for $4 million, but the price was increased to $5 million Wednesday as Mr. DeLorean sought to raise bail. Other personal holdings range from a 1.5 percent interest in the New York Yankees to Logan Manufacturing Co., a maker of equipment for ski resorts.

But Mr. DeLorean apparently was either unwilling or unable to use his personal fortune to rescue his faltering company. As his other schemes failed to materialize, Mr. DeLorean allegedly turned to what law-enforcement officials characterize as a last-ditch attempt to raise the needed funds by financing narcotics.

THE DRUG CHARGES

Documents filed in court this week assert that the automotive executive planned to import both heroin and cocaine to raise money. He was arrested in a Los Angeles hotel room on Tuesday as the result of an undercover investigation by federal officials that also resulted in the apprehension of two other men, who were charged with supplying a shipment of cocaine.

At one of four meetings secretly videotaped by FBI agents, the government says, Mr. DeLorean met with a Drug Enforcement Administration undercover agent who posed as "Mr. Vicenza." The agent said he could arrange the importation of heroin and cocaine. According to an affidavit, "the profits realized from both transactions were to be given to DeLorean." The affidavit also states that Mr. DeLorean offered the agent 50 percent of the stock of DeLorean Motor Co.

Throughout the past few months, Mr. DeLorean remained outwardly confident that he and his auto company would succeed. As recently as Monday, he told a *Wall Street Journal* reporter, "We are going to continue building and selling the DeLorean car, I can assure you of that. This is going to work out."

He probably believed that. Friends and associates of Mr. DeLorean say he was convinced that success came naturally. "I'm not a psychologist, but I can tell you that John DeLorean has an enormous ego," says Mr. Collins, the former DeLorean chief engineer. "He believed he could do anything."

DISCUSSION QUESTIONS

1. In *On a Clear Day You Can See General Motors,* John DeLorean complains bitterly about the alleged abuse of executive privilege at GM. He viewed this behavior as counterproductive and personally insulting. Now his subordinates at DeLorean Motor Co. are making the same accusations about him. What's going on?

2. Suppose John DeLorean, when he was making plans for setting up his own firm, asked your advice about how the organization could be structured so that the alleged abuses of power he had observed at GM would likely not occur. Given our discussion of this topic at the end of the chapter, what advice would you give him?

3. DeLorean's life seems to be characterized by a tragic succession of sudden successes followed by spectacular failures. What role did power play in his roller coaster management career? What can you learn from the experiences of John DeLorean that will benefit your career as a manager?

■

■ Skill Practice

Repairing Power Failures in Management Circuits

Rosabeth Kanter argues that much of what is labeled poor management in organizations is simply individuals protecting their diminished power bases.* Instead of criticizing these managers as incompetent, she proposes that one bolster their feelings of personal power. If one solved the real problem of perceived lack of power, the undesirable symptoms of poor leadership would evaporate. This point of view is consistent with the principles discussed in this chapter.

In this exercise you are asked to give advice to someone who finds himself or herself feeling powerless. In each of the situations below, one person should take the role of the powerless manager while the other person takes the role of consultant. The consultant's job is to provide suggestions to the manager about how to increase power and influence in the organization. In the dialogue, discuss the extent to which the consultant's advice is realistic, relevant, and consistent with the behavioral guidelines for gaining power. Make notes on your conversation so you can report on it to the class.

After ten minutes or so, switch roles so that the consultant becomes the manager and vice versa. Select another situation at a different managerial level and have the consultant provide advice and suggestions.

SITUATION 1—FIRST-LINE SUPERVISOR

Judy Butler had been a first-line supervisor for six months. She had thought her new position was a promotion, but she found instead that it made her feel completely powerless. She felt at a dead end in her career, and she didn't see any way to get promoted out of the job. She was not in a central part of the organization, and she felt that no one ever noticed her unless she messed up. She was expected to be supportive of her subordinates, but they never returned the favor. She was expected to absorb the flack without any recognition. Her job was extremely rule-bound, so she had little discretion in what she did or how she did it. She didn't control the pay or benefits of her subordinates, so she felt powerless to reward or punish them in ways that really mattered.

As a result, she found she was more and more apt to impose rules to get subordinates to do what she wanted. She became more and more jealous of any successes and recognition achieved by her subordinates, so she tended to isolate them from people higher up in the organization and from complete information. She lost her penchant for informality and became fairly rigid in following standard operating procedures. Unfortunately, her subordinates were becoming more resentful and less productive.

* "Power failure in management circuits," *Harvard Business Review*, July–August 1979, pp. 65–75.

SITUATION 2—STAFF PROFESSIONAL

Jake Butler had come to the organization a year ago as a staff professional. He had thought it might be a way for him to achieve a lot of visibility with the top brass, but instead he found that he felt completely powerless. As a staff officer, he had almost no decision-making authority except in his narrow area of expertise. Most of what went on in the organization occurred without his involvement. Innovation and entrepreneurial activity were completely out of his realm. While some of the line officers were given opportunities for professional development, no one seemed to care about his becoming more experienced and capable. They only saw him as a specialist. Because his job didn't require that he work with others, he had little opportunity to cultivate relationships that might lead to contacts with someone near the top.

What hurt was that a consultant had been hired a few times to work on projects that were part of his area. If consultants could be brought in to do his work, he thought he must not be very indispensable to the organization.

Jake found himself being more and more turf-conscious. He didn't want others encroaching on his area of expertise. He tried to demonstrate his competence to others, but the more he did so, the more he became defined as a specialist, outside the mainstream of the organization. He felt that he was losing ground in his professional career, rather than gaining ground.

SITUATION 3—TOP EXECUTIVE

Jodie Butler had been a top executive for three years now. When she had been given the position, she had felt that her ultimate career goal had been achieved. Now she was not so sure. She had begun to sense her powerlessness. For example, the job had so many demands and details associated with it that she never had time to engage in any long-term planning. There always seemed to be one more crisis that demanded her attention. Unfortunately, most of them were from sources she couldn't control—government regulations, stockholders' demands, union relationships, equal opportunity statutes, and so on. She had built her reputation as a successful manager on being entrepreneurial, creative, and nonroutine, but none of those qualities were desirable in this job. Furthermore, because she was so mired in operations, she had become more and more out of touch with the information flows in the organization. Some things had to remain confidential with her, but her secrecy led to others' being unwilling to share information with her. She had assistants who were supposed to be monitoring the organization and providing her with information, but she often felt they only told her what she wanted to hear.

Jodie had begun to hear rumors about certain special interest groups' demanding her removal from the top job. She responded by becoming more dictatorial and defensive, with the result that the organization was becoming more control oriented and conservative. She felt that she was on a downward spiral, but she couldn't find a way to reverse the trend.

Ann Lindner

Ann Lindner was recently hired by the Oscar Mayer Corporation as a senior marketing executive. Her previous experience at Procter & Gamble had earned her a reputation for being a creative and hard-working manager. Her department at P&G had increased in sales at least 15 percent per year over the last five years, and she had obtained a fair amount of influence in the household products division as a whole. It was precisely because of her competence that Oscar Mayer had lured her away from P&G for a substantial increase in salary and a promotion to the executive ranks.

Sixteen corporate executives attended the executives meetings at which policy and operational decisions were discussed. During her first six months in the firm, Ann contributed her opinion frequently in discussions, and she felt that because of her previous experiences, her ideas were generally well founded and important. Even so, she got the distinct impression that much of what she said was taken "with a grain of salt" or passed off without much consideration. The other two female executives participated less often, but when they did, it seemed to be with the same results.

Three or four of the executives clearly held the most power in these meetings, and they seemed to have a great deal of influence over outcomes and decisions. Even though each person on the executive committee was on the same hierarchical level and received approximately the same salary, it became clear that the power differential was great. Fairly frequently Ann found herself disagreeing with the "influentials" regarding policy or future direction, but as could be expected, they always won out.

After studying the past financial records for her division at Oscar Mayer, Ann noted that the percentage of the total budget received by her division had been steadily decreasing over the past several years. In fact, the division was so pinched that its functioning was being negatively affected. Ann suspected that this was one reason she had been hired, to get the division back on track.

She planned to ask for a substantial increase in her budget when the new biannual budget was formulated in eight months. The request was to be for the same percentage of the budget that the division had received four years ago. The problem is, if her division got more, someone else's would get less. She was sure she would encounter stiff opposition.

Assume you are on the management faculty of the small college Ann graduated from several years ago. She was your star student and you have taken great pride in her accomplishments since graduation. Ann is coming home for a visit next weekend and she called you today asking if she could spend some time with you discussing this problem. You assured her that you would be happy to discuss the problem with her Sunday afternoon at your home.

TASK 1

After thinking about this request, you have concluded that you can best help Ann by outlining several alternative approaches for her consideration. In preparation for your meeting with Ann, write out two or three scenarios that she might pursue, based on the discussion of influence strategies in the Skill Learning section. (Use Table 5.3 and the following checklist as guides.) Specifically, consider which groups in the organization she should try to influence (e.g., top management, other division heads) and the strategy that would be most effective for each group. After you have written down specific recommendations, list the key advantages and possible liabilities of each that Ann should consider in making her choice. Keep in mind the context of the problem at Oscar Mayer so your input will be both concrete and relevant. After you have completed your preparations for the meeting, discuss your recommendations in class.

TASK 2

After listening to a discussion of the various alternatives for influencing members of the executive committee at Oscar Mayer, Ann realizes that she needs to practice these influence strategies. As the newest member of the management team, she cannot afford to alienate key members of the organization.

To help with this practice, form groups of three people each. One person should play the role of Ann while another plays a member of the executive committee. Remember other managers are invested in their own budgets, but they are also reasonable. That is, they are not immune from being influenced. The third person, the observer, provides feedback to the other two (but especially to Ann) regarding the effectiveness of the influence attempts. Such questions as the following might be discussed:

1. What was the reaction of the manager to Ann's influence attempt?
2. What factors determined whether Ann and the other manager reached an agreement?
3. How could Ann's influence attempt have been improved?
4. Would another approach have been more effective?

Rotate roles so each person has an opportunity to play Ann.

CHECKLIST FOR SELECTING AN INFLUENCE STRATEGY

Retribution Strategies (coercion and intimidation)

1. Power-holder has much more power than target person.

2. Ongoing commitment to organizational goals or collaboration with powerholder is not critical.

3. Quality of workmanship, innovation, or personal judgment is not essential to job performance.

4. Time constraints are tight.

5. Request involves specific, unambiguous activities.

6. Issue in question is not vital concern of target person. It does not impinge on central values or strong convictions.

7. If issue *is* vital, possible negative consequences of hostility and alienation are acceptable (surveillance is possible, target person could be replaced if necessary, others in group have generally positive attitudes and are not likely to be adversely influenced).

Reciprocity Strategies (exchange and ingratiation)

1. Parties are mutually dependent (each can harm or benefit the other).

2. Sufficient time is available to work out agreement.

3. Rules or norms governing exchange agreements exist.

4. Commitment to long-term goals and values is not essential, only agreement to perform specific task in return for given reward.

5. Parties view each other as trustworthy. Neither is interested in exploiting other.

6. Both parties have authority and resources necessary to implement agreement.

Rational Strategies (persuasion based on facts or appeal to personal values)

1. There are few time constraints.

2. Initiative and innovation are vital ingredients of effective performance.

3. Parties have common goals or at least treat each other's perspective as legitimate.

4. Relationship between parties is ongoing, and there is not much interpersonal conflict.

5. There is high level of trust between parties.

6. It is important for other person to understand why request is being made, either because it entails personal inconvenience or because personal judgment must be used during implementation.

7. Ongoing commitment to broad goals and values is important. ■

■ *Skill Application*

Application Exercises

1. During the next week, analyze your efforts to influence other people. Catalogue your strategies, using the model discussed in the Skill Learning section. Consider why you chose each approach. Did you repeatedly use one or two strategies that are consistent with your basic personality or interpersonal style, or did you vary your approach with the circumstances? What was the outcome of each influence attempt? Did people comply with your request? What was their affective response? Select at least one person you attempted to influence with whom you have a close, ongoing relationship. Discuss the alternative influence strategies with that person and ask him or her what effect the frequent use of each approach might have on your relationship.

2. Watch at least two realistic dramas or situation comedies on TV or one movie and observe the influence strategies used by various characters. Which form of influence was used most frequently, and why? Did certain people demonstrate a preference for one strategy? If so, was this based on personality traits, sex roles, authority relationships, or other constraining factors? How successful were these influence attempts and what impact did they have on ongoing relationships between individuals?

3. Select a friend or associate who has complained to you about feeling powerless in an organizational setting. This might involve occupying a relatively insignificant leadership position in a campus organization or a low-level position in a work organization. Sit down with this individual and teach him or her the guidelines for gaining power in organizations, then design a specific plan of action for helping him or her become more powerful. Discuss the outcomes of this plan with your friend and report on his or her success.

4. Using the guidelines for gaining power, develop a plan for increasing your power in an organizational setting. Describe the setting, including the factors you feel account for your feelings of powerlessness. Describe your strategy for increasing your power in detail and report on its outcome. Also, describe the benefits of becoming more powerful in your organization. ■

6 Improving Employee Performance Through Motivation

- ■ *Skill Preassessment*

  Coming to Grips with Motivational Issues and Problems

- ■ *Skill Learning*

  Increasing Employee Motivation and Shaping Constructive Behavior

- ■ *Skill Analysis*

  Elizabeth Sternberg and Judith Greene

- ■ *Skill Practice*

  Behavior Modification at Tampa Pump & Valve

- ■ *Skill Application*

  Application Exercises

■ *Skill Preassessment*

Coming to Grips with Motivational Issues and Problems

In small groups discuss and complete one of the following tasks, as directed by your instructor.

1. Bob, a member of your staff, periodically comes to work ten to thirty minutes late in the morning. You manage a very busy, understaffed customer relations office and the phone starts ringing promptly at 8:00 A.M. When he is late for work it is necessary for you to answer his phone and this interrupts your work schedule. This morning you are particularly annoyed. He is twenty-five minutes late and the phones have been ringing like crazy. Because you have been forced to answer the phones, it will be difficult for you to complete an important assignment by the noon deadline. You are getting more upset by the minute. While you are in the middle of a particularly unpleasant phone conversation with an irate customer, you look out your window and see Bob bounding up the steps to the building. You think to yourself, "This is ridiculous. I've got to put a stop to his tardiness. Maybe I should just threaten to fire him unless he shapes up. But I must admit in every other way he is an extremely capable worker and I would hate to lose him, especially during this period of company retrenchment." In your group, generate a list of approaches to solving this problem. Discuss the pros and cons of each alternative. Agree on a general strategy and then list the specific steps you would take. Be prepared to role play your confrontation with Bob.

2. Joe joined your architectural firm two years ago as a draftsman. He came with mediocre recommendations from his previous employer, but you hired him anyway because you needed help desperately. You have been pleasantly surprised by his performance. Until recently he worked hard and consistently produced high-quality work. However, during the past few months he has definitely slacked off. He doesn't seem as excited about his work and you have noticed him daydreaming several times at his desk. You have decided it is time to call Joe in to discuss your concerns. Joe is thirty-five years old. He has been a draftsman since graduating from a tech school, right after high school. He is married and has four children. He has worked for four architectural firms in twelve years. In your group, generate several questions you could ask Joe to ascertain the cause of his apparent loss of motivation. Write these down and be prepared to role play an interview with Joe.

3. You are returning home from work one evening on the train when an article in the newspaper catches your eye. It reports that a leading psychologist argues that parents rely too heavily on punishment in training their children. This strikes a sensitive nerve, since you gave your thirteen-year-old a sharp scolding and sound whack on the rear end this morning because he refused to help his younger brother wash the dishes. You have since wondered several times if you did the right thing. Your son has become increasingly belligerent recently and you're not sure if your response this morning helped any. You are sobered by the adverse effects of frequent punishment mentioned in the article. Then you recall an incident at work today in which you docked an employee a half day's pay for violating a safety regulation, and you begin pondering the relationship between punishment at home and in the work place. You take a tablet out of your briefcase and begin listing the pros and cons of using punishment to shape behavior, along with the conditions under which you feel punishment is justified. This leads to a second list of guidelines for administering punishment to minimize adverse consequences. In your group, construct these lists and prepare to present them to the class.   ■

■ Skill Learning

Increasing Employee Motivation and Shaping Constructive Behavior

"I can't understand why we have such poor luck with Directors of Engineering. The man in there before Haverstick was technically well qualified. He'd been a good designer for us before we promoted him to be the first head of engineering. But he took to drinking heavily, and we had to relieve him of the responsibility. Then Haverstick seemed so promising. They say he is doing well in his new job at the Beta Company. But they operate much differently from the way we do. Then, Steve Spencer—he seemed to have all the qualifications we needed. And he certainly was a gentleman. But he never could get things done. Apparently he couldn't gain the respect of the design boys. So, here we are, looking for a new man. *I'm beginning to wonder whether we'll ever find him*" (Dalton, Lawrence, & Lorsch, 1970, p. 81).

So ends a popular case on organizational design, "Higgins Equipment Company." The comments of the company president reflect the frustration he has experienced trying to staff a key position in the organization. He had filled the position three times with individuals of experience and high promise but their performance was consistently disappointing. A close reading of the case reveals myriad structural obstacles facing any occupant of this position. Several subunits in the division perform production and marketing activities. The director is both the head of engineering and the director of a specified unit called "Engineering Services," which coordinates engineering and production. Finally, one department head was a "founding father" of the company and has informal direct access to the president.

The tragedy of this case is the inability of the company president to diagnose the real reasons behind the poor performance of the directors of engineering. He has ignored the structural problems and attributed the repeated failures to inadequacies in those occupying the position. No matter how well qualified and highly motivated Steve Spencer's replacement, it is highly likely that he or she will also be judged incompetent.

This example points out a critical management skill—the ability to properly diagnose and remedy poor performance. The management buzzword today is "productivity". Distressed by the recent poor performance of American businesses, many managers are frantically searching for remedies. This has led some to experiment with management techniques used in Japan in hopes of duplicating Japanese companies' remarkably high rates of productivity. However, one danger of reflexively implementing Japanese management techniques in firms that do not share Japanese cultural values and economic and technological advantages is that these techniques may appease management's compulsion to work at bolstering poor productivity but distract management from its root causes (Sullivan, 1983). Such reflexive actions suggest a Chinese proverb: "For every hundred men hacking away at the leaves of a diseased tree, only one man stoops to inspect the roots." The purpose of this chapter is to give you the skills necessary to properly diagnose the root causes of poor worker performance.

A good diagnostician needs a model to guide the inquiry process. Research by behavioral scientists on the determinants of task performance is summarized in Figure 6.1 (Maier, 1973; Lawler, 1973). According to these formulas, performance is the product of ability multiplied by motivation, and ability is the product of aptitude multiplied by training. The multiplicative function in the formulas points out that both components are essential. For example, a worker who has 100 percent of the motivation and 75 percent of the ability required to perform a task can perform at an above-average rate. However, if he or she has only 10 percent of the ability required, no amount of motivation will enable him or her to perform satisfactorily.

"Aptitude" refers to the native skills and abilities a person brings to the job. These obviously involve physical and mental capabilities, but for many people-oriented jobs they also include personality characteristics, like those discussed in the chapter on self-awareness. Most of our inherent abilities can be enhanced by education and training. Indeed, much of what we call native ability in adults can be traced to previous skill enhancement experiences, such as modeling the social skills of a parent or older sibling. Nevertheless, it is useful to consider training as a separate component of ability, since it represents an important mechanism for improving employee performance. An assessment of ability should be made during the job-matching process by screening applicants against the skill requirements of the job. If an applicant has minor deficiencies in skill aptitude but many other desirable characteristics, an intensive training program can increase the applicant's qualifications to perform the job (Wanous, 1980).

Motivation represents an employee's desire and commitment, and is manifested as effort. Some people want to complete a task but are easily distracted or discouraged. They have high desire but low commitment. Others plod along with impressive persistence, but their work is uninspired. These people have high commitment but low desire.

The first diagnostic question that must be asked by the supervisor of a poor performer is whether the problem stems from lack of ability or lack of

Figure 6.1 *Determinants of Worker Performance*

Performance = Motivation × Ability

Ability = Aptitude × Training

motivation. A University of Wisconsin social psychologist, H. Andrew Michener, and his colleagues (Michener, Fleishman, Elliot, & Skolnick, 1976) have used principles from attribution theory to help explain how this judgment is made. They proposed that a supervisor's diagnosis of poor peformance is based on four pieces of information: the difficulty of the tasks assigned to the subordinate, the known ability of the subordinate, the extent to which the subordinate seems to be trying to perform well, and the degree to which the subordinate's performance improves. In an experimental setting, they found that supervisors attributed a person's poor performance on the task of solving anagrams to lack of ability when the task was known to be difficult for most people, when the subject had a history of ineptness in solving anagrams, when the subject was obviously working hard to solve the problems, and when the subject's performance improved over several trials. In contrast, supervisors tended to attribute subjects' poor performance to poor motivation when the opposite information was communicated by the experimenter.

These results have important implications because research on power has shown that power-holders tend to select stronger means of influence if they conclude that a person's resistance is deliberate, rather than the result of external, uncontrollable forces. Managers justify their choice of a forceful influence strategy on the grounds that the subordinate has a poor attitude, is hostile to authority, or lacks dedication (Kipnis, 1976).

In the remainder of this chapter we shall examine the two components of performance in more detail. We shall discuss manifestations of low ability and poor motivation, their causes, and some proposed remedies. Overall, we shall emphasize motivation, since it is central to day-to-day manager–subordinate interactions. While ability tends to remain stable over long periods of time, motivation often fluctuates and therefore requires closer monitoring.

ABILITY

There are several reasons why a person's lack of ability might inhibit job performance. Ability may have been improperly assessed during the employment screening process, the technical requirements of a job may have been radically upgraded, or a person who performed very well in one position may be promoted into a higher-level position that is too demanding (the well-known Peter Principle).

For purposes of illustration we shall focus on the problem of mid-career obsolescence. We are not implying that all middle-aged workers are obsolete, but it is disconcerting to recognize how many are. Figure 6.2 shows a model of the typical career path. During the steep incline of the early career phase the principal concerns are "moving up" and "getting ahead." Young management trainees generally judge how their careers are progressing by tracking the progress made by other members of their training group as they spread throughout the organization. A commonly expressed fear during this stage is

Figure 6.2 *Model of Career Stages*

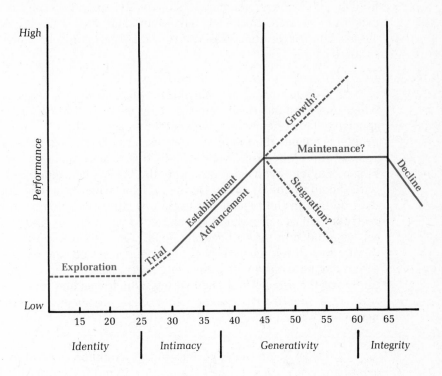

From Hall, 1976, p. 57.

being passed over for promotion. However, after several years of searching for the "fast track," most drop out of the race. They may conclude that they don't have the skills and abilities to make it to the top, or they don't want to pay the price of disrupted personal activities required in senior management positions, or they might find a task or group of people they really enjoy and decide there is no reason to move on. For whatever reason, the typical career goes through a maintenance, or steady-state, phase around middle age in which people tend to get stale in their jobs. This is often described as "job burnout." How the person and the organization act during this phase determines whether a period of decline, stagnation, or renewed growth will follow.

One critical factor influencing the outcome of the maintenance phase is whether or not the employee keeps current in terms of technical knowledge and expertise. If the leveling-off period is also associated with a gradual drift away from the mainstream of professional activities, obsolescence sets in.

Skill deterioration can occur as insidiously as physical deterioration. It progresses in such small increments that a person doesn't sense what is happening until a new opportunity opens up or an emergency arises. Then the person finds he or she has inadequate resources to respond appropriately. Tasks that used to be tackled effortlessly now seem insurmountable. Quick (1977, pp. 41–43) has cited several manifestations of managerial obsolescence, including the following:

1. *Taking refuge in a specialty.*   Managers show signs of obsolescence when they respond to situations not by managing, but by retreating to their specialty. This often occurs in general managers who feel insecure addressing problems outside their field of expertise and experience. Anthony Jay, in *Management and Machiavelli* (1967), calls this type of manager George I, after the king of England who, after assuming the throne, continued to be preoccupied with the affairs of Hanover, Germany, from whence he had come. The president quoted in the case at the beginning illustrated this pattern. He had formerly served as a prominent researcher in the company and still maintained a separate office in the engineering department. He felt most comfortable with the product development aspect of the business and spent a great deal of time discussing new ideas with young engineers. This tended to undermine the authority of the directors of engineering, which was one reason they kept quitting. This practice also made other departments in the organization feel neglected.

2. *Focusing on past performance.*   Another sign of obsolescence is measuring one's value to the organization in terms of past performance or on the basis of former standards. Some cavalry commanders in World War I relied on their outmoded knowledge of how to conduct successful military campaigns, and as a result failed miserably in mechanized combat. This form of obsolescence is common in organizations that shift their mission. For example, during the 1950s universities experienced a significant increase in enrollment. In response, they had to rapidly expand their physical facilities and hire many new faculty. These personnel were hired explicitly to teach, and so their academic credentials were not examined as carefully as their demonstrated ability to perform well in the classroom. If these instructors lived up to their potential as teachers, they were promoted and given tenure. Then the environment of the university began to shift. Enrollment pressure subsided and greater emphasis was placed on attaining a national reputation as a research institution. As a result, older faculty members found themselves being evaluated by a new set of criteria—number of scientific publications. Senior faculty members who had not kept up with recent developments in their field retreated to the security of the classroom, taught classes on their specialty, and refused to broaden their orientation.

3. *Exaggerating aspects of the leadership role.*   Obsolescent managers tend to be very defensive. This often leads them to exaggerate one portion of their managerial role. Such managers might delegate most of their responsibilities because they no longer feel competent to perform them well. Or they might become nuts-and-bolts administrators who scrutinize detail to an extent far beyond its practical value. Still others become devil's advocates, but their negativism is intended not to stimulate creativity, but to thwart efforts to change the familiar.

What remedies are available for poor performance due to lack of ability, as in the case of managerial obsolescence? The four principle alternatives are *retrain, refit, reassign,* and *release.* To begin with, once a supervisor has ascertained that lack of ability is the primary cause of poor performance, he or she should sit down with the subordinate in a performance appraisal interview and explore the *retraining* option. Unless the supervisor is convinced that the lack of ability stems from low aptitude, he or she should assume initially that it is due to a lack of training. Since an evaluation of insufficient training is less threatening than inadequate aptitude, this approach reduces the low performer's natural defensive reaction. Training programs can take a variety of forms (Schein, 1978). Many firms are using their computer technology more in education. This can involve interactive technical instruction and business games that simulate problems likely to be experienced by managers in the organization. More traditional forms of training include subsidized university courses and in-house management workshops. Some companies have experimented with company sabbaticals to release managers from the pressure of their work so they can concentrate on retooling.

Often, however, retraining is an insufficient remedy for poor performance. In this case, the next step is to explore *refitting* the poor performer to his or her task assignments. While the worker remains on the job, the components of his or her work are analyzed and different combinations of tasks and abilities that accomplish organizational objectives and provide meaningful and rewarding work are explored. In the case of the senior faculty members who lack the aptitude or inclination to become first-class researchers, this agreement might take the form of increasing a professor's teaching load. By teaching a heavier load, a classroom-oriented professor frees other professors to work longer in their laboratories. With such a symbiotic relationship, both types of faculty members use their unique abilities to help the organization accomplish its twin objectives of excellence in teaching and national prominence in research.

If it is not possible to reach an agreement on a revised job description, the third alternative is to *reassign* the poor performer. This could involve movement to a position of less responsibility or to one requiring less technical sophistication. It could also entail a lateral transfer to a part of the organization better suited to the individual's abilities. For example, a medical specialist in a hospital who finds it increasingly difficult to keep abreast of new medical procedures but has demonstrated management skills might be shifted to a full-time administration position.

The last option is *releasing.* If retraining and creative redefinition of task assignments have not worked and there are no opportunities for reassignment in the organization, releasing the employee from the organization should be considered. This option is generally constrained by union agreements, company policies, seniority considerations, and EEOC guidelines. Frequently, however, a chronic poor performer who could be released is not because his or her supervisor chooses to sidestep a potentially unpleasant task and instead opts for setting the person on the shelf—out of the mainstream of activities where he or she can't cause any problems. Even when this action is motivated by humanitarian concerns ("I don't think he could cope with being terminated."), it often produces the opposite effect. Actions taken to protect an unproductive employee from the embarrassment of termination just substitute the humiliation of being ignored. Connor and Fielden (1973) have proposed a program to prevent putting middle-aged managers on the shelf during the maintenance phase of their careers. To stimulate a period of renewed growth (rather than prolonged stagnation or decline), they urge companies to begin training employees for second careers during their thirties. The advantage of this program is that if employees reach a dead end in their organization, they have the option of changing firms, and possibly careers, before they lose labor market mobility due to advanced age. Such a program makes it much easier for a supervisor to recommend that a person search for a job in another organization for which he or she would be better suited. While a company would obviously make a substantial investment in education and training that it might never directly benefit from, it would also save a sizable sum of salary money due to increased ease in relocating unproductive workers.

MOTIVATION

The second component in employee performance is motivation. The highly skilled manager can have a greater impact on subordinates' motivation than on their ability. While it is important to see to the training needs of subordinates and to be actively involved in the hiring and job-matching processes to ensure adequate aptitude, a manager's behavior more directly affects subordinates' motivation.

Authors writing on the subject of motivation typically address two concerns: satisfaction and performance. For many years it was argued that motivation affected performance through satisfaction. If workers received lots of employee benefits, enjoyed their work, and liked their supervisors, they would be satisfied, according to this theory, and this would stimulate them to work hard at their jobs. However, more recent research has shown that there is only a weak relationship between worker satisfaction and level of job performance (Lawler, 1973). It appears that the dairy industry's motto, "Contented cows give better milk," provides insufficient guidance for the successful management of employees. For example, it is easy to imagine an organizational climate that is so satisfaction oriented that management becomes overresponsive to the needs of workers and the resulting country club-like climate hinders good performance.

While we don't want to downplay the importance of employees' feeling good about what they are doing and how they are being treated, the ultimate responsibility of managers is to hold people accountable for results. Managers should avoid the trap of working to engender high employee morale for its own sake. It is easy to be seduced by the notion that the best managers have happy people. This is only half the truth. Actually, the best managers have productive people who also are happy. The real challenge for managers is to design incentive systems that encourage high performance and also engender high employee morale (Nadler & Lawler, 1977; Lawler, 1970).

To accomplish this objective, managers should use two general approaches to employee motivation. First, they should examine the overall system of rewards in their organization from their subordinates' point of view to ascertain its potential for motivation. This is best done using diagnostic questions derived from expectancy theory. Expectancy theory basically proposes that people regulate how much effort they put into their work based on what they expect to get out of it. More specifically, it argues that employees will be motivated to perform well if they believe that highly salient outcomes will result from high performance and that there is a reasonably high probability that hard workers can become high performers (Nadler & Lawler, 1977; Mitchell, 1974; Vroom, 1964).

The second approach focuses on shaping employee behaviors so they are consistent with the expectations of management. It is referred to as operant conditioning or reinforcement theory. Several contemporary psychologists, including B. F. Skinner, have advocated operant conditioning as an approach to learning in humans (Skinner, 1963, 1967; Bandura, 1969; Luthans & Kreitner, 1975). These individuals argue that if we want to understand the causes of employee behavior, we should examine the events that occur after a behavior (reinforcers) that encourage or discourage similar future behaviors. This is in contrast to classical learning theory, which focuses attention on events that occur before a behavior (stimuli).

Expectancy theory and operant conditioning share many assumptions about human behavior and suggest similar guidelines for action in dealing with specific motivational problems (Petroch & Gamboa, 1976). However, we shall discuss them separately because they are best applied to different facets of motivation. Specifically, expectancy theory is well suited for analyzing broad, prevailing motivation problems such as the causes of general lack of motivation at the individual, group, or organizational levels. When the problem involves a specific individual, expectancy theory is best suited for situations in which the person appears to have become disenchanted with his or her work in general and seems to have run out of gas. Operant conditioning complements this broad orientation by focusing on specific behaviors. It is best applied when a specific employee is creating a hardship for others by violating rules or work norms, or a specific procedure or regulation is being ignored by an entire work crew. It is also useful for introducing new work procedures for increasing productivity and for teaching effective interpersonal skills.

In summary, these approaches to motivation are complementary in several respects. First, they address both the cognitive and behavioral aspects of motivation. The first approach focuses on the expectations of workers and the extent to which those are satisfied. Consequently, it provides useful guidelines for designing reward systems that will stimulate high performance. The second approach focuses on the way actual behaviors are reinforced and shaped through the use of incentives and disincentives. Therefore, it is more useful as a guide for improving manager/subordinate interactions. Second, they address both general and specific aspects of performance. The first approach focuses primarily on how to increase a subordinate's desire to work hard, but it does not tell how to change specific dysfunctional behaviors unrelated to effort. For example, a willing worker may have mannerisms that are so offensive to co-workers that the productivity of the group suffers. The second approach fills this gap by showing how a general willingness to work hard can be channeled into acceptable behaviors. The first approach is therefore analogous to the drive components of locomotion, while the second approach represents the steering component. The first energizes, and the second shapes or directs.

Expectancy Theory Applied to General Aspects of Motivation

Managers should examine the motivational potential of their organization's reward system for each member under their supervision. Too often managers examine the opportunities for rewards provided in their organization only at an aggregate level. For example, it is common practice to compare pay and benefit programs with industry averages, or to compare opportunities for promotion in a division with those available at its chief competitor. If the organization does well in these comparisons, managers often conclude that the system will highly motivate their subordinates. This conclusion is based on the false premise that all employees are motivated by the same reward opportunities. An evaluation of an organization's reward system at the aggregate level is an important exercise for the personnel department, but line managers should also examine the system from the perspective of individual employees.

A simplified expectancy model is shown in Figure 6.3. It depicts a causal sequence linking motivation, effort, performance, and outcomes. The model basically postulates that high motivation occurs when individuals value the specific outcomes that result from successful performance, expect that outcomes will be contingent on successful performance, and expect that high effort will lead to successful performance. If any one of these conditions is not present, motivation suffers. The model also reminds us that successful performance requires both effort and ability.

We shall discuss each of these critical conditions for motivation by framing them as diagnostic questions. First, *Are the rewards offered salient to each individual?* As we discussed in Chapter 1, employees bring a variety of personal values and needs to the work environment, expressed in the form of outcome preferences. For example, an employee with marginal skills and heavy financial obligations will be primarily concerned about job security and salary and benefits. An employee who is sharing responsibility for child care with a working spouse will probably be less concerned about financial remuneration but anxious to participate in a flextime program. Well-educated employees who have high career aspirations will be concerned about the amount of responsibility and visibility granted by their supervisors.

The proposition that different workers are motivated by different rewards runs counter to many popular management theories that advocate "one best method" approaches. Included in the list of motivational panaceas are fairness, increased responsibility, shared authority, high task variety, frequent feedback and encouragement, and enhanced promotability. In the case of Elizabeth Sternberg in the Skill Analysis section, we observe the negative consequences of management's assuming that all employees desire an opportunity for promotion. Workers' outcome preferences reflect needs that vary widely between people and often change significantly for a given person over time. Managers who ignore this diversity and fluidity and instead key their actions to the presumed needs of the "average worker" fail to achieve the maximum motivation potential from their reward system.

While the prescription to link work outcomes to the expectations of employees seems intuitively obvious, it is frequently violated, especially when subordinate feedback is not encouraged. When one-way, downward communication tends to be the norm and most supervisor–subordinate relationships

Figure 6.3   *Simplified Expectancy Model of Motivation*

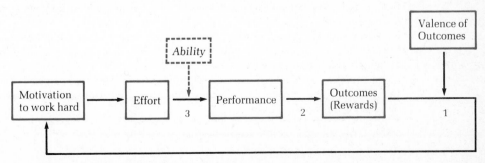

have evaluative overtones, employees become reluctant to volunteer their feelings about their work, career aspirations, and so forth. One way to overcome this problem is to separate discussions about performance from conversations about satisfaction with outcomes. In one situation the supervisor is giving feedback, in the other he or she is soliciting feedback. The second type of discussion tends to be more productive in an informal setting. It is also useful to seek this type of information indirectly, as well as directly.

Once managers determine the importance attached to various outcomes by their workers, they should ask diagnostic question 2, *Are highly valued rewards linked to good performance?* It is necessary, but not sufficient, to conclude that the outcomes desired by the subordinates are available in the organization. If rewards are dispensed to organizational members irrespective of their job performance, then good performance is not being encouraged.

This suggests a related diagnostic question, *Is the reward system equitable?* Workers place a high premium on being treated fairly (Adams, 1963, 1965). One way they judge fairness is by calculating a job-input-to-job-outcome equity ratio. That is, they add up everything they are contributing to their work, including experience, training, and effort, and measure it against the rewards they are receiving for these inputs. This assessment is compared with their perceptions of co-workers' treatment or their recollections of assessments from previous jobs. Sample items from a widely used organizational fairness survey are shown in Table 6.1.

These two diagnostic questions are closely related if we can assume that the underlying purpose of an organization's reward system is to foster good performance. If this is the case and valued outcomes are not linked to good performance, good performers are going to feel cheated. This will encourage them to search for alternative positions in which they will receive more valued rewards than poor performers receive. Managers should closely monitor

TABLE 6.1 *Sample Statements That Reflect Degrees of Organizational Fairness*

The rules for giving pay raises are not fair to some employees.

My supervisor knows who should be promoted and sees that they are promoted if he or she can.

Some employees can get away with working at a slow speed if they want to in my company.

Persons who have the same education as I have are paid more than I am being paid.

My supervisor will get after workers if they are late to work, play around in the office, or behave badly in other ways.

My supervisor tends to assign unpleasant jobs to those he or she doesn't like.

In my department, as people learn their jobs, the supervisor lets them make more and more decisions on their own.

SOURCE: The Organizational Fairness Questionnaire by John E. Dittrich.

terminations in their work group to ensure that turnover among poor performers is higher than among good performers.

Technological constraints sometimes make it difficult to perfectly link rewards and individual performance. For example, people working on an automobile assembly line or chemists working on a group research project have little control over their personal productivity. In these situations rewards should be linked to the performance of the work group to foster group cohesiveness and to partially satisfy individual members' concerns about fairness. When it is not possible to assess the performance of a work group (work shift, organizational department), an organization-wide performance bonus should be implemented. While the merits and technical details of various group and organizational reward systems are beyond the scope of this chapter, the point is that managers should seek to link valued rewards and good performance at the lowest level of aggregation possible—preferably at the level of the individual worker (Lawler, 1971). In an era of egalitarianism, managers often overlook this vital link between performance and rewards, and as a consequence find it difficult to attract and retain good performers.

This brings us to the third diagnostic question, *Can workers achieve their desired level of performance?* If highly desired outcomes are available to members of a work group and are linked to each person's performance, the task of the supervisor becomes one of facilitating good performance. Since good performance requires both high motivation and adequate ability, an attractive and equitable reward system is useless unless all organizational obstacles to personal performance are eliminated. For example, if a worker is rewarded for the number of widgets assembled each day but is having difficulty obtaining adequate supplies or works on machinery that keeps breaking down, the motivation potential of the reward system is nullified. This highlights the importance of supervisors' serving as troubleshooters by making technical adjustments in equipment, providing additional training, or resolving feuds between interdependent work groups.

Taken together, these three diagnostic questions emphasize the importance of the manager's role in an effective organizational motivation system. While line managers seldom have much input into the development of an organization's incentive system, their role in implementing the program is vital. They provide a critical bridge between employees and the reward structure and, consequently, are in a strategic position to determine where the system is failing to motivate good performance. Managers should work to ensure that the organization's reward structure is consistent with established behavior principles and then facilitate workers' efforts to obtain rewards within that system. This approach deemphasizes motivation by gimmicks, which is often interpreted by workers as thinly veiled exploitation. A motivational system should build trust in management, not erode it. When managers view themselves as facilitators, their interests are more closely aligned with those of their subordinates, and a strong working relationship is likely to result.

Operant Conditioning Used to Reinforce Constructive Behavior

A manager's responsibilities for motivating subordinates go beyond facilitating the acquisition of organizational rewards, such as pay, fringe benefits, and promotions. To the extent that major organizational outcomes are consistent with employees' expectations and are dispersed equitably (including being linked to good job performance), workers will be committed to participate in the organization and satisfactorily perform their assigned roles. However, the manager must still shape this commitment according to shifting task requirements and sustain the overall level of commitment by effectively administering local rewards within the work group.

Unfortunately, many managers do not behave as though they believed their daily interactions with work group members influenced worker attitudes and behaviors. In fact, Steven Kerr (1975) has argued that managerial actions often tend to reinforce behaviors in their subordinates that are considered undesirable. Kerr calls this "the folly of rewarding A, while hoping for B." For example, a head of R&D with a low tolerance for conflict and uncertainty may unwittingly undermine the company's avowed objective of developing highly creative products by punishing work groups that do not exhibit unity or a clear, consistent set of priorities. These actions will, over a long period of time, encourage a work group to avoid risky projects, suppress debate, and routinize task performance.

Applying Kerr's principle to the topic of planning, Marion Kellogg (1979, p. 121), a management consultant at General Electric, highlights five common mistakes made by supervisors that discourage subordinates from following the admonition to take more initiative in formulating personal work plans:

1. Asking for plans and then, when the employee presents them to you, acting as if they were unacceptable compared with those you already had in mind.
2. Insisting that the employee go about reaching his or her goals the way you would if you held the job.
3. "Rubber-stamping" subordinates' plans without critical review.
4. Pretending to know how difficult or easy plans are to meet when you have no basis for actual evaluation.
5. Changing dates arbitrarily so you can appear to be a "tough" manager.

Elaborating on these points, Kellogg proposes several key do's and don't's to encourage thoughtful, independent planning. These are shown in Table 6.2.

This example points out how supervisors continually shape the behavior and attitudes of their subordinates during the course of normal, everyday interactions. Indeed, it has been argued that "the best way to change an individual's behavior in a work setting is to change his or her manager's behavior" (Thompson, 1978, p. 52). Given the considerable leverage managers have over

TABLE 6.2 *Guidelines for Fostering Subordinate Planning*

Do	*Don't*
Do ask, "How are *we* going to do this? What can I contribute to this effort? How will *we* use this result?" thus implying your joint stake in the work and results.	Don't imply that it is the employees' total responsibility, that they hang alone if they fail. Individual failure *means organization* failure.
Do use an interested, exploring manner, asking questions designed to bring out factual information.	Don't play the part of an interrogator, firing questions as rapidly as they can be answered and usually requiring only a "yes" or "no" reply.
Do keep the analysis and evaluation as much in the employees' hands as possible by asking for their best judgment on various issues.	Don't listen to what they present and then sum up your reaction on an emotional basis.
Do present facts about organization needs, commitments, strategy, and so on, which permit them to improve and interest them in improving what they propose to do.	Don't demand a change or improvement in a peremptory tone of voice or on what appears to be an arbitrary basis.
Do ask them to investigate or analyze further if you feel that they have overlooked some points or overemphasized others and to return with their plans after factoring these items in.	Don't take their planning papers and cross out, change dates, or mark "no good" next to certain activities.
	Don't redo their plans for them unless their repeated efforts show no improvement.

their subordinates' behavior, it is important to learn how to use this process effectively to consistently produce positive results.

The process whereby managers use rewards and punishment to shape behavior is called operant conditioning. As shown in Figure 6.4, operant conditioning uses a variety of strategies involving the presentation or withdrawal of positive and negative reinforcers or no reinforcement whatsoever. Positive and negative reinforcement increases the frequency of behaviors, while punishment and extinction reduce their frequency.

Positive reinforcement consists of linking desired behaviors with positive outcomes. When a management trainee does something you would like to encourage, you should respond in a manner that is rewarding to the person. Punishment involves administering a negative reinforcer or withdrawing a positive reinforcer. Negative reinforcement is more complex. It basically entails withdrawing an aversive stimuli when a desirable behavior occurs. The classic example is a supervisor who nags until a task is done according to specifications. Subordinates learn that doing things right turns off the aversive stimuli.

It is sometimes difficult to distinguish between negative reinforcement

Figure 6.4   *Behavior-Shaping Strategies*

	Presented	Withdrawn
Positive Reinforcer	Positive Reinforcement	Punishment
Negative Reinforcer	Punishment	Negative Reinforcement
No Reinforcer	Extinction	

and punishment. When you administer an aversive reinforcer following an undesirable behavior, the other person learns not to behave in that manner. However, this form of punishment does not provide any direction regarding acceptable behaviors. By trial and error others discover what you don't like, but your reinforcement itself provides no clues about how to avoid your displeasure. ("Well, he didn't approve of those approaches. I wonder what will happen when I try this one?") In contrast, while negative reinforcement can produce an equally unpleasant experience, it does clearly communicate preferences. ("When you complete your expense report properly, I'll quit sending it back to you.")

Technically, extinction is defined as a behavior followed by no response whatsoever. However, in most managerial situations people develop certain expectations about what is likely to follow their actions based on past experience, office stories, and so forth. Consequently, it is often difficult for a "no response" not to be interpreted as either punishment or negative reinforcement. If a subordinate comes into your office complaining bitterly about a co-worker and you attempt to discourage this type of behavior by changing the subject or responding in a low, unresponsive monotone, the subordinate may view this as a form of rejection (punishment). If your secretary sheepishly slips a delinquent report on your desk and you ignore her behavior totally, she may be so relieved at not being yelled at that her tardiness is actually reinforced. Consequently, while extinction plays an important role in the learning process conducted in strictly controlled laboratory conditions, it is much less relevant as a motivational technique in organizational settings. Consequently, we shall focus our discussion on positive and negative reinforcement and punishment.

Positive Reinforcement

While positive reinforcement can be used to encourage any type of behavior, we shall apply it to the central concern of this chapter: How can you motivate a marginal performer to improve? To illustrate how positive reinforcement can be used to improve performance, we shall describe an eight-step model for shaping behavior (Hamner, 1974; Luthans & Kreitner, 1978).

1. *Clearly describe the goal or target behavior. The target should always be related to performance.*   This step represents an important modification of the classic operant conditioning model. Operant conditioning was originally developed to teach new behaviors in situations in which it was not possible to directly communicate preferences to the subject. Of course, in management situations it is not only possible, but highly desirable to communicate expectations to others. Effective managers don't force others to discover by trial and error what they consider appropriate and inappropriate behavior. Therefore, we begin our discussion of operant conditioning in organizations with this vital distinction between animal and human learning.

In deciding what behaviors you want to reinforce, the critical question is, "What specifically must this person do to become a high performer?" Answers like "be dependable," "work hard," or "take initiative" are too general. If you are designing a sales training program for new store clerks, the admonition "Be helpful and friendly to all customers" should be replaced with "When you observe customers looking over the merchandise in your department, approach them with a smile and ask if you can help them find what they are looking for."

2. *If the target behavior is actually a complex chain of behaviors, divide it into a discrete, observable, and thus measurable sequence of behavioral events or steps.*   For example, suppose you want to encourage your staff to take more initiative in solving problems. Instead of bringing certain problems to your attention, you would like them to solve these issues on their own. After discussing your wishes in detail with these individuals, you might outline the following series of steps that you could reward: (1) paying any attention at all to a problem; (2) giving more extensive attention to a problem—five minutes, ten minutes, etc.; (3) carefully studying and analyzing all facets of a problem; (4) making early attempts at actually solving a problem; (5) making successively closer approximations to a workable solution to a problem; and (6) developing final workable solutions to specified problems.

The term "behavioral chain" is used to suggest that when lower-order behaviors are reinforced, higher-order behaviors are more likely to occur. This aspect of behavior shaping is particularly important. When the initial level of desired behavior is extremely low (or nonexistent) and the manager sets the criterion for reinforcement so high that almost all of the person's responses go unrewarded, his or her efforts will gradually be extinguished from lack of reinforcement. An all-or-nothing reward contingency is much less effective than an incremental payoff schedule, in which the value of the reward is increased to match the level of performance, and the lowest reward contingency is within the grasp of the least experienced or capable member of the group.

3. Make sure the individual is capable of meeting the technical skill or ability requirements for each step. The purpose of behavior shaping is to stimulate greater effort. If low performance is due to lack of natural ability or training, a reinforcement program often creates frustration and a sense of futility. Performance standards are dismissed as unrealistic and therefore discourage greater effort. This point underscores the importance of our earlier discussion of ways to improve ability.

4. Select potentially effective positive reinforcers on the basis of the individual's history of reinforcement. This step reinforces our earlier discussion of outcome valences in expectancy theory. A basic axiom of operant conditioning is that nothing is reinforcing to all people and everything is reinforcing to some people. Further, any reinforcer can be positive or aversive, depending on the person and the situation (Thompson, 1978, pp. 14–15). While these sound like extreme statements, they underscore the importance of not taking our understanding of the values and priorities of others for granted. The manager's lament, "What does Joe expect, anyway? I gave him a bonus and he's still complaining to the other members of the accounting department that I don't appreciate his superior performance," indicates an apparent miscalculation of what Joe really values.

To illustrate how different the priorities of managers and subordinates can be, Table 6.3 shows the results of a survey conducted by researchers at the University of Michigan in which managers were asked to indicate the salience of various reinforcers from the perspective of the workers (Le Due, 1980). Specifically, they were asked to estimate how the workers would likely rank order the outcomes. These results indicate a very low correlation between workers' actual priorities and the priorities attributed to them by their bosses. It is inter-

TABLE 6.3 *Order of Importance of Various Job Factors*

Job Factors	Survey of Employees	Survey of Bosses
Full appreciation of work done	1	8
Feeling of being in on things	2	10
Sympathetic help on personnel problems	3	9
Job security	4	2
Good wages	5	1
Interesting work	6	5
Promotional growth in organization	7	3
Personal loyalty to employees	8	6
Good working conditions	9	4
Tactful disciplining	10	7

SOURCE: A. I. Le Due, Jr. Motivation of programmers. *Data Base*, 1980, 3, 5.

esting to note that the employees tended to focus primarily on rewards controlled by their immediate supervisors, while the management sample emphasized organizationally mediated outcomes. This group of managers, at least, vastly underestimated their potential for directly influencing the behavior of their workers.

In addition to miscalculating the value attached to various outcomes by others, another reason why some individuals may not respond to a "reward" is that it has lost its salience. An outcome that is initially very attractive may lose its value from overuse. The proverbial "pat on the back for a job well done" may at first be gratifying to a new employee, but after a while it is taken for granted. A similar diminution of salience can occur with annual bonuses, vacations, raises, and so forth. To overcome this problem, managers can either substantially increase the value of an old reward (three pats on the back) or substitute another reward of roughly equal value but greater appeal. Many organizations have become locked into a very expensive reward inflation spiral because they lack ingenuity in utilizing a variety of rewards. Table 6.4 lists a large number of organizational rewards, categorized as contrived or natural (Luthans & Kreitner, 1978, p. 101). Contrived rewards are not indigenous to the work setting—they must be brought in from the outside. In contrast, natural rewards occur as logical consequences of work activities. The last column contains several examples of rewards that are based on the Premack principle, named for the work of David Premack (1965). These rewards involve pairing high-probability behaviors with low-probability behaviors. If a person likes doing task B better than task A, then the manager makes task B contingent on completing task A. For example, "You can use the office computer to balance your personal checkbook after you finish logging in today's receipts." The value of this list is that it can be used for brainstorming when current rewards have lost some of their reinforcement potential. Before automatically "upping the ante" to increase motivation using the old rewards, managers would do well to consider alternative incentives.

TABLE 6.4 *Classifications of On-the-Job Rewards*

Contrived On-the-Job Rewards			Natural Rewards		
Consumables	*Manipulatables*	*Visual and Auditory*	*Tokens*	*Social*	*Premack*
Coffee-break treats	Desk accessories	Office with a window	Money	Friendly greetings	Job with more responsibility
Free lunches	Wall plaques	Piped-in music	Stocks	Informal recognition	Job rotation
Food baskets	Company car		Stock options		Early time off with pay
Easter hams	Watches	Redecoration of work environment	Movie passes	Formal acknowledgment of achievement	with pay
Christmas turkeys	Trophies		Trading stamps (green stamps)		Extended breaks
Dinners for the family on the company	Commendations	Company literature	Paid-up insurance policies	Invitations to coffee/lunch	Extended lunch period
	Rings/tie pins	Private office	Dinner theater tickets	Solicitations of suggestions	Personal time off with pay
Company picnics	Appliances and furniture for the home	Popular speakers or lecturers	Vacation trips	Solicitations of advice	Work on personal project on company time
After-work wine and cheese parties	Home shop tools	Book club discussions	Coupons redeemable at local stores	Compliment on work progress	
Beer parties	Garden tools	Feedback about performance	Profit sharing	Recognition in house organ	Use of company machinery or facilities for personal projects
	Clothing			Pat on the back	
	Club privileges			Smile	Use of company recreation facilities
				Verbal or nonverbal recognition or praise	Special assignments

SOURCE: F. Luthans and R. Kreitner, *Organizational behavior modification* (Glenview, Ill.: Scott, Foresman, 1975), Figure 5–4.

5. *Structure the environment so that appropriate antecedent conditions will increase the probability of the desired behaviors.* It is important that managers remove all roadblocks to success. In addition to lack of ability, these might include inadequate cooperation from co-workers, poor working conditions, and an undependable source of supplies. Obviously not all potential obstacles to high performance can be anticipated initially. Consequently, it is important that managers communicate willingness to assume a supportive, coaching role during the behavior change process. Periodic discussions about the person's progress, specifically focused on obstacles encountered along the way, will help ensure success. When a problem is uncovered, assistance can be provided in a variety of ways. These include modeling or role playing how to assertively state a complaint to an uncooperative co-worker, giving advice about whom to see to get faster turnaround time for computer jobs, or interceding on the person's behalf to unplug an operations bottleneck in another department.

Besides helping the person overcome obstacles, the manager should also make working toward the stated behavioral objective as appealing as possible. In the case of encouraging subordinates to take more initiative in solving problems, this might involve giving them fairly simple or very interesting problems to work on initially. The attractiveness of a given target behavior can also be enhanced by verbally pairing it with highly attractive reinforcers. For example, if you were a company president trying to encourage one of your division managers to fire several incompetent people, you might say, "You know, John, I think the manager who is willing to fire incompetent people is a rare commodity these days. He is truly worth his weight in gold to a company. Firing incompetent people is the mark of a truly professional manager." By linking the desired behavior to positive outcomes valued by John (being a professional manager, being an asset to this company, having the esteem of his boss), you can diminish his reluctance to change (Thompson, 1978, p. 177).

6. *Make all positive reinforcement contingent on successively closer approximations to the target behavior.*   The shaping process is successful only when the behavioral chain is built link by link. As we discussed earlier, when individual performance is not closely linked to rewards in an organization, high performers feel a sense of inequity and generally either lower their performance or leave the organization. A similar outcome results when manager-controlled rewards are not linked to successively higher levels of performance during the behavior-shaping process. If the employee receives the same reward from his or her manager at performance level two as at level four, the manager's reinforcement actually discourages improvement. Managers often violate this principle inadvertently. They get very busy and lose their perspective on how much of a reward the person has received up to this point. Or they quite naturally feel sorry for persons having difficulty and offer more encouragement and praise during periods of slow progress than during spurts of rapid development.

This common pitfall reminds us that effective positive reinforcement is much more than simply "being nice to people." Indeed, David Thompson, an expert on applying operant conditioning principles to management, argues that one of the most common causes of low motivation is the indiscriminate use of the "high consideration of others" management style (1978, p. 45). For example, an employee may have a habit of depreciating his or her abilities. ("I don't think I'm qualified for such a difficult task." "I didn't make a very good impression in that meeting, did I?") If his or her manager attempts to enhance the person's self-confidence by responding with very supportive comments ("What are you talking about? You always do a great job on tough assign-

ments." "Hey, don't worry about it, you did a fine job."), the inappropriate behaviors will likely increase in frequency.

One way to reduce the likelihood of a manager's inadvertently not making reinforcement contingent on continuous improvement is to set up a reinforcement schedule when the change process is initiated. Intermediate steps
can be identified and appropriate levels of reinforcement assigned to each.
This type of formal system helps the employee know what to expect at each
stage of the program and reduces the likelihood that a management oversight
will hinder the change process.

7. *Administer rewards immediately following each improvement in behavior.*   It is important to point out that all the research findings supporting
the value of operant conditioning as a motivational system assume that outcomes immediately follow behaviors. In animal studies, one can imagine how
little learning would take place if a food pellet appeared twenty minutes after
the appropriate lever was pressed. While this principle appears intuitively obvious in the context of an experiment involving learning in animals, it is frequently violated in everyday management practice. In general, most managers
give feedback on an employee's performance at the worst possible time—when
they want to, not when the employee would be most reinforced by it. Managers may feel frustrated with their personal work and this triggers a barrage
of complaints about a subordinate's poor performance. Or a manager may get
a major promotion or large bonus, which stimulates a profuse expression of
appreciation for the staff's hard work. While the feedback may be warranted
in both situations, the poor timing diminishes its impact.

Feedback on the consequences of employees' performance is also often
delayed for months by the formal administrative apparatus of many organizations. It is customary practice to restrict in-depth discussions of job performance to formally designated performance appraisal interviews, which
generally only take place once every six to twelve months. Again, this delay
between performance and feedback greatly dilutes the effectiveness of any rewards dispensed as a result of the evaluation process.

8. *During the shaping process, use a continuous reinforcement schedule.
After the target has been achieved, protect the learned behavior from extinction by gradually shifting to an intermittent reinforcement schedule.*   The
second critical aspect of reinforcement timing is consistency of reward administration. Administering a reward every time a given behavior occurs is continuous reinforcement. Administering rewards on an intermittent basis (the
same reward is always used but it is not given every time it is warranted), is
partial, or intermittent, reinforcement. Neither approach is clearly superior—
they both have trade-offs. Continuous reinforcement represents the fastest
way to establish new behavior. For example, if your boss consistently praises
you for writing reports using his or her preferred format, you will readily
adopt that style because of your desire to receive more and more contingent

rewards. However, if your boss suddenly takes an extended leave of absence, the learned behavior will be highly vulnerable to extinction. In contrast, while partial reinforcement results in very slow learning, it is very resistant to extinction. The persistence associated with gambling behavior illustrates the addictive nature of a partial reinforcement schedule. Not knowing when you will receive a payoff preserves the myth that you are only one more try away from hitting the jackpot.

This information about reinforcement schedules derived from experimental research has important implications for effective management. To begin with, it is important to realize that continuous reinforcement systems are very rare in organizations, unless they are mechanically built into the job—as in the case of a piece-rate pay plan. Seldom are individuals rewarded every time they make a good presentation or effectively handle a customer's complaint. When we recognize that most non-assembly-line work in an organization is typically governed by a partial reinforcement schedule, we gain new insights into some of the more frustrating aspects of a manager's role. For example, it helps explain why new employees seem to take forever to catch on to how the boss wants things done. It also reveals why it is so difficult to extinguish anachronistic behaviors, particularly in older employees.

This understanding of reinforcement timing is critical for a successful program of behavior modification. To enhance learning during the shaping process, managers should use a continuous reinforcement schedule. This means that managers must pay close attention to improvements and reward them immediately and consistently. If such close supervision is impractical, redundant reinforcers should be built into the system. For example, a manager might explain to a few trusted senior staff members what he or she is trying to accomplish with a new employee and encourage them to reward each manifestation of the desired behavior. This increases the likelihood that the desired behavior will be reinforced by someone each time it occurs. Once the target behavior has been reached, continuous reinforcement should continue until it is apparent that the employee regards the acquired behavior as accepted practice. Then an intermittent reinforcement schedule should be gradually introduced. For example, rewards might be administered every other time the behavior is emitted, then every third time, etc. While it is obviously difficult for busy managers to obtain laboratory-like precision in administering an intermittent reinforcement schedule, it is usually possible to establish a general pattern in which subordinates are systematically rewarded less frequently for learned behaviors.

The ultimate objective of effective management is to help employees become "self-reinforcers" so they strive to maintain their level of high performance because of the personal gratification they receive, rather than because of the praise they receive from an appreciative boss. This can be encouraged by shifting the focus of the manager's verbal reinforcement during the advanced stages of the shaping process. Instead of emphasizing how much the manager appreciates the employee's extra efforts, the feedback should help the employee appreciate the intrinsic satisfaction gained from excellent performance. This can be done using comments like, "You've completed the data entry already? How does it feel to beat your old time by an hour?" This approach to verbal commendation encourages employees to value intrinsic motivation. They become motivated by the outcomes that are produced by their performance itself, independent of how others respond. This form of motivation is an important complement to the external reinforcement techniques we have discussed for shaping behavior, but should not be viewed as a replacement for organization- or manager-administered rewards. The effective manager uses both types of reinforcement (Nord, 1969).

Negative Reinforcement

Negative reinforcement reinforces a behavior by eliminating aversive consequences. As we noted earlier, this strategy illustrates the unintended negative consequences of reinforcement conditioning. For example, nonassertiveness is negatively reinforced when it diffuses the hostility of a highly emotional and threatening co-worker, blaming one's mistakes on others is negatively reinforced when it softens the anger of a boss, and potentially debilitating management concessions are negatively reinforced when they stop a wildcat strike. As these examples illustrate, negative reinforcement is often referred to as a form of social blackmail (Luthans & Kreitner, 1975). Because it is basically a form of negative control, it produces many of the same undesirable side effects as punishment.

However, if we interpret the concept of negative reinforcement broadly, it suggests an important aspect of motivation. Technically, negative reinforcement refers to aversive stimuli that are intentionally administered by another person to influence behavior (nagging, bullying, whining). If we broaden this definition or include naturally occurring aversive stimuli (such as poor working conditions or frequent requirements to work overtime or to spend several nights a month away from home), then management can use the elimination of these aversive stimuli as an inducement to improve motivation. One successful manager asks his subordinates periodically, "If you could use the authority of my position to improve your job and working conditions in any reasonable way, what would you change?" When the ensuing discussion uncovers aversive stimuli that can be feasibly changed, the manager does what he can to remove the disincentives and thereby encourage greater commitment and dedication.

Punishment

In contrast to positive and negative reinforcement, punishment operates on the premise that the best way to modify behavior is to extinguish undesired behavior. Punishment consists of administering an aversive reward or withholding a positive reward. Punishment is the most controversial aspect of operant conditioning and is not recommended by many experts as a technique for modifying behavior (Skinner, 1953). However, for many agents of socialization (parents, teachers, managers), punishment is used far more frequently than positive reinforcement to modify behavior. In a work situation, for example, many supervisors just assume that employees fully understand what is expected of them and are self-motivated to achieve high performance. They define their role as that of a sheepdog, circling the perimeter of the group, nipping at the heels of those who begin to stray. They establish a fairly broad range of acceptable behaviors and then limit their interactions with employees to barking at those who exceed the parameters.

The problem with punishment is that it works too well. It is used frequently by managers to stop employees' objectionable behavior because it is very reinforcing to the user. For example, a manager may yell at a computer specialist for reading a book instead of coding data. If the distracting behavior is terminated as a result of the punishment, the manager's punitive approach to changing behavior is reinforced. Examining the contingencies under which administrators of punishment operate makes quite clear why punishment is so pervasive in organizational life.

While negative sanctions obviously have their place in organizations (for example, when critical safety regulations are violated), there are several liabilities to their extensive use (Maier, 1973; Bandura, 1969; Hamner, 1974).

1. *Frequently or inappropriately administered punishments may cause so much frustration and humiliation that employees become alienated and seek opportunities to "get even with the boss."* In these cases there is a tendency for punishment to become associated with the punisher. When this happens, the ongoing working relationship is seriously impaired. Immature and emotionally unstable people are most likely to respond this way, and they are also most likely to be punished frequently.

2. *Threat of punishment highlights what not to do, and in some cases this may actually suggest actions previously not considered by subordinates.* One company prominently displayed a list of thirty violations and the punishments associated with each. It is unlikely that employees could have possibly thought of so many ways to cause trouble.

3. *While punishment may extinguish an undesirable behavior, it does not provide any direction regarding more desirable alternatives.* In some cases the link between undesirable behaviors and desirable alternatives is fairly obvious, as in the case of tardiness. However, this link is much less apparent when a creative new idea is criticized in a marketing staff meeting or an engineer is reprimanded for spending too much time designing safety features of a new piece of equipment. This often leads to the next problem.

4. *Punishment is highly vulnerable to the error of overgeneralization.* If a manager repeatedly criticizes subordinates' suggestions as a way of encouraging them to sharpen their analytical and presentation skills, they may conclude that the manager does not want to hear suggestions at all. As a result, instead of working to improve the quality of their suggestions, the staff may simply stop exploring ways to make improvements.

5. *Punishment does not encourage the development of an internalized approach to behavior control.* One of the oldest studies in organizational behavior compared the impact of punitive, democratic, and laissez-faire styles of leadership on the work activities of young boys (White & Lippitt, 1967). In the punitive situation, the boys worked hard as long as the authority figure was present, but as soon as he left they began to play.

6. *Punishment encourages people to respond in kind.* The dominant mode of behavior modification used by a supervisor (either positive reinforcement or punishment) tends to become an institutionalized pattern of interaction in a work group. Therefore, when choosing between these alternatives, managers must consider not only which approach is most likely to accomplish the desired behavior-shaping objective, but which general mode of interpersonal interaction they want to encourage. The tendency is for people who are continually chewed out by their boss to vent their frustration by acting vindictively toward their subordinates or co-workers. This produces a widespread negative, hostile working environment.

If managers find it necessary to use punishment to curb undesirable behavior, they should keep in mind the following guidelines to reduce its dysfunctional consequences (Hamner, 1974; Luthans & Kreitner, 1975; Maier, 1973).

1. *Administer the punishment immediately following the offensive behavior.* This increases the likelihood that the employee will associate the punishment with the specific act, rather than viewing it as a general negative evaluation of himself as a person. ("I was penalized for being late again." vs. "He thinks I'm lazy and irresponsible.") This will reduce the hostility typically associated with being punished.

2. *Do not stop administering aversive reinforcement until the person begins engaging in constructive behavior.* Suppose an employee is being reprimanded for ignoring a direct request to perform an urgent task. A common response is to shift the focus of the discussion by blaming the problem on being overworked, not being able to obtain the help of others, or complaining that others have done the same thing and weren't reprimanded. If the manager stops applying the aversive stimuli in response to these diversions, these tactics will be unintentionally reinforced and the aversive stimuli will lose its potential for motivating better performance. To avoid this pitfall, the manager should keep the conversation focused on the seriousness of the problem until the employee acknowledges the concern and makes a commitment to change his or her behavior. Only then should mitigating circumstances be discussed.

3. *Clearly identify the desirable behaviors that should be substituted and be certain that they are positively reinforced when emitted.*   It is important that persons being punished understand how they can receive rewards in the future. This reduces the despair that occurs when people feel they will likely be punished no matter what they do. The need for positive reinforcement is especially acute following punishment because it helps convince the person that the intent of the punishment was to change inappropriate behaviors, not condemn him or her personally. Therefore, a key to the effective use of punishment is a concerted effort to help the punished individual feel successful in the future.

4. *Use punishment sparingly, and then only to accomplish a specific objective.*   Punishment is most dysfunctional when it becomes the prevalent form of reinforcement or when it is used to satisfy the needs of the manager, rather than to improve the behavior of the subordinate. Unfortunately, punishment is frequently used as a blatant act of intimidation by managers who aren't willing to spend time figuring out a way to use positive reinforcement to accomplish the same behavioral objective. Or it is used as a way of getting even with a subordinate whose errors caused the supervisor public embarrassment.

A child psychologist once gave a lecture on how to raise children without using spanking as a training device. During the question-and-answer period, parents in the audience were quick to cite dozens of examples they felt justified physical punishment (e.g., running into a busy street). Finally the psychologist replied, "You've missed my point. Seldom is spanking seriously initiated as a device for training the child. It is generally used by the parent to let off steam, to express anger or embarrassment, or to show who's boss. I'm not as concerned about the consequences of the physical act of spanking as I am about the destructive motives that usually accompany it. Spanking generally reflects the negative state of mind of the parent more than the inappropriate behavior of the child."

5. *Whenever possible, rely on natural consequences.*   The negative impact of punishment on the ongoing manager–subordinate relationship can be avoided by letting the undesirable natural consequences of inappropriate behavior serve as its own reward. The important thing is that employees learn that it does not pay to do certain things. If that lesson can be learned without the direct intervention of the boss, so much the better. When a member of an engineering research group complains to the department head that other members are not performing their fair share of the work, the manager should encourage the disgruntled worker to express his or her displeasure directly to the offending party. If the department head responds, "That strikes me as a work group problem, not a management problem," he or she encourages group members to use peer sanctions when work norms are violated. The advantage of this approach is that the manager is not pairing himself or herself with aversive consequences in the minds of the alleged offenders. As a result, the potential for damaging their relationship is avoided.

When managers cannot avoid becoming personally involved in the administration of aversive natural consequences, they should use a derivation of the Premack principle. Instead of making desirable outcome C contingent on performing undesirable task B, they should make outcome C contingent on stopping undesirable action A. In the case of excessive tardiness in a work crew, the manager might install a time clock and announce a certain wage penalty for every quarter-hour of lost work time. If the penalty is salient enough, the undesirable behavior will be extinguished without the manager's having to begin each day with a lecture on tardiness. An examination of the Premack reinforcers in Table 6.4 suggests a number of variations on this approach. The main advantage of this general strategy is that it helps depersonalize the punishment. That is, the experience of being punished does not impinge as directly on the relationship between manager and subordinate. By justifying the imposition of a formalized set of punishment contingencies on the basis of general principles or shared values (fairness, responsibility, profitability) and then making the procedures for invoking the punishment as formal and impersonal as possible (such as a computerized payroll wired directly into a time clock), one can ensure that the punishing consequences will soon be regarded as a natural part of the system.

In summary, positive reinforcement is a better approach than punishment for shaping behavior. As a motivational technique, positive reinforcement is generally sufficient to produce high performance. In addition, when used over a long period of time, positive reinforcement tends to encourage people to behave in more responsible, mature ways. It emphasizes results, rather than the acceptability of selected means, and it focuses attention on maximizing joint payoffs, rather than pitting managers against subordinates.

Empirical support for this conclusion comes from a study conducted by Greg Oldham (1976). He interviewed managers in ten stores of a national retail chain and asked them to describe the motivational strategies they used and to rate the effectiveness of each of the other managers in their store in terms of ability to motivate subordinates. He also asked them to rate the actual performance of the subordinates of each manager. After classifying the managers' motivational strategies into several categories, Professor Oldham correlated each strategy with the peer ratings for managerial effectiveness and subordinate performance. He found that what he termed the "personally rewarding" strategy correlated .43 with ratings of managerial effectiveness and .50 with ratings of employee performance. In contrast, the "personally punishing" strategy correlated −.03 with managerial effectiveness and −.16 with employee performance.

SUMMARY AND BEHAVIORAL GUIDELINES

In this section we have discussed the twin determinants of employee performance: ability and motivation. Three behavioral patterns suggest a loss of ability in mid-career employees: taking refuse in a specialty, focusing on past performance, and exaggerating aspects of the leadership role. There are four alternatives for dealing with this problem. The *retraining* approach is the least threatening because it does not imply a lack of ability. If additional training does not solve the problem, a *redefinition* of task assignment to match existing ability can be explored. If this is insufficient, *reassignment* to another position should be considered. If these alternatives have been explored unsuccessfully, *releasing* the employee from the company is the last resort.

We have focused primarily on motivation, since it is more closely linked to the interpersonal skill proficiency of managers. Specifically, we examined two key management roles that significantly affect employees' motivation to perform well: monitoring each employee's interface with the organization's incentive system to detect deficiencies in the system's ability to motivate good performance in that individual, and critically evaluating one's personal, routine interactions with subordinates to determine the extent to which they elicit desired responses. These activities are complementary and both are critical for high employee motivation. Our discussion of the first activity was grounded in expectancy theory, and our discussion of the second in operant conditioning. From these discussions we can derive the following guidelines for improving managerial performance:

1. Clearly define an acceptable level of overall performance or specific behavioral objective. Make sure the individual understands what is necessary to satisfy your expectations. Formulate a "behavioral chain" progressing from more simple to more difficult tasks leading to the objective.
2. Make sure the target performance level is obtainable by the individual. Help remove all external obstacles to reaching the objective.
3. Use reinforcing rewards that are salient to the individual.
4. Make rewards contingent on high performance or drawing nearer to the behavioral objective. Guard against unwittingly reinforcing inappropriate behaviors.
5. Minimize the time lag between emitted behaviors and administered rewards or punishment. Use continuous reinforcement to reward new behaviors, then systematically phase in intermittent reinforcement to "harden" learned behaviors against extinction.
6. Establish redundant reinforcers for critical behaviors. Avoid inadvertently extinguishing important behaviors by lack of attention.
7. When punishment must be administered, treat it as a learning experience for the individual. State specifically what the problem

is and how it should be corrected. Whenever possible, rely on natural consequences.

8. Carefully examine the behavioral consequences of your non-responses. A nonresponse is rarely interpreted as a neutral response.

REFERENCES

Adams, J.S. Toward an understanding of inequity. *Journal of Abnormal and Social Psychology,* 1963, *67,* 422–436.

Adams, J. Inequity in social exchange. In L. Berkowitz (Ed.), *Advances in experimental social psychology* (Vol. 2). New York: Academic Press, 1965.

Bandura, A. *Principles of behavior modification.* New York: Holt, Rinehart and Winston, 1969.

Connor, S. R., & Fielden, J. S. Rx for managerial "shelf sitters." *Harvard Business Review,* Nov.-Dec. 1973, *51,* 113–120.

Dalton, G., Lawrence, P., & Lorsch, J. *Organizational structure and design.* Homewood, Ill.: Irwin, 1970.

Dalton, G. W., Thompson, D. H., & Price, R. L. Four stages of professional careers. *Organizational Dynamics,* 1977, *6,* 19–42.

Hall, D. T. *Careers in organizations.* Pacific Palisades, Calif.: Goodyear, 1976.

Hamner, W. C. Reinforcement theory and contingency management in organizational settings. In H. L. Tosi & W. C. Hamner (Eds.), *Organizational behavior and management: A contingency approach.* Chicago: St. Clair Press, 1974.

Jay, A. *Management and Machiavelli, an inquiry into the politics of corporate life.* New York: Holt, Rinehart and Winston, 1967.

Kellogg, M. S. *Putting management theories to work.* Englewood Cliffs, N.J.: Prentice-Hall, 1979.

Kerr, S. On the folly of rewarding A, while hoping for B. *Academy of Management Review,* 1975, *19,* 769–783.

Kipnis, D. *The powerholders.* Chicago, Ill.: University of Chicago Press, 1976.

Lawler, E. E. *Pay and organizational effectiveness.* New York: McGraw-Hill, 1971.

Lawler, E. E., III. *Motivation in work organizations.* Belmont, Calif.: Brooks/Cole, 1973.

Lawler, E. E. Job attitudes and employee motivation: Theory, research and practice. *Personnel Psychology,* 1970, *23,* 223–237.

Le Due, A. I., Jr. Motivation of programmers. *Data Base,* 1980, 3, 5.

Luthans, F., & Kreitner, R. *Organizational behavior modification.* Glenview, Ill.: Scott, Foresman, 1975.

Maier, N. R. F. *Psychology in industrial organizations* (4th ed.). New York: Houghton Mifflin, 1973.

Michener, H. A., Fleishman, J. A., & Vaske, J. J. A test of the bargaining theory of coalition formation in four-person groups. *Journal of Personality and Social Psychology,* 1976, *34,* 1114–1126.

Mitchell, T. R. Expectancy models of job satisfaction, occupational preference and effort: A theoretical, methodological, and empirical appraisal. *Psychological Bulletin,* 1974, *81,* 1053–1107.

Nadler, D. E., & Lawler, E. E. Motivation: A diagnostic approach. In J. R. Hackman, E. E. Lawler, & L. W. Porter (Eds.), *Perspective behavior in organizations.* New York: McGraw-Hill, 1977.

Nord, W. Beyond the teaching machine: The neglected area of operant conditioning in the theory and practice of management. *Organizational Behavior and Human Performance,* 1969, *4,* 375–401.

Oldham, G. The motivational strategies used by supervisors: Relationships to effectiveness indicators. *Organizational Behavior and Human Performance,* 1976, *15,* 66–86.

Petroch, F., & Gamboa, V. Expectancy theory and operant conditioning: A conceptual comparison. In W. Nord. (Ed.), *Concepts and controversy in organizational behavior* (2nd ed.). Pacific Palisades, Calif.: Goodyear Publishing, 1976.

Premack, D. Reinforcement theory. In D. Levine (Ed.), *Nebraska symposium on motivation.* Lincoln, Nebraska: University of Nebraska, 1965.

Quick, T. L. *Person to person managing.* New York: St. Martin's Press, 1977.

Schein, E. *Career dynamics.* Reading, Mass.: Addison Wesley, 1978.

Skinner, B. F. *Contingencies of reinforcement.* New York: Appleton-Century-Crofts, 1969.

Skinner, B. F. *Science and human behavior.* New York: Free Press, 1953.

Sullivan, J. J. A Critique of Theory Z. *Academy of Management Review,* 1983, *8,* 132–142.

Thompson, D.W. *Managing people: Influencing behavior.* St. Louis: C. V. Mosby Co., 1978.

Vroom, V. H. *Work and motivation.* New York: John Wiley, 1964.

Wanous, J. P. *Organizational entry.* Reading, Mass.: Addison Wesley, 1980.

White, R., & Lippett, R. Leader behavior and member reaction in three social climates. In D. Cartwright & A. Zander (Eds.), *Group dynamics: Research and theory* (3rd ed.). New York: Harper and Row, 1967. ■

■ *Skill Analysis*

Elizabeth Sternberg and Judith Greene

Ross A. Webber

ELIZABETH STERNBERG

Elizabeth had always admired her parents. Of course she argued with them from time to time, but she loved to be home, to cook and sew, and to help with her younger brothers and sisters. To her parents, Liz was a model child. She never did especially well in school, but never received an F, either. School social life was more important than studies to Elizabeth. Yet she was a little shy, more a group follower than a leader. Although she dated frequently, most of the boys seemed too immature for her.

Liz never planned to go to college. Her real dream was to get married and have children. At seventeen, however, this seemed a way off, and after high school graduation she expected to look for a job—but not for about six months. The summer and autumn went very slowly. Many of her friends left the neighborhood; some of the boys joined the military, some traveled, others went off to college. Liz missed the excitement of the crowded halls and active conversation of high school. Finally, in November she took a clerical job in the regional office of a large insurance company.

From the beginning, Liz fit right in. She did what she was told, was polite and willing. She thought the work was fine, but she really enjoyed the beautiful new office, so clean and neat, and even more she liked the girlfriends she made, the fun of chatting and planning bridal and baby showers. Liz found herself taking a more active role in planning these affairs than she had ever done in school.

It was her social sensitivity that prompted Liz to drop a note into the suggestion box. The office had been arranged in long straight rows and columns, all rather forbidding looking. Liz suggested that the setup be modified to several semicircles. This would facilitate communicating with the group leader located in the middle and between cooperating desks. It would also create a sense of belonging (and perhaps promote gossip). Management subsequently introduced the arrangement, and everyone was pleased.

As time passed, Liz Sternberg's Prince Charming did not seem to have appeared, so she continued working. She perfected her typing, shorthand, and telephone style so much that she received several merit raises. She was even assigned a position as office claims agent and became the first female to handle

SOURCE; Ross Webber, *Management: Basic elements of managing organizations* (Homewood, Ill.: Richard D. Irwin, 1979), pp. 131–137.

routine policyholder claims over the telephone. She was flattered by the promotion, but the job did make it more difficult to keep up with her friends in the office. Nonetheless, she enjoyed talking with policyholders, who also liked to deal with her. Everyone thought she did an outstanding job.

Shortly after Liz's twenty-fifth birthday last year, her mother passed away. At first Liz wanted to quit her job to take care of the family, but her father said it wasn't necessary and she had her own life to live. It has been a rough twelve months for Liz.

Last week the regional vice president called Liz into his office, praised her, and offered her a promotion to assistant office manager in charge of hiring and training all clerical employees. The position included a private office and a salary that exceeded her father's. Liz was in a terrible quandary. She just couldn't see herself as a manager giving orders to girls like she had been herself a few years before. And she did not want to be thought of as a career woman.

JUDITH GREENE

Judith is the vice president for administration of the International Division of Trustworthy Trust Company. She joined the division as a junior analyst twelve years ago, right after she graduated from Eastern College with a B.S. in economics. She was one of the first woman analysts at the bank and is a hard worker and fast learner. These attributes always characterized her from childhood, when as a single child she helped her father with the bookkeeping in his dental practice. They spent many evenings discussing sports and investments, rather than dental medicine (conversations her mother felt rather excluded from), so Judith more naturally gravitated to economics rather than to a health care field. One of her proudest moments came in college, when her father gave her $5,000 to invest (but not spend!) in any way she desired. She still has that initial capital, which has grown considerably.

Judith has mixed feelings about her early years as an analyst. A lot of the work was boring because the tasks were routine and feedback inadequate. At times she felt like a nameless, faceless automaton, but she enjoyed the bank as an institution and initiated opportunities both inside and outside the division to talk about investments. She was very active in several professional banking and investment societies. She got along well with most of the staff, including the support personnel (apparently because she did much of her own typing, something that she saw not as a status issue but as a pragmatic opportunity: her reports would frequently be submitted while her peers were still waiting to get theirs back from the typing pool).

Judith feels that she did a better job than most analysts, but she frankly states that her break and promotion to area supervisor occurred rather fortuitously. Judith's husband, a manager for a local industrial firm, had graduated from the prestigious Old Ivy University. At an alumni dance he introduced her to Marshall Wilde, then senior vice president in the Corporate Loan Division of Trustworthy Trust, with whom Tom Greene had done business. Shortly thereafter, Wilde had been named executive vice president and head of the International Division. Wilde was a dynamic, flexible guy interested in improving opportunities for minorities. Since Judith clearly had the requisite skills and performance, she was subsequently promoted to area supervisor. Although a little younger than the other supervisors, she accepted the promotion without hesitation. Judith performed well as an area supervisor, benefiting from a number of informal conversations with Wilde.

Trustworthy Trust Company is a large, multiservice bank headquartered in a metropolitan area. Its assets rank it in the top fifty banking institutions in the United States. Its main office is an imposing granite structure in the center of the financial district. The physical setting fairly reeks of stability and conservatism. Yet it has been aggressive in opening branches and courting customers.

A business visitor is especially impressed with the dining rooms. They are like something from a Hollywood director's vision of what banks look like. There are four kinds of facilities. On the eighth floor are private rooms and the senior officers' dining room, richly paneled in walnut. Menus contain no prices. On the seventh floor is the junior officers' dining hall, also paneled, but painted. Menus contain prices (and more variety than upstairs). On the sixth floor is the general cafeteria for all employees. In fact, most of the junior officers eat here because it is quicker, cheaper, and has the most variety.

The International Division is the smallest of the bank's five major units, but it is headed by an executive vice president like the others. The division's structure is illustrated in Exhibit 1. The International Division is charged with maintaining correspondent relations with foreign banks, exchanging different currencies, and assisting its large corporate customers in raising funds and conducting business in foreign countries. The division annually hires four or five MBAs with special skills and experience (usually a foreign language and knowledge of a particular country). The executive vice president, however, is presently considering whether to hire more people right out of college rather than after graduate school. New professional employees are assigned to the analyst pool, where they write reports requested by various officers. Much of their data is gathered from the bank's extensive library, and some from a local university. Frequently they write to foreign embassies and governments. Sometimes they request division officers to gather information on their trips. The analysts are located in a common work area called the "bullpen." It is crowded, warm, and a little shabby.

After eighteen months to two years, a junior analyst is promoted to senior analyst. This means that he or she handles more difficult assignments, but work location and process are unchanged.

The first substantial promotion comes after three to four years, when a senior analyst could become a junior officer and area supervisor. In this position he or she would be in charge of four or five analysts specializing in a

Exhibit 1 *Organization of International Division*

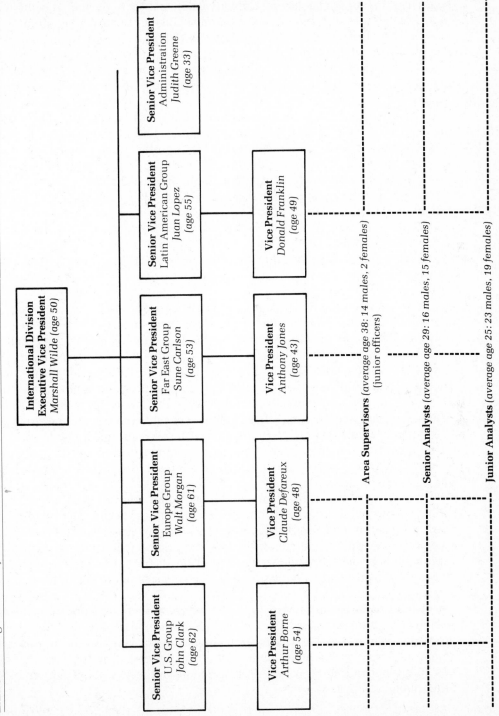

International Division Executive Vice President
Marshall Wilde (age 50)

Senior Vice President
U.S. Group
John Clark
(age 62)

Senior Vice President
Europe Group
Walt Morgan
(age 61)

Senior Vice President
Far East Group
Sune Carlson
(age 53)

Senior Vice President
Latin American Group
Juan Lopez
(age 55)

Senior Vice President
Administration
Judith Greene
(age 33)

Vice President
Arthur Borne
(age 54)

Vice President
Claude Defareux
(age 48)

Vice President
Anthony Jones
(age 43)

Vice President
Donald Franklin
(age 49)

Area Supervisors (average age 38: 14 males, 2 females)
(Junior officers)

Senior Analysts (average age 29: 16 males, 15 females)

Junior Analysts (average age 25: 23 males, 19 females)

specific country (such as France) or area (such as Central America). The area supervisor makes decisions on relatively small transactions and consults with appropriate senior officers on major matters. Once or twice a year, a junior officer makes a three- to five-day business trip to his or her geographical area of responsibility. These trips are anticipated with much interest and excitement. The junior officers' offices are located in private rooms opening into the bullpen area. Except for the lack of windows in some, they are pleasant though small.

The division's senior officers and their assistants (also senior officers) are the critical decision-makers. Their offices are located in another area opening to the public elevators. The reception space and offices can only be described as impressive and luxurious: all done in colonial decor and Williamsburg green, and with wall-to-wall carpeting. Each officer has a spacious private office with a secretary just outside the door. Exhibit 2 gives the layout of the International Division.

The senior officers specialize by areas and travel frequently. Either the senior vice president or the vice president for each area is expected to be in headquarters, but actually both are often gone on trips. About half of their time is spent traveling. They frequently complain about the onerous burden of these trips.

The Trustworthy Trust Company is a successful institution, and the International Division enjoys a high reputation. Nonetheless, the executive vice president has been concerned about the younger employees. Over one half of them leave the bank after eighteen to thirty months. Most join smaller banks, some get married and have children, and some just drop out, throw their watches away, and move around. Exit interviews produce complaints about being bored, the lousy working conditions, the crisis atmosphere, being hemmed in, and not knowing what's going on or what happens to their reports. When a consultant was called in, he administered a questionnaire to all divisional officers and managers. The results are summarized in Exhibit 3. No significant differences between male and female responses were evident within any position category.

In addition, the consultant conducted some training sessions for the senior officers which covered topics such as human needs, the meaning of work, motivation, and the generation gap. Unfortunately, several of the senior vice presidents did not attend all the meetings. Some who did took strong exception to the consultant's views on people's needs for autonomy, competence, and achievement. And a couple of senior officers seemed to sleep through the sessions.

Wilde has now promoted Judith to the newly created position of vice president of administration. He has not given an explicit job description for the new position, but he sees it as dealing with the apparently low morale among analysts and the poor administration of junior and support staff activities. Judith appears to be very enthusiastic and optimistic about the opportunities in the new post.

Exhibit 2 *Layout of International Division*

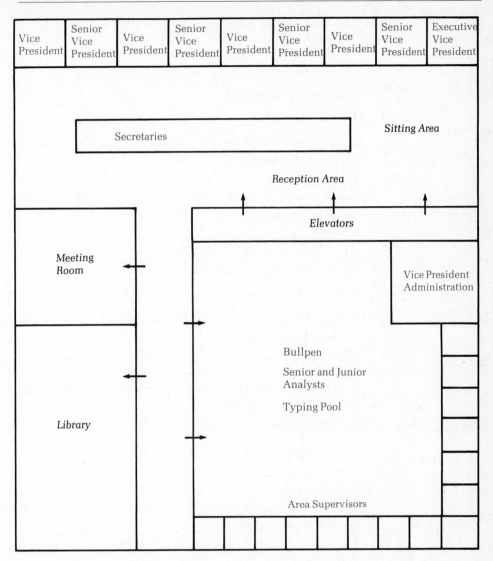

Exhibit 3   *Questionnaire Results*

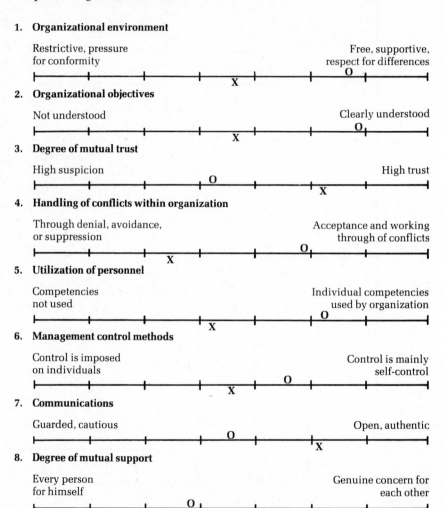

Mean response for officers: Above line, O
Mean response for non-officers: Below line, X

Perception of Organizational Climate

1. **Organizational environment**

    Restrictive, pressure   Free, supportive,
    for conformity   respect for differences

2. **Organizational objectives**

    Not understood   Clearly understood

3. **Degree of mutual trust**

    High suspicion   High trust

4. **Handling of conflicts within organization**

    Through denial, avoidance,   Acceptance and working
    or suppression   through of conflicts

5. **Utilization of personnel**

    Competencies   Individual competencies
    not used   used by organization

6. **Management control methods**

    Control is imposed   Control is mainly
    on individuals   self-control

7. **Communications**

    Guarded, cautious   Open, authentic

8. **Degree of mutual support**

    Every person   Genuine concern for
    for himself   each other

Job Attitudes

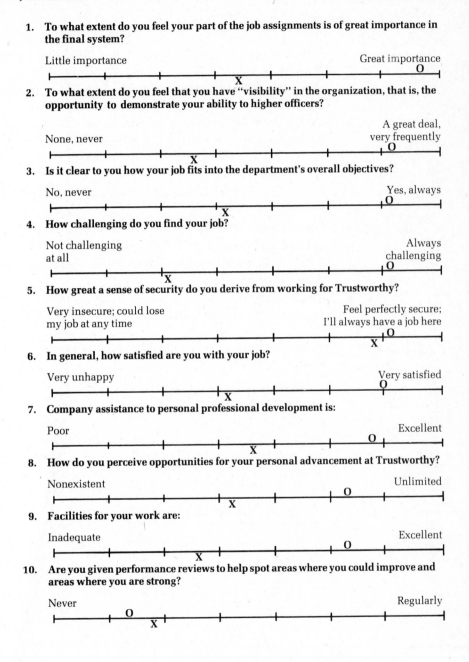

1. To what extent do you feel your part of the job assignments is of great importance in the final system?

   Little importance — Great importance

2. To what extent do you feel that you have "visibility" in the organization, that is, the opportunity to demonstrate your ability to higher officers?

   None, never — A great deal, very frequently

3. Is it clear to you how your job fits into the department's overall objectives?

   No, never — Yes, always

4. How challenging do you find your job?

   Not challenging at all — Always challenging

5. How great a sense of security do you derive from working for Trustworthy?

   Very insecure; could lose my job at any time — Feel perfectly secure; I'll always have a job here

6. In general, how satisfied are you with your job?

   Very unhappy — Very satisfied

7. Company assistance to personal professional development is:

   Poor — Excellent

8. How do you perceive opportunities for your personal advancement at Trustworthy?

   Nonexistent — Unlimited

9. Facilities for your work are:

   Inadequate — Excellent

10. Are you given performance reviews to help spot areas where you could improve and areas where you are strong?

    Never — Regularly

Answers to Question "What Is the Most Dissatisfying Aspect of Your Job?"

    A.   Analysts

        1.   The detail work involved and the constant phone calls from branches for foreign exchange rates. These jobs could be done by a clerk.

        2.   Being involved with clerical work, such as typing, and being taken for granted.

        3.   Lack of knowledge as to where my job will lead.

        4.   The close-minded narrowness of most of senior management that leads to pettiness, lack of communication, and the lack of a more democratic environment.

        5.   Lack of contact with people outside the bank. Lack of physical activity.

        6.   Lack of experience causes me to waste too much time.

        7.   Lack of sufficient time for free thinking.

        8.   The physical working conditions are intolerable in that there is too little space, no privacy, and a very high noise level.

        9.   The remuneration—the salary structure is such that it presents an unoptimistic future. If one would desire to stay, he would be passing up a great deal of financial reward. In order to financially succeed in banking, one must transfer to another bank to receive financial remuneration.

    B.   Junior Officers

        1.   Would like my boss to provide me with more constructive criticism to aid in my development.

        2.   (a) Low salary scales, (b) poor office conditions (physical), (c) government restrictions on foreign lending, (d) poor health and life insurance plans, (e) pay comparable to area wages is not good enough for an "international division," where employees have potential *national* and not just *regional* mobility.

        3.   Lack of framework in which to develop initiative and carry out duties; this creates doubt whether efforts are being properly applied.

        4.   Being susceptible to all factions of the International Division and subsequently often frustrated by what I think is a lack of concern for personnel and/or the lack of communications. I am also dissatisfied and frustrated at times by the reluctance of individuals to take the "bull by the horns" and attempt to solve problems or clear up loose ends.

Answers to Question "What Is the Most Satisfying Aspect of Your Work?"

A.   Analysts

1.   Learning something new every day and the mental challenge that is intellectually stimulating.

2.   The opportunity to pursue a field of great interest to me in a personal and flexible manner. The ability to interact in the decision-making processes on a high level.

3.   High degree of responsibility and independence to perform assignments which have to be supervised at every turn.

4.   To do my own thinking and have others rely on my judgment.

5.   The actual dealing aspect of the job. Being able to be of real assistance to customers by giving them accurate information and proper guidance.

6.   When a given project is completed and done well, which in turn receives recognition. Helping customers with problems.

7.   Customer satisfaction.

8.   The international aspect—keeping apprised of the political and economic situation in other countries, working with other languages. Secondly, learning something about finance and accounting. Thirdly, the sources of information available—the department library, our training sesions, seminars outside the bank, etc.

9.   Those few brief moments of loveliness when one is totally responsible for one's actions. . . . Those few brief moments of group interaction when people take an idea and move ahead with it, rather than get bogged down by personality considerations, biases, or insecurities in new prospectives.

B.   Junior Officers

1.   Freedom to work independently and to carry responsibility.

2.   Working with people in a function which is very important by Trustworthy's standards. Having a significant degree of responsibility and the confidence of superiors in performing these functions. It is most rewarding being involved in a number of management problems and decisions.

3.   Variety of the responsibilities and personnel reporting to one.

4.   Relative independence. Senior management's backing of the International Division. Generally good employee relations.

5.   Attracting new customers to the bank—selling the bank's international and domestic services.

DISCUSSION QUESTIONS

1. What do Elizabeth and Judy want from their work?

2. Why has each person been successful in her organization? Would she have been as successful in the other organization?

3. Why is Liz in such a quandary over her promotion? What advice would you give her?

4. Using the behavioral guidelines, analyze the effectiveness of the regional vice president of the insurance company as a motivator. What constructive feedback could Liz give this person to improve his effectiveness as a manager?

5. Using expectancy theory and operant conditioning as diagnostic tools, identify the root causes of the high turnover rate among the junior analysts at Trustworthy Trust. Examine the motivation potential of the organizational rewards, the work performed by the analysts, the physical layout of the office space, and the analysts' interactions with upper-level managers. Examine the exhibits carefully.

6. Based on your analysis, what recommendations would you give Judy for rectifying the motivation problems in her organization?   ■

■ *Skill Practice*

Behavior Modification at Tampa Pump & Valve

1. Reading over the interoffice correspondence at TP&V (Introduction) makes clear that many of the management staff are engaging in counterproductive behaviors. In small groups, review the twelve memos in this exercise and compile a list of these undesirable behaviors.

2. One theme in this chapter is that managers play an important role in shaping the behaviors of their subordinates. Indeed, an authority on operant conditioning has argued, "Any response by a subordinate that continually occurs in the presence of his or her manager is being reinforced by the manager" (Thompson, 1978, p. 50).

   In your groups, discuss how Mr. Manners could have inadvertently, or intentionally, fostered each of the inappropriate behaviors on your list. Specifically, use all four of the operant conditioning processes (positive reinforcement, negative reinforcement, punishment, and extinction) to construct scenarios that would account for the current behaviors of these individuals. In each case, specify a hypothetical action taken by the subordinate and the reinforcing behavior of Mr. Manners. Be prepared to role play one or two of your scenarios before the class.

3. Now place yourself in the position of the new plant manager, Richard West, and discuss in your groups how you would go about changing these counterproductive behaviors. Begin by considering the advantages and disadvantages of using each of the four operant conditioning approaches as a general change strategy in this situation. Next, to gain experience changing behaviors using positive reinforcement, select one of the unproductive behaviors and develop a detailed behavior modification plan using the eight-step process described in the Skill Learning section. Be prepared to have your group's plan critiqued using the following checklist. Also be prepared to role play the key elements of your plan.

CHECKLIST FOR EVALUATING PROGRAM FOR SHAPING BEHAVIOR

Evaluate the completeness of proposed programs for shaping employee behavior using the following criteria. For items 6–7, determine whether these outcomes are likely to occur.

Check if
present or
likely to occur

1. Precisely defined goal or target behavior. Related target behavior to performance. _____

2. Disaggregated complex behaviors into discrete, measurable sequence of behaviors. Constructed a "behavioral chain" progressing from simple or appealing to difficult or unappealing tasks. _____

3. Selected potentially salient positive reinforcers. _____

4. Investigated and removed potential obstacles to successful performance. Expressed commitment to facilitate improvement plan by "running interference" when obstacles are encountered. _____

5. Made all positive reinforcement contingent on successively closer approximations of target behavior. Established a graduated reward structure for each level of improvement. _____

6. Administered rewards immediately following each improvement in behavior. _____

7. Initially used continuous reinforcement to encourage learning new behavior. Used redundant reinforcers when necessary so continuous reinforcement could be achieved. After behavior was learned, gradually introduced intermittent reinforcement to "harden" behavior. _____ ■

■ *Skill Application*

Application Exercises

1. Identify a friend, co-worker, or employee who wants to engage in a program of self-improvement (such as jogging, dieting, or professional skill development) but can't seem to mount a sustained effort. Sit down with that person and design a motivational program supporting the desired behavior. Write a brief report on the success of your efforts.

2. Identify four or five situations in which you are typically provoked to exhibit punishing behavior. These might involve friends, family members, or work associates. Now design a detailed positive reinforcement system for accomplishing the same results in one of these situations. Implement your plan and report on the results.

3. Based on what you have learned about your personal needs and work expectations thus far in the course, list the characteristics of a work situation that you feel will significantly affect your level of motivation. Consider qualities of interpersonal relationships, characteristics of work activities, and opportunities for organizational rewards. Now ask a work associate or close friend to examine this list and comment on his or her impressions of its accuracy and completeness. Write down what you have learned about your personal work motivation from this experience.

4. In this chapter we have stressed the importance of training and ability as necessary prerequisities for high job performance. Identify the skills that will be essential for success in your career. To do this, first outline a realistic career path, specifying the general field you intend to pursue (for example, bank finance, management consulting, production management, hospital administration, or public accounting) and at least four positions you hope to attain during your career (beginning with a realistic entry-level position, through mid-career promotions, to your ultimate career objective). For each position, list the skills that will be essential for your success as well as a plan for gaining the necesary experience and training to qualify. If possible, ask a person familiar with these positions to comment on the accuracy of your perceptions and the practicality of your plan. ■

7 Delegating and Decision Making

- **Skill Preassessment**

  Delegating at the South Seas Gift Shop

  Inclinations Toward Delegation

- **Skill Learning**

  How, When, Why, What, and to Whom to Delegate

- **Skill Analysis**

  Case Analysis

  Minding the Store

- **Skill Practice**

  Meeting at Hartford Manufacturing Company

- **Skill Application**

  Application Exercises

■ *Skill Preassessment*

Delegating at the South Seas Gift Shop

> *This exercise requires that groups of three be formed. One person should play the role of the manager, one should play the role of the administrative assistant, and one should be the observer. After performing the exercise once, group members may switch roles so that each has an opportunity to perform each role. The purpose of the exercise is to assess how well individuals can delegate.*

SETTING

The South Seas Gift Shop has been losing money lately, mainly due to the sloppy way in which the shop has been managed. Sales are up, but problems with inventory control, budgeting, and employee supervision have caused profits to decrease over the past year. South Seas has recently hired a new manager in an attempt to turn the shop around. The manager, in turn, hired an administrative assistant to help solve some of the problems in the shop and institute some of the changes needed. The manager felt that there was just too much for one person to do.

The manager's role in this exercise is to delegate to the administrative assistant those responsibilities he or she feels the administrative assistant should have. Those responsibilities should be delegated in the most effective way possible. The administrative assistant's role is to make certain that the responsibilities are delegated effectively, that they are understood completely, and that there is a high probability of successful accomplishment. The observer is to use the Delegation Observation Form to determine how well the manager and the administrative assistant do in their delegation interaction.

THE MANAGER

On being hired at South Seas Gift Shop, you are given the following list of problems that the shop has developed over the past year. Since there are too many to handle singlehandedly, you will need to delegate some responsibilities to your newly hired administrative assistant. Determine which of the following problems you want to delegate, and then actually perform the task of delegating them to your administrative assistant.

1. The shop has poor record-keeping, but there is an estimated inventory loss of approximately 15 percent.

2. Turnover among employees has averaged 50 percent over the past two years. There are twenty-one employees.
3. Morale among the employees is very low.
4. No formal budgeting system exists for the shop.
5. There have been many mistakes on the cash registers, in inventory control, and in stock marking.
6. Shoplifting and employee pilfering have become a problem.

THE ADMINISTRATIVE ASSISTANT

You have been hired to help the manager get the South Seas Gift Shop back on its feet. You expect that the manager will delegate some important responsibilities to you, so your task is to make certain that you understand what it is you are supposed to do and then do it. Help the manager delegate effectively.

DELEGATION OBSERVATION FORM

Observe the process of delegation between the manager and the administrative assistant. Note to what extent these two people engaged in the following behaviors.

		Completely				*Not at all*
1.	Complete information was communicated about what the responsibility entails.	5	4	3	2	1
2.	It was made clear how much discretion the administrative assistant had to perform the tasks on his or her own, without checking with the manager.	5	4	3	2	1
3.	A time frame was established for task completion.	5	4	3	2	1
4.	A follow-up schedule was established for the manager to determine to what extent the administrative assistant succeeded or failed.	5	4	3	2	1
5.	The administrative assistant had some say in what was delegated to him or her.	5	4	3	2	1

6. The administrative assistant was given   5   4   3   2   1
authority to do the tasks as he or she
saw fit, not necessarily using the same
procedures as the manager would use.

After observing the interaction, give feedback to the manager and the administrative assistant regarding their behavior. Try to help them be aware of the extent to which they were effective in performing the six aspects of delegation listed above. Very few people are effective delegators without previous training, so don't be afraid to indicate where there were weaknesses.

Inclinations Toward Delegation

This instrument is designed to help you understand the assumptions you make about people and human nature. Ten pairs of statements follow. Assign a weight from 0 to 10 to each statement to show the relative strength of your belief in the statement. The points assigned for each pair must always total 10. Be as honest with yourself as you can and resist the tendency to respond as you would like to think things are. This instrument is not a test; there are no right or wrong answers. It is designed to stimulate personal reflection and discussion.

1. It's only human nature for people to do as little work as they can get
away with.   a. _____

   When people avoid work, it's usually because their work has been deprived of meaning.   b. _____

2. If employees have access to any information they want, they tend to have
better attitudes and behave more responsibly.   c. _____

   If employees have access to more information than they need to do their
immediate tasks, they will usually misuse it.   d. _____

3. One problem in asking for the ideas of employees is that their perspective is too limited for their suggestions to be of much practical value.   e. _____

   Asking employees for their ideas broadens their perspectiveand results
in the development of useful suggestions.   f. _____

4. If people don't use much imagination and ingenuity on the job, it's probably because relatively few people have much of either.   g. _____

   Most people are imaginative and creative but may not show it because of
limitations imposed by supervision and the job.   h. _____

5. People tend to raise their standards if they are accountable for their own
behavior and for correcting their own mistakes.   i. _____

People tend to lower their standards if they are not punished for their misbehavior and mistakes.

j. _____

6. It's better to give people both good and bad news because most employees want the whole story, no matter how painful.

k. _____

It's better to withhold unfavorable news about business because most employees really want to hear only the good news.

l. _____

7. Because a supervisor is entitled to more respect than those below him in the organization, it weakens his prestige to admit that a subordinate was right and he was wrong.

m. _____

Because people at all levels are entitled to equal respect, a supervisor's prestige is increased when he supports this principle by admitting that a subordinate was right andhe was wrong.

n. _____

8. If you give people enough money, they are less likely to be concerned with such intangibles as responsibility and recognition.

o. _____

If you give people interesting and challenging work, they are less likely to compllain about such things as pay and supplemental benefits.

p. _____

9. If people are allowed to set their own goals and standards of performance, they tends to set them higher than the boss would.

q. _____

If people are allowed to set their own goals and standards of performance, they tend to set them lower than the boss would.

r. _____

10. The more knowledge and freedom a person has regarding his job, the more controls are needed to keep him in line.

s. _____

The more knowledge and freedom a person has regarding his job, the fewer controls are needed to ensure satisfactory job performance.

t. _____

SCORING

To determine your scores, add up the points you assigned as follows:
    Sum of a, d, e, g, j, l, m, o, r, and s = Theory X score.
    Sum of b, c, f, h, i, k, n, p, q, and t = Theory Y score.

INTERPRETATION

The higher one's Theory X scores, the less inclined one is to delegate tasks. Theory X assumes that people are not motivated to take on responsibility unless pressured. Theory Y assumes that people seek additional responsibility and that delegated tasks will be accepted.   ∎

Adapted from M. Scott Myers, *Every employee a manager* (New York: McGraw-Hill Book Company, 1970), and David A. Kolb, Irwin M. Rubin, and James M. McIntyre, *Organizational psychology: An experimental approach,* 2d ed. (Englewood Cliffs, N.J.: Prentice-Hall, 1974), pp. 241–242.

■ Skill Learning

How, When, Why, What, and to Whom to Delegate

Organizations generally form because one person acting alone cannot accomplish a desired set of tasks. The tasks are too complex, too large, too numerous, or too ambiguous. Several individuals working together are needed to perform the work and to achieve acceptable outcomes. Coordinating a group of individuals, however, requires someone to direct the activities of the others by making specific task assignments. That is, certain tasks must be executed by some individuals while other individuals perform other tasks. This role of assigning work is one of the central duties of the manager, and the process used is called "delegation." Delegation, therefore, is one of the most basic managerial processes in organizations. Urwick (1944, pg. 51) noted, "Without delegation no organization can function effectively. Yet, lack of the courage to delegate properly, and of knowledge of how to do it, is one of the most general causes of failures in organizations."

Our purpose in this chapter is to help you improve your delegation skills and thereby contribute to the effectiveness of the organization in which you will function as a manager. You can improve these skills by becoming aware of the advantages of delegation, of the major personal and organizational obstacles to delegation, of the conditions under which delegation should and should not be practiced, and of key action steps for determining how best to delegate certain tasks. Because delegation occurs in the context of managerial decision making—that is, managers must decide when to make a decision by themselves, when to share the decision with others, when to give the decision completely to another person, and so on—we shall focus not only on helping you develop skill in *how* to delegate, but also on helping you improve your skill in determining *when* to delegate and *what* to delegate.

Unlike many other critical managerial skills, students usually have very little experience delegating. That is, while most students have asked someone to do some task for them on occasion, few have held positions in which delegating authority was a central and critical part of the job. Moreover, the delegating of work to another person often is interpreted as common-sense behavior. One MBA student, for example, described delegation this way: "As the boss, you simply tell your subordinates to do a job and they do it." It is difficult, therefore, to develop interest in or to be motivated to practice a skill that seems relevant only in a future position and appears rather easy to do anyway.

However, we shall see in this chapter that delegation is a difficult skill to develop. Moreover, McConkey (1974) has estimated that, because of personal habits, organizational constraints, and the expectations of others, it takes five years for managers to *change* their delegation practices. They find themselves locked into patterns of behavior, which were often adopted haphazardly on entering the organization, despite the current ineffectiveness of those patterns. To change delegation habits is extremely difficult. It is important, therefore, for students to become aware of, and competent in, effective delegating skills in a "safe" classroom environment so they can later perform effectively as managers.

Many practicing managers who read manuals, textbooks, and the popular press on the subject of delegation generally conclude that the authors have never been in a managerial position themselves. The simplified rules and prescriptions are seldom matched by reality. Rather than being a simple step-by-step task of assigning someone else to do part of the work, effective delegation requires a variety of managerial competencies. For example, when the work to be delegated is important or when a high personal or organizational cost is associated with failure, effective and complete delegation is one of the most difficult things a manager does, especially in small organizations. It means being willing to allow others to make a mistake with one's own money or reputation. More than that, it means encouraging others to run the risk of making mistakes and then charging the mistakes off to the experience of those others. Delegation requires a great deal of trust on the part of the manager. Furthermore, a great deal of skill is required to delegate effectively so that the probability of a successful outcome is maximized.

ADVANTAGES OF SKILLED DELEGATION

Delegation is often thought of primarily as a tool for the overworked manager. One reason for this notion is that managers, by definition, are expected to accomplish more than any one person could accomplish alone (McConkey, 1974). Most managers respond by working at an unrelenting pace, feeling more demands on their time than they can accommodate. Whyte (1954) reports that the managers he interviewed, for example, worked an average of four out of five nights. Mintzberg (1973) found that managers in his study seldom, if ever, took a coffee break or went to lunch without conducting business or holding a formal or informal meeting. Cameron and Quinn (1981) report that the families of managers suffer more dysfunction (i.e., emotional or interactional difficulties) than nonmanagers' families because of the long hours managers spend working away from home. One obvious advantage of becoming a skilled delegator, then, is to increase personal discretionary time while still meeting work demands. That is, in any organization, managers' time is constrained by a variety of factors over which they have no control. But managers can also control a variety of constraints, and it is the purpose of effective delegation to remove some of those constraints. As Oncken and Wass (1974, p. 75) put it,

> In any organization, the manager's bosses, peers, and subordinates—in return for their active support—impose some requirements, just as he imposes upon them some of his own where they are drawing upon his support. These demands on him constitute so much of the manager's time that successful leadership hinges on his ability to control this "monkey-on-the-back" input effectively.

Managers who do not learn to effectively control their own discretionary time are much less effective than those who possess effective delegation skills. But while delegation is an effective tool for overworked managers, if that is the only reason managers delegate tasks, subordinates may feel used or treated simply as a means to the manager's ends. Therefore, delegation for time management is only one of several reasons why delegation skills are critical for management success. Table 7.1 lists other advantages, each of which is discussed briefly below.

Developing Subordinates

Effective delegation involves giving subordinates authority to make decisions. It is more than just assigning tasks to be done; rather, it is giving subordinates *authority* to match the *accountability* that is associated with task assignment.

TABLE 7.1 *Advantages of Skilled Delegation*

1. Delegation increases the personal discretionary time of managers, which leads to effective time management.

2. Delegation helps develop the capabilities and knowledge of subordinates so that their own effectiveness is increased, thereby increasing the effectiveness of the manager.

3. Delegation demonstrates trust and confidence in subordinates, which leads to more effective performance and better interpersonal relationships.

4. Delegation enhances the commitment of subordinates to the task and to the organization. Participation in decision making improves morale, understanding of the work, and motivation to accomplish tasks.

5. Delegation often improves the quality of decisions by bringing to bear more information, closer to the source of the problem, than the manager has alone.

6. Delegation increases the efficiency of the manager and the organization by getting work done while expending fewer resources.

7. Delegation enhances the personal power of the manager within the organization.

Many managers find it easy to parcel out work, but they neglect to provide authority to go with it. Such a practice is not delegation at all, but servitude. When effective delegation is practiced, subordinates are given opportunities to grow, to be challenged, to "show their stuff," and to achieve recognition and status. They are supported in their mistakes so that their own skills are developed and they become more competent and effective subordinates. Therefore, they enhance the effectiveness of the manager.

Of course, managers usually do not delegate *final* accountability for the work they assign, but *prime* accountability. Final accountability is ultimate responsibility for task accomplishment, which managers cannot pass on to others. Managers, for example, are responsible for the "bottom line," even though many others may help produce that bottom line. Managers can only delegate prime accountability for tasks that lead to ultimate goal accomplishment. Delegating prime accountability requires confidence on the part of the manager that the subordinates can perform acceptably and can contribute to the accomplishment of the overall goal. It also requires that the manager extend more and more authority to subordinates who demonstrate the ability to handle it. As subordinates receive more and more authority, they are provided the opportunity to improve their own competence, as well as to more effectively accomplish tasks.

Demonstrating Confidence in Subordinates

Delegating to subordinates demonstrates trust and confidence in their abilities. This demonstration of trust by managers increases subordinates' levels of performance and engenders in them a desire to not violate that trust. Research has shown that when managers demonstrate trust in subordinates, the performance effectiveness of the subordinates is increased. For example, Parloff and Handlon (1966) and Meadow, Parnes, and Reese (1959) found that groups characterized by high trust among members were significantly more effective at problem solving than were low-trust groups. In a study of managers, Zand (1972) found similar results. Managers who demonstrated high trust in their subordinates produced work groups that were more clear about goals, better at communicating with one another, more able to process information, and better at producing creative solutions than work groups in which managers did not demonstrate high trust. Of course, managers cannot continue to demonstrate trust in subordinates if that trust is violated or not reciprocated—unidirectional trust is as ineffective as low trust (Wrightsman, O'Connor, Baker, 1972). But in general, the demonstration of confidence in subordinates through delegation improves performance.

Improving Commitment and Morale

Delegating to subordinates allows them to participate in deciding how the work will be completed. Rather than simply following the directions of others, effective delegation gives subordinates discretion and increased opportunities for decision making. The result of these opportunities for participation is increased commitment to work and higher morale. Beginning with the classic study of participation by Coch and French (1948), researchers have consistently demonstrated a positive relationship between participation and job satisfaction, low rates of turnover, good relations between subordinates and managers, high commitment to the work and the organization, acceptance of changes in tasks and in performance expectations, and a desire for more work (Levitan, 1970). Increased participation through delegation is not, of course, a panacea for all subordinate commitment and morale problems. There are some potential disadvantages of participation (to be discussed below), which the manager must be prepared to face. But the advantages accuring from subordinate participation through delegation are an important reason to become competent in this critical management skill.

Improving the Quality of Decisions

One of the most difficult tasks facing managers is acquiring enough information to make a good decision. Another advantage of delegation is that subordinates closer to the problem can often make better decisions (with less expenditure of time searching for information) than can managers. That is, when subordinates are involved directly in the work, they often have better information than the manager, so subordinates' participation in decisions affecting them frequently improves decision quality.

Delegation is particularly likely to result in improved decisions when tasks are delegated to groups of subordinates. For example, when information is not readily available to the manager, the probability that the required information exists in a group is much higher than that it exists with a single subordinate. Moreoever, groups make fewer errors using information than does one person acting alone. And the overall understanding of the problem is increased when a group of subordinates are involved in its solution. (See Huber, 1980; Maier, 1970, and Chapter 9 for a more detailed discussion of the advantages of groups versus individuals in decision making and task accomplishment.) The point is that delegation to individual subordinates or to groups may result in better decisions because of increased access to information.

Increasing Efficiency of Task Accomplishment

Efficiency is defined as the ratio of inputs to outputs. Producing more outputs with fewer inputs is an indication of relatively higher efficiency. When managers spend time on tasks that could be performed by lower-paid subordinates, the organization is lss efficient than it would be if the manager delegated. That is, when the manager performs work that could be done by a subordinate, the cost to the organization of getting that task accomplished is much greater than if the subordinate were given the work.

Sometimes an investment of time is required at the outset to train subordinates to perform the delegated tasks, and therefore the impression is that delegation is less efficient. However, after the initial outlay, organizational and managerial efficiency are far greater than if no delegation had occurred. For example, for a manager to answer routine mail, place routine phone calls, gather routine information, or spend time on other routine tasks is an inefficient use of personal as well as organizational time and resources. Others who are paid less than the manager could perform those tasks and markedly increase the efficiency of the organization. By delegating, managers free themselves to *manage* instead of serve as operators, technicians, or clerks, and it is the managerial job that is being paid for, not the clerical job. Organizational efficiency and effective delegation skills, therefore, are closely related.

Increasing Personal Power

Some managers assume that delegating authority means abdicating power. They fear that if they give others decision-making authority, it will decrease their power in the organization. As pointed out in Chapter 5, however, power is often gained by sharing it. Managers who delegate effectively to subordinates increase their own flexibility (a critical requirement for gaining power) by freeing up discretionary time. They build the commitment and support of subordinates by displaying trust in their abilities. And these managers increase their own as well as their unit's productivity, which results in increased visibility and influence in the organization (another critical requirement for gaining power). Managers who effectively use their delegation skills, therefore, are more likely to enhance their power in the organization than to decrease it.

CONSEQUENCES OF INEFFECTIVE DELEGATION

Individuals who have not developed effective delegation skills may find that their attempts to delegate produce negative consequences. They may find that, instead of freeing up discretionary time, for example, ineffective delegation results in a need to spend even more time supervising subordinates, correcting mistakes, arbitrating disagreements, or reviewing the procedures of others. These negative results are eliminated, however, when managers delegate in a skilled way. We shall explain later how effective delegation can be accomplished.

Not only can unskilled delegation lead to an increase in time constraints for managers, but managers may also find themselves out of touch with subordinates and with the tasks to be performed. Opportunities for control may be completely lost. Ineffective delegators may find that subordinates are pursuing their own goals at the expence of the organization's as they perform delegated tasks. Rather than resulting in a coordinated effort, delegation may result in a confused, even anarchistic effort within the organization, with multiple subordinates pursuing multiple goals.

Another potential negative consequence of ineffective delegation is that subordinates may come to expect that they should be involved in all decisions or all important tasks. Any autocratic decision on the part of the manager, then, could lead to accusations of unfairness, exclusivity, or Machiavellianism by subordinates.

Finally, ineffective delegation may increase the amount of time and resources it takes subordinates to accomplish a task or to make a decision. Not only would the manager be spending more time in supervision, but the subordinates would be spending more time in work-related activity. Organizational inefficiency would then be a notable consequence.

Table 7.2 summarizes these five potential consequences of ineffective delegation. Our point in enumerating these potential disadvantages is to emphasize that not only are there substantial benefits to the manager and the organization from skilled delegation, but unskilled delegation can produce harmful outcomes.

INHIBITORS TO EFFECTIVE DELEGATION

Despite the clear advantages to managers of becoming effective delegators and the potential negative consequences of not practicing good delegation, many managers still resist delegating tasks and authority to subordinates. This aversion stems largely from the *attitudes, insecurities,* and *preferences* managers have developed regarding delegation. These attitudes, insecurities, and preferences serve more as rationalizations for not delegating properly than as valid obstacles. Nevertheless, they still inhibit managers from delegating effectively. As Mooney and Reily (1931, p. 39) explained:

> One of the tragedies of business experience is the frequency with which men, always efficient in anything they personally can do, will finally be

TABLE 7.2 *Potential Negative Consequences of Ineffective Delegation*

1. Ineffective delegation may produce an increase in the amount of time required to supervise and coordinate subordinates.

2. Ineffective delegation may result in the manager's losing touch with what is going on in the organization.

3. Ineffective delegation may lead to goal displacement among subordinates.

4. Ineffective delegation may give subordinates inappropriate expectations about participation.

5. Ineffective delegation may increase the amount of time and resources required by subordinates to accomplish a task or to make a decision.

crushed and fail under the weight of accumulated duties that they do not know and cannot learn how to delegate. Whether this condition is due to egotism which manifests itself in a distrust of the relative capacity of others, or to a training which has always been confined to a narrow horizon, and has thus destroyed the capacity to envisage great undertakings, the effect is always the same. Under such conditions, growth through delegation is absolutely prevented by the character of the leadership.

The inhibitors of effective delegation discussed below are derived from surveys conducted by management consultants (Preston & Zimmerer, 1978), management theorists (Newman & Warren, 1977), and the National Management Association. They are summarized in Table 7.3.

Attitudes About Subordinates

The attitudes that managers develop about their subordinates can prevent effective delegation. One such attitude is that subordinates do not have the ability or knowledge to carry out the task. Managers may feel that they can do the job better than their subordinates, so are reluctant to delegate to them. One study showed, however, that in over 80 percent of the cases in which managers

TABLE 7.3 *Inhibitors of Effective Delegation*

Attitudes About Subordinates
1. Subordinates are not competent enough to accomplish the work.
2. Subordinates should possess the skills required by their positions, and it is not the role of the manager to train them.
3. Subordinates are unwilling to accept additional responsibility.
4. Subordinates are unable to accept additional responsibility.
5. Subordinates should not be involved in certain kinds of tasks or decisions.

Personal Insecurities
1. Managers may lose the recognition and rewards associated with accomplishing the tasks.
2. Managers may lose power if they share their expertise or trade secrets with subordinates.
3. Managers must know the details of all the work for which they are responsible so all uncertainty is eliminated.
4. Managers have to endure too high a cost as a result of mistakes made by subordinates.

Personal Preferences
1. Managers prefer to to some mundane and routine tasks.
2. Managers prefer to do the taks quickly themselves, rather than take the time to explain it to subordinates.
3. Managers prefer to put in the longest hours and do the most work of anyone in the organization.

indicated they could do a superior job to their subordinates, subordinate performance equaled or exceeded the manager's performance (Zimmerer, 1977). Instead of assuming that subordinates must be able to do the delegated task at least as well as the managers could, a more appropriate question might be, Can the subordinate do the task in an *acceptable* manner in the time allotted? This relieves managers of the burden of doing all tasks themselves unless they find a subordinate they judge to be equal or superior to themselves in competence (a situation that rarely occurs).

A second inhibiting attitude is unwillingness on the part of managers to spend the time necessary to train subordinates to accomplish a task. Managers may feel that it is someone else's job to train subordinates or that subordinates should already possess the skills required by the job. Or this attitude may mask inability on the part of managers to adequately train their subordinates in a new set of competencies. Whatever the reason for this unwillingness to train, it stands in the way of effective delegation.

A third inhibiting attitude is the belief that subordinates are unwilling to accept additional responsibilities. Douglas McGregor's (1960) classic distinction between Theory X and Theory Y assumptions about workers helps explain this attitude. Theory X assumptions, which McGregor suggests are held by a majority of managers, presume that most people do not want to work, avoid responsibility, and must be coerced, directed, or closely supervised to accomplish their tasks. Holding this view of subordinates naturally leads to reluctance to delegate.

A fourth inhibiting attitude is that subordinates are already working to capacity and therefore are unable to accept more responsibility. This, of course, can be true, but this attitude may also result from a devaluing of subordinates' capabilities or a projection onto them of the manager's own feelings of overload. Managers are unlikely to delegate to subordinates they feel are already working to capacity.

A final inhibiting attitude typical of some managers is that some things should not be the prerogative of anyone but the manager. This attitude may reflect accurately the tasks that should not be delegated (examples of such tasks are discussed below), but it also may inhibit appropriate delegation. For example, managers may feel that subordinates are too specialized and that only a generalist can perform some tasks. Or they may feel that decision making belongs at the strategic or administrative level in organizations, not the technical or production level. This general attitude that subordinates are ineligible for some kinds of tasks may serve as an artificial and inappropriate constraint on effective delegation.

Personal Insecurities

Certain fears held by managers also inhibit effective delegation. For example, managers may fear that they will lose recognition and rewards if subordinates are given some of their responsibility. Some may worry that subordinates will perform more competently than they could, thereby threatening their job security. Or managers may fear that subordinates will receive all the credit for task accomplishment while they are ignored. Livingston (1971) points out that the most successful managers are those who gain satisfaction from the achievements of their subordinates, and managers who feel competitive toward subordinates or threatened by subordinates' accomplishments are less likely to be successful. When managers feel that they must accumulate all the rewards and recognition for themselves, it is almost impossible for them to be effective delegators.

Another fear is that subordinates will learn too much about the hard-won techniques and know-how of the manager and that expertise will be lost if it is too widely shared. This leads to managers' holding back information or authority so their base of personal power can be maintained. Unfortunately, this also leads to incomplete delegation, higher rates of mistakes in tasks that are delegated, and, eventually, the feeling on the part of managers that they must perform all tasks to ensure success.

A third managerial fear results from intolerance of ambiguity. Some managers feel a great need to know the details of all work for which they are responsible. Uncertainty and ambiguity about progress toward task accomplishment or about methods being used by subordinates produce discomfort. This is especially true when the task is complex or ambiguous and the results are difficult to measure. This fear leads to overinvolvement by managers in the work they are responsible for, and produces tendencies toward close supervision and control. Rather than freeing up discretionary time for these managers, therefore, delegation adds to the managerial workload since there is a compulsion to be personally involved with and informed about everything. This fear in managers often results from not having adequate control or information in the organization.

Finally, the fear that mistakes made by subordinates will be too costly for the organization or the manager personally also leads to inadequate delegation. Intolerance of mistakes made by subordinates may lead managers to be overcritical or overcontrolling, and organizational morale may suffer as a result. This fear also may lead managers to be more interested in preserving their own reputations than in developing their subordinates or the organization. This inclination toward self-preservation may take the form of denying responsibility for errors, demeaning subordinates who make mistakes, or refusing to delegate any but trivial tasks.

Personal Preferences

The personal preferences of managers also may stand in the way of effective delegation. Some managers, for example, simply *like* to do some kinds of mundane, routine work for which subordinates are qualified. That is, despite the inefficient use of time and organizational resources, some managers refuse to delegate certain kinds of tasks to others. One manager, for example, insisted on preparing all charts and graphs for her presentations on her department's outputs. Another manager preferred to recheck by hand the calculations on the quarterly report to stockholders. Preferences for certain kinds of work that are inappropriately performed at the managerial level may therefore inhibit managers from being effective delegators.

Managers commonly prefer the short-term perspective, largely as a result of the nature of most managerial work. For example, Mintzberg (1953) has found that over half of all managerial activities are completed in less than nine minutes and only one tenth take longer than an hour. Guest (1956) and Ponder (1957) have found that first-line managers' activities averaged forty-eight seconds and two minutes, respectively. This extreme brevity of tasks leads many managers to feel that it will take longer to explain a task to subordinates than to do the task themselves. Even when it is clear that delegating work will be more productive in the long term, many managers prefer to take the short-term perspective. Thus, immediate efficiency frequently is traded off against longer-term productivity.

Finally, some managers have a martyr complex. They prefer to work long hours themselves, instead of giving more work to others. Their attitude often is, "See how hard I work. Don't you respect me for my efforts? Don't you at least feel sorry for me because I have to work so much?" Managers frequently engage in comparisons of who works the hardest and the longest—a clear case of means–ends inversion—and their guilt at not putting in inordinately long hours leads them to delegate less than they could. As was pointed out in Chapter 2, the health risks of such behavior are serious, not to mention the inefficiency of having the manager continually overloaded with delegatable tasks.

To summarize, many managers are not effective delegators because of their attitudes about subordinates, their insecurities, and their personal preferences. Even though managers may be convinced that delegation can improve their managerial effectiveness, these personal characteristics may stand in the way of effective delegation. Just being aware that these personal factors are detrimental to effective delegation is often helpful in overcoming them, but specific know-how is needed if managers are to delegate effectively and master dysfunctional attributes. The results of successful delegation tend to be reinforcing for continued delegation, so knowing how to delegate effectively can serve as a means of overcoming the inhibitors discussed above.

PRINCIPLES OF DELEGATION

In this section we shall explain the major principles of delegation. First, rules of thumb for *how* to delegate will be presented, and then *when* and *what* to delegate will be discussed. We shall present a model that has proven successful in determining precisely when and how a manager should delegate. The effective use of that model, coupled with rules of thumb for how to delegate, will help you improve your delegation skills. Table 7.4 summarizes the major principles that should be implemented in delegating tasks and authority to subordinates.

TABLE 7.4 *Principles of Delegation*

Parity of Authority and Responsibility
1. Managers should delegate sufficient authority to accomplish the task assigned.
2. Managers should not delegate too much authority—that is, authority for which there is no accountability.
3. Managers cannot delegate final accountability for task accomplishment; they can, however, delegate prime accountability to subordinates.
4. A specific time for reporting the results of the delegated tasks should always be established at the time of delegation.

Clarity and Completeness of Delegation
5. Managers must specify clearly the expected level of performance and the constraints under which subordinates will be operating.
6. Managers should specify the desired level of initiative expected of subordinates. When possible, that level of initiative should always give subordinates freedom to act and then report back only on results.
7. Managers should specify the desired type of action expected of subordinates. When possible, the type of action should allow subordinates to perform a complete task.

Levels of Delegation
8. Managers should delegate to the lowest level at which the task can be successfully accomplished.
9. Managers should not bypass their immediate subordinates in delegating to lower-level subordinates. Rather, they should delegate *through* their immediate subordinates by giving them the authority to delegate the task.
10. Managers should inform all those who will be affected by the delegated assignment that it has been delegated.

Support for Delegated Tasks
11. Managers should continually provide relevant information to surbordinates who have been delegated tasks as it becomes available.
12. Managers should publicly bestow credit when subordinates succeed at their task assignment, but not blame when they make mistakes.

Participation in Delegation
13. Subordinates should be allowed to participate in determining when and how the delegated task will be accomplished and, when possible, what the assignment will be.
14. When subordinates participate in delegation, they should be asked to make clear to what extent they understand the assignment, whether they perceive it as consistent with organizational goals and personal interests, and whether they can perform the task successfully.
15. Two-way communication should be permitted between subordinates and managers during the process of task accomplishment.

TABLE 7.4 *cont'd.*

Upward Delegation
16. Managers should avoid letting subordinates delegate their assigned work back to the manager.
17. Managers should insist that subordinates come with recommendations instead of requests for advice or problem solutions.

Accountability for Results
18. Managers should not supervise too closely after the task has been delegated. Subordinates should be allowed to make choices on their own.
19. Managers should review and evaluate the results of the delegated assigment, not the means used to accomplish the task.

Consistent Delegation
20. Managers should delegate consistently, not only when they feel overloaded or under time pressures.
21. Managers should delegate both pleasant and unpleasant tasks to subordinates.

Parity of Authority and Responsibility

The oldest and most general rule of thumb in delegation is to delegate authority to match responsibility. Subordinates should not be given task assignments if they are not also given the authority to achieve the desired results. It is sometimes easy for managers to assign work but to avoid matching the responsibilities given with discretion to make decisions and with authority to implement those decisions.

To illustrate, a mismatch between responsibility and authority occurred recently in a bargaining relationship between a teaching assistants' union and the administration at a large Midwestern university. The students involved in the negotiations were bargaining for increased salaries and smaller classes. They were given the responsibility by the union leadership to reach an agreement with the administration, but they were not given the authority to modify union demands or to commit the union to a course of action without first obtaining clearance from the leadership. As a consequence, the negotiations were so unproductive that no agreement was ever reached and a strike ensued. To be successful, the bargaining team needed authority to match its assigned responsibility.

Managers also must take care not to delegate more authority than responsibility. This mismatch leads to lack of accountability and potential abuses of power by subordinates who do not have to answer for the authority they exercise. While managers always maintain *final* accountability for delegated tasks, they must be certain that subordinates are given *prime* accountability. That is, managers are responsible in the end for task accomplishment, but delegating the task to subordinates makes the subordinates accountable to the manager for the task. A specific time for reporting on the results of the delegation should always be specified so it is clear that subordinates are accountable for their assignments.

Clarity and Completeness of Delegation

For delegation to be successful, managers must be as clear as possible about the *constraints* and *expectations* of the assigned task. To be successful, subordinates must know what is expected of them. However, it frequently is impossible to know in advance all the tasks required for accomplishing a desired goal, so managers must determine what *level of initiative* and what *type of action* they expect of subordinates. Those expectations should then be communicated clearly.

For example, in delegating the arrangements for the office Christmas party, it would not be practical or possible to specify in detail all the tasks to be performed. Instead, a specific level of initiative should be prescribed. At least five levels of initiative are possible in delegation (Oncken & Wass, 1974; Webber, 1981):

1. *Wait* to be told what to do,
2. *Ask* what to do,
3. *Recommend,* then take action on the recommendation,
4. *Act,* then report results,
5. *Act,* with no follow-up necessary.

The first level gives subordinates no control over either the content of their actions or the time when they will perform the task. The second level gives subordinates control over time but not content. The third, fourth, and fifth levels give subordinates control of both the timing of performance and the content of the task. When possible, managers should delegate at the last three levels of initiative. This reduces supervision time for the manager and helps train and motivate subordinates more than if they were constrained. Of course, not all tasks can be delegated allowing maximum subordinate initiative, but the expected level of initiative should be clearly communicated.

Managers should also be clear about what type of action is expected of subordinates performing the delegated task. There are at least five possibilities:

1. Gather information for the manager so he or she can decide what needs to be done,
2. Determine alternative courses of action for the manager to choose among,
3. Perform one part of the task at a time after obtaining approval for each new step,

4. Outline an entire course of action for accomplishing the whole task and have it approved,

5. Perform the whole task using any preferred method and then report only results.

The most preferred types of action are 4 and 5. Subordinates should be given the *complete* task to perform if possible, not just parts of it, and the opportunity to determine the method of task accomplishment. Reseach by Hackman and Lawler (1971) and others has clearly demonstrated the positive motivational benefits of allowing subordinates to see the beginning and ending of a complete task. (See Hackman, 1977, for a review of much of that literature.) Many managers tend to delegate only parts of tasks to subordinates and then take credit for the results. A senior partner in a law firm, for example, assigned various parts of the legal research and brief writing to the junior members of the firm, then stepped in to summarize the evidence and take credit for the case. Not only was this perceived to be unfair by the subordinates, but it served as a negative motivator for doing the assigned parts of the task well.

Clarity and completeness in delegation, therefore, involve being as precise as possible about the constraints and expectations associated with the assigned task. Specifying levels of initiative and types of action expected is especially critical.

Levels of Delegation

Another general rule of delegation is to delegate to the lowest organizational level at which the job can be done. This increases organizational efficiency (i.e., the task gets done for less money). Furthermore, those closer to the direct source of information often can make better decisions and do the task more quickly than individuals higher in the hierarchy. Delegating too low in an organization will likely result in inefficiency and failure, since the subordinates will not have the needed information or skill, but delegating too high is a waste of competency and results in organizational inefficiency. For example, it would be foolish to delegate the arrangements for the office Christmas party to the CEO's executive assistant when a staff secretary could do the task as competently and probably more efficiently (e.g., the staff secretary wouldn't need a secretary to type the correspondence and announcements).

One important caveat in delegating to lower levels in the hierarchy is that the delegation should follow the organizational chain of command. Managers should delegate *through* their immediate subordinates to lower-level subordinates, rather than directly to the lower-level personnel. Skipping over immediate subordinates to delegate directly to individuals lower in the organization nullifies the authority of the immediate subordinates, making it difficult for them to maintain the respect of their subordinates.

Another important caveat is that other individuals who will be affected by the delegated assignment—those who will provide information, those who will help implement actions, and those who will be influenced by the results—must be notified of the delegation. When subordinates have been given delegated authority but no one knows, the authority is essentially nullified. They are likely to encounter obstacles in preforming their assignment because the expectation is that the manager has the authority to do the task, not the subordinate.

Delegating to the lowest possible levels in the hierarchy, therefore, involves paying attention to the formal chain of command and making the delegation publicly known. This both improves the efficiency of task performance and helps train subordinates in the proper skills of delegation.

Support for Delegated Tasks

When tasks and authority are delegated to subordinates, managers must provide as much support to them as possible. This involves not only making public announcements and presenting clearly stated expectations, as discussed above, but also continually providing relevant information that may help subordinates in their task performance. Reports, recent data, clippings, articles, even random thoughts that pertain to the delegated task should be passed on both when the task is delegated and later as they become available. This support aids task accomplishment and displays the interest and concern of managers for their subordinates.

Another way managers can provide support for delegated tasks is to publicly bestow credit but not blame. Pointing out mistakes or faults in front of others embarrasses subordinates and makes them defensive, and it also creates the impression that managers are passing the buck or trying to rid themselves of final accountability. Correcting mistakes, criticizing work, or providing negative feedback regarding the task performance of subordinates should be done in private, where the circumstances are more likely to produce problem-solving behaviors than embarrassment.

Participation in Delegation

Subordinates are more likely to accept delegated tasks willingly and to perform them competently when they can help decide what tasks will be delegated to them and when. It often is not possible to give subordinates a choice about such matters, but providing opportunities to decide when the task will be completed, how accountability will be determined, when the task will be begun, or what methods and resources will be used in task accomplishment does increase motivation and morale. This participation should not be manipulative; that is, opportunities for participation should not be provided just to convince subordinates of decisions already made. Rather, managers should provide these opportunities when the task requirements allow it and when they are willing to accept the preferences of the subordinates.

Bernard (1938) formulated an "acceptance theory of authority" in which he proposed that people will accept and fulfill assignments only if four conditions are met. First, they must *understand* what they are being asked to do. Second, they must perceive that the assignment is *consistent* with the purpose of the organization. Third, they must believe that the assignment is *compatible* with their own interests. Fourth, they must be *able* to perform the assignment, physically and mentally. If one or more of these conditions is not met, according to the theory, the assignment will not be accepted. One advantage of participation by subordinates in the delegation process is that managers can determine whether these four conditions are met and the extent to which the assignment will be wholeheartedly accepted.

Another aspect of participation in delegation involves two-way communication during the process of task accomplishment. While managers should not encourage overdependence in subordinates by being available to answer every detailed question and to provide continued advice, they should be accessible for feedback or discussion. Close supervision by managers often results in subordinates' responding only when asked and providing only the information required. Managers can maintain a more participative climate and receive a better picture of what is being done if subordinates feel free to provide unsolicited feedback regarding their assignment.

Upward Delegation

Another rule of thumb for effective delegation, related to the one above, is that managers should scrupulously avoid upward delegation. Upward delegation occurs when subordinates share their tasks with managers, ask for solutions, expect managers to follow up, or in some other way tie up managers' time with their own assignments. One danger of participation in delegation is the occurrence of upward delegation. For example, suppose a subordinate comes to the manager after delegation has occurred and says, "We have a problem. This assignment just isn't turning out very successfully. What do you suggest I do?" Suppose the manager replies, "Gee, I'm not sure. Let me think about it, and I'll get back to you." The original delegated task is now the manager's problem, not the subordinate's. The manager has promised to report to the subordinate (i.e., to maintain prime accountability), and the subordinate is now in the position of following up on the manager's commitment (i.e., supervising the manager). Many managers, in the interest of trying to be helpful and available to subordinates, get themselves caught in this trap.

One way to avoid upward delegation is for managers to insist that subordinates take the initiative for developing their own solutions. Instead of promising the subordinate a report on his or her own deliberations, the manager should reply, "What do you recommend?" Rather than sharing problems or asking for advice, subordinates should be required to share proposed *solutions* or ask for permission to implement them. Managers should refuse to solve delegated tasks. For subordinates to feel that they have the initiative, managers must make clear that they expect subordinates to *take* the initiative. (Recall our earlier discussion about clarifying the expected level of initiative.) By avoiding upward delegation, managers both help train subordinates to become competent problem-solvers and avoid working on tasks for which someone else has prime accountability.

Results Accountability

Once tasks are delegated and the authority is provided to accomplish them, managers should generally avoid closely monitoring subordinates. Over-supervision makes subordinates feel incompetent, distrusted, and dependent on approval for every action before it is taken. Overdependence on managers is a frequent result.

It also is more productive for managers to review and evaluate the *results* of task accomplishment, rather than the *means* by which the task was accomplished. An acceptable result, after all, is the goal of delegation, not the use of the manager's preferred procedure. Harmful or unethical means for accomplishing tasks, of course, cannot be tolerated, but the attention of managers should generally focus on the end results, not on the subordinates' techniques.

When tasks are delegated, managers rarely need to specify the exact procedures to be used. Only when the task is precise and there is one obvious, proven method for accomplishing it, is it necessary to specify means. Allowing subordinates to determine how to accomplish delegated tasks (i.e., level of initiative 4 or 5) makes them more productive and creative. They are able to make mistakes and learn without having their behavior closely scrutinized, and they can design the task to meet their particular competencies and time frame. Managerial confidence in subordinates, as manifested by a results orientation, not a means orientation, leads to effective delegation.

Consistent Delegation

The time for managers to delegate is before they have to. Frequently, when managers have time to do the work themselves, even though it could (and should) be delegated, they spend their time doing it. There are two problems with this. First, delegation becomes only a method for relieving managers of work or reducing their pressure. The other reasons for delegation are forgotten. Subordinates begin to feel used by managers as pressure valves, rather than valued team members. Second, when delegation occurs only under pressure, there is no time to train subordinates to perform the task. Even full disclosure of relevant information may get short-circuited. Subordinates' mistakes and failures increase, and the pressure for managers to perform the tasks themselves is heightened. In other words, by waiting to delegate until they are overloaded, managers increase the pressure on themselves to perform the delegated tasks because of fear that subordinates cannot succeed.

Another key to consistency of delegation is for managers to delegate both pleasant and unpleasant tasks. Often managers keep for themselves the tasks they like to perform and pass on to subordinates the less desirable work. It is easy to see the detrimental consequences on subordinate morale, motivation, and performance. When individuals feel they are being used only to do the dirty work, follow-through on delegated tasks is less likely to occur. On the other hand, managers should not be afraid to share difficult or unpleasant tasks with subordinates. Playing the role of martyr by refusing to involve subordinates in disagreeable tasks makes the role of manager drudgery and creates unrealistic expectations in subordinates. Consistency of delegation, then, means that managers delegate tasks continuously, not just when overloaded, and delegate both pleasant and unpleasant tasks.

The principles of delegation discussed above are designed to ensure effective delegation. At least six positive outcomes should result from following these principles:

1. The delegated tasks will be accepted by subordinates.
2. Subordinates' morale and motivation will remain high.
3. The delegated tasks will be performed successfully.
4. The efficiency of task performance will be increased.
5. Subordinates will be trained in task performance as well as in successful delegation procedures.
6. Managers will have more free discretionary time.

It should be clear that delegation skills involve more than simply assigning work to other individuals. A variety of other personal and interpersonal skills are involved as well. Being a successful delegator, however, still depends on knowing *what* to delegate and *when* to delegate. In the next section we shall present a model that indicates which kinds of tasks should be delegated and which should not be, as well as when delegation should occur and to whom.

A DECISION MODEL FOR DELEGATION

Certain kinds of tasks should not be delegated to subordinates, and even tasks that can be performed by subordinates should not be delegated in some situations. Some authors have tried to generate lists of tasks that should never be assigned to subordinates (i.e., personnel appraisal, planning, conflict resolution, counseling), but managerial jobs differ so that no single list is generally applicable. Moreover, situations encountered by managers may change significantly so that effective delegation in one setting may be ineffective in another. For example, the decision to purchase new china for the White House may be delegatable in times of general economic affluence, but not delegatable when unemployment is high and the country is in a recession. What managers need is a set of guides to help them decide what to delegate, when, and to whom.

Victor Vroom has developed such a model (Vroom & Yetton, 1973; Vroom & Jago, 1974; Vroom, 1976), which was derived from empirical research into managerial decision making and delegation.

Vroom's model ignores managerial tasks in which the decision of whether or not to delegate is obvious (e.g., should managers type correspondence or make policy decisions). Instead, it deals with decisions and tasks faced by managers in which it is not clear whether or not they should be delegated, or to whom.

We introduce this model here because it has been shown to be very effective in helping managers make correct decisions about delegation. For example, Vroom (1976) has reported that when managers behave consistently with this model, there is a 65 percent probability of a successful outcome. When managerial behavior is contrary to that prescribed by the model, there is only a 29 percent probability of a successful outcome. Developing competence in using this model, therefore, enhances delegation success.

This model is based on the assumption that the most important considerations in deciding what, when and to whom to delegate are the quality that results, the acceptance by subordinates of the delegation, and the time required. Every task or decision has attributes that affect quality, acceptance, and time, and those attributes must be considered in delegation decisions. That is, it is the nature of the task to be performed that determines whether or not, and to whom, it should be delegated. Eight critical attributes are discussed below, the first three and the last of which relate to quality, and the fourth through seventh of which relate to acceptance. These attributes are termed *problem attributes* by Vroom because it is assumed that managers are not immediately clear whether or not to delegate the task, what the correct solution is, or to whom the assignment should be made. Therefore, a problem exists that requires some analysis.

Figure 7.1 lists the eight problem attributes in the form of questions to be answered when deciding whether to delegate a task and to whom to delegate. The decision tree is used to diagnose each problem and to determine whether or not it should be delegated. Vroom has identified seven courses of action managers can take regarding delegation, and the decision tree identifies which of these is best. The alternatives are presented in code form (i.e., AI, AII, CI, CII, GI, GII, DI) just below the decision tree, and each alternative is explained in detail in Table 7.5. You should familiarize yourself with the definitions of these alternatives before going on with this chapter. Basically, the alternatives suggest that managers keep the task or decision for themselves, involve and consult with subordinates but maintain final decision-making authority themselves, delegate authority to a group of subordinates and involve themselves as a group member, or delegate the decision to others and not become involved in it at all.

To use the model, several steps should be followed. First, the manager should identify the decision or task that is of concern. The second step is to determine if the task or decision is a group or individual problem. That is, will

Figure 7.1 *Model for Determining What Decisions to Delegate and to Whom*

Problem Attributes

A. Is there a quality requirement such that one solution is likely to be more rational than others?

B. Do I have sufficient information to make a high-quality decision?

C. Is the problem structured?

D. Is acceptance of the decision by subordinates critical to effective implementation?

E. If I were to make the decision myself, is it reasonably certain that it would be accepted by my subordinates?

F. Do subordinates share the organizational goals to be attained in solving this problem?

G. Is conflict among subordinates likely in preferred solutions? (This question is irrelevant to individual problems.)

H. Do subordinates have sufficient information to make a high-quality decision?

Decision Tree

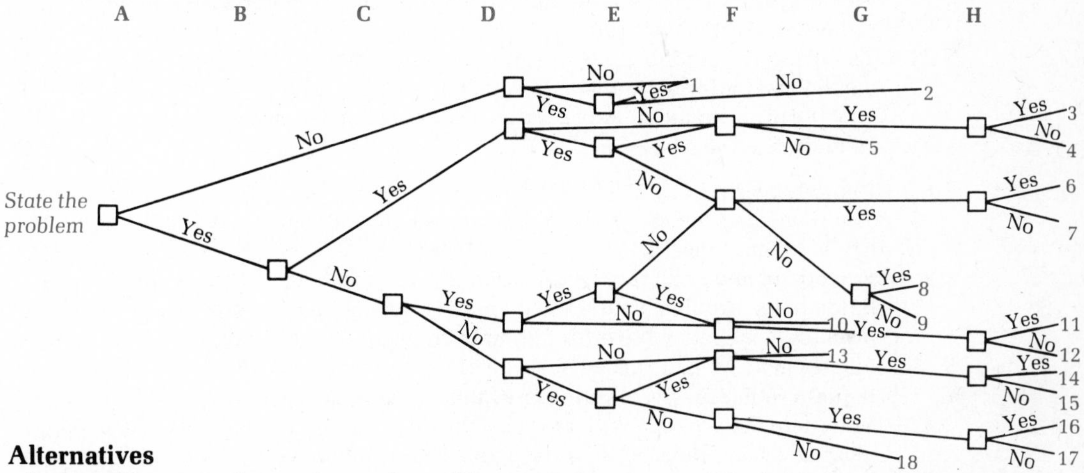

Alternatives

The feasible set is shown for each problem type for Group (G) and individual (I) problems:

1. G: AI, AII, CI, CII, GII
   I: AI, DI, AII, CI, GI

2. G: GII
   I: DI, GI

3. G: AI, AII, CI, CII, GII
   I: AI, DI, AII, CI, GI

4. G: AI, AII, CI, CII, GII
   I: AI, AII, CI, GI

5. G: AI, AII, CI, CII
   I: AI, AII, CI

6. G: GII
   I: DI, GI

7. G: GII
   I: GI

8. G: CII
   I: CI, GI

9. G: CI, CII
   I: CI, GI

10. G: AII, CI, CII
    I: AII, CI

11. G: AII, CI, CII, GII
    I: DI, AII, CI, GI

12. G: AII, CI, CII, GII
    I: AII, CI, GI

13. G: CII
    I: CI

14. G: CII, GII
    I: DI, CI, GI

15. G: CII, GII
    I: CI, GI

16. G: GI
    I: DI, GI

17. G: GII
    I: GI

18. G: CII
    I: CI, GI

From Vroom and Jago, 1974.

TABLE 7.5 *Definitions of Courses of Action in Deciding When to Delegate and to Whom*

For Individual Problems

AI   You solve the problem or make the decision yourself using information available to you at that time.

AII   You obtain any necessary information from the subordinate, then decide on the solution yourself. You may or may not tell the subordinate what the problem is in getting the information from him or her. The role played by your subordinate in making the decision is one of providing specific information you request, rather than generating or evaluating alternative solutions.

CI   You share the problem with the relevant subordinate, getting his or her ideas and suggestions. Then you make the decision. This decision may or may not reflect your subordinate's influence.

GI   You share the problem with one of your subordinates and together you analyze the problem and arrive at a satisfactory solution in an atmosphere of free and open exchange of information and ideas. You both contribute to the resolution of the problem, with the relative contribution of each depending on knowledge rather than formal authority.

DI   You delegate the problem to one of your subordinates, providing him or her with any relevant information you possess, but giving him or her responsibility for solving the problem alone. Any solution the subordinate reaches will receive your support.

For Group Problems

AI   You solve the problem or make the decision yourself using information available to you at that time.

AII   You obtain any necessary information from subordinates, then decide on the solution to the problem yourself. You may or may not tell subordinates what the problem is in getting the information from them. The role played by your subordinates in making the decision is one of providing specfic information you request, rather than generating or evaluating solutions.

CI   You share the problem with the relevant subordinates individually, getting their ideas and suggestions without bringing them together as a group. Then you make the decision. This decision may or may not reflect your subordinates' influence.

CII   You share the problem with your subordinates in a group meeting. In this meeting you obtain their ideas and suggestions. Then you make the decision, which may or may not reflect your subordinates' influence.

GII   You share the problem with your subordinates as a group. Together you generate and evaluate alternatives and attempt to reach agreement on a solution. Your role is much like that of a chairperson, coordinating the discussion, keeping it focused on the problem, and making sure the critical issues are discussed. You do not try to influence the group to adopt "your" solution and are willing to accept and implement any solution that has the support of the entire group.

DII   You delegate the problem to a group of subordinates in which you do not participate. You provide them with any relevant information you possess, and give them authority to solve the problem as a group. Any solution they reach will receive your support.

SOURCE: V. H. Vroom and A. G. Jago, Decision making as a social process: Normative and descriptive models of leader behavior, *Decision Sciences*, 1974, 5, 743–769.

more than one subordinate need to be involved with the decision, or will more than one subordinate be affected by the task or decision? If multiple subordinates are involved, the model specifies the problem as a *group problem;* if only one subordinate need be involved, it is an *individual problem.* The reason for differentiating between group and individual problems is that the courses of action for delegation are somewhat different. The third step is to identify the characteristics of the decision or task being considered by asking the eight problem attribute questions listed in Figure 7.1. This step is the most important, since the attributes of the decision or task determine the appropriate managerial alternative. To clarify these eight questions, we shall explain them individually.

A. *Is there a quality requirement for the decision or the task such that one solution is likely to be more rational than another?*   If there is a quality requirement, one solution or decision can clearly be shown to be better than another. Some criteria demonstrate the superiority of one alternative over others. An example of a problem that has a quality requirement is the decision of whether to invest in stocks or bonds. Evidence could be produced to make one choice clearly more rational than the other. An example of a problem without a quality requirement is deciding which of two brands of paper towels to buy for the office restroom (assuming equality of price and quality) or who should drive to lunch. In these cases, the alternatives selected make little difference.

B. *Do I have sufficient information to make a high-quality decision or to perform the tasks myself?*   This question refers to the amount of information possessed by the manager relative to the amount required by the problem. The manager may have more information than any subordinate but not as much as the problem requires. Therefore, the answer to this question should be based on the amount of task-relevant information possessed, not the amount of information possessed relative to subordinates.

C. *Is the problem structured?*   Structured problems are those for which the alternatives and methods for achieving them are known. For example, if the manager knew all the information needed or all possible relevant alternatives, or if it was clear exactly where to get needed information or generate the necessary alternatives, the problem would be a structured one. An unstructured problem is one for which all the alternatives are not known, the information relevant for the problem is unclear, or the boundaries of the problem are unknown. An example of a structured problem is deciding how much to bid to obtain a construction contract. An example of an unstructured problem is determining the cause of low morale among production workers in an organization.

D. *Is acceptance of the decision by subordinates critical to effective implementation?*   That is, if the manager accomplished the task or made the decision alone, would others in the organization be likely to accept that decision, or would they expect to have some say in the matter? To answer that question, the manager should determine the extent to which subordinates would have to use their initiative, judgment, or decision making to carry out the assigned decision or task, or whether they would simply have to follow a standard operating procedure for which little if any discretion or initiative would be required. The more discretion and initiative required of subordinates, the more necessary it is that subordinates accept the decision or assignment a priori. Nonacceptance could lead to refusal to perform, resistance, or even sabotage.

Another consideration is how strongly subordinates are likely to feel about the alternatives. If the decision or task has political ramifications or has clear biases attached to it, subordinates may not accept any decision made arbitrarily by the manager without their involvement. If subordinates feel strongly about an alternative or are labelled by the action they have to take when performing the delegated task, and if that action is unacceptable to them, implementation will be hindered. Therefore, decisions or tasks requiring prior subordinate acceptance are generally those in which subordinate discretion is involved in implementation and in which strong feelings are held regarding alternatives.

E. *Is acceptance by subordinates certain if the decision is made or the task performed by the manager alone?*   Subordinates are likely to accept unilateral decisions or task performances by managers if they perceive the managers to have clear authority or power (e.g., expert, legitimate, or charismatic power). The greater the power of managers, the more likely subordinates are to accept their actions. Subordinates are less likely to accept unilateral management actions when they feel they possess relevant competencies that relate to the task or decision, when they have some investment in which solution is implemented, when they want to assume more responsibility or to take more initiative (i.e., high needs for independence or control), and when they see participation in the decision or task as a means to another end (e.g., promotion). Answering this question requires prior knowledge by managers of their own power base (and their ability to "sell" their decisions and actions), as well as of their subordinates' competencies and interests.

F. *Can subordinates be trusted to share the organizational goals to be attained by solving this problem?*   Are subordinates likely to pursue their own goals in place of the overall organizational goal, or are they likely to behave as team-players? Sometimes subordinates are so interested in looking good, obtaining a reward, or winning some interpersonal competition that these side issues stand in the way of effective task performance or decision effectiveness. This question asks managers to determine if there is an overriding goal that all subordinates are committed to and that can help guide task performance and decision making. If subordinates are delegated a task, they must be trusted to act in the best interests of the organization, not in their own best interests at the expense of the organization.

G. *Is conflict among subordinates likely in preferred solutions?* This question refers to the extent to which subordinates would be in disagreement regarding the *means* for attaining a solution, not the end. The previous question relates to the extent to which subordinates accept a common goal; this question refers to the extent to which agreement exists on the various means for attaining the goal. If there is likely to be little agreement among subordinates themselves or between subordinates and the manager, then delegation and participation will likely lead to more frustration than success. No group of subordinates and managers will ever completely agree among themselves or with other groups, but if the manager trusts that subordinates can reach a decision acceptable to all concerned or that the solution reached by one subordinate will be agreed to by others, delegation and participation can more readily occur.

H. *Do subordinates possess sufficient information to make a high-quality decision?* If the task or decision were delegated to subordinates, could they effectively make the decision or accomplish the task, given their current knowledge or skill level? If managers lack the information to make a good decision but subordinates cannot help provide that information, delegating a task to them or allowing their participation in the decision is not likely to prove successful. On the other hand, when subordinates possess sufficient information or skill to make a decision or perform a delegated task, it often is inefficient for the manager to refuse to delegate to them. This question requires that managers be aware of the competencies of their subordinates so they can accurately judge what information they are likely to possess regarding the task or decision.

In deciding which decisions and tasks to delegate and to whom, managers should begin at the left side of the decision tree in Figure 7.1 and ask each question as it becomes relevant. Depending on the answer to a question, some of the problem attributes may or may not be relevant for every situation. For example, if the problem does not have a quality requirement, then whether the manager has sufficient information to make a high-quality decision (question B) and the extent to which the problem is structured (question C) are irrelevant. Since no one solution is logically better than another, the decision can be made with no information or a lot of information, and knowing none of the relevant alternatives or knowing them all. On the other hand, most decisions and tasks for which this model will be relevant to managers do have a quality requirement, so for most decisions about delegation these questions will be applicable. The model helps identify whether or not the decision or task should be delegated to others and to whom it should be assigned.

USING THE MODEL

To see how the model helps identify when to delegate and to whom, suppose you are a general plant supervisor and seven product lines involving four of your eight foremen must be disrupted to satisfy an emergency request from an important client. You naturally wish to minimize the disruption. No additional personnel are available, and time limits to complete the new project are restrictive.

The plant is new and is the only industrial plant in an economically depressed area dominated by farming. You can count on everyone pulling his or her weight. The wages in the plant are substantially above farm wages, and the workers' jobs depend on the profitability of this plant—the first new industrial development in the area in fifteen years.

Your subordinates are relatively inexperienced, and you have been supervising them more closely than you might if the plant had been in a well-established industrial area and your subordinates more experienced. The changes involve only standard procedures and are routine for someone of your experience. Effective supervision poses no problems. Your problem is how to reschedule the work to meet this emergency within the time limit with minimum disruption of the existing product lines. Your experience in such matters should enable you to figure out a way of meeting the request that will minimize the disruption of existing product lines.

This problem has the following characteristics:

Question	Attribute	Explanation
Group or individual?	Group	Task affects many subordinates
A. Quality?	Yes	One way is better than another
B. Manager information?	Yes	Manager has experience
C. Structured?	Yes	Routine changes required
D. Acceptance?	No	No discretion in implementation
E. Probability of acceptance?	Yes	Close supervision is accepted
F. Common goal?	Yes	All want to be profitable
G. Conflict?	No	No prior investment in an alternative

H. Subordinate information?	No	Subordinates are inexperienced
Problem type	4	

For each question, the list of possible behaviors a manager can select are listed below the decision tree in Figure 7.1. These alternatives are derived from a set of rules that have been found in empirical research to determine success or failure in decision making. These rules are reproduced in Table 7.6.

For problem type 4, the list of possible alternatives for a group problem includes AI, AII, CI, CII, and GII. That is, selecting any of these alternatives is consistent with the rules on which the model is based. How is a manager to decide what course of action to take when there are multiple choices? Should the manager delegate a type 4 task or decision to the group, or should an autocratic decision be made in which no delegation occurs at all? The answer to these questions lies in considering the extent to which managers want to save time, as opposed to training their subordinates. The alternative listed on the extreme left for each problem type is always the most time efficient. That is, an AI decision (autocratic, with no participation) will take less time than a GII decision (the group makes the decision). The alternative that helps train subordinates is on the extreme right for each problem type (i.e., a GII alternative helps subordinates develop more than does an AI alternative).

Research has shown that, by and large, most individuals are consistently biased in choosing the most autocratic or most participative alternatives. Few select participative and autocratic responses equally. Most managers are biased toward the time-efficient, autocratic end of the continuum, where delegation is rare, particularly to a group. However, Huber (1980) has pointed out the importance of maintaining flexibility in the alternatives selected because other situational factors may make one course of action appropriate in one setting but not in another, even though it is included in the feasible set of alternatives in the model.

Another decision tree is provided in Figure 7.2 that can be used in selecting among alternatives when several are included in the feasible set. This decision tree relates only to group problems. This is because most delegation problems faced by managers are group problems and there are more possible courses of action for managers in group problems. Figure 7.2 also lists the relevant considerations to be made in answering the questions posed at the top of the figure.

The Vroom model aids delegation decisions by *eliminating* inappropriate alternatives. However, with many problem types, managers still must choose which of several feasible alternatives to select. The model in Figure 7.2 is designed to help managers select the most appropriate alternative by taking into account several other considerations. In brief, the figure suggests that when a certain problem type has been diagnosed with the Vroom model and there is more than one alternative in the feasible set, selecting the best alternative de-

TABLE 7.6 *Rules That Determine Which Alternatives Are Appropriate for Each Problem Type*

1. *The Leader Information Rule*
   If the quality of the decision is important and the leader does not possess enough information or expertise to solve the problem alone, then AI is eliminated from the feasible set.

2. *The Subordinate Information Rule* (Applicable to individual problems only)
   If the quality of the decision is important and the subordinate does not possess enough information or expertise to solve the problem alone, then DI is eliminated from the feasible set.

3a. *The Goal Congruence Rule*
   If the quality of the decision is important and the subordinates are not likely to pursue organizational goals in their efforts to solve this problem, then GII and DI are eliminated from the feasible set.

3b. *The Augmented Goal Congruence Rule* (Applicable to individual problems only)
   Under the conditions specified in the previous rule (i.e., the quality of the decision is important and the subordinate does not share the organizational goals to be attained in solving the problem), GI may also constitute a risk to the quality of the decision taken in response to an individual problem. Such a risk is a reasonable one to take only if the nature of the problem is such that the acceptance of the subordinate is critical to the effective implementation and the prior probability of acceptance of an autocratic solution is low.

4a. *The Unstructured Problem Rule (Group)*
   In decsions in which the quality of the decision is important, if the leader lacks the necessary information or expertise to solve the problem alone and the problem is unstructured, the method of solving the problem should provide the interaction among subordinates. Accordingly, AI, AII, and CI are eliminated from the feasible set.

4b. *The Unstructured Problem Rule (Individual)*
   In decisions in which the quality of the decision is important, if the leader lacks the necessary information to solve the problem alone and the problem is unstructured, the method of solving the problem should permit the subordinate to generate solutions to the problem. Accordingly, AI and AII are eliminated from the feasible set.

5. *The Acceptance Rule*
   If the acceptance of the decision by subordinates is critical to effective implementation and it is not certain that an autocratic decision will be accepted, AI and AII are eliminated from the feasible set.

6. *The Conflict Rule* (Applicable to group problems only)
   If the acceptance of the decision is critical, an autocratic decision is not certain to be accepted, and disagreement among subordinates over methods of attaining the organizational goal is likely, the methods used in solving the problem should enable those in disagreement to resolve their differences with full knowledge of the problem. Accordingly, AI, AII, and CI, which permit no interaction among subordinates, are eliminated from the feasible set.

TABLE 7.6 *cont'd.*

7. *The Fairness Rule*
   If the quality of the decision is unimportant but acceptance of the decision is critical and not certain to result from an autocratic decision, the decision process should permit subordinates to interact with one another and negotiate over the method of resolving any differences with full responsibility on them for determining what is equitable. Accordingly, AI, AII, CI, and CII are eliminated from the feasible set.

8. *The Acceptance Priority Rule*
   If acceptance is critical and not certain to result from an autocratic decision and subordinates are motivated to pursue the organizational goals represented in the problem, methods that provide equal partnership in the decision-making process can provide greater acceptance without risking decision quality. Accordingly, AI, AII, CI, and CII are eliminated from the feasible set.

9. *The Group Problem Rule (Group)*
   If a problem has approximately equal effects on each of a number of subordinates (i.e., is a group problem), the decision process used should provide them with equal opportunities to influence that decision. Use of a decision process such as GI or DI, which provides opportunities for only one of the affected subordinates to influence that decision, may in the short run produce feelings of inequity reflected in lessened commitment to the decision on the part of those "left out" of the decision process and in the long run be a source of conflict and divisiveness.

10. *The Individual Problem Rule (Individual)*
    If a problem affects only one subordinate, decision processes that unilaterally introduce unaffected subordinates as equal partners constitute an unnecessary use of the time of the unaffected subordinates and can reduce the amount of commitment of the affected subordinate to the decision by reducing his or her opportunity to influence the decision. Thus, CII and GII are eliminated from the feasible set.

SOURCE: V. H. Vroom and A. G. Jago, Decision making as a social process: Normative and descriptive models of leader behavior, *Decision Sciences*, 1974, 5, 743–769.

pends on time, information availability, potential conflicts, motivation, clarity of the problem, and leadership.

To use the model, first ask the question, "Should I involve others in the task or the decision?" If, after considering the five factors below this question, you decide that subordinates do not possess relevant skills, their acceptance is not important, no personal development can occur, time is of the essence, or conflicts will arise among subordinates, you should answer "no" and select an AI alternative. Delegation would not be appropriate. However, if, after considering the five factors listed under question 1, you answer "yes", others should be involved, ask question 2 and consider the five factors listed below it. Answer "yes" or "no" based on those considerations and continue through the model. Any of the considerations listed below a question can result in a "no" answer. When AI is not in the feasible set of alternatives using the Vroom model—for example, as with problem type 10—the first question has already been answered "yes" because of the rules on which the Vroom model is based. The choices are among AII, CI, and CII. This also means that the fourth ques-

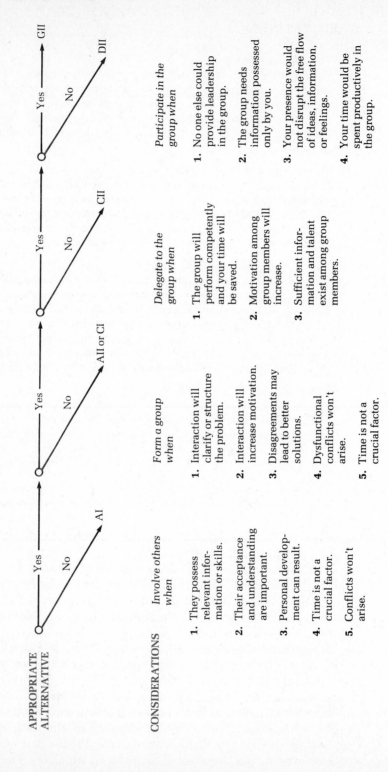

Figure 7.2   *Model for Selecting Among Alternatives When Several Are in the Feasible Set** (For Group Problems Only)

QUESTIONS

1. Should I involve others?

2. Should I direct my subordinates to form a group?

3. Should I delegate decision-making authority to the group?

4. Should I participate in the group?

APPROPRIATE ALTERNATIVE

AI   AII or CI   CII   DII   GII

(No / Yes branches)

CONSIDERATIONS

Involve others when

1. They possess relevant information or skills.
2. Their acceptance and understanding are important.
3. Personal development can result.
4. Time is not a crucial factor.
5. Conflicts won't arise.

Form a group when

1. Interaction will clarify or structure the problem.
2. Interaction will increase motivation.
3. Disagreements may lead to better solutions.
4. Dysfunctional conflicts won't arise.
5. Time is not a crucial factor.

Delegate to the group when

1. The group will perform competently and your time will be saved.
2. Motivation among group members will increase.
3. Sufficient information and talent exist among group members.

Participate in the group when

1. No one else could provide leadership in the group.
2. The group needs information possessed only by you.
3. Your presence would not disrupt the free flow of ideas, information, or feelings.
4. Your time would be spent productively in the group.

*Huber (1980) provided an elaboration of the information in this table.

tion has already been answered "no" by the model, so only questions 2 and 3 in Figure 7.2 are relevant. Alternatives GII and DII are not appropriate. In this case, begin with question 2 in Figure 7.2 and end with question 3. Depending on the factors listed below these two questions, the appropriate alternative among the three in the feasible set can be identified.

SUMMARY AND BEHAVIORAL GUIDELINES

We have argued that delegation skills are critical to management success. On the one hand, delegation frequently is perceived as a relatively simple managerial behavior anyone can perform well. On the other hand, that this is not the case is evidenced by the variety of considerations that are relevant in determining *how* to delegate, *what* to delegate, *when* to delegate, and *to whom* to delegate. Delegation is an important yet difficult skill to develop because it requires a knowledge of task characteristics, subordinate competencies, and personal inclinations. Managers face a variety of obstacles in becoming effective delegators. To help overcome those obstacles and to provide behavioral guidelines for effective delegation, we have discussed eight principles of delegation, with specific rules attached to each principle. Finally, a model of delegation was presented that helps one eliminate ineffective delegation practices and select the best alternative in determining what and to whom to delegate.

We shall conclude by summarizing the behavioral guidelines that should prove beneficial as you practice and improve your delegation skills:

1. When delegating, specify clearly and completely the expected level of performance, the constraints under which the subordinate will be operating, the level of initiative expected, and the type of action required.
2. Determine a time for reporting back the results of the delegated task.
3. Provide all information that is relevant to task accomplishment at the time delegation occurs, and pass on other information as it becomes available.
4. Inform all who will be affected by the delegation that delegation has occurred.
5. Allow subordinates some participation in determining what and when tasks are delegated to them.
6. Avoid accepting upward delegation by requiring subordinates to propose solutions and not to first ask for your solutions.
7. Evaluate results, not means.
8. Delegate consistently, not just when you are overloaded or when tasks are unpleasant.
9. Determine what tasks should be delegated and to whom by using the models in Figures 7.1 and 7.2.

REFERENCES

Bernard, C. I. *The functions of the executive.* Cambridge, Mass.: Harvard University Press, 1938.

Cameron, K. S., & Quinn, R. E. The impact of organizations on family life. *Counseling and Values,* 1981, *25,* 119–129.

Coch, L. & French, J. R. P. Overcoming resistance to change. *Human Relations,* 1948, *11,* 512–532.

Guest, R. H. Of time and the foreman. *Personnel,* 1956, *32,* 478–486.

Hackman, J. R. Work design. In J. R. Hackman & L. Suttle (eds.), *Improving life at work.* Santa Monica, Calif.: Goodyear, 1977.

Hackman, J. R., & Lawler, E. E. Employee reactions to job characteristics. *Journal of Applied Psychology,* 1971, *55,* 259–286.

Huber, G. P. *Managerial decision making.* Glenview, Ill.: Scott, Foresman, 1980.

Levitan, U. *Status in human organization as a determinant of mental health and performance.* Unpublished doctoral dissertation, University of Michigan, 1970.

Livingston, S. The myth of the well-educated manager. *Harvard Business Review,* January-February, 1971, *49,* 79–89.

Maier, N. F. *Problem solving and creativity in individuals and groups.* Belmont, Calif.: Brooks-Cole, 1970.

McConkey, D. *No nonsense delegation.* New York: AMACOM, 1974.

McGregor, D. *The human side of enterprise.* New York: McGraw-Hill, 1960.

Meadow, A. S., Parnes, S. J., & Reese, H. Influence of brainstorming and problem sequence on creative problem solving tests. *Journal of Applied Psychology,* 1959, *43,* 413–416.

Mintzberg, H. *The nature of managerial work.* New York: Harper & Row, 1973.

Mooney, J. D., & Seiley, A. C. *Onward industry.* New York: Harper and Brothers, 1931.

Newman, W. H., & Warren, K. *The process of management.* Englewood Cliffs, N.J.: Prentice-Hall, 1977.

Oncken, W. & Wass, D. L. Management time: Who's got the monkey? *Harvard Business Review,* November-December, 1974, *51,* 75–80.

Parloff, M. B., & Handlon, J. The influence of criticalness on creative problem solving in dyads. *Psychiatry,* 1966, *29,* 17–27.

Ponder, Q. D. The effective manufacturing foreman. In E. Young (Ed.), *Industrial Relations Research Association Proceedings, 10th Annual Meeting.* Madison, Wis.: IRRA, 1957.

Preston, P., & Zimmer, T. W. *Management for supervisors.* Englewood Cliffs, N.J.: Prentice-Hall, 1978.

Urwick, L. *Elements of administration.* New York: Harper and Brothers, 1944.

Vroom, V. H. Can leaders learn to lead? *Organizational Dynamics,* 1976, *4,* 17–28.

Vroom, V. H., & Jago, A. G. Decision making as a social process: Normative and descriptive models of leader behavior. *Decision Sciences,* 1974, *5,* 743–769.

Vroom, V. H., & Yetton, P. W. *Leadership and decisionmaking.* Pittsburgh: University of Pittsburgh Press, 1973.

Webber, R. A. *To be a manager.* Homewood, Ill.: Irwin, 1981.

Whyte, W. H. How hard do executives work? *Fortune,* 1954, *148,* 108–111, 150–152.

Wrightsman, L. S., O'Connor, J., & Baker, N. J. (Eds.). *Cooperation and competition: Readings on mixed-motive games.* Monterey, Calif.: Brooks-Cole, 1972.

Zand, D. E. Trust and managerial problem solving. *Administrative Science Quarterly,* 1972, *17,* 229–239.

Zimmer, T. W. How to reduce dependence on the boss. *Nation's Business,* 1977, *65,* 55–56. ∎

■ *Skill Analysis*

Case Analysis

Using the decision trees in Figures 7.1 and 7.2, read the following cases and decide on an appropriate strategy for delegation. First use the Vroom model to eliminate inappropriate alternatives; then use Figure 7.2 to determine the most appropriate alternative.

THE FINANCE CASE

You are head of a staff unit reporting to the vice president of finance. He has asked you to provide a report on the firm's current portfolio, including recommendations for changes in the selection criteria currently employed. Doubts have been raised about the efficiency of the existing system given the current market conditions, and there is considerable dissatisfaction with prevailing rates of return.

You plan to write the report, but at the moment you are perplexed about the approach to take. Your own specialty is the bond market, and it is clear to you that detailed knowledge of the equity market, which you lack, would greatly enhance the value of the report. Fortunately, four members of your staff are specialists in different segments of the equity market. Together, they possess a vast amount of knowledge about the intricacies of investment. However, they seldom agree on the best way to achieve anything when it comes to investment philosophy and strategy.

You have six weeks before the report is due. You have already begun to familiarize yourself with the firm's current portfolio and have been provided by management with a specific set of constraints that any portfolio must satisfy. Your immediate problem is to come up with some alternatives to the firm's present practices and to select the most promising for detailed analysis in your report.

Is this a group problem or an individual problem? _____

What strategy would you use in solving the problem?

Individual	AI	AII	CI	GI	DI
Group	AI	AII	CI	CII	GII	DII

What type of problem is it? (1, 2, 3, etc.) _____

SOURCE: V. H. Vroom and P. H. Yetton, *Leadership and decision making* (Pittsburgh: University of Pittsburgh Press, 1973), pp. 42–43.

THE UNIVERSAL DATA SYSTEM

You are on the division manager's staff and work on a wide variety of administrative and technical problems. You have been given the assignment of developing a universal method to be used in each of the five plants in the division for manually reading equipment registers, recording the readings, and transmitting the scorings to the centralized information system. All plants are located in a relatively small geographical region.

Until now there has been a high error rate in the reading and transmittal of the data. Some locations have considerably higher error rates than others, and the methods used to record and transmit the data vary between plants. It is probable, therefore, that part of the error variance is a function of specific local conditions, and this will complicate the establishment of a uniform system for all plants. You have information on error rates, but no information on the local practices that generate these errors or on the local conditioins that necessitate the different practices.

Everyone would benefit from an improvement in the quality of the data, as it is used in a number of important decisions. Your contacts with the plants are through the quality control supervisors, who are responsible for collecting the data. They are a conscientious group committed to doing their jobs well, but are highly sensitive to interference by higher management in their operations. Any solution that does not receive the active support of the plant supervisors is unlikely to reduce the error rate significantly.

Is this a group problem or an individual problem? _____

What strategy would you use in solving the problem?

    Individual   AI AII CI GI DI

    Group   AI AII CI CII GII DII

What type of problem is it? (1, 2, 3, etc.) _____

THE PHARMACEUTICAL COMPANY

You are executive vice president of a small pharmaceutical manufacturer. You have the opportunity to bid on a contract for the Defense Department pertaining to biological warfare. The contract is outside the mainstream of your business; however, it could make economic sense, since you do have unused capacity in one of your plants, and the manufacturing processes are not dissimilar.

You have written the document to accompany the bid and now have the problem of determining the dollar value of the quotation you think will win the job for your company. If the bid is too high, you will undoubtedly lose to one of your competitors; if it is too low, you could lose money on the program.

There are many factors to consider in making this decision, including the cost of the new raw materials and the additional administrative burden of relationships with a new client, not to speak of factors that are likely to influence the bids of your competitors, such as how much they need this particular contract. You have been busy assembling the necessary data to make this decision, but there remain several "unknowns," one of which involves the manager of the plant in which the new products will be manufactured. Of all your subordinates, only he can estimate the costs of adapting the present equipment to its new purpose, and his cooperation and support will be necessary if the specifications of the contract are to be met. However, in an initial discussion with him when you first learned of the possibility of the contract, he seemed adamantly opposed to the idea. His experience has not particularly equipped him to evaluate projects like this one, so you were not overly influenced by his opinions. From the nature of his arguments, you inferred that his opposition was ideological rather than economic. You recall that he was once involved in a local peace organization and was one of the most vocal opponents in the company of the war in Vietnam.

Is this a group problem or an individual problem? _____

What strategy would you use in solving the problem?

    Individual   AI AII CI GI DI

    Group   AI AII CI CII GII DII

What type of problem is it? (1, 2, 3, etc.) _____

Minding the Store

Analyze the following case in terms of the principles of delegation and decision making that are used successfully and that are violated.

On January 1st Ruth Cummings was formally named branch manager for the Saks Fifth Avenue store in a suburb of Denver. Her boss, Ken Hoffman, gave her this charge on her first day: "Ruth, I'm putting you in charge of this store. Your job will be to run it so that it becomes one of the best stores in the system. I have a lot of confidence in you, so don't let me down."

One of the first things Ruth did was to hire an administrative assistant to handle inventories. Because this was such an important part of the job, she agreed to pay her assistant slightly more than the top retail clerks were making. She felt that having an administrative assistant would free her to handle marketing, sales, and personnel matters—areas she felt were crucial if the store was to be a success.

Within the week, however, she received a call from Hoffman: "Say, Ruth, I heard that you hired an administrative assistant to handle inventories. Don't you think that is a bit risky? Besides, I think paying an assistant more than your top sales clerk is damaging to morale in the store. I wish you had cleared this with me before you made the move. It sets a bad precedent for the other stores, and it makes me look like I don't know what is going on in the branches.''

Three weeks later, Ruth appeared on a local noontime talk show to discuss new trends in fashion. She had worked hard to make contact with the hosts of the show, and she felt that public exposure like this would increase the visibility of her store. Although the TV spot lasted only ten minutes, she was pleased with her performance and with the chance to get public exposure.

Later that night at home, she received another phone call from Hoffman: "Don't you know the policy of Saks? Any TV appearances made on behalf of the store are to be cleared through the main office. Normally, we like to have representatives from the main store appear on these kinds of shows because they can do a better job of plugging our merchandise. It's too bad that you didn't notify someone of your intentions. This could be very embarrassing for me."

Just before Easter, Ruth was approached in the store by one of the sales clerks. A customer had asked to charge approximately $3000 worth of china as a gift for his wife. He had been a customer of the store for several years and Ruth had seen him on several occasions, but store rules indicated that no charge could be made for more than $1000 for any reason. She told the customer that she was not authorized to okay a charge of that amount, but that if he would visit the main store in Denver, maybe arrangements could be made.

Later in the day, an irate Hoffman called again: "What in the world are you thinking about, Ruth? Today we had a customer come into the main store and say that you wouldn't make a sale to him because the charge was too much. Do you know how long he has been a customer of ours? And do you know how much he spends in the store every year? I certainly hope we have not lost him as a customer because of your blunder. This makes me very upset. You've just got to learn to use your head."

Ruth thought about the conversation for several days, and finally decided that she needed to see Ken Hoffman. She called his secretary to schedule an appointment for the following day.

DISCUSSION QUESTIONS

1. What are the major problems?

2. Describe the delegation strategy of Ken Hoffman.

3. What should Ruth Cummings discuss with Ken Hoffman in her meeting with him? What specific items should be covered?

4. What is the appropriate delegation alternative for Ken Hoffman to use with Ruth Cummings?   ∎

■ *Skill Practice*

Meeting at Hartford Manufacturing Company

GENERAL BACKGROUND

Hartford Manufacturing Company is the largest subsidiary of Connecticut Industries. Since the end of World War I, when it was formed, Hartford Manufacturing has become an industrial leader in the Northeast. Its sales currently average approximately $25 million a year, with an annual growth of approximately 6 percent. There are over 850 employees in production, sales and marketing, accounting, engineering, and management.

Lynn Smith is general manager. He has held his position for a little over two years and is well respected by his subordinates. He has the reputation of being firm but fair. Lynn's training in college was in engineering, so he is technically minded, and he frequently likes to walk around the production area to see for himself how things are going. He has also been known to roll up his sleeves and help work on a problem on the shop floor. He is not opposed to rubbing shoulders with even the lowest-level employees. On the other hand, he tries to run a tight company, and employees pretty well stick to their assigned tasks. He holds high expectations for performance, especially from the individuals in management positions.

Richard Hooton is the general supervisor of production at Hartford Manufacturing. He has been with the company since he was nineteen years old, when he worked on the dock. He has worked himself up through the ranks, and now at age fifty-four is the oldest of the management personnel. Hooton has his own ideas of how things should be run in production, and he is reticent to tolerate any intervention from anyone, even Lynn Smith. Because he has been with the company so long, he feels he knows it better than anyone else, and he believes he has had a hand in making it the success that it is. His main goal is to keep production running smoothly and efficiently.

Barbara Price is the general supervisor of sales and marketing. She joined the company about eighteen months ago, after completing her MBA at Dartmouth. Before going back to school for a graduate degree, she had held the position of assistant manager of marketing at Connecticut Industries. Price is a very conscientious employee, and is anxious to make a name for herself. Her major objective, which she has never hesitated to make public, is to be a general manager or in corporate headquarters some day. Sales of Hartford Manufacturing have increased in the past year to near record levels under her guidance.

Chuck Kasper is the regional sales director for the New York region. He reports directly to Barbara Price. The New York region represents the largest market for Hartford Manufacturing, and Chuck is considered the most competent salesperson in the company. He has built personal relationships with several major clients in his region, and it appears that some sales occur as much because of Chuck Kasper as because of the products of Hartford Manufacturing. Chuck has been with the company twelve years, all of them in sales.

SETTING

This is Friday afternoon, and tomorrow at noon Lynn Smith leaves for Copenhagen to attend an important meeting with potential overseas investors. He will be gone for two weeks. Before he leaves, there are several items in his in-basket that must receive attention. He calls a meeting with Richard Hooton and Barbara Price in his office. Just before the meeting begins, Chuck Kasper calls and asks if he may join the meeting for a few minutes, since he is in town and has something important to discuss. It involves both Lynn Smith and Richard Hooton. Smith gives permission for him to join the meeting since there may not be another chance to meet with Kasper before the trip. The meeting convenes, therefore, with Smith, Hooton, Price, and Kasper all in the room.

ASSIGNMENT

Four individuals should form a group and each should take the role of one individual in the meeting. A fifth person should serve as an observer. Read the description of your role, but read *only your own role*. The exercise will be more realistic if you do not know in advance what is on everyone else's mind. Moreover, your delegation skills will be better developed if you rely only on the information associated with your own role. You will have approximately twenty minutes to conduct the role play.

ROLE OF LYNN SMITH

Three letters arrived today (Exhibits 1–3), and you judge them to be sufficiently important to demand attention before you leave for your trip. Each letter requires some immediate action, and you must decide which actions you will delegate to your subordinates and which you will keep for yourself. If you decide to delegate, you should actually do it as part of the role play. That is, practice the skills you have read about and analyzed thus far in this chapter.

Exhibit 1

T. J. Koppel, Inc.
General Accountants
8381 Spring Street
Hartford, Connecticut 06127

February 10, 198-

Mr. Lynn Smith
General Manager
Hartford Manufacturing Company
7450 Central Avenue
Hartford, CT 06118

Dear Mr. Smith:

As you requested last month, we have now completed our financial
audit of Hartford Manufacturing Company. We find accounting
procedures and fiscal control to be very satisfactory. A more
detailed report of these matters is attached. However, we did
discover during our perusal of company records that the production
department has consistently incurred cost overruns during the past
two quarters. Cost per unit of production is approximately .5
percent over budget. While this is not a serious problem given
the financial solvency of your company, we thought it wise to
bring it to your attention.

Exhibit 2

ZOKIAK INDUSTRIES
6377 Atlantic Avenue
Boston, Massachusetts 02112

February 8, 198-

Mr. Lynn Smith
General Manager
Hartford Manufacturing Company
7450 Central Avenue
Hartford, CT 06118

Dear Mr. Smith:

We have been purchasing your products since 1975, and we have
been very satisfied with both your products and your service.
However, we have had a problem of late that requires your
attention. Your regional sales director for the Boston region,
Sam St. Clair, has appeared at our company the last three times
looking and smelling like he was under the influence of alcohol.
Not only that, but our last order was mistakenly recorded, so
we received the wrong quantities of products. I'm sure you
don't make it a practice to put your company's reputation in
the hands of someone like Sam St. Clair, so I suggest you get
someone else to cover this region. We cannot tolerate, and
I'm sure other companies in Boston cannot tolerate, this kind
of relationship to continue. While we judge your products to
be good ones, we will be forced to find other sources if some
action is not taken.

Sincerely yours,

Miles Andrew
Chief of Purchasing

:ms

Exhibit 3

Hartford Manufacturing Company
7450 Central Avenue
Hartford, Connecticut 06118

"A subsidiary of CONNECTICUT INDUSTRIES"

Memorandum

TO: Lynn Smith, General Manager

FROM: Barbara Price, General Supervisor, Sales and Marketing

DATE: February 11, 198-

Mr. Smith:

As you recommended some time ago, we have instituted several
incentive programs among our sales force to try to increase sales
during these traditionally slow months. We have set up competition
among regions, with the sales people in the top region being honored
in the company newsletter and given engraved plaques. We have
instituted a "vacation in Hawaii" award for the top salesperson in
the company. And we have instituted cash bonuses for any salesperson
who gets a new customer order. However, in the last month these
incentives have been in operation, sales have not increased at all.
In fact, in two regions they have decreased by an average of 5 percent.

Since it was your initial recommendation that incentives be instituted,
what do you suggest now? We have advertised the incentives as lasting
through this quarter, but they seem to be doing no good. Not only
that, but we cannot afford to provide the incentives within our current
budget, and unless sales increase, we will be in the red.

I look forward to hearing from you.

ROLE OF RICHARD HOOTON

The backbone of Hartford Manufacturing is production. You have watched
the company grow from a small, struggling shop to a firm with a real impact on
the region because of its outstanding production processes. Your own reputation among those who know manufacturing is a good one, and you are
confident that you have been a major factor in the success of Hartford Manufacturing. You have passed up several job offers over the years because you
feel loyal to the company, but sometimes you don't seem to be afforded the respect from the younger employees you think you deserve.

The only times you have had major problems in production are when the young know-it-alls from college have come in and tried to change things. With their scientific management concepts coupled with fuzzy-headed human relations training, they have more often made a mess of things than helped improve matters. The best production methods have been practiced for years in the company, and you have yet to see anyone who could improve on your system.

On the other hand, you have respect for Lynn Smith as tha general manager. Because he has lots of experience and the right kind of training, and because he is involved in the production part of the organization, he often has given good advice to you and has shown special interest. He mostly lets you do what you feel is best, however, and he never dictates specific methods for doing things.

You suspect that this meeting is just a routine one in which some trivial assignments will be made before Smith leaves on his trip. Because you are a skilled delegator yourself, you know what kinds of questions to ask and what information you'll need to accept any assignments that may come your way. Hopefully, the meeting won't take long because you have to get back to some work that must be finished before the weekend.

ROLE OF BARBARA PRICE

You are anxious to impress Lynn Smith because you have your eye on a position in the parent company, Connecticut Industries, that is opening up at the end of the year. It would mean a promotion for you. A positive recommendation from Lynn Smith would carry a lot of weight in the selection process. Given that both Hartford Manufacturing and Connecticut Industries are largely male dominated, you are pleased with your career advancement so far, and you are hoping to keep it up.

One thing that is of current concern is the suggestion of Lynn Smith some time ago that an incentive system might be helpful for increasing sales during these slow months. You spent a great deal of time formulating such a system because you interpret a suggestion from Lynn Smith as an order. You considered a lot of alternatives and finally decided to implement three separate incentive programs: (1) competition among regions in which the salespeople in the top region would have their picture in the company newsletter and would receive engraved plaques, (2) a vacation in Hawaii for the top salesperson in the company, and (3) cash bonuses for salespeople who obtained new customer orders. The trouble is, these incentives haven't worked. Not only haven't sales increased for the company as a whole, but two of the regions are down an average of 5 percent. You have told the sales force that the incentives will last through this quarter, but if sales don't improve, your budget will be in the red. You haven't budgeted for the prizes, and the plan was for the increased sales to more than offset the cost of the incentives.

Since it was Lynn Smith's idea to get you into this incentive program, you want to get his ideas about how to get you out. The ideal situation would be for him to take the money for the prizes out of his own contingency account. You have written him a memo, and you suspect that this meeting is to reply to that memo.

You are a skilled delegator, and whenever you have received assignments from your superiors, you have known what questions to ask and what information you'll need to succeed at the assignment.

ROLE OF CHUCK KASPER

You don't get back to company headquarters very often because your customer contacts take up most of your time. You regularly work fifty to sixty hours a week, and you are proud of the job you do. You also feel a special obligation to your customers to provide them with the best product available in the most timely fashion. This sense of obligation comes not only from your commitment to the company, but also from your personal relationships with many of the customers.

Lately, you have been receiving more and more complaints about the timeliness of the delivery of Hartford Manufacturing's products to your customers. The delays between time of ordering and time of arrival are increasing, and some customers have been greatly inconvenienced by this lateness. You have made a formal inquiry of production to determine what is the problem. They replied that they are producing as efficienctly as possible, and they see nothing different from past practices. The assistant to Richard Hooton even suggested that this was just another example of the sales force's unrealistic expectations.

Not only will sales be negatively affected by a continuation of these delays, but your reputation with your customers will be damaged. You have promised them that the problem will be quickly solved and products will begin arriving more quickly. Since Richard Hooton is such a rigid person, however, you are almost certain that it will do no good to talk with him. His subordinate probably got his negative attitude from Hooton. The only alternative you see is to see if Lynn Smith can talk some sense into Hooton and get production on the ball. Hooton is so protective of his turf that the only person who can influence him is Smith.

You are a skilled delegator, and whenever you have received an assignment, you have known what questions to ask and what information you'll need to succeed at your assignment.

HARTFORD MANUFACTURING OBSERVER'S FORM

The observer's role in this exercise is to watch participants and provide them with feedback regarding the extent to which they engaged in appropriate behaviors when delegating and receiving delegation. The obligation to make delegation effective lies both with the person delegating responsibility and with the person receiving delegated assignments. If the delegator does not make the task clear, the recipient should ask questions and clarify the assignment so that each element of effective delegation is present.

Note the extent to which each of the individuals in this exercise engaged in effective delegating behaviors. Use the following scale for your ratings. At the end of the role play, provide feedback to each person, identifying what each did well and what could have been improved.

3—gave attention to this behavior; did it completely
2—gave some attention to this behavior; could have been more complete
1—gave no attention to this behavior; it was ignored

	Lynn Smith	Richard Hooton	Barbara Price	Chuck Kasper
The expected *level of initiative* was made clear.	_____	_____	_____	_____
The expected *level of performance* was made clear.	_____	_____	_____	_____
Constraints on performance were identified.	_____	_____	_____	_____
The expected *type of action* was made clear.	_____	_____	_____	_____
A *time for reporting back* was established.	_____	_____	_____	_____
Complete information relating to the task was shared.	_____	_____	_____	_____
All *others to be involved* were identified.	_____	_____	_____	_____
Participation occurred regarding what and when tasks were assigned.	_____	_____	_____	_____

Ends were given more priority than means.

   _____   _____   _____   _____

The *appropriate decision type* (e.g., AI, GII, DII) was identified.

   _____   _____   _____   _____

■

■ *Skill Application*

Application Exercises

1. Teach someone else how to delegate effectively. Discuss *how* as well as *when* and *to whom* to delegate. Describe the experience in your journal.

2. Delegate a task or receive a delegation from someone else, and note in your journal the number of key action steps that were included in the delegation process. If you are the one delegating, try to include all of them. If you are receiving the delegation, you can ask questions of the delegator to increase the number of key action steps included in the delegation. Opportunities for delegation could include your work, family, church, social clubs, and roommates.

3. Interview a manager regarding his or her delegation practices. Try to determine the general patterns of delegation that characterize the organization, as well as the extent to which the manager uses proper delegation techniques.

4. Think of a situation in your life right now in which you need to delegate. Describe how you will delegate, to whom, and what. Record your plans in your journal.

5. Identify under what circumstances these various principles of delegation and decision making would not be appropriate. ■

8 Managing Conflict

■ *Skill Preassessment*

General Strategies for Handling Interpersonal Conflicts
Where's My Talk?

■ *Skill Learning*

Interpersonal Conflict Management

■ *Skill Analysis*

The Harried Supervisor
Webster Arsenal

■ *Skill Practice*

Win as Much as You Can
Responding to Conflictual Encounters

■ *Skill Application*

Application Exercises

■ *Skill Preassessment*

General Strategies for Handling Interpersonal Conflicts

On a sheet of paper, briefly recount some of your more memorable interpersonal confrontations. Note who was involved, what happened, and what was the outcome. Next, write down how you responded in each instance in as much detail as you can. What were your objectives and how did you go about reaching them?

To determine from these specific situations your propensity to rely on different conflict management strategies, rank-order the following five approaches according to your relative use of each (1=most frequent, 5=least frequent). After you have done so, turn to Table 8.3, where the approaches are described in some detail.

I. I am generally firm in pursuing my personal goals. I try to show others the logic and benefits of my position. If they are equally committed to their position, I make a strong effort to get my way by stressing my points. I give in reluctantly.

II. I try to avoid the debilitating tensions associated with conflict by letting others take responsibility for solving the problem. If possible, I try to postpone dealing with the problem until I can cool off and take time to think it over. To reduce the likelihood of conflicts, I often avoid taking controversial positions and I try not to get uptight when others express positions different from my own.

III. I try to find a middle-ground solution. I am willing to give up some points if it will lead to a fair combination of gains and losses for both parties. To expedite the resolution, I generally suggest that we search for a compromise, instead of stubbornly holding on to my position.

IV. I try to soothe the other's feelings so the disagreement doesn't damage our relationship. I try to diffuse the conflict by focusing on points of agreement. If the other person's position seems very important to him or her, I will likely concede my own to maintain harmony.

V. I attempt to get all of the concerns and issues out into the open. I frankly describe my position and ask that the other person do the same. I favor a direct discussion of disagreements as a way of forging an agreement. It is not always possible, but I try to satisfy the wishes of both parties.

Where's My Talk?

Divide into groups of three. One person should play the role of Jan, the manager, another should play the role of Sue, the secretary, and the third should serve as an observer. All parties should read Jan's role, but only Sue and the observer should read Sue's role, and only the observer should read the feedback questions. After the role play, the observer should lead a discussion based on the questions.

ROLE OF JAN

You have been Director of Personnel for Beacon Lights for ten years. Just when you thought you had your job "down pat," the sky fell in. A strong labor union has been trying to organize your plant, the federal government recently filed a claim against your company for discriminatory hiring practices, the president and vice president of sales were forced to resign last month because of the company's poor performance, and on top of all that, your long-time secretary just died of a heart attack.

You have been asked to give a talk at a national convention on a new productivity program your company has pioneered, and you are looking forward to getting away from the office for a few days to catch your breath. You gave your talk to your new secretary, Sue, a couple of days ago so she would have plenty of time to get it typed and reproduced.

This morning you have come into the office to proofread and rehearse your talk prior to catching a plane this evening and you are shocked to find a note saying your secretary called in ill this morning. You rush over to her desk and frantically begin searching for your paper. You find it mixed in with some material for the quarterly report that should have been sent in two weeks ago, a stack of overdue correspondence, and two days' unopened mail.

As you dial your secretary's home phone number, you realize that you are perspiring heavily and your face is flushed. This is the worst foul-up you can remember in years.

ROLE OF SUE

You hear the phone ring and it is all you can do to get out of bed and limp into the kitchen to answer it. You really feel rotten. On the way home last night, you slipped on your kid's skateboard in the driveway and sprained your knee. You can hardly move today and the pain is excruciating. You are also a bit hesitant to answer the phone because you figure it is probably your boss, Jan, calling to chew you out for getting behind in your work. You know you deserve some blame, but it wasn't all your fault. Since you began working for Jan a month ago, you have asked several times for a thorough job description. You feel you don't really understand Jan's priorities or your specific job responsibilities. You are replacing a woman who died suddenly after working for Jan for ten years. You were hired to pick up the pieces, but you have found working with Jan extremely frustrating. She has been too busy to train you properly and she assumes you know as much about the job as your predecessor. This is particularly a problem since you haven't worked as a secretary for three years, and you feel a bit "rusty".

Jan's talk is a good example of the difficulties you have experienced. She gave you the talk a couple of days ago and said it was urgent—but that was on top of a quarterly report that was already overdue and a backlog of correspondence, filing, etc. You never filled out a report like this before, and every time you asked Jan a question she said she'd discuss it with you later—as she ran off to a meeting. When you asked if it would be possible to get some additional help to catch up the overdue work, Jan said the company couldn't afford it because of poor sales. This irked you because you knew you were being paid far less than your predecessor. You knew Jan faced some urgent deadlines so you had planned to return to the office last night to type Jan's speech and try to complete the report, but two hours in the emergency room at the hospital put an end to that plan. You tried calling Jan to explain the problem, only to find out she has an unlisted number.

As you sit down and prop up your leg, you wince with pain as you pick up the phone.

OBSERVER'S QUESTIONS

To what extent did the parties do the following?

1. Describe their concerns and feelings in specific, nonevaluative terms.
2. Avoid becoming defensive and overreacting to critical comments.
3. Focus on ways to solve their common problems.
4. Encourage two-way communication by asking for suggestions and reactions.
5. Show sensitivity to the other person's problems, concerns, and feelings. ■

■ *Skill Learning*

Interpersonal Conflict Management

Interpersonal conflict is an essential part of organizational life. Organizations in which there is little disagreement generally fail in competitive environments. The members are either so homogeneous that they are ill equipped to adapt to changing environmental conditions or so complacent that they see no need to improve the status quo. Conflict is the lifeblood of vibrant, progressive, stimulating organizations. It sparks creativity, stimulates innovation, and encourages personal improvement. (Robbins, 1978; Janis, 1972; Thomas, 1956; King, 1981; Kelly, 1970).

But not all conflict produces beneficial results. Some people have a very low tolerance for disagreement. Whether this is the result of family background, cultural values, or personality characteristics, a high level of interpersonal conflict saps their energy and demoralizes them. Also, some types of conflicts, regardless of frequency, generally produce dysfunctional outcomes. These include petty personality conflicts and arguments over things that can't be changed. This is especially the case when conflict is stimulated for self-serving purposes. For example, some managers feel so unsure of their qualifications and support that they continually stir up conflicts between subordinates. This reduces the threat of a coalition's forming to challenge the boss's rule, creates situations that reaffirm the boss's superior position (e.g., conflicts occur that only he or she can resolve), and provides an opportunity for him or her to berate subordinates for quarreling like children.

Consequently, while most scholars agree that some conflict is both inevitable and necessary in effective organizations, a well-known psychologist, Abraham Maslow (1965), has observed a high degree of ambivalence in our society regarding the value of conflict. On the one hand, he notes that managers intellectually appreciate the value of conflict and competition. They agree it is a necessary ingredient of the free enterprise system. However, their actions demonstrate a personal preference for avoiding conflicts whenever possible. So while they appreciate the value of conflict in the abstract, they feel uncomfortable being a part of it.

This tension between intellectual acceptance of a principle and emotional rejection of its enactment was illustrated in a study of decision making (Boulding, 1964). Several groups of managers were formed to solve a complex problem. The groups were identical in size and composition, with the exception that half of them contained a "confederate." Before the experiment began, the researcher instructed this person to play the role of devil's advocate. He or she was to challenge the group's conclusions, forcing the others to critically examine their assumptions and the logic of their arguments. At the end of the problem-solving period, the recommendations made by both sets of groups were compared. The groups with the devil's advocates had performed significantly better on the task. They had generated more alternatives, and their proposals were judged as superior. After a short break, the groups were reassembled and told that they would be performing a similar task during the next session. However, before they began discussing the next problem, they were given permission to eliminate one member. In every group containing a confederate, he or she was the one asked to leave. It is interesting that the winning groups expelled their unique competitive advantage because he or she made them feel uncomfortable. The participants in this experiment demonstrated a widely shared reaction to conflict: "I know it has positive outcomes for the performance of the organization as a whole, but I don't like what it does to me personally."

We believe that much of this ambivalence toward conflict stems from a lack of understanding of the causes of conflict and the variety of modes for managing it effectively, and from a lack of confidence in one's personal skills for handling the tense, emotionally charged environment typical of most interpersonal conflicts. It is natural for an untrained or inexperienced person to avoid threatening situations, and it is generally acknowledged that conflict represents the most severe test of a manager's interpersonal skills. The task of the effective manager, therefore, is to maintain an optimal level of conflict and to keep conflicts focused on productive purposes. The skillful manager needs to be able to effectively settle interpersonal disputes in such a way that the underlying problems are resolved and the interpersonal relationship between the disputants is not damaged. Before discussing these specific skill topics, we shall set the stage by examining various sources of conflict and generic approaches to handling conflicts.

CAUSES OF INTERPERSONAL CONFRONTATIONS

Often managers behave as though serious interpersonal confrontations were the result of personality defects. People frequently involved in conflicts are labeled as "troublemakers" or "bad apples," and attempts are made to transfer or dismiss them as a way of resolving conflict. While some individuals seem to have a propensity for making trouble and appear to be cantankerous under even the best of circumstances, "sour dispositions" actually account for only a small percentage of organizational conflicts (Schmidt and Tannenbaum, 1965).

This proposition is supported by research on performance appraisals (Latham & Wexley, 1981). It has been shown that managers generally attribute poor performance to personal deficiencies in workers (e.g., lazy, unskilled, poorly motivated). However, when workers are asked the causes of their poor performance, they generally explain it in terms of obstacles or constraints in their environment (e.g., insufficient supplies, uncooperative co-workers). While some face-saving is obviously involved here, this line of research suggests that managers need to guard against the reflexive tendency of assuming that bad behaviors imply bad persons. In fact, the aggressive or harsh behaviors sometimes observed in an interpersonal confrontation often reflect the frustrations of persons who have good intentions but are unskilled in handling intense, emotional experiences.

In contrast to the personality-defect theory of conflict, we propose four explanations for interpersonal conflict in Table 8.1. These are personal differences, informational deficiency, role incompatibility, and environmental stress.

Individuals bring to their roles in organizations different backgrounds. Their values and needs have been shaped by different socialization processes, depending on their cultural and family traditions, level of education, breadth of experience, and so forth. As a result, their interpretations of events and their expectations about relationships with others in the organization will vary considerably. Conflicts stemming from incompatible personal values and needs are some of the most difficult to resolve. They often become highly emotional and take on moral overtones. A disagreement about who is factually *correct* easily turns into a bitter argument over who is morally *right*. Such a conflict occurred in a major industrial company between a 63-year-old white executive vice president and a 35-year-old black member of the corporate legal department who had been very active in the civil rights movement during the 1960s. They disagreed vehemently over whether the company should accept a very attractive offer from the South African government to build a manufacturing facility in that country. The vice president felt the company had a responsibility to its stockholders to pursue every legal opportunity to increase profits. In contrast, the lawyer felt that collaborating with the South African government was tantamount to condoning its morally repugnant policy of apartheid.

Conflicts can also result from deficiencies in the organization's information system. An important message may not be received, a boss's instructions may be misinterpreted, or decision-makers may arrive at different conclusions because they used different sources of information. Conflicts based on misinformation or misunderstanding tend to be factual in the sense that clarifying previous messages or obtaining additional information can often resolve the dispute. This might entail rewording the boss's instructions, reconciling con-

TABLE 8.1 *Sources of Conflict*

Source of Conflict	*Focus on Conflict*
Personal differences	Perceptions and expectations
Informational deficiency	Misinformation and misinterpretation
Role incompatibility	Goals and responsibilities
Environmental stress	Resource scarcity and uncertainty

tradictory sources of data, or redistributing copies of misplaced messages. This type of conflict is very common in most organizations, but it is also easy to resolve. Because value systems are not being challenged, the confrontations tend to be less emotional. Once the breakdown in the information system is repaired, the disputants are generally able to resolve their disagreement with a minimum of resentment.

The complexity inherent in most organizations tends to produce conflict between members whose tasks are interdependent but whose roles are incompatible. This type of conflict is exemplified by the classic goal conflicts between line and staff, production and sales, production and R&D. Each unit has different responsibilities in the organization, and as a result each places different priorities on organizational goals (e.g., customer satisfaction, product quality, production efficiency, compliance with government regulations). Since this type of conflict stems from the fundamental incompatibility of the job responsibilities of the disputants, it can often be resolved only through the mediation of a common supervisor. When the disputants feel they are simply acting out the mandates dictated to them, significant incompatibilities generally must be worked out by higher authorities.

This type of conflict interacts in a significant manner with the first two. The personal differences members bring with them to an organization generally remain dormant until they are triggered by an organizational catalyst, such as interdependent task responsibilities. Also, one reason members often perceive that their assigned roles are incompatible is because they are operating from different bases of information. They communicate with different sets of people, are tied into different reporting systems, and receive instructions from different bosses.

Another major source of conflict is environmentally induced stress. Conflicts stemming from personal differences and role incompatibilities are greatly exacerbated by a stressful environment. When an organization is forced to operate on an austere budget, its members are more likely to become embroiled in disputes over domain claims and resource requests. Scarcity tends to lower trust, increase ethnocentrism, and reduce participation in decision making. These are ideal conditions for incubating interpersonal conflict.

A second environmental condition that fosters conflict is uncertainty. When individuals find it difficult to predict what is going to happen to them from month to month, they become very anxious and prone to conflict. This type of "frustration conflict" often stems from rapid, repeated change. If task assignments, management philosophy, accounting procedures, lines of authority, and so forth, are changed frequently, members find it difficult to cope with the resulting stress, and sharp, bitter conflicts can easily erupt over seemingly trivial problems. This type of conflict is generally very intense, but dissipates quickly once a change becomes routinized and individuals' stress levels are lowered.

CONFLICT RESPONSE ALTERNATIVES

As revealed in the preassessment survey, people's responses to interpersonal confrontations tend to fall into five categories: forcing, accommodating, avoiding, compromising, and collaborating (Filley, 1975, 1977, 1978; Robbins, 1974). These can be organized along two dimensions, as shown in Figure 8.1 (Ruble & Thomas, 1976). These five approaches to conflict reflect different degrees of cooperativeness and assertiveness. A cooperative response is intended to satisfy the needs of the interacting person, whereas an assertive response focuses on the needs of the focal person.

The forcing response (assertive, uncooperative) is an attempt to satisfy one's own needs at the expense of the other individual. This can be done by

Figure 8.1 *Two-dimensional Model of Conflict Behavior*

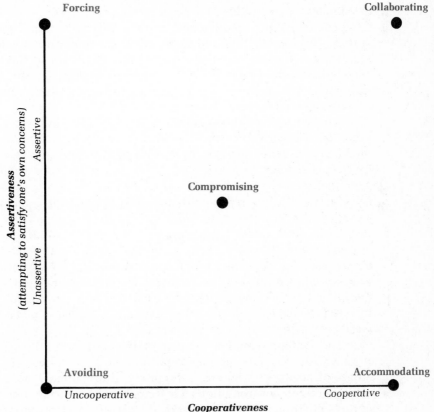

Adapted from Ruble and Thomas, 1976, p. 145.

using formal authority, physical threats, or majority rule, or simply by ignoring the claims of the other party. The blatant use of the authority of one's office ("I'm the boss, so we'll do it my way.") or other forms of intimidation is generally evidence of a lack of tolerance or self-confidence. The use of majority rule or feigned ignorance is much more subtle, but also reflects an egoistic leadership style. Manipulative leaders often appear to be democratic by proposing that conflicting proposals be referred to a committee for further investigation. However, they make sure that the composition of the group reflects their interests and preferences so that what appears to be a selection based on merit is actually an act of authoritarian rule. A related form of manipulation used by some managers involves ignoring a proposal that threatens their personal interests. If the originator inquires about the deposition of his or her memo, the manager pleads ignorance, blames the mail clerk or new secretary, and then suggests that the proposal be redrafted. After several of these encounters, subordinates generally get the message that the boss isn't interested in their ideas (Whetten & Dyer, 1975).

The problem with the repeated use of this conflict management approach is that it breeds hostility and resentment. While observers may intellectually admire an authoritarian or manipulative leader because he or she appears to accomplish a great deal, these management styles generally produce a backlash in the long run as people become unwilling to absorb the emotional costs (as we discussed in the preceding chapter).

The accommodating approach (cooperative, unassertive) satisfies the other party's concerns while neglecting one's own. This conflict-handling mode closely resembles the philosophy of interpersonal relations advocated by Dale Carnegie. In *How to Win Friends and Influence People* (1936), he argued that the key to success in working with people is maintaining a friendly relationship. This is reflected in his prescriptions for changing another person's behavior, as shown in Table 8.2. While many valid principles are embedded in these rules, the overall goal is keeping the other person happy at any cost. The difficulty with the habitual use of this approach is that it emphasizes preserving a friendly relationship at the expense of critically appraising issues and protecting personal rights. This often results in others taking advantage of you, which lowers your self-esteem as you observe yourself being used by others to accomplish their objectives while failing to make any progress toward your own.

The avoiding response (uncooperative, unassertive) neglects the interest of both parties by sidestepping or postponing the conflict. This is often the response of managers who are emotionally ill prepared to cope with the stress associated with confrontations. Or it might reflect recognition that a relationship is not strong enough to absorb the fallout of an intense conflict. The repeated use of this approach causes considerable frustration for others because issues never seem to get resolved, really tough problems are avoided because of their high potential for conflict, and subordinates engaging in conflict are reprimanded for undermining the harmony of the work group. Sensing a lead-

TABLE 8.2 *Nine Ways to Change People Without Giving Offense or Arousing Resentment*

1. Begin with praise and honest appreciation.

2. Call attention to people's mistakes indirectly.

3. Talk about your own mistakes before criticizing the other person.

4. Ask questions instead of giving direct orders.

5. Let the other man save his face.

6. Praise the slightest improvement and praise every improvement. Be "hearty in your approbation and lavish in your praise."

7. Give the other person a fine reputation to live up to.

8. Use encouragement. Make the fault seem easy to correct.

9. Make the other person happy about doing the thing you suggest.

SOURCE: Dale Carnegie, *How to win friends and influence people*, (New York: Simon and Schuster, 1936), p. 200.

ership vacuum, people from all directions rush to fill it and create considerable confusion and animosity in the process.

The compromise mode is intermediate in assertiveness and cooperativeness. A compromise is an attempt to obtain partial satisfaction for both parties, in the sense that both receive the proverbial "half a loaf." To accomplish this, both parties are asked to make sacrifices to obtain a common gain. While this approach has considerable practical appeal to managers, its indiscriminate use can produce counterproductive results. If subordinates are continually told to "split the difference" when they take a dispute to their boss, they may conclude that he or she is more interested in resolving disputes than solving problems. This creates a climate of expediency that encourages game playing, such as asking for twice as much as you need.

Collaboration (cooperative, assertive) is an attempt to fully address the concerns of both parties. It is often referred to as the "problem-solving" mode. In this mode, the intent is to find solutions to the cause of the conflict that are satisfactory to both parties, rather than to find fault or assign blame. In this way both parties can feel that they have "won." This is the only win/win strategy of the five. The avoiding mode results in a lose/lose outcome and the compromising, accommodating, and forcing modes all represent win/lose outcomes. While we shall point out later that this approach is not appropriate for all situations, when it is used appropriately, it has the most beneficial effect on the parties involved. It encourages norms of collaboration and trust while acknowledging the value of assertiveness. It constrains people to focus their disputes on problems and issues rather than on personalities. Finally, it cultivates the skills necessary for self-governance, in the sense that effective problem-solvers are less dependent on others.

TABLE 8.3 *A Comparison of Five Conflict Management Approaches*

Approach	Objective	Your Posture	Supporting Rationale	Likely Outcome
Forcing	Get your way.	"I know what's right. Don't question my judgment or authority."	It is better to risk causing a few hard feelings than to abandon a position you are committed to.	You feel vindicated, but other party feels defeated and possibly humiliated.
Avoiding	Avoid having to deal with conflict.	"I'm neutral on that issue." "Let me think about it."	Disagreements are inherently bad because they create tension.	Interpersonal problems don't get resolved, causing long-term frustration manifested in variety of ways.
Compromising	Reach an agreement quickly.	"Let's search for a mutually agreeable solution."	Prolonged conflicts distract people from their work and engender bitter feelings.	Participants become conditioned to seek expedient, rather than effective, solutions.
Accommodating	Don't upset the other person.	"How can I help you feel good about this encounter? My position isn't so important that it is worth risking bad feelings between us."	Maintaining harmonious relationships should be our top priority.	Other person is likely to take advantage of you.
Collaborating	Solve the problem together.	"This is my position, what is yours?" "I'm committed to finding the best possible solution."	The positions of both parties are equally important (though not necessarily equally valid). Equal emphasis should be placed on the quality of the outcome and the fairness of the decision-making process.	The problem is most likely resolved. Also, both parties are committed to the solution and satisfied that they have been treated fairly.

EFFECTIVE USE OF CONFLICT-HANDLING MODES

The salient characteristics of the five conflict management approaches are summarized in Table 8.3. A comparison of alternative approaches inevitably leads to the question, "Which one is the best?" While the collaborative approach produces the fewest negative side effects, all the approaches have their place. To begin with, the five modes of handling conflict are not equally attractive to all individuals. Each of us tends to have a preferred strategy that is consistent with the value we place on conflict and our dominant personality characteristics. The relationship between personality profiles and preferences for different approaches to handling conflict was investigated in a study of interpersonal bargaining (Cummings, Harnett, & Stevens, 1971) in which investigators collected questionnaire data from the participants on the following four personality dimensions:

1. Conciliation versus belligerence in interpersonal relations. Conciliators advocate responding to the needy or less fortunate with understanding. They admit their wrongs and are not motivated by revenge.
2. Risk avoidance versus risk taking. Risk-takers are adventurous, have a high activity level, and will expose themselves to dangers.
3. External versus internal control. Externally controlled persons believe that events are controlled by forces over which they have little control.
4. Suspiciousness versus trust. Suspicious persons possess paranoid-like traits of selfishness, projection of hostility, excitability, tenseness, and lack of trust.

The researchers found that by using these four dimensions, they could predict which of three bargaining styles a person would use. These approaches were described as win/lose battling, soft bargaining, and problem solving. These bargaining styles closely approximate the forcing, accommodating, and collaborating modes of conflict resolution in Figure 8.1. As shown in Table 8.4, the researchers found that the win/lose battlers were high in internal control, high in risk taking, and high in belligerence. The measure of trust or suspiciousness was unrelated to this bargaining style. Individuals using the soft, or yielding, approach to bargaining were high in external control, low in risk taking, and high in trust. The problem-solving style was found to be high in internal control, high in trusting behavior, and high in conciliation. However, it did not relate to the measure of risk taking.

The relationship between personality and conflict resolution preference has also been explored by Elias Porter (1973). This work has identified three distinct personality profiles. The altruistic-nurturing personality seeks gratification through promoting harmony with others and enhancing their welfare,

TABLE 8.4 *Personality Characteristics of Individuals Preferring Different Conflict Management Approaches*

	Characteristics	
Approach	*Cummings, Harnett, & Stevens (1971)*	*Porter (1973)*
	Win/lose battling	Assertive-directing
Forcing	High internal control	Self-confident
	High risk taking	Enterprising
	High Belligerence	Persuasive
	Soft bargaining	Altruistic-nurturing
Accommodating	High external control	Optimistic
	Low risk taking	Trusting
	High trust	Idealistic
		Loyal
	Problem-solving	Analytic-autonomizing
Collaborating	High internal control	Methodical
	High trust	Cautious
	High conciliation	Principled
		Practical
		Self-sufficient
		Self-reliant
		Logical

with little concern for being rewarded in return. This personality type is characterized by trust, optimism, idealism, and loyalty. The assertive-directing personality seeks gratification through self-assertion and directing the activities of others with a clear sense of having earned rewards. Individuals with this personality characteristic tend to be self-confident, enterprising, and persuasive. The analytic-autonomizing personality seeks gratification through the achievement of self-sufficiency, self-reliance, and logical orderliness. This personality type is cautious, practical, methodical, and principled.

When the altruistic-nurturing individual encounters conflict, he or she tends to press for harmony by accommodating the demands of the other party. In contrast, the assertive-directing personality tends to challenge the opposition by using the forcing approach. The analyzing-autonomizing personality becomes very cautious when encountering conflict. Initially an attempt is made to rationally resolve the problem. However, if the conflict becomes very intense, this individual will withdraw and break contact.

While there appears to be a strong link between dominant personality characteristics and preferred modes of handling conflict, research on leadership styles has demonstrated that the most effective managers use a variety of styles (Downey, Sheridan, & Slocum, 1976; Schriesheim & VonGlinow,

1977), tailoring their response to the demands of the situation. This general principle has been borne out in research on conflict management. In one study, twenty-five executives attending an advanced management training program were asked to describe two conflict situations—one with bad results and one with good (Phillips & Cheston, 1979). These incidents were then categorized in terms of the conflict management approach used. As shown in Figure 8.2, there were twenty-three incidents of forcing, twelve incidents of problem solving, five incidents of compromise, and twelve incidents of avoidance. Admittedly, this was a very small sample of managers, but the fact that there were almost twice as many incidents of forcing as problem solving and nearly five times as many as compromising is noteworthy. It is also interesting that the executives indicated that forcing and compromising were equally likely to produce good or bad results, whereas problem solving was always linked with positive outcomes and avoidance generally led to negative results.

It is striking that, despite the fact that it was as likely to produce bad as good results, forcing was by far the most commonly used conflict management mode. Since this approach is clearly not superior in terms of results, one wonders why these senior executives reported a propensity for using it.

The answer provided by a study of the preferred influence strategies of over 300 managers in three countries (Kipnis & Schmidt, 1983) is expediency. This study reports that when subordinates refuse or appear reluctant to comply with a request, managers become directive. When resistance in subordinates is encountered, managers tend to fall back on their superior power and insist on compliance. So pervasive was this pattern that the authors of this study proposed an "Iron Law of Power," "the greater the discrepancy in power between influence and target, the greater the probability that more directive influence strategies will be used" (1983, p. 7).

A second striking feature of this figure is that some conflict management approaches were never used for certain types of issues. In particular, the managers did not report a single case of problem solving or compromising when personal problems were the source of the conflict. These approaches were used primarily for managing conflicts involving incompatible goals and reward systems between departments.

Two conclusions can be drawn from this study. First, no one approach is most effective for managing every type of conflict. Second, while managers naturally rely on the conflict resolution strategy that is most compatible with their dominant personality characteristics, they are more effective in dealing with conflicts if they feel comfortable using a variety of approaches. These conclusions point out the need to understand the conditions under which each conflict management technique is most effective. This knowledge allows one to match the characteristics of a conflict incident with the management technique best suited for those characteristics.

The salient situational variables that should be considered are summarized in Table 8.5. These are the nature of the conflict issue, the relative importance of maintaining a supportive relationship, the nature of the formal

Figure 8.2 *Outcome of Conflict Resolution by Conflict Type and Method of Resolution*

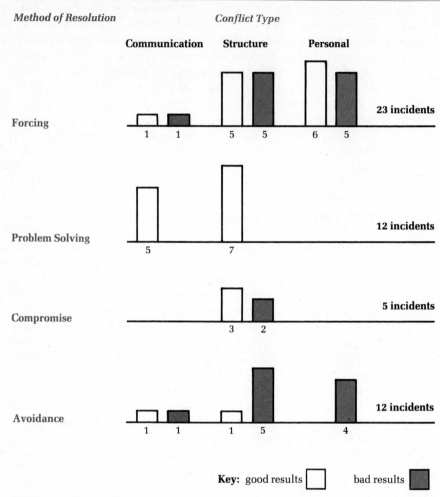

Key: good results ☐   bad results ■

From Phillips and Cheston, 1979, p. 79.

relationship between the parties, and the time constraints impinging on the conflict.

Using these dimensions, we can highlight the salient contingencies appropriate for each conflict management approach. The forcing approach is most appropriate when a conflict of values or perspectives is involved and one feels compelled to defend the "correct" position, when a superior-subordinate relationship is involved, when maintaining a close, supportive relationship is not critical, and when there is a sense of urgency. An example of this situation might be a manager insisting that a summer intern follow important company safety regulations.

The accommodating approach is most appropriate when the importance of maintaining a good working relationship outweighs all other considerations. While this could be the case regardless of your formal relationship with the other party, it is often perceived as being the only option for subordinates of powerful bosses. The nature of the issues and the amount of time available play a secondary role in determining the choice of this strategy. Accommodation becomes especially appropriate when the issues are not vital to your interests and the problem must be resolved quickly.

Trying to reach a compromise is most appropriate when the issues are very complex and critical. There are no simple solutions and both parties have a strong interest in different facets of the problem. The other essential situational characteristic is adequate time for negotiation. The classic case is a bargaining session between representatives of management and labor to avert a scheduled strike. While the characteristics of the relationship between the parties are not essential factors, experience has shown that negotiations tend to work best between parties with equal power who are committed to maintaining a good long-term relationship.

The collaborating approach is most appropriate when the issues are critical, maintaining an ongoing supportive relationship between peers is impor-

TABLE 8.5 *Matching Situational Characteristics with Conflict Management Approaches*

Approach	Nature of Issues — Critical or Complex	Not Essential or Simple	Importance of Supportive Relationship — Important	Not Important	Formal Relationship between Parties — Superior/ Subordinate	Peers	Time Pressures — Urgent	Not Urgent
Forcing	P*			P	P		P	
Accommodating		S	P		P		S	
Compromising	P		S			S		P
Collaborating	P		P			P		P
Avoiding		P	P				S	

* P = primary condition, S = secondary condition.

tant, and time constraints are not pressing. While collaboration can also be an effective approach for resolving conflicts between a superior and subordinate, it is important to point out that when a conflict involves peers, the collaborative mode is more appropriate than either the forcing or accommodating approaches.

The avoidance approach is most appropriate when one's stake in an issue is not high but the potential for damaging a critical working relationship is significant, regardless of whether the conflict involves a superior, subordinate, or peer. A severe time constraint becomes a contributing factor since it enhances the attractiveness of avoidance by default. While one might prefer other strategies, like compromising and collaboration, that have a good chance of resolving problems without damaging relationships, these are ruled out because of the time pressure.

GUIDELINES FOR RESOLVING INTERPERSONAL CONFRONTATIONS USING THE COLLABORATIVE APPROACH

From our discussion so far, we can see that part of the skill of effective conflict management is choosing an appropriate approach based on a thoughtful assessment of the situation. One characteristic of unsuccessful conflict managers is their habitual reliance on one or two strategies, regardless of changing circumstances. A second characteristic of ineffective conflict managers is the inability to effectively implement the collaborative approach. In the study by Kipnis and Schmidt (1983) discussed earlier, most managers expressed general support for the collaborative approach, but when it appeared things weren't going their way, they reverted back to a directive approach.

One important reason for this pattern is that the collaborative approach to conflict management is the most difficult to implement successfully. It requires much more skill than accommodating or forcing, for example. It is a fairly simple matter for managers to give in or impose their will, but resolving differences in a truly collaborative manner is a very complicated and taxing process. As a result, when situational conditions indicate that the collaborative approach is most appropriate, unskilled managers will often opt for less challenging approaches. To help students gain experience using the collaborative approach, the remainder of this chapter describes behavioral guidelines for effectively resolving interpersonal confrontations. The objective of this section is to enable you to register a complaint or receive a criticism in such a manner that the issue is resolved without damaging the interpersonal relationship between the disputants.

We have chosen this form of conflict because it is the most difficult form to manage in a collaborative manner. As we noted earlier, information-based disagreements in organizations are quite common, but they are also relatively easy to resolve, since the parties don't generally have a great deal invested in the outcome. Confrontations involving matters of principle or alleged personal harm are quite different. At least one of the disputants is strongly committed to winning the argument—often at any cost. It is easy to lose control of one's professional decorum in these situations. The natural tendency is to become either very aggressive or withdrawn and resentful. However, as we discussed earlier, neither response is likely to resolve this type of conflict to the satisfaction of both parties. When one feels one's rights have been violated and lashes out at the offender seeking retribution, the tendency is to be judgmental and to overgeneralize from a specific incident to a broader set of "character flaws." This negative attribution typically produces a defensive reaction (e.g., "Believe me, you're not perfect either."), which is then used to justify introducing additional criticisms into the discussion. This often results in a nasty argument that requires third-party intervention and may result in irreparable damage to the relationship.

It is important to differentiate between a complaint and a criticism. A complaint is problem focused, whereas a criticism is person focused. Complaints are descriptive, while criticisms are evaluative. It is this judgmental aspect of criticism that produces a strong defensive reaction. The other party bridles at unjustified (and often inaccurate) conclusions about his or her sinister motives or fundamental personal deficiencies. Therefore, if you are sincerely interested in solving an important interpersonal problem (versus simply trying to even the score), your best bet is to use the collaborative approach to conflict management, following the guidelines for supportive communication presented in Chapter 4.

The typical problem-solving process includes four phases: problem identification, solution generation, examination and agreement, and implementation and follow-up. In the midst of a heated discussion, problem identification is the most critical and difficult step to manage effectively. Therefore, this is the phase we shall focus on in our skill training. During this phase, your task is to identify the source of the frustration that precipitated the confrontation. This generally results from rights being violated, needs being unsatisfied, domains of activity or authority being threatened, or personal development being stymied. The behavioral guidelines to be followed by the conflicting parties at this stage are quite different. Since it is during this early phase of the confrontation that the actors' orientations are most discrepant, we shall examine the role of each participant separately.

A dyadic confrontation involves just two actors, an initiator and a responder. This might take the form of a subordinate complaining about not being given a fair share of opportunities to work overtime, or the head of production complaining to the head of sales about frequent changes in order specifications. A dyadic conflict represents a greater challenge for the responder because he or she basically has responsibility for transforming a complaint session into a problem-solving discussion. This requires considerable patience and self-confidence, since the unskilled initiator will generally begin the discussion by blaming the responder for the problem. In this situation the unskilled responder will naturally become very defensive and look for an opportunity to even the score. The result can be a serious escalation of the confrontation into a heated, lose/lose debate. If this occurs, a mediator is generally required to cool down the participants, reestablish constructive communication, and help the parties reconcile their differences. The presence of a mediator takes some of the pressure off the responder because the impartial referee provides assistance in moving the confrontation through the problem-identification phase.

PROBLEM IDENTIFICATION

The following guidelines provide a model for acting out the initiator, responder, and mediator roles in such a way that problem identification can occur. In our discussion of each role, we shall assume that the other participant in the conflict is not behaving according to his or her prescribed guidelines.

Initiator

1. *Maintain personal ownership of the problem.*   It is important that you recognize that when you are upset and frustrated this is your problem, not your boss's or your co-worker's. You may feel the other person is the source of your problem, but your frustration is the immediate problem. Suppose someone enters your office with a smelly cigar without asking if it is all right to smoke. The fact that your office is going to stink for the rest of the day may infuriate you, but the odor does not represent a problem for your smoking guest. One way to determine ownership of a problem is to identify whose needs are not being met. In this case your need for a clean working environment is not being met, so the smelly office is your problem.

The advantage of acknowledging ownership of a problem when registering a complaint is that it reduces defensiveness (Adler, 1977). If you are truly interested in getting the problem solved (rather than just griping), it is important that the respondent not feel threatened by your initial statement of the problem. By beginning the conversation with a request that the responder help solve your problem, you immediately establish a problem-solving atmosphere. For example, you might say, "Bill, do you have a few minutes—I have a problem I need to discuss with you."

2. *Describe your problem in terms of behaviors, consequences, and feelings.*   A useful model for remembering how to state your problem effectively has been prescribed by Gordon (1970): "I have a problem. When you do X, Y happens, and I feel Z." While we don't advocate the memorization of set formulas for improving communication skills, keeping this model in mind will help you implement three critical guidelines.

First, describe the specific behaviors that present a problem for you. This will help you avoid the reflexive tendency when you are upset to give feedback that is evaluative and not specific. One way to do this is to specify the expectations or standards that have been violated. For example, a subordinate may have missed a deadline for completing an assigned task, your boss may gradually be taking over tasks previously delegated to you, or a colleague in the accounting department may have repeatedly failed to provide you with data required for an important presentation after he or she promised you the information.

Second, outline the specific, concrete, observable consequences of these behaviors. Simply telling a person that his or her actions are causing you problems is often sufficient stimulus for change. In fast-paced work environments, people often become insensitive to the impact of their actions. They don't intend to cause offense, but become so busy meeting deadlines associated with "getting the product out the door" that they tune out subtle negative feedback from others. Often someone must deliberately bring to the attention of others the consequences of their behaviors to prompt them to change.

Unfortunately, sometimes problems can't be resolved that simply. At times the defender is aware of the negative consequences of his or her behaviors and still engages in them. In such cases, this approach is still useful in stimulating a problem-solving discussion because it presents concerns in a nonthreatening manner. Possibly the responder's behavior is constrained by the expectations of his or her boss or the fact that the department is currently understaffed. The responder may not be able to change these constraints, but this approach will encourage him or her to discuss them with you so you can work on the problem together.

Third, describe the feelings you experience as a result of the problem. It is important that the responder understand that the behavior is not just inconvenient. You need to explain how it is affecting you personally by engendering feelings of frustration, anger, insecurity, etc. Explain how these feelings are interfering with your work. They may make it more difficult for you to concentrate, to be congenial with customers, to be supportive of your boss, or to be willing to make needed personal sacrifices to meet deadlines.

As we mentioned earlier, you should use this three-step model as a guide, rather than as a formula. The order of the components may vary, and you should not use the same words every time. For example, it would get pretty monotonous if everyone in a work group initiated a discussion about an interpersonal issue with the words "I have a problem." Observe how the key elements in the model are used in different ways in the following examples from Adler (1977, p. 223):

"I have to tell you that I get upset [feelings] when you make jokes about my bad memory in front of other people [behavior]. In fact, I get so angry that I find myself bringing up your faults to get even [consequences]."

"I have a problem. When you say you'll be here for our date at six and don't show up until after seven [behavior], the dinner gets ruined, we're late for the show we planned to see [consequences], and I feel hurt because it seems like I'm just not that important to you [feeling]."

"The employees want to let management know that we've been having a hard time lately with the short notice you've been giving when you need us to work overtime [behavior]. That probably explains some of the grumbling and lack of cooperation you've mentioned [consequences]. Anyhow, we wanted to make it clear that this policy has really got a lot of the workers feeling pretty resentful [feeling]."

3. Avoid drawing evaluative conclusions and attributing motives to the respondent.   In presenting your problem, avoid the pitfalls of making accusations, drawing inferences about motivations or intentions, or attributing the responder's undesirable behavior to personal inadequacies. Statements like, "You are always interrupting me," "You haven't liked me since the day I disagreed with you in the board meeting," and "You never have time to listen to our problems or suggestions because you manage your time so poorly," are good for starting arguments but ineffective for initiating a problem-solving process. Another key to reducing defensiveness is not proposing a solution before both parties agree on the nature of the problem. When you become so upset with someone's behavior that you feel it is necessary to initiate a complaint, it is often because that person has seriously violated your ideal role model. For example, you might feel he or she should have been less dogmatic and listened more during a goal-setting interview. Consequently, you might express your feelings in terms of prescriptions for how the other person should behave, and suggest he or she be more democratic, understanding, or sensitive. It is important to understand that this is not a statement of your problem, but a recommendation for how the other person should solve it.

There are two disadvantages to initiating problem solving with a suggested remedy. First, it is guaranteed to produce a defensive reaction. You are implying that the other person is, by and large, responsible for the problem and that you are an expert on how he or she should behave. You have diagnosed the situation, you know exactly what the problem is, you have assessed how the blame for the consequences should be distributed, and you have discerned how to keep the problem from occurring again. The other party will certainly object strenuously at this point, sensing that you have set yourself up as the prosecutor, judge, and jury. The second disadvantage is that it hinders the problem-solving process. Before completing the problem-articulation phase, you have immediately jumped to the solution-generation phase based on the assumption that you know all the reasons for and constraints on the other person's behavior. Together you will produce better solutions that are acceptable to you both if you present your statement of the problem and discuss that thoroughly with the other party before beginning to discuss potential solutions.

4. *Persist until understood.*   There are times when the other person will not clearly receive or acknowledge even the most effectively expressed message. Suppose, for instance, that you share the following problem with a friend (Adler, 1977, p. 228):

> "I've been bothered by something lately and I want to share it with you. To be honest, I'm uncomfortable [feeling] when you use so much profanity [behavior]. I don't mind an occasional 'damn' or 'hell,' but the other words are hard for me to accept. Lately I've found myself avoiding you, and that's no good either [consequences], so I wanted to let you know how I feel."

When you share your feelings in this nonevaluative way, it's likely that the other person will understand your position and possibly try to change behavior to suit your needs. On the other hand, there are a number of less satisfying responses that could be made to your comment:

> "Listen, these days everyone talks that way. And besides, you've got your faults, too, you know!" [Your friend becomes defensive, rationalizing and counterattacking.]
>
> "Yeah, I suppose I do swear a lot. I'll have to work on that some day." [Gets the general drift of your message but fails to comprehend how serious the problem is to you.]
>
> "Listen, if you're still angry about my forgetting to pick you up the other day, you can be sure that I'm really sorry. I won't do it again." [Totally misunderstands.]
>
> "Speaking of avoiding, have you seen Chris lately? I wonder if anything is wrong with him." [Is discomfited by your frustration and changes the subject.]

In each case the friend does not understand or does not wish to acknowledge the problem. In such situations it is necessary to repeat your concern until it has been acknowledged as a problem to be solved. Otherwise, the problem-solving process will terminate at this point and nothing will have changed. Repeated assertions can take the form of repeating the same phrase several times or restating your concern using different words or examples that you feel might improve comprehension.

5. *Encourage two-way interaction.*   It is important that you establish a problem-solving climate by inviting the other person to express opinions and ask questions. Often there is a very simple explanation for the other person's behavior, or he or she may have a radically different view of the problem. The sooner this information is introduced into the conversation, the more likely the issue will be resolved. As a rule of thumb, the longer the opening statement of the initiator, the longer it will take the two parties to work through their problem. The reason for this is that lengthy statements of the problem are more likely to encourage a defensive reaction. The longer we talk, the more worked up we get and the more likely we are to violate the principles of supportive communication. As a result, the other party begins to feel threatened, starts mentally outlining a rebuttal or counterattack, and stops listening empathetically to our concerns. Once these dynamics enter the discussion, the collaborative approach is discarded in favor of the accommodation or forcing strategies, depending on the circumstances. When this occurs, it is unlikely that the actors will be able to reach a mutually satisfactory solution to their problem without third-party intervention.

6. *Approach multiple or complex problems incrementally.*   One way to cut down on the length of your opening statement is to approach complex problems incrementally. Rather than raising a series of issues all at once, initially focus on a fairly simple or rudimentary problem. Then, as you gain a greater appreciation for the other party's perspective and share some problem-solving success, you can then proceed to discuss more challenging issues. This is especially important when you are trying to resolve a problem with a person who is important to your work performance but does not have a long-standing relationship with you. The less familiar you are with the other person's opinions and personality, as well as the situational constraints influencing his or her behavior, the more you should approach your problem-solving discussion as a fact-finding and rapport-building mission. This is best done by focusing your introductory statement on a specific manifestation of a broader problem and presenting it in such a way that it encourages the other party to respond expansively. You can then use this early feedback to shape the remainder of your agenda. For example, "Bill, we had difficulty getting that work order processed on time yesterday. What seemed to be the problem?"

7. *Appeal to those things you share as the basis for working out your problem.*   Most disputants share some goals (personal and organizational), believe in many of the same fundamental principles of management, and operate under similar constraints. These commonalities can serve as a useful starting point in resolving a conflict. By explaining to the respondent that his or her behavior is causing a problem because it is inconsistent with shared values such as treating co-workers fairly, following through on commitments, and operating within budgetary restrictions, or shared constraints, such as getting reports in on time and operating within budgetary restrictions, you can keep personal animosity from creeping into your discussion. This approach is particularly effective when the parties have had difficulty getting along in the past. In these situations pointing out how the respondent's behavior is negatively affecting your shared fate will reduce his or her defensiveness: "Jane, one of the things we have all worked hard to build in this audit team is mutual support. We are all pushed to the limit getting this job completed by the third-quarter deadline next week and the rest of the team members find it difficult to accept your unwillingness to work overtime during this emergency." "Bill, we both recognize that the lifeblood of this store is customers' satisfaction with our service. When you read technical manuals and talk with the other sales personnel instead of helping customers understand the features of our new models, our sales go down."

Responder

Now we shall examine the problem-identification phase from the viewpoint of the person who is supposedly the source of the problem. In a work setting this could be a supervisor who is making unrealistic demands, a new employee who has violated critical safety regulations, or a co-worker who is claiming credit for ideas you generated. The following guidelines for dealing with a subordinate who has a complaint shows how to shape the initiator's behavior so you can have a productive problem-solving experience.

1. *Establish a climate for joint problem-solving by showing genuine interest and concern.* When a person complains to you, that complaint should not be treated lightly. While this sounds self-evident, it is often difficult to focus your attention on the problems of a subordinate when you are in the middle of writing an important project report or concerned about preparing for a meeting scheduled to begin in a few minutes. Consequently, unless the other person's emotional condition necessitates dealing with the problem immediately, it is better to set up a time for another meeting if your current time pressures will make it difficult to concentrate.

In most cases the initiator will be expecting you to set the tone for the meeting. You will quickly undermine collaboration if you overreact or become defensive. Even if you disagree with the complaint and feel it has no foundation, you need to respond empathetically to the initiator's statement of the problem. This is done by conveying an attitude of interest and receptivity through your posture, tone of voice, and facial expressions.

One of the most difficult aspects of establishing the proper climate for your discussion is responding appropriately to the emotions of the initiator. Sometimes you may need to let a person blow off steam before trying to address the substance of a specific complaint. In some cases the therapeutic effect of being able to express negative emotions to the boss will be enough to satisfy the subordinate. This occurs frequently in high-pressure jobs where tempers flair easily as a result of the intense stress.

However, an emotional outburst can be very detrimental to problem solving. If an employee begins verbally attacking you or someone else and it is apparent that the individual is more interested in getting even than in solving an interpersonal problem, you may need to interrupt and interject some ground rules for collaborative problem solving. By explaining calmly to the other person that you are willing to discuss a genuine problem but that you will not tolerate personal attacks or scapegoating, you can quickly determine the true intentions of the initiator. In most instances he or she will apologize, emulate your emotional tone, and begin formulating a useful statement of their problem.

2. *Seek additional information about the problem.* An untrained initiator will typically present a complaint that is both very general and very personal. He or she will make generalizations from a few specific incidents about your motives and personal strengths and weaknesses, and might also blame the problem on you personally. If the two of you are going to transform a personal complaint into a joint problem, you must redirect the conversation from general and personal accusations to descriptions of specific behaviors.

To do this, ask for details about specific things you have done that have led the initiator to formulate his or her judgments. You might find it useful to formulate your questions so they reflect the three-part model prescribed for the initiator's role—"Can you give me a specific example of my behavior that concerns you?" "When I did that, what were the specific consequences for your work?" "How did you feel when that happened?" When a complaint is both serious and complex, it is especially critical for you to understand it completely. In these situations, check your level of understanding by summarizing the initiator's main points and asking if your summary is correct.

Sometimes it is useful to ask for additional complaints—"Are there any other problems in our relationship you'd like to discuss?" If the initiator is just in a griping mood, this is not a good time to probe further because you don't want to encourage this type of behavior. But if the person is seriously concerned about improving your relationship, you have found that your discussion to this point has been helpful, and you suspect that the initiator is holding back and not talking about the really serious issues, you should probe deeper. Often people begin by complaining about a semiserious problem to "test the waters." If you blow up, the conversation is terminated and the really critical issues aren't discussed. However, if you are responsive to and supportive of a frank discussion about problems, the more serious issues will likely surface for discussion.

3. *Agree with some aspect of the complaint.* This is an important point that is difficult for some people to accept because they wonder how it is possible to agree with something they don't feel is true—or they are worried about reinforcing complaining behavior. In practice, this step is probably the best test of whether the responder is committed to using the collaborative approach to conflict management, rather than the avoiding, forcing, or accommodating approaches. People who use the forcing mode will grit their teeth while listening to the initiator, just waiting to find a flaw they can use to launch a counterattack. Or they will simply respond, "I'm sorry, but that's just the way I am. You'll simply have to get used to it." Accommodators will apologize profusely and ask for forgiveness. People who avoid conflicts will acknowledge and agree with the initiator's concerns, but only in a superficial manner because their only concern is how to quickly terminate the awkward conversation.

In contrast, collaborators will demonstrate their concerns for both cooperation and assertiveness by looking for points in the initiator's presentation with which they can genuinely agree. If you follow the supportive communication guidelines discussed in Chapter 4, you will find that it is possible to accept the other person's viewpoint without conceding your own position. Even in the most blatantly malicious and hostile verbal assault (which is more a reflection of the initiator's insecurity than evidence of your inadequacies), there is generally a grain of truth.

For example, a few years ago a junior faculty member in a business school who was being reviewed for promotion received a very unfair appraisal from one of his senior colleagues. Since the junior member knew that the critic was going through a personal crisis, he could have dismissed this criticism as irrelevant and insignificant. However, one particular phrase, "You are stuck on a narrow line of research," kept coming back to mind. There was something there that couldn't be ignored. As a result of turning what was otherwise a very vindictive lecture into a positive suggestion, he made a major career decision that produced very positive outcomes. Furthermore, by publicly giving the senior colleague credit for the suggestion, he substantially strengthened the interpersonal relationship.

There are a number of ways you can agree with a message without accepting its implications (Adler, 1977). You can find an element of truth, as in the incident above. Or you can agree in principle with the argument—"I agree that managers should set a good example," "I agree that it is important for salesclerks to be at the store when it opens." If you can't find anything substantive to agree with, you can always agree with the initiator's perception of the situation: "Well, I can see how you would think that. I have known people who have deliberately shirked their responsibilities." Or you can agree with the person's feelings: "It is obvious that our earlier discussion greatly upset you."

Again, in none of these cases are you agreeing with the initiator's conclusions or evaluations, nor are you conceding your position. You are trying to be agreeable—to foster a problem-solving, rather than argumentative, discussion. Generally, people prepare for a complaint session by mentally cataloging all the evidence supporting their point of view. Once the discussion begins, they introduce as much evidence as necessary to make their argument convincing; that is, they keep arguing until you agree. The more evidence that is introduced, the broader the argument becomes and the more difficult it is to begin investigating solutions. Consequently, establishing a basis of agreement is the key to culminating the first phase of the problem-solving process.

4. *Ask for suggestions for acceptable alternatives.* Once you are certain that you fully understand the initiator's complaint, you should proceed to the solution generation and examination phases of the problem-solving process by asking the initiator for recommended solutions. This triggers an important transition in the discussion by shifting attention from the negative to the positive, and from the past to the future. It also communicates your high regard for the initiator's opinions. This step is a key element in the joint problem-solving process. Some managers listen patiently to a subordinate's complaint, express appreciation for the feedback, say they will rectify the problem, and then terminate the discussion. This leaves the initiator guessing about the outcome of the meeting. Will you take his or her complaint seriously? Will you really change? If so, will the change resolve the problem? It is important to eliminate this ambiguity by agreeing on a plan of action. If the problem is particularly serious or complex, it is useful to write down specific agreements, including assignments and deadlines, as well as providing for a follow-up meeting to check progress.

Mediator

Frequently it is necessary for a third party to intervene in a dispute (Walton, 1968, 1969; Schein, 1969). While this may occur for a variety of reasons, we shall assume in this discussion that the mediator has been invited to help the initiator and responder resolve their differences. We shall further assume that the mediator is the superior of both disputants—though this is not a necessary condition for these guidelines. For example, a hair stylist in a college town beauty salon complained to the owner about the way the receptionist was assigning walk-in business. The stylist felt the receptionist was favoring other beauticians who had been there longer. Since this allegation violated the manager's policy of allocating walk-in business strictly on the basis of beautician availability, she felt it necessary to investigate the complaint. In doing so, she discovered considerable animosity between these two employees, stemming from frequent disagreements regarding the amount of work the stylist had done on a given day. The stylist felt the receptionist was keeping sloppy records, while the receptionist blamed the problem on the stylist's forgetting to hand in her credit slip when she finished with a customer. The problems between the stylist and the receptionist appeared to be serious enough to the participants and broad enough in scope that the manager decided to call both parties into her office to help them resolve their differences. The following guidelines are intended to help mediators avoid the common pitfalls of this role shown in Table 8.6.

1. *Acknowledge that a conflict exists and propose a problem-solving approach for resolving it.* It is vital that the mediator take the problems between conflicting parties seriously. If they feel they have a serious problem, the mediator should not belittle its significance. Remarks like, "I'm surprised that two intelligent people like you have not been able to work out your disagreement. We have more important things to do here than get all worked up over such petty issues," will make both parties defensive and interfere with

TABLE 8.6 *Ten Ways to Fail as a Mediator*

1. After you have listened to the argument for a short time, begin to nonverbally communicate your discomfort with the discussion (e.g., sit back, begin to fidget).

2. Communicate your agreement with one of the parties (e.g., through facial expressions, posture, chair position, reinforcing comments).

3. Say that you shouldn't be talking about this kind of thing at work or where others can hear you.

4. Discourage the expression of emotion. Suggest that the discussion would better be held later after both parties have cooled off.

5. Suggest that both parties are wrong. Point out the problems with both points of view.

6. Suggest part way through the discussion that possibly you aren't the person who should be helping solve this problem.

7. See if you can get both parties to attack you.

8. Belittle the seriousness of the problem.

9. Change the subject (e.g., ask advice for helping you solve one of your problems).

10. Express displeasure that the two parties are experiencing conflict (e.g., imply that it might undermine the solidarity of the work group).

Adapted from William Morris and Marshall Sashkin, *Organizational behavior in action* (St. Paul: West Publishing, 1976), p. 180.

any serious problem-solving efforts. While you might wish that your subordinates could have worked out their disagreement without bothering you, this is not the time to lecture them on self-reliance. Inducing guilt feelings by implying personal failure during an already emotional experience tends to distract the participants from the substantive issues at hand. Seldom is this conducive to problem solving.

One early decision a mediator has to make is whether to convene a joint problem-solving session or to meet with the parties separately. The following diagnostic questions should help you weigh the trade-off. First, what is the current position of the disputants? Are both aware a problem exists? Are they equally motivated to work on solving the problem? The more similar the awareness and motivation of the parties, the more likely it is that a joint session will be productive. If there is a serious discrepancy in awareness and motivation, the mediator should work to reduce that discrepancy through one-on-one meetings before bringing the disputants together.

Second, what is the current relationship between the disputants? Does their work require them to interact frequently? Is a good working relationship critical for their individual job performance? What has their relationship been in the past? What is the difference in their formal status in the organization?

As we discussed earlier, joint problem-solving sessions are most productive between individuals of equal status who are required to work together regularly. This does not mean that joint meetings should not be held between a supervisor and subordinate, only that greater care needs to be taken in preparing for such a meeting. Specifically, if a department head becomes involved in a dispute between a worker and supervisor, the department head should make sure that the worker does not feel this meeting will just serve as an excuse for two managers to gang up on him or her. A joint problem-solving session is particularly useful when it involves co-workers who have a history of recurring disputes, especially if these disputes should have been resolvable without a mediator. Such a history generally suggests a lack of conflict management or problem-solving skills on the part of the disputants, or it might signify attention-getting behavior. In these cases a joint problem-solving session in which the mediator takes a strong role to demonstrate to the disputants the process for resolving their conflicts can be a positive learning experience. It also provides an opportunity for the supervisor to challenge his or her subordinates to work out these types of problems between themselves in the future.

Third, what is the nature of the problem? Is the complaint substantive in nature and easily verifiable? If the problem stems from conflicting role responsibilities and the actions of both parties in question are common knowledge, then a joint problem-solving session can begin on a common information and experiential base. In contrast, if the complaint stems from differences in managerial style, values, personality characteristics, and so forth, bringing the parties together immediately following a complaint may seriously undermine the problem-solving process. Complaints that will likely be interpreted as threats to the self-image of one or both parties (Who am I? What do I stand for?) warrant considerable individual discussion before a joint meeting is called. To avoid individuals' feeling like they are being ambushed in a meeting, you should discuss serious problems with them ahead of time, in private.

2. *In seeking out the perspective of both parties, maintain a neutral posture regarding the disputants—if not the issues.*   Effective mediation requires impartiality. If a mediator shows strong personal bias in favor of one party in a joint problem-solving session, the other party may simply get up and walk out. However, this type of personal bias is more likely to creep out in private conversations with the disputants. Statements like, "I can't believe he really did *that!*" and "Everyone seems to be having trouble working with Charlie these days," imply that the mediator is taking sides, and any attempt to appear impartial in a joint meeting will seem merely window dressing to appease the other party. No matter how well-intentioned or justified these comments might be, they destroy the credibility of the mediator in the long run. In contrast, the effective mediator respects the right of each party to his or her point of view and makes sure that both perspectives are expressed adequately.

Occasionally it is not possible to be impartial on the issues. One person may have violated company policy, engaged in unethical competition with a colleague, or broken a personal agreement. In these cases the challenge of the mediator is to separate the offense from the offender. If a person is clearly in the wrong the inappropriate behavior needs to be corrected, but in such a way that the individual doesn't feel his or her image and working relationships have been permanently marred.

3. *Focus the discussion on the impact the conflict is having on performance. Keep the discussion issue oriented, not personality oriented.* It is important that the mediator maintain a problem-solving atmosphere throughout the discussion. This is not to say that strong emotional statements don't have their place. People often associate effective problem solving with a calm, highly rational discussion of the issues and a personality attack with a highly emotional outburst. However, it is important to separate these processes and outcomes. Placid, cerebral discussions often don't solve problems, and impassioned statements don't have to be negative or targeted at individuals. The critical point about process is that it should be centered on the issues and the consequences of continued conflict on performance. Even when an offensive behavior (to the other party) obviously stems from a personality quirk, the discussion of the problem should be limited to the behavior. As we stated earlier, attributions about motives or generalizations from specific events to personal proclivities distract participants from the problem-solving process. It is important that the mediator establish and maintain these ground rules. When a mediator suspects that the disputants are going to have difficulty refraining from personal attacks, it may be useful to discuss the "XYZ formula" for presenting complaints and urge the parties to adopt it in the meeting.

4. *Help the disputants put their conflict in perspective by identifying areas of agreement and focusing on one issue at a time.* Often disputants get to the point of requiring mediation simply because the disagreement has been blown out of perspective. If the disagreement has gone on for some time, solving the problem may be less important to the parties than winning the argument. Their ego is involved and they want to avoid the humiliation of being labeled a loser. Another common pitfall that frequently creates an impasse is focusing on several issues at once. Particularly when the parties have worked together for a long time, there is a tendency for them to store up problems until something finally triggers a blowup. Then they have difficulty resolving their conflict because they keep expanding the dispute to include more and more related issues.

The effective mediator helps disputants overcome both of these obstacles by breaking complex problems into smaller components. Some issues hang together and must be treated as a unit, so the objective is to carve up a problem into small enough chunks that they can be dealt with realistically without violating critical interdependencies. It is also important to help disputants distinguish between central and peripheral issues. Once this is done, it is advisable to start with one of the easier problems. This enables the mediator to demonstrate the value of collaboration and establish the groundwork for addressing particularly challenging, long-standing problems.

Another key ingredient of effective mediation is helping disputants overcome their feelings of polarization. It is common for participants in an intense conflict to feel that they are on opposite sides of all issues—that they have little in common. Helping them recognize that they agree on most things and that only a relatively small number of issues are the basis for their dispute often represents a major turning point in resolving long-standing feuds.

5. *Assume the role of a facilitator, rather than a judge.* When the parties must work closely and have a history of chronic interpersonal problems, it is often more important to teach problem-solving skills than to resolve the dispute. This is done best when the mediator adopts the posture of facilitator. The role of judge is to render a verdict regarding a problem in the past, not to teach people how to solve their problems in the future. While some disputes obviously involve right and wrong actions, most interpersonal problems stem from differences in perspective. In these situations it is important that the mediator avoid being seduced into rendering a verdict by comments like, "Well, you're the boss, tell us which one is right," or more subtly, "I wonder if I did what was right?" The problem with a mediator's assuming the role of judge is that it sets in motion processes that are antithetical to effective interpersonal problem solving. The parties focus on persuading the mediator of their innocence and the other party's guilt, rather than striving to improve their working relationship with the assistance of the mediator. The disputants work to establish facts about what happened in the past, rather than reaching an agreement about what ought to happen in the future. Simply stated, when a mediator assumes the role of judge, he or she encourages the disputants to focus on the problem; when he or she assumes the role of facilitator, they are more likely to focus on the solution. Consequently, a key aspect of effective mediation is helping the disputants explore multiple alternatives in a nonjudgmental manner.

6. *Make sure that both disputants fully support the agreed-upon solution.* A common mistake of ineffective mediators is terminating the discussion prematurely. They feel that once the problem has been solved in principle, the disputants can be left to work out the details on their own. Or they assume that because one of the parties has recommended a solution that appears very reasonable and workable, the second disputant will be willing to implement it. It is very important that the mediator insist on a specific plan of action both parties are equally willing to implement. If the mediator suspects any hesitancy on the part of either disputant, this needs to be explored explicitly—"Tom, I sense that you are somewhat less enthusiastic than Sue about this plan. Is there something about it that bothers you?" When the mediator is confident that both parties support the plan, he or she should check to make sure that they are aware of their respective responsibilities and then propose a mechanism for monitoring progress. This might involve another formal meeting or the mediator's stopping by both individuals' offices to get a progress report.

SUMMARY AND BEHAVIORAL GUIDELINES

Conflict is a difficult and controversial topic. In our culture it has negative connotations. We place a high value on getting along with people by being kind and friendly. Moreover, many people intellectually understand the value of conflict, but feel uncomfortable when confronted by it. One reason for this discomfort is lack of understanding of the conflict process, as well as lack of training in ways to handle interpersonal confrontations effectively.

Conflict can be produced by a variety of circumstances: irreconcilable personal differences, discrepancies in information, role incompatibilities, and environmentally induced stress. These causes, and the resulting conflicts, differ in both frequency and intensity. For example, information-based conflicts occur frequently but are easily resolved because the disputants have low personal stakes in the outcome. In contrast, conflicts grounded in differences of perceptions and expectations are generally very intense and difficult to diffuse.

There are basically five approaches to handling conflict: avoiding, compromising, collaborating, forcing, and accommodating. These reflect different degrees of assertiveness and cooperativeness. There is no best way to handle all conflicts. Instead, in choosing a response mode, managers should consider their dominant personality characteristics, the quality of the ongoing relationship between the actors, and the nature and seriousness of the problem. However, the collaborative approach generally has the most positive effect on the disputants. When it is used effectively, the parties tend to be most satisfied with the outcome. Unfortunately, the collaborative approach is the most difficult to implement successfully in a highly emotional one-on-one situation. It takes little skill to impose your authority on another person, to withdraw from a confrontation, to split the difference between opponents, or to abandon your position at the slightest sign of opposition. Therefore, the behavior guidelines for resolving an interpersonal confrontation related to complaint giving and receiving using a problem-solving approach have been described in detail. They are summarized below for each of the three roles in a conflict situation. These summary statements should serve as behavioral guidelines as you practice managing conflict.

Initiator

1. Avoid making accusations and attributing motives to the respondent.

2. Maintain personal ownership of the problem.

3. Succinctly describe your problem in terms of behaviors, consequences, and feelings. ("When you do X, Y happens, and I feel Z.") Use a specific incident to explore the root causes of a problem.

4. Specify the expectations or standards that have been violated.

5. Persist until understood.

6. Encourage two-way interaction by inviting the respondent to express his or her perspective and ask questions.

7. Don't "dump" all your issues at once. Approach multiple issues incrementally. Proceed from simple to complex, easy to hard.

8. Appeal to what you share (principles, goals, constraints).

Respondent

1. Respond appropriately to the initiator's emotions. If necessary, let the person "blow off steam" before addressing substantive issues. If the emotions are inappropriate, interject ground rules for collaborative problem solving.

2. Establish a climate for joint problem solving by showing genuine concern and interest. Respond empathetically, even if you disagree with the complaint.

3. Avoid justifying your actions as your first response.

4. Seek additional information about the problem. Ask questions that channel the initiator's remarks from general to specific and evaluative to descriptive statements.

5. Focus on one issue, or one part of an issue, at a time.

6. Agree with some aspect of the complaint (facts, perceptions, feelings, or principles).

7. Ask the initiator to suggest more acceptable behaviors.

8. Agree on a remedial plan of action.

Mediator

1. Acknowledge that conflict exists and treat it seriously. Do not belittle the problem or chide the disputants for not being able to resolve the conflict on their own.

2.   Construct a manageable agenda by breaking down complex or multiple issues. Help disputants distinguish central from peripheral elements. Begin working on one of the easier components.

3.   Do not take sides. Remain neutral regarding the disputants as well as the issues as long as violation of policy is not involved.

4.   Focus the discussion on the impact the conflict is having on performance and the detrimental effect of a continued conflict.

5.   Keep the interaction issue oriented, not personality oriented. Also, make sure that neither disputant dominates the conversation.

6.   Help disputants keep their conflict in perspective by identifying areas of agreement or common viewpoint.

7.   Help disputants generate multiple alternatives in a nonjudgmental manner.

8.   Make sure that both parties are satisfied with the proposed resolution and committed to implementing it.

REFERENCES

Adler, R. B. Satisfying personal needs: Managing conflicts, making requests, and saying no. *Confidence in communication: A guide to assertive and social skills.* New York: Holt, Rinehart & Winston, 1977.

Boulding, E. Further reflections on conflict management. In R. L. Kahn & E. Boulding (Eds.), *Power and conflict in organizations.* New York: Basic Books, 1964.

Carnegie, D. *How to win friends and influence people.* New York: Simon and Schuster, 1936.

Cummings, L. L., Harnett, D. L., & Stevens, O. J. Risk, fate, conciliation and trust: An international study of attitudinal differences among executives. *Academy of Management Journal,* 1971, *14,* 285–304.

Downey, K., Sheridan, J., & Slocum, J. The path-goal theory of leadership: A longitudinal analysis. *Organizational Behavior and Human Performance,* 1976, *16,* 156–176.

Filley, A. C. Some normative issues in conflict management. *California Management Review,* 1978, *71,* 61–66.

Filley, A. C. Conflict resolution: The ethic of the good loser. In R. C. Huseman, C. M. Logue, & D. L. Freshly (Eds.), *Readings in interpersonal and organizational behavior.* Boston: Holbrook Press, 1977.

Filley, A. C. *Interpersonal conflict resolution.* Glenview, Ill.: Scott, Foresman, 1975.

Gordon, T. *Parent effectiveness training.* New York: Wyden, 1970.

Janis, I. *Victims of group think.* Boston: Houghton-Mifflin, 1972.

Kelly, J. Make conflict work for you. *Harvard Business Review,* July-August 1970, *48,* 103–113.

King, D. Three cheers for conflict. *Personnel,* 1981, *58,* 13–22.

Kipnis, D., & Schmidt, S. An influence perspective in bargaining within organizations. In M. H. Bazerman & R. J. Lewicki (Eds.), *Bargaining inside organizations.* Beverly Hills, Calif.: Sage Publications, 1983.

Latham, G., & Wexley, K. *Increasing productivity through performance appraisal.* Reading, Mass.: Addison Wesley, 1981.

Maslow, A. *Eupsychian management.* Homewood, Ill.: Irwin, 1965.

Phillips, E., & Cheston, R. Conflict resolution: What works. *California Management Review,* 1979, *21,* 76–83.

Porter, E. H. *Manual of administration interpretation for strength deployment inventory.* LaJolla, Calif.: Personal Strengths Assessment Service, 1980.

Robbins, S. P. Conflict management and conflict resolution are not synonymous terms. *California Management Review,* 1978, *21,* 67–75.

Robbins, S. P. *Managing organizational conflict: A nontraditional approach.* Englewood Cliffs, N.J.: Prentice Hall, 1974.

Ruble, T., & Thomas, K. Support for a two-dimensional model of conflict behavior. *Organizational Behavior and Human Performance,* 1976, *16,* 145.

Schein, E. H. *Process consultation: Its role in organizational development.* Reading, Mass.: Addison Wesley, 1969.

Schmidt, W. H., & Tannenbaum, R. Management of differences. *Harvard Business Review,* Nov.-Dec. 1965, *38,* 107–115.

Schriesheim, C., & VonGlinow, M. The path-goal theory of leadership: A theoretical and empirical analysis. *Academy of Management Journal,* 1977, *20,* 398–405.

Thomas, K. Conflict and conflict management. In M. D. Dunnette (Ed.), *Handbook of industrial and organizational psychology.* London: Routledge and Kegan Paul, 1956.

Thomas, K. W. Toward multi-dimensional values in teaching: The example of conflict behavior. *Academy of Management Review,* 1977, *2,* 487.

Walton, R. *Interpersonal peacekeeping: Confrontations and third party consultation.* Reading, Mass.: Addison Wesley, 1969.

Walton, R. Interpersonal confrontation and basic third party function: A case study. *Journal of Applied Behavioral Science,* 1968, *4,* 323–343.

Whetten, D. A., & Dyer, W. *Leadership and Machiavellianism.* Paper presented at Meetings of the Midwest Academy of Management, Ann Arbor, Michigan, April 1975. ■

■ *Skill Analysis*

The Harried Supervisor

Al is a middle-aged supervisor of a drafting department. When one of the young draftsmen, Mel, knocks on his door to discuss a problem, Al is looking for some papers in his desk drawer.

SCENE 1

Mel: Excuse me, Al . . . Can I talk to you a minute?

Al (reluctantly, without looking up): Yeah, come on in, Mel. What's on your mind?

Mel (sitting down, obviously very nervous): Well, uh, I, uh . . . I've been wanting to talk to you about the way I feel like I'm being treated around here.

Al (absently, still intent on finding something in his desk): Oh yeah? Somebody treating you badly?

Mel: Well, I don't know if it's so much that I've, uh, been treated badly, I just feel that, uh, maybe I'm not getting the opportunities to do some of the jobs I'd like to do. I feel like, uh, maybe the work could be divided up a little bit more evenly.

Al (still searching): Oh yeah? Tell me all about it.

Mel: Well, last week that Lando job came in, uh, I noticed that Bob got it and I wondered why I didn't get it. Was I ever considered?

Al (looking at Mel, but still preoccupied): Now listen, Mel, this place is a madhouse. No supplies, and the orders are pouring in. I'm doing the best I can, kid. I mean, it's going to be all right. Don't worry about it.

Mel: I know things are busy right now, I know there's a lot of pressures, but I just want you to know that I want an opportunity to do those jobs, too. I'd like a *challenge*, Al, and I don't feel like you are really being fair.

Al (very annoyed, slams the door shut): Hey! Hey! FAIR! (Chuckles to himself.) That's all I need today. Fair! See that? These are orders that I have to fill. I can't get any supplies. There are fifty draftsmen out there and *everybody* wants to be treated fairly, and all of a sudden I get a *prima donna* in here wailing the blues. . . .

Mel (defensively): Al, I'd just like a chance to work at some of those more interesting jobs. I wonder why I'm not getting an opportunity. . . .

Al (somewhat sarcastically): Sure, Mel. OK, kid. I'll tell you what we'll do. . . . You want a challenge? All right, the next *challenging* job that

Adapted from a videotape presentation, *Listening with Understanding*, produced by Zenger and Miller, Inc., 1977. Used with permission.

comes in, I *guarantee* you will get it. And we'll see how you *handle* a challenge. Sound OK to you?

Mel (not sure how to respond): Uh, well, sure.

Al: Fine. I've got to go to a meeting now. *But I guarantee you . . . you're going to get a challenge* (gathers books and papers together) *and you'd better live up to it* (shakes his finger for emphasis).

Mel: All right.

Al: See ya.

Mel: Thanks. (After Al leaves, a look of horror comes over Mel.)

SCENE 2

Mel: Excuse me . . . Al?

Al (stops looking for papers and turns toward the door): Hi ya, Mel.

Mel: Can I talk to you a minute?

Al (gesturing to the chair next to his desk): Yeah, sure, come on in, sit down.

Mel: Thank you.

Al (intent, leaning forward in his chair): What's on your mind?

Mel: Well, I . . . I've wanted to come in and, uh, talk a little bit to you about the way I feel like I'm, uh, being treated around here.

Al (earnest, somewhat surprised): Oh, really? Something going wrong?

Mel: Well . . . I just feel like, uh, maybe if the work was divided up a little more evenly, I'd have a chance to do some jobs that would be more interesting to me.

Al: Something in particular happen? Any special job?

Mel: Well, yeah, as a matter of fact, last week that Lando job came in and I was very interested in working on it. I'm very interested in doing that kind of work, but I noticed that Bob got it. I was wondering if I was even *considered* for that job. I want a challenge, Al; I'm tired of doing the same old jobs.

Al: You want a challenge. *That is pleasant to hear.* I must say you are one of the few who have ever come in and asked me for more challenging work and I'm glad to hear it. Now as far as the Lando job is concerned, the only reason you didn't get that job is because I looked up on the records and you were busy with another job. It wasn't a question of whether or not you could handle it. (Pauses and scans a schedule on the wall.) Listen, there are a couple of difficult jobs coming up next week. I understand there are a lot of innovations in the Henderson project and I think it might interest you very much.

Mel: Yeah, it sure would.

Al (sighs, reflectively): As you know, this place has been a mess recently. We're six weeks back ordered, we can't get supplies, there are fifty men out there, and it's difficult for me to keep in touch with each of them.

Mel: Yeah, I know there's a lot of pressure right now, but I just wanted to come in and tell you how I felt about my work.

Al: That's why it's good that you did come in. I mean, how else could I know how the men feel out there? (Looks at his watch.) I have to go to a meeting now. . . . It's been prescheduled. But how about continuing our discussion tomorrow morning at 10 o'clock? Tonight I'll look up the Henderson schedule and see what I can find out about it. We can talk about it in the morning and see if it suits what you are looking for.

Mel: All right.

Al: Sound good?

Mel: Sure does.

Al: Have a good day and I'll see you at 10 o'clock.

Mel (obviously satisfied and relieved): OK, thanks a lot, Al.

Webster Arsenal

Ross A. Webber

Webster Arsenal has been one of the U.S. Army's rifle and pistol manufacturing facilities since before the Civil War. Located in central Indiana, it is the largest industrial employer in the area even though it employs only 800 persons.

The commanding officer and arsenal director is Colonel Sheridan Grant, a career Army officer. Grant has been at Webster for two years and expects to remain until his retirement in two more years because he has been passed over for promotion to general. His associate director is a civilian, William Johnson, who has spent his entire career at Webster since leaving the military twenty years earlier. Johnson was promoted to associate director last year because he had a good record as a tough production manager and was then the most senior executive. Most of the additional personnel are civilians who are members of the civil service. A few Army people occupy guard, clerical, and research positions, but their duties are essentially the same as those of the civilians with whom they work. The associate director is charged with responsibility for most day-to-day operations.

Although the arsenal is a nonprofit institution, it does have performance criteria set by the Department of the Army in Washington. Essentially these include the following:

1. Remaining within budget.
2. Meeting production quotas with necessary reliability and quality.
3. Reducing costs on standard items.

SOURCE: Ross Webber, *Management: Basic elements of managing organizations* (Homewood, Ill.: Richard D. Irwin, 1975), pp. 139–145.

4. Maintaining equipment in working order.
5. Maintaining personnel at peak efficiency.
6. Upgrading personnel skills through training.

Most of the production and testing equipment is old because the Army has not provided sufficient funds for maintenance or replacement. Washington officials have chosen to spend money on more glamorous, sophisticated, and innovative weapons systems than the simple rifles and handguns manufactured at Webster. As an apparent result of these equipment problems, the arsenal has experienced great difficulty in meeting its objectives. Prior to approximately eight months ago, the facility usually failed to achieve objectives only one or two months a year, but now it has failed four months in a row. A special problem has been inaccurate rifling (cutting the spiral grooves inside the gun barrel), which has required 30 to 40 percent reworking every month.

Colonel Grant is not a typical Army officer, or at least he does not fit the stereotype. The best physical description of him is that he is everyone's image of the kindly father—or grandfather, because his hair is all grey at fifty-one. Grant expresses great faith in people:

> I have been in the Army for almost thirty years and the number of outright shirkers and goldbrickers I have encountered can be counted on my fingers. Most men will give you honest effort if you treat them fairly, show a strong personal interest, keep them informed, and let them participate in decisions so they can affect some aspects of their work.
>
> In addition, an officer or manager should keep his objectives in view and demonstrate a sense of perspective. I never conduct inspections to demonstrate that I'm a tough officer, only to assist people in improving performance. No room has to be perfectly clean, none of that white-glove stuff, just clean enough so as not to affect product quality. In fact, my inspections here aren't really inspections at all, more like informal chats from time to time.

When William Johnson was promoted to associate director, Colonel Grant talked with him about his leadership philosophy. Johnson thought his views were fine, but he said he felt production workers needed a firm hand or performance would deteriorate.

Johnson set to work with an energy belying his years to correct the deficiencies he observed. New cleaning and inspection schedules were instituted, and a new gleam became evident in the plant. The floors and machinery definitely improved in appearance. Several training course instructors spoke to Johnson about employees' complaints that their supervisors were not allowing them to attend the training courses held on company time, but Johnson replied that the place would have to be put in shipshape order first. Then he would see that the men were allowed to attend class again (although he did wonder how much training could be accomplished in the classroom).

Several supervisors complained to the colonel during this period about how tough things had become in recent months, but Grant reassured them that things would improve when budgetary pressure let up. Meanwhile, they should give their best efforts because he, the arsenal, the fighting men, and the nation were dependent on them. At one point Grant considered talking to Johnson about the complaints but declined to do so because he believed that a subordinate should have freedom to perform a task delegated to him.

The department head in rifling is Frank Widner, the youngest supervisor in the arsenal. A mechanical engineer from the state university, Widner had spent three years in the Army as an infantry officer, with two years in Vietnam. He had been awarded a Purple Heart and a Bronze Star for bravery in action. Widner wears his hair as long as he thinks he can get away with and sports a fine mustache. His appearance is in sharp contrast to that of most of the short-haired middle-aged employees he supervises. Yet he is close to his subordinates; he plays with them on a departmental softball team and hoists a few beers several evenings a week.

Widner is having trouble, no doubt about it. Quality has been declining and he does not seem to be able to do anything about it. His men say that this is due to the old equipment, which breaks down almost every day. Frequently, the maintenance gang (which is in a separate department) doesn't have the time or can't fix it, so Widner has been repairing it himself. He really is a wizard mechanic, but he finds himself spending most of his time repairing equipment himself while his men watch.

Widner and Johnson have some conflicts. Widner can put up with the older man's wisecracking about hippies and hair, but he resents Johnson's criticism of his department. In response to Johnson's pressures to keep the department area clean, Widner has assigned two disgruntled operators as cleaners and asked the others to join in when they are waiting for their equipment to be repaired or whenever they can.

The simmering feud between Johnson and Widner exploded yesterday afternoon when Widner had his shirt off and was lying under the rifling drill replacing a stripped gear. When Johnson came in, the following conversation took place:

Johnson: Widner, where on earth are you?

Widner: Over here, under the machine, O.K.?

Johnson: Get up here. Those goldbrickers of yours are sitting in the courtyard drinking Cokes. Break time ended ten minutes ago. You can't even keep your area clean, much less meet your production goals. What are you doing about it?

Widner: Nothing! They've worked hard today; they'll be back as soon as the break is over. Besides, there's not much for them to do because of this lousy equipment. When are you going to fight for some money to replace it? That's what you should be doing, not pussyfooting around here looking for dust particles.

Johnson: O.K. wise guy, that's it. I'm going to see what the colonel thinks about this. Maybe you will be out in the park strumming a guitar with your hippie friends tomorrow.

Johnson immediately went to see Colonel Grant. When Johnson rushed into the colonel's office, the following discussion was held:

Johnson: Colonel, you've got to can Widner. His men are running wild and he's insubordinate. I want him out.
Grant: Hold on, tell me calmly what happened. Frank seems like a nice young man. I'm sure there must be some simple misunderstanding.
Johnson: Like hell, he's no leader and I think he's chicken. He does the work while his men stand around. He's afraid of them and too buddy-buddy. Unless you do something, I'm going to file a formal complaint with Washington.
Grant: Let me talk to Frank first. Then I'll get back to you.
Johnson: O.K., but I've run out of patience.

At the meeting between Colonel Grant and Frank Widner, this was the dialogue:

Grant: Frank, what seems to be the trouble between you and Johnson?
Widner: Nothing that his minding his own business wouldn't cure. He keeps butting into my department telling me to clean up a storeroom, wax the floor, cut the break time, and other picayune matters. He doesn't understand that our main problem is keeping the equipment going.
Grant: But aren't you fixing the equipment yourself too often? What of the maintenance department or your own men?
Widner: Time is too precious, I can't wait on them. There are too few maintenance men, and I need to assign my people on rework and cleaning to keep Johnson off my back. What we really need is more maintenance men and new equipment. Can you get them for us?
Grant: I'm trying but nobody seems to listen. I can't argue too strongly because we'd only make enemies and that would hurt us all. You have to go slowly on this kind of thing. I'm sure things will work out eventually. In the meantime, try to get along with Johnson.
Widner: O.K. Sure, but he'd better stay off my back.

Today William Johnson walked into the Rifling Department ten minutes before the end of the shift. Widner was conducting calibration tests on the equipment while his men were changing into their softball uniforms for a game to be held shortly after work. Johnson burst out:

Johnson: You loafers can't even keep your equipment running and you're playing games; . . . And Widner, you incompetent, you're yellow, afraid of your men. I've had it. If the colonel is too scared to act, I'm not. A complaint about you will be in Washington tonight.

Without saying a word, Widner punched Johnson in the face.

DISCUSSION QUESTIONS

The Harried Supervisor

1. Reflecting on the sources of conflict discussed in this chapter, identify the key factors that precipitated this confrontation.

2. Identify the principles of supportive communication and conflict management violated in the first scene.

3. Identify the specific behavioral guidelines for the roles of initiator and responder exemplified in the second scene.

Webster Arsenal

1. Which conflict management approaches were used by Grant, Johnson, and Widner in this case? What effect did each person's approach have on the other two? How effective was each approach in resolving the problems at Webster Arsenal?

2. What should you do when your conflict management approach differs from that used by the other party?

3. Using the behavioral guidelines discussed in this chapter, assume the role of Grant (mediator), Johnson (initiator), or Widner (responder) and be prepared to discuss how each could have handled the encounters better. ■

■ *Skill Practice*

Win as Much as You Can

William Gellermann

The object of this exercise is to win as much as you can. It is played in groups of eight (four pairs). For ten successive rounds, you and your partner are to choose an X or a Y. You can earn money depending on the pattern of choices made in your group of four pairs. The pay-off schedule is as follows:

4 X's	Each pair loses $1
3 X's 1 Y	Each wins $1 each loses $3
2 X's 2 Y's	Each wins $2 Each loses $2
1 X 3 Y's	each wins $3 Each loses $1
4 Y's	Each wins $1

There are six rules:

1. You may confer only with your partner when making a decision except for rounds 5, 8, and 10.
2. You should write down your choice as soon as you and your partner agree. Once it is written, it cannot be changed.
3. You may not talk to other members of your group except at times to be designated.
4. You should keep a running total of your winnings and losses on the following chart.
5. Note that your payoff for bonus round 5 is multiplied by 3, bonus round 8 by 5, and bonus round 10 by 10.
6. In these three bonus rounds, the four pairs of players in each group will be given an opportunity to confer with each other prior to making their individual decisions.

SOURCE: J. W. Pfeiffer and J. E. Jones, *Structured experiences for human relations training*, vol. 2 (San Diego: University Associates, 1970), pp. 62–67.

Round	Time Allotted	Confer with	Choice (X or Y)	Won	Lost	Balance
1	1½ min.	Partner				
2	1 min.	Partner				
3	1 min.	Partner				
4	1 min.	Partner				
5	1½ min.	Group				x3
6	1 min.	Partner				
7	1 min.	Partner				
8	1½ min.	Group				x5
9	1 min.	Partner				
10	2 mins.	Group				x10

Total

Responding to Conflictual Encounters

As you read each of the following situations, try to identify closely with the central character. After you have completed reading each, review the behavioral guidelines in this chapter and be prepared to role-play each situation in class. Observers should use the observation sheet to give feedback to participants.

GASPING FOR AIR

You have decided to take your family out to the local steak house for dinner to celebrate your son's tenth birthday. You are a single parent, so getting home from work in time to prepare a nice dinner is very difficult. On entering the restaurant, you ask the hostess to seat you in the nonsmoking section because your eight-year-old daughter is allergic to tobacco smoke. On your way to your seat, you notice that the restaurant seems crowded for a Tuesday night.

After you and your children are seated and have placed your orders, your conversation turns to the family plans for the approaching Christmas holidays. Suddenly you become aware that your daughter is sneezing and her eyes have become puffy and red. You look around and notice a lively group of businessmen seated at the table behind you, all of whom are smoking. As you sit for a minute pondering what to do, you realize from their conversation that they are salesmen celebrating their success in landing a major new account. Looking back at your daughter, you see that she is suffering a great deal from the smoke and you realize that you must do something quickly. You rush to the front of the restaurant and find the hostess. After you explain the situation to her, she says she is sorry but the table next to you was the last one available for seating that group. This is generally a slow night for the steak house, but a wedding party has taken up most of the space and there is a large convention in town. The hostess again apologizes for the situation but says that, because of the large line of people waiting impatiently to be served, she doesn't see what she can do. She is obviously upset by the pressure resulting from the overbooking.

CAN LARRY FIT IN?

You are the manager of an auditing team for a major accounting firm. You are sitting in your office reading some complicated new reporting procedures that have just arrived from the home office. Your concentration is suddenly interrupted by a loud knock on your door. Without waiting for an invitation to enter, Larry, one of your auditors, bursts into your office. He is obviously very upset and it is not difficult for you to surmise why he is in such a nasty mood. You have just posted the audit assignments for the next month and you scheduled Larry for a job you knew he wouldn't like. Larry is one of your senior auditors and the company norm is that they get the better assignments. This particular job will require him to spend two weeks away from home, in a remote town, working with a company whose records are notorious for being a mess.

Unfortunately, you have had to assign several of these less desirable audits to Larry recently because you are short of personnel. But that's not the only reason. You have received several complaints from the junior staff members recently about Larry's treating them in an obnoxious manner. They feel he is always looking for an opportunity to boss them around, as if he were their supervisor instead of a member of the audit team. As a result, your whole operation works smoothly when you can send Larry out of town on a solo project for several days. It keeps him from coming into your office telling you how to do your job, and the morale of the rest of the auditing staff is significantly higher.

Larry slams the door and proceeds to express his anger over this assignment. He says you are deliberately trying to undermine his status in the group by giving him all the dirty assignments. He accuses you of being insensitive to his feelings and says that if things don't change, he is going to register a formal complaint with your boss.

FIRST DAY ON THE JOB

You are Mr. West, the new manager of the Tampa Pump and Valve Company (as portrayed in the Introduction). You have just returned from your business trip to Venezuela and are midway through your first day in the office when

Pearl enters quite agitated. She says that Bill Marshall is in her office requesting an urgent meeting with you. He says he doesn't have all the budgets from the department heads and his report to the corporate comptroller is overdue. She says he is pretty upset and suggests that you meet with him. You can pretty much guess what the problem is and asks Pearl to have Bill come in.

After exchanging pleasantries, Bill comes right to the point. Tom Evert in R&D has ignored repeated requests for his departmental budget for the coming fiscal year. Bill accuses Tom of trying to make him look bad by deliberately dragging his feet. He further implies that this problem would never have occurred if Mr. Manners, your predecessor, had been a stronger leader. He urges you to come down hard on Tom to show him that office politics with the budget will not be tolerated at TP&V. You agree to look into the matter and get back to him.

After Bill leaves your office, you handle a couple of pressing phone calls and then buzz Pearl to check and see if Tom is available for you to discuss this problem with his budget. She says that that won't be necessary because she can see him coming up the hall right now towards her desk and he is obviously steamed about something. You ask her to have Tom come in when he arrives. When he enters your office, Tom skips the small talk and blurts out that he met Bill Marshall in the hall a few minutes ago and Bill told him, in a very superior tone of voice, that he had just been in to see the new boss about R&D's tardy budget and that you were going to come down hard on R&D for making the division look bad. Tom is very upset that you are taking Bill's side on this issue without first listening to his side of the story. You assure Tom that you did listen to Bill's complaint earlier in the day but your response had been only that you would look into the matter. In fact, you had asked Pearl to set up a meeting with him just before he entered your office.

After hearing that you are definitely interested in why he hadn't gotten his budget in on time, Tom proceeds to describe the running battle between R&D and Bill Marshall for the past several months. He has repeatedly requested money from Bill to explore a promising new process for extracting critical basic compounds from waste products. He speaks enthusiastically about its promise as a new product line for this division, as well as an opportunity to establish TP&V's reputation as an innovator in the industry. Then his tone turns bitter as he describes Bill's attempt to influence corporate policy by saying that this division shouldn't be getting into the chemical business. Tom claims that this refusal was a thinly disguised power play by Bill to become more influential during a transition period in the division. Tom concludes by saying he knew that the only way he could keep this promising new opportunity from being buried by an arrogant staff specialist was to hold out submitting his department's budget for the new year until he got a hearing on his request for more development funds.

It is obvious from your conversations with Bill and Tom that this problem has gotten out of hand and needs to be cleared up quickly. You also recognize that since it is the first "test of your mettle" as the new boss, you must handle this issue fairly but firmly. You assure Tom that you will get back to him soon on this matter. After he leaves, you ask Pearl to set up a meeting between you, Bill, and Tom for the next morning. You hope they will both be in better moods after thinking about the problem overnight.

The next day when Tom and Bill enter your office, you can see that your optimism was not warranted. Their expressions reflect strong feelings of apprehension, anger, and distrust. You think to yourself, "There must be a better way to break into a new job."

OBSERVATION SHEET FOR CONFLICT MANAGEMENT ROLE PLAYS

As an observer, place a check after any behavior the role players exhibit. It is preferable to focus on only one role (initiator, respondent, or mediator) at a time. Be prepared to make suggestions for improvement, as well as to identify particularly effective elements in each performance.

	Check if practiced
Initiator	
Maintained personal ownership of the problem	_____
Avoided making accusations or attributing motives	_____
Succinctly described the problem (behaviors, outcomes, feelings)	_____
Specified expectations violated	_____
Persisted until understood	_____
Encouraged two-way interaction	_____
Approached multiple issues incrementally (proceeded from simple to complex, easy to hard)	_____
Appealed to what the disputants had in common (goals, principles, constraints)	_____
Respondent	
Responded appropriately to the initiator's emotions	_____
Showed genuine concern and interest	_____
Avoided becoming defensive or overreacting	_____
Sought additional information about the problem (general to specific, evaluative to descriptive)	_____

Focused on one issue at a time ⎯⎯⎯⎯⎯

Agreed with some aspect of the complaint (facts, perceptions, feelings,
or principles) ⎯⎯⎯⎯⎯

Asked for suggestions for making changes ⎯⎯⎯⎯⎯

Agreed on a specific plan of action ⎯⎯⎯⎯⎯

Mediator

Treated the conflict and disputants seriously ⎯⎯⎯⎯⎯

Broke down complex issues, separated the critical from the peripheral ⎯⎯⎯⎯⎯

Began with a relatively easy problem ⎯⎯⎯⎯⎯

Remained neutral (facilitator, not judge) ⎯⎯⎯⎯⎯

Pointed out the effect of the conflict on performance ⎯⎯⎯⎯⎯

Kept the interaction issue oriented ⎯⎯⎯⎯⎯

Made sure that neither party dominated conversation ⎯⎯⎯⎯⎯

Kept conflict in perspective by emphasizing areas of agreement ⎯⎯⎯⎯⎯

Helped generate multiple alternatives ⎯⎯⎯⎯⎯

Made sure that both parties were satisfied and committed to the
proposed resolution ■

■ *Skill Application*

Application Exercises

1. Teach a friend the key action steps for handling personal verbal attacks. What did you learn about this skill by teaching it that you had overlooked in the classroom presentation? What have you learned about the process of mentoring? How successful was your training?

2. Serve as a third-party consultant to resolve a conflict between two individuals or groups. Describe the conflict and your intervention. How effective were you in using the behavioral guidelines? What was the outcome? Next time would you handle this type of situation differently?

3. Assume the role of consultant to a principal character in a case assigned by the instructor. Advise this person how to handle the conflict situation. Recommend the appropriate strategy and apply the key action steps. Whom should the character talk to, when, how, etc.? Adapt what you learned in this chapter to this unique situation. Instruct the person step by step.

4. Think of situations you encounter in your daily activities in which it might be inappropriate to use some of the behavioral guidelines discussed in this chapter. Describe these circumstances, as well as discussing how you would modify the guidelines so they would be more effective.

5. Find examples of individuals using the five approaches to conflict management discussed in this chapter. You might look for these in your current reading material, personal experiences with others, or simulated situations portrayed in movies or on TV. Briefly describe each situation. How closely did the situational constraints in each case match those portrayed in Table 8.5? According to Table 8.5, did the person select the appropriate approach? How effective was the person in resolving the conflict? What lessons can be learned from this experience about matching your approach to conflict management with situational factors? ■

9 Conducting Effective Group Meetings

■ **Skill Preassessment**

Johnny Rocco

■ **Skill Learning**

Improving Group Decision Making

■ **Skill Analysis**

It Wasn't "Just Another Dull Meeting"

■ **Skill Practice**

First Management Staff Meeting at Tampa Pump & Valve

Quality Circles at Battle Creek Foods

■ **Skill Application**

Application Exercises

■ *Skill Preassessment*

Johnny Rocco

Johnny has a grim personal background. He is the third child in a family of seven. He has not seen his father for several years and his recollection is that his father used to come home drunk and beat up every member of the family; everyone ran when he came staggering home.

His mother, according to Johnny, wasn't much better. She was irritable and unhappy and she always predicted that Johnny would come to no good end. Yet she worked when her health allowed her to do so in order to keep the family in food and clothing. She always decried the fact that she was not able to be the kind of mother she would like to be.

Johnny quit school in the seventh grade. He had great difficulty conforming to the school routine—misbehaving often, acting as a truant quite frequently, and engaging in numerous fights with schoolmates. On several occasions he was picked up by the police and, along with members of his group, questioned during several investigations into cases of both petty and grand larceny. The police regarded him as "probably a bad one."

The juvenile officer of the court saw in Johnny some good qualities that no one else seemed to sense. This man, Mr. O'Brien, took it on himself to act as a "big brother" to Johnny. He had several long conversations with Johnny, during which he managed to penetrate to some degree Johnny's defensive shell. He represented to Johnny the first semblance of personal interest in his life. Through Mr. O'Brien's efforts, Johnny returned to school and obtained a high school diploma. Afterwards, Mr. O'Brien helped him obtain a job.

Now at age twenty, Johnny is a stockroom clerk in one of the laboratories where you are employed. On the whole Johnny's performance has been acceptable, but there have been glaring exceptions. One involved a clear act of insubordination on a fairly unimportant matter. In another Johnny was accused, on circumstantial grounds, of destroying some expensive equipment. Though the investigation is still open, it now appears that the destruction was accidental.

Johnny's supervisor wants to keep him on for a least a trial period, but he wants "outside" advice as to the best way of helping him grow into greater responsibility. Of course, much depends on how Johnny behaves in the next few months. Naturally, his supervisor must follow personnel policies that are accepted in the company as a whole. It is important to note that Johnny is not an attractive young man. He is rather weak and sickly, and shows unmistakable signs of long years of social deprivation.

A committee is formed to decide the fate of Johnny Rocco. The chairperson of the meeting is Johnny's supervisor, and should begin by assigning roles to the group members. These roles (shop steward, head of production, Johnny's co-worker, director of personnel, and social worker who helped Johnny in the past) represent points of view the chairperson feels should be included in this meeting. (Johnny is not to be included.) Two observers should also be assigned.

After roles have been assigned, each role-player should complete the personal preference part of the worksheet, ordering the alternatives according to their appropriateness from the vantage point of his or her role.

Once the individual preferences have been determined, the chairperson should call the meeting to order. The following rules govern the meeting: (1) the group must reach a consensus ordering of the alternatives; (2) the group cannot use a statistical aggregation, or majority vote, decision-making process; (3) members should stay "in character" throughout the discussion. Treat this as a committee meeting consisting of members with different backgrounds, orientations, and interests who share a problem.

After the group has completed the assignment, the observers should conduct a discussion of the group process using the Group Process Diagnostic Questions as a guide. Group members should not look at these questions until after the group task has been completed.

WORKSHEET

Personal Preference	Group Decision	
_____	_____	Give Johnny a warning that at the next sign of trouble he will be fired.
_____	_____	Do nothing, as it is unclear that Johnny did anything wrong.
_____	_____	Create strict controls (do's and don'ts) for Johnny with immediate strong punishment for any misbehavior.
_____	_____	Give Johnny a great deal of warmth and personal attention and affection (overlooking his present behavior) so he can learn to depend on others.
_____	_____	Fire him. It's not worth the time and effort spent for such a low-level position.
_____	_____	Talk over the problem with Johnny in an understanding way so he can learn to ask others for help in solving his problems.

———   ———   Give Johnny a well-structured schedule of daily activities with immediate and unpleasant consequences for not adhering to the schedule.

———   ———   Do nothing now, but watch him carefully and provide immediate punishment for any future misbehaviors.

———   ———   Treat Johnny the same as everyone else, but provide an orderly routine so he can learn to stand on his own two feet.

———   ———   Call Johnny in and logically discuss the problem with him and ask what you can do to help him.

———   ———   Do nothing now, but watch him so you can reward him the next time he does something good.

GROUP PROCESS DIAGNOSTIC QUESTIONS

Communications

1. Who responded to whom?

2. Who interrupted? Was the same person interrupted consistently?

3. Were there identifiable "communication clusters"? Why or why not?

4. Did some members say very little? If so, why? Was level of participation ever discussed?

5. Were efforts made to involve everyone?

Decision Making

1. Did the group decide how to decide?

2. How were decisions made?

3. What criterion was used to establish agreement?
   a. Majority vote?
   b. Consensus?
   c. No opposition interpreted as agreement?

4. What was done if people disagreed?

5. How effective was your decision-making process?

6. Does every member feel his or her input into the decision-making process was valued by the group, or were the comments of some members frequently discounted? If so, was this issue ever discussed?

Leadership

1. What type of power structure did the group operate under?
   a. One definite leader?
   b. Leadership functions shared by all members?
   c. Power struggles within the group?
   d. No leadership supplied by anyone?

2. How does each member feel about the leadership structure used? Would an alternative have been more effective?

3. Did the chairperson provide an adequate structure for the discussion?

4. Was the discussion governed by the norms of equity?

5. Was the chairperson's contribution to the content of the discussion overbearing?

Awareness of Feelings

1. How did members in general react to the group meetings? Were they hostile (toward whom or what?), enthusiastic, apathetic?

2. Did members openly discuss their feelings toward each other and their role in the group?

3. How do group members feel now about their participation in this group?

Task Behavior

1. Who was most influential in keeping the group task oriented? How?

2. Did some members carry the burden and do most of the work, or was the load distributed evenly?

3. If some members were not contributing their fair share, was this ever discussed? If so, what was the outcome? If not, why?

4. Did the group evaluate its method of accomplishing a task during or after the project? If so, what changes were made?

5. How effective was your group in performing assigned tasks? What improvements could have been made? ∎

■ *Skill Learning*

Improving Group Decision Making

Few aspects of management have been criticized more than group meetings. Managers complain that they are frequently forced to sit through boring presentations, waste time discussing a decision the boss should have made alone, or interrupt important tasks to attend a meeting whose purpose is ill defined and whose duration seems interminable. Committee meetings and their decisions are the focus of office jokes. Everyone has a favorite story about a group meeting that went awry. One seasoned veteran of "blue ribbon problem-solving commissions" said of his experience with this process, "It's not just that these committees invariably miss the mark. It's worse than that. Generally they end up producing a result that is exactly the opposite of the purpose for which they were organized."

It is unfortunate that this management tool has been so broadly maligned. Properly managed group meetings can improve the quality of decision making and increase the efficient use of a managers' time. A survey of business executives in the *Harvard Business Review* concluded that "the great majority [of the suggestions from survey respondents] lead to this conclusion: the problem is not so much committees in management as it is the management of committees" (Tillman, 1960, p. 168).

The purpose of this chapter is to acquaint you with common pitfalls in poorly managed groups and techniques for avoiding them. Our discussion will focus specifically on the effective management of group meetings, rather than on the effective supervision of ongoing work groups. The basic skills required to manage work teams, such as delegation, motivation, and conflict management, have been discussed earlier. While the specific techniques outlined are frequently targeted at one-on-one, supervisor-to-subordinate interactions, when taken together they also provide a systematic, coherent framework for effectively managing ongoing work groups. Therefore, when we speak of group decision making in this chapter, we are referring not to decisions made *in* a group, but to decisions made *by* a group. Similarly, the terms "group process," "group structure," and "group leader" refer to the process, structure, and leadership of a specific group meeting. For our purposes the objective of the meeting is not critical. It might be called to inform participants, to obtain their opinions regarding an important policy decision, or to solve a common work-related problem. We shall assume that the participants have an ongoing work relationship, that they understand the purpose of the meeting, and that the meeting has been called by someone who will have presiding authority.

This type of task-related group meeting occupies a large portion of the typical manager's work week. A study sponsored by the 3M Company showed that the number of meetings and conferences in industry had nearly doubled during the previous decade and that their cost had nearly tripled (Seibold, 1979). Some sources suggest that most businesses spend 7 to 15 percent of their personnel budgets on meetings. Research shows that the amount of time an individual manager spends in meetings varies by organizational level. Middle-level managers may spend as much as one third of their time in meetings, while top management spends closer to 50 percent (Seibold, 1979). This figure increases significantly when we include the non–job-related meetings managers attend. Many managers are heavily involved in civic activities, such as those of local school boards, arts councils, youth programs, and church auxiliaries. Most business in these organizations is conducted in group meetings. A manager who spent only four hours in civic meetings each week would spend the equivalent of one year of his or her life so engaged.

These figures underscore the importance of good meeting management skills. Since managers spend so much time in meetings, their success is to a large extent determined by how effectively those meetings are managed. While ineffective stress or time management skills impede the productivity of a single manager and inadequate delegation skills create frustration for three or four subordinates, poor group meeting management skills affect the performance of everyone in attendance. As one frustrated senior executive grumbled, "To waste your own time is unfortunate, but to waste the time of others is unforgivable."

We shall focus on two critical roles, those of the meeting chairperson and individuals making formal presentations. While the chairperson controls the tempo of the meeting, presenters shape its content. Consequently, the outcome of a meeting is largely determined by how well these two roles are performed.

COMMON PITFALLS IN GROUP MEETINGS

Certain problems are frequently encountered in group meetings. Some are the result of poor leadership, while others can occur in any group meeting, but their impact can be tempered by an effective leader (Maier, 1967; Huber, 1980).

Unnecessary or Inappropriate Meetings

Sometimes a meeting is held just to satisfy routine or tradition, even though there is no important business to conduct. Unnecessary daily or weekly staff meetings often fall into this category. A regular staff meeting that is appropriate at one time, such as when a work group is first organized, may lose its utility later. Another cause of unnecessary meetings is a group leader with low self-confidence. While the alleged purpose may be to keep people informed, the underlying purpose is to test the manager's support on an unpopular policy decision, to find a solution for a tough budget problem the manager hasn't been able to solve, or to remind the staff who is in charge.

Group meetings are useful forums for insecure leaders to assert their authority. Such leaders can demonstrate their power by compelling subordinates to attend and to work on assignments made at the meeting. By sitting at the head of the table during the meeting, the leader adopts a parental role. By holding the meeting in his or her office, the leader has the "home court advantage" of familiar, supportive surroundings if a confrontation with one of the staff is anticipated. By controlling the agenda, dispensing informational handouts, deciding how much time is spent on an item, and so on, the leader reminds the staff of their subordinate role in the group. If the leader feels threatened by a rival in the group, he or she can use the meeting to publicly humiliate or browbeat. Habitually calling meetings to shore up one's personal base of power is clearly an inappropriate use of staff members' time and energy. Furthermore, it generally so alienates the group from their leader that it accomplishes exactly the opposite result—they look for opportunities to undercut the leader's authority.

It is also inappropriate to ask a group to perform a task for which they are unsuited. This is the case when group members are asked to make a highly technical decision for which they do not collectively possess the necessary information or expertise. This is also the case when a highly diverse group are asked to make a value judgment. For example, a university president might ask a group of deans to decide whose budget should be cut to compensate for falling enrollments. The business school dean would likely argue that the university should be responsive to shifting student demand for a more professional education, so the humanities and social sciences budgets should be slashed. In contrast, the liberal arts dean would argue that student preferences tend to shift every decade or two, so they represent a faulty forecasting device. Further, that dean might decry the movement toward making the undergraduate curriculum more professional since it runs counter to the traditional mission of the university to provide students with a broad range of educational experiences. Because these academic deans did not have a common view of the mission of the university, they would have considerable difficulty making a collective decision about how to allocate scarce resources.

Poorly Organized Meetings

Often the justification for a meeting is clear (e.g., our scrap rate is too high), but the group still seems to flounder, wandering aimlessly and unable to reach a consensus. Such meetings commonly begin with the boss saying, "We've got a problem that I think we all need to sit down and discuss." The chairperson erroneously assumes that because the need to meet is apparent to the participants, the meeting will be successful. As a result, he or she prepares for the meeting casually and overlooks critical factors. People come to the meeting without a clear understanding of the specific objectives. They are not informed what their specific role in the decision-making process is, nor how the decision will be made. They have not been asked to think about the problem ahead of time, so they waste time discussing ill-conceived suggestions. If the leader does not discuss the problem with his or her superiors before the meeting, the group will spend a lot of time trying to estimate how far top management will allow them to proceed on their own.

A poorly organized meeting does not always reflect a casual attitude toward meeting preparation. The inexperienced chairperson may work hard at developing meeting objectives, agendas, etc., but make some ill-advised decisions that create an unorganized meeting. For example, he or she may try to cram too much into a single meeting, scheduling too many presentations, or handing out too many documents, or trying to cover too much business. As a result, members cannot adequately discuss the topics and often leave the meeting with little sense of accomplishment: "We covered a lot of business, but didn't get closure on anything."

Inappropriate Group Composition or Size

A common planning error is to invite too many people. Thinking that it is important to obtain input from as many people as possible, the leader draws up a large, diverse list of participants. The result is a superficial discussion of the issues, since the pressure to hear from everyone prevents any one person from pursuing the discussion in sufficient depth. In addition, more points of view will likely be volunteered than the group leader can adequately consider. Also, if the group is too large, some members will simply withhold their input. In general, the larger the group, the lower is the percentage of participants that will be actively involved in the discussion (O'Dell, 1968; Hackman & Vidmar, 1970).

It is also possible to invite too few, or inappropriate, participants. If a group is too small, it will be severely handicapped in its problem-solving ability. Small, homogeneous groups have such limited personal resources that members can become easily discouraged in a problem-solving task. This is especially likely when the group task requires technical knowledge not possessed by any of the members. Despite its inherent disadvantages, some leaders prefer a small, homogeneous decision-making group. An intimate group of advisors is generally selected because they are supportive, loyal, and unlikely to produce any surprises. This type of "kitchen cabinet" possesses a certain seductive appeal since it allows the manager to avoid the inefficient and conflictual decision-making process inherent in larger, more diverse groups. The problem is that the probability of making a serious mistake is substantially increased. Indeed, an expert in corporate bankruptcy in the United States has argued that this type of group decision-making process at the senior executive level is a leading cause of business failure (Argenti, 1976).

Group Pressure for Conformity

One of the most widely documented pitfalls in group decision making is that the pressure to reach a consensus interferes with critical thinking. Irving Janis, a prominent social psychologist, has conducted extensive research on this phenomenon, which he calls "group think" (Janis, 1972). As part of his research, he examined several historic foreign policy fiascos and showed that most were made by groups exhibiting various characteristics of group think (Table 9.1). For example, Arthur Schlesinger privately expressed grave reservations about the military's plan for the Bay of Pigs invasion of Cuba, but he refrained from publicly expressing his misgivings in the planning meetings because it appeared the rest of the group firmly supported the plan.

The reluctance of members to express views contrary to the prevailing sentiment of the group is especially acute when high-status members, or formal leaders, dominate the discussion. Research on group problem solving has shown that groups tend to select the first solution that receives favorable support from opinion leaders in the group, even when solutions that are technically better are introduced subsequently (Maier, 1967). When this occurs, a basic irony of group decision making occurs. Not wanting to make a serious judgment error, a leader convenes a meeting of trusted advisors. In the process of discussing the issue, he or she expresses a strong preference for one option. Others, wanting to appear supportive, present arguments justifying the decision. One or two members tentatively suggest alternatives, but they are strongly overruled by the majority. The decision is carried out with great conviction but disastrous consequences. So while the leader brought together a group to help guard against making a bad decision, because of the high norm for conformity in the group meeting the leader actually became more vulnerable to making an error. Without the social support provided by the group, the leader would probably have been more cautious in implementing his or her preferred solution.

TABLE 9.1 *Symptoms of Group Think*

Symptom	Explanation
Illusion of invulnerability	Members feel assured that the group's past success will continue.
Shared stereotypes	Members dismiss disconfirming information by discrediting its source ("lawyers are needlessly conservative").
Rationalization	Members rationalize away threats to an emerging consensus.
Illusion of morality	Members believe that they, as moral individuals, are not likely to make bad decisions.
Self-censorship	Members keep silent about misgivings and try to minimize their doubts.
Direct pressure	Sanctions are imposed on members who explore deviant viewpoints.
Mind guarding	Members protect the group from being exposed to disturbing ideas.
Illusion of unanimity	Members conclude that the group has reached a consensus because the most vocal members are in agreement.

SOURCE: Based on Irving Janis, *Victims of groupthink* (Boston: Houghton-Mifflin, 1972).

Faulty Decision-Making Process

Since it is commonly believed that "two heads are better than one" at brainstorming, aggregates should outperform individuals at tasks requiring creative solutions. However, this is generally not the case in practice because of faulty group dynamics (Murninghan, 1981). A common pitfall is for group members to criticize one another's ideas during a group brainstorming session. They sometimes seem to compete to see who can be the first to point out why a proposal won't work. A common response is, "That's a good idea, but it won't work in this situation." As a result, the idea generation process is stifled. People are reluctant to make suggestions that are unusual for fear of being ridiculed or labeled naive. What happens in groups when an overly critical climate is allowed to develop during a brainstorming session is that members begin to censure their own ideas before they are even expressed. They think, "Joe argued that Mary's idea wasn't feasible, and my idea is similar to hers, so I guess there is no need to mention it."

A variation on this problem occurs when groups rush to resolve the first problem on the agenda before establishing ground rules. The impulse of most group members is to immediately focus on the task. The initial discussion focuses on questions like, "What do we need to decide today?" or, "What is the nature of the problem?" When groups fail to devote some time initially to process issues, it invariably takes them longer to accomplish their task. For some people this seems counterintuitive, since it appears that time spent discussing anything but the task at hand is wasted. However, research has shown that process issues will be discussed at some point in most meetings, and the sooner they surface, the less time is required to deal with them adequately (Hackman & Morris, 1975). When they are discussed at the beginning, questions about what the structure of the meeting should be, how much time should be spent discussing an item before voting on it, whether alternatives should be selected by majority vote or unanimous agreement, and so forth, can be dealt with explicitly and efficiently. In contrast, when a group jumps right into discussing the business of the meeting, process issues tend to surface in a haphazard fashion and often with considerable emotion—"Why are we spending so much time discussing this item?" or "Why don't we just hurry up and vote on the issue and move on?"

Losing Sight of Original Objectives

It is easy for members to get caught up in the dynamics of the group and become sidetracked. For example, in an organization that is having considerable financial difficulties, it is common for a problem-solving meeting to turn into a gripe session. Instead of concentrating on coming up with ideas for saving money, group members debate the merits of top management's ability to cope with the crisis.

A related dysfunctional group dynamic is the process of jockeying for positions of status in the group (Maier, 1967; Jewell & Reitz, 1981). Groups that meet frequently become a miniature organization. It is quite natural in this microcosm for a division of labor and a status heirarchy to emerge. This by itself is not dysfunctional, but, when members become preoccupied with personal concerns like "How can I enhance my status in this group?" they tend to lose interest in conducting the business of the meeting. In these cases, problem-solving meetings degenerate into speech-making sessions in which members attempt to score points with powerful interests. The meeting turns into a staged polemical debate in which antagonists strive to win arguments, rather than solve problems. When this occurs, the objective of enhancing one's personal status in the group as a powerful orator or tenacious debator subverts the problem-solving objective of the group.

THE EFFECTIVE MANAGEMENT OF GROUP MEETINGS

It is easy to see why so many group meetings generate more frustration than satisfaction. To overcome these pitfalls, managers should focus on four critical components of effective group meetings. These are arranged according to the normal chronology of events. They are written from the point of view of the group chairperson since that person contributes most to the success or failure of the group.

Deciding When to Convene a Group Meeting

As we noted in discussing the first pitfall, many meetings are held that are unnecessary or inappropriate. Unless a meeting's value can be clearly demonstrated to participants, it will not likely be successful. There are three legitimate justifications for holding a group meeting.

The first justification is when the group leader cannot make an effective decision about an important issue alone. Victor Vroom and Phillip Yetten (1973) have developed a decision-making model to help leaders decide when to involve subordinates in the decision-making process. They propose that group involvement be sought when the leader does not have sufficient information to make a good decision or when the commitment of the group to the decision will be necessary for effective implementation. A manager who lacks the expertise or data to make a well-informed decision should identify who has the necessary information and how it can best be obtained. If the information required is factual (e.g., last year's budget for project X), a phone call or memo is a more efficient retrieval device than a meeting. However, if the manager is not sure who has the information or if several people have bits and pieces of data, a meeting is probably justified. Solidifying members' commitment to the chosen course of action is especially important when the decision requires that group members change their work activities or when their reward structure is altered. Research has repeatedly demonstrated that subordinates are more likely to go along with a decision when they are involved in its formulation (Shaw, 1971; Carey, 1972; White & Ruh, 1973). Therefore, the greater the potential impact of a decision on the work activities of the group members, the more important it is to involve them in the decision-making process.

The second justification is when the group needs to conduct routine business that is more efficiently handled in a meeting than one on one. For example, in work groups performing tasks that are highly interdependent (e.g., scheduling the production of custom orders), periodic staff meetings enable members to coordinate their activities. Also, regular work meetings are useful for groups operating in rapidly changing environments, since they enable the supervisor to disseminate up-to-date information regarding changes in work priorities, emerging crises, and so forth. Daily briefings in police departments and military units serve this function. While a routine staff meeting can serve useful purposes, the group leader needs to continually assess its utility. Again, if the purpose for a meeting is not obvious to group members, they will resent management's infringement on their time, feeling that they are being required to "meet only for the sake of meeting." One time management suggestion in Chapter 2 was to cancel a regularly scheduled meeting periodically to see whether it made a difference in the group's performance. In the context of this discussion, that is a useful diagnostic tool for determining whether a routine meeting has lost its purpose.

The third justification is when tasks need to be performed that are best suited for group involvement. Groups perform certain kinds of activities better than isolated individuals, as when expertise is randomly or broadly distributed, i.e., when it is not obvious that one member of a group will perform better than others (Shaw, 1971; Maier, 1967). For example, in the popular group training exercises like "Desert Survival," "Arctic Survival," and "Lost on the Moon," members are required to rank order a list of provisions and equipment in terms of how essential each is for enhancing the survival of the group, under the premise that not all the items can be retained. In these situations it is generally not apparent at the beginning of the exercise whether one member's judgment might be superior to the others'. Consequently, the priority ranking produced after a lengthy group discussion is generally closer to the true ranking (made by outside experts) than the average of the individual rankings made by group members prior to the discussion. In fact, the group ranking is often more accurate than any individual rankings of members. In this type of task, judgment error is generally randomly distributed among group members because none of them is an expert on outdoor survival. Consequently, a group discussion is highly advantageous since it pools the members' scanty knowledge on the subject.

Groups are also superior to individuals in performing complex tasks requiring a division of labor (Filley, 1970; Jewell & Reitz, 1981; Kelley & Thibant, 1969). When several types of specialized knowledge are required to solve a problem, a well-organized group will outperform isolated individuals. Well-managed groups also outperform individuals at tasks requiring the learning of ideas or the retention of information (Davis, 1969) because groups tend to learn faster than individuals. Not only do they have a larger pool of knowledge and experience to draw from, but they are also able to recognize and correct individual errors.

Deciding Whom, and How Many, to Invite to the Meeting

When a manager decides it is necessary to hold a meeting, the next logical concern is determining the appropriate group composition and size. These are important decisions because group membership has been shown to be a strong predictor of group performance and member satisfaction (Gibb, 1951; Slater, 1958). As we noted earlier, groups that are too large or too small tend to operate inefficiently. For example, a group of three is awkward to work with because the majority is too powerful. A group of four overcomes that problem, but small, even-numbered groups tend to become deadlocked more often than odd-numbered groups. At the other extreme, studies of groups with over ten members report high degrees of alienation and low rates of participation. While large groups may be necessary in some cases because of the complexity of the problem being addressed or the need to invite a large representation of people for political reasons, managers need to closely monitor the group process to encourage broad participation. One way to do this is to break a large group into smaller working committees with specific assignments.

There is considerable evidence that five is an optimal group size. A survey of 1658 members of committees in industry showed that the average preferred committee size of the respondents was 4.6 (Kreisberg, 1950). A review of laboratory research by Alan Filley (1970) also concluded that five is the optimal size, assuming the requisite skills and knowledge are possessed by the members. In a group of this size members feel they have the resources to collectively attack a problem, while at the same time their unique contribution is still highly visible. Smaller groups tend to avoid controversial or challenging tasks, while larger ones tend to get bogged down in procedural trivia. While smaller groups tend to arrive at decisions more quickly and larger groups are better at solving complex problems, a group size of five appears to be best for general purpose meetings.

Membership composition also plays an important role in group dynamics. Aside from the obvious need to assemble a group containing the skills and knowledge required to address the business of the meeting, three other characteristics of group composition are critical for group performance. These are characterized by the following dimensions: homogeneity–heterogeneity, competition–cooperation, and task–maintenance. A homogeneous group is composed of members with similar backgrounds, personalities, knowledge, values, and so on. As one might expect, there is less likelihood of conflict during a homogeneous group's discussions, but these placid dynamics also tend to produce pretty mundane outcomes. In contrast, heterogeneous groups have great difficulty building strong interpersonal relationships, but this allows members to take greater risks and be more critical of others' ideas. Overall, it appears that heterogeneous groups are better for addressing novel, complex tasks, providing group members can cope with a high degree of conflict (Hall, 1975; Sorenson, 1973; Shaw, 1976; Collins & Guetzkow, 1965).

The empirical results regarding the effect of competitive versus cooperative orientations on group problem solving are more straightforward. Studies have consistently shown that groups whose members are working toward a common goal perform more effectively and produce higher levels of member satisfaction than groups whose members are striving to fulfill individual needs or pursuing competing goals (Hoffman, 1965; Schutz, 1958; Terborg, Castore, & DeNinno, 1976). Cooperative groups demonstrate more effective interpersonal communication, more complete division of labor, higher levels of involvement, and better task performance.

In actual practice these two factors are often linked, in that homogeneous groups tend to be more cooperative, while heterogeneous groups are generally more competitive. For example, a budget meeting of representatives from five departments will likely be less cooperative than one of five members from the same department. While not all heterogeneous groups are more competitive, they certainly place a greater burden on group leaders' conflict management skills. The challenge is to preserve the creative spark present in lively, often heated, discussions while at the same time not allowing members to get sidetracked by their own agendas for advancing personal interests at the expense of others in the meeting. One way to achieve this is by identifying a broad goal that all members can identify with. This might be getting the budget in on time or improving coordination between departments. The effective chairperson uses such goals to encourage cooperation.

Research on group dynamics has shown that effective groups contain some members who are highly task oriented and some who are concerned about maintaining the quality of the group's process (Bales, 1970; Lord, 1977). Task-oriented members have little patience with small talk and joking around. They are all business. They primarily focus on outcomes and don't worry much about members' feelings and attitudes. Meetings that are dominated by task-oriented members tend to operate very efficiently but at the expense of member satisfaction. In contrast, participants who are primarily concerned about maintaining *esprit de corps* in the group err in favor of encouraging everyone to participate, even if some have little to contribute. They are concerned primarily with members' affective assessments of the group process. They feel that making a quality decision at the expense of member satisfaction is a poor trade-off. Wanting members to feel good about their participation, they frequently interject supportive comments like, "That is a darn good idea,"

"Let's allow John to finish stating his opinion before we interrupt," "I'm interested in hearing what Mary has to say about this problem," and, "I think we have made a lot of progress on this matter." Again, the critical factor is that both task and maintenance (process) orientations be represented in group meetings.

Making Preparations for the Meeting

Several specific planning details can greatly improve the quality of a meeting. It is obviously important to make the necessary arrangements for the meeting room, visual aids, and equipment. It is also important to prepare a complete agenda and, if possible, to have it distributed before the meeting. In addition to identifying the major points of business, the agenda should specify who will be in attendance, as well as the scheduled beginning and ending times. Circling a presentation to be made by a group member on the advance agenda serves as a helpful reminder. If a business item requires advance preparation (e.g., reviewing an enclosed document), this should also be noted.

In addition to taking care of these planning details, the meeting chairperson may want to discuss specific agenda items with key members prior to the meeting. If a subordinate is making an important presentation, the chairperson might invite him or her into the office for a dress rehearsal. When a controversial policy is on the agenda, it is often advisable to discuss the matter before the meeting with key opinion leaders. This polling of sentiment is useful for gauging how much time should be set aside for discussing an issue and how it should be presented to the group. If the chairperson can obtain the support of key group members before the meeting, it is less likely that a controversial issue will dominate the group discussion to the point that insufficient time is left to discuss other agenda items.

One of the most important decisions that needs to be made before a meeting is seldom explicitly considered by managers. Several decision-making structures can be used in a group meeting, but almost all management meetings use one format. Keith Murninghan (1981) has identified five distinct decision-making procedures: the ordinary group format, brainstorming, statistical aggregation, the Delphi technique, and the nominal group technique (NGT). While at least two of these techniques do not involve face-to-face meetings, we shall discuss all five since managers should appreciate the broad range of options available for making a group decision. Each approach has advantages and disadvantages—none of them is inherently superior. Consequently, the selection of a decision-making procedure should be linked to the specific objectives of the meeting.

The ordinary group format is by far the most popular. In a sense it serves as the default option; unless a deliberate decision is made to use one of the other formats, it is adopted. Basically, it consists of the chairperson's stating a problem and then encouraging open, free-flowing discussion. When a consensus has been reached, the chairperson shifts to a new topic and the procedure is repeated.

Because this type of meeting is so unstructured, experience has shown that this decision-making process is most vulnerable to the pitfalls discussed earlier. Group members are easily swayed by social pressure, a discussion can drag on far beyond its utility, overpowering personalities can easily dominate the meeting, and few alternative solutions will likely be generated. On the other hand, because it is so unstructured, it tends to enhance *esprit de corps* among group members. Participants are able to interject humor, kid one another, and in other ways build strong social ties in an unstructured meeting. In general, because it is so unstructured, the success of the ordinary group format is highly dependent on the skill of the group leader.

Brainstorming is a well-known process for generating ideas (Osborn, 1957). People are brought together and asked to think of all the ways a problem could be solved. To conduct a successful brainstorming session, a few simple rules need to be followed. First, people should be encouraged to generate as many diverse ideas as possible. A premium should be placed on coming up with unusual alternatives. Second, and most important, members should not critique the ideas as they are proposed. Evaluation should take place after all the ideas have been generated. Third, members should be encouraged to "piggyback" on each other's ideas—"Bill's suggestion has made me think about still another alternative."

Brainstorming sessions are generally very enjoyable. Participants appreciate being asked for their input and leave the meeting with a strong sense of accomplishment. However, research has shown that brainstorming groups do not generate as many alternatives as one might expect. It is difficult for members not to violate these three rules, and as a result, the meetings often shift toward the ordinary group format (Bonchard, 1971; Taylor, Perry, & Block, 1958).

Statistical aggregation does not require a group meeting. Individuals are polled regarding a specific problem and their responses are tallied. This procedure is limited to quantitative problems, such as projections of budget overruns near the end of a fiscal year. The obvious advantage of this procedure is that it is very efficient. Participants are not required to attend a meeting and they can fit the request for information into their normal workday activities. Furthermore, individuals are not subject to social pressure in this situation, so their responses are generally more reliable. The weakness of this technique is that it is limited to a fairly narrow range of problems, those for which a quantifiable answer can be readily obtained. Also, because participants do not meet, there is no opportunity for them to strengthen their interpersonal ties.

The Delphi technique was developed at the Rand Corporation as an extension of the statistical aggregation procedure (Dalkey & Helmer, 1963). It is used extensively in the scientific community to gather information from experts around the world. To begin the process, the coordinator sends out a questionnaire stating the problem and asking for specific input from the panel.

This could involve evaluating the quality of a research proposal, making predictions about the future based on current scientific knowledge, or judging the design of a consumer product. Once the surveys are returned, the coordinator summarizes the preferences of the panel members and feeds back results to the panel. Along with the feedback report, a second questionnaire is enclosed soliciting a new evaluation based on the input. This procedure is repeated as many times as necessary to reach a consensus.

The main advantage of the Delphi technique is that it permits creation of a group of any size and composition. The principal constraints are the expense of mailing and the length of time required to complete an iteration. Obviously these parameters are highly sensitive to group size, so an upper limit of one hundred participants is generally established. While this procedure has limited application for managers, it can prove very useful when expert opinions are needed.

The nominal group technique was developed at the University of Wisconsin by Andre Delbecq and his colleagues (Delbecq, Van de Ven, & Gustafson, 1976). Commenting on this technique, Keith Murninghan (1981, p. 60) observes,

> By combining some of the characteristics of the other techniques, it takes advantage of each of their good points. It draws from brainstorming by having people generate potential solutions individually; it draws from the ordinary group procedure by allowing for some group discussion; it draws from statistical aggregation by using a formal, restrictive process for arriving at a solution; and it provides feedback concerning others' suggestions, like the Delphi technique, NGT mixes a fairly structured decision process with the interpersonal characteristics of face-to-face groups.

The NGT procedure involves several stages. After a problem has been stated, group members are asked to write down as many alternative solutions as they can. After ten or fifteen minutes, the chairperson asks members to report their ideas in round-robin fashion while a scribe records them on a flip chart or blackboard. Next, a brief discussion is held, primarily to clarify any ambiguously stated or recorded items. When this has been concluded, members are asked to vote for the alternatives they prefer. This can be done in a variety of ways. For example, each member might be given ten points to divide among all the items, or each might cast one to three votes. If an obvious winner emerges, the task has been completed. If not, the vote can be discussed and a second vote taken. This process can be repeated until a consensus emerges.

The advantages and disadvantages of these approaches are summarized in Table 9.2. On the lefthand side are criteria for judging the effectiveness of a group meeting. Depending on the nature of the business to be conducted, the participants to be included, objectives of the group leader, time and financial constraints, morale of the group, and so forth, the appropriate group decision-

TABLE 9.2 *Comparison of Group Procedures*

Criteria	Ordinary	Brainstorming	Aggregation	Nominal	Delphi
Number of ideas	Low	Moderate	NA*	High	High
Quality of ideas	Low	Moderate	NA*	High	High
Social pressure	High	Low	None	Moderate	Low
Time/money costs	Moderate	Low	Low	Low	High
Task orientation	Low	High	High	High	High
Potential for interpersonal conflict	High	Low	Low	Moderate	Low
Feelings of accomplishment	High to low	High	Low	High	Moderate
Commitment to solution	High	NA*	Low	Moderate	Low
Development of "we" feeling	High	High	Low	Moderate	Low

*NA = not applicable.

SOURCE: Keith Murninghan, Group decision making: what strategy to use? *Management Review*, 1981, 70,61.

making technique can be selected. While no approach is clearly superior on all the dimensions, this table highlights the liabilities of the ordinary group technique. For example, if the objective is to generate ideas for solving a persistent safety problem, this is the worst possible procedure to use. This awareness underscores the importance of group leaders' consciously setting priorities for their objectives and then choosing the decision-making process that is most appropriate for each topic or phase of the meeting. One underlying cause of the pitfalls of group meetings discussed earlier is the failure of the chairperson to complete this part of the meeting planning process.

Managing Dynamics During the Meeting

Initially it is important to help group members feel comfortable with one another. This is especially critical if the meeting is likely to produce emotional confrontations, the group is large, or several members have been recently added. Table 9.3 lists suggestions for helping people who have not previously worked together get acquainted. Participants in a meeting are generally reticent to get fully involved if they aren't sure where other members are "coming from" in terms of background, expertise, status, and stake in the issues on the agenda.

For example, a major athletic conference and one of its member universities were recently embroiled in a dispute over the eligibility of a star football player. Faculty representatives from each university (who serve as the governing board for athletic affairs in the conference) and the administration of the

TABLE 9.3 *Tactics for Helping Group Members Get Acquainted*

1. Before the first meeting, send each member a brief biographical sketch of the other members, perhaps in conjunction with a description of the group's assignment, schedule of meetings, etc.

2. Before the first meeting, provide an opportunity for the members to socialize, such as a coffee or cocktail hour.

3. At the first meeting, introduce each member or have the members introduce themselves. (Generally the chairperson's introductions are more informative, as the members may be too modest to say much about themselves.)

4. During long meetings, provide breaks during which members can resume the social conversations they have had to set aside while they focused on the group task.

SOURCE: George Huber, *Managerial decision making* (Glenview, Ill.: Scott, Foresman, 1980), p. 180.

university in question met several times to resolve their dispute without success. Both sides were suspicious of the others' motives, and the meetings invariably degenerated into hostile confrontations. Then, before one of their meetings, participants were invited to attend a social gathering featuring an outdoor barbeque. During this time, representatives from the conference and the university had an opportunity to get to know one another better on a personal basis. The next day at their meeting they were finally able to break the impasse and work out a solution to the problem. After the meeting, several participants credited the social gathering with playing a major role in breaking down the barriers between the two factions.

As a meeting progresses, it is important for the leader to monitor the process dynamics of the discussion, as well as to sustain the members' involvement in their tasks. Ineffective meetings generally are the result of the group's becoming either too wrapped up in their interpersonal dynamics at the expense of accomplishing their task or so preoccupied with getting their work done that they aren't sensitive to members' feelings about their role in the group. As we mentioned earlier, a balanced orientation is most likely to occur when the chairperson invites individuals who can be expected to advocate each perspective. The effective chairperson must then conduct the meeting in such a way that neither orientation is allowed to dominate the discussion. To accomplish this, the chairperson must be sensitive to the structure of the meeting, as well as to the norms that emerge.

From a large body of research on the characteristics of an effective meeting chairperson emerges what appears at first to be a paradoxical model (Maier, 1963; Prince, 1969; Huber, 1980). In our earlier discussion of the pitfalls of group discussions, we noted that poor meetings result from leaders' providing too little structure for the discussion. These leaders assumed a very passive role because they were unsure of their skills or they assumed the group would perform better if they were given a free reign. On the other hand, the research on group think argues that when a chairperson expresses strong opinions during the group discussion, members are less likely to think critically or creatively and bad decisions often result. So it appears that if a chairperson adopts either a strong or a weak leadership role, the group suffers.

This apparent contradiction is resolved when we distinguish between the leader's involvement in the structure versus the content of a discussion (Janis, 1972; Jewell & Reitz, 1981). Closer inspection of this body of research suggests that when the purpose of the meeting is to stimulate critical thinking, effective leaders take an active role in structuring the discussion but refrain from expressing strong opinions during the discussion. They work hard at facilitating the discussion but abstain from actively determining its direction. This conclusion is supported by a study of seventy-two management committees (Berkowitz, 1953), which found that a high degree of sharing of the leadership role was negatively related to member satisfaction and group performance. Groups worked most effectively when they had a "take charge" leader who provided a well-defined structure for their activities.

George Huber (1980, pp. 179–188) has outlined five steps for systematically structuring the business of a meeting.

1. *At the beginning of a meeting, review the progress made to date and establish the task facing the group.*   It is especially useful to place the current meeting in a historical context. If the purpose of the meeting is to decide how to evaluate four alternatives for cutting costs generated at the end of the previous meeting, the chairperson could begin by briefly reviewing each proposal and summarizing the pros and cons expressed previously by group members. This type of introduction has two purposes. First, it highlights the group's previous successes and demonstrates that important contributions have been made in previous meetings. Second, it ensures that members have a common understanding of the objectives of the current meeting. Once this common agreement has been established, the chairperson can refer back to it periodically during the meeting to maintain the focus of the discussion. For example, frequent statements like, "Now that we have successfully evaluated the first two alternatives, let's move on to number three," will help sustain the interest and motivation of group members.

2. *As early as possible in a meeting, get a report from each member with a preassigned task.*   This reinforces the principle of accountability and provides public recognition for the presenter. If members learn from observation and experience that they will be held accountable for tasks assigned to them, they will be more likely to accomplish such tasks in the future. It also reduces the apprehension of a presenter at the beginning of the meeting. It is very demoralizing to stay up late the night before a big meeting polishing a presentation and then find that other business has higher priority and the presentation has been postponed or, worse, forgotten. If an emergency requires that new business take priority, this should be communicated to scheduled presenters when the meeting's agenda is being prepared. If that is not feasible, the scheduling conflict should be resolved at the beginning of the meeting. Otherwise, while other business is being conducted, members scheduled to make presentations will be thinking about what they are going to say, or worrying that too little time is being left for them to cover their material, and they will not be useful contributors.

3. Sustain the flow of the meeting using informational displays. It is often difficult, especially in long, complex meetings, for participants to remain attentive to detail. It is easy to lose interest because of information overload. A useful way to sustain interest and help members process information effectively is to use displays. During a brainstorming meeting, suggestions should be listed on a blackboard or flip chart. Technical presentations should include handouts for overhead transparencies. Contingency arguments can be illustrated effectively by means of a decision tree diagram on a blackboard. Discussions about the advantages and disadvantages of a proposal or rank ordering of work objectives to allocate time also tends to flow better when a scribe is recording the group's suggestions.

4. Manage the discussion to achieve equitable participation. Group task performance and member satisfaction tend to be highest when the rate of participation of individuals in a meeting corresponds to their information and knowledge. In poorly managed meetings some members, whether due to habit, personality, desire for status, or genuine interest, participate at a rate beyond their ability to actually make a contribution.

To prevent certain individuals from dominating a meeting, the chairperson should invoke a norm of fairness. This is accomplished by the use of guiding comments. For example, the leader might tell a member that it is time to allow others to contribute by saying, "Bill, I think we understand your point of view on this matter. In all fairness, we should allow others to express their opinions." An equitable distribution should be maintained not only between individuals, but also between points of view. To keep representatives of one side of an argument from dominating the meeting, the chairperson could interject, "Now that we have heard arguments for the proposal, it seems appropriate that we hear from those who are opposed to it." Particularly in large meetings, these comments may be insufficient to draw all the members into a discussion. In this case the chairperson should formally invite noncontributors to participate. "Bob, we haven't heard from you yet. What are your feelings on this proposal?" If these guiding comments are not sufficient to ensure broad and equitable participation, the chairperson should consider a more structured form of discussion, such as the nominal group technique.

5. Close the meeting by summarizing what has been accomplished and reviewing assignments. One of the most critical functions of the leader is to help the group feel a sense of accomplishment after a meeting. This will affect their motivation to perform assignments made during the meeting, as well as their feelings about attending the next meeting. This is especially important at the end of a meeting in which progress was not obvious. If the meeting dealt primarily with examining alternatives or exchanging views, members may not recognize how constructive this process was. The chairperson can make this more apparent by pointing out how the discussion fit into the overall plan for accomplishing a task. It can also be useful to review the stated purposes or agenda items for the meeting and indicate the progress made on each topic.

Before the group breaks up, it is also important to review and clarify assignments for the next meeting. The chairperson might say, for example, "Mary, now as I understand it, you are going to examine a copy of last year's budget and prepare a report for our next meeting." Once the leader has ascertained that he or she has agreement on the nature of the task, it is also a good idea to sample members' feelings about their assignments, to probe for problems of motivation, time constraints, and work overload. This can be done in a number of ways. For example, the leader might ask, "Will you need any help in getting those materials out of the archives?" or, "Is that assignment feasible before the next meeting?"

Finally, the chairperson should review plans for the next meeting when appropriate. Just as it is important at the beginning to place the meeting in a historical context, it is useful to end the meeting by focusing on links to future activities. If the group's recommendations must be approved at a higher level, the chairperson should state plans for getting that approval and reporting back to the group. If the meeting has focused on a component of an ongoing task, it is important to point out what will be considered next. If a follow-up meeting is not regularly scheduled, plans for the next meeting should be finalized before members leave. Attending to these details at the end of the meeting ensures a smooth transition between meetings.

MAKING EFFECTIVE PRESENTATIONS

Up to this point we have focused primarily on the role of the meeting chairperson. We have emphasized this role because research on group dynamics indicates that it is the greatest determinant of task accomplishment and member satisfaction. Consequently, managers should be well prepared to effectively assume this role.

The second critical role in effective group meetings is that of the presenter. While the meeting chairperson can use the techniques we have discussed to effectively manage the discussion portion of the meeting, he or she has very little control over the meeting during formal presentations. Effective meetings require good performances by both chairpersons and presenters. This is best accomplished when these individuals recognize the interdependence of their roles. When the chairperson sets the stage for a presentation, allows adequate time for the presentation of the prepared material, and effectively manages the ensuing discussion, the presenter's contribution to the meeting is maximized. Similarly, a cogent, stimulating, concise presentation provides a change of pace in a meeting, broadens group participation, and is often the most efficient way to disseminate information during the meeting. These factors enable the chairperson to cover business with dispatch and sustain member involvement. In contrast, there is little a leader can do to salvage members' feelings about a meeting after a self-conscious, tedious, poorly organized presentation. Group members become upset, restless, and anxious to leave.

The quality of a formal presentation also has a significant impact on personal career development, particularly for newcomers in an organization. Over the course of a person's career, it is likely that more opportunities will arise to make presentations before a group than to chair meetings. Also, it is more likely that the impact on a manager's career of making a single effective presentation will be greater than the outcome of effectively chairing a single meeting. The quality of a presentation is generally attributed to the skill and knowledge of the presenter, while responsibility for the quality of a meeting will likely be shared by the members and the chairperson.

To improve the quality of your presentations ten guidelines for effective public speaking should be followed (Mambert, 1976; Barrett, 1973; Wilcox, 1967; Sanford & Yeager, 1963; Smith, 1983). Inasmuch as managers need to be prepared to make presentations in a variety of situations (from committee meetings to stockholders' meetings and business luncheons), we have included material in this section that applies to situations beyond the scope of small group meetings. At the conclusion of the chapter, a list of behavioral guidelines specifically designed for making effective presentations in management meetings will be presented.

1. *Use physical space and movement to your advantage.*   Prior to your presentation, arrange the podium area and seating in the room to remove distractions. If you are speaking in a large room, physically arrange the audience so they are not disturbed by late arrivals. Also try to group participants so there is little space between them. Eliminate unnecessary or distracting materials from the podium, such as unused equipment, signs, and displays. Keep your audiovisual material covered until actually in use and keep the chalkboard clean.

Position yourself to enhance your rapport with the audience. Do not get so close to individuals in the front that they feel threatened, or so far removed from the rear of your audience that they feel detached. Also, try to position yourself roughly in the middle of your audience from left to right, and to have the audience on either side far enough back that you can comfortably maintain eye contact during your presentation. If possible, it is desirable before your presentation to sit down at the far corners of the room to get a feel for the psychological distance your audience will be experiencing. With this in mind, you can deliberately alter your presentation style to build rapport with members of the audience seated in undesirable locations.

Arrange the podium area to accommodate your physical movement. If a microphone is needed, use a portable one so you can move freely. Physical movement can be used to punctuate important points, signal a transition in your presentation, build rapport with a person asking a question, heighten the interest of isolated segments of the audience, and help your audience stay alert by shifting their attention. It also gives you a feeling of being in command of the situation. Of course, annoying mannerisms such as pacing or bouncing around the platform should be avoided.

2. *Use gestures naturally.*   Gestures should appear spontaneous and natural so they enhance rather than distract from your message. This is likely to happen when you concentrate on your message, not your movements. As you put your whole body and personality into conveying your message, the appropriate gestures will arise. Be careful not to step out of character. Let the gesture merely accentuate your normal expression. For example, a normally conservative person should not try to become effervescent during a presentation unless he or she feels that way.

Eliminate irrelevant actions and annoying mannerisms like jingling change in your pocket, toying with notes, shifting from one foot to the other, or adjusting eyeglasses. Concentrating on the message and forgetting about yourself will help remove these manifestations of nervousness.

Use a variety of gestures and avoid repeating the same over and over. Gestures can be used to illustrate or describe, enumerate, add emphasis, and direct attention. They can also involve the entire upper body—not just your dominant hand. Be sensitive to the appearance and length of a gesture. Hand movements should be flowing and complete. Incomplete visual patterns or abrupt movements tend to be distracting. Gestures also need to be long enough in duration that they register with the audience, just as visual aids need to appear long enough for comprehension.

It is important to suit the action to your audience. Large, dramatic gestures that would be appropriate in a banquet hall would overpower participants in a small committee meeting. Also, the number and type of gestures you use will vary, depending on whether you are simply making a report or presenting an appeal for support.

3. *Convince the audience you are concerned about them as individuals.*   Prior to your presentation, learn as much as you can about the makeup of your audience. Specifically, you need to understand their background, knowledge of, and attitudes about, your subject, as well as you. A staff engineer from corporate headquarters making a presentation about the proposed introduction of a radically new production process to a group of plant managers faces a very different set of circumstances than a company president making a routine annual report to the board of directors.

Once you begin your presentation, speak directly to individuals by maintaining continuous eye contact with all members of your audience. Never slip out of focus and begin talking to the room in general. Also, pace your delivery to the audience by watching their responses. If facial expressions, questions, or other reactions indicate that an idea is not getting across, slow down. When in doubt, ask a question to see if you have been understood.

State the purpose and underscore the relevance of your message during your introduction and conclusion. Make sure your audience understands the purpose of your talk and the practical value of your message. Personalize your message by demonstrating you understand the audience's fears, needs, and desires. Effective presentations are both intellectually cogent and emotionally appealing. For example, in making a presentation advocating the adoption of a new product line, you can appeal to the comptroller on the basis of cost efficiency, to the head of production by emphasizing the small amount of retooling required, and to the president on the basis of increased profits and enhanced image. Speaking from the audience's point of view requires using their language. A speaker before an audience of naval personnel who repeatedly refers to "ropes" and "boats" instead of "lines" and "ships" is automatically an outsider with extra work to do in building a feeling of mutuality.

People are more likely to listen to someone who agrees with them. It is almost always possible to find some area of agreement with which to begin, even if it is nothing more than the audience's and speaker's joint presence. But it can usually go deeper than that. Abraham Lincoln observed, "My way of opening and winning an argument is first to find a common ground of agreement." It is also important to begin with the familiar. If you are presenting unusual or difficult material, introduce it by placing it in a context with which your audience feels comfortable. This might involve referring to a chronic organizational problem or common experience. During a presentation of unfamiliar material, you can help maintain audience interest by frequently drawing parallels to past experience or prevailing practice.

4. *Present a logically compelling argument for your proposal.* There are two basic forms of logical argument: inductive and deductive. An inductive presentation starts with several examples or a set of data and then uses them to construct arguments to support a proposal. A deductive presentation begins by outlining a set of general principles, values, or beliefs and then proceeds to show how the proposed program has been logically derived. Irrespective of which general strategy a presenter uses, it is important to build a case supporting a proposal that does not rest solely on the inherent merits of the plan. Showing how a proposal will help the audience fulfill a common objective, give expression to a salient value, or resolve a perplexing problem will substantially increase audience support.

In developing a logical argument for a proposal it is important to avoid eight common logical fallacies (Barrett, 1977):

- *Hasty generalization* (jumping to conclusions). "Because the Republicans have been elected, we can expect a more balanced budget and therefore less government demand for credit. This will result in lower interest rates for the next four years."

- *Coincidence of events* (X followed Y, therefore X was caused by Y). "Our decrease in productivity last year was the result of our poorly negotiated union agreement."
- *No relationship* (a connection of unconnectable events). "Apex Chemical just built a new office building, so they must be well managed."
- *Insufficient relationship* (false analogy). "Because New Orleans and Seattle both have important harbors, they must have similar labor problems on the docks."
- *Either-or proposal* (offering only two solutions when others are possible). "Either we increase our price or we continue to endure our current financial problems."
- *Begging the question* (false or dubious assumption). "We all know that a recession is inevitable, so let's begin planning now for the inevitable layoffs."
- *Personalizing your argument* (referring to irrelevant personal characteristics). "I urge you not to vote for Bill Ash for the school board. Just look at how he has raised his own children."
- *Arguing in a circle* (using a point to "prove" itself). "Dr. Hansen, who has lectured far and wide on robotics, is well known in his field because he talks to many large and small groups."

5. Hold your audience's attention by being vigorous and providing variety and relief. Most presentations are not intense enough. The average audience is lulled to sleep by droning monotony. If you are dull, the audience will be dull also. If you are alive, alert, intense, and enthusiastic, your audience will be compelled to listen. Your posture, tone of voice, and facial expressions are critical indicators of your attitude.

Whenever possible, make your presentation standing up, assuming an erect but comfortable posture. Do not lean on a podium or against a wall, or shift your weight from foot to foot. If you must sit down, sit erect and lean slightly forward to portray an attitude of earnestness. You should use vigorous but conversational tones of voice and inflections. Avoid "orating" or "bellowing" at the audience, but make sure that you can be easily heard and that your tone is sufficiently strong and emphatic to convey meaning effectively. Your tone of voice and facial expressions should also be used to convey an appropriate range of emotions: concern, anticipation, excitement, dismay, and so forth. As long as they are consistent with the message, using a variety of moods, voice tones, facial expressions, and physical movements enhances audience appeal.

Use novelty and uniqueness in your presentation. Alternate moving and speaking. Intersperse such things as chalkboard use, demonstrations, lecturing, audience participation, and audiovisuals so no single one occupies too long a period. Variety is especially critical during long presentations or presentations given when an audience is tired or not particularly interested in the subject.

Humor, used appropriately, is an effective source of variety and relief. Especially during a long report, the interjection of humor can ease the tension of intense concentration. However, humor should play a subordinate role and be in good taste. Rather than using planned jokes or humorous stories, the presenter should rely on spontaneous incongruities, events that may occur during the presentation that are unexpected or out of character and therefore provide comic relief. This might take the form of the presenter exaggerating or understating a point or responding in a witty manner to a question. However, it is important to avoid getting a laugh at the expense of the mistakes of audience members.

6. *Be flexible.*   Prepare more material than you can present, but don't try to include it all. Avoid content-driven presentations. Do not be so rigidly bound to a predetermined pattern that the presentation is lost because of a misunderstanding of an important point.

Prepare different approaches for presenting key points and then use the approach that suits the mood of your audience. Just because something is written in your notes doesn't mean you should feel compelled to say it. Don't be wedded to a particular form of presentation. For example, be prepared to switch off the overhead projector if your audience is becoming bored with figures, charts, and graphs.

7. *When appropriate, encourage audience participation.*   Two-way communication is superior to one-way. It allows you to check audience comprehension and heightens their interest in your message by stimulating their curiosity. Don't rely exclusively on volunteer audience participation. Be alert to possibilities for letting people in your audience act and speak. Ask questions, ask for volunteers to demonstrate, use a visiting expert, and so on. An effective way to ensure audience participation is to organize your presentation around key summary or introductory questions. When you are nervous or inexperienced, it is difficult to think of really good questions during your presentation.

The following suggestions for using questions effectively are based on Mambert (1976).

- Ask "friendly" questions. Don't use questions to embarrass or badger. Avoid known "sore spots."
- Put "you" elements into the question. Make it relevant to the respondent's personal experience.
- Limit the answer to the information wanted. Don't let the respondent wander or attempt to take control of the presentation. A

polite "Thank you, that's what I was looking for" can get you back on track.

- Make the interchange a mutually satisfying experience. Give respondents time to think and phrase their answer. If they get stuck, help them save face by summarizing what they have said so far and then asking if anyone has something to add.
- Avoid rhetorical questions. Ask interesting questions that are thought provoking but not too difficult for your audience to answer.

In your nervousness or desire to get the question answered and use the response to advance your thought pattern, you may gloss over respondents' comments to the point of almost ignoring them. Such an offense can be avoided by developing the art of exaggerated attention, even leaning forward slightly or cocking the head to emphasize that you are interested and actually want to hear what the audience member has to say. In conversing with individual members of the audience, always bear in mind that you owe them just as much attention and respect as you want from them.

8. When challenged, be candid and firm but avoid overresponding. Your evaluation of feedback must be objective and realistic. For example, if you permit an audience to anger or intimidate you or to make you feel that you are being indulged or patronized, you lose the ability to maintain control of the situation. If you do not take negative audience reactions personally, you will be less likely to permit this to happen. A look of disbelief or disapproval from a member in the front row will be duly registered, but never taken to heart. If you ask a rhetorical question and get a predictably dull reaction, you will adjust to it and continue.

Respond to objections in a positive fashion. By linking objections to positive features of your proposal, you maintain an optimistic climate in your discussion. For example, "While it is true that the initial start-up costs would be high, we project a faster than normal rate of payback."

When questions are asked, don't try to fool your audience. When you are unsure of your facts, be candid. If the answer is not known, it should be admitted and accompanied by an offer to follow up later. However, it is also important that you don't avoid being unequivocal. People respect an unequivocal message even if they don't agree. Don't be afraid to take a stand, to come right out and let your audience know that "this is the way it is." Hedging weakens your credibility and the impact of the whole presentation.

Answer questions as succinctly as possible. Long, complex answers are generally not required and tend to detract from the overall quality of a presentation. Complex answers only raise more questions, and rambling answers suggest an inability to think concisely or to feel relaxed in a give-and-take situation.

Experienced presenters soon learn that people don't always ask questions just because they want information. Audience members may ask questions to get attention or affirmation that they know something, too; to tell you something they know and thereby gain approval from the group; to lead you in a certain direction; or to defend their egos, if they resent your knowing more than they do and perceive you as a threat. Being sensitive to a person's true motive for asking a question enables you to respond appropriately.

9. *Maintain control of the meeting.*   Questioners tend to take the offensive, placing presenters on the defensive. A good presenter never stays in a defensive position too long, and avoids it altogether if possible. If you do not wish to engage in an interchange at that time, you have every right to explain the answer will be given in a moment, or to offer to discuss the matter individually after the presentation. The point is that you must retain control of the presentation. You have an objective, and you should decide what is relevant to its accomplishment. There are several rules for handling unsolicited questions from the audience (Mambert, 1976):

- Prepare completely in advance. Survey questions that might arise and be equipped with answers.
- Listen carefully to the question and think while it is being asked. Repeat the question to be sure everyone has heard it.
- Attempt to determine how sure the asker is of himself or herself. Try to determine also if the asker knows the answer and is using the question for another purpose.
- Try to draw the questioner out further if necessary. Often the best answer to a question is another question.
- Avoid a public argument. Find some basis for agreement.
- Return to your main thought sequence as soon as possible.

10. *Respond spontaneously to unexpected disturbances.*   One of the most challenging aspects of making a presentation is handling an unexpected environmental disturbance. What should you do when the mike goes dead or the air conditioner fails? To begin with, never pretend that things aren't happening. Since audience attention is directly affected by such factors as ventilation, temperature, lighting, acoustics, external disturbances, interruptions, visual aid equipment failure, late arrivals, and early departures, the obvious answer to coping with most of these factors is to prepare in advance. How you handle an unforeseen environmental occurrence will be a direct result of how well you have prepared those aspects of your presentation that can be planned in advance. Your thorough analysis and preparation will prepare you for handling the unexpected.

In general, you should do what you would do if you were not in front of an audience giving a presentation. If a window or door needs opening or closing, you can simply do it matter-of-factly, without letting it interfere with the business at hand. If a microphone goes dead, you can raise your voice and move closer to your audience. There are few rooms in which a person cannot be heard if he or she tries. Well-maintained visual-aid equipment seldom breaks down if checked just before a presentation, but if it does, it need not be a catastrophe. A good presenter knows what his or her visuals contain and can improvise if necessary.

SUMMARY AND BEHAVIORAL GUIDELINES

Six pitfalls are common in meetings: the meeting is unnecessary or inappropriate, the meeting is poorly organized, the composition or size of the group is inappropriate, group pressure for conformity suppresses valuable contrary opinions or information, the decision-making process is truncated, and group members lose sight of the meeting's original objectives.

To avoid these pitfalls, certain guidelines were presented for performing the roles of meeting chairperson and formal presenter. Behavioral guidelines for chairpersons include the following:

1. A meeting may be called for the following reasons:
   - Leader needs information simultaneously from several people.
   - Group members' commitment to decision needs to be strong.
   - Group members need thorough understanding of complex decision.
   - Complex tasks have to be performed and division of labor is feasible.
   - Activities involving several individuals need to be coordinated.
   - Expertise for solving problem is randomly or broadly distributed among group members.

2. Decisions on whom, and how many, to invite should be governed by the following:
   - The size of the group should be compatible with the task (preferably 5–7 people).
   - Individuals with strong task orientations and others with group process orientations should be included.
   - Individuals should share some goal or values.
   - All relevant expertise and knowledge needs to be present.
   - Group's composition should reflect goals of meeting (homogeneity encourages solidarity and commitment, heterogeneity fosters creativity and innovation).

3. In preparing for the meeting, be sure to do the following:
   - Provide for adequate physical space, audio visual equipment, etc.
   - Arrange for someone to take minutes, when appropriate.
   - Coordinate with individuals making presentations, special guests, etc.
   - Establish priorities for business items prior to sequencing agenda items and allotting time to each item.

- Prepare and distribute agenda before or at beginning of meeting.
- Choose most appropriate decision-making structure for each item (interactive group discussion versus nominal group discussion).

4. In managing the group dynamics of the meeting, do the following:
   - Initially allow members to become acquainted (if necessary) and make them feel comfortable.
   - Review overall purpose of meeting, specify target time length, and highlight specific tasks.
   - Get report from each member with preassigned task, preferably early in meeting.
   - When critical thinking is important, play strong role in structuring discussion, but refrain from expressing strong personal opinions.
   - Sustain flow of meeting using informational displays.
   - Encourage group not to stray from assigned tasks.
   - Manage discussion to achieve equitable participation.
   - Conclude meeting by summarizing what was accomplished, reviewing assignments, and making preparations for subsequent meetings, if necessary.

Effective meetings require both skilled leaders and skilled presenters. One without the other is insufficient. Most young members of organizations are more likely to make a formal presentation during a management meeting than to chair the meeting. Drawing on the material presented on persuasive public speaking, the following behavioral guidelines can help you make more effective presentations in group meetings.

1. Tailor your message to your audience. Understand their needs and desires, as well as their knowledge of and attitude about your subject matter. Be concrete, specific, practical, and relevant.
2. Develop a logically compelling case for your plan. Do not expect your proposal to sell itself. Demonstrate how it will resolve a pressing problem, emphasize a salient value, or help reach a common goal. Avoid the eight logical fallacies.
3. Prepare for contingencies. Allow for flexibility in your presentation so you can adjust your pace and approach to audience interest and comprehension. Anticipate difficult questions and prepare for unforeseen problems.
4. Keep graphs, charts, and other visual aids simple and straightforward. Don't let the mechanics of your presentation interfere with your message.
5. Organize your presentation in a logical sequence that is easy to follow. Initially, place your presentation in the context of the group's business. Next, explain your purpose or objective, move

from familiar to unknown subjects, use internal summaries as transitions, and conclude with a general overview, as well as a statement of "where we go from here" or a list of options if appropriate.

6. Present your program with controlled enthusiasm. Project high levels of interest and intensity without shouting or preaching. Radiate confidence in your plan, but be willing to make reasonable changes recommended by group members.

7. Use body movements and facial expressions that are natural and spontaneous. Use your body as well as the physical space to enhance rather than detract from your message. Maintain eye contact with your audience. Don't speak to the room in general.

8. Candidly discuss the pros and cons of your proposal. Begin by explaining the overall advantages, then present a realistic assessment of the risks, and conclude by reinforcing the benefits.

9. Provide variety and relief. Alternate between speech and action, lecture and audience presentation, etc., as the occasion permits. Use spontaneous humor.

10. Prepare your responses to questions as thoughtfully as you did your presentation. If you are asked a particularly difficult question, pause and organize your thoughts before replying. A very impressive presentation can be undermined quickly by careless, haphazard responses to questions. If necessary, offer to discuss a difficult or complex objection further after you have studied it in greater detail, rather than "shooting from the hip."

11. Use questions from group members to further sell your program or point of view. Answer questions candidly and positively. Use objections to underscore positive features of your proposal.

12. Maintain control of the meeting. Don't let interruptions, distractions, or objections disrupt your concentration or undermine your self-confidence. Be firm and assertive when necessary, but avoid being aggressive or defensive. Avoid circumstances that would require an apology. Be well prepared, start and stop on time, and make sure your audiovisual equipment works.

REFERENCES

Argenti, J. *Corporate collapse.* New York: Halstead Press, 1976.

Bales, R. F. *Personal and interpersonal behavior.* New York: Holt, Rinehart and Winston, 1970.

Barrett, H. *Practical uses of speech communication* (4th ed). New York: Holt, Rinehart and Winston, 1977.

Berkowitz, L. Sharing leadership in small decision-making groups. *Journal of Abnormal and Social Psychology,* 1953, *48,* 231–238.

Bouchard, T. J. Whatever happened to brainstorming? *Journal of Creative Behavior,* 1971, *5,* 182–189.

Carey, R. G. Correlates of satisfaction in the priesthood. *Administrative Science Quarterly,* 1972, *17,* 185–195.

Collins, B. E., & Guetzkow, H. *A social psychology of group process for decision making.* New York: John Wiley, 1965.

Dalkey, N. C., & Helmer, O. An experimental application of the Delphi method to the use of experts. *Management Science,* 1963, *9,* 458–467.

Davis, J. *Group performance.* Reading, Mass.: Addison Wesley, 1969.

Delbecq, A. L., Van de Ven, A. H., & Gustafson, D. H. *Group techniques for program planning: A guide to nominal group and Delphi processes.* Glenview, Ill.: Scott, Foresman, 1976.

Filley, A. Committee management: Guidelines from social science research. *California Management Review,* 1970, *13,* 13–21.

Gibb, J. R. The effects of group size and of threat reduction upon creativity in a problem solving situation. *American Psychologist,* 1951, *6,* 324.

Hackman, J. R., & Morris, C. G. Group tasks, group interaction processes, and group performance: A review and proposed integration. In L. Berkowitz (Ed.), *Advances in experimental social psychology,* Vol. 9. New York: Academic Press, 1975.

Hackman, J. R., & Vidmar, N. Effects of size and task type on group performance and member reactions. *Sociometry,* 1970, *33,* 37–54.

Hall, R. Interpersonal compatibility and work group performance. *Journal of Applied Behavioral Science,* 1975, *11,* 210–219.

Hoffman, L. R. Group problem solving. In L. Berkowitz (Ed.), *Advances in experimental social psychology,* Vol. 2. New York: Academic Press, 1965.

Huber, G. *Managerial decision making.* Glenview, Ill.: Scott, Foresman, 1980.

Janis, I. *Victims of groupthink.* Boston: Houghton-Mifflin, 1972.

Jewell, L. N., & Reitz, H. J. *Group effectiveness in organizations.* Glenview, Ill.: Scott, Foresman, 1981.

Kelley, H. H., & Thibaut, J. W. Group problem solving. In G. Lindzey & E. Aronson (Eds.), *Handbook of social psychology* (Vol. 4). Reading, Mass.: Addison-Wesley, 1969.

Kreisberg, M. Executives evaluate administrative conferences. *Advanced Management,* 1950, *15,* 15–17.

Lord, R. G. Functional leadership behavior: Measurement and relation to social power and leadership perceptions. *Administrative Science Quarterly,* 1977, *22,* 114–133.

Maier, N. R. F. Assets and liabilities in group problem solving: The need for an integrative function. *Psychological Review,* 1967, *74,* 239–249.

Maier, N. R. F. *Problem solving discussions and conferences: Leadership methods and skills.* New York: McGraw-Hill, 1963.

Mambert, W. A. *Effective presentation.* New York: John Wiley & Sons, 1976.

Murninghan, K. Group decision: What strategies to use? *Management Review,* 1981, *70,* 55–61.

O'Dell, J. W. Group size and emotional interaction. *Journal of Personal and Social Psychology,* 1968, *3,* 75–78.

Osborn, A. F. *Applied imagination.* New York: Scribner's, 1957.

Prince, G. M. How to be a better meeting chairman. *Harvard Business Review,* Jan.-Feb. 1969, *47,* 98–108.

Sandford, W. P., & Yeager, W. H. *Principles of effective speaking* (6th ed.). New York: Ronald Press, 1963.

Schutz, W. C. *FIRO: A three-dimensional theory of interpersonal behavior.* New York: Holt, Rinehart and Winston, 1958.

Seibold, D. R. Making meetings more successful: Plans, formats, and procedures for group problem solving. *Journal of Business Communications,* 1979, *16,* 3–20.

Shaw, M. E. *Group dynamics: The psychology of small group behavior* (2nd ed.). New York: McGraw-Hill, 1976.

Shaw, M. E. *Group dynamics: The psychology of small group behavior.* New York: McGraw-Hill, 1971.

Slater, P. Contrasting correlates of group size. *Sociometry,* 1958, *21,* 129–139.

Smith, C. Personal correspondence, May 1983.

Sorenson, J. R. Group member traits, group process, and group performance. *Human Relations,* 1973, *26,* 639–655.

Taylor, D. W., Berry, P. C., & Block, C. H. Does group participation when using brainstorming facilitate or inhibit creative thinking? *Administrative Science Quarterly,* 1958, *3,* 23–47.

Terborg, J. R., Castore, C., & DeNinno, J. A. A longitudinal field investigation of the impact of group composition on group performance and cohesion. *Journal of Personality and Social Psychology,* 1976, *34,* 782–790.

Tillman, R., Jr. Problems in review: Committees on trial. *Harvard Business Review,* May-June 1960, *38,* 6–12, 162–172.

Vroom, V., & Yetten, P. *Leadership and decision making.* Pittsburgh: University of Pittsburgh Press, 1973.

White, J., & Ruh, R. Effects of personal values on the relationship between participation and job attitudes. *Administrative Science Quarterly,* 1973, *18,* 506–514.

Wilcox, R. P. *Oral reporting in business and industry.* Englewood Cliffs, N.J.: Prentice Hall, 1967. ■

■ Skill Analysis

It Wasn't "Just Another Dull Meeting"

William J. Wasmuth and Leonard Greenhalgh

Marvin, the supervisor of the Accounts Receivable Department at Allied Industries, stared in disbelief at the memo on his desk. It was a notice to all supervisors, advising them that as of the end of the month, half of the parking lot would no longer be available to employees. The state was building a new roadway over the area, and the company lawyers had run out of legal steps to save the parking lot.

All of the supervisors were directed to meet with their departments to work out alternative transportation arrangements that would reduce the number of cars using the parking lot. Now, at the peak of the company's busy season, there were plenty of things to attend to without bothering with a troublesome and time-consuming problem like parking! But Marvin knew he had to give it prompt attention.

Parking had always been a problem, and many people arrived quite early, with no extra compensation, just so they could find a place to park in the company lot. The alternative was to park on the streets surrounding the plant, but employees generally hated doing this.

The plant was located in an older section of the city, and the streets were narrow and busy. Most of the streets had one-hour parking meters, and stiff fines for violations. The no-parking areas were tow-away zones, and the police patrolled the area very efficiently, and without mercy.

Because the streets were so narrow, cars were frequently scraped or dented by people backing carelessly out of driveways. To make matters worse, there was a high rate of theft and vandalism in the neighborhood.

If there was *anything* that would get employees riled up, it would be to make the already "hot issue" of parking an even bigger headache!

Marvin called a meeting right away and read the memo to the people in his department. Amid groans, they agreed to meet the next day during the noon hour to figure out what to do about it.

Everyone arrived promptly in the small conference room, and Marvin began by thanking them for giving up their lunch hour. He was outwardly congenial, although he had a sinking feeling that the long-standing parking problem was bound to stir up some strong feelings and resentment.

Marvin soon found out that his fears were justified, as Wally criticized the company management for letting the parking situation get out of hand.

"Dammit, Marvin, you and the rest of management *knew* the state was

SOURCE: William J. Wasmuth and Leonard Greenhalgh, *Effective Supervision: Developing Your Skills Through Critical Incidents* (Englewood Cliffs, N.J.: Prentice-Hall, 1979), pp. 162–167.

going to build that highway over the parking lot. Now *we've* got to figure out new ways to get to work. What a lot of bull! That's management's job, not ours!"

Wally was an old-timer who had been passed over several times for promotions. He was bitter about this, and consequently he took advantage of every opportunity to condemn the company management. But Sylvia was tired of his negative attitude.

"Come on, Wally!" she said. "Nobody knew *for sure* until yesterday that we would actually lose part of our parking area. I figure there must've been at least a fifty-fifty chance that the road would be rerouted; otherwise we'd have been told before now. And besides, if management *had* planned what to do about it, you would have complained that we never have a chance to get involved in making decisions!"

"Why don't you try to be objective about the situation?" Wally demanded, sneering at Sylvia. "Just once. That's all I ask. You're such a good company girl, you'd stick up for management no matter how badly they screwed up!"

Marvin was about to come to Sylvia's rescue, since Wally was now "playing dirty"—attacking Sylvia, rather than dealing with the point she was trying to make—when Neil intervened.

"Look, Wally, this is my lunch hour, and I've got better things to do than listen to your comments. You're not helping us solve the parking lot problem. Either try to be more constructive, or give the rest of us a chance to figure out what we're going to do."

Several others in the group nodded in agreement, and Wally sat back and folded his arms.

Marvin was glad Neil had taken the lead in using group pressure to handle a troublemaker like Wally. Otherwise, Marvin knew he would have had to do it himself, and risk losing his "neutral" role in the meeting.

Jane broke the short but embarrassing silence by offering the first constructive suggestion. "Maybe the Personnel Department could figure out which people live close together and come to work at the same time," she said, looking at Marvin. "Then it would be easy for people to get together and form car pools."

"Hey, that's a good idea," Marvin said. "I'll bet there's people working in other parts of the plant who live real close to me, and I don't even know it."

"Oh, that's just *great*," Wally said sarcastically. "*Now* the company's gonna tell me who's going to ride in my car. . . ."

"I'm in a car pool and it wasn't easy at first," Jane bravely continued, glancing around the table from one face to another, ignoring Wally's grumbling. "I guess we all like our independence."

Encouraged by Jane's boldness, another clerk, Kim, who was normally very shy, leaned forward and started to say something. But Wally cut her off with some loud remark about the young "punks" in Production he wasn't going to ride with.

"Hold on, Wally," Marvin said, raising his hand, but still looking at Kim. "Go ahead, Kim. You were going to say something?"

Kim spoke up, and turned out to have more factual information than anyone else, much of it obtained from a friend who worked in Personnel. The company had considered car pools, and had come up with some statistics. Kim explained that the 400 present parking spaces were used by 300 cars with a single driver; the other 100 were in car pool arrangements and carried about 300 employees.

Kim further added that the new road would result in losing one half of the present lot, or 200 parking spaces. If all single-driver cars were replaced by car pools averaging three people each, there would be no parking problem.

Then, before anyone could break in, she quickly added, "I know that's not entirely realistic, but I agree with Jane that at least some of the shortage could be overcome by setting up more car pools."

"That's probably going to be our only way out of this mess in the short run," Neil said, nodding in agreement and looking at Jane and Kim. "But in the longer run," he continued, turning towards Marvin, "the company might be better off buying that old vacant building across the street and tearing it down."

"There's no way," Wally said, shaking his head, "that management would spend that much money to build a parking lot for its employees."

"Hey, not so fast, Wally!" Sylvia chided him. "We're supposed to be coming up with ideas. Let's let Marvin pass along Neil's idea to top management and let *them* decide if it costs too much money. We can't make that decision."

Marvin agreed to do so. "I've got it written down. You're right. We shouldn't be trying to second-guess top management when it comes to corporate finance!" Wally got the message about killing off suggestions, and returned to sitting back in his chair with his arms folded.

"Maybe you can add a footnote to the suggestion," Kim ventured. "Maybe the company could build a multilevel parking garage and rent out spaces to the general public. That would offset the costs."

Wally slumped down into his chair and rolled his eyes, but he didn't dare say anything else negative.

As Marvin was writing down Kim's latest contribution, Brian made a joke about knocking the vacant building down for free with a gigantic office party. The laughter broke the tension that had been growing.

After the laughter, Neil suggested that they use the next few minutes to move on to figuring out some other alternatives for traveling to work.

Neil was a "bulldog" for sticking to some kind of agenda. Marvin found this role helpful in keeping the meeting moving along and agreed that more alternatives should be discussed.

After twenty minutes of discussion (during which several alternatives were discussed, including such diverse ideas as using a "commuter bus" to transport workers from the big downtown public parking lot, and putting all the office workers on the day shift and all the production workers on the night shift), it was generally agreed that car pools held the most promise for an immediate solution for the crisis.

Wally had been quietly listening to the discussion, and was still very skeptical. Living up to his reputation for "throwing cold water" on any idea that would take some extra effort, he figured that now was the time to shoot down Jane's suggestion.

"Jane," he began, in an almost insulting tone of voice, "your idea of organizing more car pools will never work. I've talked to people in Sales and around the plant, and I know that you just can't force them into using car pools. They've paid for their cars and their gasoline, and will damn well use them any way they choose. They all feel *the company* is responsible for providing them with parking spaces."

Neil turned to Wally. "How many people did you actually talk to before arriving at your conclusion about car pools? We only found out there was a problem yesterday. Have you been interviewing around the clock?"

"Well," Wally sputtered, "I don't know *exactly* how many people I talked to. At least ten. I guess I found out mostly when I used to work in the plant—but I've talked to people since."

Marvin picked up on Neil's comment.

"Let's see, Wally," he began, "if there are 300 persons not in car pools and you've only talked to ten of them, that's about 3 percent of the total. Do you think that's really a big enough sample? Especially since much of your information may be out of date?"

Wally became flustered. "I don't know why you're getting so picky about exact numbers," he retorted.

"Five years ago," Neil added, "people had different attitudes toward car pools. There weren't as many workers in the plant back then, and besides, people used to be less conscious about wasting gas and making the oil companies richer."

Everyone was silent, looking down. Kim was concealing a smile. Neil had helped Marvin make his point.

It was getting close to one o'clock. Kim quickly added that the company where her husband worked had done some successful experimenting with car pools and she would be willing to find out more about what they did, if anyone was interested. Jane then suggested they should all think about the problem some more and meet again early the following week.

Marvin took a quick poll, and set the time for the next meeting. He looked at the notes he'd made and told them that the agenda would be to look at the advantages and disadvantages of suggestions already proposed, as well as any new ideas, and then decide which ones their department would recommend for adoption by the company. Then he closed his notebook.

After they had all left the conference room to go back to their desks, Marvin sighed deeply and leaned back in his chair. He suddenly felt tired. Running a meeting, especially with so many different personalities, was hard work. It was especially difficult to separate how he felt as a car owner from how he should behave as a supervisor, setting a good example.

DISCUSSION QUESTIONS

1. Which pitfalls of group decision making were present in this meeting?
2. How well did Marvin implement the guidelines for managing effective meetings?
3. What specific recommendations would you make to Marvin for managing the next meeting on this topic more effectively?
4. Specifically, how could Marvin minimize Wally's disruptive influence? ■

■ *Skill Practice*

First Management Staff Meeting at Tampa Pump & Valve

Prior to the class period, you should assume the role of Richard (or Rebecca) West, the new plant manager at TP&V. You are on the plane, returning from your business trip to Venezuela, and you are beginning to make plans for your first meeting with your staff. You became aware of several problems at the plant through the correspondence you reviewed prior to your trip and you feel an urgent need to meet with your staff. In this first meeting, you may want to underscore points made in your memos, ask for reports on assignments made during your absence, ask for elaborations on problems mentioned in the letters, initiate new assignments, or describe your goals and management philosophy. Review the correspondence shown in the TP&V exercise in the Introduction, along with your responses, and use this information to prepare an agenda for your first management staff meeting. Using the behavioral guidelines presented earlier, decide when the meeting should be held, who should attend, how long it should last, in what order business should be conducted, and so forth. Also, anticipate any problems you might encounter during the meeting, based on your knowledge of the personalities of your staff and the potential for conflict among them, and prepare contingency plans for handling them.

After you have all completed your plans, one student should be selected to actually conduct this meeting in class, using other students as staff members. Prior to the meeting, the assigned Mr./Ms. West should take fifteen minutes to distribute the meeting agenda, arrange the physical setting, and assign seating by placing a name plate at each position. While these arrangements are being made, the assigned staff should prepare for the meeting by reviewing the agenda, as well as the TP&V case, to refresh their memories of the issues related to their roles in the company. When the arrangements for the meeting have been made, Mr./Ms. West should invite his or her staff to take their places and call the meeting to order. Assume the meeting is being held during the first week following the return of Mr./Ms. West.

Following this meeting, a discussion of what transpired should be conducted between the participants and assigned observers, using the following form as a guide.

OBSERVERS' FORM FOR RATING THE EFFECTIVENESS OF A MEETING CHAIRPERSON

Rate the performance of the chairperson using the following guidelines. If you are uncertain about any item because of lack of information, mark it with a question mark and discuss it with the chairperson after the exercise is over.

Check if
observed

1. Holding the meeting was appropriate because:

   a. The manager needed information simultaneously from several people. _____

   b. Group members' commitment to a decision needed to be enhanced. _____

   c. Activities involving several individuals needed to be coordinated. _____

   d. Complex tasks had to be performed and a division of labor was feasible. _____

   e. Expertise for solving a problem was randomly or broadly distributed among group members. _____

2. The appropriate individuals were invited to the meeting, as reflected in the fact that:

   a. The size of the group was appropriate for the assigned task. _____

   b. Individuals likely to have a strong task orientation and group process orientation were included. _____

   c. The group consisted of individuals with some common goal orientations. _____

   d. All relevant expertise and knowledge was present. _____

   e. The group's composition reflected the goals of the meeting: homogeneity→solidarity and commitment; heterogeneity→creativity and innovation. _____

3. Proper preparations were made for the meeting.

   a. Appropriate physical arrangements were provided. _____

b. The agenda was prepared and distributed before or at the beginning of the meeting. _____

c. Priorities were established for the meeting's business and these were reflected in the sequence and length of time allotted to each item (more important business was discussed early in the meeting or for a longer time).

d. The most appropriate decision-making structure was chosen for each business item (ordinary group discussion or nominal group discussion). _____

4. The chairperson managed both the task and process aspects of the meeting effectively by:

a. Allowing members to become acquainted (if necessary) and making them feel comfortable. _____

b. Reviewing the progress made to date and establishing the task for this meeting. _____

c. Getting a report from each member with a preassigned task at the beginning of the meeting or as soon as possible. _____

d. When critical thinking was important, playing a strong role in structuring the discussion but refraining from expressing strong opinions. _____

e. Sustaining the flow of the meeting using informational displays. _____

f. Encouraging the group not to stray from assigned tasks. _____

g. Managing the discussion to achieve equitable participation. _____

h. Concluding the meeting by summarizing what was accomplished and reviewing assignments. _____

Quality Circles at Battle Creek Foods

You are the Director of Personnel at Battle Creek Foods, a leading manufacturer of breakfast cereal. Productivity has been sagging industry wide and your organization is starting to see its effect on profitability. In response, you have been asked by the corporate executive committee to make a twenty-minute presentation on quality circles (QC's). The committee has heard that QC's have been initiated at several plants by your leading competitor, and it would like your recommendation as to whether Battle Creek Foods should follow suit. The only previous exposure to QC's the committee has had is what each member has read in the popular press.

Using the following reference material (as well as any other provided you by your instructor), some of you should make a presentation on quality circles. Explain the QC structure and process and the advantages and disadvantages of QC's, and make a recommendation regarding their adoption at your plants. Those not making presentations should use the following observation form to evaluate the presentations.

QUALITY CIRCLES: A BRIEF LOOK AT THE EVIDENCE

Quality control circles appear to be making a positive contribution to product quality, profits, and morale. The evidence collected so far falls short of following the scientific approach to evaluating programs, but it is based on the careful scrutiny of business people. A case in point is the quality circles at Honeywell, the high-technology electronics and computer firm.

Honeywell is currently operating about 150 quality circles throughout North America. Typically about a half-dozen assembly workers are brought together every two weeks by a first-level supervisor or team leader. "We feel that this type of participatory management program not only increases productivity," says Joseph Riordan, director of Honeywell's Coporate Productivity Services, "but it also upgrades the quality of work life for employees. Line workers feel that they are more a part of the action. As a result, we find that quality of work improves and absenteeism is reduced. With this kind of involvement, we have, in many cases, been able to increase the capacity of a line without the addition of tooling or extra shifts."

Honeywell used the quality control circle method to manage the problem of winning a renewal bid for a government contract. Other firms were making the same piece of electronic apparatus at competitive prices. "Here was a situation," Riodan relates, "where we already had cut our rejects down, where all of the learning had effectively gone out of the process." The problem was assigned to the quality circle representing that particular work area. "They came up with a suggestion for further automating the process that enabled us to improve our competitive position by about 20 percent and win the contract."[1]

Lockheed is another high-technology corporation which has achieved outstanding results with quality control circles, as reported by W. S. Rieker. The latter has been credited with introducing the QC circle concept in the

[1] This quote and the preceding ones are from Mike Michaelson, "The Decline of American Productivity," *Success Unlimited,* October 1980, p. 28.

SOURCE: Andrew Dubrin, *Contemporary Management* (Plano, Texas: Business Publications, Inc., 1982), pp. 119–123.

United States. Lockheed documented savings in the first two years with only 15 circles in operation of $2,844,000. In one operation alone, the company had reduced rejects from 25 to 30 per 1,000 hours to less than 6 per 1,000 hours. Ninety-seven percent of those employees who have participated in the quality circles have indicated a strong preference to continue with the program.[2]

A management consultant reports that numerous studies in other companies have demonstrated that quality control circles result in substantial reductions in tardiness, absenteeism, and work disruption. According to his analysis, "Typically, the break-even or payback point on the installation of a quality control circle runs somewhere between three and five months, and most companies are finding a 6 or 8 to 1 ratio to payback after the first year of operation."[3]

KEY ELEMENTS OF A SUCCESSFUL PROGRAM

Quality control circle programs show some variation from company to company. Among the points of differences are how frequently they meet, how much authority is granted to the supervisor or team leader, and how much coordination there is with the already existing quality control department. Ed Yager observes, however, that the successful programs have certain elements in common. These key elements are closely tied in with systematic application of behavioral science knowledge and/or sound managerial judgment.[4]

Quality control circles are used as a method of employee development. A key purpose of these circles is to foster personal development of the participating workers. "If the QC circle is installed as a tool for selfish gain on the part of management, they would do better not to begin."[5]

Management must be willing to grant recognition for ideas forthcoming from the circles. If management attempts to manipulate the circle volunteers or tries to take credit for improvements away from them, the program will most likely backfire. More will be lost than gained.

Membership should be voluntary. As with job enrichment and all forms of participative management, employee preference is an influential factor. Employees who desire to contribute their ideas will generally perform better than employees who are arbitrarily assigned to the QC circle.

---

[2] Reported in Ed Yager, "Examining the Quality Control Circle," *Personnel Journal*, October 1979, p. 684.
[3] Ibid.
[4] The elements are based on information presented in ibid.
[5] Ibid.

Participation from all members is essential. The leader's central responsibility is therefore to encourage all members of the circle to contribute and to facilitate free expression of ideas.

Quality circles are group efforts and not individual efforts. Recognizing this factor decreases showboating and competition, and increases cooperation and the value of interdependence within the group or department. Quality circles, not individual employees, receive credit for innovations and suggestions for improvement.

Ample training is provided. Program volunteers will often need some training in conference techniques or group dynamics. At a minimum, the circle leader will need skills in group participation methods. Otherwise he or she will wind up conducting quality improvement lectures during the sessions.

Creativity is encouraged. Brainstorming, or commonsense variations of this technique, fits naturally into the quality circle method and philosophy. For example, it is particularly important to maintain an attitude of "anything goes." If half-processed ideas are shot down by the leader or other members, idea generation will extinguish quickly.

Projects are related to members' actual job responsibilities. Quality circles are not arenas for amateur speculation about other people's work. People make suggestions about improving the quality of work for which they are already responsible. Thus, the mower manufacturers at Sterling are not plagued with sorting out suggestions from the quality circles at divisions engaged in the manufacture of something entirely different such as lawn chairs.(We are not taking the dogmatic position, however, that productive innovations in one field cannot come from people outside that field.)

Quality and improvement awareness is developed. This element might also be considered the desirable output from a quality circle program. Employees should become more committed to quality; they should see a direct relationship between their work and the quality of the product generated by their efforts.

THE ARGUMENT FOR AND AGAINST QUALITY CONTROL CIRCLES

A major argument for QC circles is that they represent a low-cost, efficient vehicle for unleashing the creative potential of employees. In the process highly desirable ends are achieved, such as quality improvement and improved quality of work life. QC circles, in fact, are considered part of the QWL movement.

Another favorable feature of these circles is that they are perceived positively by management, workers, the union, and stockholders. A firm contemplating implementing such a program thus does not run the risk of internal or external opposition. (It is conceivable, however, that opposition will be forthcoming if management fails to develop a formal reward system for quality circle contributions.)

As experience with the quality circle method increases, criticism will arise inevitably. One counterargument is that the circles do not solicit enough input from engineers and technicians. Too much reliance is placed upon practical, commonsense suggestions. We would have few high-technology innovations today if we relied exclusively on suggestions for improvement from technologically unsophisticated employees. (This argument runs counter to the good results achieved with suggestion programs.)

Quality circles may prove to be breeding grounds for friction and role confusion between the quality control department and themselves. Unless management carefully defines the relationship of quality circles vis-à-vis the quality control department, much duplication of effort (and therefore waste of resources) will be inevitable.

Exclusive reliance upon volunteers for the circles may result in the loss of potentially valuable ideas. Many nonassertive people may shy away from participation in the circles, despite their having valid ideas for product improvement.

Some employees who volunteer to join quality control circles may be doing so for the wrong reasons. It is possible that the circle will develop the reputation of being "a good way to get away from the line for a while and enjoy a coffee break and a good bull session." (To counter such an abuse of the quality circle program, QC group members might monitor the quality of input from their own group members.)

GUIDELINES FOR ACTION

An early strategic step in implementing a quality control circle is to clarify relationships between the circle and the formal quality control department. Otherwise, the quality control department may perceive the circle as a redundancy or threat. One effective arrangement is for the quality circle to complement the quality control department; the QC department does not become subject to the loss of authority.

Membership in the circle should be voluntary and on a rotating basis. In many instances a team member will soon run out of fresh ideas for quality improvement. Rotating membership will result in a wider sampling of ideas being generated.

Quality control circles should be implemented on a pilot basis. As the circle produces results and wins the acceptance of managers and employees alike, it can be expanded as the demand for its output increases.

Do not emphasize quick financial returns or productivity increases from the output of the quality control circles. It should be seen as a long-range program which will raise the quality consciousness of the organization. (Nevertheless, . . . immediate positive results are often forthcoming.)

Management must make good use of many of the suggestions forthcoming from the quality control circle, yet still define the limits of the power and authority of the circle. On the one hand, if none of the circle's suggestions are adopted, the circle will lose its effectiveness as an agent for change. Circle members will become discouraged because of their lack of clout. On the other hand, if the circle has too much power and authority, it will be seen as a governing body for technical change. Under the latter circumstances, it is also possible that people will use the circle for political purposes. A given individual who wants to get a technical modification authorized may try to influence a member of the quality circle to suggest that modification during a circle meeting.

OBSERVATION FORM FOR EFFECTIVE PRESENTATIONS

Watch for the following characteristics of effective presentations.

Check if
present

1. Tailored message to audience. Message was concrete, specific, practical, and relevant.   _____

2. Presented logically compelling case for proposal or point of view. Avoided logical fallacies.   _____

3. Prepared for contingencies and demonstrated flexibility in varying pace and approach to match audience interest and comprehension.   _____

4. Kept graphs, charts, and other visual aids simple and straightforward.   _____

5. Presented material in logically organized and easy-to-follow manner.   _____

6. Projected attitude of controlled enthusiasm, neither dull nor overbearing.   _____

7. Used body movements, facial expressions, and tone of voice that enhanced presentation.   _____

8. Candidly discussed advantages and disadvantages.   _____

9. Provided variety and relief. Alternated between speech and action, lecture and participation. Used humor well. _____

10. Handled questions and challenges thoughtfully, candidly, and assertively. _____

11. Used questions from audience to point out advantages of proposal. Maintained generally positive atmosphere. _____

12. Maintained control of meeting. There was no question who was in charge during presentation. Presenter not easily intimidated by audience or caught off guard. _____

■

■ *Skill Application*

Application Exercises

1. Go to a meeting at which someone will be making a formal presentation. This might be a faculty meeting, a local school board meeting, a political rally, or a meeting of a social club. Using the guidelines for making effective presentations, evaluate the performance of the presenter. While you are watching the presentation, look for errors you commonly make, as well as techniques you would like to emulate. If possible, discuss your observations with the presenter and review the guidelines presented here with him or her. Based on this experience, list personal goals for improving your own presentation.

2. Think of a group you belong to that has a problem it needs to address. Volunteer to serve as the leader of a meeting to discuss (and hopefully resolve) this problem. Using the guidelines in this chapter, plan and conduct the meeting. After it is over, hand out copies of the Group Process Diagnostic Questions (p. 452) and have the members evaluate the meeting. Specifically ask them for feedback concerning your performance as the group's leader using the Observation Form from the Skill Practice section.

3. Discuss the behavioral guidelines for conducting meetings. Share them with at least two persons who have experience conducting meetings. After explaining your guidelines, ask these individuals to comment on the guidelines. Are your "rules of thumb" relevant for their situation? Are they compatible with their approach to management? What modifications would they make in your guidelines to make them more useful? What points would they add to your list? Following this discussion, revise your list to reflect this input.

4. Arrange to make a presentation before a school, work, or community group on an appropriate topic. Before the presentation, hand out copies of the Observation Form to at least five members of the audience and briefly explain the guidelines. After your presentation, ask this group for feedback and collect their forms. Record this experience in your journal, highlighting your personal goals for improvement. ■

Acknowledgments

Index

Acknowledgments

Introduction

p. 11   Reprinted, by permission of the publisher, from "Improving Managerial Effectiveness Through Model-Based Training" by J. I. Porras and B. Anderson, p. 72, *Organizational Dynamics,* Spring 1981. Copyright © 1981 by AMACOM, a division of American Management Associations, New York. All rights reserved.

p. 14   "What makes a top executive?" by Morgan W. McCall and Michael M. Lombardo from *Psychology Today* Magazine, February 1983, pp. 26, 28–31. Copyright © 1983 American Psychological Association. Reprinted by permission.

p. 21   "Tampa Pump and Valve Company" by Richard E. Dutton and Rodney C. Sherman. Reprinted by permission of Richard E. Dutton.

Chapter 1

p. 42   Reprinted with permission of Macmillan Publishing Company from *The Nature of Human Values* by Milton Rokeach. Copyright © 1973 by The Free Press, a Division of Macmillan Publishing Company.

p. 45   From "The Cognitive-Development Approach to Socialization" by Lawrence Kohlberg in *Handbook of Socialization Theory and Research,* edited by D. A. Goslin, Houghton Mifflin Company, 1969, p. 376. Reprinted by permission.

p. 50   Reprinted by permission of the Harvard Business Review. An exhibit from "How Managers' Minds Work" by J. L. McKenney and P. G. W. Keen (May/June 1974). Copyright © 1974 by the President and Fellows of Harvard College; all rights reserved.

p. 53   Kolb/Rubin/McIntyre, *Organizational Psychology: A Book of Readings,* 2nd ed., copyright © 1974, p. 32. Reprinted by permission of Prentice-Hall, Inc., Englewood Cliffs, N.J.

p. 57   Reprinted from: J. W. Pfeiffer, R. Heslin, and John E. Jones, Eds., *Instrumentation in Human Relations Training,* 2nd ed., San Diego, CA: University Associates, Inc., 1974. Used with permission.

p. 64   "Interpersonal Communication, Group Solidarity, and Social Influences" by Edgar H. Schein from *Sociometry,* Vol. 23, 1960, pp. 154–155. Copyright © 1960 by the American Sociological Association. Reprinted by permission.

p. 69   From *Development in Judging Moral Issues* by James R. Rest. Copyright © 1979 by James R. Rest. Reprinted by permission of James Rest.

p. 70   From *Development in Judging Moral Issues* by James R. Rest. Copyright © 1979 by James R. Rest. Reprinted by permission of James Rest.

p. 71   From *Development in Judging Moral Issues* by James R. Rest. Copyright © 1979 by James R. Rest. Reprinted by permission of James Rest.

p. 73   From *Development in Judging Moral Issues* by James R. Rest. Copyright © 1979 by James R. Rest. Reprinted by permission of James Rest.

p. 80   From *FIRO: A Three-dimensional Theory of Interpersonal Behavior* by William C. Schutz, 1958. Reprinted by permission of the author.

Chapter 2

p. 86   Reprinted with permission from *Journal of Psychosomatic Research,* Vol. II, T. H. Holmes and R. H. Rahe, "The Social Readjustment Rating Scale." Copyright © 1967, Pergamon Press, Ltd.

Chapter 3

Chapter 4

Chapter 5

Chapter 9

Index

Ability, and motivation, 306–10
Accommodating response, and conflict management, 408, 410, 411, 415
Accuracy, in communication, 199–203. *See also* Communication
Adams, J. S., 314
Adaptability, as management skill, 3
Adler, R. B., 418
Affection, as interpersonal need, 55–56
Aggression, and stress, 92
Albert, M., 268
Albrecht, K., 89, 99, 115
Allen, J. L., 151, 162, 165
Allen, R. W., 263, 266
Allport, G., 40, 43
Anderson, B., 3
Anticipatory stressors, 93–94
Antonovsky, A., 96
Appley, M. H., 92
Aptitude, and employee performance, 305
Argenti, J., 457
Argyris, C., 96
Athos, A., 223, 227
Avoiding response, and conflict management, 408–9, 410, 411, 416
Aygen, M. M., 117

Baker, N. J., 356
Bagnell, J., 171, 173
Bandura, A., 3, 311, 327
Barnlund, D. C., 208
Barrett, H., 472, 474
Barron, F. X., 150
Basadur, M. S., 164, 165
Beary, J. F., 117
Benjamin, A., 227
Benne, K. D., 104
Benson, H., 117
Berkowitz, L., 469

Berkowitz, N. N., 262
Bernard, C. I., 369
Bersheid, E., 263
Beveridge, W., 160
Birnbaum, M., 104
Block, C. H., 465
Block, J., 47
Boje, D. M., 250
Bonchard, T. J., 465
Bonoma, T. V., 260
Boulding, E., 403
Bower, M., 150
Bowman, G. W., 199
Boyatzis, R. E., 5
Brainstorming, 170–71, 465
Brainwashing, 64–65
Bramel, D., 262
Bramwell, S. T., 95
Brass, D. J., 251
Breslow, L., 99
Broadwell, M. M., 146
Brouwer, P. J., 37
Bruner, J. S., 163
Buell, P., 99
Burke, R. J., 90
Burnaska, R. F., 3
Byrnes, A., 60

Cameron, K. S., 3, 5, 172, 354
Campbell, N., 165
Canfield, F. E., 262
Caplan, R. D., 94, 96, 112
Carcuff, R., 220
Carey, R. G., 461
Carlson, S., 94, 105
Carnegie, Dale, 408
Carpenter, L. G., 101
Castore, C., 463
Cavior, N., 264
Cayner, J. J., 3
Centrality, and power, 250–54
Cheston, R., 413
Clare, D. A., 43
Clichés, in communication, 217
Coch, L., 357
Coddington, R. D., 95

Cofer, C. N., 92
Cognitive style, 47–54. *See also* Communication
and self-awareness, 40
and stress, 102
Collaborating response, and conflict management, 409–10, 411, 415–18
Collings, B. E., 463
Commonalities, identifying in problem solving, 160–61
Communication
accuracy of, 199–203
barriers to, 203
and centrality, 250–54
and cognitive style, 47–54
and effective presentations, 471–79
and listening, 218–28
as restraining force on stress, 102
supportive, 203–18
Communication, as management skill, 6–7
Compromising response, and conflict management, 409, 410, 411, 415–16
Comstock, G. W., 102
Conceptual blocks. *See also* Problem solving
defined, 151
overcoming, 164–76
to problem solving, 151–64
Conflict management
defined, 403–4
five approaches to, 407–10
four causes of interpersonal conflict, 404–6
guidelines for collaborative approach, 416–31
as management skill, 6, 8
and problem identification, 418–31
using conflict approaches, 411–16

Confrontational response, and listening, 225

Congruence, in communication, 203–4

Connor, S. R., 310

Control, as interpersonal need, 55

Conventional level of values maturity, 44

Cooper, C. L., 100, 110

Cooper, M. J., 117

Coronary heart disease (CHD), 97–102

Coronary-prone behavior pattern, 97–99

Crichton, M., 207

Criticality, and power, 250–54

Crocker, J., 199, 218

Crovitz, H. F., 173–74

Crutchfield, R., 150

Cuming, P., 244, 269

Cummings, L. L., 411

Dalkey, N. C., 465

Dalton, G., 304

Dauw, D. C., 164

David, W. B., 103

Davidson, M. J., 103, 110

Davidson, R. J., 103

Davis, K. E., 263

Davis, J., 462

Davis, J. 462

Davis, T. R., 3

de Bono, E., 152, 169

Decision making. See also Delegation; Group meetings
delegation improving, 357
in groups, 459
as management skill, 6, 8
model, 371–83

Defensiveness, as communication barrier, 203

Delbercq, A. L., 466

Delco, J., 117

Delegation
advantages of, 354–58
decision model for, 371–83
defined, 353–54
ineffective, 358–59
inhibitors to effective, 359–63

as management skill, 6, 8
principles of, 363–71
using decision model for, 378–83

Deleo, J., 117

Dellas, M., 160, 173

DeLorean, John Z., 284–93

Delphi technique, 465–66

De Ninno, J. A., 463

DiMarco, N. J., 60

Dion, K. K., 263

Disconfirmation, as communication barrier, 203

Diverting response, and listening, 225

Downey, D. K., 412

Drucker, P. F., 148

Dutton, R. E., 21

Dyer, W., 203, 269, 408

Eckstrom, R. B., 48

Edleson, J. L., 3

Edwards, M. R., 89

Effort, and power, 265–66

Egan, E., 220, 221

Einstein, Albert, 167

Eisenhower, Dwight D., 108

Elbing, A., 144, 148

Elliot, 306

Empathy, as listening skill, 220–22

Employee performance. See also Motivation
defining, 305
diagnosing poor performance, 304–6
and mid-career obsolescence, 306–10
and motivation, 6, 8, 310–16
and operant conditioning, 316–30
remedies for, 309–10

Encounter stressors, 96

Environmental stress, and conflict management, 405, 406

Etzioni, A., 267

Evaluation response, and listening, 224–25

Expectancy theory, and motivation, 312–15

Expertise, and power, 260–61

Expressed feelings, in communication, 217–18

Falbo, T., 271

Farson, R., 220, 223

Feldman, S. D., 264

Ferris, K. R., 263

Festinger, L., 265

Feuerstein, M., 101

Fielden, J. S., 199, 310

Filley, A. C., 148, 407, 461, 462

Fixation, and stress, 92

Flanders, L. R., 5

Fleishman, J. A., 306

Flexibility
and building power base, 254–55
in communication, 210–11
in presentations, 476
in thinking, 150, 170, 172–73

Floor, E., 103

Fluency, in thinking, 170, 172–73

Fombrun, C., 250

Forcing response, and conflict management, 407–8, 410, 411

Freedman, M., 101

Freeman, M. J., 53

Friedman, M., 97

French, J. R. P., 94, 96, 112, 357

French, J. W., 48

Fromm, Erich, 36

Freud, S., 37

Gaier, E. L., 160, 173

Galbraith, John Kenneth, 207

Gamboa, V., 311

Garbarro, J., 223, 227

Gardner, J. W., 150

Gassner, S. M., 60

Ghiselli, E. E., 5

Giametti, A. B., 275

Gibb, J. R., 203, 462

Gladstein, G. A., 220

Glasser, W., 214

Goffman, E., 205, 261

Goldberg, H., 98, 114

Goldstein, A. P., 3

Gordon, A., 123

Gordon, R., 40
Gordon, T., 418
Gordon, W. J. J., 166
Greenhalgh, L., 484
Group meetings, 6, 8
  common pitfalls in, 455–60
  defined, 454
  effective management of,
    460–71
  improving, 454–55
  making effective
    presentations in,
    471–79
  managing time in, 110–11
  and quality circles, 491–96
Group think, 458
Guest, R. H., 106, 363
Guetzkow, H., 463
Guildford, J. P., 164, 170
Gustafson, D. H., 466

Haan, N., 47
Hackman, J. R., 112–13, 367,
  457, 459
Haefele, J. W., 164
Hall, D. T., 94
Hall, R., 463
Hamner, W. C., 96, 319, 327,
  328
Handleton, J., 356
Haney, W. V., 38, 199–201,
  207, 211
Hansen, D., 100
Hare, C. C., 95
Harmon, H. H., 48
Harnett, D. L., 411
Harris, R. E., 101
Harris, S., 39
Hart, D. K., 249
Hatfield, J. D., 218
Hayakawa, S. I., 36–37, 38
Haythorn, W. W., 60
Heilman, K., 220
Helmar, O., 465
Henderson, J. C., 53
Hermann, N., 163
Hewett, T. T., 60
Hickson, D., 250–51, 255
Hill, R. E., 57
Hinings, C. R., 250–51, 255
Hoffman, L. R., 463
Holmes, T. H., 95, 102, 108
Holmes, T. S., 102

Hornik, J., 60
House, R. J., 148
Huber, G. P., 148, 357, 455,
  468, 469
Human behavior, and
  operant conditioning,
  316–30. See also
  Employee performance;
  Motivation
Hunt, S. P., 101
Hurst, Richard, 234
Huseman, R. C., 218
Hutcherson, D. E., 60

Inclusion, as interpersonal
  need, 55
Incongruence, as
  communication barrier,
  203–4
Influence. See also Power
  as management skill, 6, 8
  strategies, 266–71
  transforming power into,
    266–77
  using effectively, 247–50
Information response, and
  listening, 51–52
Information, as source of
  conflict, 405–6
Initiator, in conflict
  management, 418–23
Instrumental values, 42–43
Interaction Associates, 165,
  171
Interaction conflicts, and
  stress, 96
Interchange incompatibility,
  59
Interpersonal competence,
  and stress, 100–101
Interpersonal
  incompatibility,
  analyzing, 58–61
Interpersonal orientation,
  and self-awareness, 40,
  55–61
Intimidation, and power,
  267–68
Intuitive strategy, and
  cognitive style, 50–51
Issue conflicts, and stress, 96
Ivancevich, J. M., 89, 116

Jacobson, I., 263
Jago, A. G., 372
James, William, 209
Janis, I., 403, 458, 469
Janson, R., 113
Janusian thinking, 167–68
Jay, A., 308
Jenkins, C. D., 90, 95, 97, 100,
  102, 108
Jewell, L. N., 461, 469
Jick, T. D., 90
Job burnout, 307–8
Jones, S., 262
Jourard, S. M., 39, 98, 102

Kalin, R., 103
Kalis, B. L., 101
Kanter, R., 248–49, 254, 257,
  260, 276
Katz, R. L., 5
Keats, G. R., 263
Keen, P. G. W., 48, 52, 102
Kelley, H. H., 461
Kellogg, M., 316
Kelly, J., 403
Kemball, C. P., 101
Kerr, S., 148, 316
Khedouri, F., 268
Kilmann, R., 53
King, D., 403
Kipnis, D., 247, 266, 270, 274,
  275, 306, 413, 416
Kobasa, S. C., 95, 102, 108
Koberg, D., 171, 173
Koestler, A., 153, 160
Kohlberg, L., 43, 44–47
Kolb, D. A., 48, 53–54
Korda, Michael, 248, 257
Kostrubala, T., 99–100
Kreisberg, M., 462
Kreitner, R., 311, 319, 321,
  326, 328
Kurtzberg, R. L., 264

La Gaipa, J. J., 262
Lahiff, J. M., 218
Landy, D., 263
Language
  as communication barrier,
    207–8

as conceptual block,
153–54
Lanis, I. L., 180
Latham, G. P., 3, 404
Lawler, E. E., 111, 112, 305,
311, 367
Lawrence, P. R., 112, 258, 304
Learning model, defined, 3
Leavitt, H. J., 153, 154
LeDuc, A. L., Jr., 320
Lee, C. A., 255
Levitan, U., 357
Levinson, D. J., 94
Lewin, K., 91
Lickona, T., 47
Liddell, W. W., 60
Life balance, and stress,
114–15
Likert, R., 96
Linden, W., 101
Lindzey, G., 43
Lippitt, R., 328
Listening skills, 218–28. See
also Communication
and alternative responses,
223–28
and empathy, 220–22
Livingston, J. S., 5
Locke, S. E., 103
Logical fallacies, in
presentations, 474–75
Lombardo, M. M., 14
Loomis, F., 200
Lorsch, J., 258, 304
Luthans, E., 3, 311, 319, 321,
326, 328

Mackenzie, R. A., 108
Macklowicz, M., 97, 99
Macoby, M., 277
Madison, D. L., 263, 266
Maier, A. A., 146, 170, 218
Maier, N. R. F., 148, 218, 223,
305, 327, 328, 357, 455,
461, 468
Male role, harmful aspects
of, 98–99
Mambert, W. A., 472, 476, 478
Managers. See also Conflict
management;
Delegation; Stress
attitudes about

subordinates, 360–61
characteristics of top
executives, 14–20
and cognitive strategies,
47–54
and delegation, 353–54
fatal flaws of, 15–18
and interpersonal
orientation, 55–61
and nine critical
management skills,
5–6
and sharing power, 277
values of, 43
Managing conflict. See
Conflict management
Mann, Leon, 180
March, J. G., 144, 146, 155,
169, 172
Martindale, C., 163
Maslow, A. H., 37, 163, 403
Masuda, M., 95, 108
Matteson, M. T., 89, 116
May, Róllo, 248
Mayes, B. T., 263, 266
McCall, M. W., Jr., 14
McClelland, D. C., 103, 276
McConkey, D., 354
McGregor, D., 361
McKenney, J. L., 48, 52, 102
McKim, R. H., 160, 165
McNichols, T. J., 127
Meadow, A. S., 356
Mechanic, D., 257, 262, 265
Medawar, P. B., 165
Mediator, in conflict
management, 426–31
Meditation, and stress
reduction, 117
Melhuish, A., 100
Mendelsohn, G. A., 60
Mescon, M. H., 268
Michels, R., 274
Michener, H. A., 306
Mid-career obsolescence,
306–10
Milgram, S., 47, 94
Miller, A. G., 263
Miner, J. B., 5
Mintzberg, H., 2, 5, 94, 105,
110, 354, 363
Mitchell, T. R., 311
Mitroff, I. I., 53
Moch, M. K., 251

Moral values, 43–47. See also
Values
Moriarity, R., 101
Mooney, J. D., 359
Morphological forced
connections, 173–74, 176
Morris, C. G., 459
Moses, J. O., 3
Motivation. See also
Employee performance
and ability, 306–10
approaches to, 310–12
and delegation to
subordinates, 356–57
and expectancy theory,
312–15
increasing employee,
304–6
as management skill, 6, 8
and operant conditioning,
316–30
Moyer, R. I., 262
Mulkowsky, G. P., 53
Murninghan, K., 459, 464, 466
Myers, I. B., 48

Nadler, D. E., 311
Negative reinforcement,
317–18, 326
Newman, W. H., 360
Nine critical management
skills, 5–6
Nominal group technique
(NGT), 466–67
Nord, W., 326
Nunney, D. N., 48
Nutt, P. C., 53

Obradovic, S. M., 60
O'Brien, G. E., 60
O'Connor, J., 356
O'Dell, J. W., 457
Oldham, G. R., 112–13, 330
Olton, R., 150
Oncken, W., 355, 366
Opinions, in
communication, 217
Ordinary group format,
464–65
Organ, D. W., 96
Originator incompatibility,
59
Orme-Johnson, D. W., 117
Osborn, A., 170

Pacifying responses, and
    listening, 227
Parloff, M. B., 356
Parnes, S. J., 150, 354
Partridge, K. B., 102
Payne, R., 90
Pennings, J. M., 250–51, 255
Perceptive strategy, and
    cognitive style, 48
Perceptual stereotyping, 155
Perrow, C., 255, 258
Perry, P. C., 465
Personal assessment, 11–12
Personal attraction, and
    power, 261–64
Personal stress. See Stress
Persuasion, and power,
    268–69
Petroch, E., 311
Pfeffer, J., 258, 260
Phillips, E., 413
Physical conditioning,
    99–100, 114
Plovnick, M. S., 53–54
Ponder, Q. D., 363
Porras, J. I., 3
Porter, E., 411
Porter, L. W., 263, 266
Positive reinforcement,
    317–26
Postconventional level of
    values maturity, 44
Power. See also Influence
    building strong base of,
        247–50
    defined, 248–49
    and delegation, 358
    as management skill, 6–7
    personal attributes
        fostering, 260–66
    position characteristics
        fostering, 250–59
    and stress, 101–2
    transforming into
        influence, 266–77
Preconventional level of
    values maturity, 44
Premack, D., 321
Preston, P., 360
Prince, G. M., 468
Probing responses, and
    listening, 226
Problem-solving. See also
    Decision making

and alternative
    generation, 146–47,
    169–76
conceptual blocks to,
    151–64
in conflict management,
    418–31
defining the problem,
    144–46, 165–69
implementing solutions to,
    147–48
as management skill, 6–7
model, 144–51
overcoming conceptual
    blocks to, 164–76
steps in, 144, 151
Punishment, and motivation,
    317, 326–30
Purdy, K., 113

Quality circles, 491–96
Questions, use of in problem
    solving, 161–62
Quick, R. L., 308
Quinn, R. E., 354

Rahe, R. H., 95, 102, 108
Randle, C. W., 199
Rankin, N. O., 60
Reason strategy, and power,
    266–71
Receptive strategy, and
    cognitive style, 48, 50
Reciprocal incompatibility,
    58–59
Reciprocity, and power, 268,
    269–70
Reciprocity strategy, and
    power, 166–71
Reddy, W. B., 60
Reese, H., 356
Reflective/understanding
    responses, and listening,
    223
Regression, and stress, 92
Reily, A. C., 359
Reisner, M. F., 101
Reitz, H. J., 461, 469
Reinterpretive responses,
    and listening, 226–27
Relational algorithm, 173,
    174–76

Relaxation techniques, five
    types of, 116–17
Relevance, and power,
    257–58
Renwich, P. A., 263, 266
Repression, and stress, 92
Responder, in conflict
    management, 423–26
Rest, J. R., 47
Retribution strategy, and
    power, 266–71
Rewards, and motivation,
    313–14, 317, 319–26
Ritchie, R. J., 3
Robbins, S. P., 403, 407
Rogers, C. R., 36, 203–4, 220,
    222–23, 224, 227
Rokeach, M., 40, 41, 42–43
Role conflicts, and stress, 96
Role overload, and stress,
    94–95
Rose, S. D., 3
Rosenhan, R. H., 97
Ross, J., 263
Rothenburg, A., 167, 168
Rowland, K. F., 98
Ruble, T., 407
Ruh, R., 461
Ryan, L. R., 56
Ryman, D. H., 102

Saari, L. M., 3
Safar, H., 264
Sailer, H. R., 89
Salancik, G. R., 258
Sanford, D. G., 43
Sanford, W. P., 472
Sapira, J. D., 101
Sapolsky, A., 60
Saron, C., 103
Sayles, L. R., 55, 94
Schachter, J., 94
Schachter, S., 101
Scheib, E. T., 101
Schein, E. H., 64, 94, 309, 426
Schlacter, J., 89
Schlenker, B. R., 260, 262
Schmidt, S. M., 266, 270, 413
Schmidt, W. H., 147, 404, 416
Schneck, R. E., 251, 255
Schriesheim, C., 412
Schumacher, E. F., 165

Schutz, W. C., 55, 56, 60, 96, 463
Scott, W. G., 249
Self-awareness. *See also* Values
    and cognitive style, 47–54
    interpersonal orientation, 55–61
    as management skill, 5–6
    and self-concept, importance of, 36–39
    and sensitive line, 38–39
    and stress, 101–4
    three critical areas of, 36
    and values, 40–47
Self-concept, formation of, 36–39
Self-disclosure, 39
Selye, H., 89, 92, 99
Sensitive line, and self-awareness, 38–39
Shalinsky, W., 60
Sharon, C., 103
Shapiro, A. O., 101
Shaw, M. E., 461, 463
Sheridan, J., 412
Sherman, R. C., 21
Sieberg, E., 203, 205, 208–9
Sigall, H., 263
Simon, H. A., 144, 146, 155, 169, 172
Simon, S. B., 41
Simons, H. W., 262
Singer, M. T., 43, 101
Singleton, W. T., 3
Situational stressors, 95
Siu, R. G. K., 149
Skinner, B. F., 311, 326
Skolnick, 306
Slater, P., 462
Slocum, J. W., Jr., 60, 412
Smith, C., 475
Smith, M. B., 47
Smith, P. E., 3
Smith, S., 60
Social learning theory, 3
Social Readjustment Rating Scale (SRRS), 86–87, 95, 102
Sokol, B., 98
Sokolow, M., 101
Solem, A. R., 218
Sorcher, M., 3
Sorenson, J. R., 463

Spurgeon, P., 3
Stabell, C., 54
Stammers, R. B., 3
Statistical aggregation, 465
Steil, L. K., 218
Steiner, G., 160, 164
Stereotyping, in problem solving, 155
Stevens, O. J., 411
Stone, R. A., 117
Strategic contingencies, model of power, 251
Stress
    altering reactions to, 116–18
    developing restraining forces on, 97–104
    eliminating stressors, 105–8
    and major stressors, 93–96
    management of, 6–7, 89–90, 104–18
    reaction to, 92–93
    and time, 89–90, 106–11
    understanding, 91–104
Subdivision, in problem solving, 172–73
Subordinates
    and delegation, 354–83
    management attitude toward, 360–61
Supportive communication, 203–18. *See also* Communication
Synectics, 166–67
Systemic strategy, 48, 50–51

Tannenbaum, R., 147, 404
Taylor, C. W., 150
Taylor, D. W., 465
Tedeschi, J. T., 260, 262
Terborg, J. R., 463
Terminal values, 42–43
Theory X and Theory Y, 361
Thibaut, J. W., 461
Thomas, K., 403, 407
Thompson, D. W., 316, 320
Thompson, J. D., 149
Thornton, B. B., 199
Tichy, N. M., 250
Tillman, R., Jr., 454
Time management, 105–11. *See also* Stress

Time stressors, 94
Toffler, A., 90
Torrance, E. P., 150
Troxell, J. R., 95
Truax, C. B., 220
Tuden, A., 149
Turner, A. N., 112, 162
Tushman, M. L., 250
Type A behavior pattern, 87–88
Type A personality, 97–99
Type B personality, 99

Understanding/reflective response, and listening, 227–28
Urwick, L., 353

Values
    and conflict, 405
    instrumental, terminal, 42–43
    model of values maturity, 43–47
    as restraining force on stress, 102
    and self-awareness, 41–47
Van de Ven, A. H., 466
Vernon, P. E., 40, 43, 48
Vertical thinking, 152–53
Vertinsky, I., 50–51
Vidmar, N., 457
Visibility, and power, 256–57
Von Glinow, M., 412
von Treitscheke, H., 248
Vroom, V. H., 147, 311, 372, 460
Vygotsky, L., 153

Wagner, N. N., 95
Walster, E., 263
Walton, R., 426
Wanner, E., 103
Ward, H. W., 95
Warren, K., 360
Wasmuth. W. J., 484
Wass, D. L., 355, 366
Watson, James D., 183
Webber, R. A., 334, 336, 437
Weiner, H., 101
Wexley, K., 404

Whetton, D. A., 3, 5, 250, 269, 408
White, J., 461
White, R., 328
Whyte, W. H., 354
Wienmann, J. M., 213
Wilcox, R. P., 472
Wilkinson, I., 266, 270
Williams, R. E., 101, 103
Williard, H. M., 101
Wilson, P. R., 264

Wiser, C., 275
Wiser, W., 275
Wispe, L. G., 221
Withdrawal, and stress, 92
Wolf, S. G., 95
Wolff, H. G., 95
Women, and stress, 98–99
Workaholism, 98–99
Work flow, criticality in, 250–54
Work, restructuring, 112–13

Wrightsman, L. S., 356

Yeager, W. H., 472
Yetton, P. W., 147, 372, 460
Yukl, G., 271

Zaleznick, A., 247
Zand, D. E., 96, 356
Zimmerer, T. W., 360
Zohman, B. L., 99
Zyzanski, S. J., 98